Parenting Plan Evaluations

There is really nothing like this book. What makes it especially strong is the clear and detailed background and rationales explaining why each component of a custody evaluation might be necessary and how an evaluator might make appropriate decisions about what to include in their evaluations. The breadth and depth of coverage make this book the definitive handbook for custody evaluators. It is exceptionally well referenced and will equip evaluators with the skills and information necessary to answer challenging questions, including those from hostile lawyers dissatisfied with the recommendations offered.

—**MICHAEL E. LAMB, PhD,** Department of Psychology, Sidney Sussex College, University of Cambridge, Cambridge, United Kingdom

Parenting Plan Evaluations: An Evidence-Informed Approach to Child Custody offers a sophisticated and comprehensive guide to one of the most challenging areas of family law. Grounded in the scientific process, it blends dimensional and categorical analyses with an ecological perspective. Jon Gould and Chris Mulchay have taken their guidance to the next level with new insights, data-gathering tools, and research for conducting one of family court's toughest jobs. For mental health professionals, attorneys, judges, or anyone working in the family court system, this is essential reading if you want to stay current and make decisions in the best interest of children.

—**ROBIN M. DEUTSCH, PhD, ABPP,** independent practice, Newton, MA, United States

Like Gutenberg's printing press, Edison's light bulb, and Jobs's personal computer, this magnificent volume is a game changer. Gould and Mulchay have performed a feat of alchemy: They have taken a million disparate concepts, practices, and cases and produced intellectual gold. Don't let the page count sway you. This volume distills many thousands of pages' worth of insight, concepts, and hands-on practical direction. If you read or rely on one published work in family law, this must be it. Thank you, Jon and Chris, for helping us to better help children.

—**BENJAMIN D. GARBER, PhD,** Family Law Consulting, PLLC, Hollis, NH, United States; DEFUSEdivorce.com

Parenting Plan Evaluations

An Evidence-Informed Approach to Child Custody

JONATHAN W. GOULD
CHRISTOPHER M. MULCHAY

AMERICAN PSYCHOLOGICAL ASSOCIATION

Published by
American Psychological Association
750 First Street, NE
Washington, DC 20002
https://www.apa.org

Order Department
https://www.apa.org/pubs/books
order@apa.org

Typeset in Meridien and Ortodoxa by TIPS Publishing Services, Carrboro, NC

Printer: Gasch Printing, Odenton, MD
Cover Designer: Beth Schlenoff Design, Bethesda, MD

Library of Congress Cataloging-in-Publication Data

Names: Gould, Jonathan W., 1953- author | Mulchay, Christopher M. author
Title: Parenting plan evaluations : an evidence-informed approach to child custody / by Jonathan W. Gould, Christopher M. Mulchay.
Description: Washington, DC : American Psychological Association, [2026] | Includes bibliographical references and index.
Identifiers: LCCN 2025017933 (print) | LCCN 2025017934 (ebook) | ISBN 9781433843617 paperback | ISBN 9781433843624 ebook
Subjects: LCSH: Custody of children--United States | Custody of children--United States--Psychological aspects | Parent and child (Law)--United States | BISAC: PSYCHOLOGY / Forensic Psychology | LAW / Family Law / Divorce & Separation
Classification: LCC KF547 .G69 2026 (print) | LCC KF547 (ebook)
LC record available at https://lccn.loc.gov/2025017933
LC ebook record available at https://lccn.loc.gov/2025017934

ISBN 9781433850080 (pdf)

https://doi.org/10.1037/0000474-000

Printed in the United States of America

10 9 8 7 6 5 4 3 2 1

CONTENTS

ACKNOWLEDGMENTS

We begin with our sincere gratitude to Beth Hatch and Chris Kelaher of the American Psychological Association. Chris Kelaher's belief in this manuscript was instrumental to its development and completion.

As devoted Beatles fans, we've always appreciated the genius of George Martin—the quiet architect behind so much of the Beatles music. Beth is our George Martin. She does not stand in the spotlight, but her presence was unmistakable. With wisdom, creativity, and unwavering dedication, she added depth, structure, and consistency to every sentence, every chapter. Her influence is woven through the fabric of our work—not loudly proclaimed but deeply felt.

We are also deeply grateful to our patient and supportive wives, whose steadfast belief in this project—and their understanding of the passion and enthusiasm we brought to it—sustained us through its many phases.

Jon would like to acknowledge the encouragement and input of his adult children and stepchildren. In particular, Stevi Gould, PhD, and Alyssa Levine, Esquire (now Judge Levine), offered important challenges to our work. Stevi reminded her father that family interactions must always be viewed through a complex lens incorporating multiple levels of analysis. Alyssa reminded her stepfather of the awesome challenges judges face in piecing together the mosaic of family conflict as part of the journey toward effective resolution.

Chris would like to thank Jon for his dedication to the field, along with his willingness to offer support, have an ongoing exchange of views, and tackle tough questions. Our debates and the many hundreds of draft chapters that led to this book spanned a five-year period of creative growth for us both. Given our tendency to write, challenge one another, and write some more, this book was less about the destination and more about the journey.

Our heartfelt thanks also go to the friends and colleagues who generously reviewed chapters and offered fresh insights and new directions. Among them are Michael Lamb, PhD, Benjamin Garber, PhD, Julie Goldenson, PhD, Jay Flens, PsyD, Ann Ordway, PsyD, Lynn Kamin, Esquire, Jason Bashera, Esquire, Bud Dale, JD, PhD, Eileen Kohutis, PhD, Marc Ackerman, PhD, and Madelyn Milchman, PhD. Their expertise and thoughtful feedback helped shape and strengthen this work.

As senior author, Jon wanted to add a personal note about working with Chris. We first met while on opposite sides of several custody cases. My initial impression was that Chris was one of the few younger colleagues whose passion for our discipline matched my own. At the time, I saw him as a diamond in the rough. After several years of working together, I have observed Chris becoming one of the next generation's leaders in our field. Collaborating with him has reminded me of the joy of working with someone with whom to debate, challenge, learn, laugh, and build a lasting friendship. Chris has rekindled in me the excitement of discovering new ideas and new perspectives on old ideas.

Parenting Plan Evaluations

Introduction: The Forensic Explorer

The courtroom was silent, save for the rhythmic tapping of a pen against the desk of the attorneys, the whispering of the mother to her counsel, and the icy stare of the father across the well of the court. A parenting plan evaluator sat in the witness stand, awaiting the next question. The judge listened and watched intently. The attorneys studied every expression, every breath. The evaluator, an expert witness, knew that the next words spoken could have lasting implications for a family in turmoil. This is the reality of forensic mental health professionals—social scientists navigating the challenging landscape of the legal system, interpreters of human behavior attempting to offer clarity in a storm of emotions, allegations, and uncertainty. Our work, though rooted in science, unfolds in an environment where truth is often obscured by competing narratives and high-stakes conflicts. We are explorers, charting the intricate and often treacherous territory of human relationships, child development, and family dysfunction. To be a parenting plan evaluator is to embrace contradiction. It is to balance scientific rigor with human empathy, to work methodically in the face of intense emotional upheaval, to stand firm in expertise while remaining humble in the face of ever-expanding knowledge. It is to acknowledge the limits of what we know while striving to apply the best of what we know to the unique facts of the case before us. Our task is complex: we gather data, we hypothesize, we assess, we analyze, we write, and often we testify. We leave the controlled environment of our offices and step into the lives of families in crisis. We observe their homes, speak with their children, and gather collateral data

https://doi.org/10.1037/0000474-001
Parenting Plan Evaluations: An Evidence-Informed Approach to Child Custody, by J. W. Gould and C. M. Mulchay

from teachers, therapists, and extended family members. We formulate hypotheses, test them, discard what does not hold up to scrutiny, and refine our conclusions with the methodology of a scientist and the perceptiveness of an investigator. We are not therapists in this role. We do not console, nor do we attempt to heal. Instead, we seek to investigate. We seek to understand. We seek to explain. We are social scientists who employ the scientific method to best comprehend the complexities of family systems during times of great change and stress. We visit family homes, schools, and communities to gain a more complete understanding of the best interests of the child. In this process, we become explorers of human behavior, investigators of relational dynamics, and interpreters of social science research applied to real lives. In this book, we present a comprehensive framework for conducting a parenting plan evaluation (PPE). Our approach emphasizes both the importance of the scientific process and incorporation of Bronfenbrenner's Ecological Model of Human Development. It utilizes evidence-based and evidence-informed structured data-gathering tools. It also reflects the field's shift from categorically diagnosing children and parents to a more flexible, dimensional assessment of children's and parents' behaviors. Later, we elaborate on what these things mean, define some essential terms, and explain how the volume is organized.

SCIENTIFIC PROCESS

Throughout this book, we embrace the importance of the scientific process in our evaluation work, a focus that is consistent with the needs of the court system, the admissibility of expert witness testimony, and the requirements of our ethical obligations to investigate multiple hypotheses. We emphasize the importance of transparency and thoroughness. Parenting plan evaluators are social scientists committed to the scientific process, an empirical process of gathering knowledge through observation, rigorous skepticism, hypothesis testing, analysis, and using multiple methods of independent information to confirm or disconfirm each hypothesis. Parenting plan evaluators are social scientists who employ the scientific process of data gathering and analyses to best understand the complexities of family systems during a time of great change and stress. They are field scientists who move beyond the confines of their offices to visit the family home and interview people from the child's school and community in order to best understand the psychological best interests of the child.

We agree with the intent of the historical perspective that a primary emphasis should remain on understanding the child's unique temperament, personality, strengths, and challenges, with particular attention to how parents support the child's growth and development. We expand this focus to include the myriad factors proposed in the ecological model as applied to analysis of the psychological best interest of the child.

BOOK STRUCTURE AND OVERVIEW

We identify how dimensional models allow for greater nuance in forensic opinions, acknowledging variability in personality traits, symptom severity, and contextual influences. This shift is particularly important in PPEs, where rigid classifications often fail to capture the complexity of individual and family dynamics. By moving toward dimensional assessments that emphasize behaviors rather than diagnoses, evaluators can provide courts with more precise, evidence-informed insights that better reflect the fluid nature of human behavior.

KEY CONCEPTS TO UNDERSTAND

Professionals conducting evaluations must often balance scientific research with practical judgment and real-world circumstances. The following section clarifies the distinction between evidence-based and evidence-informed approaches and how each informs evaluation practices.

Distinguishing Evidence-Based From Evidence-Informed

Throughout this book, we use two terms that need definition: evidence-based and evidence-informed. Evidence-based means "the integration of the best available research with clinical expertise in the context of patient characteristics, culture, and preferences" (American Psychological Association [APA], 2006). For example, in PPEs, an evidence-based approach uses the best available research and literature to form the methods used in the evaluation. Evidence-informed also incorporates scientific evidence, but allows for more practical experience, expert judgment, and contextual factors to guide decision making. While the APA's definition of evidence-based practice allows for clinical expertise, evidence-informed practice acknowledges that there are times in which there may not be "best available research" to guide the evaluation. Instead, the evaluator may need to rely on standards of practice or available literature. For example, an evaluator may use evidence-informed recommendations about parenting plans, adapting research-backed principles to fit the specific needs of high-conflict families. Our book is subtitled "An Evidence-Informed Approach to Child Custody" because of the complex nature of family dynamics and the lack of definitive scientific evidence on optimal parenting characteristics or child placement outcomes. The field relies on a multifaceted approach that integrates available empirical research, emerging trends, and practitioner expertise. This allows for flexibility and critical thinking in addressing the unique circumstances of each case. Unlike strictly evidence-based practices, evidence-informed evaluations can adapt to cultural backgrounds, community values, and individual preferences while still incorporating the best available knowledge. This approach acknowledges the subjective nature of interpreting family data and the need for innovation in high-conflict situations where standardized methods may fall short. Ultimately, the evidence-informed model enables parenting plan evaluators to make more nuanced and context-appropriate recommendations in the absence of clear-cut scientific guidelines.

We support the ongoing evolution of psychology, particularly in the field of forensic psychological evaluations, by emphasizing the importance of evidence-based and evidence-informed theories, models, and research. To the best of our abilities, throughout this book, we have consistently advocated for the application of scientifically grounded approaches in conducting and testifying about PPEs.

Parenting Plan Evaluations Versus Child Custody Evaluations

Unlike evidence-based and evidence-informed, the terms *parenting plan evaluations* and *child custody evaluations* are essentially interchangeable. Historically, the term "child custody evaluations" has been more common, but the field is gradually shifting to prefer "parenting plan evaluations." For instance, in 2022, while the APA released updated Child Custody Guidelines, the Association of Family and Conciliation Courts (AFCC) published revised Parenting Plan Guidelines. The AFCC replaced the term "child custody evaluations" with "parenting plan evaluations" for several reasons. One key rationale is that the term "child custody" implies possession and control rather than responsibility for a child's care (APA, 2022). Additionally, many state legislatures across the country are shifting away from the term "custody" in favor of "parenting plan," reflecting a growing emphasis on parenting access and shared responsibilities. Both the APA and AFCC guidelines center on parenting time, parental decision making, and prioritizing the child's best interests.

We will discuss the value of the scientific process as the basis of data gathering, data analysis, and opinion development. The scientific process, however, is not a test. It is a way of thinking about data gathering, data analysis, and data interpretation. Methodology identifies what we assess, not how it is assessed. The techniques and tools used to gather information in a forensic assessment include psychological tests, questionnaires, inventories, interview protocols, and observational techniques. In a parenting plan evaluation, the techniques include interviewing the parents, interviewing the child, observing the parent with the child, interviewing collaterals, psychological testing, and record review.

THE ECOLOGICAL MODEL: A FRAMEWORK FOR UNDERSTANDING FAMILIES

In order to develop a balanced and legally sound PPE, evaluators must understand *all* the systems in a child's life—from individual functioning to broad systemic influences. Thus, the underlying theory of science that guides our approach to PPEs is based on the ecological model of human development developed by Urie Bronfenbrenner (1977) and further elaborated by Jessica

Navarro and Jonathan Tudge (2023). The ecological model, shown in Figure 1, recognizes that human behavior is influenced by multiple systems that interact with each other. Families do not exist in isolation; they are embedded within broader societal, cultural, virtual, social media, and economic structures. As shown in Figure 1, the microsystem includes direct influences such as parents, siblings, and schools, while the mesosystem describes the interactions between those influences. The exosystem consists of broader social, political, and economic forces such as parental workplaces, legal institutions, and extended family, and the macrosystem represents overarching cultural values, norms, and societal expectations.

We wrote this book to honor and document both the history and evolution of the child custody field while also exploring its future through new thoughts, ideas, and evidence-informed approaches. A significant shift is occurring at multiple levels—within professional associations, case law and statutory frameworks, and peer-reviewed literature—moving from the term "child custody evaluation" to "parenting plan evaluation." As a result, we primarily use the

FIGURE 1. BRONFENBRENNER'S ECOLOGICAL MODEL

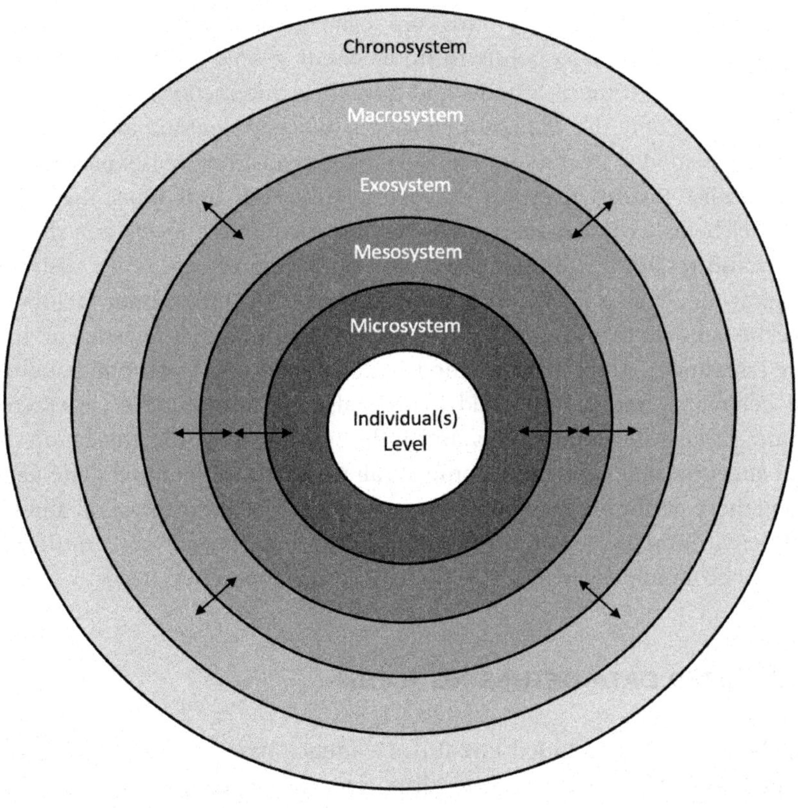

Note. From "Bronfenbrenner's Ecological Model," in Wikimedia Commons, 2020 (https://commons.wikimedia.org/wiki/File:Bronfenbrenner%27s_Ecological_Model.png). CC-BY-SA-4.0.

term "parenting plan" in this book. Historically, the term "child custody evaluation" focused on the psychological best interests of the child which were defined in psychological literature to reflect the assessment of three factors: (a) parenting attributes, (b) child developmental factors, and (c) the fit between what the parent offered the child and what the child needed. This last factor was referred to as parent–child fit. We believe that the historical focus on these three factors was too limited. As we discuss throughout the book, what is in the best interests of the child can only be understood when considering the multiple, often competing factors that affect the child, parents, family system, and other influences on the child and their family system.

When conducting a PPE, evaluators examine all levels of the ecological model. Of course, at the center of the model, the evaluator examines the child themselves—their emotional, social, and cognitive functioning and what they think and feel about their relationships with their parents, peers, siblings, etc. In the microsystem and mesosystem, the evaluator examines the parents and other close family members, and the relationships between them and with the child. In the exosystem, the evaluator assesses the child's physical and virtual communities as well as the influence of those communities on others who also influence the child. These systems would include the child's school, community, activities and friendship groups, and social media. The interactive aspect of the ecological model also points to understanding how family members and others interact with these systems and how those interactions affect the child. In the macrosystem, the evaluator considers the child's culture and history. By utilizing this model, evaluators work to avoid oversimplified explanations of family conflict. Instead of attributing dysfunction to one individual, the ecological model helps us understand how stressors at multiple levels contribute to conflict and resilience through direct and often indirect influence. Using the ecological model as a framework through which to think about factors that affect the behavior of various family members encourages a holistic and interactive assessment. The ecological model examines not just parental behaviors, child behaviors, and parent–child fit, but also the multitude of interactions within a family and interactions and influence from outside the family that might affect the child and each, some, or all members of the immediate family. Among these nonimmediate family factors that might affect the child and their family environment are community relationships and resources, cultural factors, socioeconomic pressures, and the child's developmental needs.

STRUCTURED DATA-GATHERING TOOLS

In this book, we have included a wealth of evidence-based or evidence-informed data-gathering tools, such as checklists and structured analytic techniques (SATs). These methods represent a growing trend in forensic evaluations, and they help professionals conduct systematic, transparent, and reliable assessments. Checklists are structured tools used to ensure consistency, completeness, and accuracy in data gathering by outlining key steps, criteria, or tasks that need to be completed. In professional settings, checklists help standardize procedures, minimize errors, and improve decision making. There are several advantages to the use of checklists. They can help reduce the risk of oversights and cognitive biases. They can promote systematic data collection and analysis. They can ensure consistency and transparency in decision making. SATs provide a systematic approach to decision making and data gathering that uses step-by-step methodologies to organize information. SATs reduce the influence of bias as they encourage consideration of alternative explanations. SATs also increase transparency and replicability by ensuring clear documentation of how inferences and conclusions were reached.

FROM CATEGORICAL TO DIMENSIONAL ANALYSES: A SHIFT IN FORENSIC PRACTICE

Throughout the book, we emphasize the evolving trends in the field of PPEs. One such trend is the movement from categorical to dimensional analyses of parents and children. Traditional forensic psychology relied on categorical diagnoses—placing individuals into rigid diagnostic categories based on the *Diagnostic and Statistical Manual of Mental Disorders*. However, contemporary approaches increasingly embrace dimensional analyses, recognizing that psychological characteristics exist on a spectrum rather than as binary traits. For example, as we discuss in Chapter 17, instead of labeling a parent as "narcissistic" or "not narcissistic," a dimensional perspective examines where on the narcissism spectrum a parent falls, which particular behaviors associated with narcissism affect a parent's ability to effectively parent a child, and how this influences parenting capacity, the child's perception of the parent's competence, and the ability to engage in productive coparenting communication.

This book is divided into five parts.

Part I (Chapters 1–4) lays a conceptual foundation for an evidence-informed approach to PPEs. We explore the critical shift toward scientifically rigorous forensic methods, examining both legal and scientific standards. This section also delves into key evaluation methods and addresses the increasing legal scrutiny surrounding these assessments.

Part II (Chapters 5 and 6) delves deeper into scientific standards and the application of research to individual cases. We explain the distinction between scientific and specialized knowledge, emphasizing that expert testimony must adhere to rigorous methodological standards and be clearly justified. We introduce the so-called "G2i challenge" (i.e., general-to-individual reasoning), highlighting the risks of applying research findings about broad groups to specific custody cases without careful contextual analysis. Courts often struggle with expert testimony that extrapolates from group data without demonstrating its relevance to a specific family, reinforcing the need for forensic evaluators to ensure their conclusions are both scientifically sound and case specific.

Part III (Chapters 7–9) explores how to mitigate bias in your evaluation. Bias is an inevitable human tendency, but in forensic psychology, unchecked bias can lead to significant ethical and professional concerns. Recognizing and controlling for bias requires self-awareness, consultation with colleagues, structured methodologies, and adherence to scientific principles. Common biases discussed in this part include: *confirmation bias* (the tendency to focus on information that supports preexisting beliefs while ignoring contrary evidence), *anchoring bias* (placing excessive weight on initial impressions or early data in an evaluation), and *attribution bias* (overemphasizing personal traits while underestimating situational factors in explaining behavior). Additionally, we examine the impact of sociocultural factors on family dynamics and evaluations, including race, ethnicity, language, gender identity, sexual orientation, and socioeconomic background. Recognizing and addressing these influences ensures fair and informed assessments in forensic practice.

Part IV (Chapters 10–18) covers the fundamental elements of PPEs based upon current peer-reviewed literature, professional practice guidelines, and ethical standards. These fundamental elements include parent interviews, child interviews, parent–child observations, collateral interviews, psychological testing, and records review.

Part V (Chapters 19–23) explores complex and evolving issues in child custody evaluations, including children's resistance to parental contact (i.e., parent–child contact problems), domestic violence, and parental requests to relocate.

OUR ROLE

We end this introduction chapter with a note about our role as forensic mental health professionals who work in family law. To navigate this field, one must understand not only the research and methodologies that inform best practices but also the adversarial nature of the courtroom. Unlike the collaborative atmosphere of therapy, forensic work exists within a system designed for argument, challenge, and persuasion. Attorneys advocate, judges deliberate, and evaluators must stand as neutral scientists in the midst of it all.

There is an inherent tension in this role. The families we evaluate are often desperate for an ally, for someone to validate their perspectives, their pain, and their sense of injustice. But we are not allies. We are impartial examiners who must resist the pull of advocacy and remain grounded in scientific rigor. This detachment is neither cold nor indifferent—it is a necessary safeguard against bias and emotional entanglement, ensuring that our opinions and the recommendations proffered to the court are based on evidence rather than sentiment.

This book will explore the many dimensions of forensic mental health work in family law—its challenges, its ethical dilemmas, and its profound impact on the lives of children and families. It will challenge you to think critically about your role as an evaluator, consultant, or expert witness. It will ask you to reflect on your own biases, your professional responsibility, and your moral obligation to the families you serve.

The work of forensic psychological experts takes place in a kitchen that is, indeed, very hot. The pressures are often unrelenting. The stakes are high. But for those who persist, for those who commit to the ethical pursuit of truth, the reward is immense. The work we do matters. It shapes families, influences judicial decisions, and, at its best, protects the most vulnerable among us—children who rely on the system to make sense of a world turned upside down.

To be successful in this field, one must possess a rare combination of qualities: scientific knowledge, intellectual curiosity, emotional resilience, ethical fortitude, and the ability to communicate in a clear, concise, and credible manner. One must be willing to withstand scrutiny, to defend opinions and their basis in the face of intense cross-examination, to acknowledge uncertainty where it exists, and to remain ever-vigilant against the insidious influence of bias.

Throughout this book, we will explore how to strengthen these qualities, how to refine the skills required to be an effective and ethical forensic mental health professional, and how to navigate the ever-changing landscape of family law. We will examine the scientific foundations of our work, the legal principles that shape our role, and the practical realities of working in an adversarial system.

As you embark on this work, remember that your role carries immense responsibility—not only in shaping the lives of children and families but also in upholding the integrity of the legal and psychological professions. The emotional toll of this work is real, making self-care and resilience essential to sustaining ethical and effective practice. Your words hold power, and with that power comes the duty to remain objective, evidence-based, and ever-mindful of the impact your evaluations have. This field demands both the humility to recognize when we are wrong and the courage to stand firm when we are right. Growth is continuous, and excellence requires commitment to lifelong learning, reflection, and ethical integrity.

For those who choose to enter this field, the journey is not easy, but it is meaningful. It is a journey of discovery, self-examination, intellectual challenge and excitement, and profound responsibility. And so, we begin this journey together, not as passive readers, but as explorers—searching, questioning, and discovering. For that is what it means to be a forensic mental health professional in family law. That is what it means to seek truth in a world of conflict.

Let the exploration begin.

I

CONCEPTUAL FOUNDATION FOR AN EVIDENCE-INFORMED APPROACH TO PARENTING PLAN EVALUATION

1

Daubert and the Changing Nature of Parenting Plan Evaluations

From Clinical to Forensic

Prior to the 1980s, little professional attention was focused on how to conduct a parenting plan evaluation (PPE). Most of the published literature available in the 1980s conceptualized forensic evaluations conducted for family court more like a clinical endeavor than a forensic endeavor. In 1989, the ground-breaking work of Benjamin Schutz and his colleagues was published and laid the conceptual foundation for an evidence-based approach to parenting plan evaluations (Schutz et al., 1989), although they were called "child custody evaluations" at the time. Schutz et al. were the first mental health professionals to bring the scientific process into the PPE arena. In the decades since then, important paradigm shifts have occurred in both law and mental health regarding the use of evidence-based and evidence-informed forensic psychological methods and procedures that served as a basis for trustworthy expert witness opinions (Gould, 1998, 2006). Increasingly, attorneys relied on testimony by expert witnesses in cases involving family court disputes (Dale & Gould, 2014), leading to increased attention on the selection of competent, qualified experts in family law cases.

In this chapter, we discuss how PPEs have changed in the past few decades, particularly the shift from a more clinical approach to a forensic approach. The forensic approach emphasizes the selection of data-gathering procedures that generate relevant information interpreted through the eyes of peer-reviewed literature that serves as a basis for trustworthy expert testimony. We believe it is critically important for evaluators to learn about the rules that guide the

https://doi.org/10.1037/0000474-002
Parenting Plan Evaluations: An Evidence-Informed Approach to Child Custody, by J. W. Gould and C. M. Mulchay

admissibility of their oral testimony and written reports. Mental health professionals provide services to the court within the structure of the legal system, not the other way around. That is, too often we have observed colleagues ignore or place little value on the importance of rules of evidence pertaining to the admissibility of testimony from mental health experts with the result of valuable information being excluded because of the manner in which the information was collected, organized, or presented to the court. If a therapist or an evaluator intends to provide information to the court, that information needs to be collected, organized, and presented in a manner consistent with the rules of evidence, otherwise potentially useful information will not be included in the court's deliberations. We will discuss how federal rules of evidence apply to mental health professionals who testify in PPE cases, as well as the need for standards of practice based on the best available research evidence integrated with clinical expertise.

Much of the chapter focuses on one pivotal case in 1993, *Daubert v. Merrell Dow Pharmaceuticals, Inc.*, which established several important criteria. The *Daubert* court said that judges, rather than the professional community (as had been the standard for admissible expert testimony since 1923), must act as gatekeepers to the admissibility of expert evidence. A second criterion was that the court's analyses of admissibility of expert testimony needed to follow the rules of the scientific process, a process defined by *Daubert* as examining five flexible factors. That is, *Daubert* brought into the analysis of what is admissible testimony the importance of the scientific foundation of the data gathering tools used to collect data upon which expert opinions were based. State courts have increasingly accepted the United States Supreme Court's ruling in *Daubert*; in fact, as of 2020, more than 40 states have adopted all or part of the Daubert standard.[1] We will refer to the *Daubert* case throughout this book, so it is important for readers to have a foundational understanding of this case and its enduring legacy.

---

[1]The states include Alaska (*State v. Coon*, 1999); Arkansas (*Farm Bureau Mut. Ins. Co. of Ark., Inc. v. Foote*, 2000); California (*Sargon Enters., Inc. v. Univ. of S. Cal.*, 2012; noting that California Supreme Court adopted *Daubert* as it applies to opinion testimony, except for testimony on new scientific techniques that continue to be subject to the *Kelly-Frye* general acceptance test); Colorado (*People v. Shreck*, 2001); Connecticut (*State v. Porter*, 1997); Delaware (*Tolson v. State*, 2005, p. 645); District of Columbia (*Motorola Inc. v. Murray*, 2016; adopting standards found in F.R.E. 702); Indiana (*Smith v. Yang*, 2005, p. 626; nonbinding guide for examining expert evidence); Iowa (*Ganrud v. Smith*, 1993); Louisiana (*State v. Foret*, 1993); Massachusetts (*Commonwealth v. Lanigan*, 1994); Michigan (*Gilbert v. Daimler Chrysler Corp.*, 2004, p. 408); Minnesota (*State v. Mack*, 1980); Mississippi (*Miss. Transp. Comm'n v. McLemore*, 2003); Montana (*State v. Moore*, 1994); Nebraska (*Schafersman v. Agland Coop.*, 2001); New Hampshire (*Baker Valley Lumber, Inc. v. Ingersoll-Rand Co.*, 2002); North Carolina (*State v. McGrady*, 2016); Ohio (*State v. Martens*, 1993); Oregon (*State v. O'Key*, 1995); Rhode Island (*State v. Morel*, 1996); South Dakota (*State v. Hofer*, 1994); Tennessee (*Tennessee v. Kiser*, 2009); Texas (*E.I. du Pont de Nemours & Co. v. Robinson*, 1995); Utah (*State v. Rinmasch*, 1999); Vermont (*State v. Brooks*, 1993); West Virginia (*Wilt v. Buracker*, 1994); and Wyoming (*Bunting v. Jamison*, 1999).

WHY UNDERSTANDING *DAUBERT* IS IMPORTANT

Before we explain *Daubert* and associated cases, it is important to understand why evaluators need to develop a basic understanding of relevant laws, statutes, and rules of evidence. Ethically, psychologists and psychiatrists have an affirmative responsibility to become familiar with the laws, standards, rules, and precedents that govern their participation in the legal system.

The Specialty Guidelines for Forensic Psychology's Guideline 2.04 addresses the importance of "Knowledge of the Legal System and the Legal Rights of Individuals" (American Psychological Association [APA], 2013b). The guideline reads as follows:

> Forensic practitioners recognize the importance of obtaining a fundamental and reasonable level of knowledge and understanding of the legal and professional standards, laws, rules, and precedents that govern their participation in legal proceedings and that guide the impact of their services on service recipients.
>
> Forensic practitioners aspire to manage their professional conduct in a manner that does not threaten or impair the rights of affected individuals. They may consult with, and refer others to, legal counsel on matters of law. Although they do not provide formal legal advice or opinions, forensic practitioners may provide information about the legal process to others based on their knowledge and experience. They strive to distinguish this from legal opinions, however, and encourage consultation with attorneys as appropriate. (p. 9)

The APA's (2022) Child Custody Guidelines make a similar point in Guideline 4 that addresses competence. Guideline 4 reads, in part as follows:

> Psychologists strive to gain an evolving and up-to-date understanding of the following: parenting; family dynamics and the child's place therein; child and family psychopathology; separation and divorce stress; impact of abuse, relationship conflict, and separation on children; adult development and pathology; forensic psychological assessment; relevant laws and regulations; and the specialized child custody literature (as addressed in Guideline 5). (p.7)

The Association of Family and Conciliation Courts (AFCC; 2022) Parenting Plan Guidelines devote an entire section of their guidelines to outlining evaluators' responsibilities that includes a working understanding of the law, legal system, and family court:

- Evaluators should have sufficient working knowledge to function effectively within the legal system. They are not expected to have the same degree and depth of legal knowledge as lawyers and judges. As statutes, court rules, and case law change, evaluators should keep their legal knowledge current.

- Evaluators should have a working knowledge of the governing laws, regulations, and procedures in their jurisdictions and understand the legal standards regarding the central issues in the evaluation.

- Evaluators should understand the legal criteria for original determination of a parenting plan, criteria for modifications of a parenting plan, use of parenting plan evaluations, jurisdictional requirements concerning qualifications of evaluators, and legal requirements governing the evaluation process in the jurisdiction in which they work.

- Evaluators should have a fundamental and reasonable level of knowledge and understanding of the legal rights of those whom they are evaluating and others who may be affected by the evaluative process or work product.

Section 2.2 of the Knowledge of the Law section addresses working within legal parameters. The AFCC Guideline reads as follows:

> Evaluators should seek consultation when necessary to understand governing legal parameters. If formal clarification from the court is necessary, evaluators should ensure that all parties or their attorneys are included in the request for clarification. Courts, judicial officers, and lawyers help ensure that evaluators work within those parameters by framing the purpose and scope of provisions of appointment orders or agreements to include information about the governing legal standards, and by detailing requirements for the evaluation process in the appointment order or agreement. (p. 12)

Gould has often written about the importance of understanding the rules, statutes, standards, and precedents in the legal system in terms of learning how to play in the court's sandbox (Ackerman et al., 2019; Gould, 1998, 2006; Gould & Martindale, 2007). When MHPs are invited into the legal system, we have a responsibility to learn and play by the rules that govern the legal system. It is their sandbox. They can exclude us when we misbehave.

Understanding the rules that govern how we create our work product to meet the rules governing the admissibility of scientific evidence begins with understanding your jurisdiction's rules of evidence that address qualifications and admissibility of expert witness testimony.

OVERVIEW OF *DAUBERT*

The *Daubert v. Merrell Dow Pharmaceuticals, Inc.* (1993) case is a landmark U.S. Supreme Court decision that established critical guidelines for the admissibility of expert testimony in federal courts. This case fundamentally reshaped the evaluation of scientific evidence and expert opinions presented during legal proceedings. The case involved a product liability claim where the plaintiffs, Jason Daubert and his family, alleged that prenatal exposure to the drug Bendectin, manufactured by Merrell Dow Pharmaceuticals, caused Jason's birth defects. The plaintiffs presented expert testimony based on unpublished studies, animal research, and reanalysis of existing data. However, Merrell Dow Pharmaceuticals moved to exclude this testimony, arguing that it was not grounded in scientifically valid methodology.

The trial court ruled in favor of Merrell Dow, citing the Frye standard (a precedent requiring scientific evidence to gain general acceptance in its field). The 9th Circuit upheld this ruling, which led the Dauberts to appeal to the

Supreme Court. The 1993 *Daubert* decision instructed federal trial courts to act as gatekeepers for expert evidence and to apply a set of flexible criteria to the procedures purported to have been used.

Daubert **Factors and** ***Daubert*** **Challenges**

The *Daubert* court identified five flexible factors for the court to consider when determining if expert testimony is reliable and admissible. The notion that the *Daubert* factors are flexible reflected the court's recognition that other factors might be identified in other cases as useful to the determination of admissibility of scientific evidence. The original five *Daubert* factors are as follows:

1. *Testability*: whether the expert's theory can be (and has been) tested and can be falsified.
2. *Peer review*: whether the expert's theory or technique has been subjected to peer review and publication.
3. *Error rate*: the known or potential rate of error of the technique or theory.
4. *Standards and controls*: whether the expert has maintained standards and controls for their testing.
5. *General acceptance*: whether there is general acceptance of the expert's methodology within the scientific community (*Daubert v. Merrell Dow Pharmaceuticals, Inc.*, 1993, pp. 593–594).

The Supreme Court in *Daubert* identified other relevant factors that may be applied by the trial court as part of its gatekeeping function: (a) that there be "evidentiary reliability," (b) that the expert's testimony "pertain to 'scientific knowledge,'" (c) that the "evidence or testimony 'assist the trier of fact to understand the evidence or to determine a fact in issue'" (relevance), and (d) "whether that reasoning or methodology properly can be applied to the facts in issue" (*Daubert v. Merrell Dow Pharmaceuticals, Inc.*, 1993, pp. 590–594).

Since the *Daubert* case, the term *Daubert challenge* has been used to describe when an attorney makes a motion to a judge to exclude unqualified expert witness testimony from a trial. A party can file a *Daubert* motion before or during a trial. The fundamental purpose of a *Daubert* challenge is to ensure that expert testimony presented in court is both reliable and relevant. The challenge acts as a quality control measure by filtering out unreliable or irrelevant expert opinions, thereby supporting the integrity of the legal system. *Daubert* challenges empower judges to act as gatekeepers of scientific evidence. The judge scrutinizes the methodology and underlying scientific principles of expert testimony. The intention is to exclude from evidence the introduction of pseudoscientific or unreliable expert testimony that might otherwise mislead the court. Of course, the fly in the ointment in family court is that it is often the same judge who hears both the *Daubert* challenge and the family case law.

Analytical Gap

The Supreme Court has explicitly indicated that the list of *Daubert* factors is flexible and that these or other criteria may be used by the trial courts to address the scientific validity of the evidence or testimony. In *Daubert v. Merrell Dow Pharmaceuticals, Inc.* the court emphasized that the trial judge's gatekeeping inquiry should focus on the reliability of the expert's reasoning process, stating that "the focus, of course, must be solely on principles and methodology, not on the conclusions that they generate" (509 U.S. 579, 595, 1993). This statement has sometimes been misunderstood by attorneys and psychologists as meaning that courts may not examine the expert's conclusions. In fact, the Court later clarified in *General Electric Co. v. Joiner* that judges may exclude expert testimony when there is "too great an analytical gap between the data and the opinion proffered" (522 U.S. 136, 146, 1997). Thus, while *Daubert* directs courts to evaluate the reliability of an expert's methods rather than the correctness of the ultimate opinion, subsequent case law makes clear that courts may consider whether the expert's conclusions logically follow from the underlying data and methodology.

An *analytical gap* is when the data and the expert's opinion are too far apart—in other words, when the expert's conclusion is too far of an analytic jump from the data in the report. If a court determines that there is an analytical gap, then they may not allow the expert's opinion to be admitted as evidence. Alternatively, if an attorney does not agree with the evaluator's interpretation, the difference in their interpretations of the data should not be used as the basis of a *Daubert* challenge; rather, the attorney's interpretation of the data should be the focus of their cross-examination of the expert.

Determination of the size of the analytic gap appears to be a subjective determination by the court. A primary question is whether the expert opinions are based upon reasonable inference drawn from the data. To the best of our knowledge, there has been no legal definition of the manner in which the court determines an analytic gap other than judicial judgment.

Similarly, there is no discussion in PPE literature addressing the definition or meaning of the analytic gap between data and opinion. For example, how does an evaluator determine what is and what is not too wide of an analytic gap? Although most literature describing the *Daubert* concept of analytic gap acknowledges that the trier of fact is the one who decides the size of the gap, there is no consensus in PPE literature to guide an evaluator in attempting to identify when the gap between data and opinion is useful and when that gap is too wide.

Despite the lack of consensus on what constitutes an analytical gap, there are steps evaluators can take to avoid it. To avoid analytical gap, the proponent of an expert's testimony holds the burden of demonstrating to the court that the expert opinions are relevant and reliable. Evaluators should understand that this concept places the burden upon the evaluator to show the reliability of the methods and procedures used to develop the data upon which expert opinions are based, how the gathered data are relevant to the issues at bar, and that there is a clear relationship between the expressed opinions and the data upon which those opinions are based.

Expert Testimony Versus Advocacy

Daubert also explicitly held that the goal of a trial court should be to make a definitive decision about the issues in a particular case and not, as the scientific community may attempt, to reach a consensus on an issue. Attorneys on the respective sides in a litigation might seek experts who support one side or the other of a psychological issue rather than presenting the available evidence demonstrating the lack of consensus in the psychological literature.

Experts who testify about one side of an issue become advocates, taking sides in the litigation. Advocating for research that supports only one side in a litigation is very different from citing the strengths and weaknesses of particular research findings and then testifying about why one set of research data is a better fit for the facts in the case at hand. Expert testimony that advocates for a litigation rather than advocating for the quality of research serving as a basis for an opinion runs the risk of misleading the court.

The scientific approach of presenting scientific evidence for the court's consideration is to provide interpretations of data from multiple perspectives. Psychologists have an ethical obligation to examine data from multiple perspectives and to seek reasonable alternative explanations of those data. Experts must be prepared to explain why one interpretation (or hypothesis) has greater support in this particular case than other explanations. The role of the evaluator is to provide the court with an analysis of the data gathered during the evaluation, an integration of those data with relevant professional and scientific literature, an explanation of how different rival hypotheses were considered, and a clear articulation of the basis for the expert opinion.

To be admissible, all expert testimony—whether scientific or nonscientific—must comply with *rules of evidence* that require the expert testimony to be reliable, relevant, and based upon a reliable foundation.

The Rules of Evidence

The Federal Rules of Evidence (FREs) are a set of rules that regulate the evidence that can be presented and considered in civil and criminal proceedings in federal courts. First established in 1975 and amended several times since then, FREs are designed to ensure that the evidence used by a judge or jury is reliable, relevant, and fair. Before delving into specific rules that apply to PPEs, we must first distinguish between a fact witness and an expert witness.

Any mental health professional who testifies under oath is considered a witness. Mental health professionals might play two different roles when asked to testify in court. One role is as a fact witness and the other role is as an expert witness. Most of our book (including our discussion of the *Daubert* case) pertains to testimony proffered to the court by an expert witness.

Mental health professionals need to be familiar with at least two FREs addressing expert testimony. Rule 702 addresses the qualifications of an expert and Rule 703 addresses the basis of expert testimony:

> **Rule 702.** Testimony by Expert Witnesses: A witness who is qualified as an expert by knowledge, skill, experience, training, or education may testify in the form of an opinion or otherwise if the proponent demonstrates to the court that it is more likely than not that
>
> (a) the expert's scientific, technical, or other specialized knowledge will help the trier of fact to understand the evidence or to determine a fact in issue;
> (b) the testimony is based on sufficient facts or data;
> (c) the testimony is the product of reliable principles and methods; and
> (d) the expert's opinion reflects a reliable application of the principles and methods to the facts of the case. (Federal Rules of Evidence, 2024, pp. 15–16)

Rule 702 was amended effective December 1, 2023, to fix widespread misapplication of the Rule by courts. The change requires that the proponent of expert testimony must demonstrate "to the court that it is more likely than not" that the rule's three admissibility requirements (Rule 702(b)–(d)) are met.

> **Rule 703.** Bases of an Expert's Opinion Testimony: An expert may base an opinion on facts or data in the case that the expert has been made aware of or personally observed. If experts in the particular field would reasonably rely on those kinds of facts or data in forming an opinion on the subject, they need not be admissible for the opinion to be admitted. But if the facts or data would otherwise be inadmissible, the proponent of the opinion may disclose them to the jury only if their probative value in helping the jury evaluate the opinion substantially outweighs their prejudicial effect. (Federal Rules of Evidence, 2024, p. 16)

In contrast, FREs also define the role of a fact or lay witness, which is someone who has personal knowledge of information that might be helpful to the court. FRE 701 (and the state jurisdictions that have similar rules of civil and criminal procedure) defines the role of a fact or lay witness:

> **Rule 701.** Opinion Testimony by Lay Witnesses: If a witness is not testifying as an expert, testimony in the form of an opinion is limited to one that is
>
> (a) rationally based on the witness's perception;
> (b) helpful to clearly understanding the witness's testimony or to determining a fact in issue; and
> (c) not based on scientific, technical, or other specialized knowledge within the scope of Rule 702. (Federal Rules of Evidence, 2024, p. 15)

Daubert and its progeny, as well as their respective state equivalents, have viewed the requirement of reliability for scientific evidence to extend to all expert testimony, involving technical and other specialized knowledge (e.g., *Kumho Tire Co. v. Carmichael,* 1999; *State v. Giese,* 2014; *State v. McGrady,* 2016).

LINGERING CONCERNS ABOUT *DAUBERT'S* APPLICATION TO PARENTING PLAN EVALUATIONS

It remains debatable whether PPEs are classified as scientific evidence or as technical and other specialized knowledge. The *Daubert* court did not consider this distinction, and subsequent U.S. Supreme Court decisions have not drawn a red line between hard science and social science evidence.

Some states, such as Texas and Wisconsin, have drawn a distinction between hard science and social science evidence (e.g., *Gammill v. Jack Williams Chevrolet, Inc.*, 1998). Thus, in nonscientific cases, such as a case involving the social sciences, these courts have clearly found that it is impossible to set out specific criteria for evaluating the reliability of expert testimony and that, ultimately, the trial court has the discretion to determine how to assess reliability (*Kroger Co. v. Betancourt*, 1999, p. 362). Other states, however, have not drawn a distinction between hard and social science evidence (see *State v. Kandutsch*, 2011; *State v. McGrady*, 2016). North Carolina's *McGrady* ruling suggests the application of *Daubert* criteria to both "soft" and "hard" scientific testimony.

Expert testimony must be based upon the scientific and professional knowledge of the discipline and not junk science offered to the court by the witness. *Daubert*, its progeny, and state equivalents have moved away from expert opinion testimony based upon the *ipse dixit* of the expert.[2] Psychological expert testimony must be based upon the professional and scientific knowledge of the discipline, not based upon the psychologist's unsupported or pseudoscientific opinions (Lilienfeld et al., 2012).

Conclusions and methodology are not entirely distinct from one another. Trained experts commonly extrapolate from existing data. But nothing in either *Daubert* or the FRE requires a district court to admit opinion evidence that is connected to existing data only by the ipse dixit of the expert. A court may conclude that there is simply too great an analytical gap between the data and the opinion proffered.

The concern is that expert testimony based on personal opinion and cultural myths often have masqueraded as science (Gould, 2006). Under *Daubert*, the testimony of the witness is to be "more than subjective belief or unsupported speculation" (*Daubert v. Merrell Dow Pharmaceuticals, Inc.*, 1993, p. 590). The Wisconsin Court of Appeals wrote, "No matter how good 'experts' credentials' may be, they are `not permitted to speculate'" (*State v. Giese*, 2014, p. 691)·

Testimony proffered by parenting plan evaluators is being challenged because of increased concerns over the poor quality of their reports (Feinberg

[2]*Ipse Dixit* is Latin for "he himself said it." In 1997, the U.S. Supreme Court recognized the problem of "opinion evidence which is connected to existing data only by the *ipse dixit* of an expert" (*General Elec. Co. v. Joiner*, 1997, p. 137). Likewise, the Texas Supreme Court has held "a claim will not stand or fall on the mere *ipse dixit* of a credentialed witness" (*Burrow v. Arce*, 1999, p. 235).

& Gould, 2012)[3] and the continued masquerading of personal or idiosyncratic ideas about parenting under the guise of scientific knowledge (Gould, 2006). Concern about the scientific integrity of PPEs and subsequent testimony is, arguably, critical in family law matters because the future of children is at stake (Ackerman et al., 2019; Gould & Mulchay, 2023).

There is a growing concern among attorneys and judges about the quality of PPE reports and the expert testimony provided by these evaluators. Attorneys and judges have voiced their frustrations with the inconsistent and poor quality of the information found in PPE reports, the lack of investigative rigor displayed by evaluators, and the illogical or unsupportable conclusions that are poorly tied to the data in the report (Gould & Dale, 2022).

Over the past 2 decades, legal challenges to the admissibility of PPEs are increasingly raised. Some of those challenges are based on evaluators deviating from statutory standards applied to PEEs, such as those articulated in California Family Court Rule 5.220 and Texas Family Code §107.105(b). Other challenges are based on the application of factors articulated in *Daubert* and its state equivalents to the use of psychological testing, forensic interviewing of children, and other data-gathering procedures used in forensic assessment. Still, other challenges include arguments highlighting deviations from statutory standards and deviations from ethical requirements set by both state licensing laws and national professional associations.

Among the challenges raised by colleagues about the usefulness of PPEs include questions about the reliability of methods and procedures used in gathering data during an evaluation (Garber & Simon, 2018; Gould & Posthuma, 2017; Neal et al., 2019; Rappaport et al., 2018; Turkat, 2016, 2021), the influence of various types of bias in the assessment process (Garber, 2020b; Maldonado, 2017; Milchman, 2018; Neal & Grisso, 2014), and the inconsistent quality of PPEs (Gould & Dale, 2022).

The inconsistent quality of PPEs has borne a cottage industry of consultants to attorneys focused on providing reviews of PPEs to assist the attorney in preparing for trial or to assist the court through oral testimony in understanding the strengths and deficiencies of an evaluation (Dale et al., 2021; Gould, 2018; Gould & Dale, 2022; Wittmann, 2022). Many of these retained experts hired to review the work of others analyze the PPE report through the lens of the standard of practice in PPEs. Although some respected colleagues have challenged the assertion that there is a standard of practice in regarding the methodology to be followed when conducting PPEs, there is an abundance of peer-reviewed literature supporting the assertion that there is professional consensus about what defines the methodology best suited for use in a PPE (Ackerman et al. 2021; Ackerman & Pritzl, 2011; Bow, 2006; Bow & Quinnell, 2001, 2002).

---

[3]Ms. Feinberg began the workshop describing the history of PPEs, the initial support from the courts and attorney for PPEs conducted by mental health professionals, and the current disappointment in the quality of parenting plan evaluation work products.

Methodology is defined as the specific independent areas of data collection that include developing specific questions to guide the evaluation, multiple interviews with parents, interviews with children, interviews with and document review of information obtained from collateral informants, use of psychological testing, and direct observation of parent–child interactions. We will discuss aspects of these differences throughout the book.

DEFINING STANDARD OF PRACTICE

Limited guidance is available to forensic mental health practitioners about what constitutes minimally satisfactory practice in the forensic mental health assessment arena (Heilbrun, DeMatteo, et al., 2008). In the area of PPE, there appears to be a professional consensus about what procedures are recommended for use in PPE (Ackerman et al., 2021; Ackerman & Pritzl, 2011; Bow, 2006; Bow & Quinnell, 2001, 2002). Data to support the assertion that there is a professional consensus defining a standard of practice comes from empirical studies examining what procedures are used by evaluators across the country (Ackerman et al., 2021; Ackerman & Pritzl, 2011; Bow, 2006; Bow & Quinnell, 2001, 2002), professional practice guidelines published by national associations (American Academy of Matrimonial Lawyers [AAML], 2011; APA, 2010; AFCC, 2022; Herman & AACAP, 1997), statutes, and case law. The professional consensus about procedures refers to specific independent areas of data gathering. Independent areas of data gathering include parent interviews, child interviews, psychological testing, collateral interviews, record review, and parent–child observations. Said differently, there is professional consensus about where evaluators turn to gather information sufficiently robust and diverse to allow for trustworthy expert opinions. There is no professional consensus about *how* the evaluator collects information from within each of these independent areas of data gathering. The professional consensus tells evaluators where to seek information but does not address how to collect the data other than emphasizing the use of reliable procedures when possible.

Professional standards of practice are determined by the field itself (Heilbrun, Grisso, & Goldstein, 2008). They reflect the consensus within a field. Professional standards of practice may occur informally when a particular practice becomes embraced by the general community of practitioners in that field or more formally through the development and dissemination of specific professional practice guidelines (Ackerman et al., 2019).

Professional standards of practice may reflect the industry standard, describing the customary ways of doing things in a particular field or as a set of aspirational best practice ideas in a particular field (Ackerman et al., 2019). In the field of PPE, the peer-reviewed literature reflects a consensus about the methods used by most evaluators when they conduct their evaluations (the industry standard prong of the professional standards of practice), and the professional practice guidelines promulgated by national associations reflect the consensus among the national organization about best practice. These professional practice guidelines include the APA's Guidelines for Child Custody Evaluations in Family Law Proceedings, the AFCC's Parenting Plan Guidelines, the American Academy of Child and Adolescent Psychiatry's Custody Parameters, and the American Academy of Matrimonial Lawyers' Child Custody Evaluation Standards (AAML, 2011; APA, 2022; AFCC, 2022; Herman & AACAP, 1997).

Survey data of parenting plan evaluators participating in research reveal a general consensus about the use of data gathering procedures in PPEs. Data gathering procedures include, but are not limited to, multiple interviews with parents, interviews with children, direct observation of parent–child interactions, record review, collateral interviews, and psychological testing when necessary (Ackerman et al., 2021; Ackerman & Pritzl, 2011; Bow, 2006; Bow & Quinnell, 2001, 2002).

Peer-reviewed articles and books describe a consensus in the literature about what most evaluators utilize when conducting a PPE (see Ackerman et al., 2019, for summary of articles and books). The term associated with this approach to PPE is the *forensic model* (Martindale & Gould, 2004).

It seems reasonable to conclude, therefore, that practitioners within the field of PPE have reached a general consensus of what methods and procedures should be included in a competently conducted CCE. This consensus defines the professional standard of practice in the field of PPE.

Guidance is limited about what constitutes minimally satisfactory practice in evaluation review[4] and the concomitant task of consulting with attorneys when assisting in their preparation for a family court trial (Dale & Gould, 2014; Dale et al., 2021; Gould & Dale, 2022; Gould & Nolletti, 2015). No studies have investigated how forensic mental health professionals conduct their reviews of colleagues' work products. While several articles discuss how such work *ought* to be done (Ackerman & Gould, 2015; Baerger et al., 2002; Galatzer-Levy et al., 2002, 2009; Gould, 2018; Gould & Dale, 2022; Gould & Martindale, 2013; Gould & Mulchay, 2023; McCurley et al., 2006), no published empirical research describing survey data examining how review work *is* being done in the field.

A consensus exists in the peer-reviewed articles addressing how to conduct a review in which a reviewer provides an independent analysis of another person's PPE, including analyses of the methods and procedures used in the evaluation. A reviewer may wish to examine *what* procedures were utilized and *how* they were utilized. A reviewer may wish to explore the relationship between the collected data and the expressed opinions. A reviewer may also wish to examine the evaluator's use of professional and scientific literature of the discipline as a basis for expert opinions (Dale et al., 2021; Gould & Dale, 2022; Gould & Martindale, 2008; Gould et al., 2011).

Among the unresolved questions in the literature is whether one hired to review and analyze another person's PPE report should be permitted to review materials to which the court-appointed evaluator did not have access (Gould &

[4]An evaluation review, or a work-product review, is defined as an analysis of another person's forensic psychological report.

Dale, 2022). Another unresolved question is whether the retained reviewer should be permitted to gather new information that was *not* part of the information provided to or obtained by the evaluator whose work is being reviewed (Gould & Dale, 2022).

Some scholars argue that it is appropriate for a reviewer to examine information not provided to the original evaluator (W. G. Austin et al., 2011), while others argue that a review and analysis of another evaluator's evaluation should be limited to that which was available and provided to the evaluator (Gould et al., 2011). One case addressed this issue and found that a reviewer who gathers new information—that is, information not gathered by the evaluator during the evaluation process—moved from a reviewer to an evaluator (i.e., *Grossman v. State Board of Psychology*, 2003). In *Grossman*, the Pennsylvania Board of Psychology found, in part, that psychologists retained to conduct work-product reviews ought not gather new information because gathering new data moves the reviewer into the activities of an evaluator.

We believe reviewers focus on the information provided to the evaluator, whether or not the evaluator reviewed the material that was provided for review. When a reviewer gathers new information, the reviewer moves from activities associated with that of a reviewer to those activities associated with that of an evaluator because now new information has been gathered. Once a reviewer moves into an evaluation activity, the now-evaluator must conduct a full evaluation in order to gather sufficient information upon which to base an expert opinion.

Distinguishing Standard of Practice From Standard of Care

The distinction between professional standard of practice and professional standard of care often is poorly understood. Professional standard of practice is defined by formal and informal means through development and dissemination of specific professional practice guidelines and general consensus in the peer-reviewed literature.

Professional standard of care, on the other hand, is a legal concept. Standards of care are "judicial determinations that establish minimally acceptable standards of professional conduct in the context of specific disputes" (Heilbrun, Grisso, & Goldstein, 2008). A professional standard of care requires mandatory compliance by those providing the care. Breaching the professional standard of care exposes a forensic mental health professional to liability and monetary damages. In contrast, breaching the professional standard of practice may result in a sanction or disciplinary action by a licensing board but not civil liability (Heilbrun, Grisso, & Goldstein, 2008).

Distinguishing Standard of Practice From Best Practices

We have come to believe that basing a professional standard of practice in PPEs on aspirational "best practice" guidelines sets at a higher level of practice than that which were intended by the concept of a standard of practice. Standard of practice should define a minimum level of competence. Minimal practice standards of practice ought not be defined by the professional practice guidelines and literature describing best practice. That is, what is minimal competency cannot be defined by what is best practice. This is not to say that evaluators should not aim for the highest possible aspirational goals in their forensic psychological activities, as discussed in the beginning of this chapter but there are circumstances when "good enough" might need to suffice.

This is a change of perspective for our first author. In previous writings, Gould believed strongly in using professional practice guidelines to define minimal practice standards (Gould et al., 2011). As he has participated in PPE cases across the country, he has observed the enormous variation in what evaluators do when conducting PPEs.

Both separately and together, we have observed significant variation in report quality, yet within any one specific jurisdiction, courts often have come to rely on evaluations that are very different from evaluations based upon best practice aspirational guidelines or model standards. Our collective experience has taught us that many evaluations guided by minimal practice guidelines often provide useful information to the court. As a judge once challenged, "Not everyone can buy a Mercedes. Sometimes a Volkswagen is just fine."

Despite our belief that accepting minimal practice as satisfactory is an appropriate metric, we recognize that there are many factors involved in conducting PPEs. There are some jurisdictions in which the local evaluators are doing their best to assist the court but have not attended the types of training to provide a more sophisticated basis for their forensic work. There are other jurisdictions in which there are profound restrictions on funds available to pay for an evaluation or jurisdictions in which court have opted only for psychological evaluations of parents.

Operating independently, each of us has been involved in several cases in which we have been asked to review a colleague's PPE report that was part of a malpractice action. In those cases, the alleged injured party argued that the evaluator's work was not consistent with the standard of practice in the PPE field. As we began to look at defining the standard of practice in each case, we realized that there were at least two different ways to answer the question, "What is the standard of practice in PPEs?"

One answer was based upon peer-reviewed literature, peer-reviewed survey data, published texts, professional practice guidelines and model standards, and workshop presentations. Such a level of analysis helped to define the professional standard of practice at a national level. Another answer, more commonly requested by attorneys with whom we have worked, was, "What is the standard of practice *in this community*?" The answer to this question involved examining how PPEs were conducted within a particular community. Lively discussions about how to define "community" often occupied our time, but the general approach was to review as many local reports as possible to determine what most people in that local community did when conducting PPEs. Our conclusion was that there are many different levels of quality reflected in community standards of practice and that many of those local standards of practice were viewed as acceptable by the local bar and bench.

Aspirational best practice guidelines are intended to define the highest goals of a profession, defining the ceiling of professionally responsible and competent practice. In contrast, a professional standard of practice should provide guidance about minimally satisfactory practice. Heilbrun, Grisso, and Goldstein (2008) define professional standard of practice as setting the bar at establishing a minimally satisfactory level of practice. A minimally satisfactory level of practice defines a floor, a minimal level of competently conducted professional practice. A minimally satisfactory level of practice cannot be defined by a profession's best practice aspirations. The best practice aspirational goals set the ceiling of competently conducted practice. Those who engage in providing services to the court need to strive toward those aspirational goals. At the same time, there needs to be recognition, or perhaps acceptance, that satisfactory minimal practice is not the same as best practice yet may be acceptable in many jurisdictions and may provide useful information to the court to assist in its decision making.

EVIDENCE-BASED PRACTICE AND *DAUBERT*

As the field establishes a standard of practice for PPEs, a key component should be the application of evidence-based practice (EBP). EBP should be viewed as a requirement in *Daubert* jurisdictions (Glancy & Saini, 2009). Both *Daubert* and EBP involve applying the most reliable and valid methods of data collection available and analyses as a basis of competently formulated opinions. The term EBP grew out of Sackett and colleagues' notion of *evidence-based medicine* (Sackett et al., 1996). They suggested that clinical practice needs to be based upon the best available external clinical evidence drawn from systematic research in a "conscientious, explicit, and judicious" manner (Sackett et al., 1996, p. 71).

Glancy and Saini distinguished between evidence-based guidelines and EBP. Evidence-based guidelines promulgate practice procedures, policies, and regulations to guide competent practice within a particular profession. Guidelines might provide general overviews of practice but do not "integrate knowledge with practice wisdom, client preferences, and organizational factors, including consideration of environmental strengths and barriers, which may contribute to decision making" (Glancy & Saini, 2009, p. 439).

EBP utilizes scientific research that is viewed as the most credible empirical research upon which to rely when engaged in decision making about a patient or client. Practitioners who rely on EBP attend to studies that have been replicated, not merely a single study. "The critical question concerning EBP is not whether evidence should play a role in forensic decision making but in how to establish this role efficiently and effectively" (Glancy & Saini, 2009, p. 439). At the root of EBP is the professional's commitment to "identifying and promoting methods and procedures that are efficient and effective, while discarding those that are ineffective and potentially harmful" (Glancy & Saini, 2009, p. 439). In a forensic context, EBP requires the individual who is presenting information to the court to be balanced and neutral while placing great weight on scientifically rigorous methods and procedures.

The focus in both EBP and expert testimony is that the basis of expert opinions flow from the best available evidence integrated with the expert's experience and expertise. Lack of reliable scientific findings must be presented to the court to properly advise the court of potential threats to the trustworthiness of the findings upon which the expert opinion is based.

EBP and admissibility of expert testimony need to embrace transparency so that the court can make an informed judgment of the quality of opinions drawn from the data. The expert should inform the court of the strengths and limitations of the evidence presented. "Within the best available evidence framework, *Daubert* seems to endorse EBP because of its focus on the most valid methods of collecting evidence for a particular problem or question and its emphasis on a clear and transparent appraisal process for assessing the scientific validity of the evidence" (Glancy & Saini, 2009, p. 440).

SKILLS NECESSARY FOR COMPETENT PRACTICE

A standard of practice for PPEs should include not only the knowledge base for competent practice but also the necessary qualities and skills. DeMatteo and colleagues have outlined seven fundamental domains that are considered the basis for competent practice (DeMatteo et al., 2009, 2013, 2016). These include core knowledge about forensic psychology, research design as well as conducting research, legal knowledge integrated with forensic psychology work, ethics, and training in clinical forensic work (DeMatteo et al., 2009; Goldenson et al., in press).

An examination of training models in forensic psychology revealed that there is significant variation among master's and doctoral level training programs (DeMatteo et al., 2013). Whether it is limitations in graduate school training, limitations in continuing education programs, limitations in licensing requirements, or a lack of competency based assessments about both general and specific competencies in the areas in which practitioners intend to practice, what is clear is that there are some forensic mental health examiners who do not have the minimum necessary skills to produce reliable work products and trustworthy testimony (Goldenson et al., in press).

The list of skills needed to develop professional competence in PPEs might be daunting to some who are entering the field, but there is an exciting challenge in learning from each of these information silos, integrating information between and across information silos, and achieving a competence that leads to assisting courts in their efforts to help families in conflict. One area of competence to be mastered includes application of the principles of forensic mental health assessment and behavioral science research. Another area to be mastered involves integrating clinical training with forensic training. A third area focuses on testimonial competence and report writing. A fourth area of mastery is understanding and applying ethical standards and guidelines. A fifth area includes knowing jurisdiction specific statutes, rules of evidence and civil procedures, and case law decisions relevant to the issues before the court. A final area of mastery is learning how to engage in interdisciplinary cooperation and communication with attorneys and judges. Each of these areas of professional mastery provide opportunities for professional growth, development, and fulfillment not often found in other endeavors.

APPLYING PSYCHOLOGICAL SKILLS IN PARENTING PLAN EVALUATIONS

The good news is that psychologists already have foundational skills to build upon for competent PPE practice. As clinicians and scientists, psychologists are already trained to gather and interpret data, whether from behavioral observations of parent–child interactions; interviews with parents, children, or collateral informants; results from psychological testing; past and current records addressing relevant data from third party sources; or other areas of independent data collection. The data gathered and analyzed may relate to abilities, attitudes, thoughts, feelings, behavior, and relationships. The evaluator applies this skill by organizing the data from disparate sources into a meaningful whole, which may then be presented as part of the psychological information provided to the court in its legal inquiry. In addition, psychologists are trained to be able to elaborate on those aspects of the functioning of each parent that relate to the unique needs of each child and the fit between the parenting competencies of each parent and the fit of those competencies with the psychological needs of each child.

However, applying these foundational skills in a legal context requires a certain restraint. Ethically, psychologists must limit how far beyond the data they go in predicting the future and must clearly distinguish between conclusions that are based on hard data and those that are not (APA, 2017a, Principle B, Standard 9.01(b), 9.06).

A different way to address the same question is to focus on the degree to which the underlying data support opinions proffered by the expert (in *Daubert* terminology, whether there is an analytical gap). If the question is about the individual's current psychological functioning, existing psychological tests permit a number of inferences to be developed from test data. These data points provide the basis from which an evaluator might develop hypotheses about the individual's psychological and emotional well-being. Examples would include statements regarding an individual's emotional functioning as inferred from the interpretation of the Minnesota Multiphasic Personality Inventory (MMPI), Second Edition; MMPI-2 Restructured Form; or MMPI, Third Edition scores. More difficult are questions regarding the presence of a particular state or condition (e.g., a formal diagnosis of a mental disorder) because the criteria for making many diagnoses are less explicit than are test results; that is, the psychologist must infer rather than simply report. In addition, there are considerable concerns about making inferences about an individual based solely upon inferences from psychological test scores. Experts drawing reliable conclusions about an individual's functioning in the real world based solely upon psychological test results have been discussed in the psychology and law literature since the 1980s under the terms "social framework evidence" and "diagnostic evidence" (Monahan & Walker, 1988, 1991). These concepts will be discussed later in the book.

Additionally, responses to questions involving potential dangerousness to self or others or questions asking about predictions of future parenting quality are complicated. Here, the inference is clouded by the substantial influence that environmental factors can have on how an individual responds to future situations. The quality of possible reliable predictions is, at best, equivocal and must be made with a variety of qualifying statements. In other words, the psychologist should not claim certainty about these tenuous opinions (Weiner, 1989).

Equally important, psychologists and other experts must qualify statements by identifying whether the basis for a conclusion is evidence-based, evidence-informed, literature-based, or based on their clinical judgment and experience. As we discuss more fully in Chapters 5 and 6, expert forensic psychological testimony should be based upon the professional and scientific knowledge of the discipline. For example, testimony about whether a parent engages in moral behavior is most likely outside the scope of psychological testimony. Testimony based upon common sense is not expert testimony, precisely because common sense knowledge is not beyond the knowledge of layman. In our reviews of colleagues' PPEs, we have found that often conclusions on ultimate issues (e.g., who is the better custodial parent, who is a dangerous individual) are based as much or more on moral sense or common sense as on inference based upon professional and scientific knowledge of the discipline.

Tippins and Wittmann (2005) emphasized the need to be cautious in proffering opinions about the ultimate issue. They developed a four-step clinical inference hierarchy. They suggest carefully distinguishing between and among observations (level I), inferences based on those observations (level II), the implications of those inferences (level III), and the prescriptive recommendations experts offer to the court (level IV; Tippins & Wittmann, 2005, p. 195).

When preparing reports, evaluators must remind themselves of their limitations. In discussing level I issues, even during basic data gathering, forensic mental health professionals' observations can be distorted by various cognitive biases, attribution errors, labeling effects, illusory correlations, flawed estimation rules, and so on (Tippins & Wittmann, 2005).

Inferences drawn at level II may not be reliably connected to the level III constructs that are tied to the psychological issues in dispute. At level IV, the ultimate issue(s), testifying experts may blur the boundaries between triers of fact—authorized by law to make sociomoral and socialcontrol decisions—and expert witnesses, whose role is to assist triers of fact (Tippins & Wittman, 2005, p. 214). Westen and Weinberger (2004) called attention to the fact that the vast majority of forensic psychologists offer opinions in contexts in which they do not have subsequent access to reasonably unambiguous outcome data drawn from the evidence-based literature. That is, experts often do not have clear empirically-based evidence of what has worked and what has not worked. Only with outcome data might we be able to ascertain which types of data, when attended to, lead us to accurate answers and which types of data lead us astray. In the field of forensic psychology, we lack the ability to manipulate independent variables, manage potentially confounding variables, and measure dependent variables (Ramsey & Kelly, 2004). When we are unable to resolve this inherent limitation in the data upon which we based our expert opinion, we must disclose the limitations of our data and the proffered opinions (Martindale & Gould, 2013b).

The reliability of expert testimony and limitations of current professional and scientific knowledge brings us back to an appreciation of the tensions between law and social science. We believe it is important for evaluators to develop an understanding of the needs of the legal system and, as a result, produce evaluation reports and provide expert witness testimony that conform to the rules of evidence and are based upon transparent disclosure of the limitations of the opinions we present to the court.

SOCIAL FRAMEWORK EVIDENCE VERSUS DIAGNOSTIC EVIDENCE

Forensic evaluators are social scientists. Whether the evaluator is a psychologist, psychiatrist, social worker, counselor, or some other mental health professional, the basis of their training to conduct PPEs is in the social sciences. There is a fundamental difference between the information and opinions evaluators wish to communicate to the court and how the court can accept that information and those opinions.

The professional and scientific knowledge applied by evaluators in conducting their evaluations and in formulating their opinions is based upon research findings measured at the group level. Research findings generally are described by their statistical significance. Research studies examining how children adjust to postseparation family life describe aggregate or group data. Research findings from these studies provide general knowledge about the empirical world and have been referred to as an *empirical framework* or *framework testimony* (Faigman et al., 2014). Monahan and Walker (1988, 1991) have referred to scientific testimony at the general level as *social framework evidence* to capture the use of social science research in the courts.

Both Faigman et al. and Monahan and Walker point to a fundamental characteristic of scientific or empirical research: Empirical results need to be understood at two levels of generality that are analytically separate. Empirical results can be *applied at a general level* to explain group behavior. For example, in expert witness testimony, empirical findings are useful when they are applied to similarly situated cases. Empirical results have also been *applied to specific cases* with the assumption that the general findings from group data reliably address the facts in a particular case.

The general term used by Faigman et al. to address these important conceptual areas is *G2'i* meaning general to individual. The "G" in general refers to social framework evidence and the "i" refers to diagnostic evidence. We will tackle the analytic gap between social framework evidence and diagnostic evidence in greater depth in Chapter 6.

Faigman et al. argue that "the gap between conventional scientific practice and ordinary trial practice involves the challenge of reasoning from group data to decisions about individuals" (Faigman et al., 2014, p. 420). It is the application of general research findings to explain behavior in a specific case that creates the tension between law and social science (and between law and all forms of science). Said differently, science provides results that may be generalized to the population, while expert witness testimony about scientific findings applied to a specific family moves from general notions drawn from group research to particularized application of those general findings. There is little, if any, scientific research that can address how group findings can be reliably applied to facts of a specific family system.

PARADIGM SHIFT

In the decades since the *Daubert* case, there has been a paradigm shift in both law and mental health regarding the use of evidence-based or evidence-informed expert witness opinions (Gould, 2006). Family law is increasingly influenced by social science research (Ramsey & Kelly, 2004). As a result, the courts gradually have placed greater emphasis on the scientific basis of expert testimony. To date, there is no empirical examination addressing whether the quality of PPEs and the expert testimony that flows from these evaluations reflect the courts' increased emphasis on the scientific basis of expert testimony.

Both law and psychology require that expert testimony rest on the use of reliable procedures that provide a foundation for trustworthy opinions relevant to the task at hand.[5] There is both an ethical requirement and a literature-based argument that forensic mental health professionals base upon their methods and procedures, using research to support their efficacy and show a logical relationship between the data generated by the evaluation procedures and the opinions offered to the court (Heilbrun, Grisso, & Goldstein, 2008; see also Ramsey & Kelly, 2004). Practitioners who have studied the *Daubert* decision, which made judges the gatekeepers of evidence admitted in a trial, recognize

[5]"[A]n expert's testimony both rests on a reliable foundation and is relevant to the task at hand" (*Daubert v. Merrell Dow Pharmaceuticals, Inc.*, 1993, p. 595; see also APA, 2017a).

this concept as the analytic gap between the obtained data and proffered opinions based upon it.

A careful reading of psychologists' ethical responsibilities, best practice aspirations (American Academy of Child and Adolescent Psychiatry, 1997, 2011; AAML, 2013; APA, 2022; AFCC, 2022), and documents reflecting the current state of the art in forensic mental health practice strongly suggests that evaluators need to conduct their assessments in a manner that employs the most current and well-established scientifically informed methods and procedures and interpret their findings in a manner consistent with the most highly respected professional and scientific literature in their fields. Professional and scientific literature includes peer-reviewed, published behavioral science research (Ackerman et al., 2019).

At the same time, many attorneys and courts fear that psychologists (and other mental health professionals) lack any objective criteria for their opinions and predictions and that the inferences drawn from evaluation data or observations reflect value-laden judgments without a demonstrable scientific foundation (Dale & Gould, 2014). As forensic psychology continues to develop into a unique psychological subspecialty, mental health professionals who participate in the judicial process increasingly recognize their responsibility to reexamine their methods and procedures rigorously according to the higher level of expectations now being imposed in the forensic realm.

SCIENTIFIC PROCESS

Implied in *Daubert* is a reliance on the philosophy of science and the importance of the scientific process. Science may be viewed in two ways: fact and process. We have all learned that the Earth revolves around the Sun. We do not question that the Earth revolves around the Sun. It is a fact determined through scientific observation, and the observations that form the basis of the opinion have been replicated many times. This is an example of how science can be used as a fact.

Science is also viewed as a process. It is a means of always examining alternative, rival hypotheses. Science is a means of arrogance control (Drozdek, 1994). Scientists seek to find plausible alternative explanations of their current theories to control the power of bias. Examining various alternative explanations forces one to think outside of one's pet theory. It is a method of controlling for certain types of bias (Podsakoff et al., 2012).

A critical component of *Daubert* is its recognition of the value of the scientific process as the basis of data gathering, data analysis, and opinion development. *Daubert's* emphasis on the scientific process is consistent with the ethical requirements of psychologists as described in Section 9 of psychologists' Ethics Code of the APA.

The Specialty Guidelines for Forensic Psychology stress the importance of crafting forensic reports by clearly distinguishing observations, inferences, and conclusions. Guideline 11.02 reads as follows:

> In their communications, forensic practitioners strive to distinguish observations, inferences, and conclusions. Forensic practitioners are encouraged to explain the relationship between their expert opinions and the legal issues and facts of the case at hand. (APA, 2013b, p. 16)

A key question in a *Daubert* analysis is whether the theory or technique can be (and has been) tested. "Scientific methodology . . . is based on generating hypotheses and testing them to see if they can be falsified; indeed, this methodology is what distinguishes science from other fields of human inquiry" (*Daubert v. Merrell Dow Pharmaceuticals, Inc.*, 1993, p. 594).

Looking again at the parallel between psychologists' ethical obligations and the requirements of the court's *Daubert* decision, there is an expectation that expert testimony is based, in part, on reasonable consideration of alternative hypotheses (Glancy & Saini, 2009). Some courts have determined that an expert whose testimony fails to rule out or consider alternative hypotheses or alternative causes for a condition has provided opinion testimony that is unreliable (*TXI Transp. Co. v. Hughes*, 2010, p. 23&).

Attorneys might ask for a hearing to determine the admissibility of the PPE prior to the actual family court trial. The attorney may file a *motion in limine*, a *Daubert* challenge, or some other motion in which arguments may be made about the admissibility of the evaluator's report.

In several states, a fundamental assumption in assessing the reliability of expert opinion testimony is whether the expert complied with a particular mandated statutory, regulatory, or standard of care. Mandated compliance with statutory, regulatory, or standard of practice criteria is a necessary but not sufficient component of an examination of reliability for expert testimony (Gould, 2018). Some courts have found that expert opinions that did not consider regulatory performance standards were unreliable and, therefore, inadmissible. Other courts have determined for expert testimony to be viewed as reliable, it must be predicated on "proper legal concepts" governing standard of care. In the area of PPE, the standard of practice in PPEs has been investigated in more than a dozen empirical studies (Ackerman et al., 2019).

SCIENTIFIC INQUIRY AND PARENTING PLAN EVALUATION LIMITATIONS

Evidence-based models of forensic psychological practice, whether treatment or evaluation, should be based on the best available research evidence integrated with clinical expertise (Ackerman et al., 2019). There is a multiyear history of criticism about the widespread neglect of the scientific basis for PPEs (Emery et al., 2005). It is *our* aspirational hope that books like this will help soften those criticisms by emphasizing the evidence-based and evidence-informed assessment paradigms that are able to serve the court.

One aspect of that criticism is the lack of conceptual analysis and theoretical work in the development of PPE models. A consequence of the lack of conceptual analysis and theoretical work is the acceptance by attorneys and courts of PPEs based upon unreliable methodology and acceptance of expert opinions that have little to no basis in the professional and scientific knowledge of the field.

A failure by the PPE community to develop a consensus about conceptual models and theoretical work means that attempts to bring PPEs more closely aligned with the scientific process leave the field open to justified criticisms that expert opinions are too often based upon idiosyncratic, biased, or unreliable data (Gould & Martindale, 2005; J. B. Kelly & Johnston, 2005; Tippins & Wittmann, 2005).

A pressing problem in PPE literature is the failure to ask questions about theories of parenting behavior an evaluator uses to guide their thinking and failure to require the evaluator to explain the evidence-based or evidence-informed literature upon which their opinions about the goodness-of-fit between parent and child (Gould & Martindale, 2009b). Our field has developed significant and robust literature about specific areas of concern, including resist and refusal dynamics, intimate partner violence, coercive control, gatekeeping, and relocation analysis, to name a few, and these areas of research and scholarship provide a categorical snapshot of our field. But we need more comprehensive, integrated models of the factors most relevant to assess and link those models to the peer-reviewed literature.

Our book does not provide answers to all of these pressing questions; still, it extends the work of others, including our previous work, in attempting to bring into the field professional and scientific knowledge of disciplines outside the scope of most evaluators.

As a first step, this section offers a primer on the importance of science and the phases of scientific inquiry. Throughout this book, we embrace the importance of the scientific process in our evaluation work, a focus that is consistent with the needs of the court system, the admissibility of expert witness testimony, and requirements of our ethical obligations.

The Importance of Science

Science, first and foremost, is a set of epistemic practices that focus on ways to describe, explain, predict, intervene, and control aspects of the world around us. Science is systemic, self-critical, and empirically based (T. Ward & Durrant, 2022). As Gould has written before, the scientific process acts like having a person with scientific eyes continuously looking over our shoulders.

Evidence determines whether a theory is worth pursuing or whether a specific method of measuring and interpreting evidence is trustworthy. "While science is not the only source of knowledge available to human beings, it arguably provides our most reliable way of learning about machinery of the world and deciding how best to intervene to achieve valued goals . . ." (T. Ward & Durrant, 2022, p. 2).

One of the challenges in a PPE is how best to judge the reliability of information obtained from parent, child, or collateral interviews. Data, in a strictly scientific sense, are recordings or reports that are perceptually accessible. They are observable and open to scrutiny by others (Haig, 2014).

Interviews produce data in the sense that they are recordings or reports. What is unknown, and likely never able to be known, is the internal motivation or intention behind the self-report information. In the PPE world, much of our data are based upon self-report information, and self-report information is subject to many different kinds of bias, distortions, and falsehoods. Self-report information is also subject to truthful, honest, and transparent presentation. As evaluators, we will never know the truthfulness of the self-report data. That is why it is so important to obtain relevant and comprehensive third-party information and direct observational data that serves to test the trustworthiness of the self-report information (Gould & Mulchay, 2023).

Scientific inquiry assumes that phenomena are relatively stable, recurrent features of the world (T. Ward & Durrant, 2022). In a PPE, we make similar assumptions. If a parent's self-report of parenting behavior is truthful, then such parenting behavior should be observed in a variety of different situations and observed by a variety of different people. We believe that this is the analog to phenomena as stable, recurrent features of the world.

When we obtain reports of parenting behavior from both the parent and child, observations of parent–child interactions, and independent third parties, then we are in a position to make inferences about the meaning of the parenting behavior, its effect on a child, and predictions about the fit between the parent's parenting behavior and the needs of the child.

The challenge for evaluators is to make inferences about the meaning of these behaviors that correspond to the reliable application of the professional and scientific knowledge of the discipline to those behaviors. Evaluators' inferences should be closely aligned with conceptual models of parenting. Of course, the problem with such a formulation is that there are few well-researched models of parenting.

For example, one model of parenting is reflected in the conceptual and evidence-based model of parenting style (Baumrind, 2013). Parenting style research is robust and has stood the test of time. It is a conceptual model that appears well-positioned to explain one aspect of parenting behavior. A problem with the parenting style literature—a problem that plagues most of our work—is that there are no commercially available, reliable measures of parenting style.

Similar concerns abound regarding other parenting concepts. We know that good parenting is defined, in part, by reasonable, consistent limit setting; however, there is no consensus definition of limit setting, no consensus definition of the parenting factors involved in limit setting, and no reliable assessment tools developed to measure limit setting. Yet, most evaluators know it when they see it.

Scientific Inquiry

As a result of these limitations in applying science to PPEs, evaluators find guidance in the scientific method. Yet prior to developing hypotheses to test, it is important for evaluators to identify the implicit models that guide their thinking. Does the evaluator have a model of parenting or a model of family functioning that guides their thinking about how to approach the investigative activities? A challenge in the field is that evaluators infrequently identify a model of parenting or a model of family functioning that guides their thinking. Although there is no research available, we speculate that many evaluators have not reflected on nor been challenged to articulate the implicit models of parenting, child development, and parent–child fit that guide their approach to evaluations.

When the implicit models are unknown, it is impossible to identify relevant factors to assess. The challenge for evaluators is to clarify the implicit models that guide their thinking and reflect upon the degree to which those implicit models are evidence-based, evidence-informed, or drawn from personal and professional experience. Failure to identify the implicit models that guide evaluators' approach to the assessment process may result in investigating areas of presumed family functioning that have no basis in the professional and scientific knowledge of the discipline.

The explicit framing of the problem to be addressed by the court is a critical part of the scientific process. In *Daubert* language, the question is whether the evaluator relies upon an underlying theory of science to guide the evaluation. Is there a particular theory of parenting that frames the evaluator's data collection, data analysis, and opinion formation? Explicit framing of the model imposes a conceptual and empirical boundary on the evaluator's approach to the evaluation and informs the attorneys, their clients, and the courts about the scientific basis and constraints placed on the evaluation process. The explicit framing of hypotheses to guide a PPE requires the evaluator to identify specific areas of investigation. We strongly encourage evaluators to reflect on the implicit models of parenting that are the basis for the identification of specific areas for investigation. If the implicit model has no evidence basis, then one needs to question the usefulness of the investigative question.

After defining the models of parenting, child development, etc., that will guide the PPE, the next step is to operationally define the factors identified in the theory or model used to guide the evaluator's thinking. Once the concept is operationally defined, one can then define the factors associated with the concept. Once the factors associated with the concept are defined, one can search for reliable methods of assessment. Once reliable assessment methods are found and employed, then the examination of the goodness-of-fit between the data and the conceptual model occurs.

We are a long way from being able to consistently apply the necessary components of scientific inquiry to our family court work. This book is another small step toward trying to bring together elements of scientific inquiry and previously unrelated sources of information from within the field of parenting plan evaluations.

HISTORICAL TRUTH, NARRATIVE TRUTH, AND EXPERT TESTIMONY

As you read this book and as you engage in your own scientific inquiries into family dynamics, we want you to be mindful of the differences between historical truth and narrative truth. Among the seminal articles in forensic psychology is S. A. Greenberg and Shuman's (1997) article that articulated differences between therapeutic and forensic roles and activities. They identified that among the critical differences between therapeutic and forensic psychological activities is the forensic psychologist's attention to establishing the historical truth of assertions made by litigants during interviews.

Therapists and forensic evaluators differ in the degree to which they apply scrutiny to the information utilized in their activities. The therapist is most concerned about gathering information from the person being treated with little scrutiny of that information (S. A. Greenberg & Shuman, 1997, p. 52). The forensic evaluator gathers information from the litigant and seeks information from collateral sources that either supports or refutes the assertions made by the litigant.

Gathering historical information from collateral sources has been considered a cornerstone of proper forensic psychological assessment procedures. Wesson (1985) raised questions about the limitations of historical truth that we have not seen represented in the child custody literature; questions that lead us to critically examine the potential threats to reliable expert testimony based, in part, on evaluators' reliance on what we have called "historical truth."

Wesson reminds us that courts have given expert testimony more weight than lay witnesses or give more credit to expert opinions than is appropriate. Concerns about the perceived power of expert testimony have been a source of causation in several courts. For example, in *United States v. Addison* (1974, p. 744), the court cautioned that "scientific evidence may . . . assume a posture of mystic infallibility in the eyes of a jury of laymen." Similar concerns have been raised in legal scholarly treatises (Giannelli, 1980). "The major danger of scientific evidence is its potential to mislead the jury . . . without critical scrutiny" (Giannelli, 1980, p. 1237).

Historical truth is defined as finding out what happened in the real world (Wesson, 1985, p. 331). Questions of historical truth are often a critical aspect of expert testimony, especially in child custody assessment in which the evaluator is attempting to understand both past and present parenting behavior, parent–child interactions, and coparenting behaviors.

In determining the usefulness of historical information from collateral sources, the expert must make some judgments. The judgments about historical truth from third-party interviews become part of the expert's decision making and opinion formation. Rules of evidence allow the expert to rely on such information and to make judgments, including hearsay exceptions.[6]

Judgments made by experts about the weight placed upon historical truth obtained from third parties suggest that experts are perceived to have some special expertise in the determination of historical truth (Wesson, 1985). Wesson questions whether courts are more likely than not to be influenced by those opinions precisely because they are spoken by an expert.

Experts do not have any special expertise that would lead them to be more accurate in determining the veracity of historical truth (Wesson, 1985). Experts do not have any special expertise in deciding which collateral sources to interview about historical events or observations nor do experts have any special expertise to determine how much weight to place on historical truth once it is obtained. "If we entertain this belief about witnesses with such training, we are ascribing to them powers of ratiocination that they do not have" (Wesson, 1985, p. 333).[7]

How we interpret the information gathered from historical sources is subject to "unwitting interpretations" (Wesson, 1985, p. 335) that might serve to change the meaning, the intention, or even the historical truth itself. The reporter of the historical information is subject to all of the factors that are known to affect memory function including factors that affect accurate recall of past events. Little is known about how the memories of collateral sources who describe historical events accurately correspond to the factual history of the event or observed behaviors.

One of the primary tasks of evaluators is to develop a coherent account to fit the volume of materials gathered during their data collection. Those data are continuously integrated into emerging coherent accounts about the meaning of the data that will be used as a basis for their expert opinions. (See Chapter 7 describing the coherence theory of bias.) The further evaluators move from behavioral descriptions from other sources anchored in verifiable facts to interpreting the meaning of those historical truths, the more likely that there will be modifications to the data and changes to the interpretation of the data, among other transformations known to occur to memories as a result of the passage of time. These changes, modifications, and transformations to the accurate recollection of historical data become the basis for what Wesson calls the evaluator's *narrative truth*. The evaluator's narrative truth becomes a construction of the

---

[6]Hearsay, in a legal forum, is an out-of-court statement which is being offered in court for the truth of what was asserted. Hearsay is information that a witness has heard but does not know to be true because s/he did not have personal knowledge of the event. There are exceptions to the hearsay rule. Some witnesses, such as expert witnesses, are often permitted to base their opinions on hearsay.

[7]Ratiocination is defined as reasoning, conscious deliberate inference, or the activity or process of reasoning. We figured that if we did not know the definition, others might not either!

synthesis of information obtained from sources providing examples of historical truth discovered during the data collection process. The evaluator's narrative truth is a construction not a reconstruction of the original historical truth (Wesson, 1985).

Said differently, the assumption that a forensic evaluator's task is, in part, to gather information from independent third-party witnesses who help to support or refute the picture of past events being painted by the litigant has always been viewed as a lynchpin of forensic evaluations. What Wesson is suggesting is that the collateral source who reports information about a past event provides historical truth, as defined by S. A. Greenberg and Shuman. The information of a past event that is viewed as examples of historical truth is, itself, subject to distortion, intentionally or otherwise.

The evaluator's memorialization of the examples of historical truth is also subject to distortions. The evaluator might be inaccurate or imprecise in recording the information from the historical source. The evaluator might be accurate and precise in recording the information from the historical source yet filter the meaning or intention of the historical information through the evaluator's psychological processes that influence its presentation, meaning, perceived intention, and reasonableness. The evaluator might understand certain words used by the collateral to mean something different from that intended by the collateral source.

Evaluators must continually be on the lookout for the ways in which information from sources of historical information becomes changed, distorted, or misrepresented through the naturally occurring information processing mechanisms that we all use. Evaluators whose understanding of the historical truth subsequently turns out to be inaccurate might unintentionally undermine the truth-seeking function of the court in several ways (Wesson, 1985). One way is when an evaluator misunderstands what happened during the historical event or observation. That is, the evaluator as a receptacle of the information gets it wrong. The evaluator might misunderstand the historical account. The evaluator might use language differently than the collateral source, resulting in misunderstanding of the historical information.

Beyond potential problems with understanding the literal explanation of a historical event, problems might occur in the conclusions drawn by the evaluator. When the information is inaccurate or when the conclusions are inaccurate, these unreliable data creep into the fabric of the expert opinion.

A second way is when the evaluator's erroneous understanding results in the court placing too little or too much weight on the information it rightly deserves. Inaccurate understanding of historical data might undermine the truth-seeking function of the court when evaluators convey that misunderstanding to the court. The court's truth-seeking is undermined when evaluators present their expert opinions in a manner that feeds the knowingly false yet influential belief that the expert possesses some special faculty that their version of truth is more credible than alternative versions that might be supported by the evidence (Wesson, 1985).

A third way in which an inaccurate understanding of historical data might undermine the truth-seeking function of the court is through the admissibility of expert testimony through the hearsay exceptions. The rules of evidence allow experts to base their opinions on information that would otherwise be inadmissible at trial. The special status given to expert testimony that allows reliance on hearsay might give greater weight to the expert's opinion about historical truth simply because it is said by an expert. The concern is that erroneous opinions might be given greater weight simply because they are spoken by an expert.

The conclusion drawn from this summary of Wesson's article is that evaluators need to be very cautious about the ways in which they gather, interpret, and integrate collateral information about historical events. They need to be vigilant about their understanding of the historical event. They need to be vigilant about ensuring that the language used by the collateral to describe the event has the same meaning to the evaluator. They need to be vigilant about the ways in which common memory errors might affect the trustworthiness of the collateral's recollection, might affect the evaluator's recollection of the collateral's story, and might affect the interpretation placed in the meaning of the event by the evaluator both at the time of hearing the story and at the time of integrating the historical story into the fabric of the assessment report.

CONCLUSION

Psychologists are trained in scientist–practitioner models or practitioner–scientist models, yet even the best-trained psychologist may have little training on distinguishing clinical from forensic thinking, clinical procedures from forensic procedures, and the application of legal requirements placed upon the admissibility of their oral and written testimony. Understanding the importance of reliance on the scientific process and its application to forensic psychological activities allows the evaluator to weave their expertise in working with families with the legal knowledge required to work in family court. This chapter explored the evolution of PPEs from a clinical to a forensic approach, emphasizing evidence-informed practices and the impact of legal standards like the *Daubert* factors on evaluators' forensic psychological activities.

Before the 1980s, PPEs were treated as clinical practices rather than forensic evaluations. In 1989, Benjamin Schutz and colleagues introduced an evidence-based approach to PPEs, marking a significant shift in the field. The 1993 Supreme Court ruling on *Daubert* brought an emphasis on the scientific process into judicial decision making, emphasizing the court's role as gatekeepers for the admissibility of expert evidence. *Daubert* introduced five flexible factors for assessing expert testimony: (a) testability, (b) peer review, (c) error rate, (d) standards and controls, and (e) general acceptance in the scientific community. This decision underscored the importance of admissibility standards and evidentiary reliability.

Forensic evaluators must balance legal expectations with psychological expertise, ensuring that evaluations meet scientific and professional standards for admissibility as scientific evidence. There is increasing scrutiny on the methodology and procedures employed in PPEs, placing greater concerns about the scientific integrity of report quality, control of bias factors at every step of the evaluation process, and adherence to legal rules and ethical standards and guidelines.

We made distinctions between

- Standard of practice: minimal acceptable professional conduct
- Standard of care: legal expectations to avoid liability
- Best practices: aspirational goals beyond the minimum standards

There is professional consensus on the independent sources of data gathering to be used in PPEs (interviews with parents, interviews with children, observations, collateral interviews, records reviews, and psychological testing), but the field lacks professional consensus about defining relevant parenting behaviors to be assessed and defining factors to be examined when determining child–parent fit. Evaluators face challenges ensuring their data-gathering procedures align with the legal concept of reliable principles and methods. The concept of the *analytical gap* highlights potential disconnections between data and expert opinions, which courts scrutinize to determine admissibility.

Ethical standards, professional practice guidelines, peer-reviewed literature, and evidence-based practice (EBP) integrate the best available research with clinical and forensic expertise. Transparency about reliability of data-gathering procedures and their limitations is crucial to maintain evaluator credibility and assist courts effectively. This chapter stressed the importance of integrating forensic psychological science and legal standards to enhance the credibility of the evaluator and increase the reliability of opinions in PPEs proffered to the court. Evaluators are obligated to provide courts with evidence-based or evidence-informed opinions that reflect the fairness and balance required by the courts. We call for evaluators to focus on reliability of procedures, relevance of data, transparency of the investigative process, and respect for the legal system with an eye toward supporting the integrity of our proud profession.

2

Current Expectations and Criticisms of Parenting Plan Evaluations

This chapter explores the evolving nature of family court evaluations, examining the professional practices, methodologies, and ethical considerations that have shaped this discipline. By delving into the criticisms from both legal and mental health perspectives, we aim to illuminate the areas in need of reform while underscoring the importance of maintaining the integrity and reliability of evaluations in service of the courts and the families they aim to help. As this chapter unfolds, it sets the stage for a critical discourse on how forensic mental health professionals can meet the expectations of their role while addressing the legitimate concerns raised by their methodologies and practices.

Forensic mental health professionals stand at the crossroads of law, psychology, and the evolving dynamics of family systems. They represent a critical intersection where forensic mental health professionals must navigate the delicate balance between clinical insight and forensic methodology to address the complex realities faced by families in conflict. This chapter examines the intricate tapestry of current expectations placed upon forensic mental health professionals and addresses the criticisms that have emerged over time.

We acknowledge the feedback and comments on the Structured Analytic Techniques (SATs) section of this chapter offered by Terry Kukor, PhD, ABPP (Forensic) whose excellent lecture on the use of SATs at the November 2022 ABPP conference in Chicago introduced us to the fascinating work being done in bias control within the U.S. intelligence analysts community.

https://doi.org/10.1037/0000474-003
Parenting Plan Evaluations: An Evidence-Informed Approach to Child Custody, by J. W. Gould and C. M. Mulchay

In recent decades, the field has undergone significant transformation, influenced by advancements in psychological research, legal precedent, and shifting societal norms. These changes have not only expanded the evaluative framework but have also heightened the scrutiny on the methodologies and assumptions that underpin these evaluations. The stakes are high—decisions informed by forensic mental health professionals profoundly affect the lives of children, parents, and families navigating the often tumultuous process of separation and divorce.

Forensic mental health professionals continue to organize a coherent body of literature and strive to develop a reliable methodology about how to interview, assess, integrate, interpret information, formulate expert opinions, and offer testimony in family court cases. An important change over the past 3 decades in the professional practice of parenting plan evaluation (PPE) is the increasing integration of areas of psychological study previously overlooked or simply not considered.

Among the areas of evolving interest are literature addressing developmental psychopathology, neuropsychology, executive functioning, children's use of language, use and misuse of psychological testing, domestic violence and its subtypes (e.g., coercive control), child development and psychopathology, adult psychopathology, ecological model of analysis, relationship development, cultural and ethnic differences, LGBTQIA+ factors, cognitive bias, mother parenting factors, father parenting factors, sibling factors, high conflict family factors, limitations on the use and interpretation of psychological test data, alternative models of evaluation, relevant case law, legal literature relevant to family law, and rules of evidence guiding scientific testimony.

As more and more mental health colleagues become engaged in legal issues related to divorce and custody, a wider array of skills are recommended for mental health professionals to bring to their work (Ackerman et al., 2019; Gould & Martindale, 2007; L. R. Greenberg & Gould, 2001; L. R. Greenberg et al., 2003; P. M. Stahl & Simon, 2020). Some mental health professionals may rely primarily on their clinical training when conducting PPEs. Other mental health professionals may become involved in PPEs with little forensic mental health training. Still, other colleagues may believe it proper to move from their role as the child's therapist to the court-appointed evaluator in a family court case. All are motivated by a desire to be helpful, yet in forensic mental health assessment, being "helpful" is not often the primary goal of the evaluation.

THE NEED FOR A FORENSIC PARADIGM

Paul Meehl noted that "most clinical psychologists select their methods like kids make choices in a candy store: They look around, maybe sample a bit, and choose what they like, whatever feels good to them" (as cited in Mischel, 2008, p. i). We believe that this observation applies to the ways in which many colleagues choose the methods of formal psychological assessment used in PPEs. Many currently practicing evaluators have graduate school training preparing them to be counseling or clinical psychologists. They have retrained in the practice of PPEs by attending workshops and seminars.

Still, other colleagues have not been retrained as forensic mental health specialists. They have not pursued board certification in forensic psychology or forensic psychiatry. The board certification process is one means of learning the paradigm shift from a clinical approach to assessment into a forensic approach to assessment (S. A. Greenberg & Shuman, 1997). The point to be made is not that everyone needs to obtain board certification in forensic psychology or forensic psychiatry. Rather, the point is that learning to think in a new paradigm, shifting from a clinical paradigm to a forensic paradigm, requires supervision, consultation, education, practice, and challenge from colleagues.

Without such a paradigm shift, the evaluator's mindset and assessment methodologies are derived from their training as clinical psychologists rather than from their training as forensic psychologists (Gould & Dale, 2022; Gould & Martindale, 2013; Gould & Mulchay, 2023; Martindale & Gould, 2013a). One frequent result of clinicians who retrain to conduct PPEs is their reliance upon clinical judgment, intuition, and self-reflection as trustworthy tools suitable for forensic psychological decision making. Another frequent result is a reliance upon clinically derived assessment techniques that have served the clinical psychology professional well when used in treatment, but which poorly serve the forensic psychological professional and the more stringent needs of the legal system for scientifically based procedures (Gould et al., 2018; Rappaport et al., 2018).

The gap between the use of familiar, though unreliable, methods and procedures and forensic psychology's scientific progress is cause for great concern (Emery et al., 2005). One concern is that forensic practitioners will be seen as out of touch with the legal system and its evidentiary needs. Another concern is that the families we evaluate and the courts that we serve will devalue our services because of the continued lack of predictability of the quality of PPEs and the variability in knowledge and skills displayed in the courtroom by expert witnesses. Those who utilize our services have a right to expect a higher level of competency from forensic mental health professionals who market themselves as "experts" given the stakes involved in addressing children's needs from divorcing families.

There are concerns, too, about how our legal colleagues utilize parenting plan evaluation data in the courtroom. In a recent study examining the use of psychological tests in the courtroom, Neal and colleagues (2019) reported that nearly all of the assessment tools used by psychologists and offered as expert evidence in legal settings had been subjected to empirical testing (90%). However, only about 67% were identified as generally accepted in the field. Only about 40% were reported to have favorable reviews of their psychometric and technical properties in authorities such as the Mental Measurements

Yearbook.[1] Neal and her colleagues reported that legal challenges to the admission of psychological test results are infrequent. They found legal challenges to the assessment evidence for any reason occurred in only 5.1% of cases in their sample, with a little more than half of these challenges focused on the validity of the test. When challenges were raised, they succeeded only about a third of the time. Challenges to the most scientifically suspect tools were found to be almost nonexistent. Attorneys rarely challenged psychological expert assessment evidence, and when they did, judges often failed to exercise the scrutiny required by law (Neal et al., 2019, p. 135).

CRITICISMS OF PARENTING PLAN ADVISORY REPORTS

Over the past decade, family law attorneys have begun to voice more publicly their frustration with the poor quality of parenting plan advisory reports completed by evaluators. For example, in expressing her opinion about the increasing concerns held among her attorney colleagues about the poor or inconsistent quality of PPEs, Attorney Joy Feinberg noted that attorneys helped to create the cottage industry of PPEs as early as the 1960s (Feinberg & Gould, 2012).

At the time, both courts and attorneys desperately wanted guidance from mental health professionals to better the lives of children caught in their parents' divorce. When the *quality and value* of parenting plan advisory reports had been consistently attacked, the attorneys and judges who were consumers of the PPEs work began to question the value of such reports. Their frustration was found in the poor quality of reports and the imposition of personal beliefs and bias presented to the court as if they were drawn from evidence-based or evidence-informed literature. Without quality work products, there is little need to have psychological evaluators in the system (Feinberg & Gould, 2012).

Bow et al. (2011), found that attorneys' most frequent complaints about PPEs "focused on [the] evaluator's indecisiveness, illogical conclusions, ignorance regarding the Best Interests of the Child Standard, and making or not making recommendations" (pp. 306–307). During a 2016 Association of Family and Conciliation Courts (AFCC) workshop presentation, Judge Gould-Saltman noted that what she believes the court needs most from an evaluator is a recitation of facts relevant to the issues of parenting sufficient to show that the evaluator had sufficient relevant data with which to form any opinions. She then primarily relies on the evaluator's analysis of those data based upon the evaluator's knowledge, education, and experience. It's that expert analysis that marks the difference between an expert opinion and her own analysis of those same data if it had been brought to her by testimony on a witness stand (Judge Dianna Gould-Saltman, personal communication, November 17, 2016).

[1]Buros's Mental Measurement Yearbook provides for purchase independent evaluations of many psychological tests and measures through their *Buros Online Shop* that can be accessed online (https://marketplace.unl.edu/buros/).

Our observation has been that many mental health professionals lack sufficient training to competently conduct PPEs. Our first author's conclusion (after 30 plus years of practice and review of more than 2,500 evaluations) is that many mental health professionals who become involved in PPEs are unfamiliar with research and theory about how to conduct evaluations, unfamiliar with how to integrate professional and scientific knowledge with the data created during the evaluation, and unfamiliar with how to handle themselves in the courtroom.

Many colleagues lack sufficient training to identify and evaluate the developmental factors most relevant at each stage of child development. These colleagues are often unprepared to identify and evaluate relevant parental abilities that will meet the normative and unique developmental needs of children whose families are being evaluated. Furthermore, these same mental health professionals are often poorly skilled at gathering and subsequently presenting reliable and relevant information to the court about the family, parents' strengths and weaknesses, child's strengths and weaknesses, and how these factors interact with the psychological best interests of the child.

CRITICISMS OF FAMILY LAW JUDGES AND ATTORNEYS

Our concern about poor training and preparation to conduct PPEs is not only focused on fellow mental health professionals. We have found that judges and attorneys often have little to no training in the fundamental information about child development, family systems functioning, and other relevant areas critical to understanding how best to serve children and their family's needs.

Many attorneys are unfamiliar with the behavioral science literature that forms the backbone of understanding healthy and unhealthy child development and healthy and unhealthy family functioning. We do not expect attorneys to have the same level of knowledge as a trained evaluator. However, we expect and encourage attorneys to seek out training opportunities directly addressing child development, family development, psychopathology, and other behavioral science areas relevant to their practice.

CHALLENGES TO KNOW THE LITERATURE

Forensic mental health professionals (FMHPs) have struggled with the task of how to identify and research characteristics that define competent parenting. As professionals involved in an applied field of social science, evaluators are just learning how to build a solid theoretical framework for most of our work. For example, there is little consensus in the literature about a theory of parenting and the factors to be assessed when evaluating parenting. There is little consensus about a theory of child development and the factors to be assessed when evaluating a child's developmental health. There is little consensus about a theory of how a parent's parenting abilities can be reliably matched with the developmental needs of a child, what used to be called the "goodness of fit" factor. In each of these critical areas, evaluators often do not operationally define in their reports the parent, child, and parent–child factors intended to be measured. There is robust literature available to evaluators on each of these parenting plan-related topics, yet it is a treasure of information that is seldom used to guide investigations, seldom cited by evaluators in their reports as the basis of their expert opinions, and seldom used as a basis for cross-examination of the expert.

Recently, research findings have indicated several empirically-determined positive parenting behaviors (Teti et al., 2017; Woodward et al., 2018). Later in this book we will discuss how such empirically-based information may be used to guide data collection in a PPE.

We make no attempt to portray this as the definitive work in the field because the field is dynamic, growing, and, on a daily basis, redefined through research, experience, case law, and conceptual and theoretical reformulation. Yet, we endeavor to bring new ideas by integrating areas of legal scholarship, cognitive science, and other areas of wonderfully rich ideas into the fold.

DEFINING PARENTING PLAN EVALUATION METHODOLOGY

As used in this book, methodology refers to where we look for information from independent sources. Methodology is a heuristic that reflects the scientific process. The scientific process, however, is not a test. It is a way of thinking about data gathering, data analysis, and data interpretation. Methodology identifies *what* we assess, not *how* it is assessed.

The techniques and tools used to gather information in a forensic assessment include psychological tests, questionnaires, inventories, interview protocols, and observational techniques. The techniques and tools selected to gather and analyze data from each independent information source may be subject to scientific scrutiny. For example, an evaluation that includes multiple interviews with children and observations of parent–child interactions are not scientific methods. Multiple interviews with children and observations of parent–child interactions direct us to what needs to be assessed. Multiple interviews with children and observation of parent–child interactions are areas identified as critical areas of data gathering. How we gather information and the selection of techniques and tools selected to gather data are more likely to be subject to challenges examining their reliability and validity.

The fact that an evaluator interviews a child ought not be subject to scientific scrutiny. The lack of information from child interviews may be challenged as a fatal flaw in an evaluation because the exclusion of such data may be critical to answering the questions the court expected to be addressed. The lack of information might be related to the sufficiency of data, not necessarily the reliability of how the data were gathered.

How the evaluator interviewed children is open to scientific challenges. It is important for the evaluator to employ interview procedures that have a basis in empirical research, procedures that have been demonstrated to have good reliability and can be utilized in a manner that allows for the collection of reliable, relevant information.

We include these points in an effort to anticipate some of our legal colleagues from arguing that the limitations cited in this book are *prima facie* evidence of the lack of scientific foundation for PPEs. The five independent areas of data gathering—what we are calling *methodology*—are based upon a consensus in behavioral science and legal literature addressing the most robust and comprehensive approach to gathering data in a PPE identified to date. Identification of independent areas of data gathering is separate from how to gather data from each of those areas. For example, one area of data gathering is psychological testing. Identifying the independent area of data gathering does not identify the specific test selected for use in the evaluation. An evaluator might select one or more psychological tests to administer without considering whether the tests possess the reliability and validity necessary for use in a parenting plan evaluation.

Identification of psychological testing as a necessary area of data gathering should not be subject to a *Daubert* challenge. It is the reliability and validity of the tests when used in a PPE that might be subject to a *Daubert* challenge. It is not the area of data gathering that is subject to *Daubert* scrutiny. It is the examination of the specific test's reliability and validity that are subject to a challenge regarding the scientific basis of their development and the appropriateness of their use.

CHANGES IN PROFESSIONAL PRACTICE GUIDELINES ACROSS THREE GENERATIONS

One way to think about the growth of the field is identifying trends that may be categorized as reflecting progress from early writing to more current writings. We refer to these categories as representing first generation literature, second generation literature, and the current third generation literature.

The first generation of child custody guidelines and model standards published in the 1980s and early 1990s retained elements of a clinical rather than a forensic approach to custody assessment (American Academy of Child and Adolescent Psychiatry, 1997; AFCC, 1994). The sole first-generation professional practice guideline anchored in forensic psychological practice was the American Psychological Association's (APA's) *Child Custody Guidelines* (1994) built upon the professional practice guidelines describing forensic psychological assessment, in general (APA, 2013b).

The second generation of guidelines and model standards published in the late 2000s and early 2010s (APA, 2010; AFCC, 2007) embraced the increasing consensus over what general procedures are to be used in an evaluation and an increasing awareness of the legal demands for evidence-based assessment procedures. General agreement has developed supporting the Forensic Model (Martindale & Gould, 2004) as defining the standard of practice with regard to area of data collection to be used in a PPE (Ackerman et al., 2021; Saini, 2008; Tippins, 2014).

The third generation of guidelines and standards has recently been published (APA, 2022; AFCC, 2022). Both the APA and AFCC have published new guidelines for PPEs, with APA describing them as "Child Custody Evaluations" and AFCC using the term "Parenting Plan Evaluations." We have adopted the later term, as it describes the direction the field is moving in. The revisions to professional practice guidelines are a testament to professional recognition that our field is evolving and continually refining itself. The revisions to professional practice guidelines guiding PPEs are an acknowledgment that our field is a dynamic endeavor combining changes in knowledge, changes in assessment, changes in law, and changes in ethical standards. The field is continually being revised and updated as new information is published, new theories and models lead us to more efficient and reliable assessment procedures, revised ethical standards are adopted, and new case law and statutes better define the legal expectations within which our work is intended to be proffered.

CHANGES IN PROFESSIONAL AND SCIENTIFIC KNOWLEDGE ACROSS THREE GENERATIONS

At the same time as there were three generations of professional practice guidelines, there were three corresponding generations of professional and scientific knowledge being published. The first generation of child custody texts often conceptualized the evaluation process based upon the evaluator's personal experiences and clinical judgment (Skafte, 1985; P. M. Stahl, 1994) and approached the assessment task as an extension of clinical rather than forensic psychological activities. These early books reflected how the authors approached child custody assessment with little reference to legal principles guiding admissibility of scientific evidence and little reference to the importance of integrating the professional and scientific knowledge of the discipline with assessment methodology and use of reliable procedures.

The second generation of child custody texts began to move away from a clinical psychology assessment model and toward a forensic psychology assessment model. The most important book in this second generation was Solomon Sword (Schutz et al., 1989), a conceptual precursor to the third generation of texts that have stood firmly on the application of forensic methods and procedures to child custody assessment. Among the books in the second generation that complemented the lessons drawn from Solomon's Sword were Ackerman's (1995) *Clinician's Guide to Child Custody Evaluations* and P. M. Stahl's (1999) *Complex Issues in Child Custody*.

The conceptual foundation for the application of forensic methods and procedures to child custody assessment was found in the first edition of Gould's (1998) *Conducting Scientifically Crafted Child Custody Evaluations* and further defined in Martindale and Gould's article describing the Forensic Model applied to PPEs (Martindale & Gould, 2004).

For those who were not in the field or not involved in the paradigm shift in the field from a clinical to a forensic endeavor, there were significant disagreements within the field about the application of the Forensic Model to PPEs. Professional disagreements about the usefulness of the Forensic Model turned quickly into personal attacks upon those supporting the model. Fortunately, the field has moved beyond these disagreements and embraced the relevance of the application of forensic psychological methods and procedures to PPEs (Ackerman et al., 2021).

By the time the second edition of Gould's (2006) *Scientifically Crafted* book and the Gould and Martindale (2007) *Art and Science* book were published, the clinical versus forensic challenges were largely resolved, with acknowledgments in legal and mental health journals and books that the trend toward a more evidence-based approach to assessments conducted for the court was essential.

The third generation of scholarship—empirical research and theoretical models—needs to address what factors are most relevant to investigate in a PPE and how best to assess those factors using psychometrically-sound tools. We are not suggesting that we need to define a static set of variables to be investigated in each evaluation. However, we are suggesting that evaluators need to rely more often on evidence-based and evidence-informed literature about many parenting plan-related factors that have been empirically examined. The information contained in our PPEs needs to better integrate the professional and scientific knowledge of our discipline, particularly research findings in areas such as, but not limited to, parenting, parent–child relationship, child development, and parent-to-parent communication.

One book that demonstrates the shift from one generation to the next is Ackerman and Kane's *Psychological Experts in Divorce Actions* (PEDA). First published in 1990, the book attempted to integrate legal issues, professional and scientific knowledge, and personal experience. Over seven editions, PEDA has increasingly emphasized a forensic perspective. It has been among the most comprehensive texts written about forensic psychological assessment in PPEs and related areas such as sexual abuse, alienation dynamics, use of psychological tests, assessment of drug and alcohol abuse, and domestic violence. In its most recent iteration, many of the PEDA chapters were significantly revised and updated (Ackerman et al., 2019), a process of updating chapters that has continued through each yearly update (Ackerman et al., 2024).

THE LINGERING CLINICAL EMPHASIS IN SOME PARENTING PLAN EVALUATIONS

Despite the shift in both professional guidelines and scientific knowledge being published, some evaluators continue to emphasize a clinical perspective. Over the past 30 years, our senior author has reviewed more than 2,500 evaluations. His experience and that of others who engage in work-product review has found that there remains a minority of evaluators who continue to place greater weight on their clinical judgments as the basis of their expert opinions rather than relying upon the scientific and professional knowledge of the discipline. It has been observed that many of these evaluators are finding increased challenges by both attorneys and judges because of the legal system's increased attention to reliability and relevance of information presented to the courts by evaluators.

We have also observed that the vast majority of evaluators who we review have not organized the information obtained in their data gathering around empirically-based variables found in the literature. Too often, evaluators provide little, if any, discussion of how their findings are supported by empirical research (Martindale & Gould, 2007).

The use and abuse of social science research in PPEs by advocacy and political groups have been termed *Woozles*. Originally coined by the children's fictional character, Winnie the Pooh, the term Woozles has been applied to misrepresenting research, such as recommending against shared parenting and overnights for young children in divorcing families (Nielsen, 2014). Posthuma (2016) points out that a "longstanding psychometric example of a prevalent Woozle, in both clinical and forensic literature, is the Rorschach" (p. 67). Despite many critical reviews calling into question the use of the Rorschach in PPEs, survey data reveal that it continues to be among the most widely used assessment tools in evaluations (Ackerman et al., 2021; Bow, Flens, Gould, & Greenhut, 2006; Bow, Gould, Flens, & Greenhut, 2006).

JUDGES' AND ATTORNEYS' EXPECTATIONS ABOUT PARENTING PLAN EVALUATORS

Research studies over the past 30 years have investigated the legal professions' expectations regarding what is important in selecting an evaluator. LaFortune and Carpenter (1998) found that attorneys expected evaluators to show an unbiased approach, to be competent and fair, to have earned good professional credentials, to credibly present oral testimony, and to provide timely responses to appropriate inquiries.

Bow and Quinnell (2004) found that attorneys' expected evaluators to be objective and unbiased, have relevant experience, have good communication skills and competent professional presentation, and have years of experience conducting evaluations. 51% of attorneys expected the evaluator to be a doctoral-level psychologist.

More recently, Bow, Gottlieb, and Gould-Saltman (2011) found that the biggest complaint about evaluators focused on problems with conclusions and recommendations. Attorneys also voiced frustration with the amount of time taken to complete an evaluation, problems with procedures including use of unscientific methods, failure to cross-check data, over-reliance on psychological testing results, failure to use collateral sources, failure to conduct parent–child observations or home visits, and overlooking relevant information.

Despite the concerns about PPEs and concerns about the competency of evaluators, courts continue to request the assistance of mental health professionals to conduct PPEs (Terzuoli, 2010). Some authors have argued that there is an insufficient research basis to allow for a comprehensive analysis of the contributions of PPEs to custody and decision making (R. F. Kelly & Ramsey, 2009; Tippins & Wittmann, 2005). Other authors raised questions about the appropriateness of courts ordering PPEs, adding that the legal system must also clarify the justification for imposing this extensive—and often expensive—intrusion into the privacy of parents (O'Connell, 2009). Still, others argue that PPEs are inherently unreliable and dangerous (Turkat, 2016, 2021), though such assertions have been challenged with a more evidence-based argument (Gould & Posthuma, 2017).

A primary foundation of a PPE methodology is its reliance on the scientific process. Similarly, rules of evidence guiding the admissibility of scientific evidence, such as that proffered by an expert witness who has conducted a PPE, are also guided by the expert's utilization of the scientific process. Concerns have been raised about evaluators abandoning the scientific process (Semple, 2011) and stating conclusions about their findings with a degree of certainty that is not supported either by their data, by the science underlying their opinions (S. R. Gross & Mnookin, 2003), or by the inferences drawn from those data (Tippins & Wittmann, 2005).

This mischief is exacerbated when the expert opinion is misleadingly represented or perceived as having the objective authority of science (Semple, 2011). Gould has raised similar concerns in previous works, arguing that both within the courts and within the profession of psychology, concerns continue to be expressed about clinical opinions masquerading as scientific knowledge (Gould, 1998, 2006).

To be clear, a PPE follows a scientific process of data collection, data analysis, data interpretation, and hypothesis generation. Evaluators seek information that will generate rival, plausible alternative hypotheses. They address discrepancies in the data. They articulate the limitations of their procedures and are humble about the confidence with which they proffer expert opinions to the court based upon limited scientific and behavioral data.

The legal system has responded to concerns about the quality of PPE reports and the variability in training and competency among evaluators in a variety of ways. Some courts find no value in PPEs and do not order them. Other courts limit evaluators to avoid offering opinions about the ultimate issue. We have found that within a jurisdiction, there can be a wide variety of views from the bench about the usefulness of evaluations, with a judge in one courtroom actively seeking input from evaluators, while in the courtroom next door, the judge finds no value in evaluations. Knowing your judge is critical in our work.

Some jurisdictions have established minimal standards for evaluator training, and some jurisdictions have established minimal standards for what must be included in a PPE.

Studies examining the frequency with which courts follow the recommendations of its neutral evaluators reveal that courts often follow the recommendations of psychologists and psychiatrists. Psychologists and psychiatrists who conduct evaluations and opine about custody access and decision making have been found to be accepted by courts about 90% of the time (Ash & Guyer, 1984) and recommendations from social workers are accepted about 57% of the time (Semple, 2011). Other studies have broken down judicial decision making based on evaluator recommendations into (a) orders that were exactly as the evaluator had recommended, (b) orders that were similar to the recommendation, and (c) orders that were completely counter to the evaluator's recommendations (Horvath et al., 2002). Courts continued to accept evaluator recommendations either exactly as recommended or similar to the evaluator's recommendations.

Anecdotal information paints a foreboding picture. When the first edition of Gould's *Scientifically Crafted* was published in 1998, one of the judges in his hometown immediately embraced the ideas that formed the basis of conducting a more scientifically crafted PPE. Within 12–18 months, most judges on the bench changed their expectations about the methodology to be utilized in a PPE and the importance of citing research to support expert opinions. The psychologists in his hometown who were accustomed to conducting more clinically based PPEs reacted poorly to the new model. Many colleagues viewed the forensic model as prescribing how to conduct evaluations. They voiced their concern about standardizing an evaluation process that was more art than science. In fact, in the early 2000s, the North Carolina Psychological Association was threatened with lawsuits if they published their newly revised child custody guidelines based upon the Forensic Model. The revised guidelines were never published.

Today, there is a better-informed understanding of minimal professional practice methodology to be employed in PPEs (Ackerman et al., 2021; Kirkpatrick, 2004; Patel & Choate, 2014) and related areas of evaluation (Kalich et al., 2007). Survey data have shown that most evaluators gather data from independent information sources consistent with professional practice guidelines promulgated by national organizations (Ackerman et al., 2021). Similar results have been reported for evaluators in Canada (Symons, 2010). Bala asserted that there is no single accepted methodology for conducting PPEs (Bala, 2004). Saini, citing Bala's assertion, suggested that the lack of a single accepted methodology for conducting PPEs is a "serious limitation inherent in testing the reliability of custody evaluations" (Saini, 2008).

Zumbach and Koglin (2015) conducted a systematic review of assessment methods used in PPEs. They concluded, "In general, homogeneity in the assessment methods reported was found across the reviewed studies on child custody and visitation rights, with parent interviews, child interviews, and parent–child observation and parenting skills assessment being the most frequently reported methods of assessment. Both objective and projective testing were also generally reported" (p. 230).

Based upon the survey data from the past 3 decades and the uniformity among professional practice guidelines regarding recommended procedures for evaluations, we believe there is a professional consensus about the methodology to be used in conducting a PPE. Forensic methodology applied to PPEs includes multiple interviews with each parent, interviews with the children, administration, scoring and interpretation of psychological tests when appropriate, third-party record review, collateral informant interviews, and direct behavioral observations of parent and children. (Most recently summarized in Ackerman et al., 2019, 2021; Gould & Mulchay, 2023.)

There is little, if any, consensus about the *specific information* to be gathered from each of the procedures to be used in evaluation. For example, there are few, if any, data suggesting that evaluators utilize a standard interview protocol when interviewing parents, children, or collateral informants (Emery et al., 2005). There are survey data revealing the most commonly used psychological tests in PPEs (Bow, Gould, Flens, & Greenhut, 2006; Bow & Quinnell, 2002), but significant concerns remain about the appropriate use and interpretation of psychological test data in PPEs (Emery et al., 2005; Garber & Simon, 2018; Gould et al., 2009; Rappaport et al., 2018; Zumbach & Koglin, 2015).

There are concerns about the costs and amount of time taken to complete a PPE. These concerns have resulted in an increasing recognition of the need for alternative models for PPEs that adhere to some but not all of the criteria suggested by the professional organizations and articulated in the Forensic Model (Martindale & Gould, 2004).

Saini notes that there remains less evidence regarding the efficacy of PPEs as a tool to assist the courts and families in their adjustment from marriage to divorced family systems (Saini, 2008). We disagree with Saini's conclusion about the lack of evidence regarding the efficacy of PPEs as a tool to assist courts. There is evidence that approximately 90% of PPEs lead to settlement rather than litigation. One hypothesis drawn from these data is that evaluations serve a useful purpose in assisting families in finding out-of-court solutions to their custodial disputes.

As Saini points out, there is little, if any, useful outcome data regarding the effectiveness of expert opinions about custodial placement and decision making on child adjustment, family adjustment, conflict reduction, and other related variables. However, courts may find value in different aspects of a PPE. Courts may find the data collected, analyses of the data across independent data, the integration of the data with empirical research, and the expert's opinion to be useful. None of these areas have been subjected to empirical investigation.

LIMITATIONS OF CURRENT RESEARCH

Posthuma points out many excellent examples of both legal and forensic psychological interest in developing a better understanding of scientific evidence in the courtroom (Gould & Posthuma, 2017). Faigman et al. (2014), Edmond and Roach (2011), and Haack (2013) are examples of recent legal scholars providing guidance both to the courts and forensic experts on the need for specificity in the relevance of forensic research to the issues before the Court.

Faigman, Monahan, and Slobogin (2014), writing in *The University of Chicago Law Review*, provide an excellent review of how, in response to the legal system's standards of admissibility of scientific evidence in *Daubert* jurisdictions, forensic examiners apply research findings drawn from group data to the specific individual(s) before the Court. In the *Dalhousie Law Journal*, Haack (2013) contributes a commonsense discussion clarifying many misunderstandings about what good scientific evidence is and how the courts can identify it. In a useful comment pointing out that scientific inquiry is, in fact, a more systematic process of data collection and analysis used in everyday life, Haack quotes Thomas Huxley: "the man of science simply uses with scrupulous exactness the methods which we all... use carelessly" (p. 49).

Writing from both a legal and forensic psychological perspective, psychologist John Kelly and attorney Sarah Ramsey have written about the importance of judges and attorneys developing a better understanding of social science research and the scientific processes that comprise a well-done empirical study (Ramsey & Kelly, 2004). This is particularly important in the age of *Daubert* and its progeny. They argue that judges need to understand better the methodological strengths and deficiencies of studies cited in an expert witness's oral or written testimony. They proposed a set of guidelines for judges and attorneys to follow to determine the forensic usefulness of a study drawn from behavioral science literature (Ramsey & Kelly, 2006).

Lilienfeld (2012a, 2012b), Gemberling and Cramer (2014), and Chin (2014) provide direction for forensic psychologists in ensuring the proffered evidence conforms with various indicia of scientific validity in order to satisfy the gatekeeping role performed by the judge. This healthy cross-fertilization of legal and forensic psychological research has contributed to many jurisdictions in Canada and the United States incorporating in family law legislation requirements for expert evidence to have a basis in scientific literature.

Another benefit is that the emphasis on the scientific process and, in particular, the identification of specific questions to define the scope of the evaluation, requires the expert witness to answer specific questions put forth, either by counsel or the court, which must be addressed by the expert. In many cases, this enables the expert to focus on specific issues before the court, increasing the likelihood that the evaluator will investigate issues relevant to those before the court. Forensic psychologists are more likely to find scientific support when they address specific issues described in the peer-reviewed literature than when they offer broad statements on children's psychological best interests for which there is no peer-reviewed professional or scientific knowledge (Gould & Posthuma, 2017).

There are many useful ways in which a PPE can provide reliable information to courts about a variety of issues relevant to the child's psychological best interests within the context of her binuclear family structure. There remain, however, significant shortcomings in how evaluators conceptualize the types of data to gather from different sources and how best to assess these areas of potentially rich information.

STRUCTURED ANALYTIC TECHNIQUES

Part of the fun of writing a book like this is being able to bring research and scholarship from areas that are outside the awareness of most evaluators. One area of research that has direct application to our work is drawn from the intelligence and law enforcement communities' efforts to create more accurate models of intelligence gathering and analysis (R. H. Pherson & Heuer, 2021). In the book *Structured Analytic Techniques*, R. H. Pherson and Heuer (2021) write, "The risks inherent in intelligence analysis can never be eliminated, but one way to minimize them is through more structured and disciplined thinking about thinking" (p. xv).

The structured analytic approach used by intelligence analysts in tracking threats to our homeland is based upon a context that ought to be familiar to parenting plan evaluators. The intelligence officers as provided a framework that is "a step-by-step process for dealing with the kinds of incomplete, ambiguous, and sometimes deceptive information with which analysts must work. Structured analysis is a mechanism by which internal thought processes are externalized in a systematic and transparent manner so that they can be shared, built on, and easily critiqued by others. Each technique leaves a trail that other analysts and managers can follow to see the basis for an analytic judgment" (R. H. Pherson & Heuer, 2021, pp. 3–4).

The purpose of the structured analytic approach is to improve analytic rigor, and one benefit of doing so is reducing bias. Structured analytic procedures are designed to make transparent that which is often internal mental process. The approach breaks down the analysis of problems into their component parts, requiring a step-by-step process for analyzing them.

Structured analytic techniques do not replace clinical judgment or intuition. These techniques challenge these judgments by identifying a wider range of options to consider. They require explicit identification and consideration of alternative hypotheses. A primary focus of generating alternative hypotheses is to focus on refuting rather than confirming hypotheses, which is essentially the opposite of what happens in confirmation bias. "Structured analytic techniques help mitigate cognitive biases, misapplied heuristics, and intuitive traps that analysts often fall victim to when relying only on expert-aided judgment" (R. H. Pherson & Heuer, 2021, p. 4).

There is a wonderful quote from Mark Twain that captures the challenges of our work as evaluators. Twain wrote, "What gets us into trouble is not what we don't know, it's what we know for sure that just ain't so" (as cited in R. H. Pherson & Heuer, 2021, p. 183).

The structured analytic approach helps identify multiple ways to challenge cognitive biases, misapplied heuristics, and intuitive traps, which mirrors a theme echoed throughout this book: We must always find ways to double-check our assumptions, challenge our hypotheses, and invite criticism and alternative perspectives. These techniques provide a vehicle by which we can take what we do implicitly and internally (e.g., form assumptions) and make them explicit and external, where they can be examined and challenged.

Structured Analytic Techniques contains an approach to challenging ourselves that has been found effective among those who operate in a very different social science context but who have similar goals: to gather data, effectively analyze those data into useful hypotheses, and then find ways to continuously challenge those hypotheses, especially those hypotheses that have assumed a position of being "most supported by the data." One should seek to refute as well as confirm, and then ask a trusted colleague to critically examine each assumption that serves as a basis for your preferred hypothesis. Then, treat your trusted colleague to a nice dinner as a thank you.

The ideas found in *Structured Analytic Techniques* mirror in greater detail the ways in which parenting plan evaluators ought to approach their work. What R. H. Pherson and Heuer offer is a more extensive, in-depth approach to data gathering and identifying debiasing techniques. The spirit of *Structured Analytic Techniques* is to choose the technique that fits best with the work that you are doing. We discuss the five techniques that appear most likely to apply to PPEs.

The first technique in a structured analysis is *cluster brainstorming*. Cluster brainstorming is designed to identify relevant variables, driving forces, a full range of hypotheses, and available evidence or sources of information (R. H. Pherson & Heuer, 2021, p. 36). Applied to a PPE, the evaluator identifies relevant variables by developing specific questions to guide the evaluation. Based on identification of specific questions, relevant evidence-based or evidence-informed variables can be identified. Each of the questions can be translated into a range of hypotheses.

The second technique to be considered is a *key assumptions checklist* that requires the analyst to explicitly list and question the important working assumptions underlying their analysis. Here, the analyst attempts to identify factors that might contribute to confirmatory bias, pointing the more naïve analyst down a preconceived road for which there is little external support. A key assumption check is an attempt to identify and question key assumptions that, if proven incorrect, would undermine the analysis.

Applied to a PPE, the key assumptions checklist is a reminder to make explicit the ideas, beliefs, and research basis that affect how you approach the evaluation process. We all have implicit assumptions about how the world works. We are all influenced by our personal and professional backgrounds. The key assumptions checklist is a procedure aimed at making explicit many of the implicit ideas that frame our understanding of a case and affect where we look to gather data, the ways in which we approach analyzing data, etc. Making our implicit ideas and world models explicit and open to examination by self and by others is a necessity.

Developing an explicit working model of the world knowledge brought to the specific evaluation by the evaluator might be helpful, but also challenging. For example, if the specific evaluation includes parents from a different cultural background, the evaluator might reflect on assumptions made about people of different cultures and the attributions the evaluator might have developed about the culture, the people from the culture, the parenting practices of people from the culture, etc.

Note here that we strongly suggest being aware of how bias factors such as the fundamental attribution error might influence the attributions an evaluator brings to the initial stages of an evaluation of someone from a different culture. Another example is to make explicit the theory of parenting that guides your thinking. Most evaluators do not describe the implicit model of good parenting that often guides their thinking about which factors are relevant and should be assessed. Applying the key assumption check, you could write out the model or models of good versus bad parenting that guide your thinking. Once you have made these explicit, think through these factors and reflect upon the weight you assign to each of them.

Next, talk to a colleague about your model and the factors associated with your model. Open yourself up to critical feedback about the usefulness of your implicit model. Consider integrating information from your colleague into your thinking. Then, look at peer-reviewed literature with particular emphasis on the evidence basis for each of the factors supporting your notions of good versus bad parenting. Finally, consider where to find reliable procedures to measure each of those factors. Remember, *ipse dixit* might be a fun phrase to use at a cocktail party, but it is not a term that you want attached to your expert testimony.

A third strategy to be considered is the *analysis of competing hypotheses* (R. H. Pherson & Heuer, 2021, p. 37) that requires articulating all plausible hypotheses, not just the hypotheses that appear most likely to be supported. Applied to PPE, analysis of competing hypotheses should occur periodically throughout the assessment process. Analysis of competing hypotheses occurring throughout the assessment process is tantamount to having someone constantly looking over your shoulder, challenging your assumptions and data. This is where applying efforts to refute favorite hypotheses is most useful.

A fourth strategy to be considered is *premortem analysis and structured self-critique* (R. H. Pherson & Heuer, 2021, p. 37), which requires restating the question or problem from other perspectives and continually questioning the sources of uncertainty, diagnostic evidence, critical assumptions, information gaps, and potential for deception. Applied to PPE, the evaluator must step outside of themselves to challenge assumptions. One way is to consider how the fundamental attribution error might affect the current data gathering and tentative hypotheses. Another way is to lay out an argument from one parent against the other parent against each child's perspective. A third way is to consult with colleagues, especially colleagues who are known to challenge you, perhaps because they often see things differently.

A fifth strategy is a *what if analysis* (R. H. Pherson & Heuer, 2021, p. 37) that asks the analyst to consider unexpected events and through a hindsight analysis, how it could have come about, and its potential consequences. A what if analysis creates an awareness of possible early signs of significant change and raises possible signals that the analyst's conclusions are wrong. Applied to PPE, considering a what if analysis can challenge evolving opinions about each parent's parenting abilities, each child's psychological and emotional abilities, and the fit between each child and each parent. The assumptions made about how one parent might effectively meet the developmental needs of a child can be challenged by thinking through how, if you are incorrect in your tentative conclusion, what would be the likely consequences for the parent, the child, and the family system.

HOW DO EVALUATORS UNDERSTAND THE CONCEPT OF FAMILY?

As evaluators, our task is to generate data that is integrated with behavioral science research and offer opinions about the psychological best interests of the child. Children, however, do not exist in a vacuum. Children live in families.

There is not one type of family in our culture. The concept of family has generated significant research in the social sciences, including debates over what constitutes a family, if is there is a decline in the family, if there is a demise of proper family values, who defines what a family is, who defines proper family values, and if proper family values exist, among other fascinating areas of research.

Although evaluators are charged with offering opinions about the best interests of the child, most often our examination of the child occurs within a family structure. One way to think about our task is to examine the best interests of the child within a binuclear family structure. But viewing the child as living in two different family structures still avoids addressing the question of what defines a family.

To the best of our knowledge, those who have written texts on conducting PPEs have not explored the concept of family. As evaluators, we believe it is important to reflect on the implicit model of a family that guides our thinking. Reflecting on which of the many family models guides our thinking might also reveal values and beliefs about what a healthy family model is, which influences how we approach the evaluation process. The values and beliefs associated with the healthy family model we embrace might influence the factors we choose to investigate, the weight we place on the data we obtain about those factors, the relationship among the factors, and the opinions developed from the integration of those factors.

We do not believe there is one family model that works for all children. Certainly, the concept of family has undergone significant redefinition over the past several decades. Still, we are left with the nagging thought that most of our colleagues have not explicitly identified the family model embedded in their thinking that guides their approach to the family under examination.

How do you, as an evaluator, understand the concept of family? What family factors do you choose to consider when evaluating family systems? Psychologists are not often schooled in the sociological tradition of studies of family life, and we are not here to suggest that this section of our book serves the broad, comprehensive examination of understanding family and kinship reflected in sociological research. However, reflecting on how we think about family and kinship might help to identify factors and biases that tend to guide our thinking. Another reason to reflect on how you think about family and kinship is to identify beliefs and myths about what defines a healthy family and healthy family functioning.

One school of thought focuses on whether there is a superior or natural form for the family. In that model, the male is the breadwinner, women work within the home caring for children and maintaining the home structure, and the emphasis is on the nuclear family (Smart, 2004). A prominent assumption of this family model is that the structure of a nuclear family with traditional roles will produce stable, productive, law-abiding, motivated citizens. Other schools of thought define a family as a fluid, dynamic system. Healthy family functioning is defined by the fluid, dynamic nature of relationships within that family system. Fluid family systems are defined by the dynamic, continuously-changing relationships between and among family members.

At one level, there are sections of our country that appear to remain focused on the importance of a family supporting patriarchy or capitalism or some other system outside the family itself (Smart, 2004). At another level, a useful operational definition of healthy family functioning is revealed the evolution of each family member's view of their experiences within the family.

Researchers have examined this notion of family as an evolving story. Rather than studying the respective usefulness of one family structure and its values compared to another, the University of Southern California's "Longitudinal Study of Generations" (Bengtson et al., 2007) study has examined how families worked across generations. The USC study began in 1970 as a cross-sectional study of 3-generation families. They began with 2,044 individuals from 349 families. In 1985, the study added a longitudinal element. Thereafter, the same families were contacted every 3 years. In 1991, a fourth generation was added (Generation Xers). These families have participated every 3 years and provided "one-time snapshots of different families taken in different historical periods by different researchers, guided by different research questions" (Bengtson et al., 2007). The research questions have been developed to understand both continuity and change across generations.

Many social myths about how families have changed over time are examined through the empirical data collected from these families. The USC researchers concluded that families are about raising the next generation of children and the intergenerational transmission of values, characteristics, social capital, and other important variables. Families are what families do (Bengtson et al., 2007).

The complexity and richness of the data are hard to convey in a short review, but essentially, the authors found that in relation to the most recent cohort, the Generation Xers, feelings of solidarity and closeness with parents had not changed when compared to the previous generation. In other words, they found that young people today have as much affection for and respect for their parents as their parents' generation had for their parents. They found that neither divorce nor mothers' employment affected child well-being to any noticeable degree; in fact, they argue that recent generations of mothers invest just as much in their children as did the previous generations of mothers who may not have worked outside the home. They also found that parents still influence their children and that Generation Xers model themselves on their parents just as previous generations had done.

Therefore, their data did not support the idea that parents have lost the ability to influence and guide their children. In sum, they argue that families still matter to children and that their study offers no support to those who insist that the family is in decline. However, they do not present an idealized vision of families; rather, they see families as processes that change and adapt as conditions around them change (Bengtson et al., 2007).

CONSTITUTIONAL RIGHTS, EXPERT OPINIONS, PARENTAL ACCESS, AND DECISION MAKING

We end this chapter addressing an area seldom discussed in the PPE literature: The need to understand the profound constitutional rights of parents and children whose family life is the subject of evaluators' parenting access and decision-making recommendations to the court.

Evaluators' recommendations to the court often involve parents' constitutional rights. Frequently, evaluators will offer expert opinions to the court to limit a parent's access to their children. Sometimes evaluators offer expert testimony recommending that a parent's ability to make decisions be restricted or removed. Our experience is that many evaluators do not grasp the profound constitutional issues involved in such recommendations and routinely offer opinions about custodial access and decision making that have little foundation in the data created for the evaluation proffered to the court. Most evaluators are unfamiliar with the Fourteenth Amendment and the liberty interests in parenting addressed in that amendment.

Parents' Rights

A parent's right to the development and nurturing of their relationship with their child flows from the fact that the parent's achievement of a rich and rewarding life depends, in part, on their ability to directly become involved in the rearing of their children. A child's corresponding right to protection from interference in the relationship derives from the psychological and emotional importance to them of being raised by a loving, responsible, reliable adult (*Franz v. United States*, 1983).

Parental rights in the United States are primarily protected through constitutional interpretations, proposed amendments, and recent legislative efforts. While no standalone Parental Bill of Rights exists in the U.S. Constitution, these rights derive from Supreme Court precedents and specific state and federal laws.

There is a constitutional foundation. The Supreme Court has recognized parental rights as fundamental liberties under the Fourteenth Amendment's Due Process clause. Parents have the right to direct their children's upbringing, education, and care without undue state interference, provided they meet minimum care standards (i.e., *Meyer v. Nebraska* [1923], *Pierce v. Society of Sisters* [1925], and *Troxel v. Granville* [2000]). These cases are among those that have affirmed that states cannot override parental decisions unless there is a compelling governmental interest.

There are federal legislative efforts addressing parental rights. H.R. 5 (Parents Bill of Rights Act), passed by the U.S. House in 2023, codifies five core principles regarding a parent's knowledge and right to make decisions about their child's education:

1. Right to know: Access to curricula, books, and budgets
2. Right to be heard: Engage with school boards and teachers
3. Right to transparency: Review school spending
4. Right to privacy: Protect children's data
5. Right to safety updates: Receive alerts about school violence

The bill mandates schools to publicly disclose library materials and notify parents of curriculum changes. Critics argue it could enable book bans and politicize education.

Over the years, we have noted with concern how few evaluators have understood the profound constitutional issues involved in offering expert opinions to the court to reduce or diminish a parent's right to parent their child. Our hope is that evaluators and the attorneys and judges who appoint them will reflect on the responsibility that is entailed in offering opinions to the court about curtailing or terminating a parent's right to parent their child.

Rights Are Not Absolute

Individual rights are not absolute. There are times when the State may infringe upon those rights. In family law, the court is the actor through which the state may infringe upon individual rights (S. B. Epstein & Fontana, 2010). The more important the constitutional right, the higher the burden upon the state to show why it must infringe upon that right. When a fundamental liberty interest is at issue, the state's interest must be extremely compelling and narrowly defined. The state's infringement upon a constitutional right must meet the strictest of scrutiny (S. B. Epstein & Fontana, 2010).

Evaluators must recognize that when they offer expert opinions to the court to limit or, in some other way, diminish a parent's ability to spend time with their child or to make decisions about their child, they are recommending that the court infringe upon a parent's protected constitutional rights.

Competing Constitutional Interests

The goal of granting custody based on the best interests of the child is indisputably a substantial government interest of the purpose of the Equal Protection Clause (*Palmore v. Sidoti,* 1984, p. 433). In a parenting dispute, any court solution regarding the allocation of parental responsibility balances several competing constitutional interests. One is that the government has an interest in civil order. A second interest is the parents' rights under the amendments found in the Bill of Rights as discussed above. A third interest is the child's rights as determined through a best interests analysis, which are articulated in the Bill of Rights as well.

The Power of the Court to Protect Children

Parens patriae is Latin for "father of his country." This term has come to represent the doctrine that the government is the ultimate guardian of its people under a disability. The definition of *disability* under *parens patriae* has evolved significantly from its feudal origins to modern legal interpretations, reflecting broader societal shifts in understanding vulnerability and state responsibility. Children may be viewed as being under a disability. Under *parens patriae,* in any action in which children are involved, the government retains jurisdiction until the child reaches the age of majority (removal of the disability). A court may change custody, child support, or other decisions that affect the child's best interests, no matter what the parents have previously decided, or the court has previously ruled. *Parens patriae* may be involved by the court when parents cannot agree on parenting issues (S. B. Epstein & Fontana, 2010).

Parens patriae has its origin in English common law from the 13th–17th centuries. The doctrine originated as a prerogative of the English Crown to act as guardian for "idiots" (those with congenital intellectual disabilities) and "lunatics" (those who developed mental illness later in life). The state managed their properties and derived revenue from their property, blending paternalism with financial interest. The *Prerogative Regis* (1272–1307) codified the King's authority over wards' lands and care (McGlynn, 2004).

As it is used today, the concept of disability under *parens patriae* as used in child custody disputes focuses on minor children being viewed as not legally competent, needing a competent adult as a guardian to manage their legal affairs and daily life. The state's role arises when there is no competent parent or guardian, or when existing guardians fail to act in the individual's best interest. Courts may appoint guardians or make decisions directly to ensure welfare concepts of *non compos mentis* ("not of sound mind").

When parents separate and ask the court to formally dissolve their marriage, the state has an interest in protecting the children from any harm that may result from the parents' divorce. The court (as an agent of the state) becomes a parent to oversee the best interests of the child (*Palmore v. Sidoti,* 1984).

Protecting Parental Rights

The vast majority of divorces with children are resolved by parental agreement without having the court intervene. When divorcing parents are able to agree upon parenting arrangements, they maintain their constitutional right to parent their children without infringement by the government. "The constitutional rights of a parent are clear: privacy rights and associated travel rights, and the right to raise a child with only minimal and necessary state intrusion" (Gould et al., 2016a, p. 4).

The constitutional basis for protection of parental rights has been clearly articulated in many cases. The United States Supreme Court in *Meyer v. Nebraska* (1923) held that the liberty protected by the Due Process Clause includes the right of parents to establish a home and bring up children and to control the education of their own.

The court held in *Pierce v. Society of Sisters* (1925) that the liberty interests of parents and guardians include the right to direct the upbringing and education of children under their control.

Similar decisions were articulated by the United States Supreme Court in *Prince v. Massachusetts* (1944) in which it held that there is a constitutional dimension to the right of parents to direct the upbringing of their children. The court affirmed that "It is cardinal . . . that the custody, care, and nurture of the child reside first in the parents, whose primary function and freedom include preparation for obligations the state can neither supply nor hinder" (*Prince v. Massachusetts,* 1944, p. 166).

More recently, the Supreme Court held in *Troxel v. Granville* (2000), "The liberty interest . . . of parents in the care, custody, and control of their children . . . is perhaps the oldest of the fundamental liberty interests recognized by this Court" (p. 66).

In summarizing the Court's decisions from *Myers* through *Troxel,* the Court declared, "In light of this extensive precedent, it cannot now be doubted that the Due Process Clause of the Fourteenth Amendment protects the fundamental right of parents to make decisions concerning the care, custody, and control of their children" (*Troxel v. Granville,* 2000, p. 66).

Protecting Children's Rights

It is only when parents are unable to resolve their parenting issues and bring their conflict to the attention of the court that the court assumes *parens patriae.*

> Unless fit parents disagree, the courts have no jurisdiction to become involved with a fit parent's constitutional right to direct the upbringing of the child and override that paramount parental privilege. However, when parents cannot agree, such as when a family experiences a divorce and emotions run high, they

> turn to the legal system to make determinations regarding their children. (S. B. Epstein & Fontana, 2010, p. 4)

Troxel represents an interesting potential change of direction with regard to children's rights. Acknowledging that the court has yet to describe the nature of children's constitutional interests in preserving their family relationships, Justice Stevens, writing in dissent, wrote,

> While this court has not yet had occasion to elucidate the nature of a child's liberty interests in preserving established familial or family-type bonds. . . . it seems to be extremely likely that, to the extent that parents and families have fundamental liberty interests in preserving such intimate relationships, so, too, do children have their interests, and so, too, must their interests be balanced in the equation. (as cited in *Troxel v. Granville*, 2000, p. 88)

Justice Stevens addressed the importance of including the voice of the children when their best interests are being determined.

> Cases like this do not present a bipolar struggle between the parents and the State over who has the final authority to determine what is in a child's best interests. There is at a minimum a third individual, whose interests are implicated in every case in which the statute applies—the child. (as cited in *Troxel v. Granville*, 2000, p. 86)

What is the takeaway from this discussion? Evaluators need to understand the profoundly important task they undertake when agreeing to conduct an evaluation, the purpose of which is to provide the court with expert opinions that may affect a parent's constitutional liberty interests in parenting their child. At the same time, evaluators need to be cognizant of the need to assist the court in understanding the real and potential risks to a child resulting from the parents' conflict over child-related manners they were unable to resolve without the court's intervention. We have a responsibility to ensure that the court hears the voices of the children of divorce and is able to see life through the eyes of those children.

CONCLUSION

Over the past several decades, substantial improvements have been made in defining professional practices and expanding the evidence-based foundation of family court assessments. These advancements have contributed to greater consistency, credibility, and effectiveness in PPEs and other forensic evaluations related to family law. However, despite these significant strides, the field still faces notable limitations in both professional expertise and scientific knowledge.

One critical issue is the extent to which PPEs can be considered a truly evidence-based endeavor. While efforts have been made to standardize evaluation procedures and integrate empirical research, the practice of family court assessment continues to reflect a blend of science and professional judgment (or art). In some cases, this integration is seamless, allowing evaluators to apply psychological principles and research-based methodologies effectively. In other cases, tensions arise between the objective, evidence-based aspects of forensic assessment and the subjective, interpretative nature of clinical judgment.

These challenges underscore the importance of improving the reliability and trustworthiness of evaluation reports. In the following two chapters, we will examine common errors that frequently appear in evaluation reports and explore strategies for enhancing their accuracy, consistency, and credibility and the challenges of basing evaluation procedures and expert testimony on clinical judgments. Addressing these errors is essential for fostering more evidence-based and ethically sound evaluations that can withstand legal scrutiny and serve the best interests of children and families.

3

Common Errors in Child Custody Evaluations

This chapter explores common errors in parenting plan evaluations (PPEs). By addressing these issues early in the book, we aim to provide readers with a structured framework for interpreting the information presented in subsequent chapters. Additionally, we hope that identifying these frequent mistakes at the outset will encourage readers to critically assess their own practices in light of the errors discussed.

We outline 16 common errors, offering brief descriptions of the first 15, which are from W. G. Austin (2018a). The final error, however, receives special attention as it delves into the ongoing debate over the role of clinical judgment and experience in forensic evaluations—particularly in the context of PPEs. In later chapters, we will explore specific areas such as interviewing children, adults, and collateral sources. Before delving into these topics, this chapter examines the complex challenges evaluators face and the common errors that can compromise their work. Drawing on established research and practical experience, we emphasize the crucial need for evaluators to base their assessments on a strong foundation of legal and scientific guidelines and standards.

Evaluators must navigate the intersection of legal knowledge with their clinical and forensic training. This chapter advocates for a systematic, evidence-based approach to integrating data collection into evaluations. It emphasizes the importance of grounding conclusions in peer-reviewed research, professional practice guidelines, and ethical standards while ensuring that findings are presented to the court in a clear, logical, and comprehensible manner.

https://doi.org/10.1037/0000474-004
Parenting Plan Evaluations: An Evidence-Informed Approach to Child Custody, by J. W. Gould and C. M. Mulchay

COMMON ERRORS IDENTIFIED BY AUSTIN

PPEs are among the most complex tasks undertaken by forensic psychologists. William G. Austin (2018a) described several common errors by evaluators who conduct relocation evaluations. We believe that the common errors identified by Austin can be applied to all PPEs. These evaluations demand a sophisticated understanding of not only psychology and human behavior but also the legal frameworks governing family law. Evaluators must navigate intricate intersections between statutory requirements, case law precedents, local court rules, numerous areas of behavioral science research, professional practice guidelines, ethical standards, and the unique dynamics of individual families. The stakes are high because the ways in which the court often relies on these evaluations may have profound implications for the lives of children and parents.

In this section, we identify 15 specific areas of common errors found in evaluators' knowledge bases, investigative strategies, report writing, and oral testimony.

Inadequate Knowledge of the Law

Evaluators need to develop and maintain a firm understanding of relevant statutes and case law. Evaluators must know each state's statutes regarding the best interest of the child, relocation, parenting time presumptions, and related statutes. Similarly, the evaluator must be familiar with case law addressing parenting time presumptions, relocation, best interest of the child, and related case law. For example, there is case law in some states prohibiting the admission of certain psychological tests (i.e., Millon Clinical Multiaxial Inventory, 4th ed.) or testimony about certain concepts (e.g., parental alienation syndrome).

Evaluators are wise to develop an understanding of the rules of evidence regarding the admissibility of scientific evidence. For example, evaluators should be familiar with whether their state's admissibility standards for expert testimony are guided by *Frye, Daubert,* or some mixture of these admissibility standards.

Approximately 38 states have identified best interest factors derived from statutes, case law, and court rules. Evaluators should assess the psychological components associated with each best interest factor. Similarly, in those states that have relocation statutes, case law, and court rules, the evaluator should assess both the best interest factors and the relocation factors.

INADEQUATE KNOWLEDGE OF PROFESSIONAL AND SCIENTIFIC LITERATURE

The professional and scientific literature addressing factors associated with PPE is diverse, often controversial, and lacking in consensus. There is no standard of practice supporting how best to utilize professional and scientific literature, although there are calls to provide citations to literature the evaluator relied upon in formulating opinions (Gould & Martindale, 2008; Martindale & Gould, 2007).

We believe it is important for evaluators to be familiar with literature that supports and challenges the opinions proffered to the courts. The professional and scientific literature should serve as the most reliable basis for the evaluator's opinions. Evaluators need to provide coherent arguments that support the basis for their opinions as well as provide coherent arguments that explain why reasonable alternative literature was not used as the basis of the expert opinion.

As a practical matter, the omission of literature citations likely results in increased costs to the parents or litigants. In order to obtain the literature upon which the evaluator's opinion was based, attorneys would have to conduct a deposition or go to trial in order to discover the basis for the opinions and conclusions presented in the report.

INADEQUATE FACTORIAL ANALYSIS

Many states have statutes and case law that identify specific best-interest factors that the court must consider before rendering a custody decision. There are similar statutes and case law on other issues, such as relocation, domestic violence, coercive control, and child sexual abuse. Evaluators should consider assessing each of these statutory and case law factors and discuss their findings for each factor in the body of their reports.

FAILURE TO TAKE A SYSTEMATIC APPROACH

The purpose of regulatory codes, standards of practice, and ethical standards is to help establish a minimal level of competency. Establishing a minimal level of competency allows courts and others to critically examine an evaluator's compliance with rules, standards, and guidelines through which one can evaluate the evaluation's reliability, relevance, and helpfulness. As we've noted, the field has developed a standard of practice which ensures that information from multiple, independent sources is used as the basis for expert opinions. Deviation from established standards of practice requires that the evaluator demonstrates how the novel assessment procedures are at least as reliable if not more reliable than the standard of practice procedures.

FAILURE TO ACCOUNT FOR BIAS

As we discuss in Chapter 7, bias factors affect every step of the evaluation process (Neal & Grisso, 2014). Evaluators bring their personal and professional biases into each evaluation. Parents and children, too, bring their biases to the evaluation process. So, too, do collateral informants who provide third-party information.

Bias factors might play a role in choosing psychological tests or their interpretation. Bias factors might play a role in relying on literature addressing one aspect of a concern while ignoring other, relevant aspects. For example, some people believe in the tender years doctrine, despite all 50 states having embraced the best interests standard.

We began this book asking you to reflect upon the implicit theory of parenting that guides your thinking about what is good parenting. That is a type of bias. The usual and customary bias factors must also be recognized. These include confirmatory bias, primary and recency effects, halo bias, and contextual bias, among others. Evaluators need to be aware of the various biases that parents often bring into the evaluation process, such as the tendency to present themselves in a favorable light and the tendency to minimize the other parent's parenting and maximize their parenting.

The multi-informant model (De Los Reyes et al., 2015; De Los Reyes & Epkins, 2023) reminds us that different people have different perspectives and often might have different motivations based upon the context within which they are observed. For example, a 14-year-old adolescent male might present himself in one way when observed with his mother and present himself in another way with his father. Eventually, the evaluator learns that the young male's motivation was to present himself as having a poor relationship with his father because his current girlfriend lived two houses away from his mother's home. The young man was motivated to present a negative picture of life with dad for no reason related to his father but rather his motivation to live near his girlfriend.

MISUSE OF THEORY AND RESEARCH

The misuse of theory and research is a common problem. Evaluators might speak about attachment in ways that are, at the least, distant cousins to the original attachment research. For example, Rappaport (2022) recently addressed the overuse and misuse of the concept of attachment:

> Professionals often use phrases such as "strong attachment," "healthy bond," and "well-attached," all phrases which are not in the scientific literature. Attachment has a specific definition in the scientific literature. Furthermore, other than the Strange Situation method of assessment, there are no well-research reliable and valid methods for assessing the type of attachment, as defined in the scientific literature. Until such measures exist, evaluators, therapists, and family court professionals should avoid using the term attachment to describe parent–child relationships and instead focus on functional aspects of the parent–child relationship. (p. 115)

There continues to be misuse of psychological test results in PPE reports. Aligned with the misuse of psychological test results are concerns about offering opinions about the psychological characteristics of parents that have little to no relationship with evidence-based data about how such characteristics might adversely affect parenting.

Several psychological constructs that are often referenced in reports include, but are not limited to, alienation, domestic violence, and coercive control. Similar to the concerns expressed by Rappaport regarding attachment, many commonly used psychological constructs are used inappropriately. One solution is for evaluators to operationally define the psychological constructs they intend to investigate. The evaluator should cite specific professional or scientific literature that directly addresses the construct and its factors. For example, Garber et al. (2022) wrote *The Family Law Professional's Field Guide to High Conflict Litigation* to provide such a resource. Given the obligation to consider rival, alternative hypotheses, evaluators would be wise to explain their choice of a particular construct to guide their investigation.

Once the construct is identified and defined, then the factors associated with the construct should be identified and defined. The factors should be drawn from the literature supporting the use of the construct in this particular evaluation. For example, if an evaluator is investigating a child's resistance or refusal to spend time with a parent, the evaluator needs to identify which theory will guide the investigation. Among the various theories in the current literature are the dominant factor and multiple or dimensional factors (which we will discuss in Chapters 13 and 14). Within each of these theories are specific factors that should be clearly defined and assessed based upon reliable procedures.

Employing such a procedure of identifying and defining constructs, identifying and defining factors associated with the constructs, and utilizing reliable assessment procedures reflects the scientific process we will stress in the following chapters. Identifying and defining each construct found in the professional and scientific literature of the discipline reflects the type of specialized knowledge that courts expect from evaluators.

INADEQUATE INVESTIGATION OF THE RELEVANT ISSUES

Evaluators are often challenged in court because of inadequate investigation and insufficient data gathering. The importance of an investigative approach to data collection in PPEs often is not fully appreciated (W. G. Austin & Kirkpatrick, 2004). Evaluators may fail to adequately assess the legal factors, factors indicated by research or the available forensic models, or the relative advantages and disadvantages associated with different parenting plans.

Often, there is a paucity of data, inviting the evaluator to speculate about what the missing data is likely to reveal. Such speculation is beyond the scope of an evaluator. The evaluator's responsibility is to stay within the data, not extrapolate beyond the data. Speculation and extrapolation beyond the data is more likely the role of an attorney engaged in advocacy, not the role of an evaluator providing evidence-based or evidence-informed opinions.

William G. Austin makes the point that when evaluators speculate to fill in holes resulting from a paucity of data, this "weakness usually translates to an inadequate comparative analysis in which the evaluator fails to properly help the court visualize what life would really be like for the child in the alternative residential living arrangements in the two communities" (2018a).

INSUFFICIENT ANALYSIS OF KEY VARIABLES

PPEs will often include analysis of statutory and case law factors as well as relevant psychological factors unique to the family at bar. Too often evaluators exclude analyses of key variables. For example, a history of parental communication prior to the relationship conflict that led to separation often provides important information serving as a predictor of future cooperation and communication. Similarly, gathering historical information about caretaking, gatekeeping, and related variables is often critically important in understanding the history of the child's experience with each parent, yet too often, factors such as these are either excluded or poorly investigated.

A challenge for all evaluators is to conduct an evaluation that helps the court view the current family system through the eyes of the child as well as through the eyes of each parent. Too many evaluations investigate the best interests of the child through the eyes of each parent. Helping the court see family life through each family member's eyes should be a goal of every PPE.

MISUSE OF AVAILABLE FORENSIC MODELS

Evaluators are wise to rely on the professional practice guidelines promulgated by national organizations such as the American Psychological Association and Association of Family and Conciliation Courts. The forensic model (Martindale & Gould, 2004) reflects the application of standard forensic methodology to PPE. For example, in conducting a relocation risk assessment, the relocation risk assessment (RRA) model reflects the current professional consensus about a useful forensic model. In many relocation cases we have reviewed, the RRA model is often not employed and, just as often, examination of the state's relocation factors are not addressed.

In the area of parent–child contact problems or resist and refuse dynamics, several theoretical constructs have been discussed in the literature, and survey data have revealed greater support for the multifactor or dimensional model than for other models. Unfortunately, we have observed expert opinions about alienation dynamics with little, if any, reference to or reliance upon current literature addressing assessment models.

A third example is the lack of attention to a family's gatekeeping behavior across time. We have observed very few evaluations that critically examine parental gatekeeping when the family was together and changes that occurred due to the separation.

MISUSE OF PSYCHOLOGICAL TESTING

There continues to be significant misuse of psychological test results. In many cases, test results continue to be used clinically, with the evaluator describing the test results as if they speak directly to the psychological characteristics of the parent. As will be discussed later in this book, most evaluators do not appear to appreciate or communicate the nomothetic and ideographic approaches to testing, despite these being foundational and mandatory if tests are to be utilized.

Another concern is the use of psychological tests that were never intended to be used in a forensic context. There are also evaluators who utilize measures found on the internet with little attention to the lack of psychometric support.

Psychological test data are to be used to develop hypotheses about parenting behavior. The results might also be used to develop hypotheses about how a child might experience a parent with particular psychological characteristics or the results might suggest hypotheses about the safety or predictability of a child's emotional environment based upon the parent's test results. These are only hypotheses that need to be further explored with all family members and third-party informants who have personal knowledge of family interactions.

INADEQUATE DEVELOPMENT OF PARENTING PLAN AND ATTENTION TO PRACTICAL ANALYSIS

There is little, if any, evidence-based literature to support parenting plans for children of different ages. There are several evidence-informed articles that extrapolate from child development research to crafting age-appropriate parenting plans. These parenting plans are useful ideas to guide parenting plan development, but they are not sufficiently reliable data to be used as the sole basis of an expert opinion about parenting time distribution.

The development of useful parenting plans reflects the art of the PPE evaluation process. It is unlikely that one parenting plan is sufficiently powerful enough to rule out other, alternative plans. One approach is to provide the court with two or three parenting plan options, each based upon peer-reviewed literature. The advantages and disadvantages of each plan might be discussed in a compare and contrast method, helping the court to see the similarities and differences in each plan.

FAILURE TO OBTAIN SPECIFIC QUESTIONS TO GUIDE THE INVESTIGATIVE PROCESS

In addition to the above errors identified by W. G. Austin (2018a), we include a final error that we feel strongly about: failure to obtain specific questions to guide the investigative process. We emphasize the importance of beginning an evaluation upon receiving a set of specific questions to guide the evaluation process and structure the report. If the court does not offer specific questions, the evaluator should request them.

No matter how skilled a forensic examiner may be in conducting an evaluation, the relevance of the information gathered in the evaluation is directly tied to the clarity and scope of the questions that guide the investigation. By including specific questions in court orders or stipulations, judges and attorneys increase the likelihood that evaluators will stay on course, investigate the issues of concern, and, in preparing their reports, provide information that bears directly upon the issues before the court. The identification of specific questions to guide the evaluator's investigation will lower the risk of investigative intrusion into areas of a parent's or child's life that are not directly tied to the issues in dispute before the court.

When judges fail to translate the issues in dispute into specific psychelegal questions that may be answered by evaluators, they handicap their appointed experts. When court orders do not contain specific questions, it falls to the attorneys to craft these questions for forensic examiners to investigate. Attorneys who do not provide forensic examiners with questions to guide their investigations increase the likelihood that psycholegal issues in dispute will not be directly addressed.

If evaluators do not know the specific questions to be investigated, they are unable to choose appropriate tests. Similarly, if evaluators do not know the specific questions to be investigated, they are unable to conduct focused interviews with parents, children, and collateral informants about those areas of concern. Finally, if evaluators do not know the specific questions to be investigated, they are less likely to be able to separate the wheat from the chaff as information and test data are reviewed.

CONCLUSION

In this chapter, we discussed common errors in evaluations, such as failure to address relevant statutory factors, inadequate exploration of key issues, misuse of psychological testing, and reliance on biased or unverified constructs. We also emphasize the importance of systematic approaches to evaluation, beginning with specific clear investigative questions. In the next chapter, we discuss the use of checklists and decision trees. We advocated for a transparent and methodical evaluation process that incorporates the principles of the ecological model. We want you to continue to think of these concepts as you read this book. In the remainder of the book, we will take a deep dive into specific methods (interviews, observations, psychological testing, collateral interviews, and record review) and common issues in PPEs (parent–child contact problems, domestic violence, child sexual abuse, and relocation).

4

The Role of Clinical Judgment in the Time of *Daubert*

Evaluators' reliance on clinical judgment is a common error; however, the depth of controversy over use of or reliance on clinical judgment merits a longer discussion than the errors discussed in the previous chapter. Part of the ongoing challenges to reliance on clinical judgment in parenting plan evaluations (PPEs) stems from the historical roots of clinical judgment as a cornerstone of clinical psychology treatment endeavors. Another part of the challenge is that many evaluators have not been forensically trained and, as a result, tend to rely on their clinical rather than forensic approaches to assessment. Therefore, we felt it appropriate to take a deep dive into the strengths and deficiencies of clinical judgment.

In this chapter, we take a deep dive into the role of clinical judgment in the era of *Daubert*. We examine how clinical judgment can be evaluated through the lens of the analytic gap and explore the impact of various biases on decision making. Additionally, we discuss strategies for organizing information to determine when clinical judgment serves as a valuable tool in expert testimony and when it risks creating an analytic gap that undermines reliability. The chapter concludes with practical insights into distinguishing between well-supported expert opinions and those that extend beyond a reasonable evidentiary foundation.

---

https://doi.org/10.1037/0000474-005
Parenting Plan Evaluations: An Evidence-Informed Approach to Child Custody, by J. W. Gould and C. M. Mulchay

CONCERNS ABOUT RELYING PRIMARILY ON CLINICAL JUDGMENT

The evolution of mental health practice has moved from clinical inferences and basic research studies to the systematic investigation of evidence-based practice. Evidence-based practice is an attempt to evaluate treatment effectiveness systematically. Historically, established clinicians sometimes voiced concerns about feeling slighted by evidence-based focus. Clinicians felt their decades of clinical experience were devalued or discarded by evidence-based approaches. Among the most salient objections to the evidence-based model from clinicians include concerns that clinical experience is better than standardized methods and the belief that practitioners know better than assessment tools.

There are several concerns about the use of clinical judgment and experience as the primary sources of information upon which expert opinions are based. Shuman and Sales (1999) put forth the following concerns about the reliability of expert witness testimony based upon clinical judgment and experience. First, while some expert testimony by people with scientific degrees is derived from research, the accuracy of which can be validated, much other expert testimony advances opinions derived from judgments in which accuracy rests on the expert's nonvalidated theories and skills. Second, these untested opinions are commonly referred to as clinical judgments and are defined by their reliance on personal experience rather than on statistically analyzed data drawn from valid and reliable research. Third, use of the term *clinical* refers to a method or approach of making judgments or decisions. Fourth, the growing literature on human judgment and decision making helps explain the inherent unreliability of clinical judgment and decision making. Fifth, expert judgments that are clinically derived are as susceptible to error as lay judgments and involve the use of untested procedures (strategies) in arriving at decisions that contribute to the error rate. Sixth, clinical judgments and opinions offered in court by an expert are just as flawed as any other clinical judgment. Seventh, to the extent that a scientist or practitioner relies on personal or professional experience and personal biases in drawing inferences that go beyond the data, they are engaging in clinical decision making, despite their scientific training.

PPEs are not only scientific endeavors. A degree of clinical judgment is always part of the assessment process. Gould and Martindale (2007) wrote *The Art and Science of Child Custody Evaluations* with the recognition that clinical judgment and experience affect decisions made during the evaluation process. For example, evaluators ask questions during interviews to follow one area of inquiry rather than another based on clinical judgment and experience. Evaluators do not, however, base expert opinion upon clinical judgment and experience.

If an evaluator bases one or more opinions on their clinical intuition rather than upon data collected in the investigation, should the evaluator describe in the body of the report how their clinical intuition provides a reliable basis for expert opinion? An opinion based upon clinical intuition is, by definition, an opinion based upon the interpretation of subjective information. When clinical intuition is used as a method upon which expert opinion is based, the method of data gathering is of unknown reliability. The subjective data gathering and analysis upon which intuition is based are inconsistent with the rules of evidence requiring that expert opinions are based upon data gathered from reliable procedures.

When an evaluator bases an opinion upon their subjective impressions of a parent, child, or parent–child interaction, the evaluator functions as a direct participant in the evaluation process. The evaluator is no longer an observer but has become an actor in the events of the evaluation. An evaluator who moves from an observer using reliable data-gathering methods to an actor and direct participant in gathering and analyzing data is therefore "an actor with regards to the occurrences from which the tapestry of the lawsuit was woven" (*Gonzales v. Exec. Airlines, Inc.*, 2006, p. 77). The methods that produced the subjective testimony—the clinical intuition—are not methodologically sound and, therefore, the testimony should not be characterized as expert testimony (Gordon, 2016).

CLINICAL JUDGEMENT AND THE ANALYTICAL GAP

In 2000, Gould and Stahl attempted to challenge what appeared to be efforts to discount, minimize, or exclude the application of clinical judgment and experience in PPEs by showing a way to integrate clinical acumen and clinical sensitivity into the evaluation process. Challenges to the role of clinical judgment and sensitivity were raised by Tippins and Wittmann, beginning in 2005, who brought into the field greater attention to the analytic gap between what is known in the professional and scientific literature and the empirical support or lack of empirical support for many custody and access decisions offered to the courts. Tippins and Wittmann's articles and presentations have generated important discussions about several critical issues.

Among the myriad issues raised by Tippins and Wittmann was their questioning the scientific basis for expert opinions about custody and access. Too often, evaluators offered opinions to the court that had little to no empirical support. Expert opinions about custody and access plans, in particular, were based upon speculation or personal preferences masquerading as science. They asked what expert opinions that have often been included in recommendations to the courts have a substantial enough empirical basis to serve as a foundation for reliable expert opinions. Their answer was none! They argued that expert opinions about custody and access recommendations should not be admissible because of the lack of empirical data to support those recommendations. One outgrowth of the Tippins and Wittmann argument has been ongoing questions about the role of clinical judgment in the formulation of expert opinions.

In 2007, Gould and Martindale discussed the importance of clinical training and experience as foundational skills and knowledge needed to serve as an important component of expert opinions. Throughout the multiple editions of Ackerman et al.'s *Psychological Experts in Divorce Actions* beginning in 1985 through the present, the authors struggled with how best to describe the role and potential usefulness of clinical judgment in the evaluation process and in the formulation of expert opinions.

Recently, arguments about the proper role of clinical judgment in expert opinions proffered in child custody matters and how best to apply peer-reviewed research to expert opinions have continued. The ongoing debate about these two questions is exemplified in a wonderfully dynamic exchange between psychologist Jeff Wittmann and psychologist and attorney Lawrence Braunstein in their 2023 article in *Family Court Review*.

Among the questions not addressed in the peer-reviewed research are (a) how does one define the analytic gap between data and opinion? and (b) how does one determine when the analytic gap between data and opinion is too great to allow for reliable expert opinions? Said differently, how does one identify an analytic gap between data in the report and opinions based upon those data that are too large to support a reliable or trustworthy expert opinion?

PLAYING IN THE LAW'S SANDBOX

Our intention in this book is to frequently remind the reader about the importance of evidentiary reliability, or what mental health professionals label as reliability and validity. In law, evidentiary reliability encompasses both reliability and validity and speaks to the validity of ideas brought to the attention of the court. Embedded in the notion of evidentiary reliability as validity is the acknowledgment that something cannot be valid if it is not reliable.

As evaluators, it is incumbent upon us to recognize that we have been invited into the legal system and the expectation is that we play by their rules when in their sandbox. The rules that govern the admissibility of evidence exist to ensure, to the degree possible, that trustworthy information is presented to the trier of fact. The rules that govern direct examination exist to facilitate the best possible presentation of evidence within the rules that govern admissible evidence. The rules that govern cross-examination exist to test the validity of the proffered evidence. These rules exist to ensure the proper administration of justice. "It was precisely to ensure the reliability and validity of the information placed before the factfinder that evidence doctrine was born, and it is only fidelity to that doctrine that some semblance of adjudicative integrity can be preserved" (Braunstein & Wittmann, 2023, p. 10).

Among the issues with which our field will likely continue to struggle include two questions drawn from *Daubert* that have also been foundational to the challenges raised by Tippins and Wittmann in 2003, more than 2 decades ago. The first question is what peer-reviewed literature has sufficient evidentiary reliability to serve as a basis for expert opinions? The second question is how do we develop principles or procedures to help guide the application of reliable peer-reviewed literature in the development of trustworthy expert opinions?

THE CHALLENGE OF THE ANALYTIC GAP

The backbone of the adversarial system is cross-examination. Although imperfect, it is considered the most effective way of fact finding and determining truth (J. L. Austin & Kovera, 2015). Wigmore (1978, p. 29) dubbed cross-examination "the greatest legal engine ever invented for the discovery of truth." *Daubert* held that "vigorous cross-examination, presentation of contrary evidence, and careful instruction on the burden of proof are the traditional and appropriate means of attacking shaky but admissible evidence" (*Daubert v. Merrell Dow Pharmaceuticals, Inc.*, 1993). In family court matters, cross-examinations are most useful when they assist the court with evaluating the scientific quality of expert testimony. This means that attorneys need to develop questions that are designed to help the court evaluate the reliability and relevance of proffered scientific evidence (J. Epstein, 2009). Evaluators need to prepare their reports and oral testimony by examining their reliability and relevance, knowing that their procedures and opinions will be challenged. Their expert opinions will also be scrutinized against an undefined standard: the analytic gap between data and opinions.

In most jurisdictions, many alternative dispute resolution options are available to families before the court orders a PPE. Most often, a PPE is seen as a last resort, in part, because the evaluation process is viewed as intrusive and reduces the likelihood that the parents will make final decisions about the custodial placement of their children.

Daubert was explicitly designed to help courts make individualized decisions. The court's focus on expert testimony is on the *reliability of the method* used as a basis for collection relevant data upon which the expert's opinion is based. One aspect of the court's obligation is to examine what the relevant field upon which the expert bases their opinion knows and, by extension, how that knowledge informs methods of assessment that produce reliable and relevant data upon which to base those opinions. Where evaluators often misunderstand the intention of *Daubert* is their focus on whether they used their data gather procedure correctly. This is only one part of the challenge. The other part of the challenge is whether there is sufficient evidence in the evaluator's field demonstrating that the data gathering procedure can be relied upon when used in the context for which it is being proffered (Braunstein & Wittman, 2023).

It follows, or should follow, that when data-gathering tools are of questionable reliability, expert opinions developed from them should not be presented in court. Our field has a wealth of information about a wide variety of behavioral science areas that are more likely than not to assist the court. There are also many areas in the behavioral sciences that are not ready for prime time. Part of our responsibility as testifying expert witnesses is to educate the court about the limits of our knowledge and to convey the constraints on the trustworthiness of predictions about future behavior. Psychological expert witnesses are teachers.

The specialized knowledge of psychological experts includes knowing the literature support for the selection of reliable data-gathering tools, identification of relevant information generated by those data-gathering tools, interpreting the meaning of those data in the context of the specific family under examination, integrating peer-reviewed literature with the interpretations of the data proffered to the court, and considering reasonable alternative explanation of the data.

Among the arguments in the literature is whether or the degree to which one might apply research findings as part of the basis for expert opinions. One argument is that expert opinions should only be proffered when it can be shown that the discipline has reliable research supporting the opinion being offered to the court. This is the historic battle over methodological legitimacy in the field "over which approaches 'count' as valid methods of inquiry for generating knowledge about people's thoughts, feelings, and behaviors" (Lewis, 2021a). This battle has been waged since the beginning of psychology and law.

Wittmann argues that the validity and reliability of making specific parenting time recommendations are very close to untestable. The very act of selecting an access plan implies a knowledge base sufficient for such a grand prediction, yet no such knowledge base appears to exist in the field (Braunstein & Wittmann, 2023).

Wittmann sums up a primary concern with the following question that he believes, if posed to an expert witness, cannot be answered: "Doctor, please present the literature from your field that confirms you can choose the correct factors to assess; that tells you what weight to assign to those various factors in any parenting plan matter; and that offers confirmation that your field can select a specific parent or plan with an acceptable degree of reliability and validity" (Braunstein & Wittman, 2023, p. 3).

Tippins and Wittmann (2005) have argued for 20 years that there is an insufficient empirical basis in the literature upon which to base reliable expert opinions about parenting access plans. They ask, "Where is the literature that indicates we can reliably and validly make specific custody or parenting recommendations?" (p. 3).

We agree that there is insufficient empirical research to serve as a basis for scientifically based recommendations about certain aspects of decision making and parenting time in a valid and reliable manner. However, it appears that the Tippins and Wittmann position tethers us only to what has been referred to as basic or empirical research. Psychologists' ethical code requires opinions to be based upon the professional and scientific knowledge of the discipline.

Certainly, expert opinions about decision making and parenting time ought not be based only upon an expert's clinical experience and training. Some courts have defined "pure opinion" as testimony based only on an expert's clinical experience and training and found such expert testimony inadmissible.

Pure opinion testimony "provides no insight into what principles or methods were used to reach his opinion and did not demonstrate that he applied any such principles or methods to the facts of this case" (*Giaimo v. Florida Autosport, Inc.*, 2014, pp. 387–388).

To date, there is no professional consensus in law or behavioral sciences about an acceptable definition describing how to measure an analytic gap or how to determine when an analytic gap is too great, resulting in inadmissible expert opinions. Perhaps the determination of an acceptable size of an analytic gap can only be made on a case-by-case basis. Like Potter Stuart's definition of pornography that he "knew it when he saw it" (*Jacobellis v. Ohio*, 1964, p. 197), each court might need to apply its analysis of what defines an acceptable analytic gap on a case-by-case basis. From a scientific perspective, however, the lack of an operational definition of an analytic gap goes hand-in-hand with a lack of identifying a set of factors or conceptual milestones that might help to determine when an analytic gap is too large.

SIZE MATTERS

Tippins and Wittmann appear to define very narrowly the analytic gap among data, empirical evidence, and expert opinions. Although they do not disregard the value of experience and judgment in expert witness testimony, they place little weight on its value when applied to its role in contributing to recommendations about decision making and parenting plans.

Our interpretation of the Tippins and Wittmann argument that expert opinions about certain aspects of decision making and parenting time should only be based upon empirical literature is tantamount to an evidentiary standard of beyond a reasonable doubt. We believe that the exclusion of clinical judgment and reasonable interpretation of research are too strict of a criterion regarding expert testimony.

Daubert, Kumho, Joiner, and their progeny invited professional judgment to be used in the application of empirical findings as a basis for expert testimony. The court uses its gatekeeping responsibilities as a means to allow into evidence only that which has passed the test of the "crucible of reliability." Such determination must be made in a case-specific manner.

Slobogin (2006) provides a framework for analyzing the admissibility of testimony, which involves four key issues: materiality, probative value, helpfulness, and prejudicial impact. Materiality examines if the testimony logically relates to the relevant substantive law. Probative value measures the accuracy of the expert testimony in general principles and specific application to the case. Helpfulness assesses whether the testimony provides additional insights beyond what the fact finder can determine independently. Prejudicial impact evaluates whether the testimony, despite being material, probative, and helpful, should be excluded due to potential misuse by the fact finder (Slobogin, 2006).

This framework aligns with the Federal Rules of Evidence. Rule 401 requires all evidence to be relevant, combining materiality and probative value assessments. Rule 702 mandates that expert testimony must assist the fact finder. The proposed framework integrates the reliability analysis from the amended Rule 702 into the probative value evaluation, aligning with the 401/403 balancing test and adhering to *Daubert's* requirement for demonstrating the reliability of expert testimony (Slobogin, 2006).

The basis in the foundation of the concept of the analytic gap as used in family court matters is its acknowledgment that the application of science and other forms of specialized knowledge serves to *inform* the expert's opinion. There is a recognition—indeed a trust and respect for—the ability of courts to reliably examine the fit between the facts of the case, the science that serves as a basis for the expert opinion, and the expert's application of the principles drawn from professional and scientific knowledge to the facts of this unique family system.

No two families are the same and no two-family systems operate the same way. The result is that PPEs are fact-intensive investigations into multiple levels of family functioning. Application of the ecological model to parenting plan investigations does not lend itself to the type of linear forms of empirical analysis that characterize basic research. Indeed, evaluators and the opinions that flow from the investigative process need to consider multiple levels of analyses, consider multiple hypotheses, and recognize that it is virtually impossible to know all that goes on in a family. This is why evaluations are both art and science. Evaluators interpret data. Evaluators extrapolate and apply research findings to the data gathered during the evaluation process in formulating expert opinions.

Perhaps the notion of art in the formation of expert opinions is misleading although we are hard pressed to find a reasonable alternative. It might be informative to define what we mean by art as used in the evaluation process.

As used in a PPE context, art is not abstract. It is not random. It is not intended to suggest talent, ability, or virtuosity. As used in this context, art is defined as the creative extrapolation, integration, and application of multiple variables into a coherent, trustworthy expert opinion.

We are talking about making clear how the application of facts drawn from literature, drawn from data gathering, drawn from statutes and case law are integrated into a reliable, relevant expert opinion. The steps taken between identification of data sources and development of expert opinions are revealed in the inferences that join the data with opinions.

The explicit articulation of the journey from fact to opinion is where careful exploration of the steps taken by the evaluator in piecing together the multitude of factors help to define the size of the analytic gap considered reasonable in this specific case. Too often, we have found that evaluators are unable to explain their inference process that formed the steps leading from data to expert opinion. An analogy might be to J. S. B. T. Evans and Stanovich's Systems 1 and 2 thinking (made famous by Kahneman) and the role of representative heuristics in human decision making.

SYSTEM 1 AND SYSTEM 2 THINKING

System 1 refers to the decision-making people use in the majority of their everyday lives. It is fast, automatic, and intuitive. It is a rapid, autonomous process assumed to be formulated by default responses. System 2 thinking is slow, deliberate, and conscious. System 2 thinking supports hypothetical thinking and requires significant working memory effort.

As we will describe in Chapter 7, there are a variety of cognitive biases associated with System 1 thinking. One is the availability heuristic, and another is the representative heuristic. Both are shortcuts that help people make decisions. They differ in how they predict the likelihood of future events, however both types of heuristics lead to overlooking important information used in decision making. Both are critical bias factors about which evaluators need to become aware and learn ways to identify and reduce.

Availability heuristic occurs when people estimate the likelihood of an event based on how easily relevant information comes to mind, especially recent or memorable information. Availability heuristics are likely to overestimate the likelihood of events that are easy to recall and underestimate less memorable events. Evaluators might fall prey to the influence of availability heuristics without being aware. For example, compelling information learned from one parent might serve as an anchor against which information from the other parent is compared, leading the evaluator to assign greater weight to the familiar information obtained during the first parent's interview.

Alternatively, the availability heuristic might operate when a parent describes family history experiences that are similar to those of the evaluator, leading to countertransference concerns. The shared familial experiences might be assigned greater weight because of their familiarity yet the evaluator might be unaware of how the shared information anchor might affect future data gathering and data interpretation.

The representativeness heuristic occurs when people estimate the likelihood of an event based on how similar it is to a known situation or typical case. Representative heuristics can lead to neglecting other relevant information that is likely to result in biased judgments and predictions.

Experts are vulnerable to the influence of representative heuristics in many situations in data gathering and data analyses. Typically, evaluators will examine data from interviews or test results that are similar to data from previously conducted evaluations. An example of the ways in which a representative heuristic might influence the evaluation process occurs when an evaluator makes quick judgments about the meaning of the data because of its similarity to reviewed information from previously completed evaluations or stories shared in the field.

Seasoned evaluators have developed strategies used in data collection and data integration that have been frequently practiced. These strategies are ripe for the development of availability and representative heuristics. Evaluators develop shortcuts in their data collection and data integration often without being aware of these shortcuts.

System 2 is characterized by more deliberate and hypothetical thinking. System 2 thinking is more logical and systematic than System 1. As described in Stanovich's tripartite model of the mind, System 1 uses an Autonomous Mind, while System 2 uses either a Reflective Mind or an Algorithmic Mind. System 2 thinking is slow, requires significant cognitive effort, and is less prone to error. It is not, however, foolproof.

System 2 thinking integrates logical judgment and seeks information acquired through past learning and experience (see also J. S. B. T. Evans & Stanovich, 2013; Stanovich & West, 1998) Kahneman argued that these data are processed deliberately, through an intentional application of rules, making it a much slower and cognitively demanding process but more likely to lead to better decisions.

Professional experience does not necessarily translate into better performance. Experience, without feedback or reflection, often is fertile ground for the development of faulty thinking (Choudhry et al., 2005; Ericsson, 2004).

APPLICATION OF SYSTEM 1 AND SYSTEM 2 THINKING TO THE ANALYTIC GAP

Applying these System 1 & 2 ideas to the questions we raised about the importance of articulating steps taken among data gathering, data analyses, data integration, application of relevant professional and scientific knowledge, and opinion formation, it is clear that deliberation is the critical factor in informing the court of how the evaluator moved through the opinion formation process.

Evaluators need to take time to critically examine from multiple perspectives the road traveled in the development of each expert opinion. We recommend writing out each step of the process. We provide ideas to consider but wish to stress that these questions do not exhaust the universe of questions that might need to be considered in a specific evaluation.

a. Were there specific questions identified by the court or attorneys to guide the evaluation?
b. If no, did the evaluator seek guidance from the court or attorneys about defining the scope of the evaluation?
    i. If no, why?
c. Did the evaluator answer the questions defining the scope of the evaluation?
    i. If no, why?
d. Were the questions defining the scope of the evaluation, questions that can be answered based upon the professional and scientific knowledge of the discipline?
e. What were the specific areas of data gathering during parent, child, or collateral interviews?
f. Were the data gathered during parent, child, or collateral interviews relevant to answering the questions defining the scope of the evaluation?
g. What areas of parental and child behavior were excluded and why?

    i. Is there a basis in the literature for excluding specific areas of parental and child behavior?
    ii. What is that basis?

h. What areas of parental behavior were included and why?
    i. Is there a basis in the literature for including specific areas of parental and child behavior?
    ii. What is that basis?

i. What steps were taken to confirm (support) assertions made during parent and child interviews?

j. What steps were taken to refute (challenge) assertions made during parent and child interviews?

k. What psychometric literature serves as a basis for the use of each data-gathering tool used in the evaluation?

l. What literature supports the use of each data-gathering tool?

m. What literature argues against the use of each data-gathering tool?

n. How did the evaluator decide to select and administer each data-gathering tool?

o. Did the evaluator correctly interpret the psychological test results using forensically relevant, peer-reviewed literature?

p. Did the evaluator incorporate interpretive limitations applying nomothetic or ideographic approaches and the subsequent concerns drawn from G2i concerns in the interpretation of test results?

q. What are the data that were used as the basis for the expert opinion?

r. What alternative explanations of the data were examined?

s. What was the evaluator's reasoning supporting one explanation over other explanations?

t. Has the evaluator framed opinions as statements of probability rather than statements of fact?

u. Are the data developed from the assessment tools relevant to the issues before the court?

v. Are there areas of data collection that were not pursued?

w. Were the evaluation questions investigated relevant to answering the questions of interest to the court?

x. Were there evaluation questions that were not examined?

y. Was the evaluator able to explain factors used to develop each expert opinion?

This nonexhaustive list is our attempt to bring you back to elementary school and remind you to show all your work! We believe that one way to address concerns about overreach or inappropriate application of peer-reviewed literature to the specific facts of a case is to be deliberate, specific, analytic, detail-oriented, and clear when explaining to the court as many of the factors that support and refute expert opinions as is possible to show. So, make every effort to show every step of your decision-making process.

As we will delve into more deeply in the upcoming chapters, we suggest that in preparation for writing your report, you identify specific data that you view as the most reliable upon which to base expert opinions. Next, consider specific articles found in the professional and scientific literature that seem to fit the facts of your case. Third, critically examine the literature's methodology with a particular focus on the sample. Are the characteristics of the individuals who comprised the sample used in the research similar to or different from characteristics of the individuals in the case before the court? For example, the results of a study in which the sample was comprised of South Asian parents is likely a poor fit for a family being evaluated who are from the upper Midwest or the inner city of Los Angeles.

As a final step, we recommend that you examine the manner in which you apply the literature to the facts of the case. Let humility be your guide. Evaluators are social scientists, and social scientists frame their findings, including courtroom testimony, in terms of probability statements. In a family law setting, consider using the language of the standard of evidence used in cases: Preponderance of the evidence. The application of the science being used as a basis for expert opinions is framed as "more likely than not." That is, your expert opinion is based upon a prediction that you are confident that your opinion is more than 50.1% likely to be correct.

As you read that we encourage you to be deliberate, specific, analytic, detail-oriented, and to make every effort to show every step of your decision-making process, you may wonder "How?" or "Why?" or even "Gosh, that seems like a lot of unnecessary work." If you have any of these thoughts, stick with us as we present both the rationale and how to use this book.

IMPROVING YOUR SYSTEM TO MINIMIZE ERRORS: ORGANIZATION AND CHECKLISTS

In his dissertation at Claremont Graduate University, Psychologist Geoff Smart, PhD, studied how people make difficult decisions. He grouped decision makers into different categories: airline captain, art critic, sponge, infiltrator, prosecutor, suitor, and terminator. He found that airline captains took a methodical approach by studying past mistakes and lessons from others in the field. They had a belief that accuracy was possible. They used a balanced use of multiple methods. And they had a strong commitment to systematic data analysis. They followed each step of their checklist and resisted the urge to go with their guts. Smart found that the checklist-focused airline captains made the best decisions by a landslide.

We can think of nothing more complex than building a computer circuit board, performing open heart surgery, or analyzing family dynamics. In his book on how to get things right, Surgeon Atul Gawande (2011) recalls an essay by Gorovitz and MacIntyre in which they discuss the nature of human fallibility. The authors write that we make errors due to either ignorance or ineptitude.

> Failures of ignorance we can forgive. If the knowledge of the best thing to do in a given situation does not exist, we are happy to have people simply make their

> best effort. But if the knowledge exists and is not applied correctly, it is difficult not to be infuriated. (p. 13–14)

There is nothing as complex in forensic psychology, or in psychological evaluation as a whole, as a PPE. The field is getting more complex as we are inundated with data. Evaluators identify data points and assess the degree to which those data points align. With an ever-increasing amount of data to process, we are susceptible to errors or to bias caused by irrelevant information. That is, it is impossible to conduct a PPE and avoid irrelevant information. Instead, the evaluator must sort through tremendous amounts of data and determine what is relevant.

Think about the competencies required to be an evaluator: child and family psychology, developmental psychology, abnormal psychology, interviewing parents, interviewing children, observing parent–child interactions, psychological testing, writing reports, testimony, family law, digital evidence, teleassessment, data collection, data collection, and more data collection. (Now you may be thinking that evaluators do not need to be competent in digital evidence, yet it is clear that evaluators are often required to review tremendous amounts of data from social networking sites, texts, emails, and other digital communications.)

In our experience, parenting plan evaluators analyze more data than any other psychological evaluator or forensic mental health evaluator. As the amount of data required of a parenting plan evaluator increases, so does the potential for error. Errors occur despite an evaluator's experience or knowledge.

Conducting a PPE is akin to orchestrating a symphony where the evaluator is both the conductor and an individual musician. Different evaluators may orchestrate the steps of the evaluation in a different order or manner. The end result is clear. A good evaluation incorporates the data in a coherent, fluid manner (see Chapter 10 on storytelling).

We believe parents, attorneys, and judges have been fooled by television and movies. The crime scene investigator solves the puzzle in a Sherlock Holmes–esque manner in a perfectly choreographed, 60-minute episode. Recall the hundreds of episodes of *Law and Order: Special Victims Unit* or *NCIS* and compare those shows to real life investigations of child abuse. These examples, displayed on a nightly basis to millions of viewers, lead to a misunderstanding of investigation.

The majority of families resolve conflict shortly after separation. Some families require mediation and other support. The families involved in PPE often include the most extreme behaviors, attitudes, and opinions. They are likely to be the most extreme families the field of psychology has attempted to evaluate.

WHY EVALUATORS NEED AN ORGANIZATIONAL SYSTEM

As we've discussed systems of thinking (Systems 1 and 2), evaluators should strive to reduce errors while increasing transparency. They should strive to use their Reflective Algorithmic Minds (both in System 2). Evaluators need an organizational system for a number of reasons. Evaluators need to think about archiving and managing the information they receive. Evaluators are encouraged to recognize the importance of documenting all data that they consider, with enough detail and quality to allow later scrutiny. They need to think about preserving that data in a way that demonstrates how it informed their conclusions. They need to do it in a way that other professionals, especially those who do work product reviews, can easily understand. As evaluators organize their data, they are documenting this information with an eye toward the eventual review by other qualified professionals.

If evaluators organize their information well, they can share their system and the data stored in that system when they testify. Two factors make this very difficult. First, as we've discussed, this becomes more challenging because of the amount of data evaluators are asked to process. Second, time impacts an evaluator's ability to recall information they review accurately. It is likely that when an evaluator testifies, a great amount of time has lapsed between when they originally reviewed the data.

Recall that since 1885 (see Ebbinghaus, 1885), we have known there is a primacy bias in which you may remember some of the first information you reviewed, and there is a recency bias in which you may recall the last information you reviewed. Yet both of these are likely further corrupted by time and by the likelihood that the evaluator has worked with many families in the interim, which may cause the evaluator to mix up case details.

As we conduct work product reviews, we notice that evaluators often make mistakes in remembering to incorporate all of the data. They may forget to interview an important collateral, review an important document, or misunderstand key case details. Think of a chef who forgets an important ingredient. Or think of another chef who remembers all the ingredients but not the order.

There is no consensus on how many different presenting problems an evaluator has to evaluate. There are so many complexities in our work that there are times in which even an evaluator who has specialization in a specific area may not feel their training is adequate in all areas. "The knowledge exists. But however supremely specialized and trained we may have become, steps are still missed. Mistakes are still made" (Gawande, 2011).

Terry Kukor has identified common errors in forensic evaluations to include uncritical thinking, misattribution of traits, errors of logic, not carefully weighing evidence, poorly structured arguments, and errors due to bias (Kukor, n.d.).

Specialty Guideline 1.02 (American Psychological Association, 2013b) reminds evaluators to "weigh all data, opinions, and rival hypotheses impartially." The guideline further encourages "forensic practitioners seek to represent alternative perspectives, including data, studies, or evidence on both sides of the question, in an accurate, fair, and professional manner, and strive to weigh and present all views, facts, or opinions impartially."

Evaluators' methodology should be clear and follow the scientific method: observations, developing questions, developing hypotheses, testing hypotheses, developing conclusions, and then redoing the process by continuing to be open to new observations or data. Katherine H. Pherson and Pherson (2021) expanded the scientific method into their eight steps of critical thinking strategies: (a) ask the right questions; (b) identify one's assumptions; (c) reach out to other sources; (d) evaluate the data for accuracy, relevance, and completeness; (e) assess the data and form hypotheses; (f) evaluate the hypotheses and look for conflicting data; (g) draw conclusions; and (h) present your findings.

Developing multiple hypotheses brings forward every potential explanation of family dynamics required to address the identified questions in the evaluation. The use of multiple hypotheses controls against the premature and unduly selection of one hypothesis until such time that all have been considered. It avoids simplified attribution of blame. The use of multiple hypotheses helps mitigate biases. The evaluator identifies relevant variables by developing specific questions to guide the evaluation. Based on identification of specific questions, relevant evidence-based or evidence-informed variables can be identified. Each of the questions can be translated into a range of hypotheses (R. H. Pherson & Heuer, 2021, p. 36).

One of the best ways to reduce errors is to use checklists. Checklists help us consider relevant information in a systematic manner. The checklist allows the evaluator to make explicit the data they collect from different sources. It requires articulating all plausible hypotheses, not just the hypotheses that appear most likely to be supported. Analysis of competing hypotheses should occur periodically throughout the assessment process.

You may be wondering at this point if we are going to give you a checklist to make all your troubles go away. While airline checklists may be universal (albeit slightly unique to each plane), parenting plan checklists must be tailored to each family. We recommend following our stepwise progression:

1. Read the court order and make a checklist with each question you need to answer in the court order.
2. Make a separate checklist with each action (interview, record review) you plan to conduct during the evaluation.
3. Make a checklist of the common errors you recognize are most likely to occur in your evaluations.
4. Determine whether or not the evaluation may benefit from using a decision tree, which is another form of checklist.

The process of using decision trees to reduce bias is documented by Drozd et al. (2013) in their thorough book *Parenting Plan and Child Custody Evaluations: Using Decision Trees to Increase Evaluator Competence and Avoid Preventable Errors.* They write the following:

> A key component of the proposed (decision) tree method is adopted as a habit for data analysis; the method itself provides the evaluator with the habit of thinking in parallel and complex ways. It helps the evaluator move away from simple, linear thinking. It allows for the consideration of multiple standpoints and views of a subject. The multiple hypotheses or decision tree method allows the evaluator to increase his or her capability for viewing complex issues systematically and transparently. (p. 26)

Decision trees and tables assist with organizing tremendous amounts of data. For example, a single table can document the source of the concerns, Parent A's evidence, Parent B's evidence, the child's evidence, collateral evidence, and the evaluator's evidence. These methods of organization can also aid in analyzing and synthesizing data. To date, it is unclear how many evaluators use decision trees and tables.

Evaluators also need to organize interviews with multiple people (both parents, the children, and collateral contacts).

> It is common to misconceive how checklists function in complex lines of work. They are not comprehensive how-to guides. . . . They are quick and simple tools aimed to buttress the skills of expert professionals. (Gawande, 2011, p. 120)

Without the use of mental checklists, our working memory, which is required for System 2 thinking, is likely to be overwhelmed at times which can lead to miscalculations and errors of analysis. Checklists can and should include the errors known to occur during a PPE.

> The checklist doesn't tell him what to do, he explained. It is not a formula. But the checklist helps him to be as smart as possible every step of the way, ensuring that he's got the critical information he needs when he needs it, that he's systematic about decision making, that he's talked to everyone he should. (Gawande, 2011, p. 79)

As we will describe in later chapters, there are specific times an evaluator may utilize a model or checklist in the field. For example, if there are concerns about parent–child contact problems such as resist refuse dynamics, the evaluator can use the rubric or checklist created by Benjamin Garber (2024) that includes a stepwise process of analyzing the following factors: (a) incidental sensory, temporal, and proximal factors; (b) child variables; (c) child–parent A dyadic variables; (d) child–parent B dyadic variables; (e) systemic variables; and (f) extra-systemic variables.

An alternative checklist or decision making tool for analyzing parent–child contact problems is the decision tree developed by Drozd, Saini, and Carson (2022), which includes the following steps: (a) identify issues, (b) gather information, (c) identify multiple factors leading to multiple hypotheses, (d) weigh the evidence, (e) choose among alternatives, (f) choose sequencing and timing for remedies, (g) implement targeted strategies, and (h) review your decision.

Arguably the greatest recent use of a checklist occurred over the Hudson River after U.S. Airways Flight 1549 departed from La Guardia airport. The plane collided with a flock of geese such that the birds cracked the windshield and damaged the engines with a loud explosion. With geese in two engines, they had less than 4 minutes until the plane would be on the ground. It was not enough time for the copilot (Jeff Skiles) to run through all of the checklists. He prioritized the engine failure checklists and was able to follow all of the steps to (attempt to) restart both engines, which experts would later identify as "very remarkable." He also worked through the ditching procedure checklist. As he did this, the flight attendants followed checklists to prepare the passengers for the water crash landing. After Captain Sullenberger landed the plane, all of the passengers were off the plane in 3 minutes. He later said, "First Officer Jeff Skiles and I turned to each other and, almost in unison, at the same time, with the same words, said to each other, 'Well, that wasn't as bad as I thought.'"

CONCLUSION

In this chapter we discussed concern about the reliability of clinical judgment in forensic evaluations, particularly the potential for bias, subjectivity, and variability in assessments. Unlike structured, evidence-based approaches, clinical judgment relies heavily on the evaluator's experience, intuition, and personal interpretations, which can lead to inconsistent findings across different evaluators. Additionally, cognitive biases (e.g., confirmation bias, hindsight bias) and lack of standardized methods may compromise objectivity. Forensic settings also introduce adversarial pressures, which can unintentionally influence judgment. To enhance reliability, experts emphasize using structured assessment tools, empirical research, and well-documented reasoning to support forensic conclusions.

We also described the usefulness of checklists as a means of data gathering. Evidence-based or evidence-informed checklists tend to enhance consistency, objectivity, and thoroughness. By providing a structured framework, checklists and decision trees help evaluators to systematically gather information about relevant factors, reducing the risk of oversight or bias. They improve reliability by standardizing data collection, minimizing subjective variability, and reinforcing adherence to best practices. Checklists can also facilitate clear documentation, making findings more transparent and defensible in court. When based on empirical research, checklists support evidence-based decision making.

In the following chapters, we discuss some of the areas in which evaluators are on solid professional and scientific footing in our evaluation work, as well as areas in which there is little, if any, guidance from the professional and scientific literature. We present these areas of scant professional and scientific knowledge to challenge colleagues to seek additional empirical examination of these variables to raise the scientific integrity of our work.

II

USING SCIENTIFIC KNOWLEDGE AND PROCESS

5

What Qualifies as Scientific Evidence in Parenting Plan Evaluations?

In this chapter, we address several issues regarding scientific knowledge and specialized knowledge that lie at the center of effective expert witness testimony and, by extension, lie at the center of decision making about how best to select assessment procedures that provide reliable and relevant information used as the basis of our expert opinions. As we navigate the ethical, methodological, and evidentiary challenges, we offer insights into how evaluators can meet their ethical obligations, maintain scientific integrity, and provide the court with clear, reliable, and contextually informed expert testimony. By grounding our discussions in both legal precedents and scientific best practices, we aim to equip evaluators with the tools to fulfill their roles effectively while advancing the quality and transparency of parenting plan evaluations.

Many might view our concerns about clearly defining the meaning of "specialized knowledge," "scientific knowledge," and the meaning of "science" as ivory tower pontification. We believe it is critical for forensic mental health evaluators to understand the underlying basis for the admissibility of expert psychological opinions. Understanding the basis for expert testimony should lead evaluators to choose the best available methods and procedures in the field, which we will discuss in greater detail in the following chapters. The result should lead to more trustworthy and helpful expert opinions that flow from those assessment methods and procedures.

Zervopoulos (2019) has written about three critically important components of competent expert testimony. They are "basis, basis, basis." We stand with Zervopoulos in emphasizing the overwhelming importance of expert witnesses

https://doi.org/10.1037/0000474-006
Parenting Plan Evaluations: An Evidence-Informed Approach to Child Custody, by J. W. Gould and C. M. Mulchay

being knowledgeable and articulate about the basis of their testimony. We add to this admonition the importance of understanding the legal basis of the admissibility of expert witness to assist in knowing how best to prepare reports and proffer testimony to the court.

Understanding the role of science—however it is defined—is different in the courtroom than in scientists' laboratories. Both law and science seek truth, but the quest for truth in the courtroom and the quest for truth in the laboratory differ. Scientific conclusions are continually challenged and revised based upon ongoing research. On the other hand, law requires that disputes are resolved quickly, finally, and justly (Golanski, 2001).

SPECIALIZED KNOWLEDGE

A psychological expert witness's understanding of what constitutes specialized knowledge is a critical aspect of our approach to court testimony. Psychologists' ethical code requires opinions to be based upon "established scientific and professional knowledge of the discipline" (American Psychological Association [APA], 2017a, Standard 2.04). It is our ability to communicate to the court the established scientific and professional knowledge of the discipline that defines psychologists' specialized knowledge.

Federal Rule 702 reads, "If scientific, technical, or other specialized knowledge will assist the trier of fact to understand the evidence or to determine a fact in issue, a witness qualified as an expert by knowledge, skill, experience, training, or education, may testify thereto in the form of an opinion or otherwise."

What, then, is specialized knowledge? Specialized knowledge is defined, in part, as *scientific knowledge*. The U.S. Supreme Court defined scientific knowledge in its *Daubert* decision as follows:

> The adjective "scientific" implies a grounding in the methods and procedures of science. Similarly, the word "knowledge" connotes more than subjective belief or unsupported speculation. The term "applies to any body of known facts or to any body of ideas inferred from such facts or accepted as truths on good grounds." Of course, it would be unreasonable to conclude that the subject of scientific testimony must be "known" to a certainty; arguable, there are no certainties in science...But, in order to qualify as "scientific knowledge," an inference or assertion must be derived by the scientific method. Proposed testimony must be supported by appropriate validation—i.e., "good grounds," based on what is known. In short, the requirement that an expert's testimony pertain to "scientific knowledge" establishes a standard of evidentiary reliability. (*Daubert v. Merrell Dow Pharmaceuticals, Inc.*, 1993, pp. 659–660)

Even with this definition of scientific knowledge, some legal scholars have argued that "definitions of scientific knowledge, scientific method, scientific validity, and peer review [were] matters far afield from the expertise of judges" (*Daubert v. Merrell Dow Pharmaceuticals, Inc.*, 1993, p. 599, from Chief Justice William Rehnquist's opinion concurring in part and dissenting in part).

Psychologists engaged in forensic psychological activities need to be familiar with the Supreme Court's definition of scientific knowledge as it is applied to expert testimony. We believe that scientific knowledge means that expert testimony must be based upon the methods and procedures of science. This is not to say that all psychological testimony must be based upon empirical findings but that the *basis* of the information upon which the expert opinion is derived from studies reflecting the scientific process or reliable methods. While the foundation of expert testimony is the peer-reviewed literature, the way an expert interprets and applies this information must align with the specific context of the case. This means that experts analyze the details of the current situation and apply general scientific principles to real-world circumstances. Their interpretation must remain objective and evidence-based, minimizing bias while tailoring explanations to fit the case at hand.

Daubert makes clear that expert testimony must be derived from "inference or assertion . . . derived by the scientific method." There is similar language in psychologists' ethical code requiring psychological opinions to be based upon "established scientific and professional knowledge of the discipline" (APA, 2017a, Standard 2.04).

The *Daubert* court made clear that the *general acceptance test* that was the hallmark of the *Frye* decision controlling the admissibility of expert testimony since 1923 was "not a necessary precondition to the admissibility of scientific evidence under the Federal Rule of Evidence" and that the responsibility of the trial court judge was "ensuring that expert testimony both rests on a reliable foundation and is relevant to the task at hand" (*Daubert v. Merrell Dow Pharmaceuticals, Inc.*, 1993, p. 597).

Daubert was widely interpreted as applying only to expert testimony that was based upon the "scientific context" and in which an expert "relies on the application of scientific principles, rather than on skill- or experience-based observation" (*Carmichael v. Samyang Tire, Inc.*, 1997, p. 1435).

However, *Daubert* also stressed that the court's inquiry into the admissibility of expert testimony needed to be flexible:

> Its overarching subject is the scientific validity—and thus the evidentiary relevance and reliability—of the principles that underlie a proposed submission. The focus, of course, must be solely on principles and methodology, not on the conclusions that they generate. . . . Throughout, a judge assessing a proffer of expert scientific testimony under Rule 702 should also be mindful of other applicable rules. (*Daubert v. Merrell Dow Pharmaceuticals, Inc.*, 1993, pp. 594–595)

In *General Electric Co. v. Joiner* (1997, p. 143), the court found that *Daubert* "applies as much to the trial court's decisions about how to determine reliability as to its ultimate conclusion. Thus, whether *Daubert's* specific factors are, or are not, reasonable measures of reliability in a particular case is a matter that the law grants the trial judge broad latitude to determine."

Daubert and *Joiner* left open the question of whether Rule 702 was limited only to expert testimony based upon scientific examination. Some legal scholars argued that *Daubert* would limit expert testimony that relied only upon specialized knowledge derived from scientific methods and exclude expert testimony based upon specialized knowledge derived from experience.

Kumho Tire (1999) clarified the answer to the question of whether the court's scrutiny of expert testimony using *Daubert* related factors was limited to testimony derived from a scientific context. The *Kumho* court said that *Daubert* applied to all expert testimony and that the trial court was not required to use each factor in its decision making. The *Kumho* Court noted that the language in Evidence Rule 702 makes no relevant distinction between "scientific" knowledge and "technical" or "other specialized" knowledge. It makes clear that any such knowledge might become the subject of expert testimony. In *Daubert*, the Court specified that it is Rule 702's word "knowledge," not the words (like "scientific") that modify that word, that "establishes a standard of evidentiary reliability" (*Daubert v. Merrell Dow Pharmaceuticals, Inc.*, 1993, p. 589–590). Hence, as a matter of language, the Rule applies its reliability standard to all "scientific," "technical," or "other specialized" matters within its scope. We concede that the Court in Daubert referred only to "scientific" knowledge. But as the Court there said, it referred to "scientific" testimony "because that was the nature of the expertise" at issue (*Daubert v. Merrell Dow Pharmaceuticals, Inc.*, 1993, p. 590 n.8).

The *Kumho* court also reemphasized the flexible nature of the court's inquiry into reliability and relevance as "a flexible one" (*Daubert v. Merrell Dow Pharmaceuticals, Inc.*, 1993, p. 594). The *Daubert* factors do not constitute a definitive checklist or test, and the gatekeeping inquiry must be "tied to the facts" of a particular case (*Daubert v. Merrell Dow Pharmaceuticals, Inc.*, 1993, pp. 591, 593).

The *Kumho* court determined that the specific factors articulated in *Daubert* may or may not be pertinent in assessing reliability, depending on the nature of the issue, the expert's particular expertise, and the subject of his testimony. The court recognized that some of the *Daubert* factors may be helpful in evaluating the reliability of experience-based expert testimony, while other factors might be more helpful in examining the reliability of an expert's methodology. The court concluded that determining the reliability of expert testimony in a particular case is a case-specific task, and the factors to be considered by the court when determining the admissibility of expert testimony should be tied to the methodology used in a particular case.

The *Kumho* Court stated,

> We do not believe that Rule 702 creates a schematism that segregates expertise by type while mapping certain kinds of questions to certain kinds of experts. Life and the legal cases that it generates are too complex to warrant so definitive a match. . .
>
> To say this is not to deny the importance of *Daubert's* gatekeeping requirement. The objective of that requirement is to ensure the reliability and relevancy of expert testimony. It is to make certain that an expert, whether basing testimony upon professional studies or personal experience, employs in the courtroom the same level of intellectual rigor that characterizes the practice of an expert in the relevant field. Nor do we deny that, as stated in *Daubert*, the particular questions that it mentioned will often be appropriate for use in determining the reliability of challenged expert testimony. Rather, we conclude that the trial judge must have considerable leeway in deciding in a particular case how to go about determining whether particular expert testimony is reliable. That is to say, a trial court should consider the specific factors identified in *Daubert* where they are reasonable measures of the reliability of expert testimony. (*Kumho Tire Co. v. Carmichael*, 1999, pp. 152–153)

We contend that the history of the court's thinking, beginning in its 1993 *Daubert* decision, reflects a similar evolution as occurs in the scientific context: Ideas are developed, researched, analyzed, and refined. A necessary component of the development of ideas in law and in science is reflection on how findings relate to real life. Interpretation of the meaning and usefulness of legal decisions or scientific findings is a subjective process. We believe that a reasonable reading of *Daubert* and related case law is that admissible expert testimony is derived from the expert's ability to integrate science with experience. Effective testimony should be based upon integration of evidence-based findings from past and present research with professional and scientific knowledge regarding how to apply such findings to the instant case.

The Supreme Court remanded the *Daubert* case back to the 9th Circuit, where the district court's grant of summary judgment was affirmed. What is important for psychologists to know about the 9th Circuit's decision was the judge, Justice Alex Kozinski, stating that the task for judges is to "analyze not what the experts say, but what basis they have for saying it" (*Daubert v. Merrell Dow Pharmaceuticals, Inc.*, 1995, p. 1316).

We suggest a link between the court's words "basis they have for saying it" and psychologists' ethics code requiring psychologists to articulate the data-integration processes and decision making that served as a basis for expert opinions. The ethical standard we believe is tied to Justice Kozinski's perspective is Standard 2.04 Bases for Scientific and Professional Judgments. The standard reads, "Psychologists' work is based upon established scientific and professional knowledge of the discipline."

We recognize that there are respected colleagues who might disagree with our opinions. It is precisely the debate about these challenging topics that help to move our respective fields forward, seeking better understanding of alternative arguments and integrating previously excluded ideas into an evolving understanding of how best to serve the law and science, in our case, the evidence-based and evidence-informed ideas related to child custody work.

We now move on to another somewhat controversial issue: How do we define science? There has been a controversy over the meaning of the term science in the child custody arena. We have previously written about science as facts and science as process (Gould & Mulchay, 2024). An alternative way to conceptualize these different ways of thinking about science is scientific knowledge, which refers to specific findings derived from the use of reliable research methodologies, and scientific process, which refers to the various reliable methodologies used to generate scientific knowledge.

HOW DO WE DEFINE SCIENCE?

Science is a central tenet of psychological practice (Gould & Mulchay, 2024). "In explaining, predicting, and controlling the world around us, science is by far the most powerful intellectual technique known" (Faigman et al., 2002, p. 47). Understanding human behavior begins with developing systematic procedures for reliable observation and recording. When child custody evaluators attend to the methodological integrity of their data gathering process, the court is able to place greater weight on the scientific foundation of the evaluation process (Ramsey & Kelly, 2004).

What is scientific includes both process and fact. Science is not an encyclopedic body of knowledge about the universe. Instead, it represents a process for proposing and refining theoretical explanations about the world that are subject to further testing and refinement (American Association for the Advancement of Science [AAAS], 1993).

Insomuch as science can be viewed as fact, science can be defined as the outcome of the scientific process, or an orderly body of knowledge with clearly articulated principles (AAAS, 1993). The task of Federal Rule of Evidence 702 may be best understood as regulating the supply of facts to the judge "in a manner that states a preference for science as the preeminent methods for discovering facts" (AAAS, 1993, p. 47). One important task of a child custody evaluator is as a gatekeeper of reliable psychological data upon which the court may rely. The reliability that comes from scientifically informed processes is the foundation for both psychological investigation and expert psychological testimony (AAAS, 1993).

Confusion between science as fact and science as process has created unnecessary obstacles about the role of science in PPEs. We believe, however, when the differences between *science as fact* and *science as process* are explained, there is little controversy over the importance of science as process in PPEs.

SCIENCE AS PROCESS

Child custody evaluations can be more consistent, predictable, and helpful if the evaluator uses scientific principles and methods in data gathering, data integration, and opinion formation (AAAS, 1993). Scientific method refers to "the rules or standards and community practices by which science proceeds" (Ramsey & Kelly, 2004, p. 5). Both hard science and the social sciences employ the scientific method to produce knowledge (Ramsey & Kelly, 2004).

Scientific methods and procedures are intended to reduce human error. When conducting PPEs, evaluators need to be more concerned with scientific method and process as a means of controlling for the influence of bias factors. The scientific methodology used in forensic mental health assessment, in general, and used in PPEs, in particular, places a high value on intellectual honesty (Gould & Dale, 2022). Being as objective and scientific as possible includes an explicit acknowledgment that our beliefs could be wrong and that the scientific process, with its emphasis on considering rival alternative hypotheses, is designed to protect us from fooling ourselves (Lilienfeld, 2010).

Because PPEs are viewed as the most complex and difficult type of forensic evaluation (Otto et al., 2000), they may be particularly vulnerable to the use of poor methodologies and different kinds of biases (Gould & Dale, 2022). This complexity can also make these evaluations difficult for attorneys to understand. In contrast to most examinations that focus on evaluating one person, the typical child custody evaluation involves the examination of a number of persons (e.g., parents, child or children, and potential or actual stepparents) and interviews with additional collateral informants.

Emotions typically run high in contested custody cases, further compounding what is an already complicated evaluation process (Gould & Dale, 2022). The high emotions often affect how parents behave during interviews, how they respond to psychological tests, and how they communicate with their children. Parents often attempt to paint an overly positive picture of themselves, a more negative picture of the other parent, and a glowing description of the children's experiences with them. That is, parent interviews are likely to be subject to a variety of bias factors that affect parent presentation, parent description of the information that is presented to the evaluator, and the meaning they assign to their parenting and that of the other parent (Gould & Dale, 2022).

Given the profound importance of the underlying psycholegal issues (i.e., the best interests of the children and the ability of the parents to meet those interests), the parents, children, and other caretakers must be assessed regarding a variety of behaviors, capacities, and needs. These factors affect not only parent behavior but also the evaluator's ability to accurately assess the family dynamics and assist the court in developing a parenting plan for the families' future. Forensic mental health evaluators can easily underestimate the prevalence and severity of distorting influences on their work without developing the correct safeguards for minimizing distorting biases.

APPLYING SCIENCE AS PROCESS TO THE EVALUATION TASK

PPEs conducted by psychologists in custody and parenting time disputes should be written in a manner that focuses on the reliability and relevance of the information gathered during the evaluation, the manner in which the evaluator integrated current professional and scientific knowledge of the discipline into the body of the report, and the degree to which the expert opinions proffered in the evaluation appear logically or scientifically related to the collected data.

When the task is to review another custody evaluator's report, a reviewer can examine three broad areas and, within each of these, several specific elements: (a) methodology, (b) formulation of opinions, and (c) communication of findings and opinions to the court (Gould & Dale, 2022).

Following are 20 recommendations that may help structure the evaluation process to ensure its integrity, transparency, and objectivity. These recommendations also might help increase the perception of attorneys, the court, and the parents about the diligence taken by the evaluator to respect the scientific process, ethical standards, and professional practice guidelines.

1. The evaluator should not begin the evaluation process until the court order has been received and reviewed. If the order does not include specific questions to be investigated by the evaluator, then the evaluator might

reach out to the attorneys and engage in a discussion that results in specific questions that define the scope of the evaluation.

2. At the start of the evaluation process, the evaluator should discuss with the parents information about the scope of the evaluation and other relevant information about the evaluation procedures.

3. The evaluator should also explain to the parties and their attorneys to whom the report is to be disseminated, the manner in which the report is to be disseminated, and those to whom the file will be made available.

4. Evaluators should keep notes about the sequence of activities, including when psychological testing was administered, by whom, and the order in which evaluative sessions have been conducted. The written report should include the date of the interviews and the amount of time of each interview with each parent, each child, each collateral witness, and each parent–child observation.

5. The evaluator should describe the techniques or procedures employed in interviewing the parents in the written report. There is a substantial literature demonstrating the greater reliability of using semistructured or structured interview protocols rather than clinical interview protocols. Use of a more structured interview protocol speaks to issues related to reliability of interview procedures.

6. The evaluator's file and report should reveal that each of the specific questions that defined the scope of the evaluation was systematically explored with each parent, child, and collateral informant. Gathering interview information from each parent, child, and collateral informant speaks to issues related to the relevance of interview content.

7. Interview procedures should also focus attention on obtaining pertinent historical information and current information bearing on functional abilities related to parenting. It is important that the evaluator not be distracted by information that is not relevant to the evaluative task.

8. The evaluator should examine whether each parent was asked about the allegations posed by the other parent (and collateral informants, if appropriate) and what additional collateral sources might help support their position or refute the other parent's position.

9. The evaluator should explore during interviews whether each parent has considered reasonable alternative explanations (plausible rival hypotheses) and their view of how their proposed solutions serve the best interests of their children.

10. The evaluator should show in their file or report that reasonable alternative explanations were considered. Alternative explanations should consider those that support as well as refute the tentative opinions developed from the collected data. A primary focus of generating alternative hypotheses is

to focus on refuting rather than confirming hypotheses, which is essentially the opposite of what happens in confirmation bias. Seeking challenge from others about tentative opinions "helps mitigate cognitive biases, misapplied heuristics, and intuitive traps that analysts often fall victim to when relying only on expert-aided judgment" (R. H. Pherson & Heuer, 2021, p. 4).

11. The evaluator should show in their file and report the manner by which information has been obtained from children. The evaluator must reveal the interview techniques employed and critically examine whether techniques were tailored to the child's cognitive development and expressive and receptive language abilities. We recommend audiotaping or videotaping interviews to allow for review by the evaluator and review by the court and attorneys if needed. Significant research has revealed threats to reliability from note-taking and from attempts to accurately recall who said what during an interview (Gould & Martindale, 2007). It is important that the evaluator address in the written report information about the reliability and validity of any interview techniques employed.

12. The evaluator should make clear the methods employed in conducting observational sessions between the two parents and between each parent and the children. In order to be maximally useful, observations should be conducted in some systematic manner, and evaluators should know in advance what types of information they wish to gather and that data should be gathered in a structured manner. The evaluator's parent–child observations should be structured to gather information useful in answering the specific questions guiding the evaluation. The evaluator should avoid becoming part of the parent–child observation to the degree possible. When evaluators become involved in the parent–child observation, they change the parent–child observation into a parent–child–evaluator observation. Social psychology research has shown how moving from an observer to a participant changes the attributions made about the experience (Gilovich et al., 2022; D. Walker et al., 2022). The evaluator would explain the steps taken to minimize involvement in observational interactions.

13. The evaluator should provide a list of pertinent documents that were reviewed in preparing the evaluation. This list should include documents that were utilized by the evaluator in forming expert opinions as well as those that were not relied upon. Evaluators must take great care not to view certain types of documents as constituting verification of oral reports from litigants. Some documents presented to evaluators are no more than written records of oral reports made earlier to different people. Some affidavits presented to the evaluator containing statements allegedly made by collateral informants who have personal knowledge of the parent or parent–child interactions have, in fact, been written by an attorney or the parent yet signed by the collateral informant. The evaluator must take steps to verify that the information in the affidavit does, in fact, represent the informant's personal knowledge.

14. The evaluator should make clear the manner and reason for interviewing each collateral informant. In the written report, the evaluator should also address how the reliability of information from the collateral informant was assessed and the weight the evaluator attributed to the obtained collateral information. William G. Austin and Kirkpatrick (2004) have called attention to the fact that as psychological distance from the custody dispute increases, so does objectivity. School personnel are likely to provide more objective information than neighbors. Evaluators who limit their collateral source inquiries to those who are deemed to be objective are likely to overlook information that, despite its delivery by subjective sources, is nevertheless potentially enlightening.

15. The evaluator must make clear the methods employed to corroborate information that they relied upon. Despite overwhelming evidence that psychologists are not particularly impressive as human lie detectors (DePaulo et al., 1997, 2003; Frank & Feeley, 2003; Frank et al., 2004), far too many evaluators trust their clinical intuition to tell who is being forthright and who is being disingenuous. The reviewer should examine which parent assertions were verified through third-party information.

    If the evaluator places significant weight on parent-interview data, it is important for the evaluator to explain the reasons for placing such weight on such interview data. Research has identified several powerful bias factors that operate in a forensic interview of parents involved in child custody litigation (Ackerman et al., 2019; Hynan, 2014).

16. The evaluator should identify the evidence-based criteria for selecting assessment instruments. Although in some jurisdictions, the criteria to be employed in assessing custodial suitability are statutorily defined, in many jurisdictions, evaluators must decide what constitutes effective parenting and what observable indices to utilize. Neal and colleagues (2019) recently reviewed the use of psychological assessment tools in the courtroom and concluded the following:

    > We find that many of the assessment tools used by psychologists and admitted into legal contexts as scientific evidence actually have poor or unknown scientific foundations. We also find few legal challenges to the admission of this evidence. Attorneys rarely challenge the expert evidence and, when they do, judges tend not to subject psychological assessment evidence to the legal scrutiny required by law. (2019, p. 155)

    Neal et al. reported that there is no relationship between the psychometric qualities of a test and its likelihood of being challenged in court. Their data suggested that some of the weakest tools tend to get a pass from the courts. "Our bottom-line conclusion is that evidentiary challenges to psychological tools are rare and challenges to the most scientifically suspect tools are even rarer or are nonexistent" (Neal et al., 2019, p. 154). We believe the proper use of psychological test data and its context-relevant interpretation are an important component of an evidence-based evaluation protocol (Gould, Martindale, & Flens, 2018; Rappaport et al., 2018).

17. The evaluator should have notes about the manner in which assessment instruments were administered. Evaluators should administer assessment instruments in accordance with the instructions in the manuals that accompany the instruments and should be responsive to the admonitions that appear in the Standards for Educational and Psychological Testing (American Educational Research Association et al., 1985).

18. The evaluator must be transparent about the scoring and interpretation of the assessment data. Many evaluators have become dependent upon computer-generated interpretive reports, despite the clarity of Ethical Standard 9.09(c), which reminds psychologists that they "retain responsibility for the appropriate application, interpretation, and use of assessment instruments, whether they score and interpret such tests themselves or use automated or other services" (APA, 2010a, p. 1071). Concerns about the reliability of computer-generated interpretive reports have been frequently raised in the literature for at 20 years (Gould et al., 2009, 2013; Gould & Rappaport, 2016). As far back as 1997, concerns had been raised about "intrinsic difficulties, most notably a lack of substantial empirical data to validate which the computer generates its report leads to a product that is inadequately individualized, or 'canned'" (Millon et al., p. 134).

19. The evaluator has an obligation to demonstrate efforts to protect the integrity of the evaluation process by bringing competence, transparency, objectivity, clarity of boundaries, and balancing thoroughness with the avoidance of unintended harm (Association of Family and Conciliation Courts, 2022).

20. The evaluator must comply with ethical standards, laws, and regulations governing the creation, maintenance, and production of appropriate records.

ROLE OF CRITICAL THINKING

There is an emerging concern about the lack of critical thinking in forensic psychological assessment and report writing (Kukor, 2022). Katherine H. Pherson and Pherson (2021) argue that the process of report writing has changed significantly with the wide availability of powerful search engines on the internet. We echo their concern and raise it tenfold with the introduction to artificial intelligence (AI) software that can write summaries and reports. Our concern focuses on how those writing reports search the internet and AI for information sources that address their topic, extract relevant information, copy and paste the information into their reports, and then edit and integrate the information into the body of their report. There is little demonstration that the author of the paper has engaged in any critical thinking prior to or during their inclusion of the obtained internet information to the body of their report. Another concern with the use of AI is that the author would not be able to show their work to demonstrate the basis for their expert opinion.

Katherine H. Pherson and Pherson suggest several questions that need to be asked prior to engaging in internet searches, which we have expanded to include AI software. Applied to our work, we have developed a list of questions that might be useful for the evaluator to consider when engaging in forensic assessment, report writing, and consultation with attorneys.

1. Did the evaluator or consultant develop a line of argument in preparing their report or expert opinion?
2. Were there specific questions developed to guide the evaluator or consultant in understanding the target information to be gathered during the evaluation or consultation and to be searched for online?
3. Did the evaluator or consultant carefully consider whether the questions identified by the court or attorneys were questions that are within the province and competence of the mental health field?
4. Did the evaluator or consultant consider the assumptions embedded in the questions posed for investigation?
5. Did the evaluator or consultant consider alternative assumptions and develop questions for investigation that considered these alternative assumptions?
6. Did the evaluator or consultant develop alternative hypotheses and employ reliable data-gathering procedures to examine such alternative hypotheses?
7. Can the evaluator or consultant demonstrate their methodology and show their work?

Katherine H. Pherson and Pherson stress the importance of identifying explicitly who is the primary recipient of the evaluator's work product. We believe that the primary recipient of a PPE is the court. Some evaluators write reports with the intention to assist the family move towards settlement. Our experience (and concern) is that when a custody report is written with the primary focus of assisting the family in settling their case there is a reluctance to include all relevant information in the report, particularly placing greater emphasis on strengths in the family system and minimizing challenges in the family that were important contributing factors that prevented previous ADR procedures from succeeding. When evaluators do not provide all relevant information to the court, the court's decision making might be negatively influenced by the lack of complete and transparent information about the family system. In order for answers to become clear, the questions have to be clear (Seyyedadabi, 2006).

Katherine H. Pherson and Pherson contend that too often, written analyses lack focus. In the case of child custody reports, a poorly written report that lacks focus leaves the court (and attorneys) wondering about the purpose of the report. We return to our emphasis on questions guiding the evaluation:

> A well-crafted analysis is tightly focused on a single primary message. The best way to formulate that message is to ensure that it responds to your clients' needs, answering thought-provoking questions that they are—or should

> be—asking. Questions stimulate and guide the analytic process, engaging and enabling interaction, among analysts, reviewers and clients to develop a message that will hit the target. Quite simply, questions beg for answers. (K. H. Pherson & Pherson, 2021, p. 17).

In their analysis of the importance of critical thinking, K. H. Pherson and Pherson discuss the importance of trust. Again, translating their ideas for use in child custody work, trust is defined in two ways. The first is that trust refers to how the evaluator trusts their thinking. The second way is that trust refers to whether and how much the recipients of the evaluator's work product trusts and, therefore, depend upon and utilizes the evaluator's analysis.

Katherine H. Pherson and Pherson categorize the components of trust into two factors: capability and credibility. *Capability* is defined as the knowledge, skills, and abilities that add value to one's work product (K. H. Pherson & Pherson, 2021, p. 5). Capability is measured based upon one's history of producing evaluations that have been scrutinized by the court, the weight given to each evaluation by the court, the quality of the assessments conducted during the evaluation upon which expert opinions were based, and the overall usefulness of past and present evaluations to the issues before the court.

Capability is, in part, a construct similar to psychologists' Ethical Standard 2 addressing competence. It is also similar to rules of evidence addressing the qualifications of an expert. Capability adds to our ethical standards and qualifications to be admitted as an expert, recognizing that an evaluator's past and present work products contribute to the perception that one is capable of conducting a relevant and probative evaluation that will yield helpful information to the court.

The second factor comprising trust is *credibility*, defined by an evaluator's track record and by the perception of the evaluator's work held by the parents, attorneys, and the court. Katherine H. Pherson and Pherson emphasize the importance of honesty, integrity, and intent in defining the components of credibility. In part, credibility is determined by answering two questions: "Do you do what you say you will do in serving your clients? Do you or your products have a bias or hidden agenda that diminishes their overall value and utility?" (K. H. Pherson & Pherson, 2021, p. 5).

Katherine H. Pherson and Pherson bring another interesting idea to the table. Citing the work of Carol Dweck, they suggest that people can be categorized into growth mindsets and fixed mindsets. People with growth mindsets "believe they can develop expertise in anything if they just work hard enough as opposed to those with fixed mindsets, who are convinced that their natural abilities are all they have" (K. H. Pherson & Pherson, 2021, p. 6).

Dweck's view is that competent analysis requires being open to learning new and potentially challenging ideas, learning new ways of integrating and interpreting and evaluating new tools and assessment procedures (Dweck, 2008). The growth mindset individual is "more likely to seek accurate information because (they) are looking for ways to improve and impact (their) performance and environment" (Dweck, 2008, p. 7).

Applying Dweck's view on growth versus fixed mindsets to our interest in developing greater awareness of the role of critical thinking in child custody assessment, we ask that you reflect on which mindset best describes your approach to the evaluation process. In our view, the evaluation process includes but is not limited to examination of the assessment procedures we choose, reflection on the questions we ask during interviews and how the interview structure is informed by the professional and scientific knowledge of the field, continuous review and updating of relevant peer-reviewed ideas that include evidence-based and evidence-informed data, integrating case law and statutes pertinent to the assessment process and the admissibility of the finished work product.

When considering the factors identified above that are part of the evaluation process, how do you view yourself in terms of growth versus fixed mindsets? Those with fixed mindsets are more likely to seek validation of their ideas rather than challenge their ideas with new developments. Those with fixed mindsets are more likely to view failures as disasters rather than opportunities to learn from failures, and those with fixed mindsets are more likely to avoid challenges than those with a growth mindset who seek out and relish challenges (K. H. Pherson & Pherson, 2021).

CONCLUSION

This chapter explored the foundational question: What constitutes scientific knowledge in the context of parenting plan evaluations? PPEs lie at the crossroads of science and law, where empirical rigor meets the complexities of human relationships. As expert witnesses, forensic mental health evaluators play a crucial role in helping judges bridge the gap between evolving scientific principles and the practical demands of judicial decision making. Unlike research conducted in a laboratory, the courtroom requires a different application of science, one that integrates empirical findings with real-world complexities.

The chapter began by examining how specialized knowledge and scientific knowledge are interpreted and applied in forming expert opinions. We explored key legal precedents, such as the Daubert and Kumho Tire cases, which have shaped the evolving standards for the admissibility of expert testimony. A major challenge in this process is balancing the legal system's need for timely and fair decisions with the ongoing, evolving nature of scientific discovery. This tension underscored the dual role of evaluators as both scientists and communicators, whose testimony must be both scientifically sound and practically relevant.

The chapter also addressed the ethical, methodological, and evidentiary challenges that evaluators face. It provided guidance on maintaining scientific integrity while fulfilling the evaluator's duty to offer clear, reliable, and contextually appropriate expert testimony. By grounding our discussion in legal precedents and scientific best practices, we aimed to equip evaluators with the tools they need to meet ethical obligations, maintain credibility, and provide courts with testimony that is both rigorous and accessible.

Earlier in the book, we introduced a critical challenge related to the analytic gap—the G2i challenge—which we will explore in the next chapter.

6

Applying General Scientific Findings to Individual Cases

The G2i Challenge

In legal proceedings, particularly those involving child custody and family dynamics, courts often rely on expert testimony informed by peer-reviewed literature. However, the responsible use of social science research requires careful consideration, as legal cases involve unique, context-specific factors that may not align perfectly with generalized research findings. To address these complexities, the Association of Family and Conciliation Courts (AFCC) established guidelines to promote the ethical, effective, and critical application of social science research in family law decision making. These guidelines emphasize the importance of scientific integrity, professional expertise, and contextual relevance in shaping expert opinions that assist the court in making informed, just decisions.

We begin this chapter by briefly introducing the AFCC guidelines and outlining three concerns that evaluators had in response to these guidelines. In the remainder of the chapter, we focus on the third concern: the challenge of applying group data to specific individual cases, also known as the *general-to-individual* (*G2i*) challenge. We will return to the G2i issue throughout this book and make references to social framework testimony, which we introduced in Chapter 1. Thus, this chapter is important because it explores these issues in depth and proposes a tentative solution to the bridge between social framework testimony and diagnostic testimony.

https://doi.org/10.1037/0000474-007
Parenting Plan Evaluations: An Evidence-Informed Approach to Child Custody, by J. W. Gould and C. M. Mulchay

ASSOCIATION OF FAMILY AND CONCILIATION COURTS GUIDELINES FOR THE USE OF SOCIAL SCIENCE RESEARCH IN FAMILY LAW

The AFCC developed *Guidelines for the Use of Social Science Research in Family Law* (AFCC, 2018). The purpose of the guidelines was to "promote critical thinking about effective, responsible, and ethical use of social science research in family-law related education, practices, programs, and policy making" (AFCC, 2018, p. 1). The AFCC guidelines define social science research as "knowledge claims or general assertions about children, parents, and families in their social context that are derived from data gathered using one or more of a wide range of scientific research methodologies. Recognized scientific research methodologies involve description of the population of study and systematic, transparent, and replicable methods for ethically collecting and analyzing data and reporting the results of studies" (AFCC, 2018, p. 1).

The challenge is how best to use the professional and scientific knowledge of the discipline in a responsible manner that assists the court. The diversity and heterogeneity inherent in expert testimony involving child custody matters requires critical thinking. Critical thinking involves extrapolating from the professional and scientific literature to the case at hand. Critical thinking also requires integrating relevant aspects of that literature with case-specific information. It is the integration of these elements—professional knowledge, scientific knowledge, and professional experience—that provides a reliable basis for expert opinions.

The guidelines were a response, in part, to address a controversy in the family law arena about if and when social science research should be used. Evaluators responded to the guidelines by offering at least three perspectives, each with passionate and knowledgeable colleagues arguing the relevance of their position.

One position is that the trend toward evidence-based and evidence-informed practice increases the reliability of methodology and trustworthiness of opinions offered to the court. *Daubert* and related legal trends reflect this practice and the position taken in this book. An extension of this argument is that expert testimony is an integration of scientific knowledge of the discipline with the expert's professional knowledge. Our interpretation of the Court's decision in *Kumho Tire* supports this argument.

A second position is that the currently available research is of insufficient quality and quantity to be useful as a basis for expert opinions. An extension of this argument is that expert opinions based upon the insufficient research basis might do harm by proffering opinions that are either unreliable or of unknown reliability and potentially misleading (Tippins & Wittmann, 2005). We offer a more extensive discussion of this position immediately below.

A third position is that research derived from group data and focused on majority populations may serve to reinforce the norm to the detriment of the individual child or minority groups (AFCC, 2018, p. 2). Among the many challenges to consider when offering expert opinion testimony is whether there is a reasonable basis for child custody evaluators to offer opinions drawn from group data that are then applied to a specific case before the court. This reasoning from group data to make decisions about individuals or families involved in a specific court dispute is referred to as the G2i challenge (Faigman et al., 2017).

WHAT DO AGGREGATE RESULTS TELL US ABOUT THE FIT BETWEEN THE GROUP RESULTS AND THE INDIVIDUAL?

Custody evaluators often provide testimony that applies the general knowledge of the field drawn from studies summarizing aggregate data across studies of individuals to parents, children, family systems, and other case-specific targets. G2i concerns focus on the reliability of applying findings from aggregate studies to individuals in a particular case.

One side of the G2i challenge is whether the characteristics of the individual(s) in a particular case are the same as or similar to the characteristics of the individuals who were subjects of the study or studies being applied to them. For example, if the children in a particular case are 4 and 5 years old and the subjects of the research being cited were children between 1 and 2 years old, the application of the research findings for 1- and 2-year-olds is not a proper (i.e., reliable) basis upon which to base an expert opinion about 4- and 5-year-old children.

Experts are often asked to weigh in on controversial issues in the literature. Experts frequently cite research studies that support their opinion yet exclude studies offering contrary findings. Whether the findings support or do not support the expert's opinion, significant questions often remain about whether the findings from published studies are a reliable basis for any expert opinion that the application of those findings to the particular child in the case before the court. This is the challenge of the G2i problem.

Among the areas in which much expert testimony in a custody case is often proffered to the court concerns overnight parenting time for young children. Questions about the developmental appropriateness of overnights for young children have challenged the custody field since at least 2000 most notably found in the articles by Solomon and Biringen (2001), J. B. Kelly and Lamb (2000), Lamb and Kelly (2000), and Warshak (2000).

None of the research studies that have addressed overnight access for young children have been based upon the particular child of concern in the case before the court. It is important to know whether the children in the samples used in the published research have characteristics similar to or different from the children in the case before the court. Without this information, significant questions are raised about whether the research findings from these studies can or cannot be applied to the children in the case before the court.

Experts who provide testimony that applies the results from aggregate or group data to the facts of the case before the court are likely to be unreliable precisely because of the concern expressed above. What is missing from such expert testimony is the specific history of the child with each parent, each parent's understanding of how best to calm, soothe, and generally care for the child, the degree to which each parent is appropriately responsive in a timely manner to the child's outwardly expressed and subtle signs of distress, and other factors. Said differently, whether or not there is research supporting overnights for children or not, what is most important in a particular case is the parenting history of the young child, the parent–child fit of the child, the resilience of the child, and other factors that are specific to this child in this family system with these parents and their ability to create an emotional environment in each home that facilitates the young child's ability to feel safe, secure, and loved (Gould & Stahl, 2001).

As reviewers of other psychologists' custody reports, we encounter the G2i problem most often in the use of psychological test results. Garber and Simon (2018) have expressed the concern that psychological testing is often misused in child custody assessment. We agree with their concern that many colleagues do not understand how to utilize psychological test results in a child custody context (Ackerman et al., 2019; Gould et al., 2018; Gould & Rappaport, 2016).

Among the most egregious mistakes in the use of psychological test results in a child custody context is reporting test scores and their interpretation *as if* the results and interpretation tell us something about the person who took the test (ideographic) rather than describing characteristics of people who typically produce such scores (nomothetic). That is, the scores and their interpretation tell us something about the people in the normative sample but tell us nothing about the person who took the test in the custody case. The only way to know if the group test score and interpretations fit the individual who took the test for the custody case is to gather independent, third-party information about the individual's behavior in the real world combined with self-report and other relevant information drawn from parent–child or parent-to-parent observations.

Framed in the G2i concerns, test scores and their interpretations provide information about the people in the normative sample. That is the "G" in G2i. It is unknown whether the test results and their interpretation fit the individual who took the test as part of a custody evaluation until we gather additional, case-specific information. That is the "i" in G2i. As we will discuss later, in psychological testing we refer to this as the difference between nomothetic and ideographic approaches.

WHERE IS THE LINE BETWEEN REPORTING ON THE SCIENCE AND ADVOCACY?

Another concern drawn from the G2i literature is determining when the expert witness has moved from reporting on the research and the meaning of the research findings to applying those findings to a particular case. Some argue that once expert testimony moves from describing the research findings and their meaning to applying those findings to a particular case, the expert has become an advocate offering argument.

One of the pressing questions posed by the G2i challenge is whether the scientific foundation is sound enough to permit a valid opinion about the individual case (Faigman et al., 2017). As discussed below, this distinction between providing an empirical framework of the research and its meaning and applying that framework to a specific case or individual is about social framework testimony or social framework evidence versus diagnostic testimony or diagnostic evidence.

Although we are of the opinion that social science research can be a basis for expert testimony, it is incumbent upon the testifying expert to understand the arguments challenging such testimony. The testifying expert needs to know reasonable alternative explanations and explain why the expert's opinion is a better fit for the data than the alternatives. Thus, we provide the following discussion about *social framework testimony* and *diagnostic testimony.*

SOCIAL FRAMEWORK TESTIMONY VERSUS DIAGNOSTIC TESTIMONY

Increasingly, courts are seeking reliable information from social scientists. Providing courts with evidence-based and evidence-informed information drawn from social science research can provide valuable context for deciding case-specific factual issues (Monahan et al., 2009). Expert witness testimony offers inferences and conclusions about social science research that can assist the court in its decision making. When expert testimony is based on reliable research properly applied to the facts of the case, the justice system can have greater faith in the positive contributions offered by expert testimony. When testimony is based upon unreliable or biased research findings, expert testimony is, at best, unhelpful and, at worst, misleading. Unreliable or biased research findings in expert witness testimony thwarts the court's ability to administer justice fairly, accurately, and justly (Dror & Murrie, 2018).

Historically, social science research was used to prove "legislative facts" that pertain to general questions of law or policy (L. Walker & Monahan, 1987). Social science research has been used to prove "adjudicative facts" that are applied to the case at hand (L. Walker & Monahan, 1987).

Almost 40 years ago, L. Walker and Monahan (1987) raised a third use of social science research:

> Empirical information is being offered that incorporates aspects of both of the traditional uses: general research results are used to construct a frame of reference or background context for deciding factual issues crucial to the resolution of a specific case. We call this new use of social science in the law the creation of *social frameworks.* (p. 559, italics in original)

While acknowledging the use of social framework evidence as potentially useful to the courts, Walker and Monahan also sent up a bright caution flag. They raised several concerns about the reliability of applying social science framework evidence to the facts of specific cases. Among their concerns, they questioned the relevance of group data to deciding questions applied to the facts of a specific case. They also questioned the potential for social framework evidence to obfuscate issues at trial or prejudice one party.

Often, expert witnesses offer general statements about evidence-based and evidence-informed studies. Laurens Walker and Monahan (1987) referred to this as *social framework testimony*. The results of these studies describe aggregate data across groups of individuals (Faigman et al., 2014). Courts, however, seek answers to the case at hand. Courts want to know whether the aggregate research is a reliable predictor of the individual's behavior of concern in this specific case. The challenge faced by the courts is allowing information about a general phenomenon (i.e., "G") into evidence and whether or not the particular case is an example of that specific phenomenon (Faigman et al., 2016).

A concern is that courts often do not assess an expert's ability to provide social framework testimony separately from their ability to accurately apply the social framework findings to the individual facts of the case, what is called *diagnostic testimony* (Fisher et al., 2015). Diagnostic testimony cannot be admissible if the social framework testimony is not reasonably well established in the scientific literature.

Consideration of the admissibility of social framework testimony begins with an examination of its ability to meet basic evidentiary standards. The social framework testimony must be based upon good science and be relevant to the issues before the court (Faigman et al., 2017).

The process of reasoning from the social framework research representing group data to the individual case before the court is primarily a scientific one. The expert is making an inference from the social framework research to the individual facts of the instant case. The challenge is that there is no known method or technique developed as of yet to reliably facilitate the application of the general to the individual.

FAIGMAN'S BEST PRACTICES

Faigman et al. (2017) suggest two key best practices intended to reduce the complexity of decision making about the admissibility of social science research. One key best practice is to focus attention on (a) whether the proposed scientific evidence is good science, that is "does the science meet certain evidentiary standards?" and (b) on what is it good for?

Every case involving expert testimony based upon scientific research involves two choices. The first choice is whether the court will admit testimony about the general phenomenon, i.e., overnights for young children (social framework testimony). The second choice is whether the court will admit testimony about the general phenomenon (social framework testimony) and allow its application to the specific case at hand (diagnostic testimony).

Faigman et al. argue that the first decision about social framework testimony is separate from the second decision about diagnostic testimony. They argue diagnostic testimony cannot be admissible unless the social framework testimony is found to be reliable and, therefore, admissible. "[E]vidence that something is an instance of a larger phenomenon presumes that the larger phenomenon itself exists" (Faigman et al., 2017, p. 1).

The second "key best practice" includes the process of reasoning from group data to the individual case. However, we are provided no guidance about the meaning of the term reasoning.

WHAT IS REASONING?

Reasoning is defined as the ability to assess things. In simple language, we view reasoning as the process used to put together the puzzle pieces of a complex family system. One problem with the term reasoning is that there is no universally accepted definition of its meaning and no universally accepted agreement about the process by which all people reason.

Some definitions of reasoning include the concept of rational application, while other definitions include rational application by applying logic. Each of these definitions presumes an accepted and universally agreed upon understanding of the concept of rational application and logic. Although we do not intend to dive into a discussion of the different meanings one might assign to each definition of reasoning, what is important is recognizing that these common terms used in everyday language might mean different things to different people.

For our purposes, reasoning is viewed as an internal method of integrating new and existing information to decide or solve a problem. The G2i challenge is to find ways to assess how an expert was able to reason from the general information to the specific application of that information. Applied in a forensic psychological context, reasoning provides an internal method of weighing the costs and benefits of different options. It is precisely the internal nature of reasoning that cannot be measured without relying on an individual's self-report of their internal process. It is also the internal nature of reasoning and the inference process of an individual's reasoning that is at the core of G2i concerns in applying group data to individual cases.

Like so many other important concepts in our field, the more we look at our understanding of a term, the more we realize that we do not know a lot about how the human mind works. For example, there are different types of reasoning that guide the internal decision-making process. When Faigman et al. and others talk about understanding the process of reasoning from group data to the individual case, there is an assumption that there is one "process of reasoning" that can reliably be applied to understanding the inferences made by an individual applying group data to an individual case. However, there is not one definition of reasoning and, most likely, different people might use different types of reasoning to apply to different types of problems.

SEVEN TYPES OF REASONING

Given the likely lack of consensus over the term reasoning, we have provided a brief discussion of seven different types of reason often revealed in the testimony of our colleagues. We have provided examples of each type of reasoning and a chart that summarizes the strengths and weaknesses of each form of reasoning.

Deductive reasoning follows a general legal or psychological principle and applies it to a specific case to reach a logically sound conclusion. Here are a couple examples of deductive reasoning applied to parenting plan evaluations (PPEs):

- Example 1: Applying deductive reasoning to the Best Interests of the Child Standard
  - Premise 1: Courts prioritize the best interests of the child in custody decisions.
  - Premise 2: The child's best interests include a stable home environment, emotional support, and continuity of care.
  - Premise 3: Parent A provides a more stable home environment and continuity of care than Parent B.
  - Conclusion: Therefore, Parent A is more likely to receive primary custody.
- Example 2: Applying deductive reasoning to parental fitness and substance abuse
  - Premise 1: A parent with a history of substance abuse poses a potential risk to the child's well-being.
  - Premise 2: Parent B has a documented history of substance abuse and has relapsed recently.
  - Conclusion: Therefore, Parent B may pose a risk to the child's well-being and may not be granted primary custody.

Each of these examples follows a logical structure where a general rule is applied to a specific custody situation to reach a reasoned conclusion.

Inductive reasoning involves drawing general conclusions from specific observations. Unlike deductive reasoning, where the conclusion is necessarily true if the premises are true, inductive reasoning results in probable conclusions based on patterns, trends, or evidence. Here are a couple examples:

- Example 1: Inductive reasoning applied to parenting involvement
  - Observation 1: The child consistently expresses a strong emotional bond with Parent A.

- Observation 2: Parent A attends all school meetings and extracurricular activities.
- Observation 3: Parent A has historically been the primary caregiver.
- Conclusion: Parent A is likely the more involved and supportive parent, making them a stronger candidate for primary custody.

- Example 2: Inductive reasoning applied to stability and predictability
  - Observation 1: Parent B has changed residences three times in the past two years.
  - Observation 2: The child has struggled academically and emotionally with each move.
  - Observation 3: Research suggests that frequent relocations negatively impact child development.
  - Conclusion: If Parent B continues to move frequently, the child may experience further instability, making Parent A's home the more stable option.

Analogical reasoning involves drawing comparisons between similar cases or situations to form conclusions. In PPEs, courts and evaluators may use past cases, precedents, or similar fact patterns to make informed decisions about the best interests of the child. Here are a couple examples:

- Example 1: Analogical reasoning addressing relocation and stability
  - Situation 1 (Past Case): In a prior custody case, a court ruled that frequent relocations negatively impacted a child's academic and emotional stability, favoring the parent who provided a consistent home environment.
  - Situation 2 (Current Case): Parent B has moved multiple times in the past year, while Parent A has remained in the same home and school district.
  - Conclusion: Based on precedent and similarities to Situation 1, Parent A is more likely to be awarded primary custody to ensure stability for the child.
- Example 2: Analogical reasoning in parent–child contact problems
  - Situation 1 (Past Case): In a previous case, Parent A was found to be discouraging the child from having a relationship with Parent B and the child believes that Parent B is dangerous and unfit. The court determined Parent A's parenting time with the child is under supervision and the child is now living with Parent B.
  - Situation 2 (Current Case): Evidence suggests that Parent B is undermining the child's view of Parent A as competent and fit. Parent B is also preventing the child from visiting with Parent A and making negative comments about Parent A both to the child and in front of the child.

- Conclusion: If the court follows past decisions, Parent B may face parenting time restrictions to prevent further disruption to the child's relationship with Parent A.

Abductive reasoning involves drawing the most plausible explanation or conclusion based on incomplete or uncertain information. It is often used when evaluators, attorneys, or judges must make informed inferences about a child's best interests, even when they do not have absolute proof. Here are a couple examples of abductive reasoning in child custody cases:

- Example 1: Abductive reasoning applied to child's behavioral changes and parental influence
  - Observation: The child has recently exhibited anxiety, withdrawn behavior, and emotional distress after returning from visits with Parent B.
  - Possible explanations:
    - The child may be experiencing emotional abuse or high conflict at Parent B's home.
    - The child may be struggling with adjusting to two different household environments.
    - The child may be influenced by Parent A's negative opinions about Parent B.
  - Most plausible conclusion: Given that the child was previously well-adjusted and only displays these behaviors after visits with Parent B, there is a reasonable basis to suspect that something in Parent B's household is contributing to the distress. Further evaluation is needed.
- Example 2: Abductive reasoning applied to allegations of domestic violence
  - Observation: Parent A has accused Parent B of domestic violence, but there is no police report or direct evidence. However, the child appears fearful and refuses to visit Parent B.
  - Possible explanations:
    - The child has witnessed or experienced domestic violence.
    - Parent A is coaching the child to fear Parent B.
    - The child is anxious about being away from Parent A.
  - Most plausible conclusion: Given that the child's fear seems genuine and spontaneous, it is reasonable to suspect that some form of emotional or physical conflict has occurred. A psychological evaluation and further investigation are warranted.

Cause-and-effect reasoning in child custody cases involves identifying a specific cause (an action, behavior, or circumstance) and determining its effect (the impact on the child's well-being, stability, or parental fitness). This type of reasoning helps courts, evaluators, and attorneys establish logical connections between parental actions and their consequences when making custody decisions.

- Example 1: Cause and effect reasoning applied to parental conflict and child's emotional well-being
  - Cause: Frequent and intense conflicts between the parents during custody exchanges.
  - Effect: The child becomes anxious, withdrawn, and resistant to transitions between households.
  - Conclusion: High parental conflict negatively impacts the child's emotional well-being, potentially requiring a structured custody arrangement (e.g., parallel parenting or supervised exchanges).
- Example 2: Cause and effect reasoning applied to frequent changes in custody arrangements and child's behavioral issues
  - Cause: The child has been subjected to multiple custody modifications and inconsistencies in parenting schedules.
  - Effect: The child exhibits behavioral problems including defiance, anxiety, and difficulty forming secure attachments.
  - Conclusion: Frequent disruptions in custody negatively impact the child's emotional stability, suggesting the need for a more consistent and predictable custody arrangement.

Critical thinking in child custody cases involves analyzing facts, evaluating evidence, and applying logical reasoning to determine what is in the child's best interest. It requires minimizing biases, questioning assumptions, and integrating legal principles, psychological research, and case-specific information to reach a well-reasoned decision. Below are examples of how critical thinking applies in child custody determinations:

- Example 1: Critical thinking applied to evaluating allegations of parental unfitness
  - Situation: Parent A accuses Parent B of being unfit due to alleged neglect.
  - Critical thinking approach:
    - ❑ Gather objective evidence (e.g., medical records, school reports, witness testimony).
    - ❑ Consider alternative explanations (Is the claim based on personal conflict rather than the child's well-being?).
    - ❑ Assess consistency (Has Parent B demonstrated responsible caregiving in other areas?).
  - Conclusion: Without concrete evidence, allegations alone should not determine custody; further investigation is necessary.

- Example 2: Critical thinking applied to differentiating between parental conflict and actual harm
  - Situation: Parents frequently argue, and Parent A claims this is harmful to the child.
  - Critical thinking approach:
    - ❑ Identify specific risk of harm.
    - ❑ Differentiate high conflict between parents from actual harm to the child.
    - ❑ Determine how conflict affects the child's well-being (Is the child exhibiting signs of stress or behavioral issues?).
    - ❑ Explore conflict resolution options (Would coparenting counseling or parallel parenting be beneficial?).
  - Conclusion: Not all conflict is harmful enough to warrant custody changes. Strategies may be needed to reduce conflict while maintaining parental involvement.

Decompositional reasoning involves breaking down complex issues into smaller, analyzable components to make informed decisions. In child custody cases, this reasoning helps judges, evaluators, and legal professionals assess each factor separately before forming a holistic conclusion about the child's best interests.

- Example 1: Decompositional reasoning applied to evaluating parental fitness
  - Instead of making a broad statement like "Parent A is a good/bad parent," decompositional reasoning involves breaking this assessment into distinct criteria:
    - ❑ Emotional support: Does the parent provide a nurturing environment?
    - ❑ Financial stability: Can the parent meet the child's basic needs?
    - ❑ Parental involvement: Does the parent attend school events, medical appointments, and extracurricular activities?
    - ❑ Disciplinary practices: Are they appropriate and nonharmful?
    - ❑ Mental and physical health: Does the parent's health impact caregiving ability?
  - Conclusion: By analyzing each component separately, the evaluator can form a well-supported opinion on parental fitness rather than relying on general impressions.
- Example 2: Decompositional reasoning applied to evaluating parental conflict and its impact
  - If there is high parental conflict, decompositional reasoning helps break it down:
    - ❑ Nature of conflict: Is it minor disagreements or severe hostility?

- ❑ Effect on the child: Does the child show anxiety, fear, or withdrawal due to the conflict?
- ❑ Communication barriers: Are the parents able to coparent effectively, or is communication impossible?
- ❑ Past legal issues: Have there been restraining orders or domestic violence reports?

– Conclusion: Instead of assuming that all parental conflict is harmful, breaking it down helps determine whether parallel parenting, mediation, or supervised exchanges are needed.

Each of the above reasoning types has its place, depending on the context. Deductive reasoning is great for certainty, while inductive and abductive reasoning handle uncertainty. Analogical reasoning fosters creativity but risks false equivalences. Cause-and-effect reasoning is crucial for science but can misattribute causality. Critical thinking is broadly valuable but effortful, and decompositional reasoning is great for breaking down problems but must not lose sight of the whole. Table 6.1 summarizes the strengths and weaknesses of each reasoning type.

TABLE 6.1. Comparison of Reasoning Types

Reasoning type	Strengths	Weaknesses
Deductive reasoning	Leads to logically certain conclusions; ensures consistency	Depends on the truth of premises; rigid in uncertain situations
Inductive reasoning	Useful for predictions and hypothesis generation	Conclusions are probable, not certain; prone to overgeneralization
Analogical reasoning	Helps in problem solving and understanding new concepts	Can lead to misleading comparisons or false equivalencies
Abductive reasoning	Useful in forming hypotheses and diagnosing problems	Most plausible explanation is not always correct; prone to bias
Cause-and-effect reasoning	Essential for scientific research and predicting outcomes	Correlation does not imply causation; complex interactions
Critical thinking	Reduces bias, leads to well-supported conclusions	Requires effort; can slow decision making
Decompositional reasoning	Makes complex problem-solving more manageable	May overlook the bigger picture; requires careful integration

A CHALLENGE TO YOU

We pose a challenge to you, the reader. Reflect on these different types of reasoning and apply them to your internal decision making. One question is whether you typically use one method of reasoning more than another. A second question is whether you can explain the steps taken when you reason from the data obtained in your evaluation to the opinions you proffer to the court. A third question is whether you utilize different reasoning procedures based upon different types of data (i.e., interview data, test data, record review, or observational data). A fourth question is whether you are able to identify for yourself when you employ different reasoning procedures and whether you are able to clearly explain to the court why you use one type of reasoning applied to interview data and apply a different type of reasoning to test data. Finally, are you able to reflect upon your reasoning procedures and determine whether your use of the same or different reasoning procedures for different types of data remains constant across different evaluations you have conducted?

No matter which reasoning method you use, the process of reasoning relies on inferences. Now we are going to discuss the role of inference in our decision making.

WHAT IS AN INFERENCE?

An *inference* is defined as a cognitive operation in which an individual moves from one assertion that is considered to be true to a second assertion that is assumed to also be true. Most research conducted in forensic psychology is fundamentally inferential. An experiment is conducted using a sample drawn from a larger population. When multiple studies produce similar findings, the assumption is that the reliability of the conclusions drawn from the studies represent a real world finding (Moreau, 2021). Thus, results from these experiments are used to draw conclusions about the general population. Social framework knowledge is derived from these types of studies.

Social framework research conclusions derived from such studies are often then applied to the facts of a specific case. An assumption is made that the facts in the case are similar enough to the facts in the research from which the social framework findings were drawn. The problem is that the application of social framework knowledge to facts in a specific case are applied through inferences made about the correspondence between the conditions of the study and the population used and the facts of the specific case.

Reasoning from aggregate group data to an individual case presents several problems. One problem is that the methodology of the studies is unlikely to correspond to the facts of the case before the court. Inferences are made about the goodness of fit between the general findings and the specific case. The rules governing how an expert makes those inferences are not open to examination. Inferences are, by their very nature, an internal cognitive and emotional process.

Relying on inferences from general to specific when it is not possible to examine the degree to which the inferential process reflected a reliable scientific methodology increases the likelihood of false-positive findings that cannot be easily demonstrated to the court. Expert testimony based upon false-positive inferences can mislead the court and lead to unjust decisions.

THE ROLE OF STATISTICAL MODELS

Some scholars argue that the type of inference needed to apply social framework evidence to the individual facts of a case derives from statistical inferences. Faigman and others have argued that the application of Bayesian statistical modeling might be useful in developing probability statements about the fit between social framework research and its application in a specific case. Others argue that Bayesian models are incapable of reliable predictions given the complexity of human behavior. When applied to families involved in custody litigation, the complexity of factors that operate at any one-time call into question whether any statistical model can be applied. Said differently, the hope of social framework modeling using Bayesian statistics is to provide probability statements about the fit between the general research and its application to the individual case at hand. There are three types of probability: objective, experimental, and subjective. Table 6.2 summarizes the strengths and weaknesses of each type.

TABLE 6.2. Strengths and Weaknesses of Different Types of Probability

Probability type	Strengths	Weaknesses
Objective probability (theoretical probability)	• Based on established mathematical models and logic • Consistent and universally accepted • Does not require prior experimentation	• Assumes ideal conditions, which may not always reflect real-world scenarios • Cannot account for unique or changing conditions • Not applicable when probability models are unknown
Experimental probability (empirical probability)	• Based on real data, making it more practical and applicable • Can be tested and refined with more trials • Adapts to real-world observations	• Requires a large sample size for accuracy • Past events may not always predict future outcomes • Subject to errors, bias, or limited data collection
Subjective probability	• Useful when there is not an equation, yet some data is available • Incorporates expert judgment and intuition • Flexible and adaptable to unique situations	• Requires transparency due to bias factors • Lacks mathematical rigor and consistency • Cannot be objectively verified using an equation without weighting subjective data

Objective probability (also known as *theoretical probability*) refers to the likelihood of an event occurring based on a theoretical framework or established mathematical principles. This type of probability is determined by logical reasoning, formulas, or long-term frequency distributions under ideal conditions. It does not rely on past data but rather on known probabilities derived from a model. Common examples include the following:

- The probability of rolling a six on a fair six-sided die is 1/6.
- The probability of drawing an ace from a standard deck of 52 cards is 4/52 (1/13).

Experimental probability (also known as *empirical probability*) is calculated based on actual data from observations or experiments. It depends on the frequency of an event occurring in past trials rather than theoretical models. Common examples include the following:

- If a coin is flipped 100 times and lands on heads 48 times, the empirical probability of getting heads is 48/100 or 0.48.
- If a survey shows that 30 out of 100 people prefer a certain brand, the empirical probability of preference for that brand is 30/100 or 0.3.

Subjective probability is derived from the combination of data with an individual's personal judgment, intuition, or experience rather than only by a mathematical calculation or past data. It reflects personal belief about the likelihood of an event occurring, which may be influenced by emotions, opinions, or expert knowledge. Subjective probability is vulnerable to implicit and explicit bias factors that we discuss in the next chapter. Since subjective probability is not based on formal statistical analysis, different individuals may assign different probabilities to the same event. Common examples include the following:

- A doctor estimates a 70% chance of a patient recovering based on a combination of research and his experience working with similar patients.
- A sports fan believes their favorite team has a 60% chance of winning the next match, because they win just more than half their games, and their next opponent is not very good.
- An investor thinks there's a 40% probability that a stock price will increase based on market trends and intuition.

Unlike objective or empirical probabilities, subjective probabilities are not universally agreed upon and can vary from person to person. Subjective probability is the quantified opinion of an individual (De Finetti, 1968). Subjective probability is based on the data that are available. Different individuals can estimate different probabilities for the same event or data. As Tversky and Kahneman (2005) noted, "The major contribution of this approach is that it provides a rigorous subjective interpretation of probability that is applicable to unique events and is embedded in a general theory of rational decision." So while it is possible to use Bayesian probabilities in our work, it is most likely that we would use subjective instead of objective probabilities.

If we were to use a Bayesian approach, we would be applying a numerical weight to our confidence levels:

> A wise man, therefore, proportions his belief to the evidence. . . . no testimony is sufficient to establish a miracle unless the testimony be of such a kind, that its falsehood would be more miraculous, than the fact, which it endeavors to establish. (Hume, 1777, para. 87)

While this may have its appeal, applying a numerical weight to our confidence levels also represents multiple dangers, including the concern that using such empirically unsupported numerical opinions may mislead the court. If done properly, this method would acknowledge uncertainty and incorporate scientific skepticism and systematic doubt (Mulchay & Knuth, 2023a). It would require a tremendous amount of transparency, much like the Dzozd et al.'s decision-tree model. As noted above, it is important that parenting plan evaluators continuously reevaluate their thought processes and their reasoning.

THE SEDUCTION OF AVERAGED DATA

Courts often use social framework testimony precisely because it is thought that using averaged data, that is, results from group aggregate studies, allows for inferences about the meaning of behavior in an individual case. It is difficult, if not impossible, to diagnose specific behavior in a single individual based upon group comparisons. Although useful information can be obtained from research findings based on group data, any single individual can vary greatly from the average results of the group data (Hardcastle, 2020), making inferences from the group data to the individual of unknown reliability.

Monahan et al. (2009) suggest that "general social science research can provide valuable context for deciding case-specific factual issues (but) general research findings cannot be linked by an expert witness to the facts of a specific case." They argue that linkages between social framework testimony and facts of a specific case are the province of attorneys, not expert witnesses. Said differently, Monahan et al. argue that the application of social framework testimony to the facts of a specific case is a form of argument and not a basis for expert testimony. Argument is reserved for the attorneys and the court.

NO BRIDGE FROM GENERAL TO SPECIFIC

Monahan et al. voice concern that no scientific method developed to date allows for a reliable means to cross the bridge from general empirical knowledge to its application in a specific case. Their concern is that experts rely on their professional experience or intuition to link general social science research findings to the facts of a specific case. We believe Monahan et al. would argue that *Daubert* does not allow for such reliance on professional experience or intuition and that such testimony creates too great of an analytic gap (*General Electric Co. v. Joiner*, 1997) between research findings and their application in a particular case.

Too often, experts make case-specific causal claims on the basis of extrapolation from general social science research without providing a road map to explain the scientific process used to get from the general to the specific.

ROLE OF THE SCIENTIFIC PROCESS

Monahan et al. focus attention on the scientific process placing emphasis on transparent methods. The scientific method also seeks to limit subjective judgments by making transparent the method of data collection and the inferences drawn from those data upon which the expert's opinions are based.

At the core of the concerns regarding G2i is a recognition that intuition is the expert's primary tool for making linkages between general social framework testimony and the facts of a specific case. Hart and Secunda (2009, p. 61) assert that "expert testimony lacking in a method—founded on 'expert intuition' alone—has no place under Rule 702."

Monahan et al. (2009) wrote the following:

> Experts have been qualified as experts because of their scientific training and research and knowledge of general social science research. Their court-sanctioned expertise does not arise from having conducted studies in which they accepted a set of litigation documents assembled by others and then, after reading those documents, made unaided, subjective judgments about causal relations . . . or about the match of features of this (specific case) to the features of research subjects . . ., without disclosing how those matches were made or the strength of those matches and without acknowledging the variability in behaviour and outcomes among the research subjects and explaining the implications of this variability for a supposed 'match' (indeed, such a study would not survive peer review in any journal with which we are familiar). It is a fundamental premise of federal expert witness law, post-*Daubert*, that experts are to employ the same level of rigour inside courtrooms that they do in their professional work outside courtrooms. (p. 317)

Expert opinions about the reliable application of social framework testimony to the facts of a specific case require "more of an explication by the expert than simply the statement that 'I relied on my vast experience'" (Capra, 1998).

Monahan et al voice their concern about experts offering opinions without a proper basis. Monahan et al. (2009) conclude,

> When general social science is no longer being used to provide a context for issues in the case and scientific experts are offering only personal judgments about the facts of the case, we see no reason for 'social framework' opinions to be admitted. (p. 318)

CASE IN POINT

Our first author was retained by an attorney who asked for a review of a court-ordered PPE. The parents had a preschool age child who had been living in a 2-2-3 parenting arrangement[1] for most of the child's life. By all accounts, the child was thriving in all aspects of her life.

The attorney's concern was the evaluator's conclusion was to change the 2-2-3 parenting access arrangement to provide the mother with 10 out of 14 days and the father with 4 out of 14 days. The evaluator's opinion was based upon his reading of studies conducted by Dr. Jennifer McIntosh and her colleagues. The McIntosh (2011) studies tended to find that young children did not do particularly well with frequent overnights with the noncustodial (re: father) parent.

Over the past 10 years, there has been much controversy over Dr. McIntosh's work, often focusing on the subject pool from which she gathered her data and based her opinions. Examining the subject pool used in the McIntosh studies, the parenting access plans in which the children in the study were involved, and the amount of contact the children had with their noncustodial parent *in comparison to* the facts of the case, it was clear that there was no goodness of fit between the McIntosh studies experimental context and the facts of the case. Social framework findings drawn from the McIntosh studies should never have been applied to the facts of the case because of the significant differences in the children's experiences with overnights in the experimental groups compared with those of the child in the case before the court.

MORE LESSONS FROM KUMHO

The court in *Kumho Tire* emphasized that the test for expert testimony should be a "flexible one." As the court found, "We can neither rule out, nor rule in, for all cases and for all time the applicability of the factors mentioned in *Daubert*, nor can we now do so for subsets of cases categorized by category of expert or by kind of evidence."

There is a particular place for forensic psychologists in family court. As Melton et al. point out, an important activity provided by specialized knowledge from forensic psychological experts is to assist the trier of fact, especially when they are likely to challenge factfinders' presumptions about human behavior and motivation (Melton et al., 2018, p. 19).

Not all published, peer-reviewed research is of the same quality. Some research findings have been replicated over decades of investigation, while

[1]A 2-2-3 parenting plan is a joint custody schedule where the child spends 2 days with Parent A, 2 days with Parent B, and 3 days with Parent A. The next week, the pattern reverses, so the child starts with 2 days with Parent B, followed by 2 days with Parent A, and then 3 days with Parent B. This rotating schedule ensures that both parents get frequent and continuous time with the child while maintaining stability.

other findings are based upon one recent study. There might be times when the research evidence is somewhat weak but the underlying ideas upon which the research was based provides useful guidance to the court.

Even when the research basis of opinions is weak, there may be instances in which the underlying knowledge is sufficiently great to warrant the admission of the opinions. Mental health professionals are trained and experienced in observing, explaining, and categorizing abnormal behavior. Even if these formulations are mere stories, they can provide plausible explanations that would otherwise be unavailable to the trier of fact, and that can give a defendant's behavior context and narrative coherence. If such explanations are delivered with appropriate caution, they may well assist the factfinder in reaching a judgment, even though they have not been or cannot be verified.

Over the past 20 years, significant debate has occurred in the custody literature about the degree to which expert testimony must be based upon replicated, verifiable research findings (Gould & Martindale, 2005; Tippins & Wittman, 2005). We believe that any requirement that expert testimony must only be based upon verified research is too restrictive and, in fact, runs contrary to the spirit behind expert testimony. Scientific knowledge, by definition, is continually being modified through further examination and replication. Part of the art of expert witness testimony is the expert's ability to integrate knowledge with experience.

That something is verifiable does not mean that testimony based on it will help the jury. As Melton et al. asserted and as we have promoted in this book, a nuanced approach to admissibility incorporates the scientific method. The focus should be on whether the expert has "sufficient specialized knowledge to assist jurors in deciding the particular issues in the case" (*Kumho Tire Co. v. Carmichael*, 1999).

CONCLUSION

The lessons to be taken from our discussion of social framework findings and their application to the facts of a specific case include an examination of the methodology employed in the research from which the social framework findings are based. Evaluators should scrutinize the subject pool against the individuals in the specific case. In what ways are the individuals in the specific case similar to and different from those in the experimental subject pool? This is important because any inferences about the applicability of the general findings to the specific case must consider the goodness of fit between those in the specific case and those in the subject pool. In the next section, we dive deeper into important factors to consider, such as bias, sociocultural identities, systemic inequities, gender identity, and sexual orientation.

III

MITIGATING BIAS IN YOUR EVALUATION

7

The Role of Bias in Data Collection, Data Integration, and Opinion Formation

In this chapter, we discuss the concept of bias, some of its various forms, and how each step of the parenting plan evaluation (PPE) process is vulnerable to different bias factors. We describe the origin of bias, including the cognitive foundations of bias and frameworks for understanding bias. We then discuss common bias factors in forensic work before we provide strategies to minimize bias.

There are several reasons why it is important to understand bias and take steps to mitigate its effects. First, addressing bias assists in enhancing objective decision making. Family law cases often involve high-conflict situations, emotionally charged narratives, and complex interpersonal dynamics. Evaluators working with these families must sift through subjective accounts to form reasonable hypotheses subject to further investigation. Understanding cognitive biases helps evaluators recognize when their judgments might be influenced by bias factors, allowing for more balanced evaluations.

Second, expert witnesses are perceived as neutral, but their credibility can be compromised if biases shape their assessments or testimonies. Understanding bias and taking steps to mitigate the risk of expert bias helps to maintain the expert's credibility. Professionals who are aware of their cognitive biases are better equipped to defend their methodologies under cross-examination. They can articulate how they controlled for potential biases, strengthening the perceived reliability of their work.

Third, addressing bias helps support the ethical and scientific integrity of the evaluation process. Recognizing biases aligns with ethical principles in psychology, such as objectivity, integrity, and fairness. Acknowledging one's biases

https://doi.org/10.1037/0000474-008
Parenting Plan Evaluations: An Evidence-Informed Approach to Child Custody, by J. W. Gould and C. M. Mulchay

doesn't imply incompetence; it demonstrates a commitment to self-awareness and continuous improvement—key traits of ethical practice.

And fourth, addressing bias will improve judicial outcomes. Biased expert opinions can inadvertently influence judicial decisions, affecting custody arrangements, visitation rights, and overall family dynamics. By minimizing bias, experts help courts make decisions that truly reflect the best interests of the child and the realities of family functioning.

WHAT IS BIAS?

Bias is any systematic error in reasoning and thinking that can alter an individual's memory, perception, and decision making (Chin et al., 2019). Expert witnesses are not immune to biases. While expertise enables remarkable skill specialization, the neurological and systemic architecture enabling these capabilities creates predictable bias vulnerabilities. Experts develop "cognitive schemas" from repeated exposure to domain-specific patterns, making them prone to confirmation bias and blind spot bias when novelty occurs (Neal et al., 2022; Vredeveldt et al., 2024). Said differently, experts are so well rehearsed in their approach to problem solving, they often do not take the time—and are unaware that they are not taking the time—to examine each step in their problem solving (Neal et al., 2022).

As Chin et al. (2019) warned, biased expert witnesses pose a challenge to the legal system. In civil and family law litigation, biased expert witness testimony can protract disputes, increase the cost of litigation, mislead the court, create unjust results, cause potentially life-ruining results, and undermine the public's faith in the legal system (Chin et al., 2019).

Bias can impact nearly every aspect of a PPE. Bias factors might operate in selecting questions to investigate, selecting assessment tools used to gather data, choosing what data to gather and what data to ignore, choosing procedures to analyze data, choosing among the analyzed data that will be included in a report, and that which will be excluded from a report, choosing which data to rely upon as a foundation for expert opinions, and how the expert opinion is presented both in writing and in oral testimony.

Bias factors affect how we conduct an evaluation. Bias factors do not only affect how we approach the investigative task; they also affect how we think about the ways in which we approach the investigative task.

THE EVOLUTIONARY ORIGIN OF BIAS

Human beings hold biases. We develop ways to think about ourselves, others, and the world. We are affected by our education, our family system, our current context, our perception of self and others, our understanding of our task, and many other factors. Bias allows us to use algorithms to process data more quickly. This process makes experts especially prone to bias. The most common reason evaluators experience bias occurs due to our cognitive architecture and the way information is formatted in the brain.

We can think of our brains as cognitive machinery or an adaptive toolbox. This toolbox helps us make efficient decisions even when we are faced with a variety of complex information. We process and filter tremendous amounts of information throughout the day. Without cognitive shortcuts to help us make reasonable judgments, we would be paralyzed with indecision. The adaptive toolbox creates shortcuts like heuristics and stereotypes that contribute to our efficiency while also coming with a downside that increases the likelihood of bias (Neal & Brodsky, 2016).

The efficiency of the adaptive toolbox makes us susceptible to making predictable errors and systematic errors (Kahneman, 2011). Our prior expectations shape our subsequent processing of new information (Eberhardt, 2020b). Our personal self-interest shapes our interpretation of data (Dror, 2011b).

In short, evaluators are affected by bias (Zappala et al., 2018). "Being an expert entails using schemas, selective attention, chunking information, automaticity and more reliance on top-down information, all of which allows experts to perform quickly and efficiently; however, these very mechanisms restrict flexibility and control, may cause the experts to miss and ignore important information, introduce tunnel vision and bias and can cause other effects that degrade performance" (Dror, 2011a).

Research findings have been sobering as we learn more about ways forensic psychological specialists are affected by bias. Murrie et al. (2013) suggest that retained experts are influenced by the side that retains them (retention bias and adversary bias), despite efforts to remain neutral and objective. Zappala et al. (2018) identify other possible bias factors: evaluator discipline and training, personal attitudes and values, and personality trait variations.

Despite evidence to the contrary, experts continue to believe that they can overcome such biases through mere self-reflection (Chin et al., 2019). Some scholars have suggested that simply requiring expert witnesses to be "objective" (a somewhat ill-defined term itself) is not enough.

Several questions remain unanswered. One question is how best to identify and reduce biases at various stages of the forensic psychological assessment process. Another question is, when an expert is revealed to be biased in some way, should that expert be excluded from testifying? Of course, asking if a biased expert should be excluded raises more challenging questions, such as how much bias is too much bias, who decides how much bias is too much bias, and do different types of biases affect different aspects of the evaluation and testimony process in different ways, suggesting that some biases are less prejudicial than others?

WHY UNDERSTANDING BIAS IS IMPORTANT TO THE COURT

There is a high rate of concordance between expert opinions and judicial decisions, suggesting that courts rely heavily on opinions proffered by forensic evaluators. An assumption implicit in courts' reliance on expert opinions is that such opinions have been formulated upon objectivity and accuracy (Zappala et al., 2018). Chin et al. (2019) identified an English decision from the early 1990s as the beginning of the modern interest in bias. In that case, *National Justice Compania Naviera SA v. Prudential Assurance* (1993; also known as the Ikarian Reefer case), the court was troubled by a protracted battle of expert witnesses. It laid out several duties and responsibilities of expert witnesses best summarized as encompassing *independence* and *impartiality* (*The Ikarian Reefer*, p. 565).

There are no hard and fast definitions of independence and impartiality provided by the Ikarian Reefer case. However, we find that independence and impartiality constitute general concepts to be used in guiding the ways in which various types of bias might affect our forensic psychological activities at different stages of our work. We suggest that as you read further about various types of biases, you consider how each type of bias might affect each step of the evaluation process and each step of the testimony process. Consider thinking through how you would evaluate yourself on the potential effects of each bias on various stages of your work and then consider how you would evaluate a colleague's work product using similar criteria. Remember that in a 2017 survey of forensic science examiners, approximately 71% agreed that cognitive bias is a cause for concern in forensics, but only 26% agreed that it impacted their own judgments (Kukucka et al., 2017).

Child custody evaluators are as subject to bias as anyone else. However, our training should make us aware of different types of bias and ways to control how bias affects all aspects of the evaluation process. Evaluators have an ethical obligation to be aware of their biases and how they affect their forensic psychological activities. The problem with formulating the issue in terms of evaluators being aware of their biases is that biases, by definition, are often beyond awareness. Yet, we need to find ways to identify and reduce bias.

MULTICOMPONENT MODEL

Bias has been described as the systematic deviation from the truth (West & Kenny, 2011). The multicomponent model identifies three different components that comprise bias: a cognitive component, an affective component, and a behavioral component. The cognitive component is composed of knowledge and beliefs about a person or thing. When the person or thing represents a social group, the cognitive component is composed of stereotypes (Eagly & Chaiken, 1993), which are defined as generalized knowledge about the traits, attributes, and behaviors the members of a social group share (Smith, 1998). The affective component is composed of the feelings associated with the person or thing. The behavioral component brings together two different ideas. Firstly, according to the self-perception theory (Bem, 1972), people may infer their biases from observing their behavior toward objects or persons. However, others argue that people's biases guide their behavior, and in cases of negatively evaluated groups, judgment bias or discrimination is likely to occur (Eagly & Chaiken, 1993). Hence, the relationship between biases and behavior is considered bidirectional, whereby the strength of the bias directly influences behavior and susceptibility to self-perception effects (Holland et al., 2002).

Some biases are assumed to be the result of life-long experiences with the social group (Rudman, 2004). The same assumption underlies stereotypes as the cognitive component of biases (Taylor & Crocker, 1981). However, some additional factors come into play. In the early socialization processes, children learn and adopt initial attitudes from their parents (Aboud & Amato, 2001), but in time, attitudes change according to children's own experiences. Mostly, attitudes change in a more positive direction due to intergroup contact (Pettigrew & Tropp, 2006, 2008).

DUAL MODES OF COGNITION

Jonathan S. B. T. Evans and Stanovich (2013) have articulated a dual process theory of cognition. While the reader may be familiar with System 1 and System 2 descriptions made popular by Kahneman, he adopted those terms from the work of Stanovich and West. In recent years, J. S. B. T. Evans and Stanovich have returned to using Type 1 and Type 2 terminology to clarify that these processes are not a single system with a single set of attributes, instead they are each a set of systems. Type 1 processes are intuitive and do not require working memory. They are the automatic cognitive processes we use every day and are often unaware of. For example, when we are driving and see a red light, we step on the brake without knowingly thinking about it. Another example is our automatic reactions when we hear an alarm or siren. These are automatic reactions that result in immediate responses, such as immediate reactions to situations that signal danger.

These cognitive processes evolved early in human development. They are tied to basic emotions and similar to animal cognition. Most importantly for our discussion, they are based on implicit knowledge. Type 1 cognitive processes are computationally efficient. They are almost automatic. They are unconscious and autonomous. Without the use of working memory, Type 1 processes occur very quickly and occur without knowledge. Kahneman (2011) provided the following examples of Type 1 processing: orienting to the source of a sudden sound, completing the phrase "bread and . . .," detecting hostility in a voice, answering to 2 + 2 = ?, and driving a car on an empty road.

Type 2 processes are reflective and require working memory and mental stimulation. They evolved later than Type 1 processes. Type 2 processes involve complex emotions. We believe they are distinctively human. For our discussion, you can think of Type 2 processes as being based on explicit knowledge. Type 2 processes are more reflective as they are deliberative processes that require effort and control. Most notably, they require working memory. Kahneman (2011) provided the following examples of Type 2 processing: searching memory to identify a surprising sound, focusing on the voice of a particular person in a crowded and noisy room, monitoring your behavior in a social situation, and checking the validity of a complex logical argument.

> Rapid autonomous processes (Type 1) are assumed to yield default responses unless intervened on by distinctive higher-order reasoning processes (Type 2). What defines the difference is that Type 2 processing supports hypothetical thinking and loads heavily on working memory. (J. S. B. T. Evans & Stanovich, 2013)

DUAL MODES OF BIASES

Jonathan S. B. T. Evans and Stanovich (2013) provide a list to differentiate Type 1 and 2 processes. They describe how the difference between Type 1 and Type 2 systems is more than the difference between Type 1 systems being implicit and Type 2 being explicit. (Recall that the most defining difference is the autonomous processing.) We should not, and do not, diminish the roll of implicit and explicit processes.

As will be described in more detail later, biases can be implicit or explicit. Explicit biases are believed to be conscious evaluations and the result of deliberative processes. Implicit biases are conceptualized as automatic evaluations (Gawronski & Bodenhausen, 2006) that come immediately into mind when the person or thing is present (Olson & Fazio, 2009).

Importantly, the distinction taps into the multi-component model (Eagly & Chaiken, 1993) outlined above. Hence, implicit attitudes reflect the affective component, as they are suggested to be associations between the target and its evaluations (Fazio, 2001, 2007), which is considered in all implicit methods. The assessed evaluations mirror the feelings and valences related to the object, which are the result of automatic processes. In contrast, the explicit attitudes reflect the cognitive component because these often rely on beliefs about the attitude object (Gawronski & Bodenhausen, 2007).

Another model (Olson & Fazio, 2009) suggests that biases guide behavior via two different modes. In automatic modes, implicit biases tend to guide automatic and spontaneous behavior. In the controlled mode, the explicit attitudes guide controlled and conscious behavior. Such thoughtful and effortful processes, however, can only occur when the cognitive resources are plentiful, and people have much time and motivation to extensively reflect on their behavior and attitudes (Fazio & Towles-Schwen, 1999). Therefore, people's motivation and the possibility to reflect influence which process occurs. Nonetheless, this stringent dichotomy cannot be easily maintained, as most of the processes are mixed with automatic and controlled processes and attitudes contributing to behavior (Olson & Fazio, 2009). Moreover, because of the automatic character of implicit attitudes, they are always activated in the presence of the biased object (Fazio, 2001), even when people do have the motivation and the possibility to reflect. Hence, implicit attitudes might contribute even to controlled behavior (i.e., explicit biases).

Explicit or conscious, the person is aware of their feelings and attitudes, and related behaviors are conducted with intent (National Center for Cultural Competence at Georgetown University, n.d.). Explicit bias is believed to be processed neurologically at a conscious level as declarative, semantic memory, and in words (National Center for Cultural Competence at Georgetown University, n.d.). Explicit bias is often revealed in behavior and, in the case of a parenting plan evaluator, might be revealed in the inclusion and exclusion of data in a report or reliance on one perspective in the literature while intentionally excluding information about alternative perspectives, selective attention in data gathering, or selecting specific questions to investigate.

Implicit bias is presumed to operate outside of the person's awareness and can be in direct contradiction to a person's espoused beliefs and values (Hahn & Gawronski, 2019). "What is so dangerous about implicit bias is that it automatically seeps into a person's effect or behavior and is outside of the full awareness of that person" (National Center for Cultural Competence at Georgetown, n.d.). People may hold implicit biases while not revealing any signs of explicit biases (Hahn & Gawronski, 2019). Implicit bias can interfere with selection of questions to guide an evaluation, selection of data-gathering tools, inclusion and exclusion of areas from which to gather data, analyses of data, interpretation of data from multiple perspectives, and opinion formation.

There is a distinction between attitudes and beliefs that people are unable to share and attitudes and beliefs that people are unwilling to share. There are several theoretical models explaining implicit bias. One model posits that implicit bias is based upon the notion that people are unable to share their attitudes and beliefs because they are outside of their awareness (Hahn & Gawronski, 2019).

A second model suggests that people are unwilling to report their implicit biases because of dissociations between their implicit and explicit biases as reflected in their self-presentation. That is, accurate reporting of implicit bias is influenced by the ways in which a person wants to be perceived by others (i.e., social desirability response bias; Gawronski et al., 2007).

A third model is based on the notion that people have no introspective access to the attitudes underlying their implicit biases, but that people might become aware of their implicit biases by observing their behavioral effects (Hofmann & Wilson, 2010).

A fourth model posits that implicit biases might be identified by people's spontaneous affective responses. Dissociation between people's implicit and explicit biases would be revealed in differences in the extent to which people rely on their spontaneous affective responses in their decision making (Gawronski et al., 2017).

There is no consensus about how best to help people to identify their implicit biases. Each of the theoretical models proposes a different mechanism through which a person might be able to identify their implicit biases. What is most important to take away from this discussion is that implicit biases are often unknown and might have unknown effects on how we gather, analyze, and interpret data and formulate opinions. Evaluators need to be aware that implicit biases might affect their work and need to be open to admitting that there are possible implicit bias factors operating in their work that are beyond awareness, no matter how hard they try to control bias factors.

SIMILARITY AND DIFFERENCES BETWEEN IMPLICIT AND EXPLICIT BIAS AND TYPE 1 AND TYPE 2 PROCESSING

Implicit and explicit biases relate to unconscious and conscious prejudices, respectively, while Type 1 (System 1) and Type 2 (System 2) thinking describe automatic versus deliberate cognitive processes. These concepts intersect in how they influence decision making but differ in scope and application. There are both similarities and differences.

We are not aware of implicit biases and Type I processing because they are automatic. For example, associating certain groups with negative stereotypes (implicit bias) occurs without intent, much like instantly solving 2 + 2 (Type 1). Conversely, explicit bias and Type 2 thinking involve conscious effort. For example, deliberately refusing to hire someone based on race (explicit bias) parallels complex tasks like solving 17 × 24, which require focused attention and deliberation (Type 2).

Both implicit bias and Type 1 thinking can lead to errors. For instance, implicit bias might cause an evaluator to negatively view a parent from a different culture or foreign country due to unconscious stereotypes, while Type 1 errors include jumping to conclusions without analysis. And both explicit bias and Type 2 thinking involve intentional decisions, such as discriminatory policies or logical problem solving.

Both sets of concepts are rooted in dual-process theories: Implicit and explicit bias reflects unconscious versus conscious attitudes. Type 1 and Type 2 thinking describes intuitive versus analytical reasoning.

Type 2 processing tends to mitigate implicit bias. Type 2 deliberative reasoning can override automatic stereotypes (implicit bias). For example, a hiring manager might use structured interviews to counter unconscious preferences.

In summary, implicit and explicit biases and Type 1 and Type 2 thinking share a framework of automatic versus deliberative processes but differ in their focus on social attitudes versus general cognition. Recall that "Type 2 processing is distinguished from autonomous Type 1 processing by its nature—involving cognitive decoupling and hypothetical thinking—and by its strong loading on the working memory resources that this requires" (J. S. B. T. Evans & Stanovich, 2013). Addressing biases often requires leveraging Type 2 thinking to counteract both unconscious and conscious prejudices.

WHY UNDERSTANDING BIAS IS IMPORTANT TO EVALUATORS

Forms of bias that impact how we think about our evaluation task include overreliance on memory, underutilization of base rate data, anchoring effects, overconfidence, overreliance on unique data that might affect the accuracy of evaluations, hindsight bias, fundamental attribution error, confirmation bias, and illusory correlation (Borum et al., 1993). Some readers may recall our first author devoted a full chapter to these concepts and to the Borum et al. article in both the first and second edition of *Conducting Scientifically Crafted Child Custody Evaluations* (Gould, 1998, 2006).

In forensic mental health, in particular, the research trends have differentiated cognitive heuristics and biases such as contextual effects (i.e., adversarial allegiance), representativeness, anchoring, framing, and confirmation bias. Research trends have also identified social–cognitive biases such as stereotypes, attitudes (like strong feelings), and blind spot biases. These biases will be discussed below.

CONFIRMATORY BIAS

One of the bias factors that appears to have gained significant attention in the mental health and legal literature is confirmatory bias. Confirmatory bias is selectively gathering and interpreting evidence that confirms a hypothesis and ignoring evidence that may disconfirm it (Nickerson, 1998). An example is an evaluator focusing their inquiry on confirming alienation while ignoring data that may provide reasonable alternative hypotheses. Applied to the evaluation process, this cognitive bias can lead to flawed data gathering, flawed data interpretation, exclusion of reasonable alternative hypotheses to investigate, and flawed opinion formation because it causes the evaluator to focus selectively on supporting data, creating an illusion of accuracy or objectivity. Another concern is that confirmation bias might cause an expert to give disproportionate weight to information that aligns with their initial impressions of a parent's behavior, while overlooking evidence that challenges that view. This can compromise the fairness and reliability of assessments and expert testimony.

Historically, evaluators have been concerned with how preexisting beliefs, expectations, and attitudes affect the evaluation of information. Confirmatory bias has been viewed as a type of psychological framework or set of blinders placed on the selection of information and interpretation of data. It is believed that confirmatory bias most often reflects innocent errors rather than malfeasance (Charman et al., 2019). It is assumed that most confirmatory bias types are "inherent in our human architecture and therefore reflect natural human tendencies" (Charman et al., 2019, p. 31).

Confirmatory bias might reflect both an explicit bias and an implicit bias. All evaluators bring to their work a set of attitudes and beliefs that guide their thinking. These attitudes and beliefs are based upon assumptions about the veracity of the information that serves as a basis for these assumptions. At one level of analysis, these assumptions upon which attitudes and beliefs have been developed reflect implicit biases. At another level of analysis, attitudes and beliefs might be based upon assumptions that are known and, therefore, explicit in their effect on the evaluator.

There might be a hierarchical organization of biases similar to the levels of processing model of memory. Implicit biases that are beyond awareness might have been formed early in childhood, and their influence is virtually unknown to the person. Other implicit biases that have been learned and internalized at a later stage of development might be more readily accessible through techniques aimed at increasing awareness of implicit biases (Hahn & Gawronski, 2019).

Explicit biases might have a similar hierarchical organization resulting in some being readily known and available to the person and others being known through techniques aimed at increasing awareness of them. Explicit biases are not inherently organized as hierarchical systems in the same way implicit biases often align with societal power structures (Axt et al., 2014). Explicit biases are not intrinsically organized hierarchically but often perpetuate existing hierarchies through conscious endorsement of inequitable norms. Implicit biases, conversely, are more deeply entwined with hierarchical systems due to unconscious assimilation of societal structures. Both forms of bias interact to sustain systemic inequities, but their mechanisms and solutions differ. While explicit biases are not rigidly hierarchical, they can sustain hierarchical systems. Hierarchical category systems (e.g., organizational taxonomies) amplify biases by privileging dominant-group perspectives at higher abstraction levels. Explicit biases can reinforce and perpetuate existing social hierarchies. For example, a judge in a custody case openly favoring mothers because they believe that mothers are always the better parent may seek out confirmation of their beliefs, connecting their explicit bias with a confirmatory bias.

REPRESENTATIVENESS HEURISTIC

The representativeness heuristic is the tendency to estimate the likelihood of something based on how similar it is to existing mental schemas or categories. As first described by Tversky and Kahneman (1973, 1974), the representativeness heuristic occurs when the evaluator uses similar information to make a judgment about unique data.

The representativeness heuristic in parenting plan evaluations occurs when evaluators make judgments based on stereotypes or prototypes rather than case-specific evidence. For example, a parenting plan evaluator might unconsciously favor a mother who presents as nurturing, soft-spoken, and organized because these traits match the common societal stereotype of a "good mother." Conversely, they might view a father who is assertive, works long hours, and appears emotionally reserved as less suitable, even if he is highly involved in his child's life and provides strong emotional support in ways not immediately visible in the evaluation setting.

The problem with representative heuristics is that they can oversimplify. They can ignore the complexities of parenting and the unique needs of a child. Representativeness heuristics might also lead to decisions influenced by implicit biases rather than child-focused evidence. The "representative" traits may not accurately reflect the parent's actual capabilities or the parent–child relationship quality.

When evaluators overestimate their use of similarity information, often the evaluator neglects base rate data and other information that is relevant. Base rate data tell us how often something occurs in the population. That is, base rate data answers the question: How often does something occur in the general population? Use of base rate data allows us to determine the likelihood of an occurrence. If you are hit in the head by something falling from the sky, base rate allows us to calculate the likelihood that the object that fell from the sky was a meteor or an apple. Base rate data is a form of predicting probability. When evaluating an individual's mental health, there is base rate data on schizophrenia, bipolar, and attention-deficit hyperactivity disorder.

Failing to incorporate probability estimates and applying such estimates to how often something is likely to occur can lead an evaluator to group together symptoms or data that may not be connected. An example of this mental shortcut is included in Table 6.2 (Tversky & Kahneman, 1973, p. 241).

EVIDENCE INTEGRATION

Charman et al. (2019) draw a distinction between evidence evaluation and evidence integration. They argue that much previous research examining cognitive bias has focused on a linear conceptualization, focusing on the effects of cognitive bias on individual pieces of evidence.

Evidence integration examines how combining different, disparate pieces of evidence may be subject to bias. Evidence integration involves the process of synthesizing, evaluating, and combining multiple sources of information to form a coherent, comprehensive understanding that supports decision making. In a legal and forensic context, evidence integration is the method by which legal professionals, expert witnesses, and courts systematically consider and weigh different types of evidence—such as testimonies, psychological assessments, behavioral observations, and scientific data—to reach informed conclusions. It ensures that decisions are not based on isolated facts but on a holistic view of all relevant information. In family law applications, evidence integration ensures that evaluators consider the full spectrum of data—parental behaviors, child interviews, psychological tests, and contextual factors—to provide balanced, scientifically grounded recommendations that reflect the child's best interests. Key principles of effective evidence integration include objectivity, critical thinking, transparency, mitigation of cognitive biases, and adherence to ethical and professional standards.

Snowball effect bias refers to how bias can affect all stages of an evaluation, from data collection to data analysis to opinion development. As an evaluator (or attorney or judge) accepts or builds upon the initial information, the initial information's perceived validity grows, often without critical evaluation of its accuracy. This bias can lead to self-reinforcing cycles where early impressions or minor events escalate into significant outcomes. For example, in a PPE context, an early negative impression of a parent in the initial interviews, or as portrayed in reviewed pleadings, might influence how subsequent evidence is interpreted. This anchor bias grows in its importance and often leads evaluators, attorneys, or judges to unconsciously favor information that supports that initial view. In forensic contexts, recognizing the snowball effect bias is critical to maintaining objectivity, ensuring that expert testimony and PPEs remain grounded in comprehensive, structured evidence analysis.

Biased analyses of evidence affect each stage of the evaluation process. Biased data gathering affects where we seek subsequent data. Bias affects our interpretation of the biased data gathering, leading to flawed analyses of those data. The flawed analyses of data based on biased data gathering lead to biased hypothesis generation, resulting in seeking additional information from other sources reflective of the original biased data gathering (Charman et al., 2019, p. 32). The effect of bias on one phase of the evaluation process can affect and support subsequent biases on other phases of the evaluation process, undermining the legal presumption of evidentiary independence (Hasel & Kassin, 2009).

For example, at the earliest stages of an evaluator's data gathering, a belief in the credibility of one parent over the other might lead an evaluator to erroneously interpret subsequent information and limit data gathering by ignoring reasonable alternative hypotheses that are inconsistent with the initial beliefs or evaluate neutral data in a manner that is consistent with the original belief.

In the custody literature, the prior description is discussed as an example of confirmatory bias. In a recent case in which our first author was involved, the custody evaluator determined at the early stages of the data-gathering process that one parent's 20-year-old traumatic brain injury (TBI) was the primary factor that affected the family's dysfunction. The evaluator informed the psychologist retained to conduct the psychological tests about the effects of TBI on the family system and the parent's parenting. The testing psychologist chose psychological tests seeking confirmatory data to support the evaluator's belief rather than gathering a more comprehensive, parenting-focused set of data. All collateral interviews with professionals involved with the family were structured to obtain information only about the effects of the parent's TBI. The evaluator's questions of the professional collaterals were closed-ended, yes or no questions with no opportunities for the collaterals to elaborate upon their initial answers.

At the initial stages of a PPE, much of the data gathered is ambiguous. Data from parents, children, collaterals, and record reviews are often subject to significant interpretation of their meaning. Unlike DNA analysis, data from those involved in a custody dispute is often more subjective and ambiguous.

Ambiguous and subjective data are more likely to be vulnerable to bias, especially vulnerable to beliefs and expectations brought into the evaluation process by the evaluator's expectations, beliefs, and initial responses to each party, and those initial impressions can affect every phase of the evaluation process from the initial meeting through courtroom testimony. See Chapter 10, specifically the section on storytelling development, for an elaboration of other factors that might affect how evaluators make sense of the evidence presented during the evaluation process.

Much of the bias literature in child custody has focused on the effects of evaluator beliefs, expectations, and emotional responses to the parties in the development of confirmatory bias and associated bias factors such as anchoring effects, primary effects, and recency effects. It is not just beliefs, expectations, and emotional responses that affect bias in evidence data gathering. Information that appears to imply a logical conclusion can also shape data gathering, data interpretation, and opinion formation.

Scholarship addressing bias in the evaluation process has tended to look at how an evaluator's belief leads to selectively attending to some data and not other data, seeking additional data to confirm the initial bias rather than gathering data that tests reasonable alternative explanations of the data. Implied but not often directly discussed is the power of contextual information on evaluator decision making at various evaluation processes (Dror et al., 2018).

INITIAL BIAS

Studies from criminal forensic psychology have shown how bias introduced at the beginning of a task significantly affects subsequent data interpretation, even when those subsequent pieces of information are neutral. Neutral information tends to be interpreted consistently with the initial bias introduced at the beginning of the task. For example, when a fingerprint expert is told, "We got the guy," the expert is more likely to identify the fingerprint as a match to a specific subject. Similarly, research findings have shown how retention bias—the effects on decision making when retained by one side—affects the interpretation of data. Studies of practicing forensic psychologists have revealed that strikingly different recidivism scores for sex offenders are produced when hired by the defense rather than by the prosecution (Murrie et al., 2013).

Earlier in the book we talked about anchor bias in which an evaluator relies too heavily on an initial piece of information (the anchor) when making decisions or evaluating subsequent information. This cognitive bias affects how people interpret, judge, and recall information, often leading to skewed or irrational conclusions. The initial information that forms the anchor can skew interpretation. Once an anchor is established, subsequent information is interpreted in relation to that anchor, *even if it's irrelevant*. People adjust their judgments based on the anchor, but the adjustments are often insufficient to mitigate the ways in which the investigative process has been tainted. For example, a parenting plan evaluator might initially hear that a parent was described as "uncooperative." This label can anchor their perceptions, causing them to view neutral or even cooperative behaviors through a biased lens. Another example is when an evaluator is anchored by an initial report suggesting parental alienation and, unknowingly, may unconsciously focus on behaviors that support this claim, ignoring signs that point to other dynamics, like genuine fear or trauma responses in the child.

Initial impressions that contribute to forming an anchor bias can cause individuals to focus on information that confirms the anchor while overlooking contradictory evidence. This is a selective attention process that limits robust data gathering. The selective attention acts as blinders on a horse, limiting where an evaluator looks for information. This confirmation bias reinforces the original anchor, creating a feedback loop that also involves the development of a snowball bias, discussed previously. The takeaway for child custody evaluators is how initial bias affects assessment of subsequent information and how evaluation of subsequent information in a manner consistent with the initial bias tends to reduce the likelihood of seeking information that directly challenges the initial bias.

COHERENCE

Another consideration is how the need for a coherent narrative might create bias. Although individual pieces of evidence might not be tainted by bias, how we integrate information into a coherent narrative can be subject to bias. The natural need for coherence in a narrative may affect how pieces of evidence are strung together. A narrative that allows for a coherent assimilation of information may lead an evaluator to place greater weight on the interpretation of that information relative to the value of the information, *even if the original value placed on the information was fair and balanced and free from bias.*

This bias is most likely to occur in PPEs when there is a gap in our data. For example, when a child suddenly begins experiencing enuresis, an evaluator may conclude the child was sexually abused. Another example of the need for coherence may occur when a child resists or refuses contact with Parent B and the evaluator concludes that alienation occurred even when there is no data to indicate Parent A shared unwarranted negative words, actions, or expressed emotions about Parent B. In both of these examples, the evaluator jumped to a conclusion in order to have a coherent narrative even though the data did not fully support the conclusion.

EVIDENCE INTEGRATION AND THE COHERENCE MODEL

As noted prior, bias in evidence integration refers to how the final assessment can be biased, putting together the individual puzzle pieces to form a coherent narrative. More linear models of evidence compilation suggest that the order in which the information is encountered should not make a difference. The coherence model suggests that our interpretation of the evidence is influenced by the information preceding it and by the hypotheses we develop as we encounter and evaluate those data. The coherence model is an interactive systems model. It recognizes that interpretation of evidence occurs at every stage of data collection, and interpretations of the meaning of those data are also influenced by the continuous changes in data collection and interpretation.

Charman et al. suggest that our decision making is most significantly influenced by the last information we encounter. This interpretation runs contrary to previously held beliefs that primacy and recency had relatively similar effects on memory. We discussed primacy and recency in Chapter 3.

Recall that confirmatory bias has to do with the effects of beliefs on a single piece of information at a particular point in time. Analysis of confirmatory bias has examined how a preexisting belief influences subsequent data collection and data analyses. Charman et al. argue that the evaluation task involves a more complex analysis of multiple data integrated into an evolving understanding that takes place over time.

The theoretical basis of the coherence model is various data points must be integrated over time. Each data point has a value—positive or negative. The connection between and among data points is represented as a network of interconnected nodes via a network of excitatory and inhibitory links representing positive or negative links between the nodes. There is a natural tendency to seek coherence among the nodes, leading to excitation in some nodes and inhibition in other nodes, creating a sense of a coherent narrative. There is a continuous evolution of the relationships between and among the nodes as new information enters the system or new ways of interpreting the data are introduced. The evolving relationships among nodes are bidirectional and in continuous flux, seeking the most coherent integration of information at any given time. "The very fact that the various pieces of evidence are presented within the context of a single case . . . lead the evaluations of that evidence to become correlated with one another, not because of the features of evidence itself, but because of the psychological coherence imposed upon the evaluation of those pieces of evidence" (Charman et al., 2019, p. 43).

OTHER FORMS OF BIAS

There are other forms of implicit bias that might affect our ability to conduct our work. We provide a description of some of the implicit biases that might affect each stage of the child custody evaluation process.

Allegiance bias describes the human predisposition to take positions that win social acceptance, are congruent with one's affiliations, and suit the people who are paying you.[1] The nature of legal proceedings creates "partisan bias in experts through unconscious affiliation with the side that hires them (i.e., adversarial allegiance) and by attorneys who select and pressure experts to make extreme claims" (Kellerman et al., 2018).

[1]One might attribute the chameleon child's position caught between warring parents to allegiance bias (Garber, 2014).

Allegiance bias is of concern most often when one is hired by one side to engage in forensic psychological activities. Research findings support the notion that no matter how hard one tries to control allegiance bias, mental health professionals hired by one side tend to be influenced by the side that hires them. How they are influenced and the manner in which such influence affects their work is not set in stone. Retained experts can still offer useful testimony to the court. The key is to be aware of how allegiance bias might affect one's work and take steps to reduce such bias beyond self-reflection.

Retained experts should heed the concerns expressed thus far and should prepare to be aggressively cross-examined about the ways in which allegiance bias might undermine the impartiality of testimony. In anticipation of such cross-examination, the retained expert should engage in pretrial preparation discussions that include challenges to the retained expert's testimony. At the very least, the retained expert should be able to clearly explain how reasonable alternative explanations of the data were considered and why the retained expert's opinion is more likely than any of the other alternative explanations.

> We think there are good reasons to be concerned. Scientific and clinical expertise in the courtroom is dependent on the expectancy that the expert seeks accuracy and avoids anything that may lead to bias in the collection or interpretation of data. Challenging that expectancy is a growing body of research suggesting that forensic examiners differ in the data they collect and the opinions they reach, depending on the social contexts in which they are involved in forensic cases. (Neal & Grisso, 2014)

Selection bias is evident in research that relies only on volunteers without any comparison group. An example of selection bias and how it might influence your thinking is to reflect on your experience as a custody evaluator. If a person asked for your opinion about your experience with the frequency of divorce and custody disputes, based upon your professional work, it is likely you would overestimate the frequency of divorce and custody disputes in the general population. The people with whom you work are experiencing the divorce process and engaged in custody disputes. The sample of people you work with is inherently biased toward a higher frequency of divorce and custody concerns than the general population. This is an example of selection bias.

Overreliance on memory often results from the incorrect belief that memories of past events are stored in a stable and accurate manner, easily retrieved with little or no distortion. Research has shown that memory is constructive and often nonsequential. People remember events that are more vivid or meaningful compared with events that are bland and inconsequential. "Therefore, an overreliance on memory in forensic evaluations can result not only in a decrease in information with which to make a judgment, but also in an increase in judgment bias" (Borum et al., 1993, p. 38).

Overconfidence refers to individuals expressing their opinions with more confidence than is warranted by the data. Borum et al. (1993) raised concerns about the ways in which overconfident expert testimony might mislead the court, giving the false impression that the underlying data provides a more solid basis for the opinion than is warranted.

Related to overconfidence and concerns about disregarding potentially useful data is the concept of relevance insensitivity (Hsee et al., 2019). Relevance insensitivity refers to being insensitive to the relevance of some given information. People reveal their systematic implicit and explicit biases in judgment and decision making. Many seemingly disparate biases reflect a common underlying mechanism—insensitivity to the relevance of some given information. Manipulating the relevance of the information has been shown to eliminate or even reverse the original bias. When people are made sensitive to the relevance of the information, both the original biases and their reverse biases are attenuated (Hsee et al., 2019, p. 13). When people are made sensitive to the relevance of information, they are able to overcome the initial lack of interest in the information and examine the previously disregarded information in a more balanced manner (Hsee et al., 2019).

Overreliance on unique data refers to the tendency to give excessive attention to specific behaviors that are unique, interesting, or highly unusual. This is the shiny object phenomenon. Evaluators often are drawn to that which is unusual or different and they might assume that such unusual behaviors have greater predictive validity than more familiar ones (Hsee et al., 2019).

Infrequently occurring events are difficult to predict because they are infrequent. Parenting plan evaluators are often asked to make judgments about behaviors that infrequently occur in our society. These low-frequency events occur at a low base rate–making prediction very difficult. An evaluator's failure to consider base rates when making judgments and predictions about low base rate behaviors (even when very accurate prediction techniques are used) will likely lead to overprediction of the behavior of interest with the danger of expert opinions based on those low base rate predictions misleading the court (Neal & Grisso, 2014).

Although not the focus of this chapter or book, we mention Bayesian theory because parenting plan evaluators would be well served by studying aspects of Bayesian theory as applied to base rates and prevalence estimates (Donovan & Mickey, 2019). Understanding how base rate estimates help determine likely hypotheses are critical in evaluations of child sexual abuse, for example (Kuehnle & Connell, 2009).

Hindsight bias refers to the tendency for outcome data to affect one's perception and judgment about the predictability of the outcome. Our ability to predict the outcome of an event is far more accurate once the event has occurred, and we identify variables that we now view as predictive of the event based upon the advantage of seeing the outcome of an event.

Fundamental attribution error refers to the tendency for a person to emphasize person-centered factors over contextual factors when explaining and judging the behavior of others. In a forensic evaluation, the fundamental attribution error might influence an evaluator when moving from the role of observer to the role of participant. In PPEs, evaluators sometimes engage in interviewing a parent or child while engaged in observing the parent–child relationship. The fundamental attribution error would predict that the evaluator's attributions change from attributions about person-centered factors when engaged in observation to attributions about contextual or environmental factors when engaged in parent and child interactions.

Anchoring occurs when information obtained earlier in the data-gathering process is weighed more heavily despite having information gathered later in the process that does not support the weight assigned to these initial pieces of information. Tversky and Kahneman provide many concerns about the effects of anchoring and we highlight a few here as described by Kahneman (2011). Many psychological phenomena can be demonstrated experimentally, but few can actually be measured. The effect of anchors is an exception. For example, when judges rolled a pair of rigged dice prior to sentencing a woman for shoplifting, the judges who rolled a high number sentenced the woman for longer periods of time than those who had rolled a lower number. The effect: 50% increase in sentencing!

If you read Chapter 3 closely, you may now be thinking, "Hopefully my System 2 approaches will mitigate anchoring." Kahneman (2011) addressed this: "System 2 has no control over the effect and no knowledge of it." He further described the concern:

> Anchoring effects are threatening in a similar way. You are always aware of the anchor and even pay attention to it, but you do not know how it guides and constrains your thinking, because you cannot imagine how you would have thought if the anchor had been different (or absent; p. 128).

THE IMPORTANCE OF CONTEXT

People's perceptions or decisions are systematically affected by environmental factors, often without our awareness. This is particularly true in high conflict litigation. It is important to be aware of the context of the information that's shaping how you perceive a given piece of information.

Illusory correlation refers to the tendency to see relationships between or among variables when no relationship exists. William James addressed the benefits of attention by saying, "Only those items which I notice shape my mind—without selective interest, experience is utter chaos" (James, 1890).

A critically important bias factor that is likely to affect all evaluators is *blind spot bias* (Zappala et al., 2018). Blind spot bias refers to the tendency to recognize bias in others but failing to recognize it in oneself (Pronin et al., 2002). Earlier, we described a 2017 survey of forensic science examiners in which approximately 71% agreed that cognitive bias is a cause for concern in forensics, but only 26% agreed that it impacted their own judgments (Kukucka et al., 2017). In a follow-up study, Zapf and her colleagues (2018) found that among the 1,000 mental health professionals who conduct forensic evaluations who participated in their survey, 79% acknowledged bias as a cause of concern in the forensic evaluations of their colleagues, while only 52% were concerned about bias as a concern in their evaluations. Other studies have found similar trends. Chevalier et al. (2015) reported that among 95 forensic evaluators who participated in their study, participants who reviewed reports containing PCL-R scores were concerned about retention bias among their colleagues but believed their own work would not be affected by retention bias.

Noting the robust nature of blind spot bias, Pronin and Kurgler (2007) examined strategies people use to counter the effect of bias. They found the most frequent strategy used to combat bias was self-reflection (i.e., introspection). Research has demonstrated, however, that introspection is an ineffective bias reduction strategy (Zappala et al., 2018).

Neal and Brodsky (2016) found that among the 351 forensic psychologists surveyed about strategies used to combat bias, all respondents reported using introspection to minimize bias. Zapf et al. (2018) reported a majority of respondents in their study believed they could combat bias by consciously trying to set aside their biases and expectations. Similar results were reported by Chevalier et al. (2015).

We raise these concerns about bias and, in particular, blind side bias because of its pervasiveness and the empirical findings that how most of us go about combating these biases is ineffective.

THE EMERGING SCIENCE OF MINIMIZING BIAS

We present this section as the emerging science of minimizing bias. We are not suggesting evaluators can eliminate bias. The emerging evidence-informed science has focused on the causes of errors in the observations we make and in the methods being developed to prevent or minimize them. The information we present below is emerging science, and we are not aware of its application to the field of child custody.

Research trends over the past 40 years have generated a body of knowledge that informs us about the nature, power, and limits of context or observer effects that have an impact on human perception, interpretation, and judgment. One of the early efforts to minimize bias in human judgment can be seen in the evolution of the scientific method. The scientific method is the ongoing process of observation, data gathering, hypothesis formation, hypothesis testing, data analysis, and then hypothesis refinement. The scientific method has evolved as philosophers and scientists have articulated the powers and limitations of human judgment with the help of Aristotle, Kepler, Galileo, Descartes, Sir Isaac Newton, Francis Bacon, and Karl Popper.

In an effort to minimize error and bias, researchers utilize double-blind studies. Randomized placebo-controlled trials are designed to allow researchers to control forms of error and variance (i.e., noise) in the environment, (i.e., method variance). This level of control reduces the likelihood of method variance resulting in the researchers' increased confidence in the trustworthiness of the data.

Dror (2021) recommends that a way to reduce bias is to use linear sequential unmasking, which is graded exposure to biasing information. Linear sequential unmasking aims to allow evaluators to make judgments without biasing information first when possible. So, while the evaluator would eventually see everything and hear all of the allegations, the evaluator would assess the information in a particular order. The problem that we see in applying linear sequential unmasking to child custody assessment is that data collection and data integration occur in an ongoing feedback loop. Data collected early in the process might be viewed as very important until new information is gathered later in the evaluation process. The earlier data might be of lesser importance given the new information and, as a result, the support for an initial hypothesis developed from the original data now is given less weight as subsequent hypotheses developed from the newer data become more highly weighted. This continually weighing the data and reassessing hypotheses defines the evaluation process.

LESSONS FOR PARENTING PLAN EVALUATORS

A PPE will never conform to the rigid requirements of an experimental or quasi-experimental paradigm. There are too many variables examined in an evaluation and too many ways in which the examined variables might interact with each other. However, finding ways to minimize bias is a worthy goal in PPEs. There are factors drawn from cognitive science research examining bias and human decision making that might be applied to our quest to minimize bias in our work.

Drawing on the bias and decision-making research findings, Neal and Grisso (2014) recommend that evaluators consider the following five evidence-based remedial strategies:

1. Betting the base rates is based on Amos Tversky and Daniel Kahneman's work which encourages us to find the most relevant number in our judgment. In forensic psychology, this data is most likely to be used in criminal evaluations that rely on actuarial data. In evaluating children, the importance of base rate data has been well articulated by our colleagues Eric Youngstrom and Anna Van Meter (2016) as well as Kathryn Kuehnle (1998).

2. Considering the opposite is defined as considering alternative rival hypotheses. This is a cornerstone of the scientific method in which scientists test the null hypothesis. It can be helpful to write out your hypotheses and the alternate rival hypotheses you tested. If you are retained as a testifying expert by one side, we recommend you imagine taking the other side's perspective. However, considering the opposite in an adversarial context can strengthen bias if you only consider the opposite to strengthen your original opinion. So, when considering the opposite, it is important to really test and consider the alternative hypotheses.

3. Employing checklists and structured professional tools can help you improve the quality of your methodology. Checklists are powerful tools that enhance decision making, reduce cognitive biases, and promote consistency, particularly in high-stakes environments like forensic mental health evaluations and family law proceedings. Their systematic approach ensures that critical elements are not overlooked, which is vital when providing expert testimony or conducting complex assessments. Checklists help mitigate biases such as anchor bias, confirmation bias, and availability bias by standardizing the evaluation process. This forces evaluators to consider all relevant data, even if it contradicts their initial impressions. Checklists also standardize procedures, making assessments more reliable across different evaluators and cases. This consistency is critical when expert opinions are scrutinized in court. High-stakes situations such as custody litigation often involve complex information that can overwhelm memory and attention. Checklists act as cognitive aids, ensuring no critical details are missed. Checklists align practices with ethical guidelines and legal standards, reducing liability risks. They ensure that forensic reports meet both psychological and legal requirements. When experts use checklists, their testimonies become more organized and evidence-based, aiding judges and attorneys in understanding complex psychological information.
4. Identifying and relying on five highly valid, reliable, and independent indicators can help you minimize the impact of bias. More information is not necessarily better, and it would be ideal if we could establish five indicators to focus on in evaluations. Evaluators might focus on the factors articulated by Martindale, Wittmann, and Harris-Britt (2021) as the most robust factors in a PPE. Those include

    - quality of parent–child relationship,
    - quality of coparenting relationship/level of conflict,
    - child's emotional status and special needs,
    - approach to limit setting and general parenting style, and
    - level of parental stress and social support.

    Another set of factors that should inform child custody evaluators are the best interest standards defined in statutes or case law in each jurisdiction. Following Kahneman's advice, evaluators might focus on these factors to inform their judgment.
5. Using structured and systematic methods, such as the ones in this book, will also help you minimize error. Throughout this book, our aim is to provide structured tools that can improve PPE and minimize bias.

We've mentioned introspection above, and it warrants another mention here. Recall that Neal and Brodsky (2016) found that forensic psychologists reported introspection as their primary strategy for knowing and reducing their biases, even though their study was conducted years after Pronin and Kugler

(2007) wrote that introspection does not help because it functions as blind spot bias. Multiple questions remain regarding introspection: Why is introspection ineffective? What strategy should evaluators use instead of introspection?

In order to illustrate why introspection is not effective, let's use an example familiar to parenting plan evaluators. Parent A may claim that they are not biased against Parent B because they can look inside themselves and identify their biases. Parent A further states that they work really hard to find their biases through introspection, and then they work really hard to reduce their biases toward Parent B. Why might Parent A still be biased against Parent B, despite their best intentions?

Recall that the bias blind spot is likely to prevent the success of introspection because Parent A is unlikely to be able to see what they cannot see (inside Parent B's head), and making matters worse, they are likely overconfident about their ability to control for bias. The reason Parent A can see bias in Parent B, but not in their own thoughts and behavior, is because Parent A cannot look inside Parent B's head. Parent A cannot monitor Parent B's adaptive brain architecture. Instead, Parent A can focus on Parent B's behavior and their previously developed narratives.

Evaluators can learn from this by not trusting their introspection. Instead, behavior is a better measure of bias. It is recommended evaluators look at their behavior and track it over time. If possible, it would be helpful for evaluators to track the way their decision falls in particular cases over time. This may be best accomplished in consultation and supervision with colleagues.

Another strategy to minimize bias is to attend trainings on the fallibility of introspection (Morewedge et al., 2015; Sellier et al., 2019). Yoon et al. (2021) indicate that this can be accomplished through traditional educational approaches as well as observational approaches. While these studies have not yet been applied to our field, we believe this is an area of future interest. Research has found that small changes in message framing and choice elicitation can produce debiasing effects (Morewedge et al., 2015). "Presenting information in a manner in which options are easier to evaluate generally improves decisions by making people better able to evaluate those options along the dimensions that are important to them" (Morewedge et al., 2015).

By using the tried and true methods of social learning, observing others was a highly effective debiasing intervention and may prove to be an excellent training mechanism for evaluators. Yoon et al. (2021) found that by observing others, individuals greatly reduced their susceptibility to three cognitive biases: anchoring, their ability to judge risk, and their ability to understand people's beliefs. Their research also found observational learning more effective than watching an instructional video.

The effects of observational learning appear to be so unique that they worked even when the person observed made mistakes or poor decisions. Thus, it appears that the learners benefit from observing the debiasing techniques regardless of the success rate of the teacher. Learners also got better at receiving advice and integrating new information. Yoon et al.'s study that seeing someone else use a strategy to improve their decision making suggests the importance of observational training methods for evaluators.

As discussed by Kahneman (2011), and J. S. B. T. Evans and Stanovich (2013), slowing down our thought process can improve decision making. Slowing down an evaluation to spread it out over time allows an evaluator to look at the evidence again.

Consultation and supervision can help reduce bias (Zappala et al., 2018). Consultation and supervision help as your colleague views your behavior over time. Asking for feedback about your behavior can inform patterns of behavior that can improve your methodology and make you more aware of your habits.

Moving beyond what evaluators can individually do to reduce bias, the field as a system has taken steps to improve our methodology and reduce error. Policies and procedures have been developed to improve the standard of practice. As we discussed in Chapter 1, the current standard of practice allows evaluators to obtain information from guidelines and authoritative texts. As our standard of practice continues to develop, we expect that improved methodology will continue to aid us in finding ways to identify and reduce bias.

CONCLUSION

This chapter explored how bias influences forensic psychological evaluations, particularly in expert testimony and parenting plan evaluations (PPEs). It examined the origins of bias, its impact on decision making, and strategies to minimize its effects. Bias is an inherent part of human cognition, influencing how forensic evaluators gather, analyze, and interpret data. This chapter has demonstrated that biases, whether implicit or explicit, are a hurdle for all evaluators. While self-awareness is often seen as a way to mitigate bias, research indicates that introspection alone is insufficient. Instead, structured methodologies as we will describe in the following chapters—such as using decision-making frameworks, considering alternative hypotheses, engaging in peer consultation, and employing systematic tools—are necessary to minimize the effects of bias.

This chapter underscored the importance of understanding the cognitive mechanisms behind bias, including heuristics like confirmation bias, representativeness, and anchoring. Given that courts heavily rely on expert opinions, forensic evaluators have a critical responsibility to minimize their own biases and adopt evidence-informed strategies to increase objectivity. By integrating structured methods, seeking continuous education, and engaging in transparent decision-making practices, evaluators can reduce errors and improve the reliability of their assessments. As forensic psychology continues to evolve, it is imperative that professionals remain committed to refining their methodologies to promote fairness and accuracy in the legal system.

8

Sociocultural Identities and Systemic Inequities

In this chapter, we discuss the importance of incorporating diversity, equity, and inclusion (DEI) principles into parenting plan evaluation (PPE) procedures. Inclusion of these factors enhance fairness, reduces systemic biases, and improves culturally responsive outcomes that prioritize children's best interests. We use the term "culturally responsive" PPEs or "culturally responsive" parenting plan evaluators to refer to both evaluations and evaluators who incorporate DEI factors into their investigative process.

We believe that there is an evolving set of core DEI principles in PPEs. One principle is that incorporating culturally responsive factors produces a more equity-focused assessment. Custody evaluations grounded in culturally responsive factors actively examine structural barriers (e.g., racial, socioeconomic, or cultural disparities) that may affect both the evaluator's approach to the evaluation as well as a variety of factors that affect the family system. Among the family system factors that are likely to be influenced by culture are the parent's parenting behaviors, the children's responses to those behaviors, the grandparents' involvement, the parent-to-parent communication, and the religious and community influences.

Most mental health professionals engaged in PPEs have ethical obligations to develop cultural competence. Although there is no professional consensus addressing how cultural competence is developed and maintained, a reasonable starting point is the evaluator understanding how cultural norms (e.g., communication styles, religious practices) shape parenting and child development. We recommend continuously seeking out training opportunities and

https://doi.org/10.1037/0000474-009
Parenting Plan Evaluations: An Evidence-Informed Approach to Child Custody, by J. W. Gould and C. M. Mulchay

literature reviews that address both the global factors addressing cultural competence and factors specific to parents from different cultures (e.g., literature addressing parenting among south Asian families).

Developing cultural competence also includes addressing disparities in how marginalized groups are represented in evaluations and represented in the research studies used as a basis for our expert opinions (Lewis, 2021a). Evaluators need to be sensitive to language use and communication habits among marginalized groups and among parents and children for whom English is a second language. Tools like interviews and surveys must account for linguistic diversity and nonverbal communication norms to avoid misinterpretations.

Evaluators need to gather information from children and extended family members, particularly examining how acculturation has affected the family in general and affected individual family members. Gathering information from independent third-party informants who know the family and their adjustment to the majority culture helps to contextualize family dynamics.

DEI-aligned evaluations provide judges with nuanced insights into parenting capabilities, avoiding oversimplified judgments (e.g., conflating poverty with neglect). Some states, like California, mandate higher admissibility standards for custody reports, requiring evaluators to demonstrate DEI competence. Professional guidelines (e.g., APA, AFCC) emphasize DEI as central to ethical evaluations.

There are several cautions about the ways in which DEI practices are implemented. One is that DEI practices vary widely, with some evaluators lacking training in cultural competency or antiracism. There is often a resistance to change found often in traditional evaluation frameworks that may overlook intersectional identities (e.g., race and disability). Regular training on implicit bias, LGBTQ+ issues, and trauma-informed practices is necessary. By integrating DEI, custody evaluations can better serve children's needs while fostering trust in family court systems.

UNDERSTANDING CULTURE AS DYNAMIC

A brief note on terminology is in order. The term *culture* is not a static characteristic that applies to all people from a particular region, country, or ethnic group (Barber Rioja & Rosenfeld, 2018). Culture is not a rigid or universally applied characteristic. Instead, it is fluid and varies within groups based on factors like individual experiences, socioeconomic status, generational differences, and personal choices. Stereotyping people from a particular ethnic or national background can lead to erroneous assumptions about parenting behaviors, family functioning, and other related factors.

One factor contributing to the dynamic nature of culture is acculturation, which is the process by which individuals adopt aspects of a new culture while maintaining elements of their original culture. Acculturation is a gradual and individualized process. This process is not uniform; individuals may experience it at different rates and in different ways. Acculturation tends to occur over time, yet different people use different strategies and adopt different rates of joining the dominant culture.

THE IMPORTANCE OF CULTURALLY RESPONSIVE PARENTING PLAN EVALUATIONS AND EVALUATORS

There is wide general agreement on the importance of particular methods for incorporating cultural considerations in each phase of the forensic evaluation process (Fanniff et al., 2023). However, there is not yet a consensus on best practices for incorporating cultural considerations in forensic evaluations (APA, 2017b), and there are no agreed on, evidence-based guidelines specific to culturally inclusive forensic practice (Fanniff et al. 2023). Previous chapters on common errors (Chapter 3) and bias (Chapter 7) provide a number of challenges for evaluators, and we recognize that the topic of sociocultural identities and systemic inequities may feel overwhelming. As you read this chapter, we want you to acknowledge the challenges before us and reflect on how fortunate we are to have the opportunity to learn about such unique and diverse families.

Increased awareness of the need for forensic psychologists to develop specialized knowledge in sociocultural factors is a relatively recent focus (Weiss & Rosenfeld, 2012). One area of concern is the invisibility of ethnocentric monoculturalism (Sue, 2001) that "may contribute to unintentional pathologizing of forensic examinees with a worldview based in African, Asian, indigenous, Latin American, or Pacific Islander cultures" (Fanniff et al., 2023, p. 386).

For example, the U.S. Census estimates that more than 20 million people identify as Asian or Pacific Islander.[1] These groups include people of descent from East, Southeast, South, Central, and West Asia, the Indian subcontinent, and the Pacific. The Asian American population includes more than 20 countries of origin, 100 languages, 40 ethnicities, 20 religions, and diverse personal, family, and community histories (Garrison et al., 2024). Similar to other diverse groups, there are between-group and within-group differences along a variety of values, beliefs, attitudes (Garrison et al., 2024). Previously, evaluators were provided with little guidance about how best to understand these differences, how to identify which differences are relevant to be assessed in a custody evaluation, and how to find reliable methods to assess these differences.

The dynamics of minority and majority groups are nuanced, complex, and varied (Garrison et al., 2024). Among the concerns raised by scholars raising awareness of diversity factors in forensic evaluations is the lack of training addressing historical and contemporary power asymmetry experienced by minority groups. This power asymmetry has manifested itself

---

[1]The term Asian American refers to people with ancestral roots in Asia or the Pacific Islands.

through restrictions, barriers, and limitations on freedoms that have harmed individuals and groups (Garrison et al., 2024).

Some of the power asymmetry is found in institutionalized, protected social structures that serve the majority groups. Although there is no consensus about how power asymmetry affects all minority groups, constraints on equal social power result in differing consequences depending on group membership (Garrison et al., 2024). Evaluators must gain awareness of the ways in which some people from minority groups involved in custody assessment might view the evaluation process as a representation of the majority group exercising its power over a minority group.

Forensic evaluation presents a complex intersection of psychological, legal, and sociocultural factors. As our society grows increasingly diverse, it becomes imperative for evaluators to cultivate a deep understanding of how sociocultural identities and systemic inequities shape family dynamics, parental capabilities, and the lived experiences of those involved in parenting disputes. This chapter seeks to explore the nuances of cultural considerations in forensic evaluations and to provide insight into the challenges evaluators face when navigating issues of diversity, bias, and institutionalized power structures.

Despite broad recognition of the importance of incorporating cultural awareness into forensic practice, a standardized framework for best practices remained elusive. This lack of consensus leaves evaluators with a critical responsibility: to actively engage in self-reflection, seek continuing education, and challenge ingrained biases that may influence their assessments. Yet, as we discussed in previous chapters, self-reflection and bias mitigation is often limited. The chapters preceding this one have highlighted the risks of cognitive bias, errors in judgment, and systemic imbalances within the forensic field. Building on these foundations, we now turn to the ways in which race, ethnicity, cultural identity, and systemic inequities shape parenting plan evaluations.

The future is clear to us. By integrating cultural competence into forensic psychology, evaluators can move beyond a one-size-fits-all approach and recognize the deeply personal and varied nature of identity and family dynamics. Through an exploration of ethnocentric monoculturalism, power asymmetry, and cultural socialization, this chapter underscores the importance of conducting assessments that are not only legally and scientifically sound but also culturally informed and ethically responsible.

ETHNOCENTRIC MONOCULTURALISM

Monoculturalism is defined as "actively preserving a national culture via the exclusion of external influences" (Oxford English Dictionary, 2024). Ethnocentric monoculturalism refers to the belief that one group is superior to other groups (Oxford English Dictionary, 2024). Applied to child custody assessments, ethnocentric monoculturalism refers to the ways in which the dominant white and Eurocentric culture in the U.S. influences evaluator behavior.

Sue (2004) has posited that psychologists represent a significant barrier to cultural competence because many are unaware of how their Eurocentric worldview influences their work. An unfortunate result of ethnocentric monoculturalism in psychology has been an overly narrow focus regarding not only the types of interventions implemented with culturally diverse clients but also the roles that a psychologist should fill (Sue, 2004).

Whiteness and ethnocentric monoculturalism are powerful and deeply held determinants of worldview. Sue argues that ethnocentric monoculturalism is invisible and operates outside the level of conscious awareness. One result is that evaluators who are unaware of the influence of their ethnocentric monoculturalism might negatively affect their evaluation process when working with people of color, women, and other marginalized groups in society (Sue, 2004).

Concerns about the influence of ethnocentric monoculturalism within an evaluation context include subtle ways that those who are White might gain advantages over those who are non-White. Evaluators have an obligation to develop awareness of the "invisible" effects of ethnocentric monoculturalism might affect all aspects of the evaluation process. Similar concerns about the invisibility of ethnocentric monoculturalism embedded in mainstream psychological research have been raised (Lewis, 2021a, 2021b).

In light of these and other concerns about the lack of guidance on best practices that incorporate cultural considerations, the American Psychological Association (APA) promulgated professional practice guidelines regarding multicultural practice (APA, 2017b). These multicultural guidelines were built upon the ecological model (Bronfenbrenner & Morris, 2006) that recognized the need to understand not only individual, family, and community factors that affect behavior but also the societal forces that shape experiences with power, privilege, and oppression (Fanniff et al., 2023).

The APA defines culture as "belief systems and value orientations that influence customs, norms, practices, and social institutions, including psychological processes . . . and organizations" and "the embodiment of a worldview through learned and transmitted beliefs, values, and practices, including religious and spiritual traditions" (2017b). The APA's Ethical Principles of Psychologists and Code of Conduct include the ethical principle of respecting people's rights and dignity:

> Psychologists are aware of and respect cultural, individual, and role differences, including those based on age, gender, gender identity, race, ethnicity, culture, national origin, religion, sexual orientation, disability, language, and socioeconomic status, and consider these factors when working with members of such groups. (APA, 2017a, p. 4)

FIRST STEPS TOWARD DEFINING PROFESSIONAL CONSENSUS

In an attempt to begin a systematic investigation into developing a professional consensus regarding best practices of the including culture into forensic mental health evaluations, Fanniff et al. surveyed forensic psychologists on the importance of conducting culturally informed evaluations. The study by Fanniff et al. is the first step toward a better understanding of areas for education and training. Fanniff et al. found that among their sample, "There was near universal consensus regarding the importance of considering the limits of your competence on the basis of an examinee's identities prior to accepting a referral, a practice clearly linked to Ethical Standard 2.01" (Fanniff et al., 2023, p. 396).

The subjects in the Fanniff et al. study identified 28 consensus best practices for culturally informed forensic evaluations. We've narrowed the list to 10 practices that we believe are most relevant for child custody evaluators.

1. Consider the impact of stressors associated with acculturation, racism, and discrimination.
2. Consider cultural factors in interpreting the examinee's attitude and cooperation.
3. Consider the impact of your own cultural identities on the examinee's presentation, including response style and attitude toward the evaluation.
4. Consider cultural factors in interpreting the examinee's level of insight.
5. Consider culturally normative parenting behaviors.
6. Consider how culture could have influenced the family dynamics.
7. Consider how well-established cognitive biases might manifest in the case on the basis of the examinee's cultural identities.
8. Consider within-group differences.
9. When validated measures are not available, address the limitations of each assessment used and the impact on test interpretation.
10. Consider the impact of discrimination, poverty, system-wide inequalities, and powerlessness.

Based on their results, Fanniff et al. developed a questionnaire for use in forensic psychological practice that purports to help psychologists identify and consider when conducting culturally sensitive forensic evaluations. They named their tool the Culturally Informed Attitudes, Skills, and Knowledge in Forensic Psychology (CASK-F). The CASK-F is a self-report measure "for evaluators to assess their own current practices, identify areas of strength and weakness, and seek consultation or training to address the weaknesses." The CASK-F also has a coding scheme for clinical supervisors to code reports or to track supervisee growth over time. We stress again, however, that the CASK-F is a list of possible areas of relevant exploration in conducting culturally sensitive forensic evaluations.

Martinez and Candilis (2020) expanded on Martinez's (2018) initial list of ideas that should guide forensic practice:

- To provide knowledge and understanding of persons diagnosed with mental illness within legal, regulatory, administrative, governmental, public, and clinical settings.
- To provide competent and respectful care to persons with mental illness in correctional and other clinical settings.
- To contribute to the [nondiscriminatory] truth-seeking and fairness goals of the legal system.
- To witness and narrate from forensic psychiatry's unique perspective the suffering [and inequities] that accompan[y] mental illness.
- To advocate for the de-stigmatization [and de-criminalization] of persons with mental illness.
- To advocate for alternatives to the narratives of polarization common in the adversarial system.
- To address the suffering of those with mental illness.
- To advocate for research and public policy that increase understanding of mental illness, address inequities in the behavioral health system, and move toward the development of forensic and treatment interventions that decrease suffering.

Custody evaluators can increase their sociocultural knowledge by learning about the family members' culture, language, and background. Evaluators can learn from Ethnomed (https://ethnomed.org/), the CIA World Fact Book (https://www.cia.gov/the-world-factbook/), cross-cultural journals or texts, colleagues, and community resources such as community centers and churches. There is increasing evidence-based and evidence-informed literature found in peer-reviewed journals and books.

Attendance at workshops and conferences is also an important venue for learning about sociocultural ideas. Some workshops might stress peer-reviewed research and the strengths and deficiencies in methodology. Other workshops might present various and evolving methods of assessment. Still other workshops present different cultural, ethnic, and racial paradigms that challenge the participants current thinking about sociocultural factors. Barry Rosenfield has also mentioned the potential use of individual cultural consultants, since they might provide much more nuanced information. Attending workshops and conference seminars that are taught by presenters from different cultural, ethnic, and racial backgrounds—both personal and professional—are also encouraged. Evaluators might also consider the potential use of individual cultural consultants who are likely to have more specialized knowledge and more nuanced information about a specific culture or subculture than the evaluator or information found in websites and publications (Barber Rioja & Rosenfeld, 2018).

CULTURAL GAPS IN PARENTING PLAN EVALUATIONS AND EVALUATORS

Parenting plan evaluators often come from different cultural and socioeconomic backgrounds than the families they assess. Evaluators need to be aware of how explicit and implicit bias factors might affect each stage of the evaluation process. Culture extends beyond ethnicity or immigration status—it includes religious beliefs, socioeconomic status, family structure, gender roles, and community norms. Evaluators' lack of awareness or lack of sensitivity of these factors can lead to misinterpretations of parenting behaviors and family dynamics.

Many evaluators unconsciously apply dominant-culture norms when assessing parenting capacity, attachment styles, or conflict resolution. For example, extended family involvement in child-rearing (common in many cultures) might be misinterpreted as parental detachment, parental dependence, parental incompetence, or lack of independence. Even when language barriers are minimal, cultural communication styles may differ (e.g., indirect vs. direct communication, emotional expression norms). Miscommunication may lead to misjudging credibility, cooperation, or parenting competence.

Families from marginalized backgrounds may have fewer resources (e.g., legal representation, psychological support), influencing their ability to present their case effectively. Legal and mental health professionals may misattribute stress-related behaviors (e.g., avoidance of authorities, reluctance to disclose trauma) as noncooperation.

CHALLENGES FOR THE EVALUATOR TO EMBRACE

When Gould (Gould & Martindale, 2007; Gould & Stahl, 2000) wrote about the art and science of PPEs, emphasis was placed equally on the importance of competent clinical training as well as forensic training. A core component of clinical training is the development of rapport with the individual being interviewed. Just as rapport development is essential in a clinical context, development of rapport with the interviewee in a PPE is essential. Cultural and ethnic expectations might influence the ability to create a rapport that facilitates fact-based disclosures. Evaluators need to be aware of potential challenges to the development of rapport based upon differences in education, socioeconomic background, religion, understanding and use of nonverbal cues, gender roles, appropriate clothing, role of the family, patterns of emotional expression and self-disclosure, and framing questions in culturally sensitive ways are among the many areas to be considered.

Attention to cultural and diversity factors in child custody assessment has emphasized the importance of considering context and the demands of the situation, two factors that have had little widespread focus in most custody texts. Custody evaluators need to be mindful of the ways in which individual, family, and extra-familial factors exert influence on each family member and create a unique context (Fanniff et al., 2023).

Similar to the observations of Weiss and Rosenfeld (2012) and Fanniff et al. (2023) regarding criminal and civil forensic assessment, we have observed that most custody assessment related texts written over the past 30 years have not adequately addressed factors associated with culturally sensitive and diversity informed approaches to child custody assessment. Recently, more and more workshops, articles, and books have been published in which a variety of different conceptual frameworks have been proposed to guide family-related forensic psychological assessments.

Many of the models address similar factors to be assessed. Below, we discuss many of these factors that we believe are relevant toward developing an understanding of the ways in which culture and diversity factors influence individual, dyadic, and family behavior.

NEED TO ACQUIRE BASIC KNOWLEDGE

Child custody evaluators need to develop an understanding of the variety of ways in which sociocultural identities and systemic inequities are ongoing dynamic processes that often vary both within families as well as across generations. For example, consider a family newly arrived in a Texas town from a city in Syria. Three generations (grandparents, parents, and their children) relocate to a small Texas town. The children attend school in Texas and matriculate at University of Texas, Austin. A few years later, the now young adults marry and have children. These young adult children are first-generation American. The first-generation parents divorce and a PPE is ordered.

What are some of the steps an evaluator needs to take during their psychological investigation? Among the steps to be taken include developing a knowledge of the native culture, the degree to which each parent maintains contact and identify with the native culture, the parent and grandparents embrace of their native culture and values, the ways in which the children's parents who are divorcing have been acculturated, the ways in which parents agree with how to raise their children based upon their shared cultural beliefs, the ways in which parents disagree with the degree to which their minor children should be allowed to become accultured into their community culture, and the challenges faced by the children as they develop friendships outside of their native culture and bring those influences into their familial homes.

It is not unusual that first-generation, American-born parents might have different values and beliefs about the role and importance of their cultural background than second-generation parents. The children of first-generation parents might experience acculturation into the surrounding diverse community differently than children of the second generation.

The potential conflicts between first-generation parents and their second-generation children about the ways in which acculturation into the diverse community might pull the children away from their parents' culture and values toward more community-based beliefs and values are important areas of the dynamics of family change.

Similarly, the ways in which parental conflict might emerge during divorce when one parent wishes to maintain stronger ties to their family-of-origin culture while the other parent wishes to move away from such ties are critical factors for evaluators to consider. Adding to these concerns is the ways in which children navigate where they belong in their changing family-culture when one parent seeks comfort from past cultural ties and the other parent seeks to explore new avenues. Grandparents might also exert pressure on their grandchildren to follow different developmental pathways that might result in intentional or unintentional attempts to align the grandchildren with one parent's choices.

Some authors have addressed potential trauma among those who are entering a new culture and among those who are engaged in learning how to belong to a dominant culture while maintaining connection to the source culture (B. H. Ellis et al., 2020, Introduction; Kia-Keating et al., 2023; Starck et al., 2020). Trauma and the family narratives developed from individual or shared trauma might be passed down from generation to generation (Alexander, 2015; Goodman, 2011). It is critical that the evaluator explore how family narratives that surround the stories of individual, familial, and collective trauma are maintained and serve as either obstacles or incentives toward bridging toward the dominant culture.

LANGUAGE AND NONVERBAL COMMUNICATION

Different cultural environments appear to shape thinking and language (Bettinsoli et al., 2021). It is beyond the scope of this book to address the fascinating and complex question raised almost a century ago by Vygotsky (1934) with regard to whether language precedes thought or thought precedes language. Our focus is on how culture appears to influence cognition through three distinct means: (a) the physical environment and the affordances it offers, (b) cultural values and conventions that encourage certain sensorimotor experiences while discouraging others (such as body postures of submission or pride, smiling, handwashing, and touching), and (c) cultural differences related to language, including metaphors and script direction (Vygotsky, 1934).

Inappropriate or misunderstood nonverbal behaviors may cause potential conflicts in intercultural communication (Kaushal, 2014). Effective communication is the basis of a forensic psychological interview. Effective communication in a forensic psychological interview can unfold in a harmonious and effortless manner or it can fail catastrophically (Bente et al., 2020). A critical component of effective interview communication is the ability for the interviewee and the interviewer to "click" on a nonverbal level (Bente et al., 2020). When the interviewee and interviewer "click," it is likely they are developing rapport. "In general terms, rapport is characterized as being connected, tuned-in, or in-sync" (Bente et al., 2020, p. 2).

Nonverbal communication is the transfer of information through body language, facial expressions, gestures, and vocal nuances like tone and rhythm. Nonverbal communication goes beyond oral communication. These nonverbal behaviors convey meanings critical to effective communication. There appears to be little consensus about the percentage of nonverbal versus verbal communication in American culture, but it is clear that nonverbal communication accounts for the majority of communication between and among people (Lapakko, 2015).

Nonverbal communication is dependent on expressions and physical movements as opposed to verbal communication, or the use of language to transfer information through written text, speaking, or sign language. For example, in our culture, smiling when you meet someone conveys friendliness, acceptance, and openness.

When conducting forensic evaluations of people from different cultures, differences in language use, word choice, word meaning, and other related factors influence the evaluator's accurate interpretation of the meaning of interview data. Similarly, differences in the intention and meaning behind nonverbal behavior also influence the evaluator's accurate interpretation of the meaning of interview data.

People respond to thousands of nonverbal cues and behaviors, including postures, facial expressions, eye gaze, gestures, and tone of voice. Forensic evaluators and those we evaluate are continuously responding to the nonverbal signals in the interview. Many, if not most, of these nonverbal signals are not readily observed. They are subtle and often manifest in micro-movements that are picked up and responded to without conscious awareness of the ways in which such nonverbal communications influence perception and interpretation of meaning.

Lack of recognition of the potential biases that can guide the evaluator in responding to nonverbal communication is a challenge. The study of emotion perception investigates aspects of nonverbal communication.

Emotion perception is defined as understanding the emotional meaning of another person's facial, body, or vocal behaviors (Leshin et al., 2024). Interpretation of emotion perception is a critical component to social communication. Accurate interpretation of emotion perception facilitates social connections, and inaccurate interpretation inhibits or impedes social connections.

Early theories suggested that there were universal emotions that were revealed in common facial expressions. More recent theories and behavioral evidence have shown that emotion perception is not universal but rather reflects a person's prior experiences, cultural background, language knowledge, and other variables that influence how a person perceives the verbal and nonverbal communications of others. Words that access emotional meaning are tied to the communicator's knowledge and use of language as well as tied to the listener's knowledge and use of language (Leshin et al., 2024).

When the communicator and listener come from the same or similar background, it is likely that their use of language (i.e., word choice) will be similar, the connection between word choice and emotion will be similar, and the resulting facial expressions associated with the word choice and emotions will be communicated and perceived roughly as intended through facial expression and other nonverbal communications. When a communicator comes from a different background and culture and expresses themselves using a language different (i.e., word choice) from that of the listener, it is likely that the different word choice is associated with different emotions. The communicator's different emotions tied to the particular word choice are likely to give rise to facial expressions and other nonverbal behaviors that are different from those expected by the listener (Leshin et al., 2024).

Unless the communicator and listener recognize the need to agree upon a common meaning of a particular word or concept, it is likely that a particular word that has different cultural meaning will lead to misunderstanding and miscommunication.

Misunderstanding and miscommunication that occurs in forensic interviewing will likely make the development of trustworthy rapport difficult and the resulting information provided by the interviewee less robust, less detailed, and very likely less helpful.

CULTURE-SPECIFIC PARENTING PRACTICES

Added to this complexity is the need for evaluators to become familiar with parenting practices associated with different cultures, communication behaviors associated with different cultures, emotional expression associated with different cultures, and other relevant variables.

Custody evaluators should foster an active interest in developing cultural knowledge, understanding that it is not enough to learn about one culture. Custody evaluators should learn about each family member's identity across a variety of activities, as well as the systemic pressures each individual experiences from their grandparents, church, friendships, school, workplace, and other areas that might influence them as individuals.

Consistent with the ecological model, custody evaluators should consider the family members' family structures, social roles, worldview, values, epidemiology, religion and beliefs, recent history, legal system, food, age, health, and beliefs about psychology or medicine. Communication, language, and interpersonal styles should include an analysis of nonverbal behaviors, particularly between parents and children. Custody evaluators should also learn more about the emotional journey each family member has made from the native culture to the current dominant culture, with particular attention to the challenges faced by their attempts to embrace or reject the dominant community.

ACCULTURATION

One way to think about acculturation is through a person's sense of belonging (Berry & Hou, 2016). A sense of belonging is defined as a "general feeling of inclusion and the desire to be close to a relevant social group" (Berry & Hou, 2016, p. 255). Aligned with the concept of belonging is the concept of social capital. Social capital refers to the social network of individuals. Social capital has been divided into bonding social capital and bridging social capital.

Bonding social capital refers to the individual's attempts to maintain social links with people from their native culture. Bonding social capital provides opportunities for the individual to maintain linkages with other members of the same cultural or minority group. Maintaining social contacts in this manner allows for continued identification with the source culture. Bonding social capital reinforces belonging to the source culture. It can serve as a cultural anchor to their source culture while they make the transition to a sense of belonging to the larger society (Berry & Hou, 2016).

Bridging social capital refers to developing relationships outside the source culture. Bridging social capital promotes a sense of belonging to the larger society (Berry & Hou, 2016). This enables individuals to engage with and integrate into broader social, economic, and institutional structures. Bridging social capital is a crucial aspect of acculturation, particularly for individuals and families navigating life in a new or different cultural context. Bridging social capital involves relationships between individuals from different backgrounds, ethnicities, or cultural groups. These connections help break down barriers, promote mutual understanding, and facilitate social inclusion.

Individuals who develop bridging social capital gain access to diverse perspectives, knowledge, and opportunities, such as education, employment, and community support services. Bridging social capital fosters engagement with the dominant culture, making it easier for individuals to navigate institutions such as legal systems, healthcare, and education. Societies with strong bridging social capital experience lower levels of social fragmentation, as individuals build relationships across different cultural and social boundaries. In the context of PPEs, bridging social capital plays a critical role in assessing how families and individuals integrate into their surrounding communities.

A lack of bridging social capital may lead to social isolation, limited opportunities, and difficulties navigating mainstream institutions. Conversely, excessive pressure to assimilate may create tension within families, especially if one parent prioritizes cultural preservation while the other emphasizes integration.

These two ways of developing a sense of belonging led Berry to develop a model of individual strategies for adapting to a new culture comprised of two dimensions (Berry et al., 2006; see Figure 8.1). One dimension is the degree to which people desire to maintain their heritage culture and identity. The second dimension is the degree to which people desire for involvement with the larger society into which they have moved (Berry, 2023). It is hypothesized that when

FIGURE 8.1. Berry et al.'s Model of Adapting to a New Culture

Value and maintain host culture	Value and maintain native culture: YES	Value and maintain native culture: NO
YES	Integration	Assimilation
NO	Separation	Marginalization

Note. From "Immigrant Youth: Acculturation, Identity, and Adaptation," by J. W. Berry, J. S. Phinney, D. L. Sam, and P. Vedder, 2006, *Applied Psychology, 55*(3), p. 356 (https://doi.org/10.1111/j.1464-0597.2006.00256.x). Copyright 2006 by John Wiley & Sons. Reprinted with permission.

these two dimensions are crossed, four cells are created that characterize *how* people attempt to acculturate:

- The first cell is *assimilation* and is characterized by little interest in cultural maintenance combined with a preference for interacting with the larger society (Berry, 2023).
- The second cell is *separation* and is characterized by maintaining cultural identity while seeking to avoid involvement with other aspects of the larger society.
- The third cell is *marginalization* and is found when neither cultural maintenance nor interaction with others is sought.
- The fourth cell is *integration* and is present when both cultural maintenance and involvement with the larger society are sought (Berry, 2023).

Another area to explore is how well people are able to adapt to their acculturation experience. Colleen Ward (1996) proposed two distinct ways in which people adapt to acculturating: *psychological adaptation* and *sociocultural adaptation*. Psychological adaptation refers to personal well-being, and good mental health. Sociocultural adaptation refers to an individual's social competence in managing their everyday life in an intercultural setting (C. Ward, 1996).

Berry and his colleagues found that individuals who engaged with both their native culture and the dominant culture, rather than either one alone, were found to display the most adaptive mode of acculturation and the most supportive of their overall well-being (Berry et al., 2006).

ACCULTURATION AND PARENTING PLAN EVALUATION

Berry's ideas about acculturation stressed that individuals vary in the ways in which they acculturate (Berry & Hou, 2019). Applying Berry's four acculturation strategies to PPEs in culturally diverse families, we suggest exploring how each individual in the family system employs one or more acculturation strategies and how each individual's acculturation strategy affects other members of the family.

Examining how different family members utilize different acculturation strategies might help to understand past and potential future conflicts reflective of family members' desire to move toward the larger society or maintain strong ties to the source culture. For example, intergenerational concerns might be raised when grandparents embrace a bonding social capital perspective, their adult children embrace a middle road of maintaining bonding social ties while also moving toward bridging social connections, and the grandchildren have embraced a bridging social capital connection and reject bonding connections that are so very important to their grandparents.

Another variation for evaluators to consider is when a family in which one parent is from a different culture and the other is from the dominant culture. Evaluators might examine how each parent's cultural ties influence their parenting of the children and the degree to which the children are caught in the middle of parental conflict over asking each child to choose to which culture they belong.

CULTURAL BIAS AND FORENSIC ASSESSMENT

Cultural or racial bias might affect the forensic evaluator in a number of ways (Liell, Fisher, & Jones, 2023). Social psychology research has revealed that our racial identity can create prejudice, and the existence of racial category groups also creates prejudice. The particular prejudice is the tendency for people to favor and prefer those who are similar to them over those who are dissimilar. These common, everyday biases affecting each of us have been linked to implicit bias and discriminatory behavior (Day et al., 2023).

Race has a powerful effect on our perception of our surroundings and the meanings we assign to events and to the behavior of others. People tend to be more likely to favor those who are more like themselves and less likely to empathize with those who are different, that is, who come from a different racial or ethnic group (Eberhardt, 2020a). "Our beliefs and attitudes become so strongly associated with the category that they are automatically triggered, affecting our behavior and decision making" (Eberhardt, 2020a, p. 32).

CASE STUDY: CULTURAL DIFFERENCES IN DEFERENCE TO AUTHORITY AND THE COMPLEXITY OF CULTURALLY SENSITIVE EVALUATIONS

The complexity of conducting evaluations with families from different cultures is often challenging in ways that add to the expected challenges of conducting an evaluation with a family from the dominant culture. As a result of the complexity of cultural factors in such evaluations, we take a deep dive into one factor that often varies with culture: Deference to authority, or the extent to which individuals respect and comply with figures of authority. We will discuss some of the factors that need to be considered by evaluators when conducting parenting plan investigations. We do not suggest that this one factor is a primary factor in conducting culturally responsive parenting plan evaluations. Rather, we focus on deference to authority to reveal some of the factors that evaluators need to consider when conducting evaluations with families from minority cultures.

Deference to authority varies significantly across cultures. This concept is deeply rooted in cultural values, social norms, and historical contexts. Evaluators' awareness of these differences is critical when conducting an evaluation. For example, there are high power distance and low power distance cultures. Individuals from high power distance cultures include China, India, Mexico, and Russia. In high power distance cultures, hierarchies are accepted as natural and legitimate. Authority figures are rarely questioned openly. Social roles are clearly defined, and obedience is often expected. Decisions by leaders are respected without much debate. Individuals from low power distance cultures include the United States, Australia, Denmark, and the Netherlands. In low power distance cultures, there is more emphasis on egalitarian relationships. Authority is seen as more collaborative than hierarchical. Individuals feel comfortable questioning or challenging authority figures. Decision making tends to be more democratic and participatory.

A related factor is differences among people who come from collectivist versus individualist societies. Collectivist societies include Japan, Korea, and Arab countries. Individuals from collectivist societies emphasize group harmony and respect for elders and leaders. They defer to authority because it supports group cohesion and stability. Personal opinions are often subordinated to group consensus. Individualist societies include the United States, the United Kingdom, and Canada. Individuals from individualist societies tend to value personal autonomy and self-expression. Individuals are encouraged to voice opinions, even if they contradict authority. Authority is respected, but not at the expense of personal rights.

In East Asian cultures, Confucian philosophy promotes respect for hierarchy, family roles, and societal order, leading to high deference in both personal and professional relationships. In many Middle Eastern and South Asian societies, religious teachings and traditional customs reinforce respect for elders, religious leaders, and political authorities. Societies with histories of authoritarian governance may exhibit higher deference to authority due to social conditioning, even after political changes.

Cultural differences in deference to authority will likely affect parenting behaviors during the evaluation, parenting behaviors at home, child behaviors during the evaluation, and child behaviors at home. Parenting styles may reflect cultural norms around authority, which can be misunderstood in cross-cultural custody disputes. Children's behavior towards parents and authority figures can be misinterpreted without cultural context. Often, parents and children from high-deference cultures struggle with assertiveness or expect the evaluator to take an authoritative role. Understanding cultural nuances helps evaluators to avoid imposing their own cultural values on clients.

Parents and children from high-deference cultures (e.g., East Asian, South Asian, Latin American, Middle Eastern) may be reluctant to challenge or question evaluators, even if they disagree. They might provide answers they believe the evaluator wants to hear rather than their true thoughts or experiences. Parents may expect the evaluator to act as an authority figure rather than a neutral assessor. Children may be hesitant to express opinions that contradict parental or legal authority.

Parents and children from low-deference cultures (e.g., American, Canadian, Northern European, Australian) are more likely to advocate for themselves, voice disagreements, or challenge conclusions. There may be an expectation of equal dialogue between the evaluator and the family. Children are often encouraged to express their preferences openly.

Parenting styles also differ based on cultural deference norms. In high-deference cultures, authoritarian parenting (e.g., strict discipline, respect for elders) is often viewed as appropriate, while in low-deference cultures, it may be perceived as overly rigid or harmful. Similarly, a child's deference to their parents may be interpreted differently based on cultural norms. In some cultures, a highly obedient child is seen as a sign of good parenting, while in others, it might raise concerns about autonomy and emotional well-being. Some cultures expect deference to elders in family decision making, which can create challenges in coparenting arrangements where equal input is expected. Grandparent input, religious elders' input, and other individuals from extended family and the community may also be viewed as normative and expected.

Cultural differences in deference to authority can affect how symptoms of distress, trauma, or personality traits are expressed. Individuals from high-deference cultures may be less likely to disclose mental health symptoms, family conflict, or abuse if they believe it would challenge authority figures or bring shame. A deferential communication style could be misinterpreted as passive, defensive, overly compliant, or lacking in assertiveness, potentially leading to misdiagnoses (e.g., dependent personality disorder vs. cultural respect for authority). Victims of domestic violence or child abuse from high-deference cultures may be reluctant to report abuse due to cultural expectations around obedience, loyalty, and family honor.

Cultural Influence on Interview Behavior

Cultural factors often affect how an individual presents during an interview. Individuals for whom English is a second language are often perceived as more dishonest in their presentation because of the tendency to take more time to process an answer than those for whom English is their first language (Ackerman et al., 2019). There is also the challenge for those for whom English is a second or third language to have difficulties providing coherent self-reports because of language challenges. The interviewee may also experience challenges understanding what is being asked, which may be misinterpreted as an intention to mislead or to act defensively. Differences in translating feelings and forms of expression from one language to another can also introduce obstacles to the individual clearly explaining and obstacles to the evaluator's understanding (Day et al., 2023).

Cultural norms may influence how a person presents during an interview and responds to questions and answers. Family and domestic violence might have different meanings and functions in some non-Western cultures. Expressions of shame or anger are known to be different in collectivist cultural groups compared to Western cultures (Day et al., 2023). For example, in collectivist societies (e.g., Asian, Middle Eastern, African, Latin American), shame is more public and socially oriented. It arises from the perception that one's behavior has brought dishonor or disrupted group harmony. Shame is more acceptable as an emotion because it signals a commitment to the group's values and a desire to restore social harmony. Individuals may suppress personal pride and express shame openly through nonverbal cues (e.g., bowing their head, avoiding eye contact, displaying a lowered posture) as a form of cultural humility and respect. Collectivist societies emphasize interdependent self-construal, meaning that personal identity is closely tied to relationships and social roles. As a result, shame is often externalized, meaning individuals feel accountable to their family, community, or broader social group.

In contrast, Western cultures emphasize personal autonomy and self-worth rather than group harmony. Shame in these cultures is often internalized, meaning individuals experience it as a private feeling of personal inadequacy or failure, rather than as a reflection of group dishonor. People in individualist cultures may be less likely to display overt expressions of shame, as it is often associated with low self-esteem and personal weakness. Instead, Western cultures tend to favor expressions of guilt over shame, as guilt is linked to personal responsibility and corrective action rather than collective dishonor.

As described below in our discussion of family ethnic–racial socialization, issues of trust between the person being interviewed and the interviewer might raise obstacles to accurate interpretation of the interviewee's behavior. Issues of trust might interfere with an evaluator's ability to develop an accurate understanding of the person being interviewed because of the interviewee's historically negative experiences with the legal system, with authority figures, or with mental health professionals (Day et al., 2023). How the evaluator interprets such behaviors is critically important in understanding how preconceived bias factors might color the evaluator's judgment about the interviewee. In addition, the language of traditional psychotherapy does not help because of the tendency to frame issues about trust and credibility judgments drawn from interview data in terms of defensiveness or avoidance. These inferences about internal motivation are often left unexplored during the interview and, when presented in a report or oral testimony, might serve to prejudice the court about the individual's motivation to be transparent.

Cultural Influence on the Use of Psychological Tests

For several decades, concerns have been raised about the role of bias in psychological testing. Most psychological tests used in child custody assessment have been developed for use with the dominant cultural group and then administered to those from different cultural groups without sufficient psychometric investigation (Day et al., 2023; Liell, Fisher, Jones, & Hough, 2023).

Construct bias (Pedraza & van de Vijver, 2020) refers to psychological assessment techniques informed by majority experiences and values that are likely inappropriate and unfamiliar to those from different cultures. Although robust literature describes how to use psychological test data to develop hypotheses when used in a child custody context, the results upon which the hypotheses are based are drawn from data normed on the majority culture. It is not known whether the data used to develop hypotheses about parenting from minority cultural groups generate useful hypotheses to investigate within that cultural group.

An alternative perspective is to consider that an instrument is not necessarily culturally or racially biased if one cultural group scores differently from other groups. Bias is not in the test results but in the ways in which those results are interpreted and applied (Vincent & Viljoen, 2018). It appears that the development of context-specific normative data for different cultural subgroups might assist in understanding the degree to which a test score from an individual from a cultural subgroup test score deviates from scores achieved by members of similar cultural subgroups.

Significant Cautions About Using Psychological Tests With Different Cultures

The term *construct equivalence* refers to an examination of whether a theoretical construct has the same meaning across cultures. *Construct bias* refers to comparing the definition and indicators of a construct across cultures. Evaluators need to ask those being assessed who come from different cultures what different constructs mean to them. In the context of a PPE, it would be important to ask a parent to explain their ideas about parenting, the roles played by each family member, the methods used in discipline and limit setting, and other similar constructs.

Measurement bias refers to whether an assessment tool measures the construct across cultures similarly. *Method bias* refers to whether there are similar conditions across different cultures (Schmidt et al., 2023). There is a scarcity of studies that have examined method bias among most of the measures typically used in parenting plan assessment.

Further complicating the situation is whether people from different cultures answer individual items differently from each other or answer individual items differently from the validation group. This is referred to as *differential item functioning*. Differential item functioning is another potential source of bias. When there are differences in how different cultural groups answer specific questions because they understand the item differently from the way in which the validation group answered the question, the meaning of the full scores is threatened (Schmidt et al., 2023). For example, we have comparison group data on the Minnesota Multiphasic Personality Inventory, 3rd Edition with Puerto Rican parents and we have comparison group data with American parents, yet we do not have similar data for most other tests used in parenting plan evaluations.

These concerns significantly threaten the reliable interpretation of standardized psychological test results validated on an American population yet administered, scored, and interpreted with individuals from different cultures and minority groups.

FAMILY ETHNIC–RACIAL SOCIALIZATION

Historically, child custody researchers approached the evaluation of ethnic and racially different family systems with the same or similar conceptual models based upon the prominent behavioral science literature that was most often based upon findings from studies of nonethnically diverse and nonracially diverse samples (Lewis, 2021a). Researchers are beginning to examine factors that address the ways in which evaluators need to understand socialization factors among ethnic and racial populations (Umaña-Taylor & Hill, 2020). Families play an important role in teaching their children ways to reduce the negative effects of ethnic–racial inequalities by socializing their children "to better understand their race, ethnicity, and culture, and, in effect, develop a strong sense of identity" (Umaña-Taylor & Hill, 2020, p. 244).

Few, if any, child custody assessment texts have discussed prevailing models that address relevant factors to consider when assessing a culturally, ethnically, or racially diverse family. Family ethnic–racial socialization attempts to identify the values, traditions, and practices associated with their ethnic–racial subculture (Umaña-Taylor & Hill, 2020). Evaluators need to become familiar with differences in parenting values, traditions, and practices associated with different ethnic–racial groups.

One line of research has examined the development of competencies in minority children and the role played by families in facilitating children's understanding of a socially stratified society in which everyday experiences are shaped by racism and discrimination. A theme that emerged is the important role that families play with respect to ethnicity and race as a normative aspect of effective parenting (Hughes et al., 2006).

A family ethnic–racial socialization model of four themes that serve as an organizing framework has emerged from reviews of the relevant literature (Hughes et al., 2006; Huguley et al., 2019). The first theme is *cultural socialization*, which is the transmission of cultural values, customs, traditions, history, and pride. Researchers have reported a robust and positive association between cultural socialization within the family and multiple indicators of positive child adjustment. Family cultural socialization is associated with positive self-concept, positive attributions, positive appraisals, and coping strategies. Family cultural socialization also appears important as a protective factor against the negative effects of discrimination (Neblett et al., 2012). Evaluators need to investigate the parenting attributes associated with parents' embrace of these cultural themes, how their children accept or reject these cultural themes, and extra family pressures associated with maintaining or changing the acceptance of those parenting behaviors and values tied to the cultural themes.

The second theme is *preparation for bias*. The assumption was that preparation for bias was intended to promote positive adjustment among children by preparing children for potential discrimination and skills to help cope with such discrimination. Evaluators need to examine how the family prepares its children for discrimination and how to cope with potential discrimination. Research examining the role of family preparation for bias is mixed, making it difficult to draw any reliable conclusions about the link between bias preparation and children's adjustment (Umaña-Taylor & Hill, 2020). A subset of studies found that associations between bias preparation and children's adjustment were dependent upon context. Among the context variables that influenced the relationship between bias preparation and adjustment were the quality of parent–child relationships, family context, and neighborhood factors (Umaña-Taylor & Hill, 2020).

Within each family system, it is important to investigate which family member or members are responsible for such preparation and the support provided for such preparation from other immediate and extended family members as well as support from friendship, community, and other relationships from outside the family.

A third theme is the family's *promotion of distrust*. Families tend to communicate the need for wariness and distrust of other ethnic–racial groups. Promotion of mistrust appears to be associated with greater youth maladjustment (Dunbar et al., 2015), however some research evidence suggests that promotion of mistrust is context dependent (Kiang et al., 2019). Evaluators need to investigate whether and how there is a familial culture that promotes distrust of others and, in the context of this particular family living in a specific community, does the promotion of distrust facilitate or thwart healthy adjustment and acculturation.

The fourth theme is the emphasis on *egalitarianism*, that is, promotion of equality among different ethnic–racial groups (Hughes et al., 2006). Although there is a limited research base examining the role of parents in encouraging egalitarianism, results from the few reported studies suggest egalitarianism is associated with positive child adjustment (Hughes et al., 2006).

IMPORTANCE OF OPERATIONAL DEFINITIONS AND LIMITATIONS OF PUBLISHED RESEARCH

To operationalize an example of the need to be aware of sociocultural and diversity factors, we look at the role of emotional regulation and dysregulation in a variety of different areas of family functioning among people from different cultures (Tamir et al., 2024). We recommend that evaluators examine how parents' emotional regulation and dysregulation might teach their children how to regulate their own behavior. We also recommend that evaluators examine the ways in which parental emotional dysregulation might trigger parental conflict or the ways in which children's emotional dysregulation might adversely affect parental cooperation and communication over child-related issues.

Despite the importance of evaluators understanding the role of emotional regulation and dysregulation in family systems, most emotional regulation research has been conducted within Western cultures (Tull & Aldao, 2015). There is a dearth of research and theory on culture and emotional regulation (Tull & Aldao, 2015). There is also little, if any, guidance in published child custody texts and articles addressing how cultural and diversity factors affect emotional regulation (Tamir et al., 2024).

Culture and diversity factors are likely to inform how parents and their children utilize different emotional regulation strategies that contribute to how individuals regulate their emotions and moderate the connection between emotional regulation and conflict development, conflict resolution, and conflict avoidance (Tamir et al., 2024). Evaluators need to be familiar with the literature addressing differences in how parents from different cultures express their emotional reactions to events in the family. Said differently, evaluators need to be familiar with differences in cultural variations regarding outward expressions of emotions that are different from those of the surrounding dominant culture.

Another area that has little research basis is understanding emotional regulation throughout the lifespan (Sims et al., 2015). Emotional regulation and dysregulation among young children are modulated by strategies different from their older siblings that are different from their older adolescent siblings that are different from their parents. Their parents' emotional regulation strategies are likely different from one another and are likely to have differential effects on each child within the family. Adding to this complexity is the ways in which grandparents' cultural influences about parenting, emotional regulation, and regulation strategies affect their adult children (the parents under examination).

In addition, there is a lack of research on cultural and diversity factors and parenting. There is some research addressing differences between Western parenting and Asian parenting; the problem with most of these studies is the implication that parenting within America is defined by a unitary set of parenting behaviors and that parenting within different Asian cultures is also easily defined by a unitary set of parenting behaviors. There is also an emerging literature on LGBTQIA+ parenting, yet even within that literature, there are few, if any, reliable assessment procedures. Attention has also been brought to the ways in which subcultures within larger cultures vary in their parenting behaviors, beliefs, and values (Burgamy et al., 2021; Harris-Brit & Jones, 2022). However, there are few, if any, reliable assessment procedures developed that can assist in evaluators' understanding of relevant though nuanced parenting behaviors that need to be explained to the court.

ECOLOGICAL MODEL ADAPTED FOR CUSTODY EVALUATIONS

As we've discussed family systems and an ecological model of viewing families (Garber et al., 2022; Gould, 1998, 2006), it is important to focus on the many system levels beyond the individual level (Sue, 2001). Just as we have both promoted an ecological model for evaluations, APA's Multicultural Guidelines utilize an ecological approach that incorporates context, identity, and intersectionality." The Layered Ecological Model of the Multicultural Guidelines comprises dynamic, nested systems that transact over time. Psychologists are informed by an understanding of such transactions among individuals, microsystems, exosystems, and macrosystems. We have expanded on their model to include a sixth level. We recommend thinking of the six layers as six concentric circles (see Figure 8.2). APA's layered ecological model is composed of five levels (APA, 2017b).

Level 1, the Bidirectional Model of Self-Definition and Relationships, has two inner circles that include the interaction between an individual's self-definition and relationships. The model allows for, and we suggest, evaluators to think of these circles as including the family members. It is important to remember, of course, that individuals within a family may self-define differently than one another. It is also important to remember that their socioidentity may be dynamically changing during the evaluation.

Level 2, Community, School, and Family Context, surrounds the Level 1 circles. This layer describes the influence of the community, school, and family

FIGURE 8.2. An Ecological Approach to Context, Identity, and Intersectionality

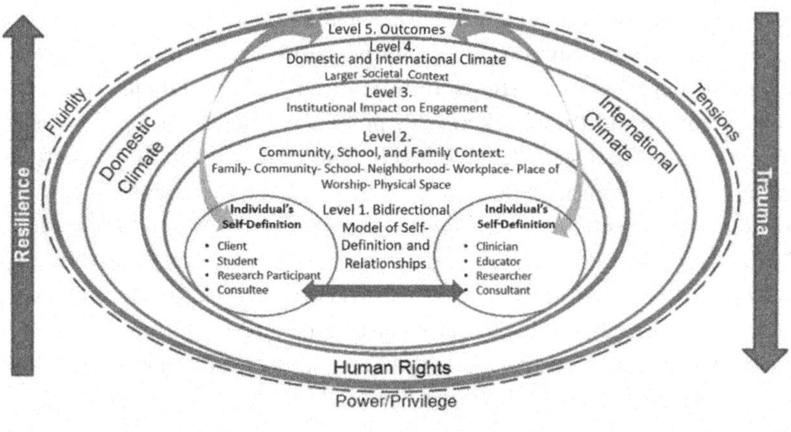

Note. Reprinted from *Multicultural Guidelines: An Ecological Approach to Context, Identity, and Intersectionality*, by the American Psychological Association, 2017, p. 97 (https://www.apa.org/about/policy/multicultural-guidelines.pdf). Copyright 2017 by the American Psychological Association.

context on individuals and their family relationships. This level can also include the influence of neighborhood, workplace, place of worship, and physical space.

Level 3, Institutional Impact on Engagement, surrounds Level 2 and "considers the influence of local, state, and federal governments; medical systems; legal systems (including law enforcement); mental and behavioral health systems; and educational systems. Level 3 examines the effects of institutional context on how clients and psychologists experience the community, school, and family contexts (Level 2) and how this experience influences both the individual's self-definition and relationships with one another" (APA, 2017b, p. 11).

Level 4, Domestic and International Climate, surrounds Level 3 and includes considerations on the impact of climate and human rights. "The psychologist is encouraged to identify and understand the ways in which the larger societal context affects the individual's self-definition and bidirectional relationships" (APA, 2017b, p. 11).

Custody evaluators should explore whether the family members' human rights are being compromised due to domestic and international climates. The APA guidelines define culture as "adaptation and maladaptation, resilience, vulnerability, and coping" (APA, 2017b, p. 71). Level 4 encourages psychologists "to seek to understand that individualism, self-reliance, self-efficacy, self-actualization, and self-care do not connote the only model in which human development and positive functioning can occur" (APA, 2017b, p. 71).

The Level 4 analysis is connected to Multicultural Guideline 8:

> Guideline 8. Psychologists seek awareness and understanding of how developmental stages and life transitions intersect with the larger biosociocultural context, how identity evolves as a function of such intersections, and how these different socialization and maturation experiences influence worldview and identity. (APA, 2017b, p. 5)

Custody evaluators are encouraged to consider the immediate social and physical environment, along with social trends and the historical period within a developmental perspective. The family members we evaluate have developed from unique experiences of cultural and social context.

Level 5, Outcomes, surrounds the four interior layers and focuses on how positive and negative interactions and experiences have impacted the family. The evaluator should then look at how power, privilege, trauma, or resilience occur within and between the five levels. The outcomes in Level 5 are influenced by interactions and experiences within and between Levels 1, 2, 3, and 4.

In summary, we encourage evaluators to consider how the family members are influenced by these five levels and the dynamic interactions they experience with the legal system. The transactions between the family members and the courts, attorneys, and evaluators are constantly shifting, creating new behavior patterns, life events, transitions, tensions, and contextual influences that occur on ever-growing timelines.

We recommend evaluators use the model we have described above to investigate each family member's sociocultural identity. After developing an understanding of each family member's sociocultural identity, the custody evaluator should assess each parent's ability to support the child's sociocultural identity. Custody evaluators should ask about each family member's experiences and assess the extent to which each parent understands the child's sense of self and the child's connection to their sociocultural identity. Custody evaluators should also be sensitive to the degree to which children have experienced racism or other pressures, and evaluators should assess to what degree each parent can advocate for the child.

EXAMPLE

Our ecological model provides a framework for understanding how different sociocultural and systemic factors influence families in parenting plan evaluations. Imagine an evaluator assessing a family involving a Mexican American mother and a White American father who are divorcing after 10 years of marriage. They have two children, ages 8 and 12. The mother emphasizes cultural traditions, extended family involvement, and Spanish-language education, while the father insists on full assimilation into mainstream American culture. The children are caught between two cultural identities, and there are allegations of bias, miscommunication, and cultural misunderstandings influencing the custody battle.

At Level 1, the evaluator examines each parent's cultural identity and how it shapes their parenting beliefs, how the children define themselves culturally (e.g., do they identify more with one parent's culture than the other?), the quality of parent–child relationships and whether either parent is discouraging the child's connection to the other culture, and how acculturation and cultural identity shifts impact family dynamics. In this hypothetical example, the evaluator learns the mother believes that maintaining strong Mexican cultural ties is essential for her children's sense of identity and family connection. The father argues that fully assimilating into American culture will help the children avoid discrimination and social exclusion. The 12-year-old child prefers bilingual education, while the 8-year-old primarily speaks English and has little interest in Spanish.

At Level 2, the evaluator examines the influence of extended family and community on the children's development, the role of schools, peer relationships, neighborhood cultural dynamics, and family support systems that contribute to or hinder stability. The evaluator learns the mother lives in a predominantly Latino community, where the children interact daily with Spanish-speaking relatives. The father has moved to a suburban, predominantly White area, where the children attend a school with few Hispanic students. The 8-year-old struggles with language barriers when visiting extended family on the mother's side, causing emotional distress. The evaluator may assess whether changes in community environment would disrupt the children's existing support systems. The evaluator may also consider whether the father's relocation would isolate the children from their maternal cultural roots.

The evaluator may also evaluate bilingual education options to bridge both parental concerns.

At Level 3, the evaluator considers how legal systems, healthcare, and social services affect the family's access to resources, bias in institutional decision making (e.g., courts, schools, law enforcement), and barriers to parental involvement due to cultural misunderstandings. The evaluator learns the mother has had limited access to legal representation due to language barriers and financial constraints. The father, a U.S. citizen with a strong financial position, has an advantage in court proceedings. School administrators tend to communicate primarily in English, leading to misinterpretations of the mother's involvement in school activities. The evaluator should recognize potential biases in legal proceedings that disadvantage non-English-speaking parents and consider whether systemic barriers prevent equal participation in custody-related decisions.

At Level 4, the evaluator looks at societal norms, discrimination, and cultural acceptance, political policies affecting immigration, language use, and family rights, and how public attitudes toward race, ethnicity, and social class influence parenting experiences. The evaluator learns the children have experienced racial bullying at school for being bilingual. The father argues that assimilating completely into White American culture will protect the children from discrimination. The mother worries that erasing their Mexican heritage will cause identity confusion and disconnect from family roots. The evaluator may evaluate the impact of discrimination, racism, and assimilation pressures on child development. The evaluator might consider whether prioritizing cultural assimilation over bicultural identity is in the best interest of the child. The evaluator might recommend interventions that promote cultural pride while ensuring social adaptability.

At Level 5, the evaluator assesses how past, present, and future interactions shape long-term family well-being, whether past experiences of trauma, racism, or systemic inequality influence parental attitudes, and the child's long-term psychological development based on parenting decisions. The evaluator learns the mother had negative experiences with institutional racism in the United States, making her reluctant to trust government institutions. The father's family has no cultural awareness of Mexican traditions, leading to tensions between extended families. The 12-year-old feels pressured to "choose" between cultures, leading to emotional distress. The evaluator might assess intergenerational trauma and its impact on parental decision making. The evaluator might explore compromise solutions that preserve cultural heritage while ensuring full social integration. The evaluator might recommend coparenting strategies that foster cultural inclusion rather than exclusion.

CONCLUSION

Culturally responsive PPEs can significantly enhance the fairness, accuracy, and effectiveness of family court decisions by addressing systemic biases and respecting diverse cultural contexts. The following are key benefits supported by research and practice guidelines:

- Culturally responsive PPEs serve to enhance accuracy in the assessment process. Evaluators trained in cultural competency are more likely to avoid misjudging parenting practices (e.g., communication styles, discipline methods) that may differ from dominant cultural norms. For example, nonverbal communication patterns in some cultures may be misinterpreted as disengagement without cultural context.
- Culturally responsive evaluators are likely to assess families' adaptation to dominant cultures, distinguishing between culturally rooted behaviors and maladaptive parenting. Such awareness often mitigates pathologizing practices like communal caregiving in collectivist cultures.
- Culturally responsive evaluations reveal sensitivity to prioritizing children's cultural heritage (e.g., language, religious practices) that tends to foster stability and self-esteem, particularly in transracial adoptions or bicultural families.
- Culturally responsive methods better identify trauma in marginalized communities (e.g., refugee families), linking families to culturally aligned support services. They tend to minimize evaluators' explicit biases (e.g., stereotypes about LGBTQ+ parents, racial minorities) and encourage the use standardized criteria to minimize subjectivity.
- Culturally tailored interviews and community liaisons improve participation from families wary of institutional systems. For example, consulting with an individual from the parents' community often helps interpret traditions like kinship care in Indigenous communities.

Our review of the current literature leaves us with significant concerns about the degree to which there is sufficient information in the peer-reviewed literature and professional training to guide evaluators in how best to conduct a reliable assessment of families from culturally diverse and from ethnic and racial minorities.

We have raised concerns about potential bias factors that might adversely affect evaluator behavior during the evaluation process. We have raised concerns about potential bias factors that might adversely affect the behavior of each family member during the evaluation process. We have raised concerns about potential biases in the use and interpretation of psychological tests. We have raised concerns about evaluators' limited knowledge of parenting practices from culturally diverse and from ethnic and racial minority families. We have raised concerns about the historical lack of information about culturally diverse and from ethnic and racial minority family systems in custody texts.

The conundrum is that our society is increasingly more diverse. There is a critical need for evaluators to become better skilled and develop greater competencies in conducting diversity and culturally informed evaluations. We encourage evaluators to adopt an ecological model that incorporates five levels and the dynamic interactions they experience with the legal system. By applying this five-level framework, custody evaluators can ensure a comprehensive, culturally sensitive assessment that goes beyond simplistic interpretations of parental conflict. The model highlights

- individual and family dynamics (cultural identity, parenting beliefs, emotional ties),
- community and educational environments (language barriers, peer influences),
- institutional biases and systemic challenges (legal barriers, social inequalities),
- wider societal attitudes and discrimination (cultural integration vs. erasure), and
- long-term outcomes (identity development, emotional well-being).

In parenting disputes involving multicultural families, this model uses an ecological approach to understand culture and the child's best interests.

9

Gender Identity and Sexual Orientation

In this chapter, we discuss gender identity and sexual orientation as areas of family life that are increasingly recognized as critical factors intersecting with family law cases, particularly in parenting plan evaluations (PPEs). As societal understanding of diverse identities evolves, parenting plan evaluators must adapt to ensure decisions are made in the best interest of the child. However, despite this growing awareness, limited specialized training is available for forensic evaluators, guardians ad litem, child representatives, and other professionals involved in these sensitive cases. This limited availability can inadvertently lead to decisions that overlook the nuanced needs of children exploring their identities, potentially impacting their emotional and psychological well-being.

Family law cases involving issues of gender identity and sexual orientation present unique challenges that require a nuanced approach. The relevance of these factors in PPEs cannot be overstated, as they directly influence a child's sense of security, self-esteem, and overall development. According to Hammer (2024), such cases demand that professionals possess specialized training to navigate the complexities associated with gender identity and sexual orientation. Unfortunately, these trainings are not yet commonplace, leaving evaluators ill-equipped to address the specific needs of lesbian, gay, bisexual, transgender, queer, intersex, or asexual (LGBTQIA+) children and their families.

https://doi.org/10.1037/0000474-010
Parenting Plan Evaluations: An Evidence-Informed Approach to Child Custody, by J. W. Gould and C. M. Mulchay

DEFINING TERMS

Before discussing selected research findings and issues related to factors that evaluators might wish to consider when conducting parenting plan assessments with LGBTQIA+ families, we define some of the terms used in the diversity and gender nonconforming literature. Many of the current terms raise distinctions between and among concepts in sexual orientation and gender identity that are poorly defined and not well understood. Here are brief definitions of some commonly used terms.

We will use the term *gender diverse* to represent those who feel or present themselves as gender nonconforming in various ways. *Gender nonconformity* refers to the extent to which a person's gender identity, role, or expression differs from the cultural norms prescribed for people of a particular sex. *Gender identity* can be defined as an individual's personal understanding and experience of their own gender, which may be influenced by socialization, environmental factors, cultural influences, psychological aspects, and their relationship with their physical body and mind, among other elements. A *transgender* person (also referred to as a *trans* person) is someone whose gender identity differs from the sex to which they were assigned at birth (i.e., the sex listed on their original birth certificate). For example, a transgender man is someone assigned female at birth (i.e., the original birth certificate says "female") who identifies as a man. A transgender woman is someone assigned male at birth who identifies as a woman. Conversely, a *cisgender* person (also referred to as a *cis* person) is someone whose gender identity is the same as their sex assigned at birth. A cisgender woman is someone assigned female at birth who identifies as a woman, while a cisgender man is someone assigned male at birth who identifies as a man. Some transgender people identify as neither male nor female; these individuals are referred to as *nonbinary* people.

Gender dysphoria refers to discomfort or distress that is caused by a discrepancy between a person's gender identity and that person's sex assigned at birth (and the associated gender role or primary and secondary sex characteristics). Only some gender-nonconforming people experience gender dysphoria at some point in their lives. Additionally, gender identity may or may not correspond with an individual's *gender expression*, which is the way an individual expresses their gender externally (including their clothing, hairstyle, mannerisms, etc.).

According to the American Academy of Pediatrics, most children have a stable sense of their gender identity by about age 4 (Steensma et al, 2013). The Canadian Pediatric Society (n.d.) notes that as puberty begins, some youth begin to recognize that their gender identity is different from their assigned sex at birth. Additionally, transgender youth have been found to often recognize their gender identity internally sometime around age 7 but may not disclose it until about 10 years later, highlighting the complex interplay between gender identity development and the onset of puberty (P. Graham, 2022).

While gender identity refers to how individuals perceive and know themselves and what they call themselves, *sexuality* and *sexual orientation* refer to one's object of desire. For example, one's sexual orientation may be gay, straight, bisexual, pansexual, queer, asexual, or numerous other variations. While core aspects of gender identity emerge in early childhood, experiences related to sexual orientation often become more prominent during adolescence, coinciding with the physical and hormonal changes of puberty.

Although gender identity and sexual orientation are different concepts, minorities in these groups are often lumped together under the umbrella term LGBTQIA+, which includes any gender-diverse or sexual minority person. In this chapter, we will use the general term "LGBTQIA+" when referring to this general category of nonheterosexual or noncisgender people. We will use the specific term "gender diverse" when referring to individuals whose gender identity or expression differs from the cultural norms prescribed for people of a particular sex, and the specific term *sexual minority* when referring to people whose sexual attraction differs from the heterosexual norm.

CHALLENGES FACED BY LGBTQIA+ PARENTS

Like LBGTQIA+ children, LGBTQIA+ parents face numerous challenges. The types of attacks targeted at LBGTQIA+ individuals are both overt (e.g., discriminatory remarks, legal challenges) and covert (e.g., microaggressions, biased assumptions). In PPEs, attacks might manifest through biased evaluations, questioning a parent's fitness based solely on their gender identity or sexual orientation or challenging the stability of nontraditional family structures. LBGTQIA+ parents might also be targets of prejudice or moral judgments. Used in this context, prejudice refers to preconceived opinions not based on reason or actual experience. Moral judgments are subjective assessments of what is "right" or "wrong," often influenced by cultural, religious, or societal norms. When evaluating parents, such biases can affect data gathering, data integration, and opinion formation that is revealed in written reports or expert testimony.

Biases against LGBTQIA+ individuals often stem from heteronormativity and gender essentialism. *Heteronormativity* is the belief that heterosexuality, aligned with traditional gender roles (male and female), is the default or preferred norm. In a PPE, such biases might influence an evaluator to prioritize traditional nuclear families over diverse family structures, implicitly disadvantaging LGBTQIA+ parents. *Gender essentialism* is the belief that gender traits are innate, fixed, and biologically determined. This perspective fails to account for the fluidity of gender and reinforces rigid roles (e.g., the idea that only a mother can be nurturing or that a father must be the disciplinarian).

IMPLICATIONS FOR PARENTING PLAN EVALUATIONS

Expert witnesses or parenting plan evaluators may, knowingly or unknowingly, allow heteronormative and gender essentialist biases to influence their assessments of a parent's capability, leading to opinions that reflect personal biases rather than evidence-informed opinions. Evaluators who testify about their reports in which one or more family members are LGBTQIA+ individuals need to be prepared for cross examinations by attorneys that might exploit societal biases, framing a parent's gender identity as inherently problematic for a child's development, despite a lack of empirical evidence to support such claims.

Furthermore, LGBTQIA+ parents—regardless of the sex, gender, or sexual orientation of their child—are wise to recognize how their gender identity or sexual orientation *as perceived by the court* might affect and influence awards of legal decision making regarding their children. For example, in cases where one or both parents are trans, there are often explicit and implicit challenges relative to contested claims of fitness for legal decision making. Arguments relative to the parents' overall mental health often arise, particularly when the trans parent previously identified in a different manner than at present (Hammer, 2024).

As evaluators, we work with children who may be exploring their identity, orientation, expression, and their sexuality prior to, during, and after the evaluation. It is, therefore, important for evaluators to understand that this process may not be linear or finalized. As we have and will continue to discuss in this and other chapters, it is also important to remember there are many reasons why individuals may hesitate to speak to evaluators during litigation.

CAUTION ABOUT RELIABILITY OF RESEARCH

We begin our summary of research on LGBTQIA+ topics with a couple caveats. Concerns raised in this "caution" might be relevant to much research in the LGBTQIA+ literature (and most likely relevant to research in general). As we have summarized some of the research below, we note that many researchers use different terminology, which leads to concerns about the reliability of the interpretation of the reported results. Many of the studies reviewed used small sample sizes and often did not operationally define terms. Multiple diagnostic criteria often introduced variability that undermined the reliable identification of specific factors being studied and made virtually impossible comparisons across independent studies purported to study the same or similar constructs. Transgender identity was defined as "dysphoria," "variance," or "diverse." These varying definitions were correlated with Autism Spectrum Condition categories of "symptoms," "traits," or "empathizing and systematizing styles of thinking" (Manjra & Masic, 2022).

In a related concern, research findings have revealed that the use of categorical versus dimensional definitions of some concepts leads to very different results. One recent study of gender identity and neurodevelopmental conditions found that categorical diagnoses were significantly less useful in identifying gender identity domains across neurodivergent and neurotypical children (Mo et al., 2024).

There are several cautionary takeaways from these studies. First is the importance of critically examining methodologies of studies used as a basis of expert opinions. Second is the importance of relying on research findings that have clearly defined the concepts being studied and the degree to which the researcher's definitions are operationalized in a manner that is both clearly defined in the study and clearly understood by the testifying expert. Third is the importance of acknowledging the limitations of research findings that result, in part, from the lack of consensus about concept definitions and the reliability of measurement techniques used to assess the concepts. Fourth, it is important to critically examine whether the operational definition being used by researchers in studies upon which expert opinions are based is categorical or dimensional. It is possible that categorical definitions that guide researchers are too global to allow for the examination of more subtle, perhaps more important factors that would be identified if a dimensional definition were utilized.

As we describe the studies below, we aim to demonstrate how evaluators should closely attend to the strengths and weaknesses of each study. We remind our colleagues that we have ethical duties to identity limitations. In the studies below, we have tried to keep the terms the studies used.

GENDER ESSENTIALISM AND PREJUDICE AMONG CHILDREN

Despite increasing support for gender equality, gender prejudice and discrimination continue to affect all levels of society (Halim et al., 2024), with many studies showing the profoundly negative effects on children. The origins of gender prejudice and discrimination appear to develop early in childhood (Halim et al., 2024).

In a study of an ethnically diverse group of young children (i.e., Asian, Black, Latinx, and White, ages 4–6 years old) from geographically diverse locations, all children showed more positive attitudes toward their gender ingroup. Children who showed more pro-ingroup attitudes were also found to hold more pro-ingroup behavioral discrimination. Girls were found to hold more ingroup favoritism than boys, no matter the ethnic or regional group membership (Halim et al., 2024).

Ingroup biases also affect adults and how they teach their children about diversity (Halim et al., 2023). Halim et al. investigated (a) whether parents' conversations with their children about gender intergroup relationships and parental modeling of such behaviors influenced children's formation of gender attitudes, status perceptions, and gender intergroup behaviors among young children (i.e., ages 4–6 years old) and (b) whether children's self-guided interests about gender socialization (self-socialization) influenced young children's formation of gender attitudes, status perceptions, and gender intergroup behaviors.

Children whose parents reported they were especially active in seeking information about gender tended to provide more resources to same-gender versus other-gender children. These same-gender children reported fewer positive evaluations of other-gender children in comparison to children who were less active. In contrast, parents' conversations with their children about gender inter-group relations and conversations about gender-play stereotypes were found to have lower associations with children's gender attitudes (Halim et al., 2023).

Children raised in homes with more traditional gender roles compared to homes with more gender equality regarding division of labor were observed to rate men as having higher status than women (Halim et al., 2023).

In a study that examined gender essentialism and prejudice against people who do not conform to gender norms among young children (i.e., ages 6–10), results revealed positive correlations between gender essentialism and prejudice against gender nonconformity. Both correlated negatively with age, showing that gender essentialism and prejudice decreased with age (E. B. Gross et al., 2024).

COMMUNITY EFFORTS PROMOTING DIVERSITY ACCEPTANCE

The communities in which LGBTQIA+ children live are frequently a source of distress, rejection, and hostility. Evaluators should investigate each child's experiences of acceptance and rejection, related emotional factors, and how such experiences affect their emotional development. Evaluators should explore how each parent understands their child's experiences in the community-at-large and the steps taken by each parent to learn about these community obstacles and steps taken to support their children in dealing with their feelings of community acceptance or rejection.

An interesting study examined factors that influenced community perception and acceptance of lesbian, gay, and bisexual (LGB) adolescents in Germany (Klocke, 2024). Community-based efforts to promote acceptance of LGB children were found to be perceived as encouraging the sexualizing of children. Study participants who understood that community efforts were intended to (a) promote acceptance of sexual diversity and not to sexualize children and (b) that children with same-sex parents are as well-adjusted as those with heterosexual parents showed higher approval of such community-based efforts compared to participants who believed that homosexuality is affected by socialization who revealed higher opposition to such community efforts.

FACTORS THAT AFFECT HOW CHILDREN REVEAL THEIR GENDER DIVERSITY

Evaluators need to gather information about how gender diverse children reveal their identities to parents, grandparents, siblings, friends, teachers, and others who play various roles in the lives of these children. As we have discussed in this book, it is important to look closely at research. For gender diverse children, "types of gender diverse children are often lumped together in research so differences among them are masked" (Martin et al., 2024). When researchers used a nuanced measure of gender self-concepts, they "compared the three types of gender diverse children and found that the types differed in their behaviors and beliefs about same- and other-gender peers in school" (Martin et al., 2024). Children who reported feeling more similar to other-gender peers described having more contact and a greater sense of inclusion with other-gender peers. Children who reported feeling more similar to same-gender peers described having more contact and a greater sense of inclusion with same-gender peers (Martin et al., 2024). It is possible that children with two atypical gender diverse patterns (cross-gender and both-gender) are more likely to experience social benefits that gender typical children do not experience.

In a study of self-socialization of gender development, findings suggest that children tend to be more influenced by people of their own gender, activities associated with their own gender, and stereotype-consistent examples in their environment (Gülgöz et al., 2024). Transgender and cisgender children were found to have better recall for activities related to their own gender. Neither group revealed better recall for same-gender characters. Transgender children revealed better recall of other-gender images (Gülgöz et al., 2024).

IMPORTANCE OF SUPPORTIVE FAMILIES

Evaluators should investigate the support that LGBTQIA+ children receive from family members. Research findings are unequivocally clear that these children need the unconditional support from their families.

Our experiences with families of LGBTQIA+ children reveal that often one parent is supportive of their children's preferences and choices while the other parent is not supportive. Evaluators need to investigate the basis for each parent's decision to accept or reject their children. Exploring parents' family of origin often will reveal generational beliefs, values, and attitudes about gender essentialism and misinformation about how LBGTQIA+ children develop their sexual preferences and lifestyles.

Evaluators might also examine each parent's relationship with each child across the child's development. Evaluators should investigate when the LGBTQIA+ individual first became aware of their nonconformity and the factors that influenced their decision to begin to explore different aspects of their identity. Some LGBTQIA+ children simply feel different from other children independent of their exposure to social influence.

LGBTQIA+ children need the support of their parents and other family members (Carone et al., 2024). In a study of lesbian, gay, and heterosexual families investigating parenting and psychological adjustment during middle childhood, no differences were reported between family types for parenting stress, parent resilience, and parent psychological distress. Lesbian mothers reported higher parental acceptance and lower parental rejection, as well as higher parent positivity, than heterosexual parents (Carone et al., 2024). No differences were reported between gay fathers and heterosexual parents on the same variables. Children's psychological adjustment (operationalized as affective, behavioral, and cognitive dysregulation), irrespective of family type, was affected by levels of parental stress and parental rejection. Parents who were more supportive and accepting of their children were found to have children with better psychological adjustment. Parents who were less supportive and accepting had more dysregulated children. The authors noted that these results support the hypothesis that family processes are more critical than family structure in influencing child psychological adjustment (Carone et al., 2024).

Another study examined the unique experiences of parenthood among LGBTQIA+ parents related to navigating (in)visibility and stigma in various contexts (Goldberg, 2023). They identified several sociopolitical events (e.g., COVID-19, the presidency) that affected LGBTQIA+ parent families, particularly those with multiple marginalized statuses (Goldberg, 2023). The researchers argued that the current sociopolitical climate has also revealed axes of privilege and oppression that impact LGBTQIA+ parents' sense of belongingness in various contexts and social groups (Goldberg, 2023). However, despite these challenges, children's positive psychological health and adjustment were found to reflect the powerful role of context and family processes in the lives and adjustment of youth raised by LGBTQIA+ parents (Goldberg, 2023).

Children's adjustment is affected by their parents' mental health and parenting quality. Psychologically healthy parents who also possess competent parenting skills have children with fewer adjustment problems (McConnachie et al., 2021). McCurdy & Russell investigated children's perceived parental social support and psychological control and their effect on psychological and emotional adjustment such as depression (2023). Results indicated joint effects of social support and psychological control predicting youth depressive symptoms. A significant interaction was reported between parenting practices and the children's reported depressive symptoms. Less social support and higher psychological control predict higher levels of depressive symptoms (McCurdy & Russell, 2023).

Several studies have investigated the effects of parental acceptance or rejection among children of sexual minorities (Bebes et al., 2015; Bouris et al., 2010; D'Augelli et al., 2008). These studies and others not cited here found that higher perceived parental psychological control was associated with higher levels of adolescent psychopathology. Children and adolescents' perception of high maternal control was more strongly associated with adolescent psychopathology than children's perceived paternal control. Children and adolescents' perceived parental acceptance was not associated with unhealthy psychological symptoms. These general findings from these studies support the view that there is a damaging effect of perceived parental psychological control on gender diverse children and adolescents and a strong positive effect for children's perception of parental acceptance.

IMPORTANCE OF HEALTHY PEER GROUP RELATIONSHIPS

Evaluators need to gather information about each child's relationships with peer groups in their neighborhood, at school, and through social media. Evaluators should be attuned to the degree to which peer group consistently supports them. Recall the research cited about ingroup influences.

Gender diverse children are well served by developing supportive peer groups. Transgender children, for example, who live in their affirmed gender are often confronted with decisions regarding concealment and disclosure of their transgender identity (Alonso et al., 2024). Alonso et al. investigated groups of cisgender, gender-diverse, and siblings of gender-diverse children about transition disclosure and concealment. All groups were found to view disclosure and concealment positively. Gender-diverse children were found to hold greater acceptance of transition concealment and held stronger positive feelings toward transition concealment. All groups also reported that they expected transgender peers to be selective about who they disclosed to, placing greater value on trustworthiness and diverse friend groups in such decisions (Alonso et al., 2024). One conclusion from the Alonso et al. study was that regardless of gender identity, children tend to be sensitive to the potential costs of disclosure and are likely to support trans children in whatever path they choose in navigating decisions about disclosure and concealment.

Exposure to diverse friendship groups has been found to elaborate children's experiences and skillsets and these positive effects have been found to remain beyond childhood (Bennet et al., 2024). Among non-White children, children's friendship groups increased in diversity and ethnic diversity but decreased in gender and age diversity. Children's early friendship group diversity (i.e., children between 2–4 years old) was positively associated with greater diversity of their peer groups among older children (i.e., children around age 6; Bennet et al., 2024).

Evaluators should be mindful of the increased parenting skills or knowledge that may support gender diverse children. Gender diverse children often pose significant challenges to their parents, and this is especially true among parents who hold more traditional ideas about gender essentialism and gender role distribution of household responsibilities. In addition, most parents of gender diverse children have little to no experience with parenting models that help to guide their decision making, relationship development, and emotional adjustment.

CHILDREN TEACH THEIR PARENTS ABOUT GENDER DIVERSITY

Evaluators are wise to examine how parents learn about their children's gender diversity and their children's experiences of being teachers to their parents. In an aptly named article, "However I Talk About It, My Kids Tell Me I'm Doing It Wrong, " Darom describes research findings showing how parents of transgender and gender diverse children "relearn from their children to fulfill their parenting role" (2023, p. 827). Mothers of cisgender teenage children living in a "progressive region" of the United States (Darom, 2023, p. 827) were found to relearn gender to parent successfully. Mothers were found to rely on their children's "generational gender literacy" (Darom, 2023, p. 827) to learn new ways of thinking about gender and parenting. Mothers who were raised to think in terms of the stable nature of gender needed to reconceptualize gender as fluid. Children have been found to have greater access to individual and institutional-level resources that guide them toward better understanding and adaptation to new gender-related ideas. One result is that children become mentors and cultural resources for their mothers. Darom suggests that gender socialization might be more likely the result of cultural fluency rather than family roles.

EMOTIONAL CHALLENGES AMONG GENDER DIVERSE CHILDREN

Evaluators must investigate the past and present emotional and psychological issues faced by each gender diverse child and each parent's awareness of their child's past and present emotional and psychological concerns. Evaluators should explore whether each parent was supportive of their child becoming involved in groups, friendships, or in appropriate psychotherapeutic support and what, if any, steps each parent took to find support and information to assist in understanding their child's emotional and psychological challenges.

Gender diverse and transgender children have been found to face several challenges that include bullying (E. B. Gross et al., 2024), difficulties in school, and perceived injustices and discrimination (Horton, 2023). In a study of 30 parents whose children socially transitioned under the age of 11, three themes emerged: Gender diverse children were consistently challenged by the cisnormativity of their schools, the failure of the schools to protect gender diverse children, and evidence of educational injustice. These experiences were associated with heightened feelings of lack of safety and contributed to school dropouts and reported trauma (Horton, 2023). "Cisnormative attitudes normalize injustice, making it acceptable for trans children to lose access to education or to experience trauma in school" (Horton, 2023, p. 73).

The stress and trauma related to challenges faced by gender diverse children have been found to be related to stress-like alterations in brain function (Loso et al., 2023). Brain function was measured by blood oxygen level dependent (BOLD) signals during task-based functional magnetic resonance imaging (fMRI; Loso et al., 2023). Based upon findings that gender diversity is broadly associated with higher victimization and mental health disparities in children aged 9–10, Loso et al. investigated the functional brain correlates of this relationship to determine if gender-diverse youth show patterns of functional activity during an emotional task consistent with those of other populations that experience heightened stress (Loso et al., 2023).

Gender diversity was associated with changes in brain function (i.e., BOLD signals in the insula or fusiform gyrus), suggesting that gender diversity is related to greater parent and school-related stress. Higher levels of stress were also found to be related to elevated mental health problems. Gender diversity was reported to be associated with increased emotional and behavioral problems, as well as problems with their parents and school-related stress (Loso et al., 2023).

Researchers appear to have identified two groups of children who present as transgender. The first group of children—called early presenters—become aware of their gender identity at about the same time as their cisgendered peers. Early presenters are between the ages of 4 and 6 and describe always knowing their gender was different than what others have told them since they were born. Pubertal presenters are between the ages of 10 and 16. Their awareness of their gender identity as different from their assigned sex at birth emerged as their sexual orientation was developing and as their bodies were changing. It is very important for evaluators not to limit their investigation to these two groups, as children can explore their orientation and identity as they age.

There is no consensus among the professional psychological community defining "gender health" in children. Professional practice guidelines exist to assist practitioners in the treatment of gender diverse children, yet no consensus exists about how best to treat gender diverse children.

COMMUNICATION AND HEALTHY FAMILY FUNCTIONING

An area of family involvement often overlooked is the ways in which the parents have created an emotionally safe, supportive environment that allows for open family discussion between and among all family members, including grandparents and other extended family members. Evaluators should examine whether and how the parents or others in the family have contributed to the creation of an emotionally safe, supportive environment that allows for open family discussion. Exploring whether some family members struggle with such openness and its effect on the gender diverse child's experience of support from that family member is also an important area of evaluation.

Parent–child sex communication is a positive strategy for adolescent sexual health outcomes (Bond et al., 2023). Few studies have examined what prompts and impedes these conversations among parents of gay, bisexual, and queer (GBQ) adolescent sons. Bond et al. found that parents are likely to engage in sex communication once they established open communication with their child, accepted their child's sexual orientation, encouraged safe sex practices, and were knowledgeable about LGBTQIA+ issues. Parents who found it difficult to communicate with their adolescent sons were unable to engage in inclusive and comprehensive sex conversations resulting in the creation of barriers to effective sex-positive communication.

CHALLENGES OF SAME-SEX PARENT UNIONS

Although we have focused our attention on LGBTQIA+ children, we are aware of the challenges of LGBTQIA+ parent unions. Evaluators need to thoroughly examine the challenges, supports, and obstacles each LGBTQIA+ parent has faced. Couples often face gendered assumptions embedded in both the law and their social experiences of marriage and dissolution (Kim & Stein, 2018). These gender roles, typically associated with different-sex couples, may be projected onto same-sex couples by society and judges adjudicating relationship dissolutions. The gender-based differences in the social and legal experiences of various same-sex couples are likely to arise due to underlying gender dynamics affecting both same-sex and different-sex marriages. Interestingly, we have found no research examining these variables among parent unions of trans individuals.

Multiple events have aided in the increasing social acceptance of families formed by LGBTQIA+ individuals (Gato et al., 2021). First, social roles of men and women have been found to be increasingly flexible compared to the more rigid sex roles of decades past. Second, the civil rights movement, including the LGBTQIA+ movement, has been an important motivator in helping to reclaim individual and family rights of sexual and gender minority individuals. Third, reproductive technologies have made it possible for the birth of children without heterosexual intercourse. Fourth, same-sex marriage and same-sex parenting have been increasingly accepted (Gato et al., 2021).

Several recent studies have investigated parenthood among LGBTQIA+ parents. Studies have examined transformations in the family-of-origin's dynamics following the coming out among LGBTQIA+ individuals and subsequent transformation in the family-of-origin's dynamics following the transition to parenthood (Giovanardi et al., 2024). Other studies have revealed an increasing interest among gender diverse couples in their desire to have children (Baiocco & Laghi, 2013; Shenkman & Abramovitch, 2021; van Houten et al., 2020), planning for children (Park et al., 2020; Rothblum et al., 2024), transition to parenthood (Rubio et al., 2020), challenges of raising children (Giovanardi et al., 2024), changes in family of origin when a previously-rejected lesbian or gay individual has a child (Giovanardi et al., 2024), and the value of family and social support in raising children (Leal et al., 2021).

Family-of-Origin's Rejection or Acceptance of LGBTQIA+ Parenthood

Evaluators might explore whether or how the LGBTQIA+ parent's family-of-origin changed as a result of the parent's pregnancy or adoption and its effect on the family-of-origin's acceptance or rejection of their LBGTQIA+ adult child or child. Often, pregnancy and birth provide opportunities for the previously rejecting family-of-origin to repair the relationship strain and for the new grandparents to accept the child and LGBTQIA+ parent.

Giovanardi et al. (2024) examined transformations in family-of-origin's dynamics following the coming out among lesbian and gay parents and subsequent transformations in family-of-origin's dynamics following the transition to parenthood. They identified three core themes. One theme was parental rejection at coming out that included how their families judged based upon heteronormativity, shaping parental prejudices regarding homosexuality. A second theme was identifying the consequences of rejection for coming out, which reflected the family's internalized homophobia. Parental or family rejection was often accompanied by significant reduction in open communications, often characterized as "silence in communication" and relocations to move away from the parents. The third theme was a type of reunification. Previously rejecting parents of their adult-child's gender diversity were found to see their adult-child's pregnancy and birth as an opportunity for relational changes. These changes tended to reflect changes that occurred when gender-diverse parents' own parents became grandparents. The transition to parenthood facilitated the repair of long-standing relational ruptures and the strengthening of bonds with gender diverse families of origin (Giovanardi et al., 2024).

Desire to Have Children

When LGBTQIA+ parents separate and divorce, there are several emotional changes that are presented, among them the parent needing to alter the narrative they have developed over their lifetime about their desire to have a child and live with their partner forever. Several studies have examined lesbian and gay individuals desire to have children (Baiocco & Laghi, 2013; van Houten et al., 2020). Changes in the evolving social acceptance of LGBTQIA+ has led to increased interest in their role as parents (Gato et al., 2021). Parenthood aspiration is one area to be explored.

Gay and lesbian individuals reported a lower estimated likelihood of parenthood than their heterosexual counterparts. The likelihood of parenthood was related to psychological well-being indicators, and this association was moderated by sexual orientation. Interestingly, heterosexual individuals anticipating parenthood compared to their gay and lesbian counterparts were found to score lower on measures of depression and reported greater life satisfaction and happiness (Shenkman & Abramovitch, 2021). Shenkman and Abramovitch opined that among the possible reasons for the differences between the two groups was that gay and lesbian individuals' psychological well-being is affected by their awareness of discriminatory local policies concerning sexual minority rights in their quest to parenthood (2021).

For many lesbians and gay men, access to parenthood is difficult, uncertain, and varies geographically. Using focus group interviews, Park et al. investigated how 36 Midwestern gay, lesbian, and bisexual young adults without children perceive gay and lesbian parenting and their own parenthood prospects (Park et al., 2020). Themes included perceptions of legal and social barriers to parenthood, assumptions of the mounting economic obstacles and constraints surrounding parenthood, and concerns with navigating legal relatedness when establishing their families (Park et al., 2020).

Grigoropoulos (2022) investigated gay fathers' desires, motivations, and experiences of having a child. Participants' challenges and concerns regarding having and raising children also were explored. Three themes were identified: (a) gay fathers' innate motives to parent and gender role strains, (b) gay fathers' concerns about stigma that included acts of rejection due to sexual orientation and traditional gender roles, and (c) gay fathers' concerns about their children's social rejection due to their parents' sexuality.

Planning for Children

Along with investigating the values, beliefs, and emotional connection to their desire to have children, evaluators might also explore the steps taken to plan for children, the emotional investment each parent had in such planning, and the changes to their narrative about becoming a parent. If the parent is a nonbiological parent who has no legal standing as a parent in the eyes of the law, the evaluator needs to explore the potential power issues associated with that parent's potential loss of contact with the child they raised with the biological parent prior to the separation. Associated areas for investigation might be how changes in the power and control dynamics between the biological parent or nonbiological parent with no legal standing affect the children.

Several studies have investigated factors associated with planning for children among gay and lesbian future parents. Park et al. (2020) found that LGB individuals reported a higher anticipation of stigma upon parenthood than their heterosexual counterparts. Concerns about social and cultural stigmas fully mediated the association between being a sexual minority and lower parenting desires and intentions. These stigma concerns also were found to partially mediate the association between being a sexual minority and lower estimated likelihood of actually becoming a parent. Among the conclusions offered by Park et al. (2020) was that LGB are significantly affected by their likely awareness of prejudice and discrimination by local legislation that prohibits or impedes sexual minorities from pursuing parenthood.

In a study that examined prospective gay fathers, Underwood (2024) found that many gay fathers carefully prepared, planned, and anticipated their parenting roles and responsibilities. Some gay men prepare for years before they become parents. He reported that some gay men pursue surrogacy, express masculine competence, and draw upon scripts of conventional fatherhood. In comparison, gay men who pursued adoption experienced a disruption in their masculine competence and tended to reflect more on their potential inadequacies as parents. Underwood opined that many of these pressures on the journey to gay fatherhood might be reduced through a queer, antiracist, and feminist consciousness.

Transition to Parenthood

LGBTQIA+ parents invest the same emotional energy and excitement into becoming a parent as heterosexual parents. Separation and divorce changes expectation about how parenting their children will likely change. Similar to the potential concerns described in the previous section, evaluators are likely to need to explore similar dynamics within the separating and divorcing family. Both parents—whether the family is in a gender diverse relationship or not—will likely have significant emotional investments in becoming a parent.

Changes to their emotional investment in becoming a parent within a family system might need to be scrutinized. The evaluator should examine each parent's understanding of how changes to their day-to-day parenting would affect them, affect their former partner, and affect each of the children.

Rubio et al. (2020) explored parental feelings during pregnancy, feelings about the parental role, perceived parental competence, the enjoyment of parenthood, expressed warmth, and emotional over-involvement among heterosexual, lesbian, and gay first-time parents who conceived using assisted reproductive technologies. Compared with lesbian parents, heterosexual parents reported fewer positive feelings in early pregnancy. Gay male parents reported fewer positive feelings at the end of pregnancy compared to lesbian parents. Gay parents also reported more positive feelings about parenthood during the first postpartum weeks than heterosexual parents. Rubio et al. reported that family type and caregiver role did not interact to affect reported feelings, perceived competence, enjoyment, warmth, and involvement.

Leal et al. (2021) investigated the role of family-of-origin support among LGBTQIA+ individuals during and after pregnancy. Results found that many pregnant and recent parents developed closer relationships to the family-of-origin and a detachment from the LGBTQIA+ community in this stage of their life cycle. Family-of-origin social support received in the transition to parenthood appeared to affect not only the psychological well-being of these parents and prospective parents but also the quality of their relationships with different support networks (Leal et al., 2021).

Adler et al. (2023) studied gay fathers' postpregnancy responses by assessing their postpartum depression (PPD). The incidence of probable PPD among gay fathers was 12% compared with 8.8% reported in heterosexual fathers. Gay fathers were found to be somewhat more often affected by PPD. Mitigating the effects of gay father's PPD was high satisfaction with family support.

Fantus & Newman (2022) developed what they termed an enhanced family model intended to address the development of the procreative identities of gay men in same-sex relationships who decide to have children via surrogacy. Given the increased interest among gay men having children, Fantus and Newman's model was intended to examine surrogacy trajectories in the context of men's same-sex relationships that ranged from examining the motivation for having a child through postbirth experiences. They suggested three factors to be examined with same-sex partnered men as an avenue to support gay men's interest in having a child. The three themes were a) procreative consciousness, b) procreative responsibility, and c) procreative transitioning, including barriers that may exert a long-term impact on fathers in same-sex relationships (Fantus & Newman, 2022).

Challenges of Raising Children

It should come as no surprise that same-sex and heterosexual parents face unexpected challenges when raising children (Giovanardi et al., 2024). Evaluators should focus attention on each parent's identified challenges when raising each child and the steps they have taken to address those challenges. Gathering data about how each child perceives each parent's challenges and the steps the child observes to address those challenges might reveal a rich area of data that speaks to, among other things, the parent–child fit.

Fortunato et al. (2023) examined lesbian mothers, gay fathers, and heterosexual parents along several psychological dimensions in relationship to raising their children. In each family, both parents reported parenting stress, parent–child relational self-efficacy, parental control, dyadic coping, and their perception of their child's emotion regulation. Fortunato et al. reported no significant differences between family types in parenting stress and the use of a controlling parenting style. Lesbian mothers reported higher parent–child relational self-efficacy compared to heterosexual parents. Lesbian mothers also reported higher dyadic coping strategies than gay fathers. Children of gay fathers showed greater emotional regulation compared to children of heterosexual parents.

Unsurprisingly, across family types, higher levels of parenting stress and dyadic coping coupled with lower levels of parent–child relational self-efficacy were associated with lower child emotion regulation (Fortunato et al., 2023). Results were interpreted to suggest that children in middle childhood in each of the examined family types displayed better emotional regulation when their parents were rated as displaying greater effectiveness in the parent–child relationship and lower parenting stress and dyadic coping. Middle childhood children are best served when their parents cooperatively manage stressors while maintaining a balanced focus on their children's resources and autonomy.

Several recent studies have investigated whether children raised by gay and lesbian parents differ in their general developmental trajectories from children raised by heterosexual parents. Although there is a multi-decade history showing no substantial differences among children raised by gay and lesbian parents compared to heterosexual parents, there remains an unfounded belief that children raised by gay and lesbian parents face developmental challenges that children raised by heterosexual parents do not face (Cerqueira-Santos et al., 2021; Gould, 2006). The authors concluded that research findings have supported the view there are no significant differences in psychological adjustment or sexual and gender behavior when comparing children in heterosexual and homosexual families. What appears to drive the unsupported concerns is the ongoing misunderstanding of conceptions of homosexuality and the explanations given to the etiology of sexual orientation and the development of behaviors and gender identities (Cerqueira-Santos et al., 2021).

Examining issues related to the development of attachment, Carone et al. (2023) examined the attachment patterns among lesbian mothers, gay fathers, heterosexual parents, and their children. Carone et al. administered the Adult Attachment Interview (AAI) to assess the parents' attachment patterns and administered the Friends and Family Interview (FFI) to assess children's attachment patterns. Results were interpreted to indicate that the distribution of AAI patterns was similar across family types and did not significantly differ from AAI international and national normative data. That is, attachment patterns were similar among gay, lesbian, and heterosexual parents.

Children's FFI attachment patterns were interpreted to reveal no significant differences among the different family types and did not significantly differ from the FFI international and national normative data referring to middle childhood samples.

In all three family types, parents with greater AAI coherence of mind scores were positively associated with increased FFI attachment security scores in their children. Said differently, children develop healthier attachment security when their parents also display healthier attachment security regardless of family type (Carone et al., 2023).

Another study explored differences among gay, lesbian, and heterosexual family types. The McConnachie et al study included data from standardized interviews, observations, and questionnaires of parental mental health, parent–child relationships, and adolescent adjustment that were administered to parents, children, and teachers between 2016 and 2018. This is among the few studies that gathered data from independent third-party collateral informants.

Similar to other studies cited above, data analyses found few differences among family types. Over the course of the study that gathered data from families for several years, children's adjustment problems increased in all family types as children moved toward middle childhood, with better parenting quality and parental mental health associated with fewer adjustment problems (McConnachie et al., 2021). These data support the hypothesis that there are no differences in children's adjustment and developmental trajectories that are unique to gay and lesbian parents or the role of parental gender in child development (McConnachie et al., 2021).

Gay and lesbian families often are faced with questions about how to convey messages of gender conformity and nonconformity to their children. Researchers have examined how gay and lesbian parents convey these messages and also have examined how their children respond to these messages (Bergstrom-Lynch, 2020). Two interrelated themes were identified that influenced how LGBTQIA+ parents' approached conversations about gender conformity and nonconformity. The first concern that affected LGBTQIA+ parents' approach to conversations with their children focused on the extent to which LGBTQIA+ parents experienced gender policing growing up, and how these lessons carry over into their interactions with their own children. The second concern that affected LGBTQIA+ parents' approach to conversations with their children was how LGBTQIA+ parents at times challenge gender conformity through their parenting practices even as they express ambivalence about gender nonconformity and transgender identities (Bergstrom-Lynch, 2020).

We have reviewed several studies that demonstrate that family type is a nonsignificant factor in children's development and that family processes are more strongly associated with individual outcomes than family structure. Despite these research findings, myths and stigmas continue to influence LGBTQIA+ parents' sense of safety and acceptance in society in general (Farr & Vázquez, 2020). Adoptive gay and lesbian parents' stigma experiences have been found to be associated with mental health, parenting competence, and parent–child relationships (Farr & Vázquez, 2020). In this study, gay, lesbian, and heterosexual parents completed assessments of mental health symptoms, adoption stigma, and perceived childcare competence. These parents also reported on their experiences of homonegative microaggressions. The children of these gay, lesbian, and heterosexual parents responded to a measure about their relationships with parents. Results revealed no significant differences as a function of parental sexual orientation and gender except that lesbian mothers, heterosexual mothers, and gay fathers all reported higher parenting competence than heterosexual fathers (Farr & Vázquez, 2020). Although parents' mental health did not significantly predict parent–child relationship quality, parents' perceived competence and gay and lesbian parents' current homonegative microaggression experiences did affect their mental health. Gay and lesbian parent–child relationships compared to heterosexual parent–child relationships were rated as showing greater parenting competence was related to greater parent–child closeness and more microaggressions were related to lower parent–child closeness.

Little research has directly analyzed the ways in which gay-fathered families navigate experiences stemming from the fact that their family type stands out and challenges heteronormative family ideologies. McKee (2022) investigated how gay fathers handle the challenges of social stigmas about their parenthood. Results revealed that fathers tended to be open and honest in addressing family, friends, and strangers who questioned or commented on their families. Many of these fathers were active in reaching out to their children's schools, urging these schools to have books and other media normalizing and explaining nonconforming families (McKee, 2022). Fathers were also found to challenge school routines that were organized around heteronormative models of education and activities.

In light of the unfounded concerns that children raised by LGBTQIA+ parents face challenges to health development compared to children raised by heterosexual parents, another question is whether their children approach notions of parenthood and becoming a parent are different from children from heterosexual family systems. Goldberg et al. (2024a) found that teenagers adopted by lesbian, gay, and heterosexual couples generally envisioned parenthood for themselves. Plans for becoming a parent varied by minoritized gender, sexual, and racial or ethnic identities. The takeaway was that adolescents who are thinking about becoming a parent and think about parenthood, in general, develop relatively independent ideas that are mostly independent from their parents' notions of parenting and parenthood.

PUBLIC POLICY CHALLENGES

No discussion of the challenges faced by LGBTQIA+ individuals is complete without some comment about current debates affecting public policy (Goldberg et al., 2024b). Over the course of the past several years, there have been legislative initiatives in several states addressing and often attempting to curtail many of the liberty interests that have been rightfully achieved by LGBTQIA+ people, including the apparent embedded threat by Justice Clarence Thomas to guide the Supreme Court toward revisiting the U.S. Supreme Court decision about same-sex marriage.

Here we focus on research that has examined the effect on the emotional well-being among LGBTQIA+ individuals who live in jurisdictions in which laws have been passed that ban schools from discussing sexual orientation and gender identity and expression, such as Florida's Parental Rights in Education ("Don't Say Gay") law and reinforce structural stigma for LGBTQIA+ people. Goldberg et al. (2024b) argue that socially imposed structural stigmas likely affect LGBTQIA+ individuals' identity disclosure or concealment processes. Socially imposed structural stigmas also affect LGBTQIA+ individuals' desire to stay in or move out of states that enact these policies.

Goldberg et al. (2024b) studied a sample of LGBTQIA+ parents who reside in Florida immediately following the expansion of Florida's "Don't Say Gay" law from K–3 to include all grades. Using thematic analyses of open-ended responses provided nuance to participants' experiences, results revealed that parents who reported higher levels of bias, identified as trans or nonbinary, and reported that signifiers of LGBTQIA+ inclusion were removed from school were more likely to report decreased outness. Those with higher socioeconomic status and those who reported no removal of LGBTQIA+ books from school were less likely to report decreased outness. LGBTQIA+ parents described worries about the law that were associated with both desire and perceived likelihood of moving. White LGBTQIA+ parents were more likely to report a desire to move. Goldberg et al. concluded that the effects of LGBTQIA+ laws have implications for LGBTQIA+ parents and families by affecting their ability to live authentically and maintain residence in their communities.

CHALLENGES FACED BY LGBTQIA+ INDIVIDUALS IN FAMILY COURT

Rebecca M. Stahl's (2024) recent article discusses challenges faced by LGBTQIA+ individuals in family court systems and offers strategies for legal professionals to be more affirming. It highlights the ongoing discrimination and trauma experienced by LGBTQIA+ clients despite recent advancements in LGBTQIA+ rights. Stahl's article focuses on three sections: the specific issues LGBTQIA+ people face in family courts, the unique aspects of the legal system that may seem more accepting than they are, and practical ways for lawyers, judges, and evaluators to support LGBTQIA+ clients. The article emphasizes the importance of understanding clients' identities, the emotional impact of legal proceedings, and the need for trauma-informed practices (see Chapter 11). Rebecca M. Stahl also provides specific recommendations for creating an inclusive environment, such as using affirming language, understanding implicit biases, and advocating for legal changes to better protect LGBTQIA+ individuals. Rebecca M. Stahl emphasizes the importance that LGBTQIA+ clients feel seen, understood, and supported throughout their legal proceedings. When evaluators make recommendations for future treatment, evaluators should carefully consider access to safer and gender-affirming care.

LESSONS FOR CHILD PARENTING PLAN EVALUATORS

We believe that organizing information about family systems using the ecological model provides a wider, more comprehensive picture of family dynamics than focusing on the individual level of analysis in which the evaluator is examining only the child or the parent. An LGBTQIA+ child will best be understood within the complex psychological and social dynamics in which the child lives. As we have argued throughout this book, the best way to understand family dynamics at all levels of family functioning that might affect a child is through the use of the ecological model.

During the evaluation, we recommend using portions of the Wright-Constantine Structured Cultural Interview (Wright et al., 2023), particularly the section on gender and gender identity and sexual orientation. The Wright-Constantine Structured Cultural Interview provides first order and follow-up questions. For example, if the parent identifies as transgender, genderqueer, nonbinary, or gender nonconforming, you may ask:

- How has being [transgender, genderqueer, nonbinary, their own words or label] affected you?
- How do you think it affects the way others interact with you?
- What was it like growing up [however they identify] in your culture, community, and family?

We then encourage evaluators to expand their interviews to include the family system using the ecological model we've discussed. As discussed in our chapters discussing interviewing in PPEs, evaluators must be cognizant of the need to create an interview context in which parents, children and collaterals feel safe enough to respond openly and honestly to relevant inquiries. Evaluators also need to embrace the investigative model (W. G. Austin & Kirkpatrick, 2004), seeking detailed information sufficiently comprehensive to paint a picture of individuals, dyadic relationships, family interactions, extended family sways, community pressures, and ethnic, religious, and cultural influences.

CONCLUSION

Court decisions about custody and access frequently fail to consider everyday issues that are integral to the experiences of children exploring their identity and sexuality. For example, when a child identifies as transgender, it is crucial for evaluators to assess how each parent supports the child's gender expression.

This includes examining factors such as clothing choices, hairstyle, physical appearance, preferred names, and pronouns. A parent's ability to affirm and respect their child's identity can significantly impact the child's mental health and sense of belonging.

Evaluators must also be vigilant in identifying potential biases—both their own and those present within the family dynamics. Implicit biases can subtly influence assessments and recommendations, potentially disadvantaging a parent who is supportive of a child's gender exploration if the evaluator lacks understanding or holds preconceived notions about gender and sexuality.

Another area of specialized training is understanding the impact of family dynamics on each person in the family system as well as the impact of relevant social systems outside of the family, i.e., extended family, school, activities. Awareness of how family and others involved with the family accept or reject gender diversity within the family influences child outcomes, with attention to the psychological effects of affirmation versus invalidation. Evaluators must also be aware of the unique stressors faced by LGBTQIA+ parents and youth, including minority stress, bullying, and societal stigma, and how these factors intersect with family law issues.

By addressing these areas, forensic evaluators and other professionals can make more informed recommendations that truly reflect the best interests of the child. As the literature in PPEs continues to address issues of gender identity and sexual orientation, it is imperative that the legal and mental health communities commit to ongoing education and reflective practice to better serve diverse families.

IV

DATA COLLECTION AND INTEGRATION

10

Using Story Development Principles to Guide Data Collection and Integration

In this chapter, we discuss the components of story development as a critical aspect of good interviewing, good report writing, and effective oral testimony. Stories resonate because they connect the audience emotionally with the experiences of each family member and with the experiences of the family. Stories frame personal and family experiences at a different level, connecting the facts of the specific case with universal themes that include, but are not limited to, love, family, struggles, triumphs, challenges, birth, death, loss, friendship, and celebrations. When we frame the family's situation accordingly, we communicate on a different level.

However, without knowing the questions that need to be answered, it is difficult to construct a compelling story. Well-crafted questions identified early in the evaluation process allow for efficient, targeted questioning of parents, children, and collaterals. Well-crafted questions also provide the evaluator with a roadmap toward building a compelling understanding of the family. Each question defines a road to follow during interviewing. The evaluator's task is to link each answer to a specific question and then to weave the answers to each question into a coherent narrative.

In the world of parenting plan disputes, developing a story is most often associated with writing a report, if it is considered at all. However, we suggest that the elements of good story development are useful ideas to apply to both data gathering *and* testifying in court. In the following section, we suggest that when applying story development factors to the nature and quality of information obtained from parents, children, and collaterals, the evaluator will develop

https://doi.org/10.1037/0000474-011
Parenting Plan Evaluations: An Evidence-Informed Approach to Child Custody, by J. W. Gould and C. M. Mulchay

a more comprehensive and complete picture, and the completeness of the picture would likely result in a more cohesive and compelling narrative to present to the court. Thus, we place this chapter at the beginning of Part IV rather than at the end of the book. We believe the principles of story development can effectively guide parenting plan evaluators in their collection and integration of data.

SENTENCES AND STORY DEVELOPMENT

We begin at the most basic level of story development: the sentence. Sentences have an internal structure (Rumelhart, 1975). Most of us have been taught in grade school or middle school how to analyze the structure of sentences. We have been taught differences among verbs, adverbs, adjectives, nouns, and other singular components that, when put together in a proper manner, make up the structure of a well-formed sentence.

Stories, too, have an internal structure (Rumelhart, 1975). However, academics who have studied the underlying structure of our language have found that few, if any, have identified a reliable way to describe a general structure for stories that will distinguish strings of sentences that form stories from strings of sentences that do not.

It appears that there is some higher level of organization that takes place in stories that does not take place in strings of sentences. Individual sentences themselves can serve as arguments for higher order predicates leading to the formation of more complex sentences, yet what defines a sentence or series of sentences that combine to form a coherent story has no reliable methodology. Said differently, stories are not a combination of pairwise relationships among sentences. Strings of sentences appear to combine into psychological wholes. When the interviewees make statements, the evaluator looks for an underlying story that unifies the ideas covered in individual sentences and works toward developing a coherent narrative.

We believe it is important to keep in mind that *how* a person tells a story often reveals nothing about who they are as a parent or anything about the nature and quality of the parent–child relationship. In other words, the individual statements made by an interviewee may not convey an accurate picture of their parenting and it might not convey an accurate or coherent narrative about the parent–child relationship. Certainly, how a parent communicates clearly with the other parent is often a factor in distinguishing effective from ineffective parent-to-parent communication. However, we wish to spend a few paragraphs addressing the importance of evaluators monitoring style over substance.

As psychologists, we have been taught the importance of clear communication. We have also been taught to recognize that the responsibility of the meaning of the communication lies with the communicator and not the listener. This notion of communicator responsibility for communication comes from our training in family systems and other psychotherapy-based training. However, when engaged in parenting plan evaluations (PPEs), we suggest that as the listener, it is the evaluator who is responsible for taking steps to ensure that the communicator's meaning is properly understood.

PROVIDING INTERVIEWEES WITH FEEDBACK ON THEIR NARRATIVE

One component of ensuring that evaluators accurately understand the parent, child, or collateral informant's statements is to repeat out loud that which is being discussed. Interviewing in such a manner might slow down the pace of the interview, however we believe that providing immediate feedback to the person being interviewed helps to correct misunderstandings as they might occur.

Brodsky and Goldenson (2022) emphasize the importance of providing the interviewee with immediate feedback about their narrative. The feedback serves to support the interviewee's need to be heard and understood. For example: "Am I correct that you spend time with your child helping them with homework every night? It sounds like it's important to you to be there for your child? Tell me how this is important?"

The feedback also provides an opportunity to slow down the pace of information gathering, providing opportunities for the interviewee to gain control over potentially powerful emotions being triggered by the interview. In the example above, it is likely that asking how doing homework with the child is important might raise powerful emotions. The evaluator can slow down the pace of the interview, change the nature and type of questions being asked, and provide opportunities for the parent to regain a sense of control over the examples being disclosed.

When the person being interviewed uses English in an unusual or idiosyncratic manner, repeating the interviewee's statements aloud provides the evaluator an opportunity to obtain feedback about the intended meaning of the communication and also an opportunity to reframe the communication into a sentence structure that reflects the evaluator's meaning structure. That is, repeating sentences aloud provides a methodology to create meaningful sentence structures that the evaluator and the interviewee can agree upon and, as a result, increases the likelihood that subsequent sentence strings will create a more coherent story (as discussed later).

MINIMIZING BIAS BASED ON VERBAL PRESENTATION OR APPEARANCE

Another important aspect of our proposal to repeat sentences is to help the evaluator identify how attributions about the interviewee based upon verbal presentation might be affecting how the evaluator judges the information from the interviewee. In Chapter 7, we discuss the *fundamental attribution error* and the ways in which observers make personality attributions compared to participants who make attributions about environmental obstacles. Most, if not all, of us make judgments about a person based upon a variety of factors that include how a person uses language. Often people make judgements about a person's intelligence, educational level, and overall competence based upon verbal presentation and the organization and coherence of their story.

We wish to stress that presentation is often unrelated to parenting competence. We also wish to stress that evaluators need to be continuously on alert for how the attributions made about a parent based on irrelevant contextual information such as sentence construction or story construction might bias the evaluator's view of the parent or bias the importance or relevance of the child or collateral informant's information.

Parenting plan evaluators tend to be educated and are more likely to make more positive judgments about interviewees perceived to be educated. The attributions we make about people we judge as being similar to ourselves might lead to untested assumptions about parenting and caretaking. Evaluators need to be aware of such predictable yet potentially biasing assumptions.

THE PROCESS OF DEVELOPING STORIES

Studies of storytelling development focus on four factors. Good stories are characterized by completeness, coherence, uniqueness, and goodness of fit. Each of these is further defined below, creating a template for how to construct a story.

Our interest in storytelling stems from the importance of narrative in our work as evaluators and attorneys. A good story—defined as a story that is compelling, consistent, and believable—is the core of a good evaluation. It is also the core of a good presentation of evidence and of an increased likelihood that the judge will find the story more probative than other stories presented at trial.

Our discussion about the development of stories is based upon research examining jurors and jury decision making. Whether you are an evaluator, a parent involved in a PPE, an attorney reviewing a report, or a judge listening to testimony, each person constructs a mental representation of the evidence and its implications. How each person puts together the representations to create a narrative is critical to the ways in which the story narrative is presented to and understood by others. We believe the value in understanding the construction of effective stories lies in understanding the social science research about how people create narratives that represent the stories they wish to present.

Pennington and Hastie (1990) found three tasks that jurors employ when developing a story of a case. The first step is the imposition of a summary structure on the information. In the case of a parenting plan evaluator, we suggest that evaluators are engaged in a continually developing summary structures that change as more and more information is brought to their attention. Pennington and Hastie described this initial narrative development as a means to manage the extensive amount of information being presented in testimony.

They found jurors tended to develop explanatory models of what had happened to produce the testimony presented at trial. We see parallels between how jurors learn to manage and make sense of evidence over the course of a trial and the ways in which evaluators take in information from multiple sources during the PPE process.

The second step of story development is a type of sorting process. As stories develop, we make decisions about facts that appear to be consistent with the emerging narrative and facts that appear to be inconsistent with the emerging narrative. Whether we are aware or not, we tend to place some information in one basket that is viewed as more important than other information. The less important information might be placed in different baskets reserved for information that is less important, less compelling, and less interesting. The trick is to remember in which basket we placed each piece of information because as more and more information comes under scrutiny, the evaluator needs to continuously reconsider earlier obtained information against the newly acquired information.

The third step is putting together the information that forms a coherent narrative. In our bias chapter (Chapter 7), we discussed coherence theory. We discussed how the development of a story narrative might be affected by the ways in which we integrate information into a coherent narrative. Human beings have a strong need to develop a consistent, logical narrative. The natural need for coherence in a narrative may affect how pieces of evidence are strung together. A narrative that allows for a coherent assimilation of information may lead an evaluator to place greater weight on the interpretation of that information relative to the value of the information, even if the original value placed on the information was fair, balanced, and free from bias.

MINIMIZING CONFIRMATION BIAS

Evaluators should be mindful of the need to check and recheck each basket that contains information we assign different weights. What must be understood is that failure to develop a consistent way of examining past information in light of new information is a critical step in challenging the potential power of earlier summaries in creating a coherent narrative that guides our data collection and data integration.

This is no easy task. One way that might help avoid getting stuck in a story narrative that is coherent, logical, and feels right yet ignores reasonable alternative narratives is to write out different story lines. This is essentially a version of hypothesis formation. If one set of facts serves as a basis for a coherent story, develop alternative stories using a combination of facts from different baskets to challenge the coherent, logical, feel-good narrative that has guided your thinking.

As Pennington and Hastie (1990) found, jurors tended to construct only one of the possible stories without considering reasonable, alternative, plausible stories that fit the evidence as well as their personal favorites. Other jurors were found to construct more than one story yet rejected all but the best account. Pennington and Hastie reported that jurors tended to engage in deliberate efforts to match their initial explanatory model against the evidence at the end of the trial, seeking a best fit between the verdict categories and their stories. We believe that there is cause for concern if evaluators follow a similar model. The potential power of the initial explanatory model might serve as a confirmatory bias filter. For example, recall our example from Chapter 7 in which an evaluator focuses their inquiry on confirming alienation while ignoring data that may provide reasonable alternative hypotheses. That is why we are proposing the development of multiple narratives that rely on different combinations of facts drawn from each of the information baskets. Only after the evaluator has developed and critically examined the cohesiveness of each narrative should the evaluator then turn to the question of goodness-of-fit with regards to the ways in which the accumulated information fits the best narrative.

DETERMINING THE BEST NARRATIVE

How does one evaluate the "best" narrative? Pennington and Hastie (1991) suggest four certainty principles that govern which story will be accepted by a juror, which decision will be selected, and the confidence or level of certainty with which a decision will be made. These four certainty principles are coverage, coherence, uniqueness, and goodness-of-fit.

Coverage refers to which story accounts for the evidence presented to the evaluator. The greater the coverage of the story, the more likely the story will be accepted as a trustworthy explanation of the accumulated data. A story that leaves much of the evidence unexplained or unaccounted for is likely to be judged as a less correct explanation of the events under scrutiny. Less coverage will likely affect the overall confidence in the story as an accurate reflection of the events.

A story's *coherence* also affects the confidence one has in the trustworthiness of the story as an accurate reflection of the events under scrutiny. Coherence is composed of three components: consistency, plausibility, and completeness. A story is consistent when it does not contain internal contradictions. A story is plausible to the extent that it corresponds to the evaluator's knowledge about what happens in the real world and does not contradict that knowledge. A story is complete when the expected story has all of its parts. Missing information or a lack of plausible inferences about one or more major components of the story structure will decrease confidence in the explanation. "Thus, the coherence of the explanation reflects the consistency of the explanation with itself and with world knowledge, and the extent to which parts of the explanation can be inferred or assembled" (Pennington & Hastie, 1991, p. 528).

The third component is *uniqueness*. If more than one story is judged coherent, then the stories will lack uniqueness. If there is more than one coherent explanation of the information, belief in any one of them over the other will be lessened. For example, suppose a parenting plan evaluator presents a coherent psychological opinion suggesting that one parent is more suitable due to stability. However, another expert provides a different but equally coherent opinion favoring the other parent. The uniqueness of either evaluation diminishes, making it harder for the court to decide based solely on either expert.

In another example, an expert witness testifies that a child's trauma symptoms are due to a parent's deliberate attempts to undermine the child's relationship with the other parent. Another expert provides an equally coherent explanation linking the symptoms to genuine abuse by the other parent. The court may struggle to determine which explanation is most useful.

Goodness-of-fit refers to the degree to which a story best fits the narrative being presented to the evaluator and the goodness-of-fit of that story with answers to the specific questions that guide the evaluation. For example, in a high-conflict divorce, a child refuses to see one parent. One parent argues the child is being alienated. The other argues that the child's reluctance stems from past emotional abuse. If the child's statements and behavioral history align more with a response to trauma rather than external influence, estrangement has a better goodness-of-fit.

Another example of goodness-of-fit involves a custody evaluator who is assessing which parent provides the most stable environment. One parent claims that they are the more nurturing caregiver, but this story does not align with documented instances of neglect. The other parent's narrative, supported by school records and therapist reports, better fits the overall picture of the child's well-being. The latter narrative has a stronger goodness-of-fit.

Story meanings are not static. Evaluators make multiple causal and intentional inferences about the meaning of information and the weight assigned to that information at different stages of information gathering. Causal reasoning begins and continues throughout the evaluation process with subsequent analyses building upon and challenging previous tentatively developed story lines.

The takeaway from this research is for evaluators to continuously check with the person being interviewed that the meaning of the story is properly understood. The evaluator should also actively ask about gaps or missing puzzle pieces. How the evaluator puts the puzzle pieces of the interview together might be different from the intention of the person being interviewed. The most direct and efficient way to control for any potential misunderstanding is to explain to the interviewee the information obtained from the interview and the meaning assigned to that information.

UNDERLYING THEORY OF SCIENCE GUIDING STORY DEVELOPMENT

The underlying assumption that guides the Pennington and Hastie work as well as our attempt to import this model into parenting plan assessment knowledge is that knowledge is constructive. Whether a juror or an evaluator, we propose that people engage in active, constructive, comprehension processes. These processes help to organize, integrate, elaborate, and interpret the nature of the information throughout the gathering of evidence.

Like jurors, evaluators are presented with large amounts of information. Information is presented from a variety of different sources and is presented over several days. The information presented to an evaluator is disconnected, presented in nonsequential, often disorganized presentations from parents, children, collateral witnesses, submitted documents, and records. There is no temporal or causal order to the ways in which information is presented to an evaluator.

The explanatory model that serves to organize information is based, in part, on reasoning from world knowledge that each evaluator brings to the task and from the evidence gathered during the evaluation process. Based upon the world knowledge that we bring to our work, some story elements are accepted as true directly on the basis of their appearance. That is, we tend to make credibility judgments about information presented based upon how we understand the world to work. Again, this is a giant warning sign. Below are two examples.

The first example finds a parent involved in a PPE claiming that the other parent is alienating the child. The evaluator, based on their knowledge of attachment theory and child development, assesses whether the child's rejection aligns more with alienation or a reasonable response to prior neglect or abuse. If the evaluator has a bias toward alienation theories, they may overweight the claim. (See Chapter 20 for more on parent–child contact problems.)

A second example is when an evaluator testifies about the impact of domestic violence on children. The judge, based on world knowledge and past cases, may accept the testimony more readily if it aligns with their understanding of trauma effects. However, if the judge lacks trauma-informed training, they may incorrectly assume that children "naturally recover" from exposure to abuse.

Evaluators cannot change how human beings process information, but they can be alert to how one's world knowledge can influence initial judgments of what does and does not make sense. That is, evaluators need to be vigilant about how they assign weight to different information and place the information into different buckets based solely on one's life experience.

The relevance of events depends on how each fact is interpreted in relation to its causal connection with other occurrences. The incorporation of additional evidence, inferred events, and causal links within a narrative arises from various deductive and inductive reasoning processes applied to both evidence and general knowledge. Analyses of inference chains leading to story events demonstrate that intermediate conclusions are formed through converging lines of reasoning, drawing on deductions from world knowledge, analogies to real and hypothetical experiences, and reasoning by contradiction (Pennington & Hastie, 1991).

Recall that we defined coherence theory as the idea that people judge the truthfulness of information based on how well it fits within a coherent story or framework rather than on objective accuracy (see Chapter 7). When different pieces of information align and reinforce each other, they are perceived as more credible, even if they are inaccurate. This can lead to confirmation bias, where individuals favor evidence that supports their existing beliefs while dismissing contradictory information. In a sense, Pennington and Hastie were articulating an early version of cohesion theory. We would add to their explanation that evaluators' analyses of inference chains are also affected by the theoretical models that guide their evaluation work, the professional and scientific knowledge of the discipline that the evaluator relies upon, their previous experiences with similar cases, and the degree to which the evaluator consults with colleagues to challenge their case formulations and opinions.

CONCLUSION

In PPEs, the application of story development principles enhances the evaluator's ability to collect, integrate, and present information in a way that is both comprehensive and compelling. By understanding the structure of story development—how information is framed, interpreted, and synthesized—evaluators can gather data that construct narratives that better reflect the complexities of family dynamics.

We believe that understanding the elements of story development helps in several areas of forensic mental health practice. During their data gathering phase, parenting plan evaluators can incorporate the various elements of story development in reviewing the nature and substance of information gathered from parents, children, and collateral informants. This will lead to more thorough interviews and a greater depth of data. During their report writing, parenting plan evaluators can incorporate the various elements of story development in creating coherent and compelling narratives about each child and each parent's experiences within the family. As we present throughout this book, it is also important for evaluators to be transparent and identify limitations. Parenting plan evaluators and other expert witnesses can incorporate the various elements of story development as they prepare for deposition and trial testimony, creating narratives about the family system and opinions about how the court can best address their unique concerns.

Throughout this chapter, we have emphasized the importance of minimizing bias, ensuring accurate communication, and considering multiple narratives before deciding which storyline has the strongest support among the variety of data collected in the evaluation process. The process of developing a well-supported narrative requires careful organization of specific information, careful organization of that information around each of the story development factors, critical examination of assumptions, and a continuous reassessment of how individual pieces of data fit into the broader context looked at through multiple, alternative perspectives.

Solid story development requires careful organization of specific information. This means collecting and structuring relevant facts, observations, and data in a logical sequence. For example, a parenting plan evaluator systematically compiles interviews, psychological test results, and school records to build a comprehensive case assessment. The evaluator must organize the gathered facts according to key elements such as context, chronology, causality, and emotional impact.

Solid story development also requires structuring information around story development factors. These elements are then organized around the four story development factors: completeness, coherence, uniqueness, and goodness-of-fit. For example, when an expert witness presents findings on a child's resistance to spending time with a parent, the expert structures the narrative by outlining the timeline of interactions, behavioral patterns, and observed psychological effects on the child. Once outlined, the expert then reviews the information organizing it around its completeness, coherence, uniqueness, and goodness of fit.

The next step is to critically examine assumptions. Look at the underlying assumptions in the opinions. Evaluate whether the underlying premises are supported by evidence rather than biases. Consider how alternative perspectives might provide reasonable explanations of the data. Decide which opinions and the assumptions upon which the opinions are based have the most support within the data. For example, a court-involved therapist might question whether a child's resistance to visiting a parent stems from actual mistreatment, external influences, or some other reason, rather than assuming one explanation is correct. The evaluator must be continuously reassessing the data and the opinions that flow from the data by examining multiple perspectives. We have encouraged evaluators to look at information from different angles, considering alternative explanations, and refining conclusions based on new data.

Ultimately, the goal of incorporating story development principles into PPEs is not to create a subjective or persuasive account, but to present a fair, structured, and evidence-based narrative that supports sound decision making. By recognizing the influence of narrative construction on our perceptions, evaluators can strive for greater objectivity, clarity, and accuracy in their assessments, thereby ensuring that the best interests of the children involved remain the focal point of the evaluation process.

11

Procedural Variables in Forensic Interviewing

In this chapter, we discuss the current literature on forensic interviewing applied to parenting plan evaluations (PPEs). Our primary focus in this chapter is to integrate mainstream forensic psychological literature into our discussion of how to approach forensic interviewing. We discuss forensic interviewing in general and provide an interview protocol to be considered when interviewing parents, children (especially young children), and collaterals.

We have broken our discussion of forensic interviewing into multiple chapters. Most literature addressing forensic interviewing of children focuses on event-specific concerns such as allegations of maltreatment. We suggest that many of the ideas in the forensic interviewing of children when there are allegations of maltreatment are also useful to guide parenting plan evaluators in their interviewing of children, parents, and collaterals.

Interviewing is a core aspect of mental health examination in clinical and forensic activities and has been characterized as a conversation in which one party obtains verbal and nonverbal information from another person for a specific purpose. Interviews are most often one-on-one exchanges, but they can be conducted with more than one person. They can be conducted over the phone, using telehealth (e.g., Zoom, Google Meet), in the natural environment, in a hospital, in a school, in a therapist's office, in a parent's home, in a child's room, on a playground, or in a forensic evaluator's office. Forensic interviews are

---

Portions of this chapter are adapted from *The Art and Science of Child Custody Evaluations*, by J. W. Gould & D. A. Martindale, 2007, Guilford Press. Copyright 2007 by the Guilford Press. Adapted with permission.

https://doi.org/10.1037/0000474-012
Parenting Plan Evaluations: An Evidence-Informed Approach to Child Custody, by J. W. Gould and C. M. Mulchay

most often preplanned, deliberate, semistructured, and are conducted in a prearranged and organized setting (J. Davies, 2019).

LIMITATIONS OF WHAT WE KNOW ABOUT INTERVIEWING IN PARENTING PLAN EVALUATIONS

There is consensus in the field of PPEs about the importance of multiple interviews with each parent (Ackerman et al., 2019; Ackerman & Pritzl, 2011; Saini, 2008). Over the course of the 40+ years in which we find survey data about how evaluators approach their evaluation task, data show an increase in the number of hours evaluators devote to parent interviews (Ackerman et al., 2019), suggesting increased interest in gathering more information from parents. There is no consensus, however, about what areas are most relevant to investigate during parent interviews, the number of interviews to be conducted, the value of joint interviews conducted during the evaluation process, and the amount of time devoted to each interview.

Some information may be gleaned from survey data indicating the average number of interviews with parents (Ackerman et al., 2019), but these survey studies do not provide data about what to ask during interviews with each parent, how long each interview should last, or the use or value of conducting joint interviews sometime during the evaluation process. The Association of Family and Conciliation Courts (AFCC) PPE guidelines come the closest to a professional consensus, stating that, "Evaluators should ensure that significant issues and allegations raised by one party are brought to the attention of the other party or parties and they are given the opportunity to respond so the evaluator has balanced information about the issue" (2022, p. 18).

As we will discuss below, the general consensus in the field is that a forensic interview differs from a clinical interview, partly in the degree to which the evaluator controls and directs the interview (S. A. Greenberg & Shuman, 1997).

THE FACTFINDING APPROACH VERSUS THE STENOGRAPHIC APPROACH

A relevant, relatively unexamined area of parent interviews is the degree to which an evaluator becomes a factfinder rather than a stenographer. We differentiate the importance of interview strategies based on an investigative model of information gathering (W. G. Austin & Kirkpatrick, 2004) rather than passively recording parent stories with little, if any, interest in understanding further the relevance of the stories. The latter, passive approach to information gathering has been termed the stenographic approach of assessment: The evaluator records what is said with little attention to mining the stories for relevant information, little attention to including only relevant information, and little concern about including hearsay, double hearsay, and other forms of irrelevant information that can influence the reader of the report (Martindale & Gould, 2012).

In contrast, the fact-finding approach of assessment demands the employment of different data-gathering techniques to marshal information relevant to answering the specific questions identified by the scope of the court's order. Objectives for the fact-finding approach may include gathering information intended to assess parenting capacity and competence, evaluating child attachment and needs, identifying potential risk factors (e.g., substance abuse, domestic violence, mental health concerns), understanding coparenting dynamics and parental conflict, or determining the feasibility of joint custody or relocation.

In the fact-finding approach, each parenting plan evaluator must pull together information about their specific issues of concern to the court. For example, relocation disputes, discussed more thoroughly in Chapter 23, may require addressing specific statutory factors and following assessment protocols developed specifically for relocation risk assessment (W. G. Austin, 2000b). High-conflict cases may emphasize gathering data on past and present coparenting behaviors, gatekeeping analyses, and children's exposure to parental conflict. Finally, allegations of abuse or parent–child contact problems may require specialized forensic assessment methodologies.

In the fact-finding approach, a forensic interviewer must have the ability to disturb conversational momentum. When those being interviewed become invested in discussing matters not directly linked to the issues that have created the need for the evaluation, the forensic practitioner is expected to re-focus the discussion so that the issues with direct bearing on the matters to be adjudicated will be dealt with.

The factfinding approach also requires the use of active listening, as opposed to passive listening. A listener can be diligent and alert yet still be passive—taking in the spoken words as a court stenographer might. An active listener views many statements as invitations to seek clarification or amplification, to challenge, and to inquire regarding the means by which information presented might be verified (Martindale & Gould, 2012). For example, when a parent states during an interview that they have experienced domestic violence, the evaluator should seek clarification and utilize methodology we present in Chapter 22. The evaluator should ask for specific behavioral descriptions of the alleged domestic violence, information about the frequency and intensity, the context within which the alleged violence occurred, whether the children were exposed to such alleged behaviors, how each parent comforted the children after the parental conflict ended, and other relevant information.

Our experience is that evaluators often do not look more closely at in-depth analyses of allegations of domestic violence by focusing on specific behaviors, the context in which such behaviors have occurred, and each parent's insight into their and the other parent's respective contributions. Evaluators need to explore each parent's understanding of the emotional triggers that are associated with elevating the situation toward violence, steps taken by each individual to step away from the violence, and actions taken to seek assistance to reduce the conflict and protect the children.

Using operational definitions helps to better illustrate the specific behaviors of concern. Another area of investigation is exploring each individual's understanding of their contribution to the conflict, the emotional triggers that are associated with elevating the situation toward violence, and steps taken by each individual to step away from the violence.

The factfinding approach incorporates interview questions intended to gather information to answer specific questions that guide the evaluation. We present sample questions in Chapter 12. As we've discussed in Chapter 3, parenting plan evaluators should never begin an evaluation without knowing the purpose of the evaluation. Specific questions define the scope of the evaluation (Ackerman et al., 2019; Gould, 1999; Gould & Martindale, 2009b).

Relevant information is obtained in PPEs when the evaluator gathers information that answers the questions the evaluator has been directed to address. Defining the nature and scope of the evaluation provides clear guidance on what areas are to be investigated in interviewing parents, children, and collaterals. At the same time, evaluators need to gather data about relevant parenting factors, integrating information about salient parenting factors into their answers to the specific questions guiding the evaluation.

STRUCTURING INTERVIEWS AROUND EVIDENCE-BASED AND EVIDENCE-INFORMED FACTORS

Evaluators should structure information gathering during parent interviews around empirically-based positive parenting factors. Listed are 10 empirically derived positive parenting factors. These evidence-based or evidence-informed parenting factors are often useful organizing concepts around which the evaluator structures the interviews:

- Parents' expressions of warmth and responsiveness as well as each child's experience of their parents' warmth and responsiveness. Secure attachment is fostered by consistent emotional warmth, sensitivity, and responsiveness to a child's needs. Positive parent–child interactions (e.g., active listening, validation, and affection) enhance emotional security and resilience (Chen, Haines, et al., 2019; Chen, Kubzansky, et al., 2019).
- Parental consistency and developmentally appropriate discipline. Positive discipline strategies (e.g., setting clear expectations, using natural consequences, and reinforcing desirable behavior) promote self-regulation and responsibility. Harsh or authoritarian discipline (e.g., corporal punishment) is associated with negative outcomes for children's short- and long-term life adjustment, while consistent, nonpunitive guidance fosters cooperation (Kuppens & Ceulemans, 2019).
- Parental monitoring and supervision of their children. Age-appropriate monitoring of a child's activities, friendships, and online presence reduces risky behaviors and fosters safety. Authoritative (not authoritarian) supervision promotes independence while maintaining protective oversight (Prime et al., 2023).

- Parental emotion coaching and social–emotional learning. Evaluators should gather data about how each parent engages in teaching their children to recognize, label, and manage emotions. Such teaching supports emotional intelligence and resilience. Gathering data from direct observation and collateral information about observed parental modeling of healthy coping skills and stress management helps to determine parents' abilities to foster adaptive emotional regulation (Neppl et al., 2020).
- Parental encouragement of children's autonomy and problem solving. The evaluator needs to gather information about how each parent provides age-appropriate choices and encourages independent decision making. Such parenting behaviors help build children's confidence and problem-solving skills (Kuppens & Ceulemans, 2019).
- Healthy parent–child communication. Evaluators need to gather data about parent–child communication in a variety of different situations and activities to determine the parent's ability to encourage open, age-appropriate discussions about emotions, relationships, and values, each of which strengthen family bonds and trust. Among the behaviors to be assessed include parents' active listening and nonjudgmental communication, each of which helps to create an environment where children feel safe expressing themselves (Centers for Disease Control and Prevention, 2021).
- Parents' positive role modeling. Parents who model healthy relationships, coping skills, and conflict resolution influence children's social and emotional development. The evaluator should gather data about parents' observed demonstrations of empathy, respect, and ethical behavior that are known to reinforce positive values (Bandura, 1977; Grusec & Hastings, 2015).
- Stress reduction and parental self-care. Parental well-being directly affects parenting quality. Parental stress management and self-care enhance a parent's ability to be present and engaged. Among the factors evaluators should gather information is from coparents, family, and professionals who have personal knowledge of each parent's self-care activities (Crnic & Low, 2002; Mikolajczak et al., 2019).
- Healthy coparenting and family relationships. Cooperative coparenting, even in separated families, provides children with stability and reduces conflict-related stress. Further, reducing children's exposure to high-conflict dynamics protects children's emotional well-being (Emery, 2011; Sanders & Turner, 2018).
- Parents' cultural responsiveness and inclusive parenting. Parents who recognize and value a child's cultural background, identity, and experiences promote a strong sense of self. Inclusive parenting embraces diversity, equity, and belonging and may be parental role modeling of tolerance and acceptance of others (Foulidi & Papakitsos, 2022).

These 10 factors do not define the universe of relevant parent factors to examine. However, these factors align with leading research from developmental psychology, attachment theory, and family systems models, providing a strong foundation for parenting assessments in legal and clinical contexts.

AN EVALUATIVE AND CRITICAL STANCE

Consistent with the fact-finding model, a parenting plan interview is an investigative interview. The role of the forensic evaluator is similar to that of an investigative journalist (W. G. Austin & Kirkpatrick, 2004). The evaluator actively seeks information from various sources. The evaluator does not wait passively for information to be provided. The evaluator advocates for the results and defends the chosen procedures to assist the court in understanding the strengths and deficiencies of the methodology and the relationship between the data obtained from that methodology and the expert opinions developed from those data.

An evaluator assumes an evaluative and critical stance toward information obtained from all sources, particularly from parents and those with an emotional tie to the parents. There are times when an interview may become challenging and adversarial because the goal is obtaining an accurate understanding of the family system and is not helping the parent or litigant feel better or change behaviors. It can help to explain to the parent or litigant the nature of the forensic role, especially if they expect empathic support, similar to therapy.

The evaluator continually applies scientific skepticism and the scientific method by testing reasonable alternative explanations of the data. As the evaluator gathers information, "the need for historical accuracy in forensic evaluations leads to a need for completeness in the information acquired and for structure in the assessment process to accomplish that goal" (Gould & Martindale, 2009b, p. 53).

THE ROLE OF EMPATHY

One area of challenge to many forensic evaluators is the role of empathy in interviewing. The American Psychological Association (APA) Ethics Code, as well as APA and AFCC guidelines, instruct evaluators to inform the parties about the purpose of the evaluation and the limits of confidentiality. They must explain how information will be disseminated and to whom.

During exchanges between the parent and the evaluator, a relationship develops, and often, an evaluator expresses or is perceived to express empathy. A person involved in a forensic interview who experiences the evaluator as displaying empathy might come to believe the evaluator is pursuing that parent's best interests rather than maintaining a neutral position (Vera et al., 2019). Of particular concern is the possibility that the evaluator's perceived empathy will lead parents to reveal potentially prejudicial or disadvantageous information about themselves (e.g., negative attitudes or experiences) and their legal cases.

> [T]he concern is that evaluators might use empathy as a "seductive power" to create a false sense of therapeutic alliance and "induce an inappropriate level of trust in the evaluee." (Vera et al., 2019, p. 56)

Evaluators must strike a balance between empathic understanding and investigative challenge.

TRAUMA-INFORMED FORENSIC INTERVIEWING

PPEs can be stressful for all members of a family. For family members who have experienced events resulting in trauma, the evaluation context, in general, and the interview process, in particular, might result in the triggering of emotional associations that affect the individual's presentation, ability to think and speak clearly, ability to participate meaningfully, and regulation of emotions.

Goldenson asserts there has been a long-standing effort to integrate trauma-informed (TI) practices to psychological activities and more recently to forensic psychological activities (Goldenson et al., 2022) and has drawn into focus how aspects of the forensic mental health evaluation process might adversely affect those who have been traumatized (Goldenson, 2024; Goldenson et al., 2022). Goldenson suggests that forensic evaluators have an ethical obligation to be aware of how the forensic evaluation context has the possibility to retraumatize litigants and that evaluators need to be aware of the need to monitor litigant behaviors for signs of emotional distress (Goldenson, 2024). Goldenson explains that such monitoring can assist in the management of the interview and be useful clinical information about the litigants' mental health and general functioning (J. Goldenson, personal communication, January 12, 2023). Goldenson suggests the reluctance among forensic psychologists engaged in forensic assessment to employ TI interviewing procedures stems from TI's close association with clinical treatment literature.

The application of a TI approach in parenting plan interviews does not change the procedure into a therapeutic endeavor. At its core, a TI approach to forensic interviewing is a mindset that the evaluator brings to the interview context. The evaluator needs to be mindful of the inherently stressful nature of the forensic evaluation process, how the stressful nature of the evaluation process might result in retraumatization of a parent or child, and how such stressors and potential retraumatization might alter the nature, quality, and completeness of information gathered from the individual.

Goldenson identified three areas to integrate into conventional forensic interviewing procedures. First, the evaluator develops an understanding of the general literature related to the biopsychosocial impact of trauma, including how trauma can shape brain development, psychological functioning, and social functioning (Goldenson, 2024). Second, the evaluator develops a familiarity with the growing body of literature on trauma-related conditions as they apply to forensic evaluations, and competence in applying this knowledge in forensic interviewing (Goldenson, 2024). Third, the evaluator uses trauma-related knowledge to create the type of interview context that promotes optimal parent and child engagement in the assessment and reduces the likelihood of retraumatization (Goldenson, 2024).

PROCEDURAL CONSIDERATIONS

How the interview process begins might set the stage for the parent or child's sense of safety and transparency. Harris and Fallot (2001) proposed five guiding principles to TI work: (a) facilitating a sense of safety (physical and emotional); (b) being trustworthy; (c) working collaboratively; (d) providing choice to individuals, to the degree possible; and (e) empowering individuals. Evaluators should explain to the parent or child at the beginning of the interview that the process will involve being asked questions about their histories and that the questions could cause some degree of distress.

The situational demands of the assessment can be dysregulating for the parent or child. Evaluators often probe for evocative information and do so in a high degree of detail over the course of a brief period of time (Rocchio, 2020). It is also important to monitor shifts in arousal that can inform the pacing of the assessment to avoid undue retraumatization of the parent or child (Rocchio, 2020).

Goldenson raises concerns about possible disempowerment, loss of agency, and loss of control as common experiences among those involved in forensic assessment who have experienced childhood abuse. Goldenson describes how a TI forensic interviewer can empower the examinee by providing opportunities to make choices throughout the assessment, such as deciding where to sit, when to take breaks, and the order of material to cover. Rocchio (2020) suggests consent or assent might need to be repeatedly obtained over the course of the assessment to ensure the parent or child is attending to the information provided. Providing parents or children with a choice about pacing can give them some degree of control and opportunities to regulate.

ESTABLISHING A BASELINE

A useful first step to assist in monitoring later shifts in arousal is to establish a baseline of parent or child presentation in a less aroused state. Starting the interview with neutral material (rather than inquiries about trauma-related experiences) can be helpful both in terms of building rapport and a working alliance and in providing a sense of the individual's general presentation (Goldenson, 2024).

Baseline information helps the interviewer identify hyperarousal, hypoarousal, and dissociation states and provides information for the evaluator to monitor corresponding changes in behavioral, cognitive, and affective characteristics. Attending to signs of dysregulation and carefully noticing shifts in arousal can assist the evaluator in managing the pace of the interview, which can also reduce distress and retraumatization without therapeutic intervention (Goldenson, 2024).

Checking in about levels of distress when observing shifts in arousal, particularly when engaging in challenging lines of questioning, and providing the parent or child with some control over the tempo of the interview can enhance the examinee's ability to self-regulate (Brand et al., 2017). Some parents or children might be able to describe their traumatic experiences in one sitting, while others might find it necessary to take breaks. The evaluator might move between inquiries about the events associated with challenging life events with less evocative material.

Some parents or children have never before told another person about their abuse experiences or have not had their stories validated. Experiencing invalidation or a lack of support can exacerbate the effects of the traumatic experience and can lead parents or children to hold ongoing assumptions that they are unlikely to be taken seriously, believed, or treated fairly by others (Goldenson, 2024). The result could be a reduction in the completeness, cohesiveness, and uniqueness of the story being told by the parent or child.

AMERICAN PSYCHOLOGICAL ASSOCIATION AND ASSOCIATION OF FAMILY AND CONCILIATION COURTS GUIDELINES ADDRESSING FORENSIC INTERVIEWING

The APA (2022) custody guidelines provide guidance about how best to conduct forensic interviews of parents and children. Guideline 13 reads,

> Psychologists remain aware that interviewing children requires specific knowledge and skills. They strive to utilize approaches consistent with each child's age, language ability, and developmental level. Psychologists seek to be aware of the concerns that may be engendered by such factors as repeated questioning or subtle suggestibility that may influence children's responses. Psychologists seek to avoid exacerbating a child's distress during this process, and they aim to remain sensitive to any inadvertent risk of harm that may be occasioned by the evaluation process itself. (p. 16)

APA (2022) Guideline 14 encourages, "When interviewing parents, psychologists strive to collect and assess information relevant to parenting strengths and weaknesses, to ascertain the best interests of the child" (p. 17).

The AFCC (2022) guidelines provide more information about forensic interviewing of parents and children. The AFCC provides two broad guidelines that address forensic interviewing of parents and children:

> Guideline 6.5: Evaluation of all Adults in Parenting Roles: Evaluators should seek the voluntary participation of any adult who performs a parental caregiving role, even if the individual is not a party to the case, such as stepparents and significant others. This includes adults living in, or expected to be living in, the home with the children and performing ongoing care of the children.
>
> This section is not intended to apply to nannies, daycare providers, or other employed caregivers, who may be important collateral sources of information, but not subject to evaluation.
>
> Evaluators should conduct forensic interviews and assessments of adults in a culturally sensitive and trauma-informed manner.
>
> Evaluators should clearly articulate the limitations of their data and opinions when nonparties decline participation.
>
> When an appointment order specifies the individuals to be evaluated but does not include individuals the evaluator believes are appropriate to evaluate, evaluators may
>
> - seek the court's authorization to evaluate the additional individuals;
> - seek the consent of the nonparties to be evaluated;
> - decline the appointment; and
> - clearly articulate the limitations of their data and opinions in light of being unable to evaluate the individuals. (p. 19)
>
> Guideline 6.6: Evaluation of Children: Evaluators should interview children in a developmentally appropriate, culturally sensitive, TI manner using empirically-informed interview techniques. If an evaluator chooses not to interview a child, the evaluator should explain the reason for this decision in the report.
>
> Evaluators should interview all children who reside in the home, including stepsiblings, half-siblings, foster siblings, or other children, if appropriate given the issues under evaluation.
>
> Evaluators should obtain written authorization to interview children who are not subjects of the evaluation prior to conducting the interviews.
>
> In their reports and testimony, evaluators should describe the factors that influenced the weight that was given to the child's input and expressed wishes, including, but not limited to the child's developmental stage, emotional and cognitive maturity, independence, temperament, impact of trauma, experiences, cultural considerations, and role in family dynamics. (p. 20)

The AFCC provides additional guidance on the competencies that evaluators should obtain prior to engaging in forensic interviewing of children. The AFCC (2022) also provides ideas about how best to structure the child forensic interview:

> Guideline 7.1: Competence in Forensic Child Interviewing: Evaluators should have knowledge of evidence-informed forensic child interview procedures and be able to articulate the evidence-informed strategies they used to elicit information from the child, such as the use of free recall methods.
>
> Evaluators should have knowledge of the numerous factors that can affect the reliability and validity of children's statements, such as the effects of various forms of questions, multiple interviews, repeated questions, the presence of others.
>
> Evaluators should be skilled in conducting culturally sensitive and TI interviews with children. (p. 20)
>
> Guideline 7.2 Structuring of Child Interviews: Evaluators should recognize that the purpose of interviews with children is to gather information from the child about the nature and quality of a child's relationships, life and family experiences, perspectives on family issues, wishes, and preferences;

> Evaluators should plan and structure interviews with their purpose in mind, and consider the child's age, developmental stage, language abilities, culture, any disabilities, and any known traumatic or adverse experiences; (p. 20)
>
> Evaluators should inform children in a developmentally appropriate manner of the purpose of the interview and that what they say is not confidential; (p. 20)
>
> Evaluators should strive to gather sufficient information to be able to consider a range of hypotheses about the issues central to the evaluation. (p. 20–21)

CLINICAL VERSUS FORENSIC INTERVIEWING

A clinical forensic interview is defined as "an interview undertaken with an individual who is subject to some form of legal process which serves a clinical purpose (e.g., to inform diagnosis, treatment)" (Goldenson, 2024, p. 3). A forensic evaluation interview is intended to develop evidence that is subject to confirmation or disconfirmation from independent third-party sources and is part of the data on which expert opinions are based to inform a legal process (Goldenson, 2024).

In their seminal article describing components of a forensic evaluation interview, S. A. Greenberg and Shuman (1997) identified ten differences between therapeutic and forensic relationships (see Table 11.1). We believe these differences help define the structure for conducting a forensic interview with parents, collaterals, and children.

FAVORABLE PRESENTATIONS

Research has consistently demonstrated, over the past 60 years, human beings—including parenting plan evaluators—cannot accurately determine credibility in face-to-face interviews (DePaulo et al., 1997; Ekman & O'Sullivan, 1991; Feely & Young, 1998; Frank & Feeley, 2003). Evaluators need to be aware of this bias factor and resist the potential lure of responding to the intuitive appeal of someone they feel is credible. Their responsibility is to investigate and understand the power of intuitive thinking and develop strategies to move to deliberative thinking (Kahneman, 2011).

As discussed in Chapter 7, many evaluators believe bias affects other people but not themselves. This is called the *blind spot bias* (Zappala et al., 2018) There are unsupported beliefs that knowing one's biases and how to control for them are sufficient to control for bias (Zappala et al., 2018). Research has revealed, however, that self-reflection as a means of bias control does not work well (Zappala et al., 2018).

Parents interviewed in PPEs tend to present themselves in a favorable light (Bathurst et al., 1997; Gould et al., 2018). Evaluators need to be aware of this biasing factor and seek information from independent data sources to reduce the influence of this "faking good" bias factor. For example, if there are allegations that a parent's symptoms of depression impact their ability to get the child to school on time, yet the parent denies the allegations, the evaluator can review school attendance records and speak to the staff at the school.

TABLE 11.1. Ten Differences Between Therapeutic and Forensic Relationships

Differences	Care provision	Forensic evaluation
1. Whose client is the patient/litigant?	The mental health practitioner	The attorney
2. The relational privilege that governs disclosure in each relationship	Therapist–patient privilege	Attorney–client and attorney work-product privilege
3. The cognitive set and evaluative attitude of each expert	Supportive, accepting, empathic	Neutral, objective, detached
4. The differing areas of competency of each expert	Therapy techniques for treatment of the impairment	Forensic evaluation techniques relevant to the legal claim
5. The nature of the hypotheses tested by each expert	Diagnostic criteria for the purpose of therapy	Psychological criteria for purpose of legal adjudication
6. The scrutiny applied to the information utilized in the process and the role of historical truth	Mostly based on information from the person being treated with little scrutiny of that information by the therapist	Litigant information supplemented with that of collateral sources and scrutinized by the evaluator and the court
7. The amount and control of structure in each relationship	Patient structured and relatively less structured than forensic evaluation	Evaluator structured and relatively more structured than therapy
8. The nature and degree of "adversarialness" in each relationship	A helping relationship; rarely adversarial	Evaluator relationship; frequently adversarial
9. The goal of the professional in each relationship	Therapist attempts to benefit the patient by working within the therapeutic relationship	Evaluator advocates for the results and evaluations of the evaluation for the benefit of the court
10. The impact on each relationship of critical judgment by the expert	The basis of the relationship is the therapeutic alliance and critical judgment is likely to impair that alliance	The basis of the relationship is evaluative and critical judgment is unlikely to cause serious emotional harm

Note. Reprinted from "Irreconcilable Conflict Between Therapeutic and Forensic Roles," by S. A. Greenberg and D. W. Shuman, 1997, *Professional Psychology: Research and Practice, 28*(1), p. 52 (https://doi.org/10.1037/0735-7028.28.1.50). Copyright 1997 by the American Psychological Association.

Parents tend to maximize their parenting competencies and minimize the other parent's competencies (Ackerman et al., 2019; Hynan, 2014). Parents often view themselves as doing more with the children and around the house than the other parent because they are always aware of their activities and are not always aware of the other parent's activities. This is called the *egocentrism bias* (Hynan, 2014). Recall classic studies that looked at the attribution bias (Ross & Sicoly, 1979; Thompson & Kelley, 1981). When researchers ask parents about their household contributions, mothers claim to do 90% of the work, while fathers claim approximately 40% of the work. As these studies are replicated, the numbers may not always be a 90/40 split; however, the total is always more than 100%. This is an example of remembering one's own contribution, while dismissing the other parent's contribution. Evaluators need to be aware of this bias factor and thoroughly investigate each parent's *unique contribution* to parenting through information obtained from independent data sources.

These research findings argue strongly for evaluators to adopt an investigative model of assessment to obtain information from independent third-party sources that may determine whether the information from parent interviews is or is not an accurate description of past and present parenting behaviors observed outside of the evaluator's office (W. G. Austin & Kirkpatrick, 2004).

AUDIO AND VIDEO RECORDING

Research on human memory, cognitive bias, and other relevant areas of human information processing shows video recording or audiotaping interviews create a more reliable record than note-taking (Gould & Martindale, 2007), yet there seems to be resistance to making video or audiotape parent interviews standard. The reliability of the evaluator's interview data and interpretation of interview data are increased when there is an audio and video record.

Some colleagues might be concerned about how being recorded may alter the interviewee's behavior, transparency, or comfort during the evaluation. This is a clinical, not forensic, concern. PPEs seek to obtain historical and present information about parenting and related concerns.

Placing emphasis on in-office interview behavior should not be a particularly important aspect of the PPE process, unless genuine mental health concerns are observed. Even then, however, the evaluator needs to be concerned that the observed behavior is not an artifact of the evaluation process. Again, the evaluator seeks independent verification of the observed behaviors. If the behaviors are not observed outside the interview, then questions need to be considered that the unusual behavior is associated with the interview process and not with parenting behavior.

Another reason for the pushback against creating an audio or video record of the evaluation is that it can significantly increase the cost of the evaluation. When considering whether to litigate, the attorneys would need to review the video recordings as part of their decision making. If there were a decision to proceed to trial, then the video records would need to be reviewed in preparation for deposition and trial. The evaluator, too, might need to spend time reviewing the video record prior to deposition or trial. Each of these activities increases the cost of the evaluation process.

Some tensions between law and forensic procedures cannot be easily resolved, and the manner in which such tensions are resolved seldom have an empirical basis. We place the scientific integrity of forensic psychological assessment above the attorney's concerns about cost, recognizing the value judgment in choosing one perspective over the other.

One way to resolve the questions about whether or not to video record an evaluation and concerns about costs associated with video recording is to consider bringing the issue before the court. A court might direct an evaluator to video record to maintain the integrity of the interview data, thereby resolving the conflict. A court might also direct an evaluator not to video record, citing concerns about cost. In either situation, it would be important for the evaluator to explain to the court the potential threats to reliability, making sure that there is a record of reasoned concern about choosing not to video record and an acknowledgment by the court that the lack of a video (or audio) record will not be used at trial to challenge the integrity of the evaluator's procedures.

Regarding cost, it is noteworthy that during COVID-19, many evaluators used video-based telehealth interviews to conduct their interviews (Dale & Smith, 2021). Software, such as Zoom, provides an easy way to record interviews. As described in Mulchay and Knuth (2023b), while there is not data specific to interviewing parents during a PPE via telehealth, a fair amount of data exists supporting the use of telehealth to conduct forensic interviews with adults.

Some parents ask to audiotape their interviews with the evaluator. There is no consensus in the field about whether to allow a parent to audiotape an interview, as there may be some challenges. Prime among these challenges is how to ensure recordings are not edited or changed, as it is both easy and free to edit audio recordings. There may as well be unique concerns about what the parent does with the interview data. Of particular concern, albeit rare, is the parent who shares sensitive family information on social media. In these situations, a protective order may be necessary. Making the interview process transparent by allowing the interview to be recorded should serve everyone well, and transparency during the interviews is best achieved when there is an audio or video recording of the interview.

REMOTE ASSESSMENT

The APA has published Guidelines for the Practice of Telepsychology, which are helpful for parenting plan evaluators to consider prior to conducting remote assessments. Guideline 1 states the following:

> Psychologists who provide telepsychology services strive to take reasonable steps to ensure their competence with both the technologies used and the potential impact of the technologies on clients/patients, supervisees, or other professionals. (Joint Task Force for the Development of Telepsychology Guidelines for Psychologists, 2013, p. 793)

Evaluators who conduct remote assessments should know where the people they interview are located to adhere to the second APA guideline for telehealth, which is the standard of care. Evaluators should also work to address threats to confidentiality, with particular emphasis on whether the person they are interviewing is alone, has privacy, and feels safe.

Mulchay and Knuth reviewed the available literature and categorized custody evaluation data-gathering procedures by best practice, sufficient practice, and insufficient practice. After a careful analysis of the case-dependent details, "evaluators will need to be prepared to defend their decisions to employ (or not employ) telehealth and explain why the decisions they made still produce reliable data, just as evaluators need to defend any other tools they use during evaluations (e.g., face-to-face interviews, telephone conversations, psychological testing)" (Mulchay & Knuth, 2023b).

When evaluators conduct PPEs, collected data typically comes from one of the following categories: direct interviews with parents, direct interviews with children, observations of the child or children with the parent, psychological testing, interviews with collaterals and third parties, or record review. As summarized by Mulchay and Knuth (2023b), there is considerable data to support the reliability of the use of remote procedures used in psychological, neuropsychological, and forensic evaluations of adults.

As summarized by Mulchay and Knuth (2023b), the data regarding interviewing children is much less established. The National Children's Alliance created guidelines for conducting remote forensic interviews with children. Their guidelines group three methods of interviewing children by how likely they are to recommend an interview setup. Their guidelines follow a three-prong categorization (i.e., *more likely, sometimes,* and *very rare*) as follows::

- More Likely scenario: occurs when the evaluator and the child are in the same building but in different rooms. In this setup, the child is interviewed via a video feed. We call this remote-in-office evaluation.
- Sometimes scenario: occurs when the child is in the office, clinic, or hospital room while the evaluator is at home or in a different location.
- Very Rare scenario: occurs when the child is at home and the evaluator is at their home or at their office. (Mulchay & Knuth, 2023b)

There is emerging research that explores the benefits and risks of remotely interviewing children to investigate allegations of sexual abuse (Brown et al., 2021; Dickinson et al., 2021; Miyamoto et al., 2014). There is no data on remotely interviewing children during a PPE. Even if an evaluator utilizes the Very Rare scenario setup, the evaluator does not know who else is in the room, whether someone is influencing the child's responses, whether or not a parent said before the interview, "I'll get to listen to you," whether the parent has a listening device in the room such as a baby monitor, or whether the parent may be able to eavesdrop (Mulchay & Knuth, 2023b).

There are many ways to conduct remote observations; however, "of all the aspects of a PPE to do digitally, observations are probably most poorly suited for telehealth" (Mulchay & Knuth, 2023b), because it may be impossible for the evaluator to control for or assess many context specific threats to the observation.

More than a decade ago, the APA published guidelines on remote psychological testing. There have been longstanding guidelines on the use of remote testing. Guideline 7 states the following:

> When a psychological test or other assessment procedure is conducted via telepsychology, psychologists are encouraged to ensure that the integrity of the psychometric properties of the test or assessment procedure (e.g., reliability and validity) and the conditions of administration indicated in the test manual are preserved when adapted for use with such technologies. (Joint Task Force for the Development of Telepsychology Guidelines for Psychologists, 2013, p. 798)

When evaluators decide to administer psychological tests, evaluators cannot ensure that the conditions are proper and maintained if they are not witnessing the individual complete the test (Mulchay & Knuth, 2023b). Ben-Porath (2020) published a paper on the steps evaluators can follow to ensure they are administering the Minnesota Multiphasic Personality Inventory appropriately via telehealth, which includes the need to maintain visual and auditory connection with the individual throughout the evaluation to ensure that they are not coached or interrupted. The steps include the following:

- Use secure online platforms approved for psychological testing
- Monitor technical issues that may affect test validity
- Conduct preassessment screenings to determine if remote testing is appropriate for a given individual
- Ensure the test taker is in a distraction-free environment
- Ensure the test taker does not have unauthorized assistance
- Monitor response consistency and be vigilant about signs of test-taking irregularities

Evaluators have traditionally utilized remote assessment techniques to gather collateral data. Collateral interviews, which can be done in-person, via telehealth, or on the phone, will be discussed in detail in Chapter 18.

CONCLUSION

Forensic interviewing is a crucial aspect of PPEs, requiring evaluators to apply both structured and flexible methodologies to gather accurate, relevant information. This chapter has emphasized the distinction between forensic and clinical interviewing, underscoring the need for an investigative approach rather than a passive, stenographic model. The fact-finding framework, which encourages evaluators to actively question, challenge, and verify information, is essential for maintaining objectivity and reliability in forensic assessments.

We have examined key limitations in current forensic interviewing practices, including inconsistencies in interview structure, biases that may influence assessments, and the complexities of implementing trauma-informed approaches. While a trauma-informed perspective is not a therapeutic endeavor, it enhances engagement and accuracy in information gathering while minimizing the risk of retraumatization. Additionally, we discussed ethical considerations and procedural safeguards critical to maintaining the integrity of forensic evaluations. These include the benefits of audio and video recording, adherence to APA and AFCC guidelines, and the increasing role of remote assessments. As technology continues to reshape forensic evaluations, maintaining empirical rigor and ethical sensitivity remains imperative. Ultimately, forensic evaluators must balance empathy with investigative rigor, ensuring that interviews are conducted with scientific skepticism while upholding ethical commitments to transparency and accuracy. In the following chapters, we will explore specific forensic interviewing methods in greater depth.

12

What to Ask About in Forensic Interviews

Forensic interviewing plays a crucial role in parenting plan evaluations (PPEs), yet there has been limited guidance in the literature on how to conduct these interviews effectively. While a substantial body of research exists on interviewing children in cases of alleged child sexual abuse, there remains a significant gap in resources addressing forensic interviews in the broader context of child custody disputes. Evaluators often struggle with determining what to ask, how to ask it, and which factors are most critical when assessing children's experiences, parental capabilities, and the overall family dynamic.

This chapter seeks to address that gap by providing structured guidance on forensic interviewing techniques for children, adolescents, and adults involved in parenting disputes. While providing a sample of questions to guide interviews, we explore psychological and developmental factors that influence children's responses, including memory processes, loyalty conflicts, and the impact of parental influence. We also discuss best practices for interviewing adolescents, taking into account the complexities of adolescent brain development and decision making. Additionally, we outline the critical areas to explore when interviewing parents, with an emphasis on assessing historical and current parenting behaviors, coparenting relationships, and potential risk factors such as intimate partner violence and child safety concerns.

This chapter provides a framework for evaluators conducting interviews. Our goal is to equip evaluators with the necessary tools to obtain reliable and relevant information. As we reviewed the commercially available books and

https://doi.org/10.1037/0000474-013
Parenting Plan Evaluations: An Evidence-Informed Approach to Child Custody, by J. W. Gould and C. M. Mulchay

peer-reviewed articles in the field, we were surprised to learn that none of the previously published material provided much guidance on interviewing. Gould's 2006 book provided guidance about topics to address when interviewing parents, and Gould's book with Martindale (2007) provided a conceptual model to guide forensic interviewing of young children, but there has been little guidance in more recent literature on forensic interviewing of adolescents and adults. There is little current information about theoretical or conceptual models to guide forensic interviewing, and little practical advice about what to ask, how to ask, or the areas of most importance to examine. Although there is ample peer-reviewed literature on forensic interviewing of young children, most of that literature is drawn specifically from forensic interviewing of children in cases of alleged child sexual abuse. Parenting plan evaluators need more general guidance for forensic interviewing in PPEs.

In this chapter, we seek to fill that gap in the literature. We identify factors to consider when preparing to interview young children, preadolescent children, and adolescent children. Although our discussion on memory and interviewing is more likely to be a concern with young children, these factors matter when interviewing children of all ages. The previous chapter placed greater attention on process variables that might affect the reliability of interview data. This chapter addresses the content of, structure of, and conduct in the interview.

LIMITATIONS

There is consensus about the importance of interviewing children. Survey research reveals most evaluators interview children at least twice, once during their parenting time with Parent A and once during their parenting time with Parent B (Ackerman et al., 2021). There is no consensus about what parenting, child development, or parent–child relationship factors are most important to investigate during interviews with children. We believe guidance about areas to investigate in child interviews is drawn directly from the specific questions that define the evaluation's scope.

We explore the importance and relevance of using specific questions to guide areas of interview focus during child interviews. Evaluators too often rely on general questions such as asksing the child to make "three wishes" and other nonspecific areas of inquiry. Although children may provide useful information in response to general questions, more relevant information would be obtained by developing age-appropriate questions to gather information used to answer the specific questions identified at the beginning of the evaluation process.

Returning to limitations in research about child interviewing, there is no consensus about how long child interviews should last, no guidance about where to interview children (home vs. office), and no guidance about what empirical factors are most relevant. For example, what are the salient factors to examine in the life of a 4-year-old compared to the salient factors to examine in the life of a 15-year-old?

Strong empirical findings describe reliable procedures to be used in child interviews. Few, if any, parenting plan texts direct evaluators to employ reliable interviewing procedures when interviewing children, although Gould and Martindale (2007) devoted several chapters to research addressing reliable interview procedures, children's use of language, and empirically based areas to guide child interviews. Given the increased emphasis on evidence-based procedures, evaluators should employ child interview techniques that increase the reliability of children's responses and reduce the likelihood that interviewer techniques introduce errors that result in less reliable child interview data.

Most literature on child interview procedures addresses sexual abuse. As discussed in the previous two chapters, child forensic interview protocols have been developed and empirically examined for their effectiveness in reducing interviewer-imposed error and increasing the reliability of children's self-report data (Lamb et al., 2018; Poole, 2016).

We propose evaluators bring into their PPE procedures techniques proven to reduce error and apply those procedures to child interviews in family court matters. Although the content areas to be explored in a PPE would be different from the content areas explored when engaged in sexual abuse investigations, the principles guiding the nature of how an evaluator interviews a child involved in a parenting plan assessment would be the same. Child forensic interviewing in the context of a PPE would continue to emphasize the importance of open-ended, nondirective questions.

FORENSIC INTERVIEWING OF CHILDREN

Memory and Interviewing

Recency and proximity effects may impact an interview (see Chapter 7). Many children feel a strong sense of loyalty to their parents. Some children mostly feel loyal to one parent, often the parent whom the child has most recently visited. Thus, evaluators need to be aware of how loyalty, alignment, and the motivation to be fair to both parents might influence a child.

Many children display loyalty, alignment, and fairness to their family system, such that "context is identity. This means that every professional tasked to interview a child must take into account where that child woke up on the morning of the interview, who drove the child to interview, how the child understands the interview process, how the child understands the limitations of privacy or confidentiality, whether the child believes that the accompanying parent is nearby and listening in, and what the child anticipates about the drive home" (Garber et al., 2022). These dynamics have been described as the bookends of the interview (Martindale, 2019).

Recency and proximity variables can contaminate a child's presentation in an interview. Each evaluation should be designed so as to minimize and mitigate recency and proximity effects. For example, many evaluators who conduct in-office interviews of the children interview the child at least twice, having each parent transport the child to the interview one time. Early in the interview, the evaluator should ask the child what happened before the interview. The evaluator should inquire as to the child's presession activities, with particular attention to what the child was told prior to the interview. The evaluator should also ask what the child anticipates will happen after the interview.

Kuehnle et al. (2004) suggested the strength of the evidence basis of forensic interviewing in the child sexual abuse arena was sufficiently reliable and robust to be applied to child custody assessment. The overall structure of a forensic interview of minor children engaged in a PPE should include the following:

1. Develop rapport.
2. Assess ability to answer questions and provide details.
3. Provide ground rules.
4. Practice nonessential questions.
5. Introduce substantive topics with open-ended questions, then move to more directive questions.
6. Interview closure.

Kuehnle et al. suggest setting clear *ground rules* for children during the beginning of interview sessions to help children understand what is expected of them. The evaluator should describe the basic rules of the interview:

- The evaluator is clueless, meaning that the evaluator has no information about an alleged event.
- There is no confidentiality, meaning that the evaluator will share information with others such as the judge and attorneys.
- Questions must be answered honestly.
- The evaluator should be corrected if mistaken.
- If a question is not understood, the evaluator should be made aware.

The evaluator should follow forensic interviewing procedures:

- Use open-ended inquiries
- Avoid yes or no questions
- Avoid multiple-choice questions
- Exercise great care with syntax
- Limit the use of pronouns

A Smart Approach to Interviewing Children

More than 20 years ago, psychologist Carol Smart (2002) conducted innovative research on how children of divorce think about living in each parent's home. She noted a growing awareness of the need to talk to children about their wishes and feelings, or at the very least, to ascertain through other means, children's wishes and feelings about changes in their lives resulting from their parents' divorce. Smart wrote, "There is, for example, the fear that listening to children will become a kind of token process, a box that needs to be ticked rather than a genuine consultation. . . . [T]here are problems of how to hear what is being said and then what to do with the diversity of accounts likely to be expressed" (2002, p. 307).

Smart conducted several studies that involved speaking with children of divorce and their parents. "One of the most significant outcomes' for us was the way in which talking to children, and analyzing their stories, had the effect of jolting us into a child's worldview. . . . [W]e were acutely aware of how different the experiences of the 'same' divorce was for parent and child. . . Even the most caring parent could find it very difficult to see divorce from the standpoint of [their] child" (2002, p. 308).

When adults attempt to place themselves into the shoes of children, they often project memories of their own childhoods onto the children. They hear children's stories as reconstructions of their own childhoods, recalled through many layers of personal history. Evaluators need to be aware of the need for reflection and sensitivity to children's stories: "It is not simply a matter of allowing the child to speak; it is also a matter of being attentive to what it is that we hear the child say" (Smart, 2002, p. 309).

Smart found that children and their parents often offered vastly different accounts of many aspects of family experiences: "It is not that children's accounts obliterate or correct the parents' accounts; nor is it the other way around. Rather, it is to acknowledge that people stand in different relationships to one another, have access to different resources, and regard different things as important" (2002, p. 309).

Children's accounts of family life frequently were overshadowed by their parents' interpretations of family events. Smart argued that taking children's stories seriously means giving legitimacy to their experiences on the same level as that given to parents' experiences. One is not necessarily more important than the other. Each experience needs to be thoroughly understood.

Factors to Examine

Smart (2002) proposed that among the most relevant factors to examine when talking with children about their experiences in a divorced family are (a) physical space, (b) emotional space, (c) psychological space, (d) equal time, (e) time apart, (f) time to oneself, (g) time and hurting, and (h) time in sharing.

Physical space refers to the practical issues of getting from one place to another. Physical space includes examining concerns that the child has about organizing clothes, toys, and schoolwork. It entails letting children's friends know where they are and letting children voice concerns that they have about remembering where to be at certain times. The following questions can be used to examine the child's experience of the physical space at each parent's home. These questions assume that a child lives with their mother in one residence and with their father in another residence. These questions may be altered to fit any situation in which the child has two caretakers:

1. Tell me where you live.
2. You live with your mother some of the time?
3. Tell me about your mother's home.
4. Tell me about your bedroom at your mother's house.
5. When you get ready to spend time with your father, tell me who helps you get ready?
6. What does your mother do to help you get ready to visit with your father?
7. What clothing do you like to bring to your father's home?
8. Who helps you pack your clothes?
9. What are you not allowed to bring to your father's home?
10. What do you talk with your mother about as you get ready to stay with your father?
11. Who helps you with your homework?
12. What do you like about the way that your mother/father helps you with your homework?
13. What would you like to change about the ways in which your mother/father helps you with your homework?
14. Tell me about your favorite toys.
15. Tell me how your mother/father plays with you.
16. Which is your mother/father's favorite toy?
17. What is the best part about playing with your toys when you are with your mother/father?
18. What does your mother/father do when one of your toys is broken?
19. What is your mother/father's favorite game?
20. What is your favorite game?
21. What is the best thing about playing with your mother/father?
22. When you are playing with your toys, what is your mother/father doing?
23. What would you like your mother or father to do with you when you play with your toys?

Emotional space refers to different emotional climates that exist at each parent's home. Children move from one physical home to another and from one emotional landscape to another. Children may react to changes in emotional climate between parents' homes. The geographic distance between parental homes can create an emotional distance between the child and parent. Even children who are equally happy to be with either parent or equally happy to be in either parent's home experience transitions between homes as emotional journeys that require regular emotional adjustment. Children's emotional reactions can be misread or misinterpreted by the parents, causing them to advocate for a custodial or visitation schedule that may not be in the children's best interests and may not be responsive to the children's actual needs. The following questions can be used to examine the child's experience of the emotional space at each parent's home:

1. I understand that when you go from your mother's home to your father's home, you ride in your mother/father's car?
2. Tell me where you sit (front or back).
3. Tell me what you talk about on the drive to your mother/father's home.
4. Is it a long drive?
5. What does it feel like to drive to your mother/father's home?
6. Who do you talk to about your feelings?
7. What feelings are you able to talk about with your mother/father?
8. What feelings does your mother/father talk about with you?
9. What can your mother/father do to make the car ride better (more comfortable, more fun, less boring, more exciting, etc)?

Psychological space refers to differences in household structure, organization, and functions. There may be changes between homes in routines, codes of behavior, expectations, standards of living, and other functional differences. Children may find it difficult to adjust to a home that does not fit their psychological narratives about who they are and where they are supposed to live. The following questions can be used to examine a child's experience of differences in the psychological space between family homes:

1. Tell me about the rules at your mother's home.
2. Tell me about the rules at your father's home.
3. Tell me how the rules at your mother's house are different from the rules at your father's house.
4. What chores do you have at your mother/father's house?
5. You used to live with your mother and father? What is different about your mother's house?

6. What is different about your father's house?
7. What is different about the rules at your mother/father's house?
8. What rules do you like? Why?
9. What rules do you not like? Why?
10. When you don't like something at your mother/father's house, who do you talk to?
11. What do you like best about talking with your mother/father?
12. What would you like your mother/father to do differently?
13. When you come back from time with your mother, what does your father talk with you about?
14. When you come back from time with your father, what does your mother talk with you about?
15. Is it difficult to go back and forth from your mother's house to your father's house?
16. Tell me more about that.
17. Who do you talk to about your feelings about going back and forth?

Equal time refers to parents', judges', and attorneys' tendencies to think about parenting in exact amounts of time. Whether children spend one week with one parent and another week with the other or spend 4 days with one parent and 3 days with the other, the rigidness of time-share schedules often affect children's needs for flexibility between homes. For example, a child scheduled with their father might need to spend time with their mother on a particular day, and the rigidness of the access schedule can be a more valued decision-making element than the child's needs. Smart reported children can feel frustrated with the rigidness of access schedules and may be reluctant to talk about these frustrations with their parents. Children may be aware of their parents' competing needs for the children's time and do not want to disappoint either parent or cause tension. The following questions can be used to explore children's perception of equal time:

1. Do you have any thoughts that you want to share with me about how much time you want to spend at each parent's home?
2. Tell me more about why you think that this arrangement is a good arrangement for you.

Time apart refers to children's time away from one parent. Smart (2002) referred to this time away from the residential parent as a "sabbatical." Some children do not like time away from a particular parent, and other children may feel forced to spend time with a parent. Some children may like time away from the residential parent to gain some perspective on the nonresidential parent.

Some children worried about one parent when they were with the other parent. Children may worry about parents who do not have romantic partners and feel time away from a single parent means that the parent will be lonely. Children have also reported time passes more slowly at one parent's home than it does at the other's, usually because one parent was less available, less involved, or had a home with fewer creature comforts. The following questions can be used to discuss a child's experience spending time away from one parent:

1. Tell me about what you like about spending time with your mother/father.
2. When you are with your father, tell me your understanding of what your mother is doing.
3. How do you know what your mother/father is doing when you are with the other parent?
4. Which parent has more rules around the house?
5. Tell me about the rules.
6. What rules do you like?
7. What rules do you think make sense when you are at home?
8. What feelings do you have about your mother/father being at their home while you spend time with your father/mother?

Time to oneself refers to children's private time. Children of divorce may feel their time was always scheduled. They have less time for themselves and to spend with their friends. The following questions can be used to explore a child's perceptions of time to themself:

1. Tell me about the time that you spend in your room.
2. What do you do in your room?
3. Tell me about the toys in your room.
4. Tell me who spends time with you in your room.
5. When you are with your father/mother, tell me what you like to do with your mother/father?
6. Tell me about the playdates you have when you spend time at your father/mother's house.
7. Do you go to sleepovers?
   a. If yes, tell me about the sleepovers.
8. Do you have friends come over to play?
   a. If yes, tell me about the friends you have come over to play.
9. Tell me what you do?

10. Do you have sleepovers at your house?
11. What do you like most about having friends over?
12. What does your mother/father say about having friends come over and play?

Time and hurting refers to an experience of children who have to wait for the nonresidential parent to visit them or take them out. These children often feel powerless and can view time spent waiting for their parent as a measure of how much that parent cares. The following questions can be used to explore a child's perception of having to wait and how waiting affects them:

1. When your mother/father says they will pick you up at a particular time, are they on time?
2. Do you often wait for your mother/father to pick you up?
3. What do you do when you are waiting for your mother/father to pick you up?
4. What does your father say when your mother is late?
5. What does your mother say when your father is late?
6. When your mother is late picking you up, what does she tell you about why she was late?
7. What does she ask you about your feelings about her being late?
8. What do you say to your mother/father when they are late picking you up?

Time and sharing refers to situations where both parents enjoy ample time with their children, are on good terms with each other, and regularly share parenting time. Children may feel happy with time-sharing arrangements because of the quality of their relationships with each parent, as they may feel the most important issues are sustaining and managing their relationships with their parents. The following questions can be used to examine the child's perception of sharing time with their parents:

1. Tell me how you feel about spending time with your father.
2. Tell me how you feel about spending time with your mother.
3. When you are with your mother/father, what is your understanding of what your mother/father does at their home?
4. How do you feel about your mother/father being home at their place when you are with your mother/father?
5. What does your mother/father say when you leave to go to the other parent's home?
6. What does your mother/father say when you come back from spending time with the other parent?

7. Is your mother/father worried about you when you visit the other parent?

    a. If yes, tell me what they say worried them.

Smart's (2002) research can remind evaluators that a true understanding of a child's experience of divorce comes from seeing the world through the eyes of the child. Recognizing parents' tendencies to project adult interpretations of children's experiences on to parents' narratives may help evaluators focus attention on factors associated with children's experiences of divorce through their perspectives. When added to the evaluator's emerging understanding of children's use of language as described in the following section of this chapter, evaluators should find themselves becoming increasingly child-centered in evaluating children's emotional, developmental, and psychological experiences of their new lives.

OTHER QUESTIONS

Our previous interview questions flow from Smart's (2002) findings and are research informed. Other experts have proposed questions that flow from their clinical experience and knowledge of the literature. For example, Ackerman (2006) has offered these questions to guide child interviews:

1. When your mother talks about your father, what does she say about your father?
2. What did your mother/father tell you to be sure to tell me today.
3. What do you like best about your mother/father?
4. What would you like to change about your mother/father?
5. Tell me something that makes you happy/sad/mad/worried.
6. How would you feel if the Judge said you should live with your father and visit your mother? And vice versa.
7. Has your mother/father ever hurt you?
8. Has your father ever hurt your mother?
9. Has your mother ever hurt your father?
10. When you think about your mother and father:
    a. Who laughs the most?
    b. Who cries the most?
    c. Who yells the most?
    d. Who helps most with homework?
    e. Who buys you clothes?
    f. Who cooks your meals the most?

g. Who goes to school conferences?
h. Who takes you to the doctor?
i. When you have a problem, who do you talk to about your problem?

Garber (2007) created the Query Grid, which is "designed to assist interviewers in eliciting accurate reports from court-involved children aged four through twelve years old" (p. 4). The grid is separated into four columns: happy, sad, mad, and scared. The grid has different rows of contexts: home-with-mom, home-with-dad, and school (with more that can be added by the interviewer). The evaluator asks the child to fill in each square with an event. For example, something that makes the child happy at their home with their mother. The evaluator can then structure an interview with the child around each event, exploring the specifics of the event and seeking additional information about other related, relevant experiences.

FORENSIC INTERVIEWING OF ADOLESCENTS

While many of the provided interview questions in the previous section will work well when interviewing adolescents, there are some special considerations. The emerging neuroscience of adolescence has changed the way we understand adolescence, a period of brain development that has been expanded to include ages 11–24: "Today adolescence begins much earlier, it ends much later, and it is far more important in determining health, success, and happiness in adulthood than it has ever been" (Steinberg, 2014).

The Adolescent Brain

Steinberg (2014) teaches that our actions depend on two things: a) the strength of our emotion and b) our ability to manage it. To understand the teenage brain, it is important to understand some neuroscience, particularly the functions of the prefrontal cortex and the limbic system. The prefrontal cortex oversees organizing, self-regulation, and rational thinking. The prefrontal cortex may not be fully developed until an adolescent reaches their mid-20s. The limbic system plays an important role in generating emotions. The story of adolescence is the story of how the prefrontal cortex and limbic system work together.

Steinberg (2014) describes how the prefrontal cortex and limbic system work together in three stages. In phase one, adolescents are driven by emotions. They exhibit irrational thoughts and behavior, impulsivity, and recklessness. In phase two, the brain has improved self-regulation—though it is not consistent. In phase three, the adolescent has consistent self-regulation.

In situations that are emotionally charged, adolescents in phase one do not have capacity for self-regulation. They are also very vulnerable to peer influence and immediate incentives, so the interviewer needs to be vigilant about how the adolescent's interview data might be more influenced by the last person with whom they spoke than influenced by a reliable, fact-based assessment of their experiences.

Adolescents also often lack time perspective, which impairs the adolescent's ability to make judgments and decisions that require future orientation. Interviewers need to conduct multiple interviews in order to control for threats to the reliability of the information being provided by the adolescent. They also need to delve more deeply into the adolescent's intention and meaning rather than accept judgment statements without understanding the basis or motivation of the judgment.

Adolescents develop physically, emotionally, cognitively, and socially at rates unique to the individual. For example, 15-year-old Billy may display cognitive maturity, executive functioning immaturity, psychosocial immaturity, emotional immaturity, and physical maturity, while 15-year-old Stephen may display cognitive immaturity, executive functioning immaturity, psychosocial maturity, emotional maturity, and physical immaturity. Because of the various emotional experiences each exerts upon the adolescent's understanding and perspective, an adolescent could display cognitive maturity about the relationship with their father yet display cognitive immaturity about their relationship with their mother.

The adolescent's varied maturity levels can impact their understanding, reasoning, reward sensitivity, time orientation, emotional responsiveness, risk perception, suggestibility, abstract thinking, impulsivity, perceived autonomy, self-regulation, and their reaction to peer influence. For example, adolescents at different maturity levels may have varying abilities to comprehend the implications of parenting time arrangements, such as a more mature adolescent might articulate their needs and preferences clearly, while a less mature one may struggle to grasp long-term consequences.

Another example has to do with whether the adolescent is highly sensitive to rewards and has a lower perception of risk, as they might be more prone to favoring the "fun" parent over the more structured or disciplinary one. A younger adolescent with a short-term perspective might prioritize immediate gratification over stability, which could influence their stated preferences in custody proceedings. Adolescents with a strong sense of autonomy may resist authority and seek greater control over their living arrangements. However, their sense of independence may not always align with their actual ability to manage responsibilities effectively.

Evaluators should also ask the adolescent about their peer relationships. Peers play a crucial role in an adolescent's life, and a child might prefer a parenting time arrangement that aligns with maintaining friendships rather than what is best for their overall well-being.

Factors to Examine

Moran and Weinstock (2011) created the Parenting Competence 3 Child Interview to assess the adolescent's perception of their parents' parenting skills.

Moran and Weinstock grouped parenting skills into three categories (i.e., nurturing skills, teaching skills, and coparenting skills).

Nurturing skills include:

1. Shared affection: offering physical contact and affection; participating in activities with the child; expressing enthusiasm and approval
2. Responsiveness: sensitivity to the child's subjective experience and behavioral signals; empathic responding; helping the child identify and express emotions
3. Protection: providing physical, emotional, and cognitive resources; learning developmentally appropriate expectations; ensuring physical, emotional, and interpersonal security

Teaching skills include:

1. Communication: clarity about expectations, rules, and values; active listening; minimal use of negative talk such as loud, demanding, threatening, or hostile speech; teaching problem-solving and critical-thinking skills
2. Managing: structuring routines, monitoring academic progress in a nonintrusive manner, social involvement, and exposure to social environments including the media and internet
3. Discipline: setting developmentally appropriate goals; establishing clear and consistent limits, boundaries, rules, expectations and consequences; using praise, positive reinforcement, planned ignoring, and time-outs
4. Modeling: mood management, impulse control (e.g., anger, use of mood-altering substances), rule-compliance, conflict management, time management

Coparenting skills include:

1. Communicating with the coparent about the child's medical needs, school performance, recreational activities, friends, disciplinary incidents, daily routines, etc.
2. Encouraging the child's relationship with the coparent by refraining from criticism of the coparent; supporting the coparent's authority; flexing the parenting timeshare schedule; acknowledging the coparent's resources and benign intentions; supporting the relationship with the coparent's extended family and social network.

Moran and Weinstock (2011) asked adolescents to grade their parents on the above categories using their Parenting Competence 3 grid. Beyond these inquiries, it is also important to ask the child about their health:

1. Have you had any recent doctor visits?
2. Have you had any significant illnesses or injuries?

3. Do you take any medications? Now or in the past?
4. Do you have any challenges with vision and hearing?
5. Describe your sleep schedule.
6. What are the bedtime rules at your mother's house?
7. What are the bedtime rules at your father's house?
8. Are there any exceptions?
9. Approximately how many hours of sleep do you get a night?
10. When do you wake up?
11. How often do you wake up in the middle of the night?
12. How long does it take you to fall back to sleep?

The evaluator should also understand the child's academic history:

1. What is your current school? Grade or level?
2. Pretend we had a time machine, how would a teacher in elementary school describe you?
3. How would a teacher in middle or intermediate school describe you?
4. If I were to ask your present teachers, how would they describe you?
5. What is or are your favorite class or subjects?
6. What is the most difficult classes or subjects?
7. Do you get any extra help with these subjects? Who helps you? How do they help you?
8. What were your recent grades?
9. Describe for me your recent experiences with homework?
10. What are the rules regarding homework at your mother's house?
11. What are the rules regarding homework at your father's house?

Adolescents are constantly rewriting the scripts that comprise their identities. Interviewers should ask about the adolescent's strengths, interests, and engagement:

1. What are some things you like to do or think that you are good at?
2. How do you like to spend your free time?
3. What are ways you have of relaxing and having fun?
4. What are your favorite hobbies, sports, music and movies?
5. How do you relax and have fun with your family (including common interests and activities)?

As we have described above, a major component of adolescent development is the ability to self-regulate. The following questions address self-regulation:

1. How do you calm yourself down when upset or angry?
2. How do you calm yourself down at your mother's house?
3. How do you calm yourself down at your father's house?
4. How do you handle difficult or stressful situations? Give an example of the last difficult situation you faced and how you handled it.

The influence of peer relationships is a cornerstone of adolescence, and the following questions can be used to explore those relationships:

1. What are your friends like?
2. What are some things you like to do together?
3. What do your friends think of your family?
4. Whom are you closest to in your family?
5. When you get into trouble at home, how do your parents handle it?
6. How would your friends' parents handle that same situation?
7. Who in your life helps you reach your goals or explore your interests?
8. Name some people whom you respect or whom you see doing things you like or appreciate. What kinds of things do they do?
9. Do you belong to any clubs, teams, community organizations, or churches (synagogues, temples, etc.)?

Noting that an adolescent's goals and aspirations may change frequently, it is important to understand how they envision themselves and their future. The following questions can be used to explore adolescents' vision for their future:

1. If things went well for you over the next month, what would be different?
2. How do you see yourself in a year?
3. How about when you are an adult?

Adolescence is a time of transition, and it is a time in which their developing brains are ultrasensitive to change. The following questions can be used to explore transitions:

1. Did you recently change schools or are you planning to change schools?
2. Have you changed houses or are you planning to move soon?
3. Have there been any big changes in your family recently?
4. Have there been any big changes with your friends recently?

Since adolescents have challenges with time-perspective, they may speak in highlights that do not allow for understanding context or their day-to-day lives. It may be necessary to ask the child to walk you through their daily schedule:

1. Think of a regular day for you. Tell me what you do first thing when you get up. What's next? And after that? (Have the child describe what they do from waking up to going to bed at night.)

While there are many psychological tests and screening instruments, we recommend screening for social-emotional challenges during the interview:

1. Tell me how you have been feeling:
    a. Over the past year.
    b. Over the past month.
    c. Over the past week.
2. Tell me about your interests, hobbies, and activities.
3. Tell me what you enjoy about those interests, hobbies, and activities.
4. Have you noticed any change in how often you engage in each of these interests, hobbies, and activities?
5. Tell me your understanding of why these changes have occurred.
6. How is your appetite?
7. What kinds of things do you like to eat?
8. Have you gained or lost weight lately?
9. How well do you sleep?
10. About how much do you sleep each night?
11. Have you noticed any change in your sleep habits or behavior?
12. Do you often have trouble paying attention to details?
13. If yes, how long have you had difficulties paying attention?
14. Give me an example.
15. Are there particular situations in which you have more difficulties paying attention than other situations?
16. Tell me about what you view as the differences between situations in which you have difficulties paying attention versus those in which you have fewer difficulties.
17. Are you told to sit still a lot?
18. Do you usually get upset and lose your temper if things don't go your way?
19. Do you talk back or argue with your parents or teachers a lot?

20. Do you worry more than other kids your age? If so, do you worry as often as every day or every other day? What do you worry about?

It is important to understand the adolescent's access to technology. It is also important to understand how the adolescent perceives how their parents manage, supervise, and limit their use of technology, which can be explored with the following questions:

1. What technology (phone, tablet, computer, video game system) do you use?
2. What social media do you use?
3. What are your favorite apps, games, things to do?
4. What are the technology rules at Parent A's house?
5. What are the technology rules at Parent B's house?
6. How does Parent A respond if you don't follow those rules?
7. How does Parent B respond if you don't follow those rules?
8. Does Parent A know how to monitor or limit your tech?
9. Does Parent B know how to monitor or limit your tech?
10. What limits or restrictions or monitoring does Parent A place on technology?
11. What limits or restrictions or monitoring does Parent B place on technology?
12. What's your favorite video game?
13. How many hours have you logged on that game?
14. Who do you communicate with over your video games/apps/social media?
15. Does anyone monitor these communications?

INTERVIEWING ADULTS

Forensic interviewing of adults includes parent, stepparent, grandparent, and collateral interviews. The focus of the adult interview is to obtain information directly related to answering specific questions posed at the beginning of the evaluation. Interviews of adults involved in the caretaking of minor children need to address a wide variety of areas. The evaluator should seek to verify answers to each of the areas examined in the interview from independent informants or records. Interviewers should remember that a fundamental basis of a forensic interview is to seek out historical truth (S. A. Greenberg & Shuman, 1997); that is, the evaluator is seeking information from third party' sources that support or refute the assertions made during the interviews with the parents and child.

Obtaining information about past and current parenting behavior is critical. As we describe in Chapter 20, gatekeeping analysis is one method to obtain such information. A gatekeeping analysis includes information about childcare activities from birth through present. Gatekeeping refers to the degree to which each parent has provided the other parent access to their child and provided opportunities to engage in childcare activities. Gatekeeping is a dimensional concept in which the dimension exists between flexible and restrictive (inflexible) gatekeeping.

William G. Austin and Rappaport (2018) suggested that gatekeeping is more than just physical access to the child. A parent might engage in restrictive gatekeeping with regards to the time the child is allowed to spend with the other parent while being flexible about sharing information about the child. Alternatively, a parent might be a restrictive information gatekeeper about educational or medical information yet be flexible in sharing information about the child's activities.

Families differ in terms of how active and involved each parent has been in the day-to-day caretaking of children. Often, there is an unspoken social contract between the parents about their respective roles and activities in the family. These unspoken social contracts about each parent's roles and activities frequently are based on models of parenting responsibilities drawn from their families of origin. Gathering information about past generations' ideas about the role and activities of mothers and fathers often provides useful information about the ideas, beliefs, values, attitudes, and behaviors that guide the parents' current ideas about parenting responsibilities.

In some families, there is a conscious effort to change the influence of how past generations have distributed parenting responsibilities. Gathering information about how each parent contributed to the development of parenting responsibilities helps to establish the structure of parenting activities in the family prior to its dissolution.

The next step is to investigate whether and how respective parenting responsibilities have changed over time beginning with changes that occurred when the parents were together and extending to changes that have occurred since the parents separated. As the evaluator examines these changes, they should focus attention on the parents' involvement and agreement with changes in parenting time and parenting activities. Some parents report unilateral decisions about changes in parental access, parental activities, or parental responsibilities. Other parents report a cooperative approach to distribution of parental responsibilities.

Parallel to a gatekeeping analysis is the evaluator's development of a timeline of legal maneuvers that can be charted by monitoring motions to and orders from the court. Developing a chronology of legal motions and court orders and comparing those legal actions against changes in parental access and responsibilities is often a useful area for analysis.

During the parent interviews, evaluators should seek information about a range of parental involvement with each child, including engagement in child-related activities and descriptions of the parents' perceptions of the nature and quality of interactions with each child. Too frequently, evaluators neglect to report information about the nature and quality of parent–child interactions.

Knowing which activities to which a parent might shuttle a child says little about the nature and quality of the interactions before, during, and after the chauffeuring.

We believe that descriptions of the nature and quality of parent–child interactions provide information that might be used to address the third American Psychological Association factor that seeks to establish the fit between parental parenting abilities and the emotional and developmental needs of the child. Evaluators might gather information about each parent's perception of their behavior with each child, parenting philosophy, parenting behavior reflective of the philosophy, disciplinary philosophy, and disciplinary behaviors. Evaluators are ethically obligated to consider the historical context of the matter at hand (Association of Family and Conciliation Courts, 2007; American Psychological Association 2017a; King, 2013). Understanding the historical context includes collecting and creating a timeline of events relevant to the present evaluation and a history from each caregiver (Gould & Martindale, 2007; Garber, 2020; Hynan, 2014). As this history is taken, we encourage evaluators to also ask the parent their perception of the other parent's perspective. The following are prompts that can be used:

1. Summarize the major aspects of the current situation from your perspective.
2. Summarize what you think the other parent would describe as the major aspects of the current situation.
3. Describe the events which have led up to the current legal dispute.
4. Describe what you believe the other parent believes are the events which have led up to the current legal dispute.

Information About the Child

Evaluators are encouraged to gather information about each parent's description, along a variety of dimensions, of each child. This might include information about the child's daily routine, friends, activities, social strengths and challenges, academic progress, and related areas of child development.

Interviews should also explore each parent's perception of the nature and quality of their relationship with the child. Evaluators should seek as much detail as possible to gain an understanding of each parent's grasp of the complexity and uniqueness of each child. A similar examination should be undertaken about the parent's relationship with each child.

Interviewers need to understand historical and present conditions. Among the areas to explore are the nature and quality of sibling relationships, changes to the sibling subsystem resulting from parental separation, and each parent's understanding of similarities and differences in sibling behavior between the two parent's homes.

Understanding extended family involvement often leads to information about the degree to which extended family involvement has played a role in the family conflict. Grandparents often provide a needed haven for children whose parents are engaged in conflict. Exploring each parent's relationship with both maternal and paternal grandparents might reveal important information related to factors associated with the current parental conflict.

The following are among the questions that might guide a parent interview about each child:

1. Describe your child's early developmental history.
2. Did your child experience any developmental or medical challenges before they were born?
3. Did your child experience any developmental or medical challenges when they were an infant?
4. When did they begin to walk?
5. When did they begin to talk?
6. Has your child received any special services for speech, hearing, sight, or movement?
7. Do you believe the child(ren) could benefit from any special services related to speech, hearing, or sight problems, or from other physical or psychological problems, developmental or educational delays, or chemical addictions?
8. Does your child need or receive any specialized support now?

It is also important to ask about the child's social and emotional development, which can be done with the following questions:

1. What is your understanding of your child's feelings about their relationship with you?
2. What is your understanding of your child's feelings about their relationship with the other parent?
3. How does your child interact with children their age?
4. How does your child manage their emotions on a daily basis?

To learn about the parent's perception of their child's abilities to cope with challenges, consider the following questions:

1. How does your child manage disappointments?
2. How does your child manage stress?
3. Has your child experienced any regressions in which they have acted younger than their chronological age or in which they had a skill that they then lost?
4. How do you believe your child behaves differently at school?
5. How do you believe your child behaves differently in the community?
6. How do you believe your child behaves differently at the other parent's house?

Mirroring Smart's (2002) inquires, we have modified the following questions about the child's physical space to questions about the parent's perception of the child's physical space:

1. Tell me about your home and your neighborhood.
2. What is the parenting time schedule?
3. What is the child's schedule when they are with you?
4. Tell me about the child's bedroom.
5. When your child gets ready to spend time with the other parent, tell me who helps them get ready?
6. How do you prepare for transitions?
7. What do you need to bring?
8. Are there any items that are not allowed?
9. Tell me about the conversations you have with your child around transitions.
10. Who helps your child with homework?
11. What are your child's favorite toys.
12. How do you and your child play?
13. What is your favorite game?
14. What is your child's favorite game?

Another area to examine, which can be done with the following questions, is the parent's perception of the children's experience of the *emotional climate* at each parent's home:

1. Tell me about the child's experiences transitioning between homes.
2. How does the child behave in the car before and after parenting time with the other parent?
3. Tell me what you talk about on the drive.
4. Does your child talk to you about their feelings?
5. Do you talk to your child about your feelings during transitions? If so, what do you say?
6. What feelings does your child express?
7. What do you do to make the transitions better?

The parent's perspective of the *psychological space* between family homes can be explored with the following questions:

1. Tell me about the rules at your home.
2. Tell me about the rules at the other parent's home.

3. Tell me how the rules are different at each home.
4. What chores does the child have at your house?
5. What would the child say is different about each house?
6. How would the child describe the different rules at each house?
7. Who does the child communicate with at your house?
8. Who does the child communicate with at the other parent's house?
9. What does your child like best about you?
10. What would your child like you to do differently?
11. Does your child think it is difficult to go back and forth between homes?

Next, we encourage the evaluator to ask about the parent's understanding of the child's perception of equal parenting time with the following questions:

1. Does your child express any thoughts about how much time they want to spend at each parent's home?
2. Does your child's physical behavior suggest they have opinions about how much time they want to spend at each parent's house?
3. Tell me what you think your child believes is the best arrangement.

The next area of inquiry is how their child handles the separation from the other parent, which can be explored with the following questions:

1. Does your child ask about the other parent during your parenting time?
2. Does your child call or FaceTime with the other parent during your parenting time?
3. Does your child worry about the other parent during your parenting time?
4. What do you believe your child thinks the other parent is doing during your parenting time?

The following questions explore the child's schedule:

1. How is the child's schedule determined?
2. What is your child's understanding of the parenting time schedule?
3. How does your child keep track of time?
4. During your parenting time, how do you communicate the schedule?
5. Does the child have a different schedule with each parent?
6. Does the child have a voice in determining their weekly schedule?
7. At your home, does the child have private time in their room?
8. Does your child have playdates during your parenting time?
9. Does your child have sleep overs? If so, tell me about the sleepovers.

Another area of interview focus is on children's sense of powerlessness, which can be explored with the following questions:

1. How often are you or the other parent late to pick up your child?
2. What do you tell your child when you are late?
3. What does the other parent tell you or the child when they are late?

To ask about the parent's understanding of their child's concern with both parents, consider the following questions:

1. Describe your understanding of your child's concerns, if any, about custodial placement with you.
2. Describe your understanding of your child's concerns, if any, about custodial placement with the other parent.

It is important to ask about resist and refuse dynamics. The following questions can guide that conversation:

1. Do you believe that the other parent is attempting to negatively influence the child(ren) against you?
   a. If so, tell me how.
2. Do you believe that the other parent has intentionally interfered or attempted to interfere with your ability to see the child(ren)?
   a. If so, tell me how.
3. Tell me about your children's access to the other parent.
4. Have they been able to see the other parent consistently over time?
5. What obstacles have gotten in the way of the children spending time with the other parent?
6. Tell me about each child's interest in spending time with the other parent.
7. When one of your children indicates concern or hesitancy about spending time with the other parent, what have you done?
8. Tell me why you believe your actions are best for your child.
9. Have you stopped your children from seeing the other parent?
   a. If so, why?

Information About the Parents

The evaluator should understand the history of the parents' relationship prior to separation. The following questions can guide that conversation:

1. How did you meet?
2. What drew you to the other parent?

3. How did you decide to marry?
4. What were the expectations about marital life?
5. What were the expectations about parenting roles?
6. How did you and your coparent talk about each of these expectations and roles?
    a. Tell me about your family-of-origin influence regarding communication, affectionate style, attachment style, etc.
7. What were some challenges that developed during the marriage and how were they addressed?
8. When did the marriage begin to deteriorate?
9. What steps were taken to address the problems?
10. When did you realize the marriage was broken?
11. How did you present this to the other parent?
12. Describe the major strengths or significant assets that you feel existed during your marriage to the other parent.
13. Describe the major weaknesses or challenges that you feel existed during your marriage to the other parent.

Too often in high conflict families, each parent is highly polarized and stuck in blaming the other parent for their children's challenges. Attempt to gain understanding into each parent's ability to see beyond their anger and polarizing blame by asking each parent about their respective contribution to the problems in the marriage and since the separation:

1. How did the other parent contribute to the problems in the marriage?
2. How did you contribute to the problems in the marriage?
3. How has the other parent contributed to the problems since the separation?
4. How have you contributed to the problems since the separation?

Research on attachment and early development has illuminated patterns and the organization of attachment relationships on adults' future emotional regulation, social relatedness, access to autobiographical memory, and the development of self-reflection and narrative (Cicchetti & Toth, 1995; Main et al., 2005; Siegel, 2020; Sroufe, 2005). The adult parent's security of attachment "appears to convey a form of resilience—at least for offspring—even in the face of trauma or loss" (Siegel, 2020). We await the day when the adult attachment interview has been studied in PPEs. Until then, it is important to ask about the parent's relationship and attachment history, and the following questions can be used:

1. Describe your parent's marital relationship.
2. How long were they married?

3. How many separations did they have?
4. How would you characterize the way they showed each other love and affection?
5. How would you characterize the way each parent showed you love and affection?
6. How would they respond to you when you needed them?
7. How would you characterize the way they dealt with marital problems such as disagreements or conflict?
8. How would you characterize the stability of their marital relationship?
9. Describe your father's temperament and personality.
10. Describe your father's style of parenting.
11. Describe your father's style of discipline.
12. Describe your relationship with your father during childhood, your teenage years, and now.
13. Describe your mother's temperament and personality.
14. Describe your mother's style of parenting.
15. Describe your mother's style of discipline.
16. Describe your relationship with your mother during childhood, your teenage years, and now.
17. Describe how your family was organized. For example, who was in charge and how was that shown? Who was the favorite and how was that shown? Who was out of favor, why, and how was that shown?
18. Were there any other family members (like grandparents) or friends who had a role in your childhood?

The parent's mind and the patterns of their communication directly shape the organization of the developing child's mind (Siegel, 2020). Experienced and unresolved trauma is likely to impact parents' emotional regulation. A parent's preoccupation with past childhood disappointments or trauma can continually intrude on the parent's present perceptions (Siegel, 2020; J. Walker, 2007): "Life narratives are not merely accumulations of autobiographical detail, but are driven by both explicit memory and implicit recollections of repeated experiences" (Siegel, 2020). It might be relevant to inquire about each parent's development, resiliency, and relationships. The following questions can be used for such inquires:

1. How would you describe yourself as a person?
2. Describe how you felt about yourself during your childhood.

3. Describe how you felt about yourself during your teenage years.
4. Describe how you felt about yourself during your young adult years.
5. Describe how you felt about yourself during your marriage.
6. Describe how you feel about yourself now.
7. How do you think other people describe you?
8. How do you generally feel about yourself?
9. What are your relationships with people other than the other parent like?
10. Who are the most important people in your life?
11. What is your relationship with them like?
12. How well do you think you understand yourself?
13. How well do you understand other people?
14. How do you deal with having strong feelings about things?
15. How do you deal with people who have different opinions?

To understand the parent's parenting beliefs and knowledge, consider the following questions:

1. What do you believe is the purpose of parenting?
2. What is your parenting philosophy?
3. What are your strengths as a parent?
4. What are your challenges as a parent?
5. What are the other parent's strengths as a parent?
6. What are the other parent's challenges as a parent?
7. Tell me about your ideas regarding disciplining your child.
8. Please describe the books, magazines or other materials you have read about parenting.
9. What did you learn from those sources?

The parent's medical history can be explored with the following questions:

1. Have you had any significant illness, injury, surgery or other medical procedure?
2. Are you anticipating any significant illness, injury, surgery or other medical procedures in the future?
3. What medications are you taking?
4. What medications have you taken?

The parent's substance use can be discussed with the following questions:

1. Describe your alcohol use.
2. Describe your history of marijuana use.
3. Describe your history of cocaine use.
4. What over the counter medicines do you take?
5. What over the counter medicines have you taken?

Information should also be gathered about each parent's mental health history. It can be useful to compare each parent's explanation of their mental health history with their medical and mental health records, with an eye toward the parent's realistic assessment of what, if any, mental health issues have been (or are currently) relevant to their parenting or coparenting abilities.

Screening for Domestic Violence, Intimate Partner Violence, Coercive Control, and Trauma

As described in the Association of Family and Conciliation Courts Guidelines for Examining Intimate Partner Violence (2016), "Allegations of intimate partner violence are common among custody-litigating families, and custody evaluators face special challenges when conducting evaluations in this context." Model Standard 5.11 and the guidelines provide direction to help the evaluator in identifying intimate partner violence and examining the possible effects on children, parenting, and coparenting. While we have a chapter devoted to this topic, here we include some questions that can be used to explore this area:

1. Describe what you and your former spouse would argue about.
2. Might concerns or allegations about coercive, intimidating, aggressive, violent or hostile behavior on your part be raised by the other parent as part of this evaluation?
3. Might concerns or allegations about coercive, intimidating, aggressive, violent or hostile behavior on the part of the other parent be raised as part of this evaluation?
4. If there was hostility, did the hostility include financial manipulation or control, strong expressions of dislike, verbal violence or abuse, violence toward or destruction of property, alienation of children's affection, threats of personal physical violence, withholding access to children, actual personal physical violence, or custodial interference or kidnapping of children?
5. Did the hostility include
   a. physically aggressive behaviors, which involve the intentional use of physical force with the potential for causing injury, harm, disability, or death;

b. sexually aggressive behaviors, which involve unwanted sexual activity that occurs without consent through the use of force, threats, deception, or exploitation;
c. economically aggressive behaviors, which involve the use of financial means to intentionally diminish or deprive another of economic security, stability, standing, or self-sufficiency;
d. psychologically aggressive behaviors, which involve intentional harm to emotional safety, security, or well-being; or
e. coercively controlling behaviors which involve harmful conduct that subordinates the will of another through violence, intimidation, intrusiveness, isolation, or control.

6. If the parent reports any behaviors listed above, inquire about
   a. frequency,
   b. recency,
   c. severity,
   d. directionality,
   e. pattern,
   f. intention,
   g. circumstance, and
   h. consequence.

Risks to Children

Evaluators should ask each parent about their perception of potential risks to the child in any and all aspects of their lives. In most high-conflict families, one or both parents often identify potential risks of harm originating from the other parent's behavior. Interviewers should explore specific examples of potential risks of harm with prompts such as the following:

1. I note that there are concerns in the pleadings about risk to the children. Tell me about your concerns.
2. Tell me your understanding of the other parent's concerns.
3. Describe how each child has experienced these specific concerns.
4. Tell me a few specific examples of each concern.
5. Do you believe that the child(ren) is/are at risk?
6. Are there allegations or concerns about physical, emotional, verbal, or sexual abuse toward the children by the other parent?
7. Are there allegations or concerns about physical, emotional, verbal, or sexual abuse toward the children by anyone else who you or the other parent knows?

8. To the best of your knowledge, has anyone in your family (including you) been victim of any form of abuse, neglect or exploitation?
9. To the best of your knowledge, has anyone in the other parent's family (including the other parent) been victim of any form of abuse, neglect or exploitation?
10. To the best of your knowledge, has any child been victim of any form of abuse, neglect or exploitation?

CONCLUSION

Forensic interviewing is a crucial element of PPEs, yet the field has long lacked comprehensive, structured guidance on what to ask and how to ask it. This chapter aims to bridge that gap by providing a framework for conducting child and adult interviews in forensic contexts.

We have outlined key considerations for interviewing children at different developmental stages, recognizing that factors such as memory, emotional responses, and loyalty conflicts can significantly impact the reliability of their statements. Evaluators must carefully assess influences such as primacy and recency effects, parental narratives, and the child's lived experiences in both households. Similarly, when interviewing adolescents, evaluators must account for the complexities of adolescent brain development, peer influences, and evolving identity formation. Adolescents may present unique challenges in forensic interviews, requiring careful questioning to accurately assess their perceptions of family dynamics, parenting, and personal needs.

For adults, interviews should be structured to explore historical and current parenting practices, coparenting dynamics, and potential concerns regarding parenting capacity. A forensic evaluator must balance the perspectives of both parents, distinguishing between subjective narratives and verifiable accounts. Additionally, specialized inquiries into topics such as domestic violence, coercive control, and child safety risks are essential in high-conflict cases. While these issues will be discussed in detail in the following chapters, we emphasize the importance of focusing interviews on the child's best interests and the broader family dynamics.

Ultimately, the questions and approaches outlined in this chapter serve as flexible tools that must be adapted to the specifics of each evaluation. Effective forensic interviewing requires a balance of structured inquiry, professional judgment, and an understanding of the psychological and developmental factors influencing both children and adults. The questions provided here are not intended as a rigid checklist but rather as a sampling of inquiries that should be tailored to the unique details of each case. By employing evidence-based interviewing techniques, evaluators can enhance the reliability and validity of their assessments, ensuring that their conclusions are well-supported and truly serve the best interests of the child. In the next chapter, we will take a deep dive into interviewing younger children.

13

Special Considerations for Interviewing Young Children

In this chapter, we delve into the critical considerations forensic interviewers must address when working with young children, particularly in legal contexts involving allegations of abuse or other sensitive matters. Given children's developmental stages, cognitive abilities, and vulnerability to external influences, forensic interviewing requires a nuanced, research-informed approach to elicit accurate and reliable information while minimizing the risks of contamination, coercion, or misinterpretation.

The discussion begins by exploring the unique challenges associated with interviewing young children, including the impact of memory development, suggestibility, language skills, and emotional regulation on their ability to recall and communicate experiences. Special attention is given to the risks of leading questions, interviewer bias, and external influences that may distort children's accounts. The chapter then examines evidence-based methodologies designed to enhance the integrity of forensic interviews. Drawing on established research in developmental psychology, cognitive science, and forensic best practices, we highlight techniques that foster open-ended responses, minimize suggestibility, and create a supportive environment that encourages children to disclose information accurately. Strategies such as the National Institute of Child Health and Human Development (NICHD) Investigative Interview Protocol, the use of structured yet flexible questioning frameworks, and rapport-building techniques are discussed in detail.

We greatly appreciate the comments and ideas provided by Michael Lamb, PhD.

https://doi.org/10.1037/0000474-014
Parenting Plan Evaluations: An Evidence-Informed Approach to Child Custody, by J. W. Gould and C. M. Mulchay

Additionally, the chapter underscores the importance of specialized training and continuous professional development for forensic interviewers. We emphasize the role of ongoing quality assessment, peer review, and supervision in ensuring ethical and effective interviewing practices. A key focus is placed on the necessity of maintaining an open, neutral stance to reduce bias and safeguard the credibility of the child's narrative. By integrating research on best practices in forensic interviewing—particularly in cases involving allegations of sexual abuse—this chapter provides a comprehensive set of guidelines aimed at enhancing the accuracy and reliability of children's statements. The insights presented here are especially relevant to parenting plan evaluations (PPEs), where children's perceptions of family dynamics, attachment relationships, and past experiences can significantly influence legal determinations regarding custody and visitation.

Our review of empirical literature and forensic case studies is intended to equip professionals with the knowledge, skills, and ethical considerations necessary for conducting legally defensible and developmentally sensitive forensic interviews with young children. By bridging psychological science and forensic practice, this chapter aims to support evaluators in adhering to evidence-based and evidence-informed procedures of data collection.

CHALLENGES IN THE FORENSIC INTERVIEWING OF YOUNG CHILDREN IN PARENTING PLAN EVALUATIONS

The forensic interviewing of young children, defined as children 6 years old and under, presents a unique set of challenges, requiring specialized training, knowledge, and sensitivity. Despite its critical role in forensic mental health and legal proceedings, this area remains poorly understood, with significant gaps in practitioner training outside the narrow task of interviewing children when there are allegations of sexual abuse. The complexities of interviewing young children arise from their developing language skills, cognitive abilities, and susceptibility to suggestion, all of which impact the reliability of the data gathered from the interview.

Few forensic mental health areas are as poorly understood or in which deficiencies in practitioner training are as apparent as the interviewing of young children. One reason is that the literature summaries describing the forensic interviewing of young children often provide little information about how children use language and how children view their unique worlds. Gould and Martindale devoted several chapters to research addressing conducting interviews through the eyes of children (Gould & Martindale, 2007).

Questions concerning the reliability and credibility of children's accounts often have emerged in adversarial legal proceedings, fostering a highly contentious debate about the value and limitations of children's testimony. Ceci and Bruck (1995) warned that the field of forensic interviews of children is expanding so quickly that reviews of the literature published only a few years ago may now be out of date. Evaluators must maintain awareness of current literature (Gould & Martindale, 2007).

INTERVIEWER TRAINING

Evaluators should obtain training, experience, and supervision in forensic interviewing, and they must be mindful of the research demonstrating the limited effectiveness of training programs in forensic interviewing. For example, one line of research has been focused on teaching interviewers to reduce the number of leading questions and yes or no questions. After attending a 10-day professional training seminar conducted by prominent child witness researchers, about 70% of participants' interview questions were yes or no questions (Gilstrap et al., 2001; Warren et al., 1999). Gilstrap et al. found 34.6% of questions asked were categorized as suggestive. Lamb et al. (2000) reported forensic interviewers in child abuse cases are inaccurate 66% of the time concerning the format of the questions they asked. The researchers also found that interviewers inflated estimates of open-ended questions asked during the interviews. Warren and Woodall (1999) found that even when interviewers had their interview notes available, they had difficulty reconstructing interview data.

Evaluators need training. We particularly recommend training that involves active practice and continuing quality assessment and review, since lecture-type training tends to have limited and often short-term impact (Lamb et al., 2018). Evaluators also need to remember to continuously monitor the format of their interview questions with children. As we will describe later, due to the research that indicates interviewer notes are not very accurate and the many challenges interviewing children, evaluators will be best served by audio or videotaping interviews.

RESEARCH TO GUIDE OUR UNDERSTANDING OF INTERVIEWING CHILDREN

It can be difficult for evaluators to conduct child interviews because there are no reliable procedures used to identify the credibility of children's statements during forensic interviews. Most research examining the credibility of children's statements during forensic interviews is found in the child sexual abuse literature (Blasbalg et al., 2021; Hershkowitz & Lamb, 2020). There is no reliable method to accurately distinguish between true and false statements, and increasing evidence raises doubts about professionals' ability to judge the trustworthiness of children's testimony (Hershkowitz & Lamb, 2020). Furthermore, several recent studies have shown that children, especially young children, are often reluctant to accurately report their experiences of abuse when they are formally interviewed, even when the allegations of abuse are valid (Hershkowitz & Lamb, 2020). When children are reluctant to disclose information about their experiences, it may compromise the quality and accuracy of information provided to forensic interviewers and the courts (Blasbalg et al., 2021).

While previous research has largely concentrated on cognitive strategies to enhance children's recall, Lamb and his colleagues have undertaken a series of studies aimed at improving the overall quality of children's self-reports. Their work extends beyond cognitive mechanisms to explore socioemotional factors that can hinder children's willingness to disclose information, particularly in sensitive contexts such as forensic interviews. By identifying and addressing these barriers—such as fear, anxiety, loyalty conflicts, and social pressures—they have contributed to the development of more effective interviewing techniques that facilitate accurate and comprehensive disclosures. Their research emphasizes the importance of creating a supportive and developmentally appropriate environment that encourages reluctant children to share information while minimizing the risks of suggestibility or external influence (Blasbalg et al., 2021).

The evidence-based factors found to decrease children's reluctance and enhance their cooperativeness nonsuggestively can be applied to forensic interviewing of children in PPEs. Children are especially reluctant to disclose abuse by family members, such that as many as half of suspected victims of abuse are reluctant to talk about their abuse (Blasbalg et al., 2021). Children caught in high-conflict custody battles might be reluctant to disclose information about their experiences with each parent and information about their experiences in the family system. We recognize that no research directly addresses this hypothesis, but we believe it is a reasonable inference drawn from the research on children's reluctance to disclose.

Specific expressions of omission, such as "I do not know" or "I do not remember," that occur early in the forensic interview, before the topic of abuse was broached, predict the failure to disclose substantive aspects of the child's experience (Hershkowitz et al., 2006). Other research has found that similar types of omissions by children were negatively correlated with children's overall forensic informativeness (Hershkowitz et al., 2015). One hypothesis drawn from these studies is that many omissions reflect children's reluctance rather than only their expressions of ignorance (Blasbalg et al., 2021).

Research trends suggest interviewers have been found to respond to children's reluctance by being less, rather than more, supportive. Interviewers may ask more intrusive questions, be less supportive, and prematurely ask questions about suspected abuse (Hershkowitz et al., 2006; Lewy et al., 2015). One hypothesis drawn from these data is that interviewers' counterproductive responses to children's reluctance are likely to have increased the child's reluctance to disclose and reduced their cooperation during interviews.

Supportive interviewer behavior is defined as a form of social interaction with children that fosters a feeling of well-being in the child. Supportive interviewer behavior includes being warm and friendly, smiling, maintaining eye contact, adopting open postures toward the child, and expressing interest in what the child is discussing. Supportive interviewing was found to predict more rather than less accurate information than did neutral or nonsupportive interviewing, even in response to suggestive questions (Saywitz et al., 2019). Thus, evaluators should adopt a supportive stance when engaged in forensic interviewing of children.

Research findings over the past 3 decades have identified certain interview conditions that create a high risk of contaminating young children's reports. Contrary to previously held beliefs, errors made by children in reporting sexual abuse are not limited to errors of omission (i.e., failure of the child to report important events). Under certain conditions, young children can also make errors of commission about personally experienced events involving their own bodies (e.g., reporting that an event occurred that, in fact, did not occur). Young children, especially preschoolers, are more likely than older children to respond erroneously to suggestive questions about their experiences and to select erroneous options when responding to forced-choice questions. Young children tend to remember less information, and they provide briefer accounts of their experiences than older children—yet their reports are no less accurate (Lamb et al., 2018; Poole, 2016).

Oral testimony from children, especially young children, may be influenced by the number of interviews, the number of interviewers, the types of questions, and the types of responses to answers expressed by the interviewer. Custody evaluators need to explore how many times a child has been involved in discussions with each parent, grandparent, and others. If possible, it is also important for evaluators to investigate how, if at all, the child's attitudes and feelings about each parent has changed over time after discussions with others.

MONITORING WHO IS PRESENT IN THE INTERVIEW ROOM

Most empirical studies of forensic interviewing of children have explored interviews conducted by one interviewer. Some interviews might involve more than one interviewer examining a child during an interview. Ferra et al. (2022) examined the effects that the number of adults present (in such interviews) had on young and older children's recall. Young children were between the ages of 5- and 7-years-old and older children were between the ages of 10- and 12-years-old.

Ferra et al. found that the number of adults present during an interview had an effect on the quality and quantity of the information children provided. When children of both age groups were interviewed by a single interviewer with no one else present, the children provided lengthier and more accurate accounts, in comparison to when children were interviewed by an interviewer in the presence of either one or two additional adults. Children who were interviewed by a single interviewer produced more correct and fewer incorrect answers. Compared to older children, younger children produced fewer correct answers and more incorrect and "I don't know" responses. Older boys and younger girls were only slightly affected by interviewing condition (i.e., single interviewer versus single interviewer with one or two additional adults). There was only a slight increase in the number of responses provided by children, regardless of their age, when they were interviewed in the presence of three adults. When interviewed by a single interviewer, young girls performed slightly worse than young boys. However, when in the presence of three adults, young boys fared worse. In contrast, older boys' performance was poorer when interviewed by a single interviewer while older girls performed poorer than older boys when interviewed in the presence of three adults.

EVERYDAY CONVERSATIONS BIAS CHILDREN, TOO

In most forensic interviews of children, children almost always talk with one of their parents or other concerned adults about an alleged transgression. These initial parent–child conversations often take place before authorities are contacted. How initial parent–child conversations about alleged maltreatment might influence subsequent forensic interview data from children was not well understood—until now.

In a recent study, Principe and London (2022) summarized several of their findings examining how mothers' everyday conversations with their children include factors likely to undermine the reliability of the child's self-report in a forensic interview, such as how mothers teach their children about language use, narrative formation, storytelling, and other commonly relied on factors that in a formal forensic interview format are known to influence children's self-report. Findings showed that exchanges between parents and their children play a central role in the development of autobiographical memory (Principe & London, 2022). Parents scaffold their children's narratives, teaching them about the structure and function of storytelling; that is, parental scaffolding teaches children how to tell others about their experiences with others (Principe & London, 2022). Parents serve as a filter through which children learn about past events through discussions. Parents teach children what is and what is not important in their lives by molding conversations that tend to reflect the beliefs about others and also beliefs about what their children have experienced (Principe & London, 2022). When parents hold beliefs about what their children have experienced, parent communications tend to mold their conversations to bring out children's reports that are consistent with those beliefs (Principe & London, 2022).

Parental scaffolding helps children to develop autobiographic skills by helping children draw out additional details, validate and expand on what children report, and provide connective threads among responses (Principe & London, 2022). Children's tendency to rely on their exposure to parents' discussions of the events in their lives serves to create a scaffold to both how to recall and what to recall about different events. Children's abilities to retrieve and relay their experiences to others are likely influenced by how those experiences and the stories created around those experiences have been reconstructed in prior conversations with parents (Principe & London, 2022, p. 291).

The concern over parental influence on development of children's storytelling of past events is a critical component in child custody interviews. It is highly likely that children have a significant number of conversations with one or both parents about the dissolution of the family. Parents might intend these conversations to convey openness, sincerity, and clarity about changes in their family. Each of these conversations might result in children developing new, possibly false narratives about events in their family, possible false narratives about experiences about which they have personal knowledge that has been altered—intentionally or otherwise—through interactions with each parent.

Everyday parent–child conversations are characterized by types of prompts, leading questions, directive questions, and suggestive questions that in a forensic context would result in a biased interview. What is among the unique aspects of the Principe and London (2022) studies are demonstrations of how everyday conversations that might occur with no intent to teach children a false report of an event or experience influence children's memory in informal, everyday conversations as well as influence children to offer a false report during formal investigative interviews. In everyday conversations, parents who are focused on obtaining accurate accounts of their children's experiences were found to produce more false information from their children. The key factor is that parents' motivations to elicit accurate information has the paradoxical effect on children of obtaining more false information. When these children are later interviewed by unfamiliar persons in more formal interviews who employ neutral, open-ended questioning strategies, the parents' earlier influence results in false information from the children. Children who were asked to recall about their earlier conversations with parents were unable to recall much of the conversations, even when the conversations were highly suggestive.

EXAMINING RELIABILITY OF INTERVIEW DATA

In forensic and psychological contexts, *reliability* refers to the consistency and stability of a child's narrative across multiple tellings. A reliable statement is one that remains coherent and retains key factual details over time, regardless of variations in questioning or the setting in which the disclosure occurs. Reliability does not speak to accuracy. One can tell a consistent story over multiple interviews, yet the accuracy of the story can be incorrect. When evaluating the reliability of a child's account, professionals consider:

- Internal consistency: The degree to which the child's story remains stable across different recountings without significant contradictions or spontaneous alterations in core facts.
- External consistency: How well the child's narrative aligns with corroborative evidence, independent witness accounts, or other reliable sources.

- Developmentally appropriate recall: Whether the level of detail and complexity in the child's account aligns with their cognitive and linguistic abilities.
- Resistance to suggestibility: The extent to which the child's account remains unaffected by leading questions, external influences, or pressure from authority figures.

While consistency is a key indicator of reliability, forensic experts must also recognize that minor inconsistencies—especially in peripheral details—are common in truthful accounts due to memory processes, stress, and developmental factors. A rigidly identical retelling across multiple interviews may, in some cases, raise concerns about rehearsed or coached statements. Therefore, reliability is best assessed in conjunction with credibility factors and scientific principles of memory and disclosure patterns in children.

If a child has been repeatedly interviewed using leading, directly suggestive, coercive, or suggestively manipulative interview techniques, the child's memory of alleged events may be altered in ways that change their meaning. When this happens, the child's statements are judged to be not reliable.

Timeline analysis entails following the chronology of a child's statements over time. Evaluators should examine the conditions under which the interview was conducted, the number of interviews or conversations in which the child participated with formal forensic interviews as well as informal conversations with people in the child's life, and how the child's description of the alleged events evolved over time, including how the child's relationship with each parent has changed over time. Most parents do not engage in coercive manipulation of their children but may engage in suggestive manipulation that influences the child's construction of reality and construction of their relationship with each parent.

As Underwager and Wakefield reminded us in 1998, more than 2 decades ago, "When the person's memory of events is changed or lost, the person may not know what is true or false. When the person then gives unreliable information, the person may not be aware of it. In such cases, the person cannot be said to be lying. A child who has been suggestively interviewed may be unable to distinguish the memory for a real event from the one that has been taught by the interviewer. Therefore, the testimony the child gives is not reliable."

Several factors affect the likelihood of children giving misinformation about personal events. Among those most often cited are interviewing methods used in obtaining the testimony. Repeated questioning, delayed questioning, suggestive and misleading interviewing, the emotional tone of the interview, and the status of the person conducting the interview can all have a significant negative impact on the accuracy of the testimony obtained from the child. The preexisting beliefs on the part of the interviewer will often affect the interviewer's methods of questioning, thereby influencing the child's response (Lamb et al., 2018; Zappala et al., 2018).

Evaluators should work to distinguish between suggestive conversations with parents that often are not intentionally suggestive but are suggestively manipulative versus suggestive interviews by professionals. This distinction will serve two purposes. The first is to draw attention to how conversations with parents and others in the child's life might contribute to tainting the child's memory. The second is to help the court broaden its understanding that children's accurate memories can be influenced by any conversation, not just those conducted by professionals.

METHODS AND CONDITIONS THAT NEGATIVELY AFFECT CHILDREN'S TESTIMONY

Research findings have revealed that many forensic interviews of children are often conducted using improper interviewing techniques. Most of these studies have examined forensic interviews of children alleged to have experienced some form of maltreatment. To the best of our knowledge, no similar studies have been conducted in which the forensic interviewing methods of parenting plan evaluators have been examined. We believe, however, that many, if not all, of the same factors that can influence forensic interviewing in maltreatment cases, will also affect children being interviewed in other forensic psychological investigations, including parenting plan assessments. In this section, we describe several factors shown to be useful in competently conducting an interview of a young child. We draw a distinction between forensic interviews designed to elicit information about specific events such as incidents of alleged maltreatment and one designed to explore information about general circumstances or patterns of experiences, such as the interview format described in the previous chapter.

Repeated Questions

Among the challenges faced by forensic interviewers is determining when an interview is or has been contaminated. A *contaminated child interview* refers to a forensic interview in which external influences have compromised the accuracy, reliability, or integrity of the child's statements. Contamination can occur through suggestive questioning, repeated exposure to misinformation, external pressures, or improper interview techniques that distort the child's memory or narrative. When contamination happens, it becomes difficult to determine whether the child's statements reflect genuine experiences or are the result of external influences.

Much of the research has divided children into two age groups. Younger children are usually defined as 6 years old and younger, and older children are usually defined as later elementary school or older. When young children are provided with information during a contaminated interview, they often understand that the information does not come from memory. This is called *source monitoring*. Children are able successfully to identify the source of the information that formed the memory. Upon retesting, young children accurately recall the information provided during the initial interview but do not accurately recall whether it came from memory or from someone else. This is called *source misattribution* and refers to children's inability to accurately recall the original memory source (Ceci & Bruck, 1995; Lamb et al., 2018).

In general, younger children, as contrasted with older children, are more likely to accept someone else's interpretation of an event if it bears a resemblance to the original event (Poole, 2016). Young children, as contrasted with older children, are less capable of recalling the sources of their memories. Therefore, what children recall in a third interview, may be intrusive memories that that they now believe are their own. Once a memory has been contaminated, it is not possible to determine what components are accurate representations of an event and what parts are contaminated representations that a child falsely believes are accurate representations of an event.

Several studies have shown that asking children the same question repeatedly within an interview and across interviews often results in children changing their answers (Lamb et al., 2018). Preschool-age children are particularly vulnerable to the contaminating effects of repeated questioning. Children seem to reason: "The first answer I gave must be wrong, that is why they are asking me again. Therefore, I should change my answer" (Ceci & Bruck, 1995, p. 279). Several studies have shown that some interviewer techniques result in children quickly changing their stories to conform to the suggestions and beliefs of the interviewer. Suggestions planted in the first interview were quickly picked up and the stories told during the second interview reflected changes congruent with the earlier placed suggestions.

Lyon argued that the introduction into evidence of research on the suggestibility of child witnesses is not of assistance to triers of fact. Lyon is critical of a large body of research conducted by Stephen Ceci, Maggie Bruck, and others. Lyon's primary criticisms are: (a) that the researchers have overstated the frequency with which suggestive questioning occurs and, in their proposals for methodological changes, have failed to address the risk that abusers will be acquitted; (b) that research conditions conducted over the past 25-years conditions have failed to replicate real-world phenomena closely enough, thereby making it unreasonable to presume that we have gained meaningful knowledge of the real-world phenomena through the research on their artificial analogs; (c) that Maggie Bruck, in particular, has erred in statements made during testimony and that her decision to offer didactic as opposed to case-specific testimony is flawed; and (d) that jurors are already aware that children are suggestible and that testimony concerning the research causes jurors to over-estimate the probability that testimony from a particular child witness has been distorted by suggestive questioning (Lyon, 1999, 2001, 2002b).

Martindale pointed out that some of the emotional distress experienced by children involved in forensic interviews is attributable to the methods employed in the course of interviewers' interactions with them (Martindale, 2001, Fall). Skilled interviewers are likely to obtain more reliable information and do minimal harm. Unskilled interviewers can cause significant harm and have unreliable information to show for their efforts. We are strong supporters of didactic testimony (also referred to as framework testimony), in which the testifying expert endeavors to educate the trier of fact concerning phenomena with which the court or jury may be insufficiently knowledgeable. Such testimony provides a context within which evidence can be evaluated. Regarding the need for such testimony when children have testified concerning their memories, Martindale observed, "It has been well established that a proffer of evidence must be accompanied by confirmation of its authenticity. It must be shown that it is what it is presented as being. Suppose the prosecution wishes to introduce testimony concerning what is purported to be a memory of an actual event. In that case, the defense should be afforded the opportunity to question the authenticity of the memory" (Martindale, 2001, Fall, p. 10).

Repeated interviewing is far more likely to be the rule rather than the exception in investigations of allegations of child maltreatment. The evaluator should also obtain and review copies of all video or audio tapes of the interviews. In a PPE, the evaluator should follow a similar approach by aggressively exploring who interviewed the child, how often the child was interviewed, how the child's story changed, if at all, and the degree to which the child's recollection of family events corresponds to information obtained from third party sources (De Los Reyes et al., 2015; De Los Reyes & Epkins, 2023).

Accusatory Emotional Tone

Children respond to the tone of an interviewer's questions (Ceci & Bruck, 1995). Children may provide incorrect information in response to misleading questions when the interviewer creates an emotional tone of accusation (A. M. Crossman et al., 2002). Lamb et al.'s revised protocol (2018) is designed to help distinguish between suggestive and nonsuggestive support. Their research showed it is possible to be supportive without doing harm to the reliability of children's memories. For this reason, we strongly advocate creating an audio tape or video tape record of the interview to allow for a proper examination of such tonal factors.

High-Status Interviewers

Young children are sensitive to the status and power of their interviewers (Lamb et al., 2018). Particularly because young children are more likely to believe adults than other children, young children may be more likely to comply with the implicit and explicit agenda of high-status interviewers, sometimes incorporating adults' beliefs into their reports (A. M. Crossman et al., 2002; Lamb et al., 2018). Evaluators must be vigilant about the importance of maintaining a neutral attitude when interviewing children.

Biased Interviewers

Confirmatory bias refers to the process of selective attention to information that is supportive of a preconceived idea about what has happened. Some people may approach an interview with a child with a preconceived belief about the child's experience in the family system. The concern is that these evaluator-based preconceived ideas might result in the belief that the preconceived family events or relationships have been reported. Some interviewers focus the search for information in a manner that virtually assures uncovering information supportive of their only hypothesis. In *Daubert* jurisdictions, the court expects that the expert witness has considered reasonable alternative explanations of the data. An investigative approach using a single hypothesis to guide the evaluation is contrary to the required admissibility criteria for expert witness testimony.

Though there is always some risk that inaccurate information will be obtained during interviews with children, several studies have shown that children interviewed by biased interviewers are more likely to offer inaccurate information than children interviewed by neutral evaluators. When an interviewer's belief was contrary to what the child experienced, interviews were characterized by an abundance of misleading questions, leading children to provide highly inaccurate information (Lamb et al., 2018; Poole, 2016).

The most reliable and accurate information is obtained from children responding to open-ended questions designed to elicit free narrative accounts of events they have experienced (Lamb et al., 2018; Poole, 2016). Direct questions are best presented as nonsuggestive as possible, using developmentally and individually appropriate vocabulary and sentence construction. Repeated questions, leading questions, or suggestive questions asked in an accusatory manner are most likely to promote distortion on the part of the child. The child's responses to these types of questions may result in the introduction of details that are incorporated into and contaminates subsequent accounts.

Lamb and his colleagues have developed a reliable structured investigative protocol that enhances young children's responses to free recall prompts in the course of forensic interviews (Lamb et al., 2018; Orbach et al., 2000; Orbach & Lamb, 2000, 2001). A similarly innovative approach is the Cognitive Interview modified for use with children. The Cognitive Interview purports to improve the quantity of useful information gained from children 7- to 12-years-old without creating heightened inaccuracy (Camparo et al., 2018; Saywitz, 1992; Saywitz & Camparo, 1998; Saywitz & Geiselman, 1998; Saywitz et al., 1999). Although originally developed for use with abused children, the Cognitive Interview minimizes interview-related influence and may help children elaborate upon memories that are somewhat more difficult to recall.

An alternative approach, based upon the Cognitive Interview and Narrative Elaborative Training research and experience, is the Narrative Elaboration Technique. Research findings of this technique have revealed that preschool and school-aged (typically developing and learning-disabled, average- and lower-intelligence) children, from middle- and low-socioeconomic status communities, were found to increase the amount of accurate, but not inaccurate information, as well as the quality of children's autobiographical narratives (Saywitz et al., 2015).

Children's Lack of Metasuggestibility and Metacognition

Most cited research about children's suggestibility in child custody cases describes the wealth of research studies examining suggestibility in young children. Other areas that need greater attention include research examining suggestibility of older children and research examining metasuggestibility in children.

Metasuggestibility is defined as "an awareness of factors and situations that can taint memory and/or event reports" (London et al., 2011, p. 146). One aspect of metasuggestibility is the development of understanding that questions or statements from some individuals can influence other individuals to inaccurately report their experiences. Conversational pressures can lead someone to make a false report, but metasuggestibility allows someone to understand that false statements can develop from compliance with suggestive questions (London et al., 2011). Children's lack of metasuggestibility makes them less likely to detect when an interviewer is asking leading questions or statements. This inability to detect leading questions and statements increases the likelihood of false statements (London et al., 2011).

Metasuggestibility is one aspect of *metacognition,* which is the awareness of and understanding of one's own thought processes. Metacognition is composed of two factors. The first factor is declarative metacognitive knowledge and is defined as one's knowledge of one's own capabilities. There is an awareness of variables that affect performance, including task characteristics and demands of the immediate situation. Declarative metacognitive knowledge in a young child is often limited to the young child's elementary understanding of concrete factors that might affect memory while also holding unrealistic beliefs about the infallibility of their memories. As children develop, they learn that several variables affect memory acquisition and retention. They understand that their memories are fallible and are best served by developing strategies to remember (London et al., 2011).

A second component of metacognition is cognitive monitoring: the ability to self-monitor one's cognitive process. Cognitive monitoring is often referred to as learning how to think about the thinking process, also known as self-reflection. Cognitive monitoring is one's awareness that something is not well understood or that one needs to remember through the "ability to deploy and execute performance-enhancing strategies" (London et al., 2011, p. 147).

Young children are unlikely to develop and deploy strategies to preserve a memory if they do not believe they will forget, a common belief among young children. Young children are also unlikely to be aware that memories from different sources might cause confusion. If a young child is not aware that memories from different sources might cause confusion, then it is unlikely that the young child would actively attempt to develop memory retrieval strategies that might reveal the source of a memory.

Young children are unable to recognize that suggestion can affect autobiographical reports. If a young child does not understand or recognize that suggestion can affect memory, there is no need for the child to develop strategies to resist suggestion.

> The argument is that children must realize that memory is fallible in some way before they will actively employ some cognitive strategy. For example, if young children do not realize their memory is not a perfect recording of information, they will not employ strategies intended to promote memory (such as spending time studying to remember information). Similarly, forensic interviewers sometimes instruct children that they can say 'I don't know' or 'that didn't happen' if interviewers give them misleading information. But in order to benefit from these instructions to protect their memory reports from suggestion, it seems logical that children must recognize that these reports could be influenced by interviewers' suggestions. (London et al., 2011, p. 147)

The importance of understanding metasuggestibility in our work is assessing whether a child has developed the ability to realize that (a) their reports are not necessarily accurate representations of reality, (b) their reports can change independent of the original reality, and (c) their reports can be influenced by someone else's alternative representation (i.e. two people can provide different descriptions of events, one of which is incorrect).

We found only one study in the American Psychological Association PsycNET database that was identified using the search terms "metasuggestibility" or "metasuggestion" related to child's memory. London et al. examined the development of children's understanding of interrogative suggestibility, one aspect of metasuggestibility. They found children's understanding of suggestibility develops over time, with the youngest children correctly answering less than 30% of the two initial questions about why a child actor had made a false allegation. Almost 50% of the children in this age group failed all questions (London et al., 2011, p. 151). It was not until children were 8 and 9 years old that they were able to perform at a 50% level on most measures of being able to identify why a child actor made a false allegation. Children who were 12 and older could accurately identify why a child actor made a false allegation, readily identifying that it was the social pressure of the interviewer who influenced the child actor to make the false allegation. The authors showed school-age children, ages 7- to 10-years-old, were found to be suggestible, even when they were exposed to explicit and seemingly obvious suggestive questions and even with warnings about suggestive questions (London et al., 2011, p. 151).

London et al.'s study points to the need for evaluators to develop awareness of when children develop metacognitive abilities that influence suggestibility and the evolving cognitive skills of reflecting upon how their memories of events might be influenced by others or various contextual variables. If a child does not believe memory is fallible, it is likely that the child is unable to reflect upon how memory might be influenced by others or different contextual factors. Further, even when school-age children develop the ability to reflect upon some of these factors that might influence accurate memory, they are still inconsistent in their application of cognitive strategies used to increase retention of relevant memories or in development of other memory strategies.

MEMORY

Memory is the basis for the retention of experience and is essential for functioning and development (Ceci et al., 2003). The memory system has three stages. The first stage is encoding, in which we determine how the events we witness are stored in memory. Encoding is also influenced by the level of detail of the event. The second stage is storage and involves how memories are stored, encoded into short-term memory, and then transferred to long-term memory. The third stage is retrieval of stored information, what we often call remembering. Each of these stages of memory change over time during development.

Ceci et al. (2003) identified three factors that change with development and influence encoding, storage, and retrieval. The first factor is children's existing knowledge. The second factor is children's awareness and application of mnemonic strategies that assist in remembering. The third factor is metamemory. Metamemory refers to understanding the properties of memory and what strategy or strategies are needed in a situation to facilitate retrieval.

In forensic interviewing of children, it is critical for evaluators to understand how various factors might influence children's encoding, storage, and retrieval of memories of past events. One such factor is suggestibility: children's tendency to change memories and beliefs in their retrieval of memories. A second factor is the development of children's language competence, both receptive and expressive language abilities (A. G. Walker & Kenniston, 2013; A. G. Walker & Warren, 1995). A third factor is the developmental trajectory of children's confidence in the accuracy of the events or encounters they experience.

DEVELOPMENTAL TRAJECTORY OF CONFIDENCE

A frequent finding in metacognitive research is that children overestimate their ability to accurately recall events. The *developmental trajectory of confidence* is viewed as a reflection of metacognitive processes that involve memory retrieval (Roebers, 2002). Roebers revealed that when presented with a neutral event and then questioned using misleading questioning, children's monitoring skills were seriously impaired. In contrast to misleading questions, when children were asked suggestive questions, their metacognitive differentiation was positively associated with recall accuracy. Misleading questions can negatively affect children's use of their metacognitive abilities, while suggestive questions can allow for children to use their metacognitive abilities to determine accurate from inaccurate information.

When asked about events using *unbiased* questions, children provide higher confidence ratings that their recollections are accurate after correct rather than after incorrect answers (Roebers & Howie, 2003). When asked *misleading* questions, children's abilities to differentiate accurate from inaccurate answers was undermined. Children tended to give similar accuracy confidence ratings to their answers when the interview contained a mix of misleading and unbiased questions. Further, when the interviewer bombarded the children with an uninterrupted series of misleading questions, children's abilities to provide accurate answers to questions were even more negatively affected. Roebers and her colleagues (2020) stressed the importance of critically examining the ways in which questions are asked of children.

RISKS OF INACCURACIES IN EVALUATORS' RECORDING OR RECOLLECTION OF CHILD INTERVIEW DATA

Since the 1980s, when bizarre allegations about preschool children being sexually abused became national news (Ceci & Bruck, 1995), concerns about the accuracy with which child statement evaluators record or recall have prompted demands that investigative interviews be recorded electronically (Ceci & Bruck, 2000). In testifying about children's statements, mental health professionals and child welfare workers often refer to contemporaneously taken notes or to notes entered after an interview with the child. Often, this practice is deemed acceptable, because it is assumed that such notes are relatively accurate representations of the information exchanged during the investigative interview. However, research increasingly demonstrates that when testifying experts rely on this type of note, the resulting testimony can be highly inaccurate (Gould & Martindale, 2007; London et al., 2011).

Errors made in the course of note taking can significantly affect the nature, quality, and accuracy of information presented to the court leading to demands that investigative interviews be recorded electronically (Ceci & Bruck, 2000). In one study, mothers were asked to recall recent conversations they had with their children. The mothers were told in advance they would be asked about their conversations. Foreknowledge that they would be asked questions concerning their conversations did not improve the mothers' performance. The mothers' memories for general meaning (gist memory) were better than their memories for the exact wording or structure of the conversation (verbatim memory). The mothers had difficulty recalling how information was elicited from their children, specifically whether their children's statements were spontaneous or prompted, and whether specific utterances were spoken by the mothers or by the children (Bruck et al., 1999).

In a related study, mental health trainees who interviewed four children about experienced events had difficulty remembering which children made certain statements. These trainees could not remember which details were spontaneously produced and which details were prompted using leading questions (Ceci & Bruck, 2000). In another study, experienced interviewers who participated in an analog study claimed to have asked few if any leading or even specific questions of the 5-year-old children they interviewed, although a review of tape recordings of the interviews revealed that more than 80% of the questions they asked were specific or leading. In addition, notes made shortly after the interview included only 20% of the questions that the interviewers actually asked (Warren & Woodall, 1999).

Another study examined verbatim contemporaneous accounts—that is, a record in which the interviewer attempts to record every word—of 20 investigative interviews compared with audio-taped recordings of the same interviews (Lamb et al., 2000). Of particular note in this study was the nature of the sample. All interviews were conducted by eight of the most senior and experienced forensic interviewers in Israel who knew that the interviews were being audio taped and were therefore motivated to record the interviews as accurately as possible. Investigators' notes misrepresented the information elicited from the young interviewees and how information was elicited. "An alarming number of incident-relevant details (25% of the total) were not recorded at all in the investigators' notes, with 17.8% of the central, i.e., allegation-specific details not reflected in the investigators' notes. [M]ore than half of the substantive interviewer utterances were ignored completely, and the types of prompts used to elicit information from the children were misrepresented" (Lamb et al., 2000, p. 704). The researchers concluded, "Such errors very likely distort judgments about the extent of interviewer contamination, the accuracy of children's testimony, the validity of children's allegations, the severity of the alleged abuse, and perhaps even children's credibility" (Lamb et al., 2000, p. 704).

There are several primary dangers when hearsay is received as trial evidence (McGough, 1995):

- Faulty memory: The danger that the child reporting the information to another person will forget key material
- Ambiguity: The danger that the meaning intended by the child will be misinterpreted by the witness, and hence, reported incorrectly by the witness to the fact finder
- Misperception: The danger that the child misjudged, misinterpreted, or misunderstood what she heard or saw
- Lack of candor: The danger that the child will consciously lie

Evaluators should be concerned about faulty memory, ambiguity, and misperception. Lack of candor may be a concern when conducting parenting plan interviews, but we are also concerned about how children's descriptions of their experiences may reflect faulty memory or interpretations of family events that are unique to the child but different from other family members. We address the challenges posed by discrepant information from various family members in Chapter 18 on collateral data collection and interviewing describing the multi-informant model.

Faulty Memory

Several researchers have provided evidence about the potential danger of faulty memory on the part of the child witness (Lamb et al., 2018; Poole, 2016). There is also concern about the possibility of faulty memory on the part of the mental health professional reporting to the court. Bruck and Ceci pointed out that a child's statements and reporters' accounts of a child's statements are likely to be affected by faulty memory (Bruck & Ceci, 1995). Adult interviewers are often inaccurate in recalling what was said or what took place in an interview. Inaccuracies may be found in reports offered from memory and in notes taken contemporaneously. Adult memories of interviews are often inaccurate. When asked to recall conversations, most adults recall the gist of the conversation, but they often do not recall the exact words used or the sequences of interactions between speakers. Bruck and Ceci observed that written summaries of unrecorded interviews are subject to several distortions, and they concluded summaries of missing interviews do not substitute for an audio or video recording.

Ambiguity

Ambiguity is another danger affecting hearsay testimony. Children do not use language in the same ways that adults use language (A. G. Walker & Kenniston, 2013). Children may provide ambiguous responses to interview questions. For example, a child may state that they were "touched on their private parts" or that a parent "rubbed their bottom." The meaning of the communication may be clear to the child, while its meaning is unclear to an interviewer. Unless the child can provide a detailed description of the actions, the interviewer makes an inference about the meaning of these statements that may or may not be accurate interpretations of the child's statements. Interviewers should ask the child developmentally appropriate follow-up questions to facilitate the child's recall of more detailed information. For example, an unreliable response is likely when a mental health professional asks a 4-year-old child if they have been "touched" by a particular person. A 4-year-old often cannot distinguish an affectionate touch from a sexualized touch. Indeed, children may not distinguish appropriate from inappropriate touch (Bruck, 2009). The child may honestly reply, based on a concrete interpretation of the word "touch" that they were "touched." The investigator may interpret this to mean that the child was touched in a sexual way, whereas the child may have been referring to a nonsexual touching. Ambiguity is also present in questions such as, "Did they hurt you?" "Was it a good touch or a bad touch?" or "Did the hug make you feel yucky?" When the results of such ambiguous questioning in an interview are presented at trial, the risks of inaccuracy are increased. Often what follows is an allegation of sexual abuse, with tremendous personal and social costs to all involved.

A child's denial of nonmemorable experiences might lead interviewers to use suggestive questioning techniques that further cloud the reliability of the child's statements. Nonmemorable experiences refer to routine, emotionally neutral, or developmentally unremarkable events that a child may not encode in long-term memory. For example, if an interviewer asks a child about what happened on a particular date weeks or months ago, the child may genuinely not remember, even if something significant did occur. This lack of recall can sometimes be misinterpreted as avoidance, deception, or reluctance, leading interviewers to apply pressured or leading techniques in an attempt to extract information. However, such techniques can distort a child's memory, compromise the credibility of their statements, and ultimately affect legal or investigative outcomes.

Misperception

A third threat to the accuracy of hearsay evidence is misperception, which refers to the risk that an individual misjudged, misinterpreted, or misunderstood what they heard or observed. This issue is particularly concerning in forensic child interviews, where both the child's cognitive limitations and the interviewer's biases can shape the content and interpretation of statements.

As discussed throughout this book, research has consistently demonstrated that interviewer bias can influence multiple aspects of forensic evaluations. Bias can affect how an evaluator structures and conducts interviews, potentially leading to suggestive questioning or reinforcement of certain narratives. Interviewer bias can determine what information is included or excluded in reports, potentially omitting critical context or alternative explanations. The way evaluators process and analyze children's responses can be shaped by preexisting assumptions, affecting the perceived credibility of statements. Bias in data collection and interpretation can lead to misinformed expert conclusions, which may impact judicial decision making and case outcomes.

A reasonable control on evaluator misperception is using audio or video recordings of interviews. Without audio or video recordings of interviews, it is impossible to accurately assess the reliability of a child's subsequent statements or the accuracy of the evaluator's notes from the interview. The absence of recorded documentation raises at least three concerns about reliability of data collection. The first concern is whether leading questions were asked and, if so, how frequently and in what manner. The second concern is whether interviewer influence shaped the child's responses, either through reinforcement, pressure, or suggestibility. The third concern is whether inconsistencies in the child's statements emerged due to contamination during the interview.

ONE MORE CALL FOR MEMORIALIZING INTERVIEWS

Until recently, audio and video recording of interviews did not have substantial support from a legal viewpoint. To date, there is little authority from U.S. Supreme Court precedent to support an assertion that a prosecutor has a constitutional duty to (mechanically) record and preserve an account of a pretrial interview with a potential child witness. The Supreme Court did not find it violated due process to fail to record interviews (*Idaho v. Wright*, 1990) or discard investigators' notes (*Arizona v. Youngblood*, 1988).

Several states have seen decisions to require recordings. For example, the Supreme Court of Florida decided that

> Experts generally agree that contacts between a child and an expert evaluating the child for sexual abuse should be videotaped to ensure the trustworthiness of the communications and to ensure that the expert did not lead the child during the evaluation . . . [W]e can only hope that in the future greater care will be taken to properly preserve testimony in this type of case and that judges will carefully adhere to the trustworthiness and reliability requirements set forth in [our statutes]. (McGough, 1995, p. 379)

Similarly, the Idaho Supreme Court considered the failure to preserve any reviewable record of an evaluative interview with the child to be unprofessional conduct and explained that failure led to the inclination to find the hearsay report of the child's allegation to be untrustworthy and inadmissible. These decisions call into question the reliability of hearsay testimony taken from investigative interviews of children.

From scientific and legal standpoints, audio or video recording is advisable. Bruck and Ceci (1995) assert that "the failure to record initial interviews with child witnesses rules out the possibility of ever reaching any firm conclusion as to whether any abuse actually occurred. In other words, the primary evidence has been destroyed" (p. 272). Because of the ample research on the unreliable nature of notetaking and the inherent problems with human memory, audio or video recordings should be seriously considered.

RECOMMENDATIONS FOR EVIDENCE-BASED FORENSIC INTERVIEWING

There appears to be a worldwide recognition of the importance of developing a set of rules or recommendations governing forensic interviewing of children. We end this chapter summarizing ten evidence-based recommendations for conducting forensic interviews with children recently published by the European Association of Psychology and Law (Korkman et al., 2024). Each of these recommendations reflects important guidance consistent with current professional and scientific literature for forensic interviewers in the United States as well as other countries (Korkman et al., 2024):

1. **Understand child victims and witnesses**. Forensic child interviews should be conducted by professionals with specialized training that includes an understanding of developmental issues, suggestibility, memory, and language, factors influencing disclosure and the importance of creating rapport with and supporting the child throughout the interview.

2. **Use evidence-based child-interviewing protocols**. Interviews in cases of suspected child abuse should be conducted according to evidence-based

interview protocols, such as the NICHD interview protocol or other protocols based on scientific evidence, in which the emphasis is on obtaining as much information as possible about the events investigated in a nonleading manner.

3. **Follow the phases of the interview and adequately prepare the child witness**. Interviewers should strive to conduct the interviews following the general principles of phasing the interview (introduction, ground rules, practice interview in a child-friendly way, including making efforts to build adequate good rapport with the child).
4. **Maintain an open mindset and test hypotheses**. Interviewers are advised to engage in hypothesis testing when planning, conducting, and assessing the interview to reduce the risk of bias.
5. **Record interviews**. It is essential that the interview is electronically recorded, to see how the child's account has evolved, assess interview quality as well as for evaluation purposes.
6. **Limit the number of persons present at the interview**. It is recommended that only the child and the interviewer are present in the interviewing room during the interview, while other professionals monitor the interview (e.g., via a video-link).
7. **Consider cultural aspects and interpretation in the interview**. Interviewers are advised to take cultural aspects into account, and in interviews where interpreters are required, interviewers should prepare the interview jointly with the interpreters and where possible, interpreters should have specialized training in child interviewing.
8. **Avoid dolls, body diagrams, and drawings in the interview**. The use of dolls or props is not recommended in the interviews, and doll play or drawings should not be used to make interpretations of possible abusive experiences by the child.
9. **Keep an eye out for evidence-based recommendations for online child interviewing**. Online interviewing shows promising results also with regards to child witnesses, but more research is warranted before conclusive recommendations can be made.
10. **Receive appropriate training**. Interviewers should receive specialized training, including continuous assessment and feedback on their interviewing style for quality assurance.

We hope that as you read these recommendations, you drew connections to many of the previous sections of this book. As we have presented an ecological, child-centered focus to the evaluation, we encourage you to use multiple hypotheses to investigate different levels of influence.

CONCLUSION

Forensic interviews with young children require specialized training, evidence-based methodologies, and a deep understanding of the risks associated with suggestibility, contamination, and memory distortion. Given the significant impact of children's statements on legal and investigative outcomes, interviewers must be equipped with the skills and knowledge to elicit accurate, developmentally appropriate, and legally defensible accounts. This chapter explored the core considerations in forensic interviewing, emphasizing the necessity of interviewer expertise, adherence to structured protocols, and sensitivity to developmental and socioemotional factors that influence children's disclosures. When forensic interviews are conducted without careful attention to these elements, the risk of compromising the reliability of a child's statement increases significantly.

We have addressed some of the risks of improper forensic interviewing to the reliability of information from child interviews. We discussed several pitfalls that can undermine the integrity of forensic interviews with children, including:

- **Leading and suggestive questions**: Directing the child toward specific answers can introduce false information, shaping their recall in a way that aligns with the interviewer's expectations rather than the child's actual experience.
- **Repeated questioning**: Asking the same question multiple times can lead children to believe their initial response was incorrect, prompting them to alter their statements to satisfy the interviewer.
- **Interviewer bias**: Preconceived notions about the case can subtly influence how questions are framed, how responses are interpreted, and which details are emphasized or ignored in forensic reports.
- **External influence**: Conversations with parents, caregivers, or other third parties before the forensic interview can contaminate a child's memory, making it difficult to distinguish genuine recall from suggestively introduced details.

Given children's developing cognitive abilities and increased vulnerability to social pressure, these factors pose a substantial risk to the credibility and evidentiary value of their testimony. This underscores the critical need for forensic interviewers to rely on empirically validated protocols designed to minimize such risks.

We addressed best practices concepts for conducting reliable forensic interviews. We discussed the use of evidence-based protocols such as the NICHD Investigative Interview Protocol that provides structured guidelines that help minimize suggestibility and interviewer influence. We stressed the importance of interview procedures that focus on open-ended, nonleading prompts (e.g., "Tell me everything you remember about what happened") rather than "Did someone touch you?" We also argued strongly for the use of video or audio recordings of interviews because of the important role they can play as critical safeguards, allowing evaluators, attorneys, and courts to review the interview process for accuracy, interviewer conduct, and potential contamination.

The lessons learned from forensic child interviewing research should extend beyond abuse investigations to all forensic settings, including PPEs and collateral interviews with children and adults. By implementing structured, scientifically supported methodologies, professionals can enhance the credibility, accuracy, and forensic value of the information obtained. Ultimately, the integrity of forensic child interviews depends on the interviewers' commitment to best practices, continuous training, and adherence to neutral, nonsuggestive techniques. By applying these principles consistently, forensic evaluators can improve the quality of the evidence gathered, contributing to fairer, more informed judicial decisions that serve the best interests of children and families.

14

Parent–Child Observation

Parenting plan evaluation (PPE) guidelines direct evaluators to observe parent–child interactions (American Academy of Matrimonial Lawyers, 2011; American Psychological Association [APA], 2022; Association of Family and Conciliation Courts [AFCC], 2022). Direct observation of parent–child interactions is also a key component of the standard of practice among parenting plan evaluators (Ackerman et al., 2019, 2021a) and an essential component of a comprehensive assessment (Ackerman, 2006; Ackerman et al., 2019; Gould, 1998, 2006, Gould & Martindale, 2007, 2013; Hynan, 2003; Schutz et al., 1989; P. M. Stahl, 1999). Surveys with evaluators have emphasized the importance of observing parent–child interactions, second only to conducting forensic interviews with parents and children (Ackerman et al., 2021; LaFortune & Carpenter, 1998).

Parent–child observations play a crucial role in PPEs, offering direct insights into family dynamics, parent responsiveness, and the quality of parent–child relationships. These observations help evaluators assess how parents meet their children's needs, how children respond to each parent, and whether any potential risks or concerns exist within the family structure. Although professional guidelines emphasize the necessity of such observations, there remains a lack of uniformity regarding the methods, settings, and evaluation criteria.

Despite their importance, the validity and reliability of parent–child observations have been questioned, particularly regarding the extent to which they reflect real-world behavior. Some researchers argue that being observed may alter family interactions, necessitating multiple observations across varied

https://doi.org/10.1037/0000474-015
Parenting Plan Evaluations: An Evidence-Informed Approach to Child Custody, by J. W. Gould and C. M. Mulchay

settings to obtain a more accurate picture. Additionally, parenting plan evaluators must navigate numerous challenges, such as the choice between structured and unstructured observations, home versus office settings, and the presence of third parties.

This chapter explores the theoretical foundations, methodologies, and best practices for conducting parent–child observations in PPEs. It reviews professional guidelines, empirical research, and observational models that inform these assessments. The chapter also highlights the importance of ecological validity, the use of multiple informants, and considerations for ensuring fair and comprehensive evaluations. By synthesizing research and practical recommendations, this chapter aims to guide evaluators in refining their observational techniques.

THE NEED FOR VALID, RELIABLE OBSERVATIONS

Bricklin (1995) raised concerns about the degree to which parent–child observations were representative of real-world behavior, arguing that parent–child observations were "tainted as sources of information" (p. 58) because the family's knowledge of being observed was likely to change the nature of the interactions. Based on the lack of subsequent articles supporting Bricklin's position, Bricklin's arguments do not appear to reflect a consensus position in the custody field. His caution, however, is relevant and underscores the importance of conducting multiple observations across various situations and obtaining observation data from collateral informants with personal knowledge of parent–child interactions.

Despite the importance of conducting observations of parent–child interactions, parent–child observations remain largely unstudied (Saini & Polack, 2014), with a lack of standard procedures for conducting reliable and valid observations, a lack of consensus about dimensions to assess, or the means to gather information about how to best assess parent–child interactions in the context of custody disputes (Hynan, 2003).

Saini reminds evaluators about the need to look at the social science research specific to what we know and don't know in terms of structured or unstructured observations, duration of the observation, location of the observation, number of people present and their relationship to the child, and factors that might affect the observation because of the setting, (i.e., office, home or park; M. Saini, personal communication, April 25, 2004). The evaluator also needs to consider the type of observation that is best for the particular family being evaluated. For example, would the child be more comfortable or familiar with the parent–child observation occurring at a familiar park because that is where the visits have taken place for the past 6 months or at the parent's home?

Schutz et al. (1989) provided a detailed procedure for conducting parent–child observations. He identified specific factors to assess, factors that Schutz et al. identified as having an empirical basis in the custody and child development literature. They provided recommendations for other areas to observe systematically and for observational tasks that included free play, cooperative, structured activities, and problem solving.

Schutz et al. suggested conducting parent–child observations at each parent's home, a procedure that we believe generates observational data that is likely to be more representative of real-world behavior compared to the information obtained from observations conducted in the evaluator's office.

During COVID-19, we saw evaluators become more flexible in conducting observations. We believe the evaluator should attempt to create a context that represents how the parent and child interact in the real world as closely as possible. When entering a parent's home was not an option, evaluators observed parents outside at a park or in the parent's backyard. Some of our colleagues suggested we observe parents in their home with the use of a video feed such as that provided by Zoom. Researchers have begun to study video telehealth's viability as a tool for the collection of qualitative data because of its relative ease of use, cost-effectiveness, data management features, and security options (Dale & Smith, 2021). As noted above, it also makes it easy to record the session.

Our second author argued for remote-in-office observations. Inspired by his previous work conducting parent–child interaction therapy using a one-way mirror, he suggested that evaluators could use technology such as video cameras to observe the parent and child in a separate office in the same building. While the parent and child would still know they are being observed, this protocol allows the evaluator to control the setting and limit distractions. It also has the potential to reduce the observer effects a child may experience when the evaluator is in the same room. However, observing interactions through a video feed may limit an evaluator's sense of the relationship between the parent and child.

Although the use of remote-in-office observations has not, as of yet, been empirically examined for its effectiveness as a forensic assessment methodology, it has been described in the literature on interviewing children when there are allegations of sexual abuse, and it reflects our emphasis on using evidenced-based and evidence-informed data to support our methods. Not all components of a PPE can be empirically investigated using experimental and quasi-experimental procedures. However, structured clinical judgment methods are being applied to forensic data-gathering procedures yielding useful data. We believe that continued refinement of the use of remote-in-office observations is an exciting, innovative direction for future research.

THEORY AND RESEARCH

Hynan (2003) proposed integrating theory and research about parent–child interactions from outside the custody realm. Hynan rightly criticized the existing literature at the time for providing little guidance about how to conduct parent–child observations. He cited the family systems work of Beavers and

Hampson (1990, 2003) and others who have been systematically investigating factors associated with healthy and unhealthy family functioning.

A critically important contribution of Hynan's article was his attention to the importance of identifying a theory of science that addresses factors to be assessed in parent–child observations. Hynan advocated anchoring observational methods on empirically derived assessment techniques and assessing factors articulated in the identified theory. The parent-child interactive therapy research mentioned above provides another theory of science that can guide parent–child observations (Hembree-Kigin & McNeil, 2013).

Garber (2016) suggested that parent–child observations often fail to consider interactions in the context of the family system. "[A] best interest analysis must balance the quality of the child's relationship *within* each dyad with an understanding of how the child experiences the larger family system, that is, those between-parent variables, including how the child manages separations from, and reunions with, and transitions between the parents' care. Thus, [PPEs] must include observations of the child both within and between relationships" (Garber, 2016, p. 262).

Garber's distinction of within-parent–child relationship observation and between-parent–child relationship observation is an interesting way to frame the move toward a family systems model. Garber made an analogy to an analysis of variance procedure in which researchers examine main effects and interaction effects. This model is a useful analogy when one recognizes the importance of vertical and horizontal interaction effects.

When using Garber's idea of within- and between-parent–child observations, it is important to think beyond the family system level. Within- and between-levels of analysis might need to include extended family members, caretakers and nannies, or other people who are involved in the day-to-day care of the children and who affect the family's functioning.

Garber argued, in part, that evaluators need to apply both linear analyses characterized by parent child interactions and configurational analyses characterized by the complex interactions that exists within family systems and between family systems and other systems that influence family functioning such as those described by Bronfenbrenner's ecological model.

Slaven's (2001) survey of 518 custody evaluators found a lack of uniformity regarding how evaluators conduct parent-observations and minimal attention toward a standard methodology used to gather parent–child observational data. Bow and Quinnell (2004) reported that almost half of the custody evaluation reports they reviewed did not provide sufficient detail regarding the parent–child observation to classify the observation according to whether the visits were structured or unstructured. The majority of evaluators did not indicate the length of time spent observing the parent–child interaction within the custody evaluation report. When the length of time spent observing parent–child observation was reported, times ranged from 20 minutes to 8 hours per session.

THE IMPORTANCE OF PARENT–CHILD OBSERVATIONS

There is consensus about the importance of parent–child observations (Ackerman et al., 2021.) There are some survey data that address how long evaluators engage in parent–child observations, but these data do not tell us how long the evaluator observes at each home or whether the evaluator's total time represents two, four, or more observations (Ackerman et al., 2021; Bow, 2006; Bow & Quinnell, 2001). There is a paucity of survey data describing the number of observations conducted during an evaluation, the length of time observing each observation, and the involvement and degree of involvement of the evaluation in the parent–child observation in each home.

Ackerman's series of studies provide information about preferences and expectations among evaluators, judges, and attorneys regarding parent–child observations. For example, Ackerman et al. reported that 100% of surveyed psychologists who conduct PPEs observe parent–child interactions. Family law judges expected the parenting plan evaluator to provide information about parent–child observations based upon the age of the child. More than 80% of surveyed family court judges expected to read about parent–child interactions when the child is 12 and under. Seventy percent of judges expected to read about parent–child observations when children were over 12 (Ackerman & Drosdeck, 2010).

PROFESSIONAL PRACTICE GUIDELINES AND MODEL STANDARDS

The AFCC (2022) Parenting Plan Guidelines addresses the importance of conducting parent–child observations in Guideline 8.1:

> (a) Evaluators should observe each parent and their children together, regardless of the child's age, unless doing so creates a significant risk to the child's physical or emotional safety or when such observations are impossible, such as when a parent is incarcerated or otherwise unable to participate in a parent–child interactive session.
>
> (b) Evaluators should conduct their observations to view samples of interactions between and among the children and their parents and to obtain data reflecting on each parent's skills and ability to respond to the children's needs and manage their behavior. In assessing each parent's skills and abilities and the reciprocal relationship between parent and child, evaluators should be attentive to:
>
> 1. Signs of reciprocal interaction and attention;
> 2. Parent's communication skills with the child;
> 3. Methods by which parent manages the interaction and influences the child's behavior, thoughts, attitudes, and feelings;
> 4. Parent's demands and expectations relating to developmentally appropriate behavior;
> 5. The appropriateness of any materials brought to the interactive sessions; and
> 6. Developmental appropriateness of child's language, behaviors, and reactions in the presence of each parent.

(c) Evaluators should be mindful that their presence and the presence of others in the same physical environment as those being observed may influence the behaviors and interactions that they are observing.
(d) Evaluators should specifically describe the behavioral interactions between parents and children and differentiate their impressions and opinions from their observations.
(e) When parent–child observations have not been conducted based on risk to the child, or when conducting such observations are impossible, evaluators should clearly note this in the record and articulate the basis for their decision to not conduct parent–child observations in their report.
(f) Evaluators should articulate the limitations of their opinions and recommendations when observations of each parent with the children have not been completed. (p. 21)

The APA Child Custody Guidelines also address the importance of including behavioral observations as a core component of a parenting plan assessment. Similar to the more comprehensive information included in the 2022 AFCC guidelines, the APA guidelines also provide more comprehensive information about conducting parent–child observations. Guideline 18 reads:

> Psychologists strive to include an observation of parent–child interactions when conducting child custody evaluations.
>
> **Rationale**
>
> Observing parent–child interactions often provides highly relevant information for determining the best interests of the child and can increase the ecological validity and scientific rigor of the overall assessment process (Saini & Polak, 2014). This approach may also offer a valuable opportunity to assess the statements that were made by parents and children when those parties were interviewed separately, and to assist in the formulation of questions for follow-up interviews.
>
> **Application**
>
> Psychologists endeavor to understand the importance of prioritizing the child's safety and well-being when gauging the appropriateness of observing parent–child interactions. In child custody evaluations, observation techniques generally focus on developmentally and scientifically informed parent and child variables that may have particular meaning to the court and that can serve to clarify the fit between a child's needs and an adult's parenting attributes. Observations may occur in a variety of settings, such as the home or clinical office. When observations are slated to occur in public or quasi-public settings—such as airports, schools, or waiting rooms—psychologists strive to consider with special care the confidentiality and informed consent ramifications (see Guideline 7) of these arrangements, as well as the impression management inherent in public social encounters.
>
> When observing parent–child interactions, psychologists seek to focus on elements that may include (but need not be limited to) the nature of the parent's guidance, limit setting reflected in the parent's attempts to redirect the child, the supportive aspect of the parent's role in collaborative undertakings, the parent's evident affection for and sensitivity to the child, the extent to which the child heeds the parent's guidance and redirection, the child's willingness to collaborate affirmatively with the parent, the child's subtle ways of demonstrating the quality of connection to the parents and the child's evident affection for, and search for reassurance by, the parent.

> Psychologists take into consideration cultural factors that may influence the way parents demonstrate these aspects (APA, 2019). Psychologists strive to report these interactions as behavioral observations, and to take care that methods of documenting these interactions are both valid and reliable. Psychologists remain aware that some behaviors may reflect an acute awareness of being observed (Goodwin et al., 2017; Henry et al., 2015).
>
> Familiar with professional literature on different approaches to observation, psychologists' endeavor to explain why parent–child interactions were arranged in a particular manner for the evaluation (e.g., structured, unstructured, with siblings present, with both parents present, with the psychologist physically in the room). Psychologists may postpone or opt against observing parent–child interactions to protect the child's safety, based upon such factors as the parent's problematic presentation, the child's expressed wishes, or situations in which the child has never met or has no recollection of the parent. Psychologists strive to understand the impact of such factors on the resulting opinions.
>
> Observations of parent–child interactions are not in and of themselves "attachment" evaluations (as the latter concern the quality of the organization of the parent–child relationship), which require special training and settings (Isaacs et al., 2009). When the situation requires a formal attachment evaluation, psychologists' endeavor to make a referral for this type of procedure if they do not have the formal training to conduct one themselves. (APA, 2022, pp. 17–18)

It is important for custody evaluators to assess the degree to which their observations of parent–child interactions are an accurate representation of how the family functions in the real world. This is a question of ecological validity.

ECOLOGICAL VALIDITY

Ecological validity refers to whether the evaluator's observation of parent–child characteristics, behaviors, and interactions in the real world are accurately captured within the observation (e.g., a scheduled home visit).

A similar term, *external validity*, refers to the extent to which research results can be generalized to others, a task that would be nearly impossible to do within this context due to the diversity of families (Saini & Polack, 2014).

> An ecologically valid observation is the balance of developing rigorous methods for observing parent–child relationships while remaining cognizant of the contextual factors at play during these observations that can influence the transferability of observations to real-life situations when these parents are not observed by the custody evaluator. (Saini & Polack, 2014, p. 185)

Saini and Polack point out that evaluators must be aware of the potential influence of several factors prior to giving significant weight to results obtained based on the observations. For instance, parent–child interactions can be affected by observer behavior and biases (e.g., the evaluator); the setting of the observation (e.g., parent–child observations in the home, office, or public space); the presence or absence of family members and significant others; the timing of observations (e.g., during mealtime vs. early mornings); racial, cultural, and ethnic differences; and the duration of observations. These are important factors that need to be considered when assessing the relative weight given to the data obtained and its ecological validity (Saini & Polack, 2014).

PRESUMPTIONS UNDERLYING OBSERVATIONAL DATA

Achenbach et al. (1987) conceptualized a fundamental debate about whether behavior is determined by situational factors or by personality factors that remain stable across situations. It is clear that people have general tendencies toward behavior across situations. It is equally as clear that there are situational influences on behavior. Behavior in one setting does not necessarily predict behavior in a different setting. This has been called a cross-situational assessment.

Achenbach et al. (1987) argued that questions about situational specificity are critical to consider when assessing children's physical and emotional behaviors. They argued that the only way to capture a useful picture of a child's functioning is to gather information from a cross-section of environments that include, but are not limited to, home, school, neighborhood, therapists, coaches, and neighbors. Cross-situational assessment requires information from mothers, fathers, stepparents, teachers, neighbors, coaches, mental health and medical professionals, and children. The challenge is to assess children across a variety of environments, engaged in a variety of activities and diverse relationships.

Achenbach et al. (1987) raised concerns about the lack of reliable information obtained from different observers of children's behavior. Parents view their children in particular settings and make attributions about their behavior based upon factors that are different from other observers. It is the differences among observers that have been found to have low correlations. The low correlations between observed children's behavior and different informants have tended to cast doubt on one or both informants. The assumption has been that at least one of the informants has provided unreliable information about the child's behavior rather than recognizing that different informants' validity contributes to different information. "Low correlations between informants may indicate that the target variables differ from one situation to another, rather than that the informants' reports are invalid or unreliable" (Achenbach et al., 1987, p. 213).

Achenbach et al. (1987) concluded that assessment of most children must take into account the effects of different situations and informants. Children's behavior may be situation-specific, but it is also dependent upon the informant and a variety of cognitive and attitudinal variables that each person brings into the situation being observed.

Different informants have different information about a child. The informants are likely to have an effect on the child being observed. A child being observed by a parent might behave differently at home compared to a child being observed by a coach on the soccer field. A child being observed with a parent by an evaluator might behave differently than when that child is observed with that same parent by a therapist or pediatrician or neighbor.

Achenbach et al. (1987) note the importance of obtaining information from more than one informant observing the child in the same or similar situation. They argue that each type of informant uniquely affects the nature of the child-observation and that the uniqueness of the ways in which one informant affects an observation is very likely different from the ways in which a different informant might affect the child in the same situation, resulting in different observations.

Achenbach et al. (1987) found that informants who observed children in the same context tended to report higher agreement in their behavior observations (e.g., parents observing the child at home; teachers observing the child at school) compared to informants observing the same child in different contexts (e.g., parents observing the child at home and teachers observing the child at school). These data strongly suggest that who observes the child and where the child is observed are separate sources of variance to be considered.

A second finding was that informants were more consistent in their behavior observations of younger children compared to their observations of older children. Achenbach et al. (1987) were studying children and adolescents' mental health problems. They hypothesized that younger children might be more constrained than older children to display mental health problems in different contexts. To date, little research has been conducted examining a similar paradigm among children without mental health concerns; however, the Achenbach et al. findings suggest that evaluators become aware of the possibility that the age of the child may affect what different informants' observe and how where evaluators observe a child might affect what behaviors the child displays or what behaviors the informant notes as remarkable.

The final finding from Achenbach et al. (1987) was informants' reports of children's behavior were more consistent when directly observing externalizing behavior than reporting on children's internally experienced behaviors which are thus less directly observable.

We note two statistical findings of great interest. One result was that children's self-reports could not substitute for reports by other informants. Children's self-reports were found to have a relatively small relationship to information obtained from parents, teachers, and mental health workers (i.e., $r = .22$). The second result was that different informants observing the same child contribute uniquely to information about the child. There was a mean correlation of $r = .28$ between different types of informants, suggesting that each informant brings a unique perspective.

MULTI-INFORMANT APPROACH

One of the fascinating developments over the past 30 years has been the increasing frequency of inter- and intra-disciplinary information exchange. Of particular interest is the integration of the robust literature on the multi-informant approach to assessing child and adolescent mental health to the methods and procedures utilized in parenting plan assessment.[1]

De Los Reyes and colleagues (2015) conducted a follow-up meta-analysis to the Achenbach et al. (1987) discussed prior. De Los Reyes et al. were interested in the reliability of the multi-informant data gathering approach to assessing children's and adolescents' mental health. Similar to the argument put forth by Achenbach et al., De Los Reyes et al. argued that not all situations elicit children's mental health concerns to the same degree. Children may display maladaptive behaviors in one context but not others. Behavior variations associated with different situations occur within a variety of mental health domains. Children might display social anxiety in one situation and show no signs of maladaptive behavior in other situations.

The applicability of these findings to PPE should be readily apparent. Children's behavior might change as a result of context. A child might behave one way with their mother and another way with their father. That same child might behave one way when their siblings are around and another way when their siblings are absent. The application of the multi-informant model to parenting plan assessment and gathering collateral information, in particular, was recently presented in an AFCC podcast (Gould & Flens, 2020).

INTERNAL CONSISTENCY

Garber (2016) addresses the importance of internal consistency "as one method with which to infer the validity of an observation or a report" (p. 270). Mirroring the general approach to data gathering in parenting plan assessment, he notes that evaluators are often encouraged to conduct multiple observations or interviews to establish consistency across time and situations.

Garber (2016) argues that consistency across multiple interviews or multiple observations might lead to greater confidence in the representativeness of the information, while inconsistency is confounded by intervening events. Consistency in data across multiple independent data sources has been viewed as a high mark of reliability in parenting plan assessment. Garber notes that inconsistency across multiple observations might lead to a higher likelihood of false negatives, i.e., incorrect claims that the inconsistency is the result of lying.

Questions about the importance of information consistency across multiple observations, multiple collateral interviews, or multiple interviews have often been viewed as the holy grail in parenting plan assessment. But does inconsistent information really mean that the discrepant data are unreliable?

One of the fascinating challenges in parenting plan assessment is obtaining accurate and reliable reports about children's behavior when spending time with each parent. Children may, in fact, behave differently at one parent's home compared to the other parent's home. Alternatively, children might behave the

[1]See Hynan (2003) for an example of interdisciplinary integration proposals.

same way at each parent's home, yet each parent perceives their children's behavior differently.

Children might also behave differently at the same parent's home because of factors that affect the child but have nothing to do with the nature and quality of the parent–child relationship. See Chapters 19 and 20 for more.

Similarly, observational effects may impact our perspectives. Children might behave the same way with each parent when observed, yet the informant observing the interaction perceives differences based upon cognitive bias factors that the informant brings to the observation. Children might behave differently with each parent when observed, yet the informant observing the behaviors perceives similarities based upon a different set of cognitive bias factors.

Adding to the complexity is both parents' and children's view of themselves in each situation, how each person wants to be perceived by the other person as behaving, and how each person wants to be perceived by the informant observing the interactions. There are times when children's behavior might be affected by age-appropriate attitudes toward parents that affect their behavior toward that parent. A preadolescent boy might wish to display his movement toward independence by deliberately challenging the parent while the same child observed as a 15-year-old teenager might have a more sophisticated grasp on his need for independence and to recognize the need to display cooperation and caring toward a parent rather than independence.

PARENTAL INSIGHT AND UNDERSTANDING OF CHILD NEEDS

How a parent understands the interface between the requirements of a parent–child observation during an evaluation and how their child's level of development might become a factor in the child's observed behavior is also an important area of consideration. Although parent–child observations are an essential component of PPEs, these observations are influenced by multiple factors, including the child's developmental stage.

Evaluators need to be aware of the tension between developmental expectations and evaluative demands. For example, a child's behavior during an observation is not just a reflection of parenting but also of their cognitive, emotional, and social development. A younger child may show separation anxiety or clinginess that could be misinterpreted as insecurity in the parent–child relationship. An older child, particularly a teenager, may display resistance or detachment due to developmental independence rather than parental inadequacy or due to the older child's preference for one parent over the other being demonstrated by disruptive behavior during the observation.

Another factor that evaluators need to consider is the tension between a child's situational reactivity compared with the child's everyday behavior. For example, observations sometimes take place in an unfamiliar setting, often under artificial or stressful conditions. A child might behave differently due to anxiety, reluctance, or confusion about the evaluation process.

Parents may also feel pressure to "perform," impacting their natural parenting responses. Gathering relevant third-party information is critical in helping to determine whether the child's behavior, the parent's behavior, or their interaction is reflective of situational reactivity or are examples of their everyday behavior.

Parent–child observations, especially with children 6 and under, are likely to offer information about parental insight and adaptability. For example, observations can help determine a parent's ability to recognize and respond appropriately to their child's developmental stage, a key indicator of effective parenting. If a parent lacks insight into why their child behaves a certain way during the evaluation, it would be important to gather relevant third-party information about the parent's ability to develop healthy, age-appropriate attunement with the child in the outside world.

Evaluators must contextualize observed behaviors within a developmental framework rather than making blanket interpretations. Evaluators should be cautious about over-reliance on one-time observations without considering broader developmental and contextual factors.

Evaluators are best served when they develop strong clinical skills upon which forensic psychological acumen is built. Forensic psychological methodology has always been informed by assessment models drawn from clinical assessment models. A basic assumption in clinical-child and clinical-adult assessment is gathering information from multiple informants.

MULTI-INFORMANT MODEL

The multi-informant approach assumes that informants each carry unique and valid perspectives of the people to whom services are being provided (De Los Reyes et al., 2015). To maximize the clinical value offered by the multi-informant model, informants who provide information to the assessment team should differ in their opportunities to observe the client across different situations, different activities, and with different people.

In clinical assessment, integrating multiple distinct pieces of information improves clinical decision making compared to more limited information (De Los Reyes et al., 2015). The multi-informant model in assessments is particularly valuable in PPEs, because it allows for a more comprehensive understanding of a client's psychological functioning and behavior across different contexts. The following are examples of how different informants contribute unique perspectives:

- It is not uncommon for Parent A to report on the child's behavior at home, emotional responses to transitions, and interactions with family members, while Parent B provides a potentially different perspective on the same behaviors, often influenced by different parenting styles and environments.

- Teacher observations provide information about the child's social interactions, academic performance, and emotional regulation in a structured setting that is different from the parent's observations of the child in each home.
- Therapists (either the child's therapist or a parent's therapist) can assess emotional and psychological well-being, attachment patterns, and coping strategies during sessions.
- Extended family (e.g., grandparents, stepparents) can offer insight into the child's adaptability and relationships in nonprimary home settings.
- Neighbors or friends who have personal knowledge of parent–child interactions can provide observations on parenting practices and social behavior outside of formal settings.
- Medical and mental health professionals often offer insight into physical injuries, health neglect, or developmental concerns. Pediatricians often have notes about parental involvement in the child's medical and observations of parental medical decision making observed during office visits.

By diversifying informants, the evaluator can triangulate data, thereby reducing bias and increasing the reliability of findings.

CONTEXTUAL VARIATIONS IN PARENT–CHILD OBSERVATIONS

There are contextual variations in observations. Different informants might respond differently to the same observational setting, and the reasons for these different reactions may or may not reflect differences in the context in which the child was observed. Informants differ in their perceptions of observed behavior. They may differ in their interpretation of the same events. They may focus attention on different events during the observation. They may assign different weights to the behaviors being observed. As we discussed in Chapter 8, sociocultural factors may affect which behaviors are viewed as healthy versus unhealthy parenting.

Discrepancies in informants' observations may result from differences in observers' relationship with the one being observed. Parents have a different relationship with their children than their teachers. Mothers have different relationships with their children than their fathers. A math teacher might develop a different relationship with a child compared with a history teacher who is also the child's football coach. Observational differences between parent and child may result from differences in cognitive abilities. Informants may be influenced by social desirability factors, too.

The literature has addressed issues about threats to the reliability of data gathering from multi-informants from the perspective of reporting biases and measurement errors (De Los Reyes et al., 2015). What we find fascinating about the multi-informant model of information gathering is its recognition that divergent observations do not necessarily represent unreliable information. Divergent observations may represent highly reliable information that is viewed through an alternative perspective.

HOME VERSUS OFFICE OBSERVATIONS

Using nondivorced samples, several older studies reported differences in the rates of child compliance in office clinic settings compared to home environments. Children have been observed to display higher rates of noncompliance in office environments. Studies also found mothers tend to use more restraint in directing their children in the clinic compared to the home environment (Saini & Polack, 2014). Thus, observations should occur in both the office and the home. If there are financial limitations or time limitations, each parent's home is more likely to be an ecologically valid location for the observation.

DURATION OF OBSERVATIONS

There are suggestions in the literature about the number of observations and the amount of time to be devoted to parent–child observations (Ackerman & Ackerman, 1997; Ackerman et al., 2021), but no data on the duration of each observation. Hynan (2003) posits a minimum of two 45- to 60-minute observation sessions with each parent. Ackerman et al. reported evaluators spend about 4 hours engaged in parent–child observations. Martindale (2005) indicated that the evaluator needs to make a judgment about whether the observation was sufficient to accurately assess the family situation.

Benjamin et al. (2018) suggested that the adequacy of the duration of the observation can be determined by whether the parents believe the observations produced an accurate representation of their parenting abilities and interactions with their children. However, findings from the De Los Reyes et al. (2015) research consistently reveal the following: parents are poor reporters of the quality of their parenting, parents' perception of their parenting is different from their children's perception of their parenting, and parents' perception of their parenting is different from collateral informants' observations of parenting.

PLANNED VERSUS CONVENIENCE SCHEDULING

Garber observes that most evaluators appear to schedule interviews and observations based on convenience to parents' or the evaluators' calendars (Garber, 2016). The parent–child observation should occur with little interference from the evaluator. The purpose is to obtain a set of data against which the evaluator compares these observations to those obtained from other sources. After the observation, both parent and child should be asked about the degree to which the parent–child observations were representative of a typical day in their lives.

When an observation includes others besides each parent, we recommend conducting several observations. One observation must be with each parent and the child or children. Additional observations might occur, but the evaluator needs to gather information about the unique interactions between and among each parent and child separate from observational data about the children's behavior (and the parent's behavior) when other people are included in the observation.

RECOMMENDATIONS FOR EVALUATORS

Some evaluators endorse the use of established observational techniques such as the strange situation or Parent Child Interaction Therapy. We caution against using these techniques as they do not offer forensic comparison samples or a reliable way to integrate the information in a parenting plan evaluation. Rather, we summarize recommendations from other evaluators.

Saini and Polak

Saini and Polak (2014) offer the following considerations:

- Plan for observations during naturally-occurring family interactions (e.g., meal times, homework). Planning for naturally-occurring interactions can provide the evaluator with an opportunity to observe typical everyday family interactions and behaviors (F. Gardner, 2000).
- Conduct the observation in a comfortable setting. Observations should be conducted in a location that is comfortable for the parents and children. Ideally, this would include home observations to observe parent–child interactions in their typical surroundings. If observations are conducted in the office setting, special attention must be made to ensure that the space is child-centered with a range of age-appropriate activities for children and parents to engage in while being observed.
- Observe all significant parties. Parent–child observations may include each parent with each child, but it should also include a period of time where the parent is observed with all children together. Stepparents and partners who live together should be included in the parent–child observations.
- Use introductory engagement methods for the first 5 to 10 minutes of the observation (e.g., asking for a tour of the home, informal conversations about family activities). Spending the first part of the observation engaging the family may help to reduce any anxieties about the observation, which would then allow the family members to more freely participate in the observation.

- Choose activities that are familiar to the children and parents. Activities that are familiar to the children and parents can assist in observing more typical interactions. Evaluators may consider asking the family about the activities they typically engage in or enjoy doing (e.g., board games, cards, puzzles) such that the observation meeting can be structured around those activities.

- Use both structured and unstructured activities. Parent–child observations should include both structured and unstructured activities or tasks during the visit (Ackerman, 1995). Structured visits are important because they allow a greater opportunity to observe the parent and the child working toward a goal together (Bow & Quinnell, 2001). Evaluators must be vigilant to the potential of observer reactivity effects as such influences can limit the validity of an evaluator's observations. If structured tasks are introduced into the observation, the evaluator should ensure that the family is adequately comfortable with the evaluator's presence before initiating any structured activities.

- Use culturally appropriate methods for observing. There are no template answers to being culturally sensitive during observations. It is important in multicultural societies that the evaluator develop the capacity to accommodate the diversity of families, respecting differences and making genuine efforts to explore cultural realities. Within ethnic groups, there will be many variations in customs and degrees of adherence to traditional ways between the genders, age groups, class groupings, and ethnic or regional groupings from their countries of origin. Evaluators need to be aware of these variations and plan their observations accordingly.

- Spend sufficient time observing. Although there is no set standard for the duration of an observation visit, prolonged engagement in the observation can increase the representativeness of the parent–child interactions. Observations longer than an hour in duration, for example, can provide children and parents some time to become more comfortable with the presence of the observer, which can result in a more fair and accurate representation of the parent–child interactions. The evaluator may consider an observation lasting 1.5 hours as sufficient to provide a credible and representative sample of the parent–child interactions.

- Check-in with parents. Assess the accuracy of the observation by asking parents whether the duration of the observation provided a fair and accurate representation of their parent–child interactions.

- Conduct further observation(s) if necessary. There may be situations when one observation is insufficient to assess the representativeness of the parent–child interactions due to the timing of the observation (e.g., the child was ill, tired, hungry, distracted). Asking the parent about the representativeness of the observation can allow the evaluator to determine whether it is necessary to conduct a follow up observation.

- Use methods consistently with both parents. Whenever possible, the methods for conducting the observations should be the same for the observations with both parents. If the observation with one parent occurs at meal time, the observation with the other parent should also occur at meal time. Any deviation from the method of the observation with one side of the dispute should be clearly explained in the report and any limitations related to this deviation should be explained.
- Document the methods for conducting the observation. To ensure transparency of the selected methods for conducting the observations, evaluators should document the conditions of the observation (e.g., time of day, day of the week, location of the visit, family members present, duration of the visit, the number of visits).
- Document all deviations and report limitations. If the methods chosen by the evaluators for observing parent–child interactions are atypical and not consistent with the natural occurring family interactions (e.g., at a supervised access center, office observation), this information may be useful for assessing parent–child interactions in these specific circumstances, but these observations may be limited by their representativeness of the parent–child interactions outside of these conditions. Therefore, the evaluator should clearly and transparently describe any limitations of the representativeness of the observations in the custody evaluation report.

Behaviors to Observe

Again, there is little guidance from professional practice guidelines about specific behaviors that should be assessed during parent–child observations. A single observation session is insufficient for making reliable inferences about a family's typical interaction patterns. However, conducting numerous observational sessions may be impractical and financially burdensome. A reasonable approach is to conduct at least two observation sessions, each lasting 45 to 60 minutes, with each parent to ensure a more accurate assessment of parent–child dynamics (Hynan, 2003).

We are not recommending that evaluators need to identify only one theory of family functioning to guide their parent–child observations. We are, however, recommending that evaluators, when possible, identify a theory or model that has been empirically examined, extract from the model those behaviors that (a) have an empirical basis and (b) are relevant to the case at hand. It is possible to assess several different factors drawn from different models or theories.

PARENTAL META-EMOTION PHILOSOPHY MODEL

The parental meta-emotion philosophy (PMEP) model (Gottman, Katz, & Hooven, 1996) is a framework for understanding how parents process and respond to both their own and their child's emotions. PMEP consists of the following three fundamental components:

- **Awareness of Emotions**—This refers to how well parents recognize and understand both their emotions and those of their child. Parents who are highly attuned to emotions can better respond to their child's needs and foster a sense of security.
- **Acceptance of Emotions**—Some parents view all emotions (both positive and negative) as natural and valuable, while others see certain emotions as problematic or unnecessary. Acceptance of emotions allows for healthy emotional processing, whereas suppression or dismissal can lead to emotional difficulties in children.
- **Coaching or Dismissing**—This aspect differentiates between parents who actively guide and validate their child's emotional experiences (emotion coaching) and those who minimize, ignore, or even punish emotional expression (emotion dismissing; L. F. Katz, Maliken, & Stettler, 2012).

PMEP plays a critical role in shaping children's emotional development and has significant implications in family law, particularly in custody evaluations. Thus, PMEP can provide data useful toward understanding parental fitness, the quality of parent–child relationships, and a child's overall emotional well-being.

There are four primary types of PMEP: emotion-coaching parenting, emotion-dismissing parenting, emotion-disapproving parenting, and laissez-faire parenting. Specific behaviors associated with each parenting philosophy are presented as follows (Gottman et al., 1996):

1. **Emotion-Coaching Parents**
   - See emotions as an opportunity for teaching and connection, and
   - Help children identify and label their feelings, guiding them toward emotional regulation and problem solving.
2. **Emotion-Dismissing Parents**
   - Perceive emotions as insignificant or problematic, and
   - Tend to downplay or ignore their child's emotions, sometimes redirecting or distracting the child rather than engaging with their feelings.
3. **Emotion-Disapproving Parents**
   - Actively discourage or punish emotional expression, believing that emotions should be controlled through discipline, and
   - Often react negatively to emotional displays, sometimes responding with criticism, scolding, or even shaming the child.
4. **Laissez-Faire Parents**
   - Allow their children to express emotions freely, but
   - Do not teach coping strategies or emotional regulation techniques.

The impact of PMEP on children is profound (Eisenberg, 2020):

- **Positive PMEP (Emotion Coaching)**
  - Leads to stronger emotional regulation, social skills, and resilience;
  - Reduces the likelihood of anxiety, depression, and behavioral issues; and
  - Strengthens the parent–child relationship, fostering trust and emotional security.
- **Negative PMEP (Emotion Dismissing/Disapproving)**
  - Can lead to emotional dysregulation and difficulty in forming healthy relationships,
  - Increases the risk of both externalizing behaviors (e.g., aggression, defiance) and internalizing behaviors (e.g., anxiety, depression), and
  - May contribute to long-term mental health struggles and difficulties in coping with stress.
- **Laissez-Faire Parenting**
  - Can lead to emotional dysregulation, where children struggle with intense emotion, leading to emotional instability (Merchant, 2024).

PMEP can be assessed through multiple methods, including structured interviews, direct observations, collateral interviews, and psychological testing. In structured interviews, evaluators ask targeted questions about:

- **Parental Awareness of Emotions**:
  - How do you recognize when your child is experiencing an emotion?
  - How do you respond when your child is upset, sad, or angry?
- **Parental Beliefs About Emotions**:
  - Do you believe all emotions are acceptable, or should some be suppressed?
  - What role do emotions play in your child's development?
- **Emotional Coaching versus Dismissal**:
  - Can you describe a time when your child was emotionally distressed and how you handled it?
  - What do you do when your child cries or expresses frustration?
- **Conflict Resolution & Emotional Modeling**:
  - How do you handle emotional conflicts with your child?
  - What do you do when you feel overwhelmed or frustrated as a parent?

In direct observations, evaluators may

- Observe how parents respond when their child expresses emotions, looking for validation versus dismissal;
- Assess nonverbal behaviors such as comforting gestures, eye contact, and tone of voice; or

- Examine coparenting interactions to identify patterns of emotional validation or invalidation.

In collateral interviews, evaluators examine

- The degree to which collaterals have observed how a parent responds when the child expresses emotions;
- The degree to which collaterals have observed a parent's nonverbal behaviors such as comforting gestures, eye contact, and tone of voice; and
- The degree to which collaterals have observed coparenting interactions, and the details of those interactions.

In psychological testing, evaluators use standardized tools such as

- The Behavior Assessment System for Children, Third Edition (BASC-3) Parent Rating Scale, which measures the degree to which the parent is aware of the child's strengths and challenges;
- The BASC-3 Self Report of Personality, which contains a Relations with Parents scale which "provides an objective evaluation of the child's regard for the parents while also considering the child's feelings of being esteemed by the parents" (Reynolds et al., 2021);
- The BASC-3 Self Report of Personality, which also contains a Locus of Control scale to gather data on the child's perception of how much control their parents place on them; and
- The BASC-3 Teacher Rating scales, which provide for collateral data of the teacher's observations, which can then be compared to the data collected from the child, the parents, and other collaterals.

In summary, identifying risks associated with emotionally dismissive or disapproving parenting and risks associated with laissez-faire parenting is essential. Chronic emotional invalidation can contribute to anxiety, depression, and attachment issues, particularly in high-conflict custody cases. In contrast, emotion-coaching parenting serves as a protective factor, supporting a child's psychological resilience during family transitions.

Garber's Process-Oriented Systemic Observation Protocol

Garber's (2016) process-oriented systemic observation protocol lists a set of behaviors that, according to attachment theory, are critical for understanding the quality of the parent–child relationship. This protocol incorporates interviews with the children, observations of each parent with the children, observation of a child's transition between the parents, and multiple parent–child separations and reunions. With Garber's protocol, there are eight "landmark, process-oriented" areas for observation: (a) transition into interview in the company of Parent A, (b) separation from Parent A, (c) reunion with parent A, (d) transition out of Parent A's care and into Parent B's care, (e) acclimation to

Parent B, (f) separation from parent B, (g) reunion with Parent B, and (h) departure. The goal is to understand "how the child manages a succession of stresses not unlike those stresses [they] must manage in the postseparation world" (Garber, 2016, p. 264).

There are four planned separations. As Garber describes, "Separation opens a window on the proximal parent's capacity to respond sensitively to the child's need for predictability and structure. On this basis, the evaluator may be able to draw hypotheses about how the particular parent–child pair manage anxiety" (Garber, 2016, p. 265). The evaluator should also look at how the child regulates their emotion, how the parent regulates their emotion, and how they coregulate (i.e., how they help each other manage their feelings and behaviors). There are also opportunities for reunions, as the evaluator will observe three reunions. Garber's protocol becomes more complicated with larger families, and he notes the risk of evaluator fatigue. Our second author has found this protocol to provide an abundance of data in an efficient manner.

Imagine that the child has time with Parent A and will transition midday to Parent B. Here is how Garber's model would work with that transition:

9:00 a.m. Parent A delivers the child to the office; introduction and orientation.

9:10 a.m. Parent A is excused to waiting room/lobby. First interview with the child begins.

10:10 a.m. Parent A joins the child in meeting room. Observation of the child and Parent A begins.

11:10 a.m. Parent B arrives and joins us in the meeting room. Parent A packs up and departs. Observation of Parent B and the child begins.

12:10 p.m. Parent B is excused to waiting room/lobby. Second interview with the child begins.

1:10 p.m. Parent B joins and we begin to clean up.

1:20 p.m. Parent B and the child depart.

For each stage, Garber provides the following between-parent observations of interest:

1. Transition into interview
    a. How does Parent A facilitate or inhibit the child's transition?
    b. How does the child use Parent A to manage anxiety?
2. Separation from Parent A
    a. How does Parent A facilitate or inhibit the child's transition?
    b. How does the child use Parent A to manage anxiety?
3. Reunion with parent A
    a. How does Parent A facilitate or inhibit the child's transition?
    b. How does the child use Parent to manage anxiety?

4. Transition between parents

    a. How does Parent A facilitate or inhibit the child's transition?
    b. How does Parent B facilitate or inhibit the child's transition?
    c. How does the child use Parent A to manage anxiety?
    d. How does the child use Parent B to manage anxiety?
    e. How do the parents respond to one another around the child?
    f. How does the child respond to the parents' interaction?

5. Acclimation to Parent B

    a. How does Parent B facilitate or inhibit the child's transition?
    b. How does the child use Parent B to manage anxiety?

6. Separation from Parent B

    a. How does Parent B facilitate or inhibit the child's transition?
    b. How does the child use Parent B to manage anxiety?

7. Reunion with Parent B

    a. How does Parent B facilitate or inhibit the child's transition?
    b. How does the child use Parent B to manage anxiety?

8. Departure

    a. How does Parent B facilitate or inhibit the child's transition?
    b. How does the child use Parent B to manage anxiety?

As the evaluator charts these interactions, transitions, and reunions, they have the opportunity to gather a wealth of data. We applaud Garber's protocol and encourage you to read more in his paper or attend his workshops, where he describes how he incorporates both structured and unstructured activities during his observations. After each parent leaves, the evaluator should ask each parent to write a summary of how the day went with specific attention to what was similar or unsimilar to the child's usual behavior.

Our model incorporates his in-office observation protocol with home visits to each parent's house. We recommend asking the child to give a tour of the house before the evaluator settles in to an observer role, not participating with the family. The combination of Garber's protocol with observational visits at the home provides a wealth of information, including multiple interviews with the child, separations and reunions with each parent, and the child's transition between the parents.

CONCLUSION

In this chapter, we discussed the importance of parent–child observations in PPEs. Observations help to evaluate ways a child responds to each parent during an observation that can provide insights into both the child's needs, preferences, and potential emotional difficulties and each parent's understanding and parenting to support those needs, preferences, and potential difficulties. Observations help evaluators assess which parent is better equipped to meet those needs. Observations allow for a more holistic understanding of the family dynamic and the child's well-being. Parent–child observations also serve as a way to corroborate or clarify the information provided during interviews and written reports. In some cases, parents may not be fully aware of how their behavior impacts the child, and observations can provide a more objective basis, particularly with regard to transitions, reunions, and parenting time exchanges.

Evaluators can also compare the information obtained from the parent–child observations against independent third-party informants who have personal knowledge of each parent's interactions with the child. As discussed, the multi-informant model reminds us about potential variability in children's presentation. Obtaining information about parent–child behaviors across different activities observed by different people helps to broaden an evaluator's understanding of the reliability of their observation data.

Observations offer a unique, real-time perspective that can help create more accurate, fair, and child-centered parenting plans. They are critical in ensuring that the best interests of the child are fully considered in the legal process. We have discussed earlier in the book the importance of evaluators clearly articulating the theory of science that guides thinking about salient parent variables, child variables, parent–child variables, and extra-familial variables. To the best of our knowledge, Hynan's was among the first articles to recommend integrating empirical investigated models of parent–child observations into the assessment procedure (Hynan, 2003), and Garber's article was the first to identify a specific theory of child development as a basis for his identifying factors to be assessed in a PPE (Garber, 2016). Garber et al. (2022) address these challenges by integrating more factors to consider in assessing relationships. The critical importance of Garber's contribution is his reliance on an established theory of science, identification of factors drawn from the theory, and a procedure for how to gather data about those salient factors.

While concerns regarding observer effects, ecological validity, and inter-informant reliability persist, structured methodologies, such as those proposed by Garber (2016), provide a framework for more comprehensive assessments. Dedicating a significant amount of time to interviewing the child and observing the child with both parents in a single day provides a unique window into the life of the child. As evaluations become longer and more costly, observing the child with both parents, observing how the child transitions between the parents, and interviewing the child multiple times should be at the top of every evaluator's priority list.

15

Usefulness and Limitations of Psychological Testing and Assessment

In this chapter, we discuss the cautious usefulness of properly selecting, administering, and interpreting psychological test data in parenting plan evaluations (PPEs). We also address some of the reasons that feed the controversy over the use of psychological test results. We begin this chapter by clarifying the distinction between psychological assessment and psychological testing. Although the distinction between the two has been made before (Meyer et al., 2001) and has been applied to parenting plan assessments before (Ackerman et al., 2019; Gould, 2006), the distinction is critical, and we believe we can add to earlier discussions.

Next, we address the controversies often raised in the literature about the use of psychological tests. Some colleagues argue about whether psychological tests ought to be used at all in PPEs (Emery et al., 2005). Concerns have been focused on the lack of validation data drawn from custody samples, calling into question the usefulness of interpretations. However, we believe that these concerns have been adequately addressed in the literature by stressing the need to develop hypotheses from test data rather than any conclusions from those data. Most current arguments about the usefulness of psychological test data in PPEs appear to confuse how colleagues utilize psychological test results in misleading and often incorrect ways from the proper ways in which to use psychological

---

Portions of this chapter are adapted from *The Art and Science of Child Custody Evaluations,* by J. W. Gould and D. A. Martindale, 2007, Guilford Press. Copyright 2007 by the Guilford Press. Adapted with permission.

https://doi.org/10.1037/0000474-016
Parenting Plan Evaluations: An Evidence-Informed Approach to Child Custody, by J. W. Gould and C. M. Mulchay

test results in a parenting plan assessment (Garber & Simon, 2018; Rappaport et al., 2018).

Lastly, we reemphasize the purpose and usefulness of psychological testing in PPEs using current assessment models. In the upcoming chapters, we will discuss the usefulness of evolving dimensional assessment models, such as the hierarchical models of dysfunctional personality and psychopathology (Kotov et al., 2017, 2018). Among the reasons we prefer using dimensional models of assessment such as the Alternative Model for Personality Disorders and the Hierarchical Taxonomy of Psychology (discussed in Chapter 17) is their stronger empirical bases than the current categorical models often used for interpretation of test data.

DISTINGUISHING PSYCHOLOGICAL ASSESSMENT FROM PSYCHOLOGICAL TESTING

Psychological testing is not the same as psychological assessment. In *psychological testing,* a particular test is administered to obtain a specific score. A descriptive meaning can be applied to the score based on normative group findings (Meyer et al., 2001). This type of evaluation has been called *nomothetic,* meaning "relating to, involving, or dealing with abstract, general, or universal statements or laws" (Merriam-Webster, n.d.-b), because the test score describes only how the individual compares to the norm. The interpretation does not describe a particular individual's score within the context of the person's life. The sole purpose of the evidence-based interpretation of the test score is to provide a description of the meaning of the data relative to a normative group. These data might be used to develop hypotheses about whether the individual being assessed displays any of the behaviors suggested by the test score interpretations. However, the test score does not tell us anything about the particular person being assessed. The evaluator needs to gather additional independent third-party information to determine whether the data from the test accurately captures the individual's behavior in real life.

In contrast, *psychological assessment* is a broader process in which the evaluator obtains and analyzes a variety of data from multiple sources and methods. Psychological assessment procedures are empirically based data-gathering methods intended to help organize and guide the evaluator's conceptualization of the family system and the development of hypotheses (Weiner & Kleiger, 2021b). The evaluator "considers the data in the context of history, referral information, and observed behavior to understand the person being evaluated, to answer referral questions, and then to communicate findings . . ." (Meyer et al., 2001, p. 131). A fundamental assumption of psychological assessment is that there are aspects of our functioning that we are not entirely aware of or cannot effectively articulate (Wright, 2020). Since the people we evaluate are not entirely aware of their functioning, evaluators gather information from multiple sources to create a more robust data basis upon which to base expert opinions (Wright, 2020). This type of evaluation has been called *ideographic*, meaning "relating to or dealing with something concrete, individual, or unique" (Merriam-Webster, n.d.-a) because the assessment task is to understand the psychological test score within the context of the specific person's life.

It is vital that all testing psychologists, and particularly forensic evaluators, closely attend to both nomothetic and idiographic approaches with every test score. Evaluators often misuse psychological test results by not attending to idiographic data. The assessment task is to combine data from evidence-based or evidence-informed psychological measures with multiple sources of information, which might include historical data, presenting concerns, direct observations, interview results, information from past and present record review, and interviews with third parties. The evaluator's task is to systematically examine each hypothesis looking for the best fit of the data to each hypothesis. The process of ideographic evaluation is far from simple and requires a high degree of skill and sophistication to be implemented properly (Meyer et al., 2001; Weiner & Kleiger, 2021b).

CONTROVERSIES ABOUT THE USE OF PSYCHOLOGICAL TESTS

Among the longstanding controversies in PPEs is the use of psychological tests. Thomas Grisso (1986) described the debate as follows:

> Psychological testing of parents in custody cases (for intelligence, personality, and/or psychopathology) has been described variously as of no utility, of dubious value, potentially useful when performed selectively and only when a clear need is identified, and one of the better indicators of a parent's true feelings and intentions. Rarely are opinions of this type offered with any empirical support or with reference to any particular psychological tests. (p. 229)

Below we review the main concerns about the use of psychological tests in PPEs.

Criterion-Related and Construct-Related Validity

One criticism of psychological testing in PPEs relates to validity. In graduate school, we learned the distinction between criterion-related validity and construct validity; however, the distinction seems to have been often overlooked when evaluators consider the meaning of test scores, and the terms have been updated in 1985 and again in 1999. As we will describe in the next chapter, we have more precise validity terminology. Yet, the distinction between criterion-related validity and construct-related validity continues to be important.

Criterion-related validity addresses the extent to which scores correlate with some condition of the subject or some predicted aspect of their behavior. *Construct-related validity*, on the other hand, addresses the degree to which a theoretical formulation can account for relationships between test scores and some condition or behavior. In the case of the use of psychological tests in PPEs, construct-related validity would address the conceptual or theoretical relationship between a model of parenting behavior and test scores.

Our field has been slow to examine the relationship between specific psychological test results and parenting behavior. In the case of criterion-related validity, few studies have explored parenting correlates associated with scores on specific scales. Similarly, we know of no studies that have examined the construct validity of predictions drawn from parenting theories to specific psychological test results. To the best of our knowledge, we know only of a few studies that have demonstrated an empirical relationship between scores on specific NEO Personality Inventory and NEO Personality Inventory-3 dimensions and specific parenting behaviors. Despite the usefulness of these criterion-related validity data, we have found no studies that have examined the construct validity of specific theories of parenting behavior and specific psychological tests. For example, the data on the NEO are not interpreted to address specific parenting style factors nor are NEO scores shown to be predictive of specific behaviors that are part of a specific parenting style factor.

These concerns about the lack of criterion-related and construct validation studies vis-a-vis parenting theories and models lead us to caution evaluators about the degree to which one might draw inferences from test data that are not supported by empirical studies. Framed within a *Daubert* perspective, evaluators need to be wary of developing inferences and proffering testimony built on those inferences about parenting behavior, parent–child interactions, and parent-to-parent communication and cooperation based upon psychological test results that create an indefensible analytic gap (*General Electric Co. v. Joiner*, 1997) between data and opinions.

In all psychological assessment procedures, we are wise to remember that "no self-report is made without bias and blind spots, no test has perfect reliability and validity, and no single method of measurement should be taken as gospel. The validity of every single test in existence has been challenged" (Wright, 2020). Further, in PPEs, context may impact validity. "The validity-scale elevations can reasonably be understood as resulting from the demands of the test situation, and conclusions about client traits based on these elevations may be unfounded" (Carr et al., 2005).

Stages of Inference

Weiner and Kleiger (2021a) described a stage model of inferences to be applied to the interpretation of psychological testing data. They also described the levels of confidence assigned to each inference stage. The first stage of inference is called the *representative inference* and is closely tied to test scores. Representative inferences "exemplify the psychological functions we seek to assess" (Weiner & Kleiger, 2021a, p. 9).

Second stage inferences, called *symbolic inferences*, are steps taken beyond those made with the representative inference. They often reflect stepping beyond the test results and interpreting the meaning of the results within the context of a theory or concept that is intended to extend or elaborate the original inference.

> Higher order inferences integrate test findings and enable assessors to make inferences about the presence and severity of clinical syndromes and the disorders to which they may be linked. Representative inferences are the scaffolding on which higher order, diagnostic inferences may be made. (Weiner & Kleiger, 2021a, p. 9)

As we will discuss later in the chapter, most of the controversy about the use of psychological test results focus on *symbolic* or *second-stage inference*. Most evaluators we have reviewed do not attempt to tie hypotheses developed from test scores to specific theories of parenting, concepts about parenting, or specific parenting behaviors.

Some readers might question whether any inferences drawn from test data should be included in an evaluation given the lack of criterion-related and construct-related validity data. We believe there are empirical data about many parenting-related behaviors associated with behaviors measured on psychological tests. For example, there is substantial literature addressing how parental depression is associated with various problematic parenting behaviors. When a parent's psychological test results reveal concerns about depression, evaluators should be aware of the parenting correlates associated with depression, such as increased irritability, increased use of corporal punishment, and decreased supervision of children. Test scores do not tell us much, if anything, about parenting behavior. Test scores might provide direction, pointing to an examination of evidence-based literature associated with specific psychological problems or psychopathology that allows for the development of hypotheses to be further investigated.

Psychological Test Results Can Be Used in Incorrect Ways

Despite the clear need to understand the psychological dynamics within the context of the person's life (Eyde et al., 1993; Gould, 2006; Meyer et al., 2001), psychologists misuse tests when they incorrectly apply nomothetic and idiographic approaches, and when they do not interpret the results within the context of the family dynamic. In clinical contexts, psychologists err when they do not use multiple sources of assessment data. It is not appropriate to base important decisions on the result of one assessment (Reynolds et al., 2021). This is most likely to occur when one parent or one teacher identifies an issue with attention (i.e., attention-deficit/hyperactivity disorder) or social reciprocity (i.e., autism) that is not corroborated in other contexts. Psychologists also err when they offer interpretations that are too far removed from the data, which in a *Daubert* analysis would be an issue concerning an analytic gap (*General Electric Co. v. Joiner*, 1997). This is most likely to occur when an evaluator bases their opinion on their experience instead of the data.

In forensic contexts, psychological tests can be misused in the same ways as discussed above. More than 30 years ago, Brodzinsky (1993) warned, "Although psychological testing can play an important role in custody and visitation evaluations, psychologists routinely misuse test data." Brodzinsky described reasons psychologists misuse psychological tests. He noted that lawyers and judges have an unrealistic view of what psychological testing can accomplish such that they believe psychological tests allow the evaluator to be "truly objective and therefore unbiased." There is also the perception that psychological tests measure traits that cannot be uncovered through other procedures, as testing magically allows the psychologist to learn hidden truths and read people's minds. Brodzinsky also noted that psychological testing is a key aspect of professional identity and it allows evaluators to bill for more time.

Another way psychological tests can be misused is when they serve to exacerbate the adversarial positions (Posthuma, 2016). Test results may be used to pejoratively describe a parent or may be used aggressively in cross-examining the expert. Test results may be taken out of context. They may be misunderstood. They may be misrepresented, particularly when psychologists only apply a nomothetic approach. When dealing with psychological test results in the courtroom, the evaluator and the expert hired to review the evaluator's work, need to have exquisite knowledge of the research being cited in the court proceeding (Posthuma, 2016).

These concerns have been consistently raised for the past 35 years. The use of psychological testing in PPEs was recently criticized based, in large part, on the inaccurate interpretation of psychological test results presented to the courts. Concerns are focused on the leap from inference drawn from test data used to expert opinions that address the ultimate question regarding allocation of parenting rights and responsibilities for which there is virtually no empirical support (Garber & Simon, 2018; Tippins & Wittmann, 2005). Recall our discussion of the nomothetic and idiographic approaches. We welcome our colleagues' encouragement to use "cautiously and carefully crafted, systemically-informed, empirically-grounded, and child-centered qualitative observations, inferences and recommendations" (Garber & Simon, 2018, p. 327).

THE USEFULNESS OF PSYCHOLOGICAL TESTING DATA

Psychological tests provide a wealth of information that is unavailable from interview data alone. Because patients are notoriously poor historians, tests assess many characteristics and traits often overlooked during interview assessment, provide quantitative information that allows for precise measurement of characteristics, and help ensure multiple sources of data are collected (Reynolds et al., 2021). Brodzinsky noted the clear need for psychological tests that would help in PPEs, while he also noted that the tests were designed for clinical purposes. He noted that these tests "must have proven reliability and validity for forensic purposes" (Brodzinsky, 1993). Later we elaborate on specific benefits of psychological testing in PPEs and suggest ways to improve validity in these tests.

Psychological Testing Generates Hypotheses

Careful interpretation of psychological test data should lead to the development of hypotheses worthy of further investigation or consideration (Melton et al., 2018). Recall that a hypothesis is a "tentative explanation" based on observation and inferences (Campbell, 1996). Evaluators employ the hypothesis-testing model that incorporates developing hypotheses, testing those hypotheses, and using multiple methods of independent information to confirm or disconfirm each hypothesis.

For example, suppose a psychological test indicated that a parent had clinical-level anxiety. We believe the evaluator should review the psychological test results with each parent in order to understand whether the results might reflect factors associated with the litigation context rather than factors associated with their real-life functioning. Many of the widely used psychological tests list test responses endorsed by the test taker. On the Minnesota Multiphasic Personality Inventory (MMPI), 2nd Edition (MMPI-2); MMPI-2, Restructured Form (MMPI-2-RF); and MMPI, 3rd Edition (MMPI-3) these are the "critical items." On the PAI, they are found in the "critical item endorsement." On the Millon Clinical Multiaxial Inventory (MCMI), 3rd edition (MCMI-III), and MCMI, 4th edition (MCMI-IV), they are found as "noteworthy responses." The process of interviewing clients about these specific responses is called a *critical item analysis* of the client's responses.

Oftentimes, a parent will endorse items that elevate scales that measure paranoid thinking. Closer inspection of the item responses may reveal that the parent's answers are related only to the conflict involving the current custody dispute rather than revealing a true paranoid response set. We explain such test results as reflecting the parent's nonparanoid responses to the litigation process rather than reflecting paranoid functioning.

Psychological Test Batteries Provide Uniquely Useful Data

Forensic testing can circumvent problems commonly associated with clinical assessment by imposing somewhat greater structure and direction on the accumulation of data. One such structure is the use of a psychological test battery. Meyer et al. (2001) identify several reasons why the use of psychological tests in a comprehensive psychological assessment provides a genuinely unique data set. Their criteria for the use of psychological tests in a clinical evaluation assessment are applied in the following to the use of psychological tests in a forensic assessment.

A psychological test battery provides an empirically based set of data that allows for more precise measurement of individual characteristics than is usually obtained from interviews alone. The use of multiple tests that comprise a test battery allows for cross-checking of hypotheses. By incorporating multiple measures of multiple dimensions, the evaluator can gather a wide range of information to facilitate understanding the parent or child as well as to facilitate an understanding of the comparative strengths and limitations of each parent or child, both against each other and against a group of peers.

Another advantage to using a psychological test battery is the generation of data from a large number of personality, cognitive, emotional, or other dimensions simultaneously. Test batteries tend to be inclusive and cover a range of functioning domains, many of which may be overlooked during less formal evaluation procedures.

A third advantage to psychological tests is standardized administration and scoring procedures. Each parent or child is presented with a uniform stimulus that serves as a common yardstick to measure their characteristics. Standardization also may reduce legal and ethical problems because it minimizes the prospects that unintended bias may adversely affect the individual or the evaluator's interpretation of the individual's responses.

A fourth advantage to the use of psychological tests is the comparison of the parent's or child's scores to norms, permitting each individual to be compared with a relevant group of peers. For personality tests like the MMPI-3, the information obtained from such normative comparison allows the evaluator to formulate refined inferences about the strengths and weaknesses of a parent compared with a relevant group of peers. For example, the MMPI-2, MMPI-2-RF, MMPI-3, Parenting Assessment Inventory Plus, and the MCMI-III have data reported for custody litigants. Use of these comparison groups allows the evaluator to consider the degree to which a particular parent's scores deviate from the norm group. An experienced evaluator is able to take the obtained data and examine subtle differences in it, which may be relevant to questions about individual functioning along relevant dimensions associated with parenting in order to develop hypotheses suitable for further investigation.

Psychological tests used in a forensic evaluation ought to have information about reliability and validity. Such psychometric information allows the evaluator to consider the strengths and limitations of the information obtained from the test. Without such information, evaluators have little ability to gauge the accuracy of the data they process when making judgments.

A fifth advantage is the ability to gather data from multiple sources. For example, when a child completes the Behavior Assessment System for Children, Third Edition (BASC-3), each parent completes a BASC-3 about their perception of the child, and the teacher completes a BASC-3 about their perception of the child, we have multiple sources of data that each can be compared to norms. The data can also be compared to one another such that we learn how either parent or the teacher may have a similar or different perception of the child than the child has of themself.

Psychological Testing Contributes to Multitrait or Multimethod Assessment

Forensic assessment is premised upon the idea of convergent validity. A competent forensic evaluation is based upon multiple sources of information from independent sources of data, which includes psychological testing. This is referred to as the multitrait or multimethod model of assessment. A critical issue in the use of a multitrait or multimethod model is the extent to which distinct assessment methods provide unique versus redundant information. It is important to recognize that more data does not always mean more accurate results. For example, when using tests that are intercorrelated, it is possible that the predictive power of the two tests combined is lessened compared with the predictive power of the psychometrically more powerful test.

The idea behind multitrait or multimethod assessment is to increase the predictive power of the data. If a method does not increase the ability of the data to predict the behavior of interest, then there is no incremental validity derived from the use of the method. If there is no incremental validity, there is no reason to administer the test.

However, it is critical to remember that the use of the same method obtained from different sources of data may produce unique observations. For example, self-report questionnaires which are completed by parents, siblings, aunts, uncles, teachers, coaches, youth counselors, therapists, and other people outside the family system may provide very different descriptions of the identified behavior (See Chapter 18 on Collateral Information).

Validity Tests Can Detect "Faking Good" and "Faking Bad"

"People are not very good at judging other people objectively, and most 'non-test' assessment procedures involve subjective judgment" (Reynolds et al., 2021, Chapter 15). It is the fallibility of human judgment (Reichardt, 1992) that has led to the increase in psychological testing.

Parents are notoriously poor historians and present biased information, intentionally or otherwise. Some parents will attempt to minimize their difficulties in order to appear more competent or socially acceptable. This is referred to as "faking good." Other parents may exaggerate their symptoms in hope of gaining a financial reward, such as those involved in personal injury evaluations. This is referred to as "faking bad."

These tendencies to misrepresent one's true characteristics are typically referred to as response biases or response styles. To address these, many contemporary tests incorporate specific validity scales that are designed to help the clinician detect a response bias and when present, consider its impact on test scores. How validity scales tend to influence psychological test scores in PPEs has been recently addressed (Gould et al., 2018).

The process and content of forensic interviews and observations often vary considerably from parent to parent, from parent to child, from child to child, and from each of these family members to collateral informants. For example, an evaluator might deviate from a set of semistructured questions posed to each parent, asking one set of follow-up questions to one parent and an entirely different set of questions to another. In contrast, psychological tests have standardized stimuli (i.e., questions or items), administration (e.g., instruction and time limits), and scoring procedures. Since all those who are tested are presented the same stimuli under the same conditions with the same scoring criteria, we can have increased confidence that observed differences are the result of true differences, not simply differences in the questions they were asked.

LESSONS FOR USING PSYCHOLOGICAL TESTS IN PARENTING PLAN EVALUATIONS

Heilbrun, Rogers, and Otto (2002) suggested three categories into which psychological tests and measures fall. The first category is clinical assessment instruments (CAIs). CAIs are psychological and medical tests and other assessment techniques that aid in assessment, diagnosis, and treatment planning in therapeutic contexts. Often, these measures and techniques have been carefully developed with strong evidence-bases for their use in particular situations or with particular populations. Data from CAIs might be helpful in formulating hypotheses about a parent or child's psychological and emotional functioning that could bear on the psycholegal questions of concern. Data from these measures and techniques might also be helpful in formulating hypotheses about behavioral correlates associated with parenting behavior, parent-to-parent communication and decision-making abilities, and parent–child interactions.

None of the CAIs typically used by parenting plan evaluators have been developed for use in parenting plan assessment. As a result, results from these measures do not speak directly to questions of parenting, parent-to-parent communication, or parent–child interactions. Framed within the Weiner two-stage inference model, data from these measures are useful when integrated with symbolic or second-stage inferences. The evaluator might integrate the primary data—representative inferences—with specific theories or constructs associated with parenting, parent-to-parent communication, or parent–child interactions—symbolic inferences. When providing interpretation of test results within the context of specific theories or constructs, it is critical for the evaluator to be clear about the inferential steps being taken. The evaluator must be clear that the interpretations being offered are based upon inferences drawn from theoretical models or constructs applied to test results and not directly from the test results themselves.

It is also important for the evaluator to clearly state in the report that all inferences taken from psychological test results, whether they are representative or symbolic inferences, are explanations based upon nomothetic data, which describe data from the normative group. More data must be collected from independent information sources before an evaluator can make reasonable ideographic interpretations.

Heilbrun et al. (2002) describe a second category of tests and measures as forensically-relevant instruments (FRIs). FRIs measure constructs most relevant to the specific psycholegal questions of concern, i.e., psychopathy, response style. FRIs are less frequently used by mental health professionals who are not involved in forensic psychological activities and, as a result, tend to be less well researched (Melton et al., 2018).

The third category is forensic assessment instruments (FAIs) that are designed for use in the legal process. FAIs assess relevant psycholegal capacities, abilities, and knowledge (Melton et al., 2018). Although several FAIs have been developed for use in criminal and civil proceedings and have reasonably good psychometric integrity, FAIs developed for use in the parenting plan field have been shown to have weak or nonexistent psychometric integrity (i.e., ASPECT or the Bricklin Scales).

The challenge in parenting plan assessment is to utilize data from CAIs in a manner consistent with their intended use as supported by the test manual or evidence-based research and to develop inferences and hypotheses about the meaning of these results that are reasonable and supported by independent information sources.

CONCLUSION

In order to understand an individual's functioning, forensic psychological evaluators must extend their data collection far beyond what the individual can self-report. People are not fully aware of their own behaviors, motivations, or psychological states, making it necessary for evaluators to employ a multimethod approach. This approach integrates self-reports, collateral information from third parties, objective psychological testing, and direct behavioral observations to form a comprehensive picture.

Psychological testing plays a crucial role in hypothesis generation, rather than serving as definitive proof of a person's psychological state. Evaluators follow a hypothesis-testing model, in which they propose initial explanations, systematically test them, and then use independent sources of information to confirm or refute these hypotheses. This method ensures that assessments remain grounded in empirical evidence rather than subjective judgment.

Yet, despite the utility of psychological testing, diagnoses alone do not define a person. Individuals are not simply distinguished by clinical labels but rather by their behavioral traits and how they function in their relationships. Evaluators must carefully differentiate between temporary, situation-driven behaviors (states) and long-term personality traits, a distinction critical in forensic assessments, particularly in PPEs. This necessity for a multisource, multimethod approach has long been recognized in forensic mental health assessment, where the stakes are high, and judicial decisions must be informed by reliable expert testimony. By utilizing diverse sources of information, evaluators enhance the reliability of their findings. The process often involves ruling out hypotheses rather than confirming them, as definitive proof is rarely attainable in complex human behavior. However, when multiple sources of data align and provide converging evidence, the case for a given hypothesis becomes significantly stronger.

The strength of an evaluator's conclusions lies in the robustness of the evidence supporting them. In legal contexts, where expert testimony influences life-altering decisions, the credibility of an opinion depends not on assertion but on the weight of the scientific evidence behind it. In the next couple of chapters, we'll dive deeper into psychological testing.

16

Selecting and Using Psychological Tests

Previously, we discussed how psychological testing plays a crucial role in parenting plan evaluations (PPEs), serving as one of multiple sources of data that inform evaluators' assessments. Alongside interviews with parents and children, observations of parent–child interactions, and collateral reports, psychological tests provide valuable insights that can guide evaluators in forming and investigating hypotheses about parenting capacity and child well-being. In this chapter, we address key considerations in the selection, administration, and interpretation of these tests. This includes the validity and reliability of commonly-used assessment tools, the interpretation of test results in the context of parenting behavior, and the integration of test findings with other sources of information. We also examine some of the ongoing debates surrounding the use of projective techniques, the selection of scientifically-supported tests, and the role of validity scales in assessing response style.

SELECTING RELIABLE AND RELEVANT ASSESSMENT TOOLS

Many who are writing in the field have stressed the importance of selecting psychological tests for which there is empirical support for use in a parenting plan context (Ackerman et al., 2019; Gould et al., 2011; Otto et al., 2000; Rappaport et al., 2018). The *Standards for Educational and Psychological Testing* (American Educational Research Association et al., 2014) identify five categories of evidence that are related to the validity of test score interpretation. One area,

https://doi.org/10.1037/0000474-017
Parenting Plan Evaluations: An Evidence-Informed Approach to Child Custody, by J. W. Gould and C. M. Mulchay

evidence based on relations to other variables, includes evidence based on examination of the relationship between test performance and external variables or criteria, like parenting.

Until recently, survey research revealed many colleagues continue to use assessment tools of weak or nonexistent psychometric integrity. "The forensic use of psychological tests needs, not only research support on the specific application but also clarity in demonstrating the best interest of the child or children. In other words, forensic custody testing needs to have the type of research support of risk assessment now commonly part of police investigations and court proceedings" (Posthuma, 2016, p. 67). The most recent survey data suggest parenting plan evaluators are more mindful of administering psychological tests perceived to pass a *Daubert* challenge (Ackerman et al., 2021).

Examining how psychological tests were used in courtrooms across the country, Neal et al. (2019) reported that nearly all the assessment tools used by psychologists and offered as expert evidence in legal settings had been subjected to empirical testing (90%). However, only about 67% were identified as generally accepted in the field, and only about 40% have favorable reviews of their psychometric and technical properties in authorities such as the *Mental Measurements Yearbook.* Furthermore, Neal et al. (2019) reported that legal challenges to the admission of psychological test results are infrequent. They found legal challenges to the assessment evidence for any reason occurred in only 5.1% of cases in their sample, with a little more than half of these challenges focused on the validity of the test. When challenges were raised, they succeeded only about a third of the time. Challenges to the most scientifically-suspect tools were found to be almost nonexistent. Attorneys rarely challenged psychological expert assessment evidence, and when they did, judges often failed to exercise the scrutiny required by law (Neal et al., 2019, p. 135).

Another important finding in the Neal et al. (2019) study was the frequent use of psychological tests for purposes the test was not developed to assess. This is referred to as *context-relevant validation studies.* A test developed for one purpose may not be appropriate for use in another context. Data need to be available demonstrating the test's reliability and validity when used with the population under scrutiny. That is, are there data to support an evidence-informed understanding of the meaning of test results with a particular population? The Minnesota Multiphasic Personality Inventory (MMPI), 2nd Edition (MMPI-2); MMPI-2 Restructured Form (MMPI-2-RF); MMPI, 3rd Edition (MMPI-3); Personality Assessment Inventory (PAI) Plus; Millon Clinical Multiaxial Inventory, 3rd Edition (MCMI-III); and Parenting Stress Index, 4th Edition have normative data describing male and female custody litigants' performance. Similar data should be available for each of the measures employed by the evaluator.

As evaluators determine which tests to administer, we remind them of American Psychological Association (APA) Ethical Standard 9.02:

> (a) Psychologists administer, adapt, score, interpret, or use assessment techniques, interviews, tests, or instruments in a manner and for purposes that are

> appropriate in light of the research on or evidence of the usefulness and proper application of the techniques. 9.02(b) Psychologists use assessment instruments whose validity and reliability have been established *for use with members of the population tested* [emphasis added]. When such validity or reliability has not been established, psychologists describe the strengths and limitations of test results and interpretation. (APA, 2017a, 9.02 Use of Assessments section)

Neal et al. (2019) reported that there is no relationship between the psychometric qualities of a test and its likelihood of being challenged in court. Their data suggested that some of the weakest tools tend to get a pass from the courts. "Our bottom-line conclusion is that evidentiary challenges to psychological tools are rare, and challenges to the most scientifically suspect tools are even rarer or are nonexistent" (Neal et al., 2019, p. 154).

VALIDITY

Validity refers to "the degree to which evidence and theory support interpretations of test scores for the proposed uses of the test" (Reynolds et al., 2021, p. 185). Validity is not binary as many evaluators write or testify. Instead, validity exists on a continuum. If you think about how accurately a test measures a concept, such as depression, the validity of an evaluator's interpretation of the results is dependent upon how closely the test taker matches the standardization sample. When the test taker and their responses match those in a comparison group, psychological testing can be very accurate. In fact, psychological tests often provide results that equal or exceed the validity of medical tests (Meyer et al., 2001).

While reliability is easily defined as the stability, consistency, and accuracy of test scores, validity has often been broken down into different types, even though validity has been identified as a unitary concept for more than 20 years (Reynolds et al., 2021). While we no longer discuss validity by defining its content, criterion, and construct, we now focus on five categories of evidence:

- Evidence based on test content includes evidence derived from an analysis of the test content, which includes the type of questions or tasks included in the test and administration and scoring guidelines.
- Evidence based on response processes includes evidence derived from an analysis of the processes engaged in by the examinee when answering test items, or by the examiner when recording or judging the examinee's performance on the item.
- Evidence based on internal structure includes evidence regarding relationships among test items and components.
- Evidence based on relations to other variables includes evidence based on an examination of the relationships between test performance and external variables or criteria.

- Evidence based on consequences of testing includes evidence based on an examination of the intended and unintended consequences of testing. (American Educational Research Association et al. 2014; Reynolds et al., 2021).

As you read these examples of how the validity terminology has changed, we hope you will notice that the language is directly related to forensic pursuits. This language should aid forensic experts by directing their focus to types of validity evidence.

SENSITIVITY AND SPECIFICITY

To describe sensitivity and specificity, we will take a quick detour to the airport. There are sensitivity settings on airport metal detectors. Sensitivity is when the metal detector correctly sounds the alarm when a person is carrying a weapon. If the alarm goes off when a person does not have a weapon, it is a false positive, or a type I error—in this case, the metal detector is sensitive but not specific. However, when a person is carrying a weapon and the alarm does not sound, it is a false negative, which is called a type II error—in this case, the metal detector is neither sensitive nor specific. Specificity occurs when a person does not have a weapon, and the alarm does not sound (Martindale, 2017).

Test authors attempt to find the right balance by calibrating their metal detectors with the best setting (cut scores). As is much of what we do, this decision is context specific. For example, the goal of screening measures is designed to identify everyone who might have a diagnosis and may need further evaluation, so screening measures emphasize sensitivity over specificity. If, however, the context does not require the test to identify everyone who might have a diagnosis, the test might emphasize specificity. This would lead an evaluator to be more confident in the results they get, even if it means the test results may miss some individuals with the symptoms.

RESPONSE STYLE AND PARENTS' MOTIVATION TO PRESENT AS VIRTUOUS

Discussions of the use of psychological testing in parenting plan assessment often focus on how best to interpret clinical scale results. Little attention has been paid to the importance of understanding validity scale results as they affect accurate interpretation of clinical scales. It is critically important that evaluators understand better how validity scale data influence evaluators' ability to provide accurate explanations of the meaning of the clinical test data (Gould et al., 2018).

An important factor in parenting plan assessment is awareness that the parent/litigant approaches the assessment process with a motivation to present themself in a favorable light. Tests used in parenting plan assessment need to include measures of response style to assess whether the parent has attempted to place themself in a favorable light, and if so, the degree to which the parent is attempting to present a more favorable picture of self.

The meaning that a custody litigant or parent's response bias may have on the interpretation of other scales on a psychological test is critical to an accurate understanding of the meaning of test results. At the broadest level, response bias may be categorized as faking good, faking bad, or open and responsive to the context of the evaluation. In the parenting plan arena, most parents approach the test with the motivation to fake good. They wish to convince the evaluator and the court that they are psychologically healthy and emotionally capable of parenting their child or children. It is very unusual in a PPE to find parents who fake bad.

RESPONSE STYLE ISSUES

The first step in the interpretation of a parent's psychological test responses is an analysis of the validity scales. This initial phase involves determining how the individual approached taking the test by examining the parent or child's response style. Several different response styles are discussed in the literature, including malingering, defensiveness, irrelevant responding, random responding, honest responding, and hybrid responding (Heilbrun, 2001). Research examining how custody litigants perform on the MMPI-2, MMPI-2-RF, MMPI-3, and the PAI suggest that there are two common response styles: defensive responding and honest responding (Rappaport et al., 2018).

Parents in litigation often have more defensive responses than the normative group, although their results may not meet specific cutoffs. It is not surprising that parents will appear defensive on the testing profiles. Most parents are motivated to present themselves in a favorable light. Historically, this was particularly true after reviewing the item content of the validity scales for the MMPI-2, MCMI-III, and PAI and examining some of the scales of the MMPI-2 and the commonly elevated scales on the MCMI-III. This is often called a *defensive response style* or a *fake good response style*. A fake good response style is more difficult to detect than a fake bad response style (Baer et al., 1992). This dilemma is aptly described by J. R. Graham (2000):

> It is not possible to tell if such a profile is indicative of a well-adjusted person who is motivated to appear even more well [sic] adjusted or of a poorly adjusted person who is trying to appear to be well adjusted. (p. 58)

Response style issues help evaluators determine how much confidence and certainty can be placed in their interpretation of the test data (Bathurst et al., 1997; Butcher et al., 1997; Gould et al., 2018; Heilbrun, 2001). Response style can influence scale elevations and profile configurations. For example, it is likely that the influence of a fake good response style on clinical scales is to underestimate the parent's true score. When a person intentionally presents a favorable picture of themself, it is likely that items that measure pathology will be intentionally underreported in an effort to present a consistent fake good profile. Failure to take response style into account may result in erroneous interpretations, faulty opinions, and unsupportable recommendations.

A review of the item content from the MMPI-2, MMPI-2-RF, MMPI-3, MCMI-III, MCMI-IV, and PAI will quickly show many of the items are quite transparent. Evaluators sometimes describe these items as face valid, an outdated term that is not actually a form of validity. While face validity is desirable in therapeutic settings (as it increases cooperation, investment, and motivation), it is not ideal in forensic settings. When the validity scales suggest these fake good attempts, the clinical scales are unlikely to accurately represent the mental health of the parent.

Items on standardized tests measure aspects of the mentally healthy individual and aspects of abnormal or psychopathological functioning. The defensive individual is likely to address items measuring healthy and abnormal functioning by developing a response style consisting of two elements: assertion of mentally healthy attributes that are inaccurate; denial of characteristics that are accurate but less than desirable.

Nichols and Greene (1997) noted the following about the defensive test-taker:

> They may endorse items not merely to conceal symptoms and maladjustment, but to assert a degree of soundness, virtue, prudence, strength and well-being that is, if anything, superior to "normal" levels . . .. In child custody, the evaluator is likely to see underreporting by a mix of trying to conceal any indication of psychological distress (dissimulation) and trying to assert superior adjustment simulation. (p. 254)

These authors suggest the defensive individual uses a combination of dissimulation, *"concealing what one believes to be true,"* and simulation, *"displaying what one believes to be false"* (Nichols & Greene, 1997, p. 252).

Exner et al. (1963) noted more than 50 years ago that these tests rely heavily on the test-taker's willingness to answer the items honestly:

> Thus the total usefulness of the device as a diagnostic instrument, particularly when used for screening or in situations where social desirability is an important element, seems to be dependent largely upon the honesty of the subject or on the ability of the interpreter to detect willful attempts at dishonest responding. (p. 91)

Response style issues help the evaluator determine how much confidence and certainty can be placed in their interpretation of the test data (Bathurst et al., 1997; Butcher et al., 1997; Gould et al., 2018; Heilbrun, 2001). Response styles also can affect scale elevations and profile configurations on the clinical scales of a test. As we will discuss, the prudent evaluator must take into consideration how validity scale scores affect clinical scales. Failure to consider how validity scale scores may affect clinical scale scores increases the likelihood that the evaluator will develop erroneous interpretations of the test data, which can lead to faulty expert opinions.

PROJECTIVE TECHNIQUES

The tension between traditionally trained clinicians and forensic psychologists is never as intense in psychological testing as the debate over the use of projective techniques, such as those used in the house-tree-person task. A key distinction between clinical psychology and other mental health practices is the use of formal assessment tools that are psychometrically validated. We have argued throughout this book that the selection of psychological tests must be grounded in the methods and procedures of science, a position that is reflected in the standards for ethical conduct articulated by the APA and the *Daubert* decision. Historically, clinical psychologists have incorporated projective techniques into comprehensive diagnostic assessments, particularly when evaluating children (Chandler, 2003). Some researchers, such as McClure et al., (2002), argue that while projective techniques may be less well-validated, they can still provide valuable insights into an older child's internal world, including developmental, relational, cultural, and contextual factors. However, the use of projective techniques in clinical child assessments has faced increasing scrutiny. Incorporating projective methods into evidence-based assessment models is increasingly viewed both as problematic (C. M. Lee & Hunsley, 2003) and inconsistent with ethical standards (Gould et al., 2013). Many projective techniques commonly used in child assessments fail to meet established scientific standards for psychological testing. Furthermore, over recent decades, reliance on time-intensive, clinician-administered personality assessment tools has declined (Meyer et al., 2001). Despite this shift, projective techniques—many of which have questionable reliability and validity—remain widely used (Chandler, 2003).

The foundation of projective techniques lies in the projective hypothesis (Chandler, 2003; Gould et al., 2013), yet critical aspects of this hypothesis have not been empirically validated. Even Chandler (2003), a proponent of projective techniques in child assessments, acknowledges the ongoing validity concerns. He notes that without a clear consensus on appropriate outcome measures for projective assessments, these methods will continue to be poorly understood.

The use of psychological tests in a forensic context such as PPEs requires selection of measures that are consistent with the five *Daubert* factors. When we evaluate projective techniques against the five *Daubert* factors, we find that most, if not all, projective techniques have insufficient basis in science and therefore are likely inadmissible.

1. Testability—Psychological tests should be based on theories that have undergone empirical examination and rigorous scientific challenge. Virtually no projective techniques have undergone such examination.

2. Peer review—The validity of tests should be supported by critical peer review, though the quality of peer review varies. Some journals may lack true scholarly rigor, allowing flawed research to pass. However, within the

field of forensic psychology in general and within parenting plan evaluation literature, in particular, there is no peer-reviewed support for the use of projective techniques as a psychological test.

3. Error rate—The reliability of psychological tests should be assessed based on their error rates, including false positives and negatives. Psychological scoring incorporates confidence intervals to account for measurement error. Virtually none of the commonly used projective techniques used in child assessment have information about their reliability, validity, or error rate.
4. Standards and controls—Tests should have manuals with standardized procedures for administration and scoring. Some projective techniques have manuals describing their use; however, some practitioners fail to follow prescribed methods, using outdated manuals, personal modifications, or impose their idiosyncratic interpretation of the meaning of subject responses.
5. General acceptance—While general acceptance is a criterion, it is not always the strongest measure of validity. Tests should be reviewed favorably in respected peer-reviewed journals. When the general acceptance factor is applied, we believe it is important to look at whether the field of forensic psychology and/or the field of parenting plan evaluations is defined as the community within which test use is examined. None of the peer-reviewed literature in either area finds that the use of projective techniques as a psychological test is accepted by the general community.

The key takeaway is that when applying the *Daubert* factors to the selection of projective techniques identified as psychological tests in parenting plan evaluations, there is virtually no support for their use as psychological tests and, therefore, testimony based upon data or opinions drawn from their use are likely inadmissible.

We strongly believe that there is no place in any forensic psychological evaluation to utilize projective techniques as psychological tests. The lack of reliability and validity data, the lack of a scientific basis of a theory of science, and the lack of support in the forensic psychological literature are among the reasons we reject the use of projective techniques as psychological tests in PPEs. We also believe that projective techniques would fail a *Daubert* challenge, failing to meet any of the five flexible factors identified by the *Daubert* court.

We do not place the Rorschach in this category. The Rorschach is an open-structured, performance-based cognitive perceptual problem-solving structured task with standardized scoring methods (Lilienfeld et al., 2000). The fact that the Rorschach measures performance rather than projection is significant. As Table 16.1 shows, projective measures rely on ambiguous stimuli and subjective interpretations to reveal deeper psychological processes, whereas performance measures utilize structured tasks with objective scoring to evaluate specific capabilities.

TABLE 16.1. Projective Measures Versus Performance Measures

Aspect	Projective measures	Performance measures
Stimuli	Ambiguous images or prompts (e.g., inkblots, ambiguous pictures)	Well-defined, structured tasks or problems (e.g., puzzles, standardized tests)
Response format	Open-ended, free responses encouraging personal interpretation	Constrained responses with clear right or wrong answers; empirically based interpretations
Scoring	Subjective interpretation by the clinician, often qualitative	Objective, standardized scoring methods
Purpose	To explore hidden or unconscious aspects of personality and emotion	To assess specific abilities, skills, or knowledge
Examples	Thematic Apperception Test (TAT)	Rorschach, IQ tests, academic performance assessments, cognitive ability tests

Despite the fact that the use of the Rorschach remains controversial, the published peer-reviewed literature contains useful arguments on both sides of the issue to render its use appropriate by those who are competent to administer, score, and interpret within the context of a parenting plan assessment (Mihura et al., 2013). In fact, the Rorschach controversy extends past the decision to administer it during a PPE. Among psychologists, there continues to be great debate between the two Rorschach scoring systems. Some Rorschach supporters are excited about the Rorschach Performance Assessment System (R-PAS) scoring system, while many continue to advocate for the use of the comprehensive (Exner) scoring system. Gacono and Smith (2020) document significant concerns that suggest the following: the R-PAS has altered administration procedures, there are significant concerns about the meta-analyses used to create variables, and the data used to norm the R-PAS is no longer available in "their original format." There are concerns about the lack of forensic samples or comparison groups. "Other than 15 adult and 15 adolescent sex offenders and a few forensic case studies, no forensic samples exist from R-PAS administered protocols" (Gacono & Smith, 2020). We recommend that those using the Rorschach be familiar with these concerns as well as the counterarguments presented by Erard and Viglione (2014) and Viglione et al. (2022).

SPECIFIC TESTS

In the following sections we discuss four of the most commonly selected psychological tests used in parenting plan evaluations: The MMPI-3, PAI, MCMI-IV, and the Behavioral Assessment System for Children (BASC), 3rd edition (BASC-3). We also present information on the NEO Personality Inventory-3 (NEO-PI-3) that we believe will become more frequently selected in the years to come. Are there other tests? Yes. Should evaluators employ other tests?

Maybe. The tests we discuss have a recent literature basis. Many other tests that could be used are either outdated or have weak validity, reliability, or comparison group data. If an evaluator is to use another test, they are wise to recall APA Ethical Standard 9.02b:

> (b) Psychologists use assessment instruments whose validity and reliability have been established for use with members of the population tested. When such validity or reliability has not been established, psychologists describe the strengths and limitations of test results and interpretation. (APA, 2017a, 9.02 Use of Assessments section)

Therefore, if an evaluator uses a test that does not have validity, reliability, or comparison group data for parenting plan evaluations, the evaluator should describe the rationale for using the test as well as the limitations of the test in their report.

Minnesota Multiphasic Personality Inventory, Third Edition

The MMPI is a widely used psychological assessment tool that has evolved significantly since its initial publication in 1943. Its primary purpose is to provide data about personality and psychopathological characteristics of an individual. It has been updated three times: MMPI-2, MMPI-2-RF, and MMPI-3. The updates provided updated and enhanced psychometric properties, validity, and applicability across various domains, including forensic psychology and parenting plan evaluations. In parenting plan evaluations, data from surveys indicate that MMPI instruments have been used in over 95% of evaluations over the past 15 years (Ackerman et al., 2021), demonstrating their dominance in this area.

The original version of the MMPI, published in 1943, was designed to aid in the differential diagnosis of mental disorders. It became widely used in clinical settings due to its empirically derived scales, which allowed for the identification of psychological conditions based on statistical patterns of responses rather than theoretical assumptions. The MMPI-2, published in 1989, introduced new normative data, improving the test's applicability across different populations. New items were added to enhance the content coverage, ensuring that the test remained relevant as psychological research advanced. The MMPI-2-RF, published in 2008, improved the test by reducing item redundancy and enhancing validity measures. The MMPI-2-RF introduced a comprehensive set of psychometrically robust scales, making it more effective for assessing personality and psychopathology. The MMPI-3, published in 2020, was built on the foundation of the MMPI-2-RF. The MMPI-3 further expanded the test's normative database and updated its content coverage. The MMPI-3 incorporated responses from 28,000 individuals, including a normative sample of 3,423 participants. With 52 validity and substantive scales, the MMPI-3 offers a more comprehensive assessment tool while maintaining continuity with the MMPI-2-RF forensic literature.

There are comparison data describing how child custody litigants' (CCLs') scores on the MMPI-3 compared to the normative sample. The use of comparison group data enhances the MMPI-3's utility by allowing evaluators to compare litigants' test results against a relevant reference population, improving the accuracy and interpretability of findings in family court cases. The child custody sample produced scores that were similar to the MMPI-3 normative sample, with a few notable differences, such as mean scores on the lie scale (L; 58.02T) and the defensiveness scale (K; 55.91T) were meaningfully higher in the CCL samples (Whitman et. al, in press). Comparison group data also indicated scores on some externalizing scales were meaningfully lower (behavioral and externalizing dysfunction, hypomanic activation, impulsivity, aggression, cynicism, and aggressiveness) The substantive scales were similar to the normative sample profile. All of the CCL women and half of the CCL men produced mean scores at least a half (5T) below the normative sample on externalizing scales in regards to social desirability (Whitman et. al, in press).

There is also data comparing a CCL group to a parental fitness litigant group. Comparison group data produced very similar profiles, with CCL samples slightly higher on L and K, and the greatest differences being in anxiety-related differences (higher in the CCL sample) and disconstraint (higher in the PFE sample; Whitman et. al, in press).

There are several strengths of the MMPI-3. Compared to other psychological assessments used in forensic evaluations, the MMPI-3 is particularly strong in its validity measures. Its sophisticated system of validity scales helps detect response biases such as exaggeration, minimization, or inconsistency, which are crucial considerations in custody disputes. The MMPI-3 also brings dimensional interpretations into focus. Results are discussed in terms of higher-order scales, which provide a broad conceptual framework for understanding test results. These scales should be the starting point for interpreting any valid profile, as they offer insights into major psychological domains:

- Emotional and Internalizing Dysfunction: Assesses difficulties related to mood and affect regulation, such as depression and anxiety.
- Thought Dysfunction: Evaluates issues associated with disordered thinking, such as paranoia or cognitive distortions.
- Behavioral and Externalizing Dysfunction: Measures problems related to impulse control, aggression, and rule-breaking behavior.

These higher-order scales are linked to the Hierarchical Taxonomy of Psychopathology, an advanced dimensional model of mental disorders that aligns with contemporary research in psychopathology. This connection strengthens the MMPI-3's scientific foundation, ensuring that evaluators can rely on robust, evidence-based interpretations.

One major advantage of the MMPI-3 is the ability to analyze raw responses, as Pearson—the company that markets the MMPI-3—allows evaluators to download and print item-level data. This feature enhances the assessment process by enabling evaluators to engage in content-based questioning, where test takers can explain their rationale for specific answers. This process allows for a more nuanced understanding of their psychological profile, improving the overall quality of forensic reports.

Additionally, the MMPI-3 can be administered via telehealth, following guidelines established by Corey and Ben-Porath (2020; see Chapter 11). This capability ensures accessibility for individuals undergoing evaluations remotely while maintaining the test's reliability and validity.

In sum, the MMPI-3 represents the most advanced iteration of the MMPI series, incorporating modern psychometric advancements, updated norms, and forensic-specific applications. Its strong validity scales, reliance on higher-order dimensions, and ability to compare results against a child custody litigant comparison group make it a useful tool in parenting plan evaluations.

Personality Assessment Inventory

The Personality Assessment Inventory (PAI) is a well-established personality assessment tool that has been widely used in clinical and forensic psychology since its introduction in 1991. It is known for its strong psychometric properties, detailed subscales, and applicability in both diagnostic and forensic contexts, including parenting plan evaluations. With the advent of the PAI Plus scoring system, the test has been enhanced with digital scoring, new malingering and distortion scales, and alignment with *Diagnostic and Statistical Manual of Mental Disorders*, 5th Edition (*DSM-5*) criteria. These updates strengthen its application in forensic evaluations, particularly in child custody cases where response bias and impression management are common concerns. As we write this book, we are told Psychological Assessment Resources, the organization behind the PAI, is updating the PAI.

Among the updates found in the PAI Plus scoring system are its digital scoring and child custody comparison group. The child custody comparison group was developed based on research conducted by Hynan (2013) in his private practice. These context specific comparison group data allow evaluators to compare a parent's results with a reference sample of parents undergoing custody evaluations, improving the accuracy and contextual relevance of interpretations. For example, among child custody litigants, there are elevated positive impression management scores often exceeding 60T compared to the national sample, in which the average score is 50T. There are also modest elevations on the treatment rejection scale. Of most importance is that the efforts to minimize symptoms as found on the positive impression management scale have an effect on the clinical scales, with parents scoring average clinical scale scores of 45T compared with the national sample in which the average score is 50T.

The PAI Plus scoring system has been updated to correspond with *DSM-5* diagnostic criteria. The updated structure ensures that scale interpretations are consistent with current psychiatric classifications, making the PAI Plus scoring system more useful in forensic evaluations, particularly when assessing personality pathology, substance use, and other clinical concerns.

The PAI Plus scoring system introduces four new malingering and response distortion scales, addressing two types of bias: negative distortion and positive distortion. The negative distortion scale was developed to identify individuals who may be malingering or exaggerating symptoms. Although most parents undergoing PPEs tend to present themselves in a favorable light, some parents might be motivated to show how living in an abusive environment has affected their emotional well-being. The negative distortion scale is useful in cases involving allegations of psychological instability, posttraumatic stress disorder, or severe mental illness, where one parent might claim the other is unfit due to psychopathology. The Positive Distortion Scales are comprised of two subscales, similar to the L and K scales on the MMPI-3. Positive distortion scales help assess positive impression management and defensive responding. These are particularly relevant in PPEs, where litigants may attempt to present themselves as overly virtuous, free of any psychological issues, or as the superior parent.

The PAI Plus also introduces new measures for aggression and violence risk, which are crucial for cases involving allegations of domestic violence, coercive control, or potential harm to children. Key new scales include:

- Violence and aggression risk index—Assesses overall risk for aggressive or violent behaviors.
- Reactive aggression scale—Evaluates impulsive aggression and emotional reactivity.
- Instrumental aggression scale—Measures premeditated, goal-driven aggression, which is particularly relevant in cases involving coercive control or manipulation.
- Treatment rejection scale—Assesses resistance to psychological treatment or interventions, which can be relevant when courts mandate therapy, coparenting counseling, or anger management programs.

In sum, the PAI is ideal for detailed inquiry into specific personality traits, malingering, and aggression risks. In contrast, the MMPI-3 is better suited for broad psychological assessment with strong validity scales and higher-order interpretations. In parenting plan cases, many evaluators use both tests together to gain a comprehensive view.

Millon Clinical Multiaxial Inventory, Fourth Edition

Unlike instruments such as the MMPI-3 or the PAI, which are designed to measure both clinical and subclinical traits, the MCMI-IV is specifically designed to assess pathological personality patterns. The MCMI-IV was developed for clinical, not parenting plan, populations. The MCMI-IV was normed on 1,547 individuals in a clinical setting. Parenting plan litigants do not necessarily represent a clinical sample. While some may have psychological issues, many are functioning individuals caught in high-conflict situations. The base rate scoring method used in the MCMI-IV assumes a higher prevalence of pathology than is likely present in nonclinical populations. When applied to family court litigants, the MCMI-IV is likely to inflate the appearance of psychopathology, leading to potentially incorrect misinterpretations and unreliable opinions. This distinction is critical because in parenting plan evaluations, the focus should be on functional capacity as a parent, not necessarily on the presence of a pathology or a personality disorder. Courts expect scientifically valid and legally defensible assessments and using a test outside its intended purpose raises concerns about admissibility under *Daubert* and *Frye* standards as well as ethical concerns.

The MCMI-III and MCMI-IV have shown some concerning elevations. The MCMI-III has been found to overpathologize litigants, especially women. The testing company addressed this concern by combining male and female test results but to date, how the integrate of scores was done has yet to be peer-reviewed.

It appears that the MCMI-IV has taken steps to eliminate the concern about gender differences that had no basis in research, however there are other significant concerns about the use of the MCMI-IV. Similar to the MCMI-III, the MCMI-IV reveals elevated scores on histrionic, narcissistic, and compulsive scales among people who do not show personality dysfunction. This has been called the healthy triad because healthy individuals often score highly on these three scales. Further, elevations on these scales can be interpreted as either strengths or deficits. Without reliable third-party information about the parent's functioning in the real world, it is not possible to know whether the three elevated scores suggest healthy or problematic functioning. We have observed that among parenting plan evaluators who use the MCMI-IV, elevations on these three scales are almost always interpreted incorrectly, over pathologizing parent scores that are, in fact, typical of healthy functioning individuals.

The most powerful argument against the use of the MCMI-IV in PPE comes from the test developer, Seth Grossman, who has explicitly discouraged its use (Sellbom et al., 2022). Grossman and others stated that there was insufficient evidence-based support for the use of the MCMI-IV in PPE.

Behavior Assessment System for Children, Third Edition

The Behavior Assessment System for Children, Third Edition (BASC-3) is a widely used tool in child psychology and in PPEs. The BASC-3 is not a personality measure like the tests discussed above. It is a multi-informant system designed to assess children's emotional, behavioral, and adaptive functioning from multiple perspectives—parents, teachers, and the children themselves.

There are several strengths of the BASC-3. The tool comes with teacher rating scales that help assess the child's behavior in an academic setting, providing an objective comparison to peers. There are also parent rating scales (PRS) that allow evaluators to compare how each parent perceive their child's emotional and behavioral state. These data can also be used to compare each parent's perception of their child against that of an independent third-party observer (i.e., the teacher). The BASC-3 also includes a self-report of personality measure that provides insight into the child's own perception of their experiences, including their relationship with each parent. The SRP includes a locus of control scale, which examines the child's perception of how much control they perceive each parent to exert over their life. This can be useful in understanding parenting styles, enmeshment, or autonomy issues. The BASC-3 parenting relationship questionnaire provides data on parents' perceived attachment, communication, discipline, involvement, and parental confidence. These elements can be helpful in evaluating the quality of parent–child relationships. The BASC-3 data helps to identify discrepancies between parents based on the BASC-3 ratings. This is helpful because a common occurrence in PPEs is significant discrepancies between parental ratings. The BASC-3 also provides opportunities to interpret behavioral variability across settings. Children may behave differently with each parent, teachers, or evaluators. Another use of BASC-3 results is in identifying children's special needs. The BASC-3 teacher rating scales can help in identifying potential learning disabilities, attention-deficit/hyperactivity disorder, or other special needs.

In sum, the BASC-3 is not a standalone custody evaluation tool but can provide valuable data when combined with interviews, observations, and collateral sources. It offers a structured, norm-referenced assessment, but lacks a custody-specific comparative sample. Interpretation should focus on patterns and consistencies across multiple raters rather than isolated scale scores. As we have noted multiple times, these tests can help generate hypotheses.

NEO Personality Inventory

We believe that over the next several years, there will be increased interest in the use of the NEO-PI-3, even though the NEO does not have validity scales. If used in conjunction with the MMPI-3, the MMPI-3's validity scales can identify under-reporting on concurrently administered measures (Holmes et al., 2024). The NEO-PI is a psychological assessment tool designed to measure the Big Five personality traits. The NEO-PI is the only psychological test that has been found to have empirical associations to parenting behavior. Research has explored how personality traits assessed by the NEO-PI relate to parenting styles, parent–child relationships, and child outcomes. Here's a breakdown of how each Big Five trait may influence parenting:

- Openness to experience
  - High openness: Parents who score high on openness tend to be more creative, flexible, and open to new parenting approaches. They are more likely to encourage intellectual curiosity, exploration, and diverse experiences in their children.
  - Low openness: More traditional and structured, preferring routine and established parenting norms. They may resist new parenting techniques or perspectives.

- Conscientiousness
  - High conscientiousness: Predicts consistent discipline, structure, and organization in parenting. These parents tend to enforce rules, set high expectations, and prioritize responsibility and academic success.
  - Low conscientiousness: May struggle with maintaining consistency in discipline, setting routines, or enforcing household rules.
- Extraversion
  - High extraversion: Extroverted parents are typically energetic, engaging, and sociable with their children. They encourage social activities and interactive play.
  - Low extraversion (introversion): May prefer one-on-one interactions or independent activities with their children, potentially fostering deeper but fewer social connections.
- Agreeableness
  - High agreeableness: These parents are warm, nurturing, empathetic, and supportive. They foster secure attachments and positive emotional climates in the home.
  - Low agreeableness: Can be more critical, controlling, or less emotionally available, which may contribute to authoritarian parenting styles or high-conflict coparenting dynamics.
- Neuroticism
  - High neuroticism: Parents high in neuroticism are more prone to stress, emotional reactivity, anxiety, and mood instability. This can affect their ability to handle parenting challenges calmly and may contribute to inconsistent discipline or overprotective tendencies.
  - Low neuroticism: More emotionally stable, resilient, and less likely to react negatively to stress, fostering a calm and predictable parenting environment.

Research has demonstrated significant correlations between the Big Five personality traits and various parenting styles. A study by Ramesh and Ramana (2023) found that individuals high in agreeableness are more likely to adopt an authoritative parenting style, which is characterized by warmth and structure and is often considered the most effective. Conversely, those with high levels of neuroticism and low conscientiousness tend to exhibit authoritarian or permissive parenting behaviors. Further research by Tomšik and Čerešník (2017) indicated that integrative and liberal parenting styles are associated with higher levels of conscientiousness, extraversion, and openness in adolescents. In contrast, autocratic and indifferent parenting styles toward adolescents were linked to increased neuroticism. Additionally, a study by Yao et al. (2023) explored the impact of discrepancies between maternal and paternal parenting styles on the Big Five personality dimensions. The findings suggested that inconsistencies in parenting approaches are associated with lower levels of conscientiousness, agreeableness, openness, and extraversion in offspring.

These studies collectively highlight the intricate relationships between parental personality traits and parenting styles, emphasizing the influence of the Big Five traits on parenting behaviors and, subsequently, on child development. Parenting style dimensions are associated with the following specific NEO-PI factors:

- Authoritative parenting (best outcomes for children)
  - High conscientiousness (structured and responsible)
  - High agreeableness (nurturing and responsive)
  - Moderate openness (adaptive to child's needs)
  - Low to moderate neuroticism (emotionally stable)
- Authoritarian parenting (rigid and controlling; worst outcomes for children)
  - Low openness (strict, less flexible)
  - Low agreeableness (demanding, less nurturing)
  - High conscientiousness (rule-oriented)
  - High neuroticism (emotionally reactive)
- Permissive parenting (lax and indulgent; potentially problematic for children)
  - Low conscientiousness (inconsistent rules)
  - High agreeableness (overly indulgent)
  - High openness (flexible but lacking structure)

The NEO-PI-3 can provide insight into a parent's personality traits, emotional stability, and interpersonal functioning. However, it is not a direct measure of parenting capacity or mental health disorders. It should be interpreted alongside other assessments, records, and collateral data.

Comparison Among the NEO Personality Inventory, Minnesota Multiphasic Personality Inventory-3, and Personality Assessment Inventory

The NEO-PI-3, MMPI-3, and PAI are all widely used personality assessments, but they differ significantly in their theoretical foundations, intended applications, and utility in forensic and clinical contexts. We do not provide a comparison of the BASC to these personality measures because, as stated above, the BASC measures children's emotional, behavioral, and adaptive functioning from multiple perspectives, not adult personality dimensions. Table 16.2 provides a comparative analysis of the NEO-PI-3, MMPI-3, and PAI.

When choosing which test to use, consider the purpose. Use the NEO-PI-3 when assessing normal personality traits (e.g., occupational settings, therapy clients). It is not a diagnostic tool and is generally not recommended for forensic

TABLE 16.2. Comparisons of the NEO-PI, MMPI-3, and PAI

Feature	NEO-PI-3	MMPI-3	PAI
		Theoretical foundations	
Model	Big Five personality traits	Psychopathology-based (empirical criterion keying)	Psychopathology & personality (Theoretical & Empirical)
Primary focus	Normal personality traits	Clinical and forensic pathology	Clinical and forensic pathology
Approach	Descriptive (nonclinical)	Diagnostic (clinical and forensic)	Diagnostic (clinical and forensic)
		Structure and scales	
Items	240 (full version), 60 (short version)	335	344
Main scales	5 broad traits (neuroticism, extraversion, openness, agreeableness, conscientiousness) with 6 facets each	10 validity scales, 3 higher-order scales, 8 restructured content scales, 26 specific problem scales, and 5 Psy-5 scales	4 validity, 11 clinical, 5 treatment, 2 interpersonal
Response format	5-point Likert scale	True or false	4-point Likert scale
Validity scales	None	Extensive (e.g., inconsistency, response bias, overreporting, underreporting)	Moderate (e.g., inconsistency, positive/negative impression management)
		Intended uses and applications	
Clinical use	Limited clinical application	Strong clinical and forensic use	Strong clinical and forensic use
Forensic use	Not well-suited for forensic cases	Frequently used in forensic settings (custody, criminal, disability)	Frequently used in forensic settings (custody, criminal, disability)
Occupational/ Workplace	Used in personnel selection & leadership	Limited use	Some use in high-risk professions
Custody evaluations	May provide personality insights but lacks forensic validation	Extensively used to assess psychological functioning in legal cases	Often used for psychological and forensic evaluations
		Strengths and limitations	
Strengths	Well-validated for Big Five personality factors; useful in occupational settings	Strong forensic utility; extensive validity measures; updated norms	Balances clinical diagnosis and personality assessment; shorter than MMPI
Limitations	No validity scales; not designed for detecting pathology	Long administration time; requires extensive interpretation training	Moderate validity scales (less robust than MMPI-3)

Note. NEO-PI = NEO Personality Inventory; NEO-PI-3 = NEO Personality Inventory (3rd ed.); MMPI-3 = Minnesota Multiphasic Personality Inventory (3rd ed.); PAI = Personality Assessment Inventory; Psy-5 = Personality Psychopathology-Five model.

use. Use the MMPI-3 for forensic evaluations, especially in custody disputes, criminal cases, and high-stakes legal contexts. It is the gold standard for assessing psychopathology and malingering. Use the PAI when you need a clinically and forensically valid tool that is easier to interpret than the MMPI-3, while still capturing pathology, treatment considerations, and personality functioning.

CONCLUSION

Psychological assessments play a crucial role in PPEs, serving as one of the primary data-gathering tools alongside interviews, observations, record reviews, and collateral interviews. However, many evaluators tend to interpret psychological test results through a clinical lens rather than linking them directly to parenting behaviors. This disconnect can result in missed opportunities to develop hypotheses about how a parent's psychological profile may impact their parenting capacity.

The selection of psychological tests in forensic contexts is of particular concern. While best practices emphasize the importance of using assessments with strong empirical support, some evaluators continue to rely on tools with weak or nonexistent psychometric integrity. Despite these concerns, legal challenges to the admissibility of psychological test results remain rare. Even when challenges occur, courts often fail to scrutinize the scientific validity of the assessments in question.

Validity, a core principle in psychological testing, is not a binary concept but rather exists on a continuum. It is assessed through multiple categories of evidence, including test content, response processes, internal structure, relationships to external variables, and consequences of testing. While attorneys and judges have the authority to challenge the admissibility of psychological test results, research indicates that this rarely happens, even when questionable tools are used.

Another key issue in PPEs is response style, particularly the tendency of parents to present themselves in an overly favorable light. Since most custody litigants want to appear as psychologically healthy and competent as possible, defensive responding—sometimes called "faking good"—is a common challenge for evaluators. This response style can distort test results, leading to an underestimation of potential psychological concerns. Therefore, evaluators must carefully analyze validity scales to determine how response bias may influence their interpretations.

Among the most widely used psychological tests in PPEs, the MMPI-3 stands out as the most scientifically supported, with robust validity scales and a strong research base. The PAI Plus offers new response distortion scales and forensic comparison groups, though some concerns remain about its forensic applicability. The MCMI-IV, however, is not recommended for PPEs due to its reliance on clinical norms rather than a general population sample. The BASC-3, while primarily used for assessing children's emotional and behavioral functioning, provides valuable insights when multiple informants (such as parents and teachers) contribute perspectives.

Ethical considerations are paramount in forensic evaluations, as outlined in professional guidelines. Evaluators must ensure they use psychological tests appropriately and transparently report any limitations related to validity and reliability. Test results should not be interpreted in isolation but instead integrated with observations, interviews, and collateral information to form well-supported conclusions.

Ultimately, the effectiveness of psychological assessments in PPEs depends on the evaluator's ability to critically analyze test data, consider response styles, and apply findings in a way that directly informs parenting-related concerns. As courts continue to rely on psychological expert testimony, it is crucial that both evaluators and legal professionals remain vigilant in ensuring that only scientifically sound assessment tools are used properly as a part of a multimethod, multisource approach.

17

The Shift From Categorical to Dimensional Diagnostic Models

A diagnosis describes a pattern of thoughts, feelings or behaviors within an individual. A categorical model of diagnosis, which has historically dominated psychiatric diagnosis, operates like an on/off switch—where a disorder is either present or absent based on predefined criteria. In contrast, a dimensional model views psychopathology as existing on a continuum, much like a dimmer switch that reflects varying degrees of severity, symptom expression, and functional impairment.

Over the past few decades, parenting plan evaluations (PPEs) have increasingly moved away from categorical models toward dimensional models. This paradigm shift has profound implications for clinical practice, forensic evaluations, and parenting plan assessments. Traditional diagnostic categories, while useful for communication and treatment planning, often fail to capture the complexity of psychological functioning. Categorical labels may oversimplify dynamic psychological processes, pathologize normative variations in personality, and overlook the contextual factors that influence behavior. In forensic contexts, particularly in PPEs, a rigid diagnostic framework can lead to misleading conclusions about parental fitness, risk assessment, and the psychological well-being of children. A dimensional model, on the other hand, allows for a more comprehensive, behaviorally specific, and scientifically valid approach that aligns with contemporary research in psychopathology.

This chapter explores the shift from categorical to dimensional diagnosis in PPEs, emphasizing the alternative model for personality disorders (AMPD) and

https://doi.org/10.1037/0000474-018
Parenting Plan Evaluations: An Evidence-Informed Approach to Child Custody, by J. W. Gould and C. M. Mulchay

the Hierarchical Taxonomy of Psychopathology (HiTOP) as scientifically supported alternatives to traditional *Diagnostic and Statistical Manual of Mental Disorders* (*DSM*) classifications. We begin by examining the core differences between categorical and dimensional models, highlighting both their advantages and limitations. Then, to highlight the need for dimensional models, we consider the shaky research supporting the preeminent categorical model of mental health diagnosis, the *DSM*. Next, we introduce the AMPD and HiTOP frameworks, discussing their hierarchical structures, empirical foundations, and how they refine our understanding of personality pathology and mental disorders. The AMPD, integrated within the fifth edition of the *DSM* (*DSM-5*), provides a dimensional approach specifically for personality disorders, whereas HiTOP offers a broader, transdiagnostic framework that reconceptualizes mental illness beyond traditional diagnostic silos.

Finally, we explore the practical applications of HiTOP in forensic contexts, particularly in PPEs. By utilizing a dimensional approach, forensic mental health professionals can assess parental functioning in a way that is more behaviorally anchored and context-sensitive, reducing the risk of overpathologizing individuals based on rigid diagnostic criteria. This shift also encourages a focus on specific functional impairments, coping mechanisms, and interpersonal dynamics, rather than simply assigning diagnostic labels that may lack predictive validity in legal decision making.

By moving beyond traditional categorical diagnoses and embracing a dimensional framework, forensic evaluators and mental health professionals can adopt a more nuanced, evidence-based, and ecologically-valid approach to forensic assessment. This perspective fosters a deeper understanding of psychological functioning within family systems, ultimately leading to more informed judicial decisions that prioritize the well-being of children and families.

CATEGORICAL VERSUS DIMENSIONAL APPROACHES

Human beings often categorize people by their behaviors. We previously discussed the fundamental attribution error and the tendency for people who observe others to make personality attributions to explain their behavior. These personality attributions often serve as anchors. Diagnostic labels are a type of personality attribution. A concern about the use of diagnostic categories in PPEs is that they serve as anchors for evaluators, attorneys, judges, parents, and others. These diagnostic anchors tend to affect the manner in which experienced mental health professionals perceive and process additional information (Martindale, 2005). Recall our discussion of anchor bias in Chapter 7 and Kahneman's warning that humans "do not know how it guides and constrains (their) thinking, because (they) cannot imagine how (they) would have thought if the anchor had been different (or absent)" (p. 154, this volume).

For example, a parenting plan evaluator reviews prior records stating that a parent has borderline personality disorder (BPD). This diagnosis becomes an *anchor*, shaping how the evaluator perceives the parent's behavior throughout the assessment. The anchor bias influences the evaluator unconsciously by filtering new data and observations through the lens of BPD, interpreting emotional reactions as manipulative or unstable rather than considering situational stressors (e.g., high-conflict custody battle).

The anchor bias often leads to confirmation bias. In the example above, when the parent displays distress over allegations, the evaluator perceives this as confirmation or support for the hypothesis that the parent is displaying emotional dysregulation rather than a normal response to stress. Adding insult to injury, the anchor bias that leads to the confirmation bias often results in the evaluator ignoring evidence that refutes the BPD hypothesis. Despite third-party evidence that the parent demonstrates consistent stability in work, family relationships, and coparenting interactions, the evaluator assigns less weight to these data and observations, reinforcing the initial diagnostic impression. The evaluator's anchored perspective may lead to opinions proffered to the court that limit the parent's custody or require unnecessary interventions (e.g., extensive therapy, supervised visits). The court may rely on this biased assessment, unfairly impacting the parent's rights and the child's relationship with them.

In contrast to the categorical model, which we described as similar to the on/off function of a light switch, the dimensional model of psychopathology is like a dimmer. The dimensional model identifies psychological problems as existing on a continuum or a spectrum (Hopwood, 2018; Krueger & Hobbs, 2020; Widiger & Hines, 2022). Plotting psychological challenges, like anxiety, on a spectrum acknowledges that all people can experience anxiety, and the degree of anxiety might vary from mild to severe. Anxiety might also vary based upon different contexts, different relationships, and other external factors. In contrast, the categorical model of anxiety disorders classifies anxiety as present or absent.

Recall Guideline 10.01 from the Specialty Guidelines for Forensic Psychology: "Forensic practitioners are encouraged to consider the problems that may arise by using a clinical diagnosis in some forensic contexts, and consider and qualify their opinions and testimony appropriately." A similar warning about the use of diagnostic labels is found in the Association of Family and Conciliation Courts (2022) custody guideline 11.1 (e):

> Evaluators should recognize that use of diagnostic labels to describe the functioning of the parties can divert attention from the focus on their abilities and capabilities as parents. For these reasons, evaluators are cautious when using diagnostic terms, and should provide behavioral descriptions of any significant personality characteristics they note that bear upon the issues before the court. (p. 25)

In a dimensional classification system, there is no clear bright line distinction between "normal" and "abnormal" psychological functioning (Lahey, 2021). Psychological problems are, in large part, problematic ways of thinking, feeling, and behaving that lie on continuous dimensions from minor to severe.

THE ROOTS OF CATEGORICAL CLASSIFICATION: THE *DIAGNOSTIC AND STATISTICAL MANUAL OF MENTAL DISORDERS*

To emphasize why dimensional models are needed for diagnosing mental health problems, we will consider the research on the preeminent categorial model, the *DSM*. The *DSM* of the American Psychiatric Association has been the bedrock of mental health diagnoses for more than 75 years. A primary assumption of the *DSM* is that mental health problems can be classified into discrete diagnostic categories in a manner similar to medical problems. This binary approach identified mental health problems as either completely present or completely absent. The light switch is either on or off. However, current theory and research suggest we should take another approach.

The first edition of the *DSM* was published in 1952 (Grob, 1991). It provided a classification framework for mental health problems. In the late 1970s, concerns were raised about the low interrater reliability of *DSM* diagnoses (Spitzer et al., 1978). Research findings revealed that patients with the same symptoms were diagnosed differently in New York than in London. Based upon the mounting concerns about the lack of reliability of *DSM* diagnostic classification, the developers of the next version of the *DSM* took on the task of codifying the diagnostic categories. Theodore Millon, PhD, who would go on to create the Millon Clinical Multiaxial Inventory, described the lack of research upon which earlier versions of the *DSM* were based.

> There was very little systematic research, and much of the research that existed was really a hodgepodge—scattered, inconsistent, and ambiguous. I think the majority of us recognized that the amount of good, solid science upon which we were making our decisions was pretty modest. (Spiegel, 2005, January 3)

Accumulating research has exposed additional significant limitations of this categorical model, including diagnostic overlap, arbitrary symptom thresholds, and the failure to capture the complexity of mental health conditions (Kotov et al., 2017). Thus, while the use of categorical classification worked well for research purposes, the research basis for many of the diagnoses in the *DSM* continues to reflect Millon's concerns (Caspi et al., 2014; Insel et al., 2010; Reiger et al., 2013).

OVERVIEW OF THE ALTERNATIVE MODEL OF PERSONALITY DISORDERS AND THE HiTOP TAXONOMY OF PSYCHOPATHOLOGY

In response to the criticisms of categorical diagnostic systems, researchers have developed dimensional approaches. Two complementary approaches with particular relevance to PPEs are the AMPD and the HiTOP. Below we provide a brief overview of the similarities and differences between the two models. In subsequent sections, we provide a more detailed description of each model.

The AMPD and HiTOP share several important similarities:

- **Dimensional approach.** Both models move away from categorical diagnoses and embrace a dimensional understanding of personality and psychopathology. This approach recognizes that traits and symptoms exist on a continuum rather than as discrete categories.
- **Hierarchical structure.** While the AMPD is specifically focused on personality disorders, HiTOP provides a broader framework for all psychopathology, including personality. HiTOP organizes psychopathology into a hierarchical structure, with more specific symptoms and traits at lower levels and broader dimensions at higher levels.
- **Trait models.** The AMPD's Criterion B, which describes pathological personality traits, aligns closely with the trait model in HiTOP. These five domains in the AMPD are considered maladaptive variants of the Big Five personality traits:

    1. Negative affectivity
    2. Detachment
    3. Antagonism
    4. Disinhibition
    5. Psychoticism

    However, the HiTOP model uses the term spectra rather than traits. HiTOP spectra are broad dimensions of psychopathology that form a key level in the HiTOP model that will be discussed in the following section. These spectra represent larger constellations of related syndromes and subfactors, providing a comprehensive framework for understanding and classifying mental health issues.

    Spectra reflect continua of psychopathology rather than discrete categories, allowing for a more nuanced understanding of mental health. Spectra sit at a higher level in the HiTOP framework, above syndromes and subfactors but below superspectra. The spectra are based on observed patterns of co-occurrence among symptoms and syndromes; that is, they are empirically based.

    Although they do not perfectly map onto the AMPD and the Big Five, HiTOP includes similar spectra that correspond to personality pathology:

    1. Internalizing (related to negative affectivity)
    2. Thought Disorder (related to psychoticism)
    3. Disinhibited externalizing
    4. Antagonistic externalizing
    5. Detachment

- **Integration of personality functioning.** The AMPD's Criterion A, which assesses impairments in personality functioning (identity, self-direction, empathy, and intimacy), has been proposed to be integrated into the HiTOP model. Some researchers suggest that personality functioning could be mapped onto the general psychopathology factor in HiTOP.

While there are many similarities, the models are not identical. HiTOP is a broader framework that includes nonpersonality psychopathology, whereas the AMPD is specifically focused on personality. Ongoing research is exploring how to best integrate these models:

- Some studies suggest that certain aspects of personality functioning (Criterion A) may align with specific HiTOP spectra, while others may be more general markers of overall psychopathology (Kerber et al., 2024).
- Researchers are investigating how to incorporate the AMPD's emphasis on self and interpersonal functioning into the HiTOP framework (Bottesi et al., 2024).
- There is ongoing debate about whether personality functioning should be considered distinct from traits or if it can be fully captured by trait models (Pianowski et al., 2019).

While the AMPD and HiTOP share many conceptual similarities, especially in their dimensional approach to personality pathology, research is ongoing to determine how best to integrate these models for a comprehensive understanding of personality and psychopathology. The alignment between these models represents a broader shift in the field towards dimensional, empirically based approaches to mental health classification.

DIAGNOSTIC AND STATISTICAL MANUAL OF MENTAL DISORDERS ALTERNATIVE MODEL OF PERSONALITY DISORDER

The *DSM-5* included a section describing an AMPD. This dimensional model attempted to address the many challenges with the DSM categorical system. The AMPD model is framed around two criteria. Criterion A concerns deficits and impairments in the *sense of self* and *interpersonal relatedness*. This is a psychodynamic concept, which is evaluated on a continuum. An individual's self-functioning involves their identity and self-direction, whereas their interpersonal functioning involves empathy and intimacy. The *DSM-5* and *DSM-5* Text Revision (*DSM-5-TR*) provide the Level of Personality Functioning Scale, in which each of the four categories (identity, self-direction, empathy, and intimacy) can be differentiated by five levels (Level 0 to 4) of impairment from healthy/adaptive functioning to extreme impairment.

Imagine Parent A who presents as having consistent and self-regulated self-esteem with accurate self-appraisals, and is capable of experiencing, tolerating, and regulating a full range of emotions. This would be identified as Level 0 (little or no impairment) in identity. Consider Parent B who presents as excessively dependent on others, and with vulnerable self-esteem, such that their emotional regulation depends on positive external appraisal and threats to their self-esteem may lead to strong emotions such as rage or shame. This would be identified as Level 2 (moderate impairment) of identity.

Those same parents may present with different levels of empathy, such that Parent A may be somewhat compromised in their ability to appreciate and understand their child's experiences and may wish to control their child's behavior. This would be identified as Level 1 empathy. Whereas Parent B who is quite dependent on others may be capable of accurately understanding others' experiences and motivations in most situations. They may comprehend and appreciate other's perspectives, which would be identified as Level 0 (little or no impairment) in empathy.

Intimacy is another Criteria A level of personality that is often relevant to parenting plan matters. At one end of the continuum, Level 0 of intimacy is identified as maintaining multiple, satisfying and enduring relationships in personal and community life; desires and engages in a number of caring, close, and reciprocal relationships; and strives for cooperation and mutual benefit. While on the other end of the spectrum, Level 4 (extreme impairment) the parent's engagement with others is detached, disorganized, or consistently negative. At this level, relationships are conceptualized almost exclusively in terms of their ability to provide comfort or inflict pain and suffering.

Differing greatly from the psychodynamic approach of Criterion A toward a research based organization of personality traits, Criterion B is composed from meta-analytic reviews and empirical data. Criterion B consists of 25 maladaptive personality traits that are divided into five domains: negative affectivity, detachment, antagonism, disinhibition, and psychoticism (Hopwood, 2018; Krueger & Hobbs, 2020; Widiger & Hines, 2022).

There are a number of personality traits in Criterion B that might be relevant in PPEs. They include separation insecurity, hostility, perseveration, withdrawal, suspiciousness, antagonism versus agreeableness, impulsivity, rigid perfectionism, and negative affectivity versus emotional stability. Recall that this model does not ask for binary responses of whether the parent is antagonistic or not. Instead, the model acknowledges that a parent may have impulsivity at a specific time and for a specific reason, yet it is only when the behaviors become a pattern that they would qualify as traits, which are more stable. This differentiation is significant in PPEs, as parents may behave differently due to the stress of litigation or the conflict with their coparent than they would in other situations and contexts.

Using the Criterion B model, the evaluator would inquire into all five domains: negative affectivity, detachment, antagonism, disinhibition, and psychoticism by using the Personality Inventory for *DSM-5*. The evaluator would then take that trait based data, develop hypotheses, and investigate to what degree do these traits appear to impact parenting and the child's best interests.

HiTOP MODEL

The HiTOP is an empirically-developed diagnostic framework developed through factor analyses of data from multiple studies across multiple populations (Lahey, 2021). The HiTOP model redefines psychopathology into a classification system organized around vertical and horizonal dimensions of normal to abnormal behavior developed through evidence gathered from statistical modeling and validation studies (Kotov et al., 2020).

The HiTOP system was developed to address the limitations that hinder psychology, psychiatry, research, and treatment by organizing mental health behavior as a spectrum or existing along dimensions. Classifying mental health behavior as dimensional removes the *DSM's* artificial boundaries of mental illness that made traditional diagnoses more definitive yet less accurate representations of what people experience (Kotov et al., 2018).

Traditional *DSM-III* diagnoses require a priori assumptions. The HiTOP Model relied upon independent work from multiple researcher groups, which has been described as a quantitative rather than qualitative movement of researchers gathering data from factor analytic studies of normal personality (Kotov et al., 2020).

A primary problem with the *DSM* classification system is the lack of independence between and among diagnostic categories. For example, a parent may display signs of an anxiety disorder while also displaying signs of depressive affect. Some of the behavioral characteristics the comprise diagnostic prongs defining anxiety might also be found among the diagnostic prongs defining depression. The symptom overlap makes reliable differentiation between diagnostic categories virtually impossible. There are similar concerns when attempting to make reliable diagnostic distinctions between and among various personality disorders. Several of the diagnostic prongs that define BPD are also among the diagnostic prongs that define narcissistic personality disorder, antisocial personality disorder, and histrionic personality disorder. Recognition of the lack of diagnostic independence among personality disorders is, in part, the basis for the personality clusters described in current *DSM* editions.

The HiTOP approaches these classification challenges by identifying evidence-based behaviors that characterize psychopathology structures starting from the most basic building blocks and proceeding to the highest level of generality. The HiTOP classification model first combines individual signs and symptoms into homogeneous components or traits. Next the HiTOP model assembles these homogeneous components or traits into empirically derived syndromes. Finally, the HiTOP model groups these empirically derived syndromes into psychopathology spectra (e.g., internalizing and externalizing; Renaissance School of Medicine, 2024).

A primary goal of the *DSM* categorical model is to identify a specific diagnosis so that specific treatment can be prescribed. The utility of the *DSM* categorical model becomes more difficult as a tool for identifying specific treatments when an individual's symptoms meet the criteria for multiple diagnoses. Co-occurring diagnoses are one of the most significant challenges to the *DSM's* categorical approach.

The HiTOP system simplifies the categorical approach to diagnosis by identifying psychopathology dimensions at multiple levels of hierarchy. The result is that it allows for a finer description of symptom detail while it also allows for a broader view of the dynamics. The HiTOP allows for multiple levels of classification and, subsequently, multiple levels of treatment. The HiTOP model integrates the most recent scientific evidence, which is fundamentally different than the process in which the *DSM-III* was created. This is to say its foundation is less reliant on expert opinion and more reliant on research (via factorial analysis).

The HiTOP is derived from research that differentiates into six dimensions (see Figure 17.1), two of which have been identified in the research since the 1960s: The internalizing and externalizing dimensions. Internalizing is best thought of as what occurs in one's inward focus of attention or one's internal processes. Internalizing dimensions are represented by mental health concerns such as depression, anxiety, and posttraumatic stress disorder (PTSD). Externalizing is best thought of as behaviors outwardly displayed by a person. Externalizing dimensions are represented by behaviors such as substance use disorder, attention-deficit hyperactivity disorder (although there are internalizing aspects of ADHD), conduct disorder, or oppositional defiant disorder.

Subsequent research differentiated the externalizing dimension into either disinhibited or antagonistic dimensions. Both the HiTOP and *DSM-5* define disinhibition as "orientation toward immediate gratification, leading to impulsive behaviour driven by current thoughts, feelings, and external stimuli, without regard for past learning or consideration of future consequences" (American Psychological Association, 2013a, p. 780). Antagonistic externalizing is related to childhood conduct problems, interpersonal problems, and criminal behavior.

The remaining three dimensions of the HiTOP model are thought disorder, somatoform, and detachment. These are distinct but interrelated constructs in the HiTOP model. Thought disorder encompasses psychotic like symptoms, including delusions, hallucinations, and disorganized thinking. Thought disorders are strongly associated with schizophrenia-spectrum disorders that often include traits like cognitive-perceptual dysregulation, suspiciousness, and unusual beliefs. Each of these areas of concern exist on a continuum from mild cognitive distortions to full-blown psychosis. Somatoform represents symptoms of somatic distress, including excessive concern with physical symptoms and unexplained medical complaints. Somatoform overlaps with somatic symptom disorder, illness anxiety disorder, and conversion disorder. Individuals with high somatoform traits may frequently seek medical attention and experience bodily symptoms without an identifiable medical cause. Detachment captures emotional and social withdrawal, reduced affect, and lack of pleasure from social interactions. It is related to schizoid, avoidant, and depressive personality traits. Individuals high in detachment may struggle with emotional engagement, lack motivation for social contact, and exhibit anhedonia (inability to experience pleasure). Detachment is strongly linked to negative affectivity and introversion.

Looking at the HiTOP model in Figure 17.1, the six spectra (somatoform, internalizing, thought disorder, disinhibited externalizing, antagonistic externalizing, and detachment) are broken down into subfactors. Subfactors refer to grouping small clusters of strongly related symptoms or syndromes into more

FIGURE 17.1. Spectra of the Hierarchical Taxonomy of Psychopathology

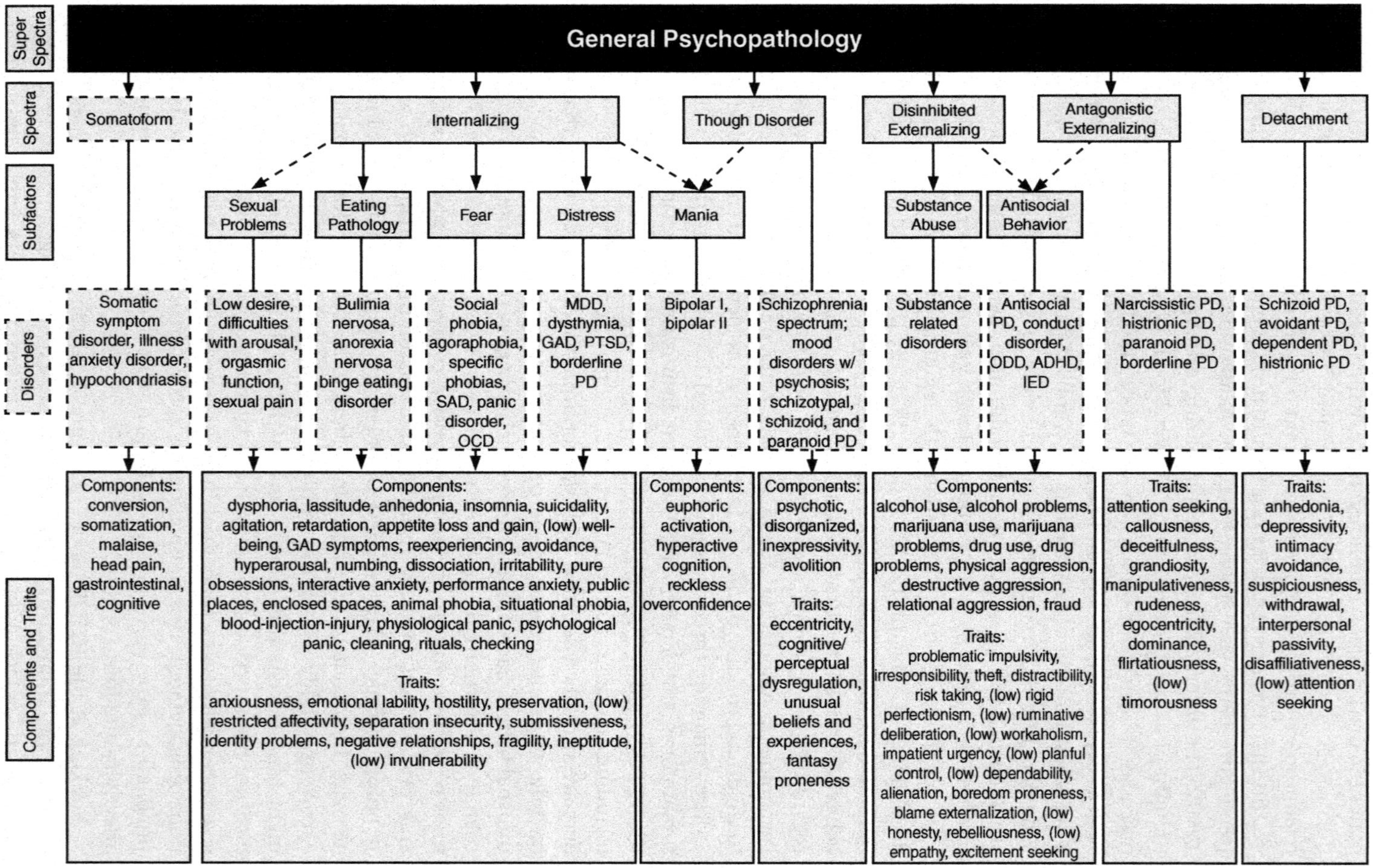

Note. Dashed lines indicate elements of the model that were included on provisional basis and require more study. Disorders with most prominent cross-loadings are listed in multiple places. Minus sign indicates negative association between histrionic personality and detachment spectrum. See the online article for the color version of this figure. Adapted from "The Hierarchical Taxonomy of Psychopathology (HiTOP): A Dimensional Alternative to Traditional Nosologies," by R. Kotov, R. F. Krueger, D. Watson, T. M. Achenbach, R. R. Althoff, R. M. Bagby, T. A. Brown, W. T. Carpenter, A. Caspi, L. A. Clark, N. R. Eaton, M. K. Forbes, K. T. Forbush, D. Goldberg, D. Hasin, S. E. Hyman, M. Y. Ivanova, D. R. Lynam, K. Markon, K., . . . M. Zimmerman, 2017, *Journal of Abnormal Psychology, 126*(4), p. 462 (https://doi.org/10.1037/abn0000258). Copyright 2017 by the American Psychological Association.

general classification terms. The next level of the hierarchy identifies disorders or what used to be called diagnoses. Disorders organize groups of symptoms and traits that often occur together. The terms used in the HiTOP model at the disorders level of classification are similar to those found in the *DSM*. The lowest level of the model identifies specific signs or symptom components and maladaptive traits of behavior.

One way to use the HiTOP model is to analyze behaviors from specific behaviors to the spectra level. If a parent presents with specific behaviors characterized by anxiety, hostility, or emotional liability, each of these behavioral characteristics is found at the specific signs or symptoms level of analysis.

HiTOP provides guidance for evidence-based hypotheses testing based on empirical research. Once sufficient data are gathered to differentially group the behaviors into a specific disorder, then the subfactor identification becomes easier, leading to the identification of more specific treatment options.

INCORPORATING HITOP INTO PARENTING PLAN EVALUATIONS

If you are unclear how you might incorporate the HiTOP into your PPEs, there is a good chance that you already have been using dimensional assessment tools (Kotov et al., 2017), such as the Minnesota Multiphasic Personality Inventory (MMPI; Hathaway & McKinley, 1943; specifically the MMPI-2RF and MMPI-3), or the Personality Assessment Inventory (PAI; Morey, 1991, 2007). For example, the PAI assess both traits and symptom component measures. Kotov et al. (2017) document that the PAI assesses the following dimensional symptoms:

> 15 broader syndromes and 30 more specific components/traits: Eight clinical syndromes (somatic complaints, anxiety, anxiety-related disorders, depression, mania, paranoia, schizophrenia, and aggression) containing three components each, three clinical syndromes without specified components (suicidality, alcohol problems, and drug problems), two personality syndromes (borderline features and antisocial features) containing three subtraits each, and two personality syndromes without subtraits (dominance/submission and warmth/coldness modeled after the interpersonal circumplex; Leary, 1996). (p. 466)

When conducting PPEs, we believe that description of specific behaviors and their impact on parenting and related concerns rather than providing DSM diagnoses is more helpful to the consumer of the report. Behavior descriptions provide opportunities for the evaluator to focus on the dynamics between people and the fit between the child and each parent.

To assist in applying the HiTOP model to parenting plan assessment, we have created a graphic that highlights some of the components and traits often seen in parenting plan and child custody evaluations (see Figure 17.2). We have kept the same language from the original HiTOP factor analytic research. We have also taken the liberty of applying the HiTOP model knowing that the HiTOP research was gathered from people representing general population trends rather that specific child custody sample populations. Currently, there

FIGURE 17.2. Adaptation of the HiTOP Model for Parenting Plan Evaluations

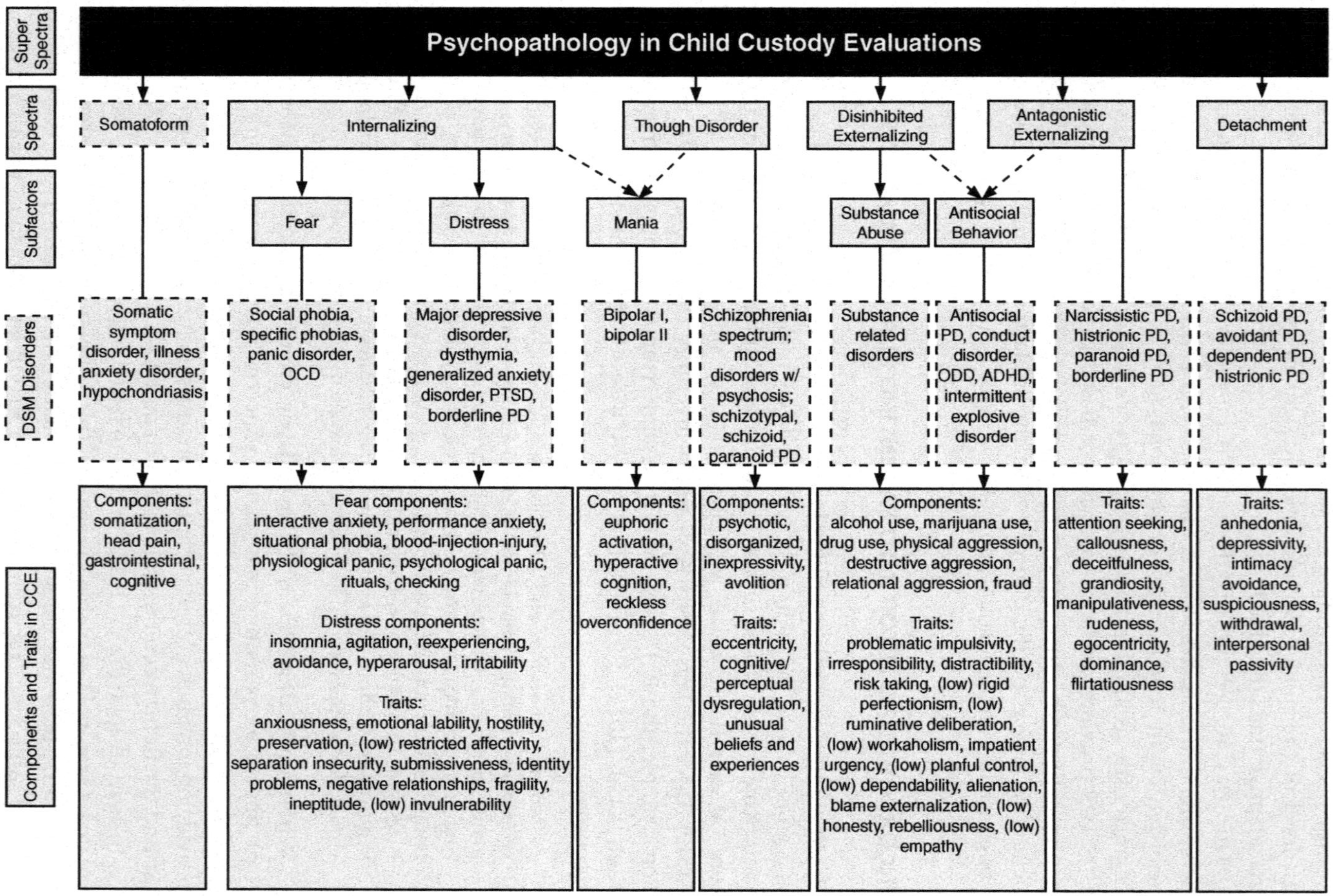

Note. Dashed lines indicate elements of the model that were included on provisional basis and require more study. Disorders with most prominent cross-loadings are listed in multiple places. OCD = obsessive-compulsive disorder; PTSD = posttraumatic stress disorder; PD = personality disorder; ODD = oppositional defiant disorder; ADHD = attention-deficit/hyperactivity disorder.

are no factorial analyses of parents in child custody disputes using the HiTOP model. We also have deemphasized the somatoform spectra and traits as they are less likely to be identified in a PPE. Therefore, we discuss this model as an evidence-informed application of the HiTOP to PPEs.

Applying the HiTOP to data gathered during a PPE the evaluator who is evaluating a parent who carries a diagnosis of generalized anxiety disorder (i.e., disorders level of analysis) would focus attention on specific behaviors identified in the component and traits level of analysis. The specific behaviors identified at the components and trait level can be used as a basis for development of specific hypotheses about the parent's behavior and its effect on each child. These specific behavior-based hypotheses guide the evaluator in seeking information about the observation of each behavior from each parent, each child, each collateral informant, and document review. For example, a parent who carries a *DSM-5* diagnosis of social anxiety may be identified using the HiTOP model as having mild discomfort in specific situations, such as when they see their ex-partner during parenting time transitions.

Using the HiTOP model as an organizing heuristic, assume that a parent carries a diagnosis of BPD. The diagnostic label is likely to be prejudicial while also conveying little, to no, information about specific behaviors that are alleged to pose a risk to the minor children in a custody dispute. Using the HiTOP model, the evaluator can identify and differentially classify the parent's fear components (psychological panic), distress components (agitation, irritability), and traits (emotional lability, hostility, negative relationships, and limited vulnerability). Each of these behavioral descriptions can be used as a basis for targeted, specific hypothesis investigation.

A third example of the use of the HiTOP model is applied to ADHD. ADHD is a common disorder that often conjures up an image of a young child with Dennis-the-Menace-like behavior. Characterizing a child or parent with ADHD in a PPE is likely to elicit a similar Dennis-the-Menace image for the judge and attorneys. Such general media portrayals are one way that diagnoses might be prejudicial. Avoidance of the potentially prejudicial effects of a diagnostic label is to provide information about specific behaviors. An individual with ADHD is likely to display observed behaviors such as impulsivity, distractibility, risk-taking, poor planning or poor dependability. Each of these behaviors are likely to be observed in the child or parent's daily lives and witnessed by collateral informants with personal knowledge of the specific behaviors and their observed effect on the child or on the parent–child interactions.

CHILD DEVELOPMENT AND THE HITOP

A primary way in which people experience and observe emotion in others is through nonverbal behavior such as eye movement, facial expressions, body tone, voice tone, and physical reactions. Children are influenced directly and indirectly by witnessing the emotional behaviors and reactions of their parents and others.

Children are hardwired to closely attend to their parent's nonverbal behavior. Their monitoring of their parents' emotional verbal and nonverbal expressions and behaviors is related to their appraisals of the safety, security, and predictability of their emotional and physical environments.

Children need affection, attention, and acceptance. Children shape their behavior by watching others. In order to understand social interactions and anticipate a parent's behavior, a child must observe their parent's behavior, interpret their parent's intentions, and monitor their parent's attentional focus (Siegel, 2020).

Children's reactions to their perception and interpretation of their parents' verbal, expressions, and emotional behavior provide a basis for the development of parent–child attunement. Parent–child attunement to the safety, security, and predictability of the emotional and physical environment serves as a basis for the development of children's attachment. As we have discussed earlier in this book, there are different types of attachment styles associated with the children's perception of the safety, security, and predictability of their environment and relationship with each parent. No matter the type of attachment a child develops, attachment processes provide "increasingly complex layers of external and then internal security for the growing child as he encounters an increasingly challenging world… The child's system requires the parent's attunement to help organize the child's own mind" (Siegel, 2020).

Development of children's social and cognitive structures are intimately tied into the nature and quality of their relationship with each parent. Young children continually monitor their parent's eye contact, facial expression, emotional reactions, and other verbal and nonverbal behaviors as a primary means through which to develop a model of the safety (or lack of safety) of the world.

As children grow and develop in relation to their parent's behavior, it is important for evaluators to examine how each parent's behavior is likely to affect each child. Evaluators need to explore the parent's behavior, the child's reaction to that behavior, and how those changes affect parent–child interactions. For example, the ADHD trait of problematic impulsivity can be identified as poor inhibitory control (an individual's ability to manage their impulses). A parent with poor impulse control may struggle to control their behavior in a socially appropriate manner. An impulsive parent might have difficulty controlling their immediate response to their child's behavior. When Sally makes a simple mistake, an impulsive parent may respond too harshly in their tone or in their physical discipline. Sally might internalize her parent's harsh words, causing her to feel anxious. Her anxiety would likely lead her to make more mistakes because her anxiety might interfere with her behavioral controls because her focus of attention is on her anticipation of her parent's impulsive reactions rather than attending to the tasks at hand. The parent who struggles with inhibitory control is likely to struggle continuously to handle these situations well. As the dynamic continues, Sally's sense of safety and security would likely be negatively affected, the nature of the parent–child relationship would likely be negatively affected, and Sally might be at higher risk of developing anxiety.

The coparenting relationship is likely to be negatively affected, too. The other parent observing the impulsive parent's harsh response to their child is likely to create conflict. Parent-to-parent conflict over different parenting styles might then infect the emotional environment of the home, affecting Sally and the other children.

When we interview the impulsive parent, we may hear that Sally sometimes makes careless mistakes. The parent may even acknowledge that they sometimes respond strongly to Sally's errors. As evaluators we need to understand the dynamic between the parent and the child, and we need to understand how the dynamic may continue to impact their relationship. Too often, we have observed evaluators accurately identify the parent's behavior and the child's behavior but neglect to critically analyze the ways in which the parent–child fit is affected and neglect critical analyses of how the impulsive parent–anxious child dynamic affects the parental relationship and permeates the emotional environment of the family system.

Parents are role models for their children, whether or not the parents recognize their role as role models in their children's eyes. As children grow older, they continue to closely watch their parent's behavior. Children who observe healthy prosocial interactions between their parents and their parents' interactions with others, including their other children, are most likely to emulate those behaviors. Children who observe unhealthy behaviors are more likely to internalize the unhealthy behaviors modeled by their parents and display those behaviors in their interactions within the family and in their relationships with others outside the family, including but not limited to, school relationships and friendship group relationships.

Poor parental behavior serving as a model for their children is likely to create a feedback loop in which an already under resourced parent is called upon to respond to their child's negative behavior, which, if done ineffectively, may lead their children to demonstrate more negative behavior not only within the family but in other areas of their lives. This negative feedback loop often results in the under-resourced parent responding more often to negative behavior and missing opportunities to address their children's positive behavior. The feedback loop focuses the parent on their children's negative behavior, which serves as an anchoring bias that goes unnoticed by the parent but is strongly felt by the children. Ultimately, this loop creates a system in which the parent shames the child for negative behavior more often than the parent can praise the child or listen to the child. The system becomes unbalanced. Both the parent and the child experience less affection, less positive attention, less acceptance, and more parental rejection.

In another example, we meet Susan, a parent who acknowledges that she is being treated for depressive symptoms. Using the HiTOP model, we identify that the HiTOP trait that appears to most impact her parenting is restricted affectivity.

If we define restricted affectivity as a clear reduction in the expressive range and intensity of affects, we can hypothesize that limited affect can impact a child who is searching for connection. Restricted affectivity would likely have more significant effect on young children (Zahn-Waxler et al., 2002). When Joe does not see his mother smile at him, he might not feel attuned with her, and the relationship suffers. Further, restricted affect expression might also suggest parental depression. Young children raised by depressed mothers have been reported to develop a more depressed view of the world based upon the cues and behaviors observed during parent–child interactions and child observations (Zahn-Waxler et al., 2002).

Research suggests there is a clear association between children's exposure to parental restrictive affectivity and children's physical health impact. Results from a UCLA study reported that children who have less affection and love experience with their parents were found to have worse physical health later in life (Carroll et al., 2013). Most interestingly, the study also reported that parental warmth and affection was associated with greater protection of a child from the effects of toxic childhood stress (Carroll et al., 2013). Other studies have drawn links between parental warmth and affection and children's improved health later in life (Chen, Kubzansky, et al., 2019). These examples demonstrate how the AMPD and HiTOP can be used as part of an ecological evaluation of the family.

CONCLUSION

The AMPD and HiTOP models illustrate a paradigm shift in how we conceptualize mental health, moving beyond rigid categories to a more flexible, scientifically grounded, and useful framework. In the context of child custody litigation, applying dimensional diagnostic models could enhance forensic evaluations, improve expert testimony, and support more precise intervention planning. Dimensional models offer expert witnesses a scientific basis for explaining psychological traits in a less stigmatizing and more precise way than using more categorical models such as the *DSM*. Instead of stating a parent has a personality disorder, testimony can frame concerns in behavioral terms. For example, an evaluator might explain that a parent exhibits traits of emotional instability, impulsivity, and interpersonal antagonism, which may lead to inconsistent discipline and emotional unpredictability in parenting interactions. By shifting language away from rigid diagnostic labels, the AMPD and HiTOP models can help judges and attorneys better understand psychological findings in a clear, empirically derived manner.

Of course, a central theme in our book is the connection between research and practice. As we discussed, there are many areas in which we may be tempted to use measures or research that do not yet have sufficient empirical support or evidence-informed guidelines. While we write this book, articles are being published on how to integrate the AMPD and the HiTOP models into clinical practice. While they have not yet been directly applied to PPEs, they hold significant potential for forensic mental health professionals tasked with assessing parents, children, and family dynamics in litigation settings. As research on HiTOP and the AMPD continue to evolve, parenting plan evaluators should consider integrating their principles into parenting plan assessments, testimony, and court-involved therapy.

18

Collateral Interviews and Record Review

Forensic evaluators are tasked with uncovering historical truth—an objective reconstruction of past events and family dynamics based on verifiable evidence (S. A. Greenberg & Shuman, 1997). In high-conflict custody disputes, the narratives presented by parents and children may be influenced by personal perspectives, emotions, or even intentional distortions. To navigate this complex landscape, forensic evaluators must rely on independent sources of information that extend beyond the direct statements of the involved parties (W. G. Austin & Kirkpatrick, 2004). Collateral interviews and record reviews serve as critical investigative tools in this process, allowing evaluators to cross-check claims, identify patterns of behavior, and reduce reliance on subjective accounts. By examining school records, medical history, legal filings, and professional observations from educators, mental health providers, and other relevant third parties, evaluators can move beyond surface-level assertions to construct a well-supported, evidence-based assessment.

However, the effectiveness of these tools depends on the depth and rigor of the evaluative process. Evaluators must approach collateral interviews with precision and neutrality, seeking behavioral observations rather than general impressions. Similarly, record reviews should be conducted systematically to ensure that past events are contextualized appropriately. Without these safeguards, forensic evaluations risk becoming unsubstantiated opinion exercises rather than reliable guides for judicial decision making.

In this chapter, we explore how collateral interviews and record reviews contribute to the search for historical truth in forensic evaluations. By examining

https://doi.org/10.1037/0000474-019
Parenting Plan Evaluations: An Evidence-Informed Approach to Child Custody, by J. W. Gould and C. M. Mulchay

best practices, common challenges, and the importance of investigative rigor, we aim to highlight the essential role these methods play in producing fair, accurate, and scientifically grounded assessments.

HISTORICAL TRUTH AND THE PURPOSE OF COLLATERAL INTERVIEWS AND RECORD REVIEW

In their seminal article on the irreconcilable differences between therapeutic and forensic activities, S. A. Greenberg and Shuman held that a primary responsibility of evaluators is to gather information that might help to explain "historical truth" (S. A. Greenberg & Shuman, 1997, p. 52). The purpose of information gathering in a forensic evaluation is the pursuit of validating historical truth. Evaluators work towards validating the historical truth of assertions made by parents, children, or others. That is, evaluators seek past and present information from independent, third-party sources. Whereas a therapeutic investigation is more concerned about the patient's perception of their world and less concerned about the accuracy of the information brought into the treatment session, parenting plan evaluations (PPEs) offer opinions to the court regarding historical truth and the validity of the psychological aspects of a litigant's claims (S. A. Greenberg & Shuman, 1997).

In our review of other evaluators' reports, we have observed some colleagues approach their work with the belief that parents will provide evaluators with all the information needed, and that evaluators have no obligation to engage in the active pursuit of third-party information. In Chapter 10, we referred to this as the stenographic model of assessment. The model that we will discuss next, which we have referred to as the factfinding model of assessment, runs contrary to the idea of a forensic evaluator as a passive recipient of information. Evaluators should engage in the active pursuit of information.

Evaluations rely, in great part, on information obtained from third-party sources. Survey data (Ackerman & Ackerman, 1997; Ackerman & Dolezal, 2006; Ackerman et al., 2021; Bow & Quinnell, 2001, 2002, 2004) and professional practice guidelines (American Psychological Association [APA], 2022; Association of Family and Conciliation Courts, 2022), child custody textbooks (Ackerman, 2006; Gould, 2006; Gould & Martindale, 2007; Hynan, 2013; P. M. Stahl, 1999), and peer-reviewed articles (W. G. Austin & Kirkpatrick, 2004; Gould & Martindale, 2013; Gould & Mulchay, 2023) provide overwhelming support for the use of collateral information in child custody evaluations. Obtaining collateral information is viewed as an important component of the standard of practice in child custody assessment.

There is consensus across disciplines (America Academy of Matrimonial Lawyers, 2013; APA, 2022; Hernan & American Academy of Child and Adolescent Psychology, 1997) about the importance of gathering information from third parties, both from those who are independent sources of information with no apparent emotional ties to family members and from those who may have emotional ties to one or both parents. Collateral interviews may include information from daycare workers, nannies, neighbors, family members, pediatricians, therapists, teachers, coaches, and other people who have direct observational knowledge of parent–child interactions.

William G. Austin and Kirkpatrick (2004) illustrate how a third-party informant's emotional distance from the case impacts their credibility. See Figure 18.1. The innermost circles represent individuals with strong emotional alignment or bias toward a specific person. The outer circles represent individuals with less emotional involvement, making them more objective and credible as sources of information. This is not to say a parent's mother or best friend may not provide useful information. Instead, the concentric circles emphasize that evaluators are more likely to get reliable information from professionals who do not have a stake in the game, such as teachers and coaches.

Collateral interviews should focus on gathering information to answer the specific questions guiding the evaluation. Similar to interview procedures used when interviewing each parent, evaluators should employ interview procedures that minimize leading, suggestive, and directive questions while at the same time focusing the informant on providing answers useful in answering specific questions that define the scope of the evaluation.

FIGURE 18.1. Concentric Circles of Collaterals

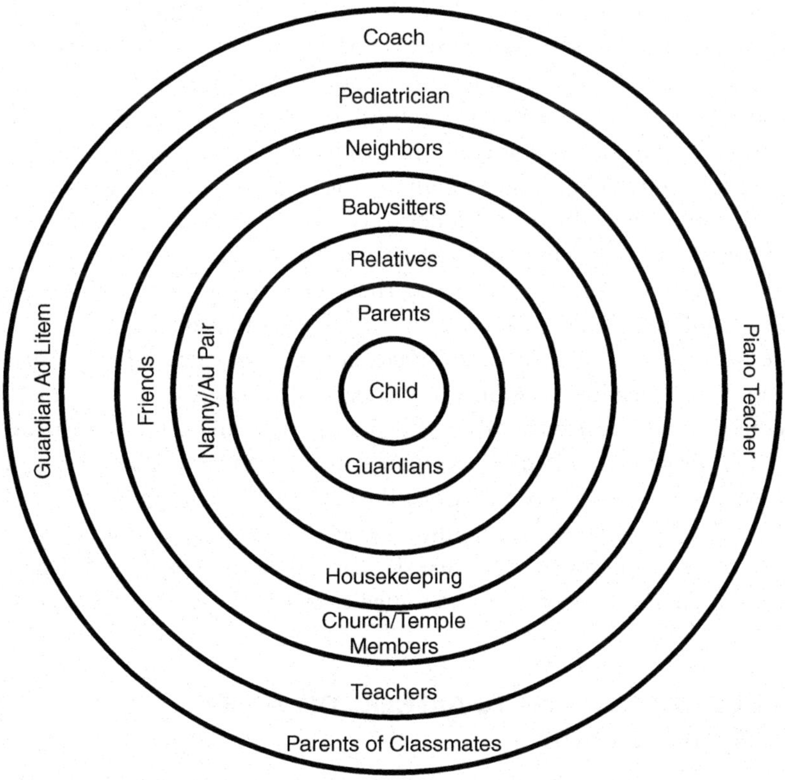

Note. Validity tends to increase the further you move from the center. From "The Investigation Component in Forensic Mental Health Evaluations: Considerations for Parenting Time Assessments," by W. G. Austin and H. D. Kirkpatrick, 2004, *Journal of Child Custody: Research, Issues, and Practices, 1*(2), p. 34 (https://doi.org/10.1300/J190v01n02_02). Copyright 2004 by Taylor & Francis. Reprinted with permission.

CONCERNS ABOUT COLLATERAL INTERVIEWS

Among areas of concern is the evaluator's lack of attention to gathering collateral witnesses' descriptions of observations of specific parent–child behaviors. Too many evaluators do not ask during interviews for the collateral informant to provide examples of observed behavior. The collateral informant often expresses an opinion about the parent (e.g., "She is a wonderful mother" and "He is a loving father"). Seldom does the evaluator provide data in the report to help the reader understand what observations served as the basis of the opinion that the parent is "wonderful" or "loving." In many evaluations, the evaluator does not direct the collateral informant to provide specific examples of observed behavior, and the collateral informants are generally unfamiliar with providing behavioral descriptors rather than expressing opinions. The collateral informant usually believes they are providing useful information when they describe a parent as loving, playful, and engaged. They are unfamiliar with the level of analysis needed in evaluations: behavioral observations.

Another concern is that collateral interviews often take place after the evaluator has completed parent and child interviews. When the collateral interview occurs after parent and child interviews are complete, there is no opportunity for the evaluator to query the parent or child about the collateral information, thereby providing an opportunity for a challenge to the collateral information through the identification of additional informants or records. The failure to provide litigants with opportunities to respond to information provided about them by collateral sources increases the probability that collateral sources who have provided information relied upon by the evaluator will be subpoenaed as fact witnesses. An evaluator who does not allow a parent to respond places greater weight on the collateral sources and records than they may have done if they had counterbalanced the data. The process of restricting either parent from responding most likely reduces the reliability of his data.

The Association of Family and Conciliation Courts *Parenting Plan Guidelines* (2022) instruct, "Evaluators should use a balanced process to enhance objectivity and equity." The *Guidelines* continue, "Evaluators should ensure that significant issues and allegations raised by one party are brought to the attention of the other party or parties and they are given the opportunity to respond so the evaluator has balanced information about the issue." This process of seeking balanced information also allows for the inclusion of additional collateral information sources that might not have been identified earlier in the evaluation process.

USING QUESTIONNAIRES TO GATHER COLLATERAL OBSERVATIONAL DATA

Evaluators have historically gathered collateral data on the telephone, through email, or through the mail. Each of those data-gathering procedures are memorialized through written notes or audiotapes whether the third-party source is a family member, friend, neighbor, or professional. For collaterals to share their observations, our second author has created a form in the electronic medical record he uses to send out Health Insurance Portability and Accountability Act (HIPAA)–compliant questionnaires to collaterals. He then follows up with a phone call or a telehealth interview. The following list of questions is a template that should be modified to address case-specific questions:

1. How do you know Parent A?
2. What is the relationship that you have with Parent A?
3. How do you know Parent B?
4. What is the relationship that you have with Parent B?
5. Describe what you have observed about Parent A's parenting of the child. Provide specific examples.
6. Describe what you have observed about Parent A's daily caretaking of the children?
7. Who have you observed to assist Parent A in caretaking of the child?
8. What have you observed these other people to do in their caretaking of the child?
9. Describe what you have observed about Parent B's parenting of the child. Provide specific examples.
10. Describe what you have observed about Parent B's daily caretaking of the child?
11. Who have you observed to assist Parent B in caretaking of the child?
12. What have you observed these other people do in their caretaking of the child?
13. Describe what you have observed of how the parents communicate with each other. Provide specific examples.
14. If you have observed the parents arguing, have the children been present? If yes, please describe your observation of how the children responded to the parents' arguing.
15. If applicable, describe how each parent behaved toward each child during the observed parent-to-parent arguing.
16. If applicable, describe how each parent involved each child during the parents' arguing.
17. Describe what you have observed regarding Parent A's treatment of Parent B. Provide specific examples.
18. Describe what you have observed regarding members of Parent A's family's treatment of Parent B. Provide specific examples.

19. Describe what you have observed regarding Parent B's treatment of Parent A. Provide specific examples.
20. Describe what you have observed regarding members of Parent B's family's treatment of Parent A. Provide specific examples.
21. Describe what you have observed about how Parent A or Parent B disciplines the child.
22. Describe your observations of Parent A's or Parent B's use of force such as slapping, physical or verbal threats, hitting, pushing or any other like behavior.
23. Do you have any concerns about Parent A's or Parent B's parenting skills?
24. Is there anything you would like to share with me about the parent that I have not asked?
25. Is there any other person you think would be useful for me to talk with?
26. What has Parent A or Parent B said to you about the other parent?
27. Describe your observation of each parent's use of alcohol and drugs when the children are physically present.

RECORD REVIEW

There is consensus about what records most evaluators ask to review (Ackerman et al., 2021). Past and present records may include review of documents such as police reports, school records, military records, medical records, personnel files, athletic team attendance, credit card bills, check stubs, changes in one's resume, depositions, witness statements, and any other possible sources of information about the parent's pre- and postseparation thoughts, emotions, and behaviors. Recently, evaluators have been asked to review emails, text messages, and social media posts, which can all be described as electronically stored information (ESI).

Parenting plan evaluators are often faced with a complex question: *How much weight should be given to a parent's historical mental health records?* The answer is not always clear, and there is no universal consensus on how to interpret past diagnoses in the context of parental capacity. In family law cases, it is not uncommon for one party to introduce mental health records as evidence, hoping to demonstrate a history of psychological instability, emotional distress, or psychiatric disorders. However, a diagnosis is not predictive of parenting ability. A parent with a history of depression, anxiety, or even more severe mental health conditions may still function as a capable, loving, and attuned caregiver. Similarly, the absence of a diagnosis does not automatically indicate that a parent is fit to provide a stable environment.

Furthermore, while a record may document a psychiatric condition from years ago, it often lacks essential information: How was this diagnosis determined? What alternative hypotheses were considered at the time of the examination? Has there been any attempt to explore how this reported condition affects the parent's ability to meet their child's emotional, physical, and developmental needs? How does it impact the quality of parent–child interactions or coparenting dynamics? A past diagnosis, standing alone, does not answer these questions, and assuming otherwise can lead to misinterpretations and unjust outcomes in custody determinations. Recall our earlier discussion of how diagnosis can lead to an anchor bias, which snowballs into a gross misrepresentation of a parent's behavior. This is why parenting plan evaluators must exercise caution when incorporating historical records into their assessments. Best practices suggest that record reviews should not replace direct forensic evaluation, collateral interviews, psychological testing, and behavioral observations. Whenever possible, evaluators should seek clarification by discussing the contents of the records with the parent involved—ensuring that the information is contextualized and not taken at face value.

Evaluators must also recognize that mental health conditions exist on a spectrum and can be influenced by treatment, life circumstances, and resilience factors. A person diagnosed with bipolar disorder, for instance, may have once struggled with mood instability but may now be well-regulated through therapy, medication, and strong social support. In contrast, a parent with no formal psychiatric history may exhibit coercive control, poor emotional regulation, or high-conflict behaviors that are far more detrimental to a child's well-being than a treated mental illness.

Some evaluators require attorneys to provide the information shared for the record review. Some evaluators also require that when attorneys submit information to the evaluator for a record review, they also share the documents with opposing counsel. In this scenario, opposing counsel and, subsequently, the client may learn the contents of the record review. In other situations, the parents may not know what is being reviewed. Our view is that evaluators should provide parents and children with opportunities to review collateral information and opportunities to respond to that information. While these records offer valuable insights, they are often imperfect, incomplete, or open to interpretation. Additionally, the individuals being evaluated—parents and children—may not have had the opportunity to clarify, challenge, or provide context to the information contained within these reports. A therapist's note from years ago, for example, may describe a parent as "struggling with emotional regulation," but without an update, it fails to reflect the parent's progress in treatment. Providing parents the chance to review and clarify such records helps ensure that evaluators are working with the most accurate and current data. This lack of procedural fairness can lead to inaccurate conclusions and biased assessments. If a parent is judged based on information they have never seen or had a chance to refute, this can create an unfair process. Allowing for review and response aligns with principles of due process and ensures that evaluations meet ethical standards.

Throughout the evaluation, the evaluator should be gathering information from collateral informants and gathering information from the review of records. Too often, evaluators wait until the last stages of the data-gathering process to interview collaterals or review records. Information learned from these third-party sources needs to be discussed with the parties and, if appropriate, with the children. In our review work, we have observed that evaluators often take one of two paths that compromise the evaluation process. Some evaluators conduct third-party interviews at the end of the data-gathering process and do not allow the parties or their children to respond to the information learned from third-party sources. Other evaluators conduct third-party interviews and record review yet never talk with the parties or children about what was gleaned and, once again, do not afford the parties or their children opportunities to respond.

Waiting until the later part of the evaluation process is a flawed methodological approach because the evaluator often does not use the obtained collateral information as a basis for interviewing the parents. Interviewing the parents based upon collateral information gathered from interviews and record review allows the parent to provide an alternative explanation of the allegations or assertions. Interviewing the parents based upon collateral information gathered from interviews and record review also allows the parent to provide the evaluator with other potential collateral information sources that might refute the third-party information.

Obtaining information from third-party sources is overwhelmingly important in any forensic psychological evaluation and, in our view, especially important in child custody assessment. Parents and children bring a variety of explicit and implicit bias factors into the evaluation process. Among the bias control procedures most useful to balance the influence of various bias factors is seeking third-party information. Remember what we discussed in the section on structured analytic techniques: It is as important to seek data that refutes your evolving hypotheses as it is to seek information that confirms your evolving hypotheses.

It is wise to seek information from objective collateral contacts, including school records, legal records, police records, or other records. Testimonials from relatives of a parent are often filled with accolades for that parent, however, relatives may be able to provide useful observations about parent–child interaction, information about who attends to the child and when, information about who the child seeks out when upset, tired, or frightened, and other areas of parenting that are often not observed by people outside the family or extended family system. Relatives may also provide information about the degree to which other family or extended family members may contribute to the on-going conflict. The parents should be invited to tell the evaluator whom they want to have interviewed, the gist of what they expect each person to say, and to provide contact information for each person. It is not necessary for the evaluator to interview each person suggested, but having that information will make some collateral contacts easier. The evaluator may, of course, interview people not on either parent's list.

Common Sources of Records

Records that evaluators may want to review include:

- **School records**. School records should be utilized to understand the child's performance and behavior. School records are also utilized in an effort to determine whether a child has performed better while living with one parent or the other, whether there has been a substantial change in academic performance during the pendency of the divorce, or whether teacher comments on school reports suggest any concerns. Teachers may also be useful sources of information about what the child may say at school about family life and what each parent may be saying to the teacher about the other parent.
- **Criminal records**. The issue of recency and frequency is also important when reviewing criminal records. In an illustrative case, the stepfather was found to have a 14-year criminal history, including felony convictions for crimes against both property and person. This history weighed much more heavily than another individual's history of one property offense occurring many years ago.
- **Medical records**. Medical records are important to review, especially pediatric records for each child. Information about who brought the child, how often the child was brought, and why the child was brought to the doctor may be useful. Learning how each parent talks to the physician or staff about the other parent may also provide helpful information. For cases with concerns about maltreatment or abuse, medical records may need to be reviewed by a consulting physician who may assist the evaluator in understanding the medical concerns described in the file. The evaluator should also have access to any hospital records of the parents.
- **Mental health records**. It is important that the evaluator obtain the mental health records of each child. Mental health record review is part of the larger picture of understanding each parent's and each child's overall physical and emotional well-being. For parents, the extent of the outpatient and inpatient history, the frequency of the contacts, and the recency of the episodes must be considered. The data obtained in the records should be compared with the information provided in the parent interview. One psychiatric hospitalization 10 years prior to the evaluation for a problem that has been completely resolved should not carry the same weight as a number of hospitalizations in recent years. The evaluator should also have access to psychotherapy records, if any, of the parents, as well as the written consent by each parent, if relevant, to talk with their therapist.

If either parent refuses to provide authorization to release medical or mental health records to the evaluator, a court order for the records and interview may be sought. Similarly, each parent should provide written consent to mental health and medical providers to release their entire file to the evaluator. This would include obtaining copies of children's psychotherapy records and permission to conduct an interview with the treating therapist. Far too often, therapists assert privilege on behalf of clients when they refuse to disclose therapy records. Recall that privilege belongs to the patient, and the therapist cannot assert privilege if the client has waived it or if there is a court order. The evaluator should consider whether it is in the best interests of the child for the evaluator to access the child's therapy records and interview the therapist, or whether it is more likely in the best interests of the child for that therapy to be kept out of the evaluation process.

One of the challenges involved in third-party record review is to obtain information about the basis of the diagnostic information found in the written record. Just as the evaluator's responsibility is to testify to the information upon which expert opinions are based, the evaluator needs to explore the information upon which past mental health diagnoses were based.

The evaluator is a type of psychological information gatekeeper. If a previous mental health diagnosis was based solely upon the previous provider's initial impressions rather than based upon the use of a reliable data-gathering procedure, then it is possible that the evidence-basis of the past diagnosis is unreliable. As the person who will testify to the court, the evaluator needs to know how the previous mental health diagnoses were determined. Too often, a previous mental health diagnosis based upon an initial, 30-minute intake is entered into a hospital record and years later, that initial diagnostic impression is used to argue that a parent is mentally ill or that a parent carries a DSM diagnosis suggestive of harm to children. Evaluators need to scrutinize the data upon which previous diagnoses were based, seeking to confirm that the diagnostic label was based upon more than an initial impression at intake without a more formal diagnostic workup.

Extent of Records Requests

We believe that evaluators request as much collateral information as possible in all PPEs, to avoid the possibility of missing essential information or being confronted with surprise information during court testimony. Even though a considerable amount of extraneous material may be provided, at least it should be the evaluator who determines what will be reviewed.

Collateral sources have become an important part of the evaluation process. Ackerman and Ackerman (1997) found that parenting plan evaluators spent approximately 21.1 hours completing PPEs. The number of hours spent per custody evaluation has largely increased, as Ackerman et al. found that psychologists reported spending an average of 64 hours per custody evaluation, including an increase in time spent reviewing collateral materials (Ackerman et al., 2021).

Bow divides collateral contacts into several different categories: parent documents, child documents, parent collaterals, and child collaterals (Bow, 2010). Bow points out that the interview technique for collateral sources should be similar to that of other interviews, starting with open-ended questions seeking information relevant to the specific questions guiding the evaluation, followed by more focused and direct questions (Bow, 2010).

ELECTRONICALLY STORED INFORMATION AS A COLLATERAL INFORMATION SOURCE

While many evaluators may advocate for reviewing the collateral information to guide interviews with parents, this does not always occur due to the organizational demands required to integrate substantial amounts of information. Evaluators may be asked to review volumes of ESI: emails, texts, or social media posts. Data from emails, texts, audio recordings, video recordings, and social networking sites are considered records, and best practices for record collection should be applied to ESI. Compared to other psycholegal referrals, forensic psychologists are most likely to review social media evidence when conducting a PPE (Coffey et al., 2018). The use of ESI data is becoming commonplace in PPEs. Sean Knuth (2020) proposed a model suggesting four areas of parent functioning as providing data obtained through ESI.

Knuth's four areas of examination are:

a. How the parent communicates with others and how they interpret communication from others.
b. Whether the parent possesses insight into how their actions potentially benefit or harm the relationship between the minor children and themselves or the opposite parent.
c. How well a parent understands social networking and technology.
d. Whether the parent effectively monitors and controls a minor child's access to information in an appropriate manner.

We applaud Sean Knuth, who appears to be the first to suggest ways to utilize ESI data in PPEs. Recall that among the points raised throughout this book is the importance of relying on the scientific process. Mulchay and Knuth (2021, 2022a, 2022b, 2022c) have developed a structured approach to gathering, investigating, and analyzing ESI data. We have expanded their model on how to think about the value of ESI information.

Here, we propose a structured professional judgment tool to obtain reliable information from parents involved in child custody assessment. We begin by discussing reliability. Then, we describe emerging research. We conclude by providing factors and questions to guide the investigation.

Reliability

Like with all record review, ESI data can provide evaluators with a source of information they can use to inform their evaluation. Like data from any other source, data from ESI can help an evaluator generate hypotheses for investigation and can provide an evaluator with data that lends support or argues against hypotheses. Like data from any other source, data from ESI is rarely in and of itself dispositive. Data from ESI are only reliably interpreted when considered within the context of all collected information.

Further complicating the reliability of ESI data is how easy it is to fabricate. As Mulchay likes to demonstrate in his workshops, it is quite easy to fabricate text messages, emails, Facebook posts, and other documents. It is also now becoming easier to fabricate audio and video recordings with inexpensive software. Our recommendation, which we described above in reference to reviewing records, is for evaluators to interview parents about the content and context before interpreting the data. By asking each parent about the ESI data, the evaluator makes the review of ESI a multisource, multimethod process. Interestingly, by asking each parent about the submitted ESI data, our second author has often found that the data has only been partially provided. Or the data has been manipulated. For example, when Parent A provides 20 pages of text messages and Parent B is asked about this exchange, Mulchay has found that Parent B is often able to point out that Parent A edited or removed messages from the provided excerpt. At other times, Parent B may show that the conversation moved from text to email or Facebook. Without asking each parent about the content of the submission, the evaluator cannot reliably interpret the content and the context.

Another threat to reliability is that the evaluator does not know who might have written the communication. As more parents ask their attorneys to edit or write their emails and Our Family Wizard replies, and there are new apps that will edit the parent's responses, we have increasing concerns about authorship. At a recent Association of Family and Conciliation Courts conference, we noticed a company advertising a service that would edit or take over the parents' written communication.

It is important for evaluators to remember that in an evaluation, there are at least four types of records. First, there are the records that an evaluator does not have access to. Second, there are unsolicited records that are provided by one side. Third, there are solicited records that the evaluator requests. And finally, there are meaningful or probative records. It is this fourth category that may overlap with each of the first three categories, such that there may be meaningful or probative records that the evaluator does not have access to (the first type of records), there may be meaningful or probative records that the evaluator did not request but received (the second type of records), and there may be probative records that the evaluator requested (the third type of records). It is important for evaluators to understand that they may never have all of the probative data.

Attorneys can hire a forensic technology company to evaluate the authenticity of the ESI on the device that created it prior to providing it to the evaluator. Once the evaluator has the ESI data to review, their best course of action is to use the forensic method to interview both parents (and possibly the children or collaterals) about the data.

A key factor in our investigation of reliability is the degree to which ESI data has impacted the child. Survey data suggests that 8 of 10 children have their parent's passwords and pin codes (Choong et al., 2019). It is, therefore, important for evaluators to investigate what ESI data the child knows.

Before we discuss how to gather information from collateral informants about family member's ESI use, we summarize some of the emerging literature about the potential benefits and risks associated with social networking sites use across the lifespan.

Potential Benefits and Risks of Media Use Among Young Children

Digital media are integrated into the everyday lives of young children, adolescents, and adults. Emerging research is revealing how digital media exposure has different potential impacts on children's cognition, psychosocial functioning, and physical health (Canadian Pediatric Society, 2019; Coyne et al., 2017). Among the potential benefits of children engaging in digital media use include watching age-appropriate cable or online programming. Such media watching might occur with family and can serve important roles in sharing common experiences, teaching children about aspects of life that are outside of their daily lives, and creating a shared history with family members (Canadian Pediatric Society, 2019; Coyne et al., 2017).

Certain types of media can improve children's academic performance, enrich knowledge and literacy skills, and help develop positive relationships with teachers and other students. Some media experiences encourage autonomous functioning, while other media experiences encourage collaboration. Children engaged in media play have been found to make friends and maintain those friendships, and, interestingly, those friendships appear to be more diverse and gender-inclusive than friendships developed offline (Canadian Pediatric Society, 2019; Coyne et al., 2017).

Cooperative and competitive video games can provide health benefits. Playing video games with family and friends can provide opportunities to engage with family and friends who are geographically distant, reflect and function as a type of traditional play, and offer opportunities for developing identity, developing cognitive skills, and engaging in social skill building (Canadian Pediatric Society, 2019; Coyne et al., 2017). Additionally, recreational screen time at low levels (1 hour per day) has been associated with lower depression risk compared with no screen time (Canadian Pediatric Society, 2019; Coyne et al., 2017).

Among the risks posed by digital media use include exposure to age-inappropriate or violent content, cyberbullying, and sexting. Having a television in a child's room has been found to negatively affect development and behavior. For example, children who watch television for 3 or more hours a day at 5 years of age have been observed to have an increased risk for conduct problems at 7 years of age.

Heavy use of social media is associated with poorer mental health and relationships, as well as involvement in risky behavior (Wallace, 2021). Higher rates of recreational screen use have been found to be associated with higher rates of depression and lower levels of physical activity among children. It appears that children from economically disadvantaged homes and minority students and their families tend to consume significantly more media overall, with associated increases in depression and decreases in physical activities (Canadian Pediatric Society, 2019; Coyne et al., 2017).

Significant concerns have been raised about the degree to which children of all ages are unsupervised in their digital use. Unsupervised media use significantly increases the risks of exposure to negative, inappropriate, or harmful content. Some research has found that children might be overconfident in their ability to protect themselves from said content (Canadian Pediatric Society, 2019; Coyne et al., 2017).

Children, especially young children, attempt to divide their attention between two or more tasks (i.e., media multitasking). Research data suggest that children who engage in media multitasking have more difficulty learning. Media multitasking has an immediate negative effect on both concurrent learning in the home or classroom and negatively affects academic achievement in children 12 and younger.

Potential Benefits and Risks of Media Use Among Adolescents

Adolescents spend an extraordinary amount of screen time per day, with high school students reported to average about 7.5 hours per day on various screens. Research findings suggest that older children, i.e., teens, are less likely to be as negatively affected by high levels of screen time as young children. Teens who engage in excessive screen time appear more vulnerable to the negative effects of media use compared with teens who engage in moderate screen time, defined as between 2–4 hours per day.

The Centers for Disease Control and Prevention published a data brief in November 2024 examining the relationship between screen time and mental health among teenagers aged 12–17 (Zablotsky et al., 2024). The study found that approximately 50% of teenagers reported engaging in 4 or more hours of daily screen time. Notably, about 27.1% of these teens experienced anxiety symptoms, and 25.9% reported depression symptoms within the past 2 weeks. In contrast, among teenagers with less than 4 hours of daily screen time, 12.3% reported anxiety symptoms, and 9.5% reported depression symptoms. This suggests that higher screen time is associated with increased mental health challenges among adolescents.

Adolescents spend an extraordinary amount of screen time per day, with high school students reported to average about 7.5 hours per day on various screens. Research findings suggest that older children, i.e., teens, are less likely to be as negatively affected by high levels of screen time as young children. Teens who engage in excessive screen time appear more vulnerable to the negative effects of media use compared with teens who engage in moderate screen time (Zablotsky, et al., 2024).

While the Center for Disease Control and Prevention's study highlights the negative impacts associated with excessive screen time, it does not specifically address the effects of no screen time or moderate screen time. However, other research has explored these aspects. For instance, a study published in *BMC Psychology* in April 2024 reviewed associations between screen time and mental health in adolescents (Francisquini et al., 2024). The findings indicated that both excessive and minimal screen time could be linked to negative psychological effects, suggesting that moderate screen time might be less harmful.

These studies collectively suggest that while excessive screen time is linked to increased mental health challenges, moderate screen time may be less detrimental. However, individual experiences can vary, and it's essential to consider personal circumstances when evaluating screen time's impact on mental health.

On the positive side, adolescents engaged in social media use may profit from increased social connections with peers, developing a sense of identity, increasing independence from family, learning how to navigate the sociocultural world, and developing increased autonomy. Of course, each of these positive aspects might also turn negative depending upon the people with whom the teen engages. In addition, being continually online can contribute to increased feelings of aloneness, social alienation, and social exclusion and can negatively affect the development of healthy social engagement skills (Canadian Pediatric Society, 2019; Coyne et al., 2017).

The risks of violent media and violent video games on aggression have been well documented. The APA Task Force on Violent Media found strong correlational data that suggests parental monitoring is important.

> On the basis of our review of the literature directly addressing violent video game use, we concluded that violent video game use has an effect on aggression. This effect is manifested both as an increase in negative outcomes such as aggressive behavior, cognitions, and affect and as a decrease in positive outcomes such as prosocial behavior, empathy, and sensitivity to aggression. (APA, 2015)

Excessive screen time was associated with a heightened risk of obesity and other cardiometabolic issues, mental health challenges, unhealthy eating habits and disorders, as well as developmental and parent–child relationship difficulties. Additionally, it negatively impacted sleep, physical activity, vision, headaches, and musculoskeletal health (Priftis & Panagiotakos, 2023).

Screen time usage should now be a focus of many evaluations and evaluators should ask if either parent identifies it as a significant issue. Evaluators should also ask the children about their usage.

Factors to Examine With Collaterals With Personal Knowledge of Minor Children's Social Media and Digital Exposure

Coyne et al. (2017) assert that understanding family dynamics is a critical step in understanding how children use media, and the effects media use has on each child, familial relationships, and other relevant child-development concerns. Child characteristics, parent–child relationship factors, parental mediation practices monitoring and supervising children's social media use, and parents' own media use are all factors that can influence children's social media use, their attitudes toward social media use, and the effect of social media on children (Coyne et al., 2017).

Among the child characteristics associated with social media use that appear to affect healthy development include children who have difficulties with emotional regulation and poor self-regulators. Parents of children who have difficulties with emotional regulation and poor self-regulators have been found to give their children mobile devices to calm them down or keep them quiet. One result is that these children have been observed to exceed the media guidelines of the American Academy of Pediatrics. The guidelines were developed based upon research that exceeding the recommended screen time had a negative effect on a wide range of developmental milestones.

The relationship between parental restrictive media monitoring and children's self-regulation has been explored in various studies. For instance, research indicates that children with better self-regulation abilities tend to experience lower levels of parental restrictive media monitoring. This suggests that as children develop stronger self-regulation skills, parents may feel less need to impose strict media restrictions (Coyne et al., 2017). Additionally, a study found that adolescents' self-regulation was associated with lower levels of parental cocooning, a form of restrictive mediation, suggesting that parents might adjust their media monitoring strategies based on their perception of their child's self-regulatory capabilities (Padilla-Walker & Coyne et al., 2011). These findings suggest a bidirectional relationship where not only can parental monitoring influence a child's self-regulation, but a child's self-regulation abilities can also inform parental monitoring practices.

Parental mediation regulation refers to parents who set rules about appropriate content to be viewed or the time spent engaged in screen time. Researchers have found parents to fit into two groups: autonomy-restrictive or autonomy-granting behaviors. Some parents discipline their children by rewarding or punishing through media access. Parents who engage in e-discipline, as it is called, allow access to screen time as a reward for good behavior and prohibit access as a punishment for inappropriate or bad behavior (Coyne et al., 2017).

Some parents engage in active mediation, defined as parent–child conversations about media use, including parental attempts to provide children with critical viewing skills. Other parents engage in *coviewing*, defined as parents and children participating together in viewing or using social media but do not necessarily discuss the context of the shared media viewing (Coyne et al., 2017).

Parents who exercise low control over their children's screen time are more likely to allow their children to engage in excessive screen time. Parents who exercise more control while still being supportive of their children are more likely to engage in active and restrictive screen time allowances (Coyne et al., 2017).

Recent research has suggested that on average, parents monitor their child's social media access once a week (Wallace, 2021). The study found that mothers spoke to their adolescents more often about social media, mothers were more likely to punish their children for breaking social media rules, and mothers used more intrusive strategies such as tracking apps. The study also found that "adolescent gender also influenced patterns in parental monitoring" such that parents were more likely to monitor social media use if their adolescent was their same gender.

In some families, parents are more media-centric (about 11 hours a day) and as a role model, tend to have children who engage in more daily screen time and are more likely to have a television in their room, although these days iPads and screens often have more capabilities than televisions. Media-centric parents are more likely to use social media as a means of keeping up with and connecting with their children (Coyne et al., 2017).

In some families, parental media use might interfere with or interrupt family time. Family time and routines have been found to be protective factors for child development, school success, and resilience. Interruptions to family time and routines have been found to adversely affect those factors. Parent mobile media use has been associated with fewer mother-child interactions (Coyne et al., 2017). A nationally representative study found that adolescents report that their parents are less warm or connected because their parents are distracted by their phones (Stockdale et al., 2018).

A Structured Approach to Evaluating Electronically Stored Information in Parenting Plan Evaluations

As digital communication plays an increasingly significant role in family law disputes, forensic evaluators must adopt a structured approach to analyzing ESI. To ensure fairness, reliability, and contextual accuracy, our approach to evaluating ESI can be categorized into four investigative areas: communication, insight, monitoring, and context. Each category offers a distinct lens through which evaluators can assess parental behavior, coparenting dynamics, and potential risks to the child's well-being. To enhance the depth of evaluations, targeted interview strategies should be incorporated to gather context and clarify digital evidence.

Communication

One of the most valuable aspects of ESI is its ability to provide a real-time record of how parents interact with each other and their children. Text messages, emails, social media exchanges, and call logs offer insights into coparenting relationships and parental conflict. Evaluators must consider whether communication between parents is collaborative and child-focused or marked by hostility, manipulation, and gatekeeping. For example, a series of text exchanges may reveal a parent consistently refusing to facilitate visitation, engaging in derogatory comments about the other parent in the child's presence, or demonstrating an unwillingness to coparent effectively. However, evaluators must take great care not to overemphasize isolated messages or emotionally charged moments. A single heated exchange does not define a pattern, and evaluators should seek broader context by examining multiple interactions over time.

To assess digital interactions between parents and children, consider the following interview questions:

- Can you describe a typical exchange between you and the other parent regarding the child's needs? (Assessing overall communication patterns)
- Have there been times when digital communication escalated into conflict? What happened next? (Exploring conflict resolution)
- How does the other parent respond to concerns or requests made via text or email? (Assessing responsiveness and cooperation)
- Are there messages you feel have been misinterpreted or taken out of context? Can you explain? (Evaluating reliability of presented evidence)

By reviewing ESI data and interviewing the parents about the content, we can learn how parents communicate with others and interpret communication from others.

- Are messages reported as antagonistic or patronizing but do not appear to be so?
- Is a parent able to maintain a rational and calm style of communication in the face of clearly antagonistic behavior?
- Are the content and tone of the parent's messages with others consistent with how they represent their communication style during the interview or consistent with how collaterals report a parent's communication?

Insight: Understanding Parental Attitudes and Emotional Stability

Beyond direct communication, ESI can provide deeper insight into a parent's attitudes, beliefs, and emotional stability through social media posts, blogs, online forums, and other forms of digital expression. Evaluators should consider whether a parent's online behavior reflects a stable, responsible approach to parenting or raises concerns about impulsivity, hostility, or an inability to support the child's relationship with the other parent. For instance, a parent who frequently posts derogatory comments about their coparent on social media, encourages public disparagement, or engages in hostile online exchanges may demonstrate an ongoing pattern of conflict that could impact the child's well-being. Additionally, social media activity may provide insight into a parent's lifestyle, including substance use, risky behavior, or extreme ideological views that could affect their parenting capacity.

To assess parental attitudes and emotional stability, consider the following interview questions:

- Can you explain your approach to social media and how you decide what to share? (Assessing awareness of digital footprint)

- Have any online interactions caused conflict in your coparenting relationship? How was it addressed? (Identifying conflict dynamics)
- How do you discuss or reference the other parent in digital spaces where the child may be exposed? (Evaluating disparagement risks)
- Do you feel your online presence accurately represents you as a parent? Why or why not? (Exploring digital self-presentation)

Insightfulness is a parents' capacity to see and feel things from the child's point of view (Drozd et al., 2016). Rooted in Ainsworth and Bowlby's work, the research on insightfulness has grown and been applied to child custody evaluations. "Parental insightfulness provides the basis for sensitive caregiving and for secure child–parent attachment" (Drozd et al., 2016, p. 56). By interviewing parents about ESI data, we can learn whether they demonstrate insight into how their actions potentially benefit or harm the relationship between the minor children and themselves, the minor child and the other parent, or the minor child and their social circles.

- Do they make blatant public posts denigrating their ex?
- Are they publicly members of online communities that could directly or indirectly harm the opposite parent's relationships?
- How, if at all, do they modify their online presence in response to being made aware of the implications of such behavior?

Monitoring: Evaluating Surveillance and Parental Oversight

As technology enables greater digital monitoring, evaluators must be attuned to cases where a parent's use of surveillance crosses the line into behaviors that may be one aspect of coercive control. Global positioning system (GPS) tracking apps, spyware, excessive digital restrictions, and unauthorized access to the other parent's private communications can indicate an unhealthy dynamic that affects both the parent–child relationship and coparenting interactions. A parent who routinely monitors their coparent's social media activity, hacks into email accounts, or installs tracking software on the child's devices may be engaging in controlling behaviors that warrant closer scrutiny. Similarly, excessive restrictions on a child's digital access—such as blocking all communication with the other parent without a justified reason—may raise concerns about parental alienation or undue influence.

However, evaluators must also distinguish between reasonable parental oversight and inappropriate monitoring. Parents have a legitimate interest in ensuring their children's online safety, particularly with younger children, and the use of parental controls or location-sharing apps is not inherently problematic. The key factor is whether monitoring behavior is necessary, proportionate, and in the child's best interest rather than a means of exerting control over the coparent.

To assess surveillance and parental oversight, consider the following interview questions:

- How do you monitor or oversee your child's digital activity, and what is your reasoning behind it? (Assessing parental intent)
- Does the other parent have access to your child's digital communication? If so, under what circumstances? (Exploring boundaries and access)
- Have there been disagreements over monitoring practices? How were they addressed? (Assessing parental cooperation)
- What guidelines or digital rules does your child follow in both households? (Identifying consistency or conflicts in parenting approaches)

Context: Understanding the Significance of ESI

Perhaps the most critical aspect of evaluating ESI is ensuring that digital evidence is authentic, reliable, and contextually relevant. Misinterpretations, selective presentation, and fabricated evidence are common challenges in family law cases, making it essential for evaluators to apply a rigorous verification process. Before drawing conclusions, evaluators must assess whether messages, social media posts, or other digital evidence have been altered, whether screenshots reflect full conversations, and whether timestamps indicate consistent patterns rather than isolated incidents. Additionally, evaluators should consider the motivations behind digital disclosures—whether evidence is being presented objectively or strategically to support a particular narrative.

Another crucial aspect of understanding ESI is recognizing its limitations. Digital communication does not capture tone, intent, or the full context of an interaction. For example, a sarcastic or joking message may appear hostile when read without context. Similarly, a single angry exchange may not reflect the overall nature of the parent–child or coparenting relationship. Evaluators must rely on multiple data points, including collateral sources, behavioral observations, and historical patterns, to ensure that digital evidence is interpreted accurately.

To understand the context of the ESI data being examined, consider the following interview questions:

- What do you believe is the most important digital evidence in this case, and why? (Assessing parental perceptions)
- Do you feel any digital evidence has been misrepresented? How so? (Evaluating claims of manipulation)
- Can you provide additional context for certain digital exchanges that have been questioned? (Clarifying intent and tone)
- How has digital evidence influenced this custody dispute? Have any decisions been made based on ESI? (Understanding legal and emotional impacts)

Since children often understand technology better than their parents, it is often the case that children have their parents' passwords (Choong et al., 2019) and access to their online communication. While there are not yet studies to inform us how much children know of their parents' emails with attorneys, texts with the other parent, or other online behavior, the emerging research suggests that children know a tremendous amount. Therefore, not only do we recommend reviewing ESI data with both parents, we also recommend asking the child open-ended questions about their access to technology and their parent's attempts to monitor their access.

Applying a Balanced and Ethical Approach to ESI in Forensic Evaluations

The rise of digital evidence in family law evaluations presents both opportunities and challenges. While ESI can provide valuable insights into coparenting dynamics, parental behavior, and potential risks to the child, it must be analyzed critically, contextually, and ethically. By categorizing digital evidence into communication, insight, monitoring, and context, evaluators can apply a structured approach that enhances the reliability of forensic assessments while mitigating risks of bias and misinterpretation. Additionally, incorporating targeted interview strategies ensures that evaluators gather crucial contextual information, cross-check digital data with lived experiences, and provide courts with well-supported, objective recommendations that prioritize the best interests of the child.

There are at least two ways to apply the structured factors described prior into a parenting plan interview. One way is to develop a set of hypotheses, and the other way is to develop a set of custody specific questions.

Hypothesis Testing

Using hypothesis testing (in which the null hypothesis is that the data does not inform us about parenting), we encourage evaluators to assess ESI data with these questions:

- Does this inform us on the parent's communication with others? (Fuhrmann & Zibbell, 2012, p. 170)
- Does this inform us about the parent's interpretation of information?
- Does this inform us on the parent's insight? (Koren-Karie & Oppenheim, 2018; Oppenheim & Koren-Karie, 2012, 2014)
- Does this inform us on the parent's understanding of social media? (Canadian Pediatric Society, 2019; Coyne et al., 2017)
- Does this inform us on how effectively a parent monitors their children's social media? (Canadian Pediatric Society, 2019; Coyne et al., 2017)

Our second author has presented a structured protocol for organizing ESI data into eight categories. Evaluators are encouraged to organize the ESI data they review into these categories for future interviews:

- Examples of how each parent communicates with others
- Examples of how each parent interprets communication from others
- Examples of each parent's parenting skills, as described or evidenced in social media
- Examples of each parent not acting in the child's best interest, as evidenced by not following medical, psychological or educational recommendations
- Examples of each parent's insight, or lack thereof, into how their actions potentially benefit or harm relationships with the children
- Examples of each parent's insight, or lack thereof, into how their actions potentially benefit or harm relationships with the other parent
- Examples of each parent's understanding of social networking and technology
- Examples of how well each parent monitors and controls a child's access to information

We emphasize that data from ESI is rarely in and of itself dispositive. Therefore, we have documented ways in which an evaluator can use a multimethod, multisource process for investigating ESI data. When there are concerns about how children and adolescents are exposed to social media, monitored regarding screen time use, and are influenced by their parents' social media involvement, evaluators might structure interviews around the ideas presented above. Evaluators might begin by talking with each family member about their respective social media use. What do they use? When do they engage in each of the identified social media platforms? How often do they utilize each social media platform? What feedback has each family member provided to other family members about their social media involvement?

On the positive side, the evaluator might examine the benefit of social media use by each family member. In some families, it is likely that everyone will have the same positive experiences of social media use while in other families, social media use is a source of conflict. The evaluator should explore with each family member their respective experience of their own social media use and their experience of social media use by each family member.

Investigating the rules around social media use is also important. Exploring how, if at all, each person's social media use is monitored or supervised is important. Using the category system described above, evaluators might want to categorize parents into autonomy restrictive versus autonomy granting rules. How, or whether, parents use social media as a reward or punishment might also be informative. Talking with each child about their experience of each parent in their application of social media as a reward or punishment might yield useful information. Seeking information about how, or whether, social media use has been a source of parental conflict or a source of parent–child conflict or a source of sibling conflict are also areas ripe for examination. Categorizing parental monitoring and supervision of children's social media use might also be viewed along a continuum from high to low control, as described above. How social media is used to monitor or supervise each child and whether the monitoring or supervision of social media use is consistently enforced is an additional area to examine.

Investigating parental social media use and children's feelings and experiences about it might yield interesting data about family functioning and parent–child relationships. Knuth (2020) suggested examining how emails, texts, and other forms of social media are increasingly used in parent-to-parent communication and in parent-to-child communication. We have taken his ideas of examining parents' emails, texts, and other forms of social media used in custody litigation and suggested that evaluators can gain significantly important information from collateral informants who have personal knowledge of parent, child, and parent–child use of social media.

CONCLUSION

Collateral interviews and record reviews are essential to ensuring that PPEs are based on verifiable evidence rather than subjective accounts. By integrating third-party observations, historical and current records, and ESI, evaluators can enhance the reliability of their PPEs and minimize the likelihood that biases could otherwise distort findings. A well-conducted evaluation requires an investigative approach rather than passive acceptance of parental reports. Evaluators should seek collateral data from diverse sources, including teachers, medical professionals, and childcare providers, using structured interviews that focus on behavioral observations rather than opinions. Reviewing school, medical, legal, and mental health records can help identify patterns that provide insight into family dynamics, parental capacity, and potential risks to the child. Ensuring that both parents and children have an opportunity to respond to collateral information strengthens the fairness, transparency, and validity of the assessment.

As digital communication increasingly plays a role in family disputes, evaluators must be diligent in analyzing ESI, such as text messages, emails, and social media posts. While such evidence can offer valuable insights into parental behavior and parent–child interactions, evaluators must consider authenticity, authorship, and context before drawing conclusions. Selective or manipulated digital evidence can create misleading narratives, and evaluators should take a structured approach to its review, ensuring that findings are supported by corroborating information rather than isolated messages.

To enhance fairness and accuracy, evaluators must be mindful of potential biases and apply a trauma-informed perspective, particularly when assessing cases involving abuse or coercive control. Actively seeking information that challenges initial impressions, rather than reinforcing preexisting assumptions, helps prevent or control confirmation bias. By adopting standard protocols for ESI analysis and refining interview techniques, evaluators can gather a more comprehensive understanding as an element of their multimethod, multisource evaluation.

V

COMMON ISSUES IN PARENTING PLAN EVALUATION

19

Early Conceptualizations of Parent–Child Contact Problems

Over the past several decades, much has changed in how mental health professionals conceptualize issues involving disruptions in children's relationships with their parents, what is now referred to as parent–child contact problems (PCCP). Earlier texts and chapters we have authored, as well as those by others, focused primarily on alienation dynamics (Ackerman et al., 2019; Galatzer-Levy et al., 2002; Gould, 2006; Gould & Martindale, 2007; P. M. Stahl, 1999) or conceptualizing the analysis of alienation along an abuse versus estrangement versus alienation continuum (Drozd & Olesen, 2004). Today, there is an increased awareness that disruptions to children's relationships with their parents have their roots in a variety of reasons, only one of which may be alienation dynamics (Drozd et al., 2016; Garber, 2024; Saini et al., 2017).

This chapter examines the historical evolution of PCCP, tracing the trajectory from early models that focused on parental alienation syndrome (PAS) to contemporary, multidimensional approaches that integrate insights from psychological science, forensic assessment, and family systems theory. The chapter explores the contentious debates surrounding PAS and the broader implications of diagnostic labeling in family court proceedings. Given the complexity of these cases, a movement toward behavior-focused evaluations—rather than rigid diagnostic categories—has gained traction, with professionals emphasizing the importance of assessing both parental and child contributions to contact resistance. Through a critical examination of contemporary research, clinical practices, and forensic methodologies, this chapter aims to provide professionals with the tools to navigate the evolving landscape of PCCP. By laying the

https://doi.org/10.1037/0000474-020
Parenting Plan Evaluations: An Evidence-Informed Approach to Child Custody, by J. W. Gould and C. M. Mulchay

groundwork for subsequent discussions on assessment, intervention, and legal decision making, this chapter sets the stage for a more sophisticated, evidence-driven approach to addressing parent–child contact problems in family law cases.

A BRIEF HISTORY OF HOW PROFESSIONALS VIEW PARENT–CHILD CONTACT PROBLEMS

In both mental health and family law, there has been a continuous and often profound evolution in how professionals conceptualize and address disruptions in parent–child relationships. Once predominantly viewed through the lens of parental alienation, these disruptions—now more broadly referred to as PCCP—are increasingly recognized as multifaceted issues arising from a complex interplay of psychological, relational, and situational factors.

The field has progressed from the early 1980s conceptualization of PCCP as the result of the mother influencing her child to view the father as unfit, unsafe, dangerous, and unloving (R. A. Gardner, 1987) to the early 1990s in which PCCP was viewed as the result of either parent negatively influencing a child (R. A. Gardner, 1998). The early 2000s brought a reconceptualization of PCCP that included the need to understand family relationship history, child developmental factors, and family system influence (J. B. Kelly & Johnston, 2001). The mid-2000s saw a refinement that included a procedure to differentiate PCCP from abuse (Drozd & Olesen, 2004). The most recent evolution of PCCP builds upon both the family systems perceptive of earlier work integrated with an ecological model (Garber, 2020a; Johnston & Sullivan, 2020). While earlier frameworks primarily focused on distinguishing what was then called alienation from estrangement or abuse, contemporary perspectives advocate for a more nuanced, evidence-based understanding that accounts for the diverse pathways leading to a child's resistance or refusal to maintain contact with a parent (Garber, 2020a; Johnston & Sullivan, 2020; Judge & Deutsch, 2016).

The shift in professional discourse reflects a growing awareness that PCCP cannot be fully understood or addressed through a singular explanatory model such as the dominant factor theories (Bernet & Baker, 2024; Garber & Simon, 2024) that we will discuss in this and the next chapter. Historically, the field was shaped by theories that positioned parental alienation as a primary explanation for contact resistance (R. A. Gardner, 1987). About 25 years ago, a multidimensional perspective was introduced that provided a conceptual framework about relationship development that ranged from healthy relationships to aligned relationships to allied relationships to estranged relationships to alienated relationships (e.g., J. B. Kelly & Johnston, 2001). Integrating the multidimension perspective with concerns about abuse, the abuse-estrangement-alienation continuum (Drozd & Olesen, 2004) provided essential conceptual tools for distinguishing abuse from alienation in these complex cases. However, as research expanded and evolved, it became evident that disruptions in parent–child relationships could stem from a range of influences, including family conflict, attachment dynamics, parental behaviors, child temperament, developmental factors, and even broader contextual stressors such as litigation-induced pressure (Johnston & Sullivan, 2020).

The five-factor model (FFM) of personality (Soto & Jackson, 2013)—not to be confused with the five-factor model of PCCP dynamics—offers a structured framework for evaluating claims of alienation, ensuring that conclusions are drawn based on empirical evidence rather than assumptions. The ecological model (EM) we have been presenting in this book highlights the multiple interacting layers—ranging from family dynamics to social and legal systems—that shape a child's experience and perception of parental relationships. Additionally, the multifactor model (MFM) emphasizes the necessity of considering case-specific nuances, reinforcing the importance of individualized assessments rather than one-size-fits-all solutions.

Broadly speaking, the change in how professionals view parent–child contact problems represents a move away from adversarial, zero-sum perspectives to more integrative, family-oriented solutions. The legal system's adversarial structure can exacerbate polarization between parents, fostering narratives that position one parent as entirely good and the other as entirely bad, rather than recognizing the more complex and dynamic nature of parent–child relationships. We support the move toward a more collaborative approach that prioritizes the best interests of the child while fostering healthier parent–child relationships whenever possible.

PARENTAL ALIENATION SYNDROME

In our opinion, part of the contentious debate has come from arguments about the concept of alienation and the tendency to formulate concerns about children's resistance to spend time with a parent as either alienation or abuse (Drozd & Olesen, 2004). Since 1985, when Richard A. Gardner brought attention to the concept of parental alienation syndrome and the controversies surrounding the initial formulations, professionals on both sides of the controversy have poorly served parents, attorneys, and the courts by turning an important scientific observation about the extent to which some parental behavior has negatively influenced children's perceptions of and behavior toward the other parent exist into a strawman argument.

We support those in the custody world who are bringing ideas into the marketplace of ideas that focus attention on the myriad of possible ways that children might resist or refuse contact with a parent, with alienation being only one of many possible reasons (Garber, 2004). The heated controversies over single factor versus multifactor models of resist and refusal dynamics often overlook the similarities in their respective conceptual models (Warshak, 2020b).

Many colleagues who continue the contentious debate about alienation—as distinct from those who are attempting to find common ground and seek family-oriented solutions—appear engaged in a zero-sum game. Zero-sum games need a winner and a loser. We know of no mental health training program that uses a zero-sum game approach to psychotherapy or research. The attorneys, however, approach the litigation context being trained as zero-sum game thinkers. Attorneys are often trained from the first day in law school to think in terms of winners and losers. Similarly, parents engaged in high conflict custody litigation fall into zero-sum game thinking: What is good for the mother is bad for the father.

In contrast to a zero-sum approach, mediation is based upon a win-win approach to problem solving. The goal is for each parent to feel that the agreed upon solution was a win-win for each parent and a win for the children. How the important theoretical, conceptual, and research models examining PCCP have evolved into a zero-sum game is of great concern.

For more than 60 years, some social scientists and legal professionals have questioned the legitimacy of parental alienation as a concept and its admissibility in child abuse and child custody litigation (Milchman et al., 2020a, 2020b). We continue to be amazed at peer-reviewed articles that have persisted in their arguments over whether Gardner's original formulation of PAS is a viable, evidence-based model. As far back as 1993, Myers argued about the challenges to the admissibility of syndrome evidence (Myers, 1993), citing concerns about the evidentiary basis of Gardner's 8 symptoms that defined PAS. Given the increased attention to evidence-based testimony required in states that are controlled by *Daubert* and its progeny, we believe that empirically based challenges to syndrome models such as PAS would undergo significantly more scrutiny today than was reflected in Myer's concern in 1993.

Some scholars have provided balanced, nuanced, and evidence-informed models of PCCP factors, stressing the need to move beyond arguments over labels (Garber, 2020a) and toward research that systematically investigates the evidence-basis of different conceptual family systems models. Gould described behaviors that interfered with or thwarted a child's relationship with one or both parents rather than in the legal or political debate about whether or not the observed behavior was or was not an example of PAS (Gould, 1998). Similar arguments continue to be made by present-day scholars about the need to focus attention on developing a vocabulary that reliably and validly describes family system dynamics rather than focusing attention on diagnostic labels (Gould, 1998). We support those authors who make similar arguments about the need to address behaviors rather than diagnostic labels (Garber, 2020a; Garber et al., 2022; Milchman et al., 2020a).

THE IMPORTANCE OF FOCUSING ON BEHAVIORS, NOT DIAGNOSES

Kleinman reminds us about the importance of operational definitions. Providing clear definitions of concepts drawn from emerging models to explain behaviors that have yet to be tied to evidence-based or evidence-informed theoretical models is critical in order to avoid misunderstandings (Kleinman, 2021). The language used to describe emerging concepts needs to be defined to reduce the likelihood of misunderstanding (Kleinman, 2021). When the consumer of information is the court, incorrect or imprecise language might lead to the court's misunderstanding or misinterpretation of the concept, incorrect or unreliable application of the concept to the facts of the case, and misguided and untrustworthy expert opinions (Toby Kleinman, personal communication, May 17, 2024).

Milchman et al. (2020a, p. 340) take Kleinman's concern a step further focusing on the problems created in child custody evaluations by including "evaluative labels or diagnoses instead of descriptions of behavioral functioning." Although Milchman's concern is with the "oversimplified beliefs, implicit or explicit, about alienation that support such practice" (Milchman, 2022b, p. 101), her concerns about the problematic use of diagnostic labels should be generalized to other mental health concepts that have found their way into our vocabulary. Many commonly used diagnostic-sounding terms found in custody reports are often poorly defined or reflect a simplicity that does a disservice to the complexity of behaviors seen in conflicted family systems.

"Professionals demonstrate oversimplified beliefs that lend unjustified credibility to alienation claims when they assert or imply that they observed alienation directly rather than inferring it from behavioral observations; that their inferences are unambiguous in their meaning; and that the validity of their inferences is not compromised by difficult-to-detect risks to the child" (Milchman, 2022b, p. 101).

Our concern is that presenting expert testimony that oversimplifies beliefs or is based upon poorly defined concepts is likely to have undue influence on the court. Given what is known about the weight often given to expert testimony by the courts (Faigman et al., 2016), it should be an obligation of all testifying experts to describe psychological concepts that are the basis of testimony in a manner consistent with the evidence-based definition of those terms.

Milchman's second point is the inherent dangers in offering expert testimony-based inferences drawn from assertions or implications that a particular problematic behavior must be the result of some insidious parental actions without tying the assertions or implications to specific behaviors. Recall our discussion earlier in the book about the importance of tying opinions to observable behaviors. Expert opinions that have no clear link to observed behavior are likely to be challenged by cross examining attorneys with regards to the analytic gap between opinions and the data—or lack of data—upon which the opinion is based. Basing expert opinions on inferences that are coupled with the presentation that inferences are ambiguous does a disservice to the court.

Scientific inquiry seldom, if ever, produces unambiguous results. The purpose of science is to continually challenge previous findings in order to test, support, and challenge hypotheses. Unambiguous conclusions might be the province of attorney-based advocacy. Unambiguous conclusions stated in psychological expert testimony are likely spoken by someone who does not understand the scientific process or who places advocacy ahead of the cautiousness inherent in competent scientific testimony.

Science is a form of arrogance control. Expert testimony based upon scientific knowledge should reflect the understanding that scientists speak in terms of likelihood or probability (Stebbins, 2001). There are no unambiguous expert opinions in child custody matters (S. R. Gross & Mnookin, 2003).

Garber has been among the most prolific voices to date drawing attention to the potential multiple reasons why children might resist or refuse contact with a parent (Garber, 2020b, 2024). Potential harm exists when one assumes that a child's resistance or refusal to spend time with a parent is the result only of alienation dynamics operating in the family system. "The custody evaluator who approaches these matters through a deductive process, seeking data that support an a priori theory (that the child is alienated), is vulnerable to confirmatory bias and doing harm to the child whose interests are paramount" (Garber, 2020b, p. 386). Garber proposes 13 variables, which are not mutually exclusive, to be considered by evaluators in order to more fully identify why a particular child is resisting or refusing contact with one parent.

We address Garber's model in greater detail later.

INTENTIONAL OR UNINTENTIONAL NEGATIVE INFLUENCE ON CHILDREN

Some parents in conflicted separation or divorce situations engage in a process in which they intentionally and negatively influence their children's perception of the other parent. Some of these intentional acts thwart the child's perception of the other parent. There is not a single motivation that characterizes all parents who engage in such acts. For example, some parents might engage in these intentional acts to thwart their child's perception of the other parent out of fear that the child will align with the other parent. Other parents might act out of deep-seated dependency needs, feeling a need to create an enmeshment (defined later) between parent and child. A third motivation to intentionally thwart a child's perception of the other parent might lie in unresolved anger and vengeance toward that parent.

Some parents are unaware of the ways in which their behaviors toward the other parent might influence a child to align or to take sides in the marital conflict. Subtle, unspoken attitudes and opinions about the other parent that a parent believes are not displayed to their child might also influence the child's perception (Principe & London, 2022).

Several studies have shown that children are influenced by one parent's feelings, attitudes, and beliefs about the other parent despite parental attempts to shield their children from such influence. These studies have shown that children develop and hold ideas about the other parent consistent with the parent's beliefs (Principe & London, 2022). Parents who provide their children with more structure and control in discussions about the other parent and their binuclear family increase the likelihood of children developing a false narrative about family events. When parents are motivated to provide their children with accurate accounts of family experiences, paradoxically, children have been found to produce more false information:

> The influence of parents' contributions is evident not only during parent–child discussions but also later during formal interviews with children by an unfamiliar person who employs neutral open-ended questioning strategies. Importantly, children may recall little about the initial parent–child conversations, even if the conversations were highly suggestive. Young children are unlikely to recognize the suggestive nature of even highly leading conversations. (Principe & London, 2022, p. 289)

Regardless of whether it is intentional or unintentional, behaviors that negatively influence children's perception of the other parent and result in resistance or refusal to spend time with that other parent, thwarting parent–child relationships is, by definition, not in the psychological best interests of the child.

PARENT–CHILD CONTACT PROBLEMS AND ATTACHMENT

Alienating behavior interferes with the attachment process and, therefore, is a primary risk to children's best psychological interests (Garber, 2004, 2009). When a parent engages in behaviors that have the potential to adversely affect children's relationship with the other parent, they are often conceptualized as alienating strategies. These strategies may be seen as tools that interfere with the developing or existing attachment relationship between the child and the target parent.

Current attachment theory and research suggests that infants are best served with strong emotional ties with each parent, who ensures infants' safety by inducing them to seek closeness with them when there is perceived or real danger (Madigan et al., 2024). Certain biologically determined experiences are believed to activate the attachment system, resulting in the infant seeking comfort and closeness to the caregiver who historically has provided safety and comfort when needed, such as during illness, darkness, being alone, being in an unfamiliar environment, and when strangers are present. When these signals of potential danger are triggered, the infant seeks proximity and comfort from the attachment figure. If that figure is appropriately responsive to the infant's comfort-seeking behavior, they learn to trust that person and continue to seek comfort from that person in the future. *Safe haven* has often been used to describe the child's perception of the safety, security, and trust of the parent.

When the attachment figure is not emotionally or physically available, the infant either becomes preoccupied with gaining such comfort from that parent (if the parent is unpredictably available) or accepts that the parent is not available and ceases seeking to gain comfort from that parent (if the parent is predictably unavailable). For infants to desire comfort and closeness to the care-taking adult, they have to develop a sense over time that the adult is emotionally and physically available. As children develop and mature, the types of situations that activate the need for comfort and proximity to a caregiver change, but the underlying function of the attachment relationship remains the same (Ackerman et al., 2019).

Parents who interfere with the young child's ability to form and maintain continuous contact with the other parent appear to intuitively understand that a child's experience of the other parent as a safe haven is to discourage the child to believe that the target parent is not emotionally or physically available. One result would be that the child would cease seeking comfort from and contact with the target parent. Safe haven parents often give the opposite message, namely that the target parent is untrustworthy, unsafe, and unavailable and limits contact between the child and target parent which impedes that parent's function as an attachment figure. The target parent has fewer opportunities to provide comfort to the child, to take care of the child when ill, to soothe the child when afraid, and to be with the child as a primary care-taking parent.

Often it is concluded that the safe haven parent engages in alienating behaviors. The alienating parent creates a narrative that teaches the child that their primary attachment figure (the custodial parent) would be less emotionally and physically available if the children developed a positive relationship with the target parent. The child's insecurity is thought to become about their relationship with both the target parent and with the custodial parent. Insecurity in the custodial parent–child relationship is reduced when the child pleases that parent by turning against the target parent, thereby removing the threat of the custodial parent becoming emotionally or physically unavailable. Children receive double messages from the alienating parent: (a) the target parent is not safe and is unavailable for the child with whom to have a relationship, and (b) pursuing a relationship with the target parent would entail loss for the child of the relationship with the custodial parent.

FALSE NARRATIVES

An additional concern is the child's development of a false narrative that, when repeated often enough without challenge, becomes the child's belief that both parents are rigidly positioned to reflect the alienating parent's view of each parent. When children are brought into mental health treatment by the alienating parent with the intention of helping the child and without the frequent input from the target parent, the treatment becomes a tool used by the alienating parent to solidify the false narrative (L. R. Greenberg et al., 2003). In therapy, the child discusses the false narrative and develops a fear of the factors and people contained in those narratives.

Many clinically trained therapists are unfamiliar with the research on children's suggestibility and the literature describing the dynamics of high conflict families and the treatment of children living in those families (L. R. Greenberg et al., 2003). One result is that therapists often unknowingly contribute to the child's negative perception and false narrative about the target parent (L. R. Greenberg et al., 2003). It is also not unusual for these narratives to contain unsupported allegations of domestic violence, intimate partner violence, or coercive control which the child embraces as part of their history. The child's embrace of the false narrative often leads to the development of fear responses that are interpreted by the therapist and parent as reasons to suspend or limit the child from spending time with the target parent. These responses are often viewed by therapists as indicators of a trauma reaction. The child is treated as a victim of trauma and the source of the child's trauma—the false narrative that Parent B is the danger—must be avoided.

There is an alternative literature that questions the robust findings from children's suggestibility literature, among them Thomas Lyon, Karen Saywitz, and Gail Goodman (Lyon, 2002a; Saywitz & Lyon, 2002; Saywitz et al., 2002). What is fascinating about this literature as represented by Ceci, Lamb, Poole, Bruck, Lyon, Saywitz, and Goodman is their recognition that each is looking at the same behavior and each developing reasonable, evidence-based perspectives that capture the pros and cons of this challenging area of research.

A minority opinion challenges the development of false narratives in PCCPs. Blizard and Shaw argue that "studies on the suggestibility of children show that they cannot easily be persuaded to provide detailed disclosures of abuse" (Blizard & Shaw, 2019, p. 20; Shaw, 2019). Review of their articles and the reference sections in their articles reveals that they included none of the research conducted by Stephen Ceci, Michael Lamb, Maggie Bruck, or Debra Poole about children's suggestibility (Brown & Lamb, 2019; Bruck et al., 2008; Ceci & Bruck, 2006, 2007; Ceci et al., 2016; LaRooy et al., 2013).

The exclusion of research by these and other scholars, who have systematically examined children's suggestibility, suggests that the Shaw material is an advocacy argument rather than a review of scholarly research. As discussed previously in this book, an important part of the scientific process is to seek out information that refutes as well as supports one's position. Exclusion of alternative perspectives on the development of false narratives is contrary to the importance being voiced in this book and contrary to how expert witnesses need to be prepared for trial testimony. Remember, *Daubert* requires that an expert has considered reasonable alternative explanations of the data.

One common theme among many researchers is how the historical basis of alienation dynamics and its binary position continues to raise its head in peer-reviewed publications. We believe a careful reading of many of the primary authors in the field such as Baker, Bernet, Deutsch, Garber, Johnston, Joshi, Milchman, Pruett, Saini, Sullivan, and Warshak find similar attention to the multiple causes that creates problems in children's relationships with their parents. Most of the differences are more apparent than real accentuating differences that reflect matters of degree rather than kind.

There are, and will likely continue to be, arguments about what models best capture various dynamics that characterize different PCCPs. Part of the problem in the field is the assumption that a single model can capture all or most types of PCCPs. As Warshak noted, "It is not surprising that multiple threads form the tapestry of a child's irrational aversion to a parent; this is true for nearly every psychological disturbance in childhood" (Warshak, 2015). No one solution will fix all possible problems.

CURRENT CONTROVERSIES IN PARENT–CHILD CONTACT PROBLEMS: THE FIVE-FACTOR MODEL, THE ECOLOGICAL MODEL, AND MULTIFACTOR MODELS

The Spring 2024 issue of *Family Transitions* published a series of articles addressing conceptual similarities and differences in the five-factor and multifactor models. The FFM has been described as the single factor theory, more accurately described as the dominant factor theory (Drozd et al., 2022), is based on the FFM of parental alienation. The FFM is based upon the belief that there are five factors used to diagnose parental alienation. These factors are

- The child's resistance or refusal to have contact (i.e., a relationship) with one of the parents;
- The presence of a prior positive relationship between the child and the now-rejected parent;
- The absence of abuse, neglect, or seriously deficient parenting on the part of the now-rejected parent;
- The use of multiple alienating behaviors on the part of the favored parent; and
- The presence of many of the eight behavioral manifestations of alienation on the part of the child (Bernet, 2020).

Garber and Simon's (2024a) recent critique of the FFM was thoughtful and a useful contribution to the field. They raised important challenges to the FFM. Bernet and Baker's response brought to light alternative arguments.

Garber and Simon (2024b) posit that the underlying science model best equipped to investigate PCCP is the EM that we have discussed throughout this book. Recall that the EM posits that an individual's environment is a nested arrangement of structures, each contained within the next. These structures are the microsystem, mesosystem, exosystem, macrosystem, and chronosystem. Each system is organized according to their presumed effect on the individual. The five systems are interrelated and the influence of one system on a child's development depends on its relationship with the others.

The elegance of the EM is its attention to multiple levels of potential influence on various aspects of family life. As we have discussed, the EM might examine an individual's behavior, a parent–child relationship, a family relationship, the influence of extended family, the influence of a community, the influence of culture, and other levels of potential influence on any one or more of the levels within the family system. It is a dimensional framework that acknowledges how multiple factors are likely to affect behavior and that the behavior that is affected by each or many of those multiple factors might lead to varied outcomes. The idea that similar experiences might lead to different outcomes and different experiences might lead to the same outcome is fundamental to the ideas of developmental psychopathology. That human behavior is determined only by dynamics within a dyad is contrary to the theoretical assumptions about what influences behavior.

Bernet and Baker (2024) argue that comparing the MFM to the FFM is inappropriate. The FFM was developed to look at a narrow issue: "While the EM broadly considers 15 or so reasons for PCCP, the FFM is narrower and pertains to only one of those scenarios, i.e., parental alienation." Bernet and Baker suggest that the EM might be best to examine "the broad, general analysis of all the reasons why a child might refuse to have contact with or have a relationship with one or both of their parents." Supporting Garber and Simon, Emery (2024) argues that the FFM reduces the complexity of family dynamics "to a simple either-or question: Is my ex-wife at fault for my bad relationship with my kids?"

Bernet and Baker argue that there are unique situations in which PCCP are the result of one parent's adverse influence on a child that results in that child's refusal or resistance to having contact with a parent. The FFM captures what they believe to be the most relevant factors to assess in those unique situations in which alienation is operating. Assuming that our interpretation of Bernet and Baker's argument is correct, we offer five questions to be examined in future research:

1. How does one determine that the five factors used to examine the child and the child's relationship with each parent are comprehensive enough to explain to the court the most relevant factors influencing the child?

2. What data support that these five factors contribute the most toward prediction of a reliable opinion that a child has been alienated?

3. Does it matter whether an evaluator employs the FFM or the MFM if the bottom line is identification of parental behavior that negatively affects the child, whether or not other factors are also contributing to the PCCP?

4. Does an evaluator's reliance on what Garber, Simon, and Emory view as an oversimplified understanding of the complexity of family dynamics mislead the court?

5. If the FFM provides the basis for a reliable opinion about PCCP but is based on fewer areas of functioning than the multifactor theory, is it ethical to provide expert opinions based upon a model that uses fewer data points as a basis for an expert opinion compared to a model that uses more data points drawn from factors that potentially paint a broader picture of family dynamics and influence?

It is likely that the ethical answer is "yes." Framed differently, minimal levels of reliable evaluative procedures are likely just as admissible as maximal levels. The question then becomes a moral question, not an ethical question: Should an expert opinion be based upon less than the best evidence?

Bernet and Baker appear to confuse the EM with the MFM, and that confusion may be due, in part, to the ways in which Garber and Simon discuss EM. The MFM of PCCP is based upon the EM but is designed to look specifically at PCCP. In their article, Garber and Simon appear to use the EM and the MFM of PCCP interchangeably, yet the components of the MFM examine the cause or causes of PCCP in the broader EM.

The challenge in the field is not the uncertainty of definition or the continued examination and reexamination of ideas. The challenge is finding ways to engage in constructive discussions about how best to assess PCCP while controlling the emotional and reactive responses that have often accompanied professional differences. There are some situations in which a parent engages in behaviors that damage their child's relationship with the other parent. In such situations, parental alienation, as originally defined and currently represented by the FFM, might be an accurate description. In other cases, the MFM characterized by the contributions by each family member or context and situational factors, might apply. Additional factors that influence a child's resistance to spending time with a parent might be independent of the factors described in the FFM or the MFM.

PCCP occur in complex cases (Fidler & Bala, 2010). Often, alienation is alleged when, in fact, alienation has not occurred, and alienating dynamics are not operating in the family system. When there is a factual basis to conclude that one parent is engaged in attempts to alienate a child from the other parent, interventions will vary depending on the degree of the alienation (Fidler & Bala, 2010). PCCP exist on a continuum from none to mild to moderate to severe. More severe alienation cases are unlikely to be responsive to therapeutic or psycho-educational interventions (Fidler & Bala, 2010). The mental health field continues to struggle to find therapeutic or psychoeducational interventions that move the family system from polarized and polarizing dynamics to healthier family dynamics.

Fidler and Bala (2010) argued that "the too often strongly gendered polemic on alienation and abuse is polarizing and needs to be replaced with a more nuanced and balanced discussion that recognizes the complexity of the issues so that the needs of children and families can be better met." It appears that Fidler and Bala were among the first to coin the term PCCP to capture the complexity of parent–child contact problems.

Warshak (2020a) suggests that PCCP is likely not the best descriptor of problems in contact. He cites to the manifest focus of the PCCP definition on behavioral problems. Problems in parent–child contact also include cognitive and affective dimensions.

Warshak (2020a) raised concerns about the limitation of the concept of PCCP when parent–child contact problems are revealed in fact-based alienation dynamics. When a child is unwilling to spend time with a parent and rejects that parent, the parent understands that the reason for the child's behavior is more than simple avoidance. Such behavior illustrates the child's distorted thoughts, feelings and memories about that parent and saying that the child is physically avoiding a parent misses the psychological components because the resistance includes those attitudes, feelings and negative thoughts about that rejected parent (Warshak, 2020a).

Understanding how children develop and maintain false narratives is an often-overlooked factor in attempts to help children remediate factually false narratives about the other parent. One frequent dynamic is that one parent will allege abuse and the other parent alleges alienation. More than 15 years ago, Gould and Martindale (2007) raised concerns about protecting a child from allegations of abuse might place the child with a parent who is nurturing a false narrative that becomes very difficult for the child to unlearn.

When there are competing allegations of abuse and alienation in high-conflict family matters, the court often will protect the child from the alleged perpetrator with little awareness that the determination to maintain the child with the abuse-alleging parent is, potentially, a biased perspective. In an emergency hearing in which the well-intentioned court moves to protect the child from alleged abuse, placement with the abuse-alleging parent places greater weight on the abuse allegation than the weight placed on an alienation allegation. In those cases, in which abuse is unfounded or unsupported, the child may have been exposed to multiple interviews, therapeutic intervention, and home-based discussions of the now unfound abuse allegations that the child views as their historical reality.

Evaluators must recognize that what is initially labeled as alienation might represent other, reasonable factors that affect a child's comfort and safety with a parent. As evaluators approach cases in which there are disruptions to parent–child relationships, whether or not the disruptions result in contact problems, it is important for evaluators to consider multiple causes of the behaviors of concern. Reflecting the ecological framework, systematically assessing each family member at the individual, dyadic, and family level by gathering data from multiple sources is critical. Formulation of multiple hypotheses that would include, but not be limited to, consideration of child physical abuse, child emotional abuse, exposure to various forms of violent and nonviolent aggression (i.e., domestic violence, intimate partner violence, and coercive control), reactive or poor parenting, parent–child mismatch regarding parenting attributes and child needs, and other rationally derived hypotheses.

JOHNSTON AND KELLY'S ALIENATED CHILD CONCEPT

Joan B. Kelly and Johnston (2001) proposed the concept of the *alienated child* as a more useful and robust conceptualization of alienation dynamics at work in high conflict families. They placed the emphasis on the child and their relationship with parents and recognized that there are many different factors at work in a family system that influence child behavior. They refocused alienation dynamics to examine the child, their observable behaviors, and parent–child relationships. They argued that the emphasis on an alienating parent wrongly focuses our attention on adult behavior when primary concern should be on how the child is influenced and how the child's relationships with each parent are affected. The child alienation model brought attention to the need to develop multiple alternative hypotheses to examine when there are allegations of alienation.

Distinguishing Alienated Children From Other Children Who Resist Parenting Time

An important task for evaluators is distinguishing the alienated child (who persistently refuses and rejects visitation because of unreasonable negative views and feelings) from other children who also resist contact with a parent after separation but for a variety of normal, realistic and developmentally predictable reasons. The frequency with which children are inappropriately labeled *alienated* and how a parent's questioning of the wisdom of visitation often is labeled as an *alienating parent*. They cite several hypotheses to consider explaining why children may resist visitation, emphasizing that "only in very specific circumstances does this behavior qualify as alienation" (J. B. Kelly & Johnston, 2001, p. 251). Among the reasons children may resist visits are

- concerns rooted in normal developmental processes (e.g., normal separation anxieties in the very young child),
- concerns rooted primarily in the high conflict marriage and divorce (e.g., fear, or inability to cope with the high conflict transition),
- concerns rooted in a child's response to a parent's parenting style (e.g., rigidity, anger, or insensitivity to the child),
- concerns rooted in the child's concern about an emotionally fragile custodial parent (e.g., fear of leaving this parent alone), and
- concerns rooted in the remarriage of a parent (e.g., behaviors of the parent or stepparent that alter willingness to visit).

A Continuum of Child–Parent Relationships After Separation and Divorce

Joan B. Kelly and Johnston (2001) brought into the PCCP discussion the importance of thinking dimensionally. They proposed a continuum of child–parent relationships after separation and divorce. Their five-point continuum ranges from positive to negative, with the most negative being alienation.

Positive Relationships to Both Parents

At the healthiest end of the continuum are the majority of separated children who have positive relationships with both parents. They value both parents and wish to spend significant (often equal) amounts of time with each parent.

Affinity With One Parent

The next step along the continuum are children who have an affinity for one parent while also desiring continuity and contact with both parents. Affinity for one parent is characterized by children feeling closer to one parent than the other. It may result from temperament, gender, age, shared interests, sibling preferences of parents, and parenting practices. Such affinities may shift over time with changing developmental needs and situations. These children may occasionally express an overt preference for a parent, but they still want substantial contact with and love from both parents (J. B. Kelly & Johnston, 2001).

Allied Children

The third step along the continuum are children who have developed an alliance with one parent. During the marriage or separation, these children demonstrate or express a consistent preference for one parent over the other. They often want limited contact with the nonpreferred parent after separation. Allied children generally do not fully reject the other parent, nor do they seek to terminate all contact. They tend to express some ambivalence toward this parent, including anger, sadness, and love, as well as resistance to contact.

Such alliances may have their roots in family dysfunction that preceded the divorce. Children may have been encouraged to take sides or to carry hostile messages between the parents. Alliances appear to occur more often in older children in response to the dynamics of the marital breakup. Older children tend to make moral assessments and judgments about which parent caused the breakup, who is most hurt, who is most vulnerable, and who needs and deserves the child's unfettered help and support. These strong alliances, and children's accompanying expressions of moral outrage and contempt, are usually short-lived if the child has an opportunity to process the separation with a therapist or trusted adult, or when the conflict subsides. Some of these children may also develop more hardened alignments or even resistance or refusal of contact with one parent in the context of a bitter divorce with protracted litigation and may result in strong resistance to visiting.

Evaluators need to distinguish aligned children from those who are alienated. Most aligned children acknowledge (sometimes begrudgingly) that they love the other parent yet focus attention on not enjoying time with that parent. These aligned children do not engage in the fierce, brittle remonstrations and cruel behaviors toward the rejected parent commonly observed in the alienated child. They often protect the preferred parent, who they perceive as wounded and needing their full attention.

Estranged Children

A fourth step along the continuum finds children who are realistically "estranged" from one of their parents as a consequence of that parent's history of family violence, abuse, or neglect. These children need to be clearly distinguished from alienated children. They have taken sides in the family because of a fact-based history of observing repeated violence or explosive outbursts of a parent during the marriage or after separation. Sometimes these children have been victims of violence and abusive behavior from an abusive parent. The only time they feel safe enough to reject the violent or abusive parent is after the separation when protected by their protective custodial parent.

These children do not have to directly witness violence. They may witness the aftermath of intimate partner violence or be traumatized by an act of violence that from an adult's perspective may not have been very serious or injurious. "The mix of intense anger towards the abusive parent, and phobic reactions to that parent caused by subconscious fear of retaliation looks like alienation. But unlike alienated children, the estranged children do not harbor *unreasonable* anger and/or fear" (Mercer & Drew, 2022).

Children who have suffered exposure to or been victims of abuse generally suffer from some type of traumatic stress reaction. Evaluators need to assess for trauma reactions, a theme emphasized in later PCCP writings by Milchman and others in the book edited by Mercer and Drew (2022). If no trauma reaction is identified, then one might wish to consider alienation among other possible alternative hypotheses.

The reasons children become estranged from a parent include

- severe parental deficiencies including persistent immature and self-centered behaviors;
- chronic emotional abuse of the child or preferred parent;
- physical abuse that goes undetected;
- characterologically angry, rigid, and restrictive parenting styles; and
- psychiatric disturbance or substance abuse that grossly interferes with parenting capacities and family functioning.

The responses of these realistically estranged children following separation are commonly and incorrectly interpreted and played out in custody disputes as alienation cases. The deficient, abusive, or violent parent frequently accuses the protective parent of alienating the child against them. They do not acknowledge how marital violence or severe parenting deficiencies negatively impacted their parent–child relationship. Subsequent research suggests that it is likely that children are unaware of how they might have been influenced by exposure to parental comments and actions (Principe & London, 2022).

The Alienated Child

At the extreme end of the continuum are children who are alienated from a parent after separation and divorce. They tend to express their rejection of that parent

1. stridently,
2. without apparent guilt or ambivalence, and
3. strongly resisting or completely refusing any contact with that rejected parent.

Often, a target parent has been less involved in the children's lives compared with the other parent or the target parent displays less robust parenting competencies. The children's complaints and allegations about the rejected parent may reflect some true incident that has been grossly distorted and exaggerated, resulting in the children holding highly negative views and feelings. It is the gross distortion and exaggeration without reality-based foundation that makes this a *pathological* response. Child alienation is a severe distortion on the child's part of the previous parent–child relationship. These children display an intensity, breadth, and ferocity of behaviors toward the parent they are rejecting that goes far beyond alliance or estrangement. They are responding to complex and frightening dynamics within the divorce process itself that includes an array of parental behaviors combined with their own vulnerabilities that make them susceptible to becoming alienated. Bona fide child alienation most often occurs in high conflict custody disputes and is an infrequent occurrence among the larger population of divorcing children, a fact too often lost among those engaged in custody litigation.

Kelly and Johnston's Evaluation Model

Joan B. Kelly and Johnston (2001) recommend an evaluation model based upon family systems theory. They propose a variety of factors to investigate as well as a set of reasonable alternative hypotheses, a requirement under *Daubert* for experts to demonstrate to the court that they have considered reasonable alternative explanations of the data.

Background factors are viewed as directly or indirectly impacting on the child. These may include, but are not limited to,

- history of intense marital conflict;
- a humiliating separation;
- subsequent divorce conflict and litigation that can be fueled by professionals and extended kin;
- personality dispositions of each parent; and
- child-related factors such as age, cognitive capacity, and temperament.

Intervening variables might moderate or intensify the child's response to critical background factors. Intervening variables may include

- parenting beliefs and behaviors,
- sibling relationships, and
- child's own vulnerabilities within the family dynamics.

Some children may be groomed to be alienated. Children may be exposed to several of these factors resulting in an increased risk for alienation in the future. Evaluators need to fully assess the influence of these alienating processes for preventive action to be taken, especially when children are younger. The presence of alienating processes and the display of typical alienating behaviors of parents do not reliably predict that a child will become alienated. It is hypothesized that alienation results from the intensity and longevity of children's exposure to these alienating processes in combination with other important parent and child variables.

Joan B. Kelly and Johnston (2001) suggest a set of "risk factors that potentiate alienation" (p. 255). Among these risk factors are

- triangulation of child in intense marital conflict;
- child experiences separation as deeply humiliating;
- parents are involved in highly conflicted divorce and litigation; and
- tribal warfare or the contributions of new partners, extended kin, and professionals.

Common Behaviors and Organizing Beliefs of the Aligned Parent

The continuous and negative representation of the other parent undermines the child's relationship with, confidence in, and love for the rejected parent. One result is intolerable confusion for the child that is most easily resolved by the child choosing to take sides with one parent rather than the other parent. The influence of these alienating behaviors on a child constitutes a form of emotional abuse because the effect of the parental behavior is intended to disrupt a child's healthy relationship development with a parent.

There are several *organizing beliefs* held by the aligned parent that help alienate the child from the other parent. These organizing beliefs are borne out of the aligned parent's deep psychological issues and reflect the aligned parent's deep distrust and fear of the ex-spouse. Often, the aligned parent is "absolutely convinced that [they are] at best irrelevant and at worst a pernicious influence on the child" (J. B. Kelly & Johnston, 2001, p. 257).

1. The first major organizing belief is that children do not need the other parent in their lives.
2. The second major organizing belief is that the aligned parent often fervently believes that the rejected parent is dangerous to the child in some way, either violent, physically or sexually abusive, or neglectful.
3. A third major organizing belief of the aligned parent is that the rejected parent does not and has never loved or cared about the child.

Aligned parents often create alliances with professionals who often mobilize and enable these parents to present themselves in a coherent, organized manner. In addition, the very nature of the adversarial process tends to polarize positions and parties, leading to increased hostility and dualistic thinking with little challenge. There is often significant pathology and anger in the aligned parent that encourages the child to reject the other parent. Often the aligned parent has problems with boundaries and differentiation from the child, severe separation anxieties, impaired reality testing, and projective identifications with the child all of which negatively affect the child's ability to remain on a healthy developmental trajectory.

Normal parenting does not include encouraging the complete rejection of the other parent. Even when there is history of child abuse, a history of parental mental illness, or when the child's safety is endangered, the average parent will seek different avenues and more rational means of protecting the child. Most parents recognize that their child loves the other parent despite the destructive behavior (J. B. Kelly & Johnston, 2001).

Behaviors of the Rejected Parent That Contribute to Child Alienation

Although lightly touched upon in previous formulations of alienation, J. B. Kelly and Johnston (2001) focus attention on the contribution of the rejected parent to the alienation process. They contend that the rejected parents' behaviors do not by themselves warrant the disproportionately angry response of the child nor the refusal to have contact. The rejected parent's involvement and parenting capacities are generally within a normative range though the rejected parent's parental-functioning may have become compromised by marital conflicts, divorce disputes, and the child's problematic response.

Several characteristics of the rejected parent may contribute to the alienation process. Among them are

- a tendency to become passive and withdraw in the face of conflict;
- a tendency to react to their child's harsh and unjustified treatment by becoming highly affronted and offended by the lack of respect and ingratitude afforded them;
- display of a parenting style characterized by a harshness, lack of empathy, and rigidity in their parenting style that does not, however, rise to the level of emotional or physical abuse;
- a tendency to display a self-centered, immature personality;
- a history of having displayed critical and demanding behaviors in parent–child interactions during the marriage leading to the aligned parent counterreacting to the perceived harshness and overcompensating by becoming even more lenient or overprotective with the child; and
- a tendency for the rejected parent to have difficulty in differentiating the needs and behaviors of the alienated child from the motivations and behaviors of the aligned parent.

Joan B. Kelly and Johnston (2001) provide a more thorough explanation of each of these tendencies and how both the alienated child and the aligning parent may react to the rejecting parent's behaviors. It is the richness of the family systems interpretation of each family member's interaction that moved the field toward a significantly more complex and subtle understanding of alienation dynamics.

Developmental Stage and Vulnerability of the Child to the Alienation Process

Another unique contribution of the child alienation model was recognition that not all children are subject to alienation. There are certain individual differences that may make one child more vulnerable to an alienation process. These may include differences in children's psychological, cognitive, and developmental strengths and vulnerabilities, and by external arrangements involving the rejected parent (J. B. Kelly & Johnston, 2001).

Among the most critical are

- the child's age and cognitive capacity;
- the child's feeling of abandonment by the rejected parent;
- the child's temperament and personality style;
- other parent–child relationship factors that may include the dependency of the child on the aligned parent, threats of abandonment by the aligned parent, the child's belief that she needs to protect and take care of the aligned parent, and an enmeshed parent–child relationship; and
- lack of external support for the child, including the child not being allowed to spend time with the rejected parent or his extended family.

Reflecting their family systems' approach, J. B. Kelly and Johnston (2001) also describe how the target parent may respond to a child's rejection of them. They note that the rejected parent, extended family, and other adults knowledgeable about the prior parent–child relationship are often confused about the change in the parent–child relationship. Most often, rejected parents have had at least an adequate relationship with these children, and the angry rejection is disproportionate to the context of the challenges faced by the child and by the context.

Joan B. Kelly and Jonston (2001) identified several common behaviors among alienated children as follows:

- The child strongly expresses resistance to visiting the rejected parent, and in more extreme cases, absolutely refuses to see the parent in any setting, including a therapeutic one, and a desire to unilaterally terminate the parent–child relationship.
- The child only wishes to talk to lawyers who represent their viewpoint, and to those custody evaluators and judges whom they believe will fully support their efforts to terminate the parent–child relationship,
- The child's manner of telling their story reveals replicas or slight variants of the aligned parents' allegations and stories about the rejected parent yet has little if any underlying substance, texture, or detail to support the allegations.

- The child may act towards the rejecting parent, grandparents, and other relatives in a hostile and disrespectful manner.
- The child often idealizes or speaks glowingly of the aligned parent as an adult and parent and refuses to consider any information that might undermine this viewpoint of their perfect companion and parent. The child vigorously rejects any suggestion that their obsessive hatred of the rejected parent has any relationship to the views or behaviors of the aligned parent.
- The child's social relationships are often impaired due to their polarized thinking style. They are likely to hold simplistic, black and white views of the world. They may express harshly strident views and feelings towards others that are reflected in their dealings with their peers as well as those in authority.
- The child's behavior in the rejected parent's home is severely problematic.

Foundation for Subsequent Innovations in Theory and Treatment

The Kelly and Johnston child alienation model set the stage for several profound changes that have emerged since its publication. One change is the increasing focus on differentiating what was then called alienation from other PCCP that result in children's resistance or refusal to spend time with a parent. A second change is the increasing focus on more complex models through which to examine PCCP. As we discussed last chapter, the current prevailing model—Bronfenbrenner's ecological model—offers avenues of investigative consideration incorporating multiple variables at multiple levels of individual, dyadic, family, and community functioning. A third change is the increasing attention on distinguishing different subtypes of behaviors within established categories (i.e., multiple factors that might create circumstances leading a child to resist contact with a parent yet not be alienated). A fourth change is the continued development of models that are intended to help distinguish alienation from abuse. Although more sophisticated models have built upon the original Drozd and Olesen model that we discuss below, the elegance and complexity of their model identifies areas of relevant investigative focus that serve evaluators well today. A fifth change is the continued scholarship and research into PCCP models. For example, see recent journal publications devoting significant amounts of space to discussion of PCCP such as the April 2020 issue of *Family Court Review* and the February 2024 issue of *Family Transitions.*

GATEKEEPING

The original research examining gatekeeping focused on intact families. Gatekeeping behaviors were conceptualized as the mothers' ability to regulate fathers' involvement with children (W. G. Austin, Fieldstone, & Pruett, 2013). Subsequent ideas elaborated to define maternal gatekeeping as a set of complex behavioral interactions between parents that examined mothers' regulation of father involvement through their use of controlling, facilitative, and restrictive behaviors. Initial views described gatekeeping behavior reflecting a mother's behavior directed at a father's childrearing and interactions with their children, either through the mother's support for or thwarting of the father–child interaction.

William G. Austin, Fieldstone, and Pruett (2013) were the first to apply the gatekeeping literature to matters involving child custody and parental access. Parental gatekeeping refers to parents' attitudes and actions that are intended to influence the quality of the other parent's relationship and involvement with their child. Parental gatekeeping was viewed as consistent with the common statutory best interest factor with regard to each parent supporting their child's relationship with the other parent. Parental gatekeeping was viewed as a critical factor to examine not only in child custody disputes, but also in relocation cases (W. G. Austin, 2011; W. G. Austin et al., 2016; W. G. Austin & Gould, 2006).

The W. G. Austin, Fieldstone, and Pruett (2013) parental gatekeeping model as applied to custody disputes has been conceptualized along a continuum varying from very restrictive to very facilitative in coparenting attitudes and actions. Austin argues that research examining restrictive gatekeeping is a basis for a general prediction of potential harm to the child (W. G. Austin, 2015a). For example, restrictive gatekeeping in a custody context often affects children's access to valuable social capital through the parents' restriction of contact with the other parent. One significant result of social capital restriction is the children's loss of contact with people and opportunities associated with the target parent and the myriad experiences from which the children might find valuable growth experiences but for the restrictions.

Austin stresses the importance for evaluators not to confuse restrictive gatekeeping attitudes and behaviors. At the time the Austin et al. model was developed, it was believed that restrictive or negative attitudes are normative among custody litigants and are unlikely to create risk of harm for the children unless directly exposed to such attitudes. More recent research by Principe and London (2022) has shown that children can be and often are influenced by exposure to attitudes, values, and beliefs whether or not they are directly exposed.

It is the behaviors associated with restrictive gatekeeping that are more likely to cause harm by interfering with children's abilities to form and maintain healthy contact with the target parent. It is more likely that children's adjustment will be affected more by the level and quality of parental involvement than by parental gatekeeping attitudes. Evaluators are encouraged to identify specific gate-closing and gate-opening behaviors in a gatekeeping assessment (W. G. Austin, Fieldstone, & Pruett, 2013).

An alternative model that has not yet entered into the child custody literature is the Puhlman and Pasley (2013) model. This model introduced a more nuanced dimensional model based on an eight-type model of parental gatekeeping reflecting three factors: control, encouragement, and discouragement. Their dimensional model expands on traditional gatekeeping concepts by showing how different levels of these dimensions influence a parent's involvement in coparenting. Here's an overview of the eight types:

1. *Facilitative encouragement* reflects high encouragement, low control, and low discouragement. For example, a parent actively supports and encourages the other parent's involvement in parenting with minimal restrictions.
2. *Passive encouragement* reflects moderate encouragement, low control, and low discouragement. For example, a parent allows and supports the other parent's involvement but does not take an active role in facilitating it.
3. *Active gate opening* reflects high encouragement, high control, and low discouragement. For example, a parent actively encourages and ensures the other parent's involvement while maintaining some control over parenting decisions.
4. *Inclusive gatekeeping* reflects moderate encouragement, moderate control, and low discouragement. For example, a parent supports the other parent's involvement but maintains an equal or slightly dominant role in decision making.
5. *Ambivalent gatekeeping* reflects low encouragement, moderate control, and moderate discouragement. For example, a parent is inconsistent, showing both support and restriction toward the other parent's involvement.
6. *Passive gate closing* reflects low encouragement, low control, and moderate discouragement. For example, a parent does not actively prevent involvement but creates barriers by being unresponsive or indifferent.
7. *Active gate closing* reflects low encouragement, high control, and high discouragement. For example, parent actively restricts and discourages the other parent involvement while maintaining strict control over parenting decisions.
8. *Exclusive gatekeeping* reflects low encouragement, high control, and high discouragement. For example, a parent fully excludes the other parent from parenting, maintaining all decision-making power.

Puhlman and Pasley's (2013) model highlights how one parent's behaviors are likely to influence the other parent's involvement. Despite its apparent appeal and the introduction of a dimensional model into the gatekeeping literature, surprisingly this model has not yet been integrated into parenting plan evaluations within family law.

The apparent lack of integration of the Puhlman and Pasley model into the custody literature is a good example of the ways in which professional subspecialties tend to stay within their information silos. The Puhlman and Pasley model was intended to offer a new definition and an expanded conceptual model of maternal gatekeeping derived from the extant literature and critiques offered by scholars and applied to fathering. From our perspective, it should have been a logical next step to incorporate this model into the Austin et al. gatekeeping model.

Integrating this framework into the currently dominant Austin et al. gatekeeping model could improve parenting plan evaluations by helping to more precisely categorize parental behavior along a dimension from supportive and restrictive gatekeeping behaviors. The newly integrated model might also aid in identifying the impact of parental control, encouragement, and discouragement on coparenting.

Evaluators are strongly recommended to examine the coparenting relationship with regards to the family history of gatekeeping from early in the child's life through the current custody dispute. Within an intact family, the social contract (Sager, 1976) between the parents regarding division of labor might be a useful focus of examination. Evaluators should investigate parental gatekeeping behaviors, attitudes, and beliefs held and directed by one parent that regulated the other parent's relationship with the child during the marriage. This historical perspective might provide insight into whether what is seen today is, in fact, restrictive gatekeeping or a continuation of a previously agreed upon (often unspoken) social contract of parenting responsibilities that one parent wishes now to be changed.

Exploration of each parent's basis for gatekeeping behavior during the marriage and postseparation might yield information about attitudes, values, and beliefs about gender roles and other relevant ideas. The set of theoretical perspectives most often used as the basis for examining gatekeeping behaviors is gender perspectives (Schoppe-Sullivan & Altenburger, 2019). Gender perspectives tend to emphasize the social construction of gender. Evaluators might examine the significance of prescribed gender roles for men and women within the marriage and how, if at all, the acceptance and embrace of those gender roles remain relevant in their postseparation ideas about parenting (Schoppe-Sullivan & Altenburger, 2019). Separation and divorce often lead one or both parents to reflect upon the extent to which their marriage-based ideas about parenting responsibilities need to be modified, given the substantial changes in family structure following separation.

ASSESSING FOR GATEKEEPING

Gatekeeping analyses must be conducted in all cases. It begins with data drawn from the history of caretaking of the child from birth to the present, parenting models and gender roles in family systems. Understanding how a parent's family of origin might have influenced current parenting and coparenting behaviors might lead to a better understanding of current conflicts related to differences in parenting models based on their respective families of origin. Gathering data about past parental involvement should also include information about each child's recollection of each parent's caretaking, availability or accessibility, engagement in activities, and other areas in which the child might recall both the activities shared with each parent but also the child's emotional experiences of time spent with each parent. Children's perception of life in different homes also might contribute to a child's comfort spending time with each parent. Smart's conceptual framework developed from analyses of children's experiences in binuclear families is an instructive guide for data gathering (Smart, 2002). We discuss the Smart conceptual framework in the chapters addressing interviewing children.

William G. Austin and Rappaport (2018) improved upon the original Austin et al. gatekeeping model by suggesting that gatekeeping might occur with some behaviors and not with others. They also introduced the idea that one parent might engage in one type of gatekeeping such as restricting the flow of information to a parent while the other parent might engage in financial or visitation restrictive gatekeeping. The novelty of the Austin and Rappaport model is their identification of behavioral domains in which parents exchange information and assess access to their children. Each family might have a variety of domains in which they share information about their children or coordinate and determine parental access that is unique to their family culture. Identifying these domains is an important evaluation task. Flexible gatekeeping might be found between mother and father along medical information but not access to children's activities. In the same family, father might engage in restrictive gatekeeping around information about children's daily activities when with him yet display flexible gatekeeping when exchanging children around holiday times.

Gathering information from independent third parties with personal knowledge of each family member's behavior with each child and with the other parent is also a critical aspect to a competently conducted evaluator. The De Los Reyes et al. (2015) multi-informant model reminds us that all family members have ideas, feelings, and agendas that vary with each situation or person. A parent being interviewed by an evaluator might behave differently than that parent participating at a school board meeting. Similarly, a child might behave differently when interacting with a teacher at school compared with interactions with parents of their best friend. Each of these third-party observers might have personal knowledge of the child, the parent, or their interactions that vary with the context. This is why gathering information from multiple collateral sources across a variety of situations and activities is likely to provide more reliable data than limited collateral information.

Fidler et al. (2010), Milchman (2018), and Milchman et al. (2020a) maintain that parent–child contact problems have a variety of sources and are often based upon very complex historical and current factors. In the next chapter, we will explore how to develop an assessment methodology robust enough to address the multiple issues that might be an area of concern in an evaluation.

CONCLUSION

This chapter has explored the evolving professional understanding of PCCP, charting a path from early, often divisive constructs such as parental alienation syndrome toward more sophisticated, evidence-based frameworks. Contemporary models—like the EM and the MFM—offer a more accurate reflection of the multifaceted nature of modern family systems. These approaches move beyond simplistic, binary explanations and instead highlight the dynamic interplay of individual characteristics, relational patterns, and broader systemic factors. As the field has matured, there has been a growing emphasis on conducting ecologically valid evaluations, using precise and nonstigmatizing language, and developing a deeper appreciation for the complex dynamics that shape family functioning. This shift reflects a commitment to both scientific rigor and clinical sensitivity. In the next chapter, we will continue to build on these developments, further examining how these evolving frameworks can inform practice and improve outcomes in high-conflict family law cases.

20

Modern Conceptualizations of Parent–Child Contact Problems

Over the past 2 decades, research on parent–child contact problems (PCCP) has evolved significantly, moving from early conceptualizations of child alienation toward more comprehensive, multifactor models. Scholars such as Kelly and Johnston laid the foundation by redefining alienation, while later contributions from Drozd, Olesen, Garber, Milchman, and others have refined the understanding of why children resist or refuse contact with a parent postseparation. This chapter explores various conceptual frameworks that differentiate between distinct causes of PCCP. Rather than relying on a singular diagnostic approach, contemporary research emphasizes an ecological perspective, recognizing the interplay of child-specific factors, parental behaviors, systemic influences, and external pressures.

The importance of distinguishing between alienation and other legitimate causes of parent–child contact problems cannot be overstated. Misidentifying the underlying issue can lead to misguided interventions that may either reinforce harmful dynamics or fail to protect the child from potential abuse or neglect. By critically reviewing these models, we aim to provide professionals in family law, forensic psychology, and mental health with a deeper understanding of the theoretical and practical considerations necessary for assessing and addressing PCCP.

https://doi.org/10.1037/0000474-021
Parenting Plan Evaluations: An Evidence-Informed Approach to Child Custody, by J. W. Gould and C. M. Mulchay

DROZD AND OLESEN'S MODEL FOR DISCRIMINATING ALIENATION FROM DOMESTIC VIOLENCE

Few investigation questions are as difficult to examine in child custody evaluations as distinguishing among allegations of child abuse, forms of domestic violence (DV), and a child's unnecessary alienation from an otherwise good parent. On the one hand, to place a child with a violent, intimidating, or abusive parent while severing ties with the more nurturing and more protective parent may result in harsh consequences for the child and is counter to the child's best interests. At the same time, limiting or eliminating a child's contact with a good enough parent, based on the other parent's allegations that the good enough parent is dangerous or evil, results in similarly harsh consequences for the child and also is considered counter to the child's best interests. In the latter case, the child's experience of reality becomes distorted. Their ability to judge the quality of relationships with others becomes impaired and the child's experiences of being with other people become impaired. These concerns continue to be raised in our literature (Bernet & Freeman, 2013; Freeman, 2020; Garber, 2004, 2012; Garber et al., 2022; Garber & Simon, 2024a).

Drozd and Olesen (2004) recommend an evaluation strategy for distinguishing among allegations of child abuse, DV, and a child's unnecessary alienation from an otherwise good parent. The first step is to assess the nature of the child's attachment to and relationship with each parent. The evaluator should take an extensive history from each parent and from each child. Then, the evaluator should gather information of past and current observed child problem behaviors. The evaluator should directly observe the child across several settings to determine whether or not the alleged distressing behavior represents bona fide child rejection of the parent or whether it represents some other form of disruption in the parent–child relationship, that is, in the child's attachment to either parent. For example, in a recent case, historical information revealed that the toddler experienced several residential moves, several changes in babysitters, and several significant disruptions to her daily routines. Several hypotheses were generated to explore the toddler's display of distress, among them were her developmental age; her reaction to externally imposed stressors that resulted in her significantly reduced sense of safety, security, and predictability; or her temperament, a factor that may be independent of the contextual changes she has endured.

It is important for evaluators to determine whether a child's behavior problems are artifacts of the current situation such as a child's reaction to her parent's separation. The evaluator should examine factors that operate across other levels of system functioning such as individual, relationship, family, and extended family factors. Evaluators may also ask questions that probe deeper into each of these areas. That is, the evaluator may need to probe both across a broader set of factors and must probe deeper within each factor.

If there are problems with a child's relationship with either parent or if a child is displaying behavior problems, the evaluator then must investigate whether there is a realistic basis for the child's behaviors. There are many types of family situations and parenting behaviors other than alienating parenting behaviors that may lead a child to refuse contact with or to express anger and rejection toward a parent. There are situations in well-functioning families that could result in a child's behavior change. There may have been preseparation family dynamics characterized by one parent's physical or emotional absence from the family that resulted in a child developing an insecure attachment to that parent.

Evaluators need to examine how infants and toddlers developed attachments to each parent. Subsequent to the publication of the Drozd and Olesen model, models developed to examine how parental gatekeeping functioned before and after the relationship dissolution have guided evaluators toward examination of the role of parental gatekeeping from birth through the present (W. G. Austin, 2018b; W. G. Austin & Drozd, 2013; W. G. Austin, Fieldstone, & Pruett, 2013; Saini et al., 2020). Gatekeeping analyses shed light on the family culture regarding gender roles; parental access; parental involvement; parental social contracts involving distribution of family responsibilities, vis-à-vis childcare, and work outside the home; parent-to-parent decision making; and other historical factors.

Applying Gatekeeping Analyses

In the previous chapter, we discussed the concept of gatekeeping as how one parent facilitates or restricts the other parent's involvement in a child's life. We expand on the concept of gatekeeping to show how it evolves over time, particularly after separation or divorce. Analyzing a family's history of gatekeeping helps determine whether current behaviors are consistent with past patterns or if they have changed due to conflict or other factors.

You will recall that gatekeeping falls on a spectrum from flexible to restrictive, influencing a child's access to both parents:

- *Flexible gatekeeping*. In some families, both parents actively share child-rearing responsibilities. If this pattern continues after separation, both parents support frequent and meaningful contact between the children and the other parent, ensuring stability.

- *Restrictive gatekeeping*. In other cases, one parent (often the mother) may shift from a flexible approach to a more restrictive stance after separation, limiting the other parent's involvement. This can create a false impression in court that the restricted parent (often the father) was never actively engaged, painting them as uninvolved or unfit.

By assessing past and present gatekeeping behaviors, evaluators and courts can better understand whether a parent's restriction of access is based on legitimate concerns (such as safety or prior neglect) or a reaction to conflict, resentment, or control dynamics. It is critical that evaluators examine whether parents who engage in restrictive gatekeeping prioritize the child's best interests, rather than serving as a tool for parental conflict or a legal advantage.

One example is a shift from flexible to unjustified restrictive gatekeeping. Before separation, Sarah and David coparented their two children with a flexible gatekeeping approach. Both participated in daily childcare, with Sarah handling school-related tasks and David managing extracurricular activities. They made parenting decisions together and ensured both had quality time with the children. After separation, Sarah became increasingly restrictive in allowing David access to the children. She began canceling his scheduled visits last minute and insisting that the children were too busy to see him. In court, Sarah framed David as an uninvolved father, pointing to his absence at recent school events—events from which he had been excluded. Over time, the children's relationship with David weakened, and they expressed reluctance to see him, mirroring their mother's concerns. This case illustrates how restrictive gatekeeping can distort the perception of parental involvement, potentially leading to a parent–child contact problem based on exclusion rather than genuine disengagement.

In contrast to the first example, here is an example of consistent flexible gatekeeping despite the divorce. Before separation, Mark and Julia had a balanced parenting arrangement, where both were equally involved in their children's upbringing. Mark worked late on weekdays but spent quality time with the children on weekends. Julia, who had a more flexible work schedule, managed school pickups and daily routines, but she respected and encouraged Mark's role in parenting. After separation, both parents maintained a cooperative, flexible gatekeeping approach. Julia ensured that Mark remained actively involved by encouraging the children to spend weekends and holidays with him. Mark reciprocated by keeping Julia informed about the children's activities and major decisions. The children adjusted well, experiencing minimal disruption in their relationships with both parents. This example demonstrates healthy coparenting where gatekeeping remains flexible postdivorce, allowing children to maintain strong relationships with both parents.

Why Children Might Have Favorites

Children's feelings toward each of their parents are shaped by a complex mix of emotional, psychological, and situational factors. Some children naturally gravitate toward one parent more than the other, while others experience a deep divide in their affections due to specific family dynamics, past experiences, or external influences.

A child's attachment to a parent often begins in early childhood, influenced by the level of care and emotional responsiveness they receive. If one parent has historically been the primary caregiver—providing comfort, structure, and stability—that parent may become the child's preferred source of emotional security. Conversely, if another parent has been less present or inconsistent in meeting the child's needs, the bond may not be as strong.

Parenting styles also play a critical role in shaping a child's feelings. A nurturing and emotionally available parent may foster warmth and trust, whereas a parent who is overly strict, emotionally distant, or unpredictable in their reactions may create feelings of fear, resentment, or detachment. Children, particularly as they grow older, are highly perceptive of the way they are treated and often form preferences based on how supported and understood they feel.

Family conflict can further complicate a child's emotional landscape. When exposed to parental disputes, particularly if one parent is more aggressive, emotionally volatile, or critical of the other, children may align with the parent they perceive as safer or more understanding. In cases where one parent actively attempts to turn the child against the other, the child's perception of the targeted parent can become distorted, leading to rejection or estrangement.

The consistency of a parent's presence in a child's life also has a lasting impact. A parent who is actively involved in daily routines, school events, and personal activities tends to create a deeper bond than one who is frequently absent due to work demands, travel, or disengagement. Over time, a child may come to associate stability and reliability with the parent who is more present, regardless of the absent parent's intentions.

Sometimes, a child's preference is shaped by personality compatibility. They may feel naturally more aligned with the parent who shares similar interests, temperament, or communication style. When a parent understands and validates a child's emotions, the child is more likely to seek comfort and connection from them. On the other hand, when misunderstandings arise or a child feels unseen by a parent, emotional distance can grow.

Life changes, such as divorce, remarriage, or the introduction of new siblings, can also shift a child's relationship with each parent. If one parent moves away or starts a new family, the child may feel a sense of abandonment or resentment. In cases where a parent's actions have caused direct harm—whether through neglect, substance abuse, or past trauma—children may develop an emotional barrier as a means of self-protection. Even when the parent expresses regret or seeks reconciliation, trust may take time to rebuild.

As children grow, their developmental stage influences how they perceive their parents. Younger children often seek comfort and security from the parent who provides the most nurturing care, while older children and teenagers may critically assess past experiences and form independent opinions. Peer influence, siblings, and extended family members can also subtly shape a child's feelings, reinforcing their attachment to one parent over the other.

Ultimately, the way a child feels toward each parent is rarely simple or static. It evolves over time, shaped by lived experiences, emotional connections, and the environment in which they are raised. For professionals working in family law and mental health, understanding these dynamics is crucial when assessing a child's needs and ensuring that their emotional well-being remains at the center of any legal or therapeutic intervention.

Evaluators might consider assessing individual factors such as a child's temperament or a child's affinity for one parent over the other parent that contributes to the child's feeling significantly closer to one parent. Sometimes, a parent may feel particularly possessive of a very young child because of the child's preexisting illness, disability, or vulnerability yet the parent may not be actively attempting to interfere with the child's relationship with the other parent. There may be efforts by extended family members, stepparents, and other people who have influence over parental decision making.

In addition to the nonpathological causes of a child's refusal to visit or have contact with one parent, there are cases in which the child's avoidance of a parent is a reasonable, healthy, and rational response to dysfunction in the family and its resulting trauma. Abusive relationships, relationships in which children feel unsafe, or relationships experienced by the child as emotionally unpredictable are among those that might contribute to a child's strong desire to avoid contact with a parent.

Among the insights gained since the publication of the Drozd/Olesen model is increasing recognition of the multiple ways in which definitions of "good parenting" might be tied to cultural context. What is viewed as "good parenting" in one cultural context might be viewed differently from another cultural context (see Chapter 8). Another more recent insight is increased recognition of violent and nonviolent coercive control (CC) factors that affect family systems (E. Katz, 2019, 2022; Stark, 2023a) and the significant developmental harm that exposure to family-based CC has upon children (E. Katz et al., 2020; Stark, 2023b; Stark & Hester, 2019).

Questions About the Child's Behaviors and Relationships

Evaluators might need to examine allegations of DV, intimate partner violence (IPV), CC, reactive parenting, immature parenting, and other behaviors that might cause a child to feel unsafe, fearful, and resist wanting to spend time with a parent. These are among the questions we believe are critical to ask in a competently conducted evaluation:

- Are there any problems with the child's behaviors?
- What type of problems?
- Under what conditions or context are the behaviors observed?
- During what time are the behaviors observed?
- Who has observed the behaviors?
- How often have the behaviors been observed?
- How consistently over time and place have the behaviors been observed?
- Where and when do these behaviors occur?
- Under what circumstances are the behaviors not observed?
- Who observes and reports them?
- Are there any problems with the child's relationship with either parent? If yes, what type of problem?
- When did the problem behaviors start?

Once the evaluator has gathered information that leads to preliminary hypotheses that a child displays problematic behaviors or that there is a problem in the parent–child relationship, the next area of investigation is whether there is a factual or reality-based reason for the problems. The following are among the questions to ask:

- Has the child been exposed to any kind of abuse—as the direct victim or as a secondary victim?
- Has there been child abuse?
- Has there been alcohol or drug abuse?
- Has there been family violence?
- Has there been emotional or psychological abuse?
- Has there been physical abuse?
- Has there been sexual abuse?
- Has the child interpreted an event as abusive?
- If there is abuse, who is the alleged aggressor?
- Who is the alleged victim?

It is important to recognize that seeking a "fact-based reason" includes both whether specific events occurred that can be verified as well as the child's perception of events as problematic. There is significant variability in how children perceive their reality based on their developmental level, their linguistic competence, their construction of meaning from their reality, reliability of experiences from past events, their recognition of how recollection of past events might be influenced by others, and other similar factors that introduce potential threats to the reliability of children's self-reports.

When there are allegations of abuse or a child's apparent display of trauma symptoms, a thorough assessment of all elements of the alleged concerns is critical. This includes the particular dynamics and behaviors of alleged abuse along dimensional terms. That is, examination of allegations of abuse is not a binary determination. Abuse can be real or perceived. What is experienced by one person as abuse may be viewed by another child as unremarkable. There is a critical need to move away from the label of "abuse" toward a behavioral description of the alleged behaviors, examination of motivation and intention on the part of the alleged victim, alleged perpetrator, and, in the cases in which allegations of abuse have been reported to child protective services, the reporter of the alleged abuse.

In cases in which there are written records such as child protective services files, pediatric files, hospital reports, we have found that it is critically important to review the primary, underlying description of the alleged behavior. Not infrequently, we have found an initial statement that serves as the basis of the investigation to be vague and missing clearly articulated behaviors. In its place, we have found that a frontline interviewer inferred abuse behaviors without clear statements from the alleged victim. For example, the frontline worker may report that a child has been abused and is at risk of harm, yet the behavioral basis of the concern is never identified.

Evaluators need to aggressively examine files to ensure that the initial report that lead to a determination of abuse was based on clearly defined behaviors described by the alleged victim. Our experience is that conceptual leaps from vague allegations to findings of abuse occur most often in high conflict families with young children with age-appropriate language development in which statements such as "I was touched" are the basis of an abuse conclusion without in-depth investigation of the child's use of language (A. G. Walker & Kenniston, 2013), the context within which the alleged outcry occurred (Kuehnle & Connell, 2013; Kuehnle et al., 2016; Lamb, 2018), and consideration of reasonable alternative explanations.

Drozd and Olesen (2004) recommend that among the factors to be investigated are abuse severity, chronicity, and context. Children exposed to abuse are affected differently based upon their age and their stage of development, based upon support that they have from others in their life, and based upon their general level of resilience. Evaluators should assess the ways in which the child is safeguarded by the protective parent and the risk posed to the child by the alleged abusive parent.

After careful evaluation of the basis for the child's rejection of a parent, evaluators need to look more broadly at both parents and their parenting of the child in question. Such behavior should be investigated using careful interviews with the parties, collateral witnesses, and written records of letters, faxes, voice mail messages, and electronically-stored information. Any investigation of alleged alienating behavior by one parent toward the other parent should be separate from an investigation of the behavior of the alleged abusive parent. What follow are among the questions the evaluator should consider regarding parental rejection:

- Has the child been exposed to a campaign of denigration about the other parent?
- Has one parent engaged in any behaviors associated with alienation of the child from the other parent, such as a parent rejecting the child when the child expresses love for the other parent?
- Does the parent believe the things they are saying about the other parent?
- Are they genuinely frightened and protective, even if mistakenly so?
- Is there a financial or another kind of gain that would help explain the reason for the behavior if genuine fear does not seem to be present?
- Is there a personal or family history of rejection being repeated in the current family system?

- Is the parent displaying polarized thinking for reasons not related to a past or present history of abuse?
- Does the parent see most things as win–lose or all-or-nothing?
- Is there documented psychopathology that would explain any existing problems with flexible and clear thinking?
- Is the parent prone to form enmeshed relationships?
- Does the parent tend to view the child as an extension of themself? If there is no campaign of alienation, the evaluator should consider examining questions such as:
  - Is the observed child problem behavior or the observed problem parent–child behavior associated with situation specific factors around separation?
  - Is there a greater affinity for one parent because of gender, shared interests, or temperament?

Relationship Typology

Drozd & Olesen (2004) propose a classification system for pathological and nonpathological parent–child relationships, pointing to the ways in which both abuse and alienation may lead to PCCPs. Medical problems, developmental difficulties, psychological issues, school or learning problems, or family problems may cause or may contribute to relationship problems (J. B. Kelly & Johnston, 2001). Drozd and Olesen also propose four nonpathological and six pathological parent–child relationships.

The nonpathological parent–child relationships include the following:

- **Equal**. Many, if not most, children in nonabusive families have equal relationships with their parents—relationships that are not identical but relatively equal.
- **Affinity**. A child is emotionally closer to one parent than to the other, perhaps because the parent to whom the child feels closer has interests that are more in tune with the child's interests. It is likely that the child also has a strong and positive affectional bond with the other parent.
- **Alignment**. In families where there is no abuse, the child may have an exaggerated connection with one parent at the expense of the other parent. The affectional bond with one parent is strong and the affectional bond with the other parent is weaker or the affectional bond is nonexistent. It is possible that the parent with whom the child is aligned has neither directly nor indirectly promoted or manipulated the child into the alignment, and if this is the case, most likely the alignment is nonpathological. A pathological alignment not caused by direct parental abuse or alienation occurs when the child is unable to tolerate tension surrounding their parent's high conflict

divorce. The child may opt out of the unbearable conflict by choosing sides in the conflict, thereby reducing the child's sense of conflict.

- **Protective parenting**. Some parents' concerns and fears about the safety of their children are reality-based. A victim–parent may engage in healthy protective parenting to keep a child out of harm's way. The evaluator should assess the parent's ability to protect the child in healthy ways. When protective parenting inhibits a child's normal development, it is important that evaluators provide recommendations about how a parent can learn healthy protective parenting behaviors.

Pathological parent–child relationships include the following:

- **Identification with the aggressor**. Identification with the aggressor refers to a type of alignment that occurs in abusive families and often begins with a child being fearful of the aggressor–parent. The child may or may not be aware of their fear. The child then has a counter-phobic reaction to the fear and they align with the aggressor. Often, the abuser promotes this kind of alignment and might also actively capitalize on the child-victim's identification with the aggressor by encouraging the child to view Parent A as weak and disempowered and by encouraging the child to dislike Parent A or view the parent as an incompetent or unfit parent.
- **Estrangement as a result of abandonment or poor parenting**. There are situations in nonviolent families where a child may develop an estranged relationship with a parent. For example, estrangement may occur when a child has not seen their father for 2 years because he was stationed overseas during wartime. From the child's perspective, the parent has abandoned her. Another form of estrangement may result when a parent abuses drugs and the effects of that substance abuse is to make that parent emotionally unavailable to the child. From the child's perspective, the parent has abandoned her.
- **Estrangement in abusive families**. Some children may not develop emotional attachments with one parent for good reasons. A parent may have abused them or may have abused their other parent. These children may be traumatized from what they have been exposed to, from what they have experienced, or from what they have witnessed. They may be afraid of the abusive parent, and they have little or no positive emotions toward that parent usually while maintaining a relationship with the other parent. The child's reasons are reality-based. Cases of estrangement with DV are most at risk of being mislabeled as cases of alienation. The abusive parent claims that the victim–parent has made the children not want to be around them by making allegations of abuse. They do this to take the focus off them and to put the blame for the child's rejection of them back on the victim parent.
- **Alienation in its pure form in nonabusive families**. Alienation is a process through which a child expresses, freely and persistently, unreasonable

negative feelings and beliefs (such as anger, hatred, rejection, or fear) toward a parent that are significantly disproportionate to a child's actual experience with that parent. The child develops strong and nonambivalent feelings towards the targeted or rejected parent. Although the rejected parent has not been abusive, the child refuses contact with that parent for irrational reasons. There is no reality-based reason for the child's rejection of the parent. Bona fide cases of alienation are rare.

- **Alienation by the abuser in DV families**. Another type of alienation in families with DV or abuse occurs when the abusive parent alienates the child against the victim–parent. The abuser is in a better position to promote a division that might be developing between the victim parent and the child because the abusive parent holds the power in the family system. To the evaluator, the abusive parent appears as the calm, rational, and good parent, while the victim appears emotionally distraught and inadequate in their parenting.
- **Alienation by victim mothers in DV families**. Some parents may be more pathological, and more entrenched in their hatred of the abusive parent. In these cases, the victim–parent engages in protective parenting and alienating behaviors.

DROZD, OLESEN, AND SAINI DECISION-TREE MODEL

The Drozd et al. (2013) decision tree is a structured framework designed to assist custody evaluators, forensic mental health professionals, and family court practitioners in assessing and making recommendations in cases involving high-conflict custody disputes, IPV, CC, child abuse allegations, and other factors that impact child safety and parental capacity.

Its key features include an empirical and theoretical basis. Recall our discussion of decision trees in Chapter 4. The decision-tree concept integrates psychological research, forensic best practices, and legal considerations to guide evaluators through complex cases. It helps professionals weigh the risks posed by a parent's behavior and the protective factors that may mitigate harm to the child, and it assists in determining appropriate custody and visitation recommendations based on evidence rather than subjective judgment.

There are four steps in the decision tree:

1. **Screen for family violence and CC**. Evaluators assess the history, patterns, and severity of IPV, including physical violence, emotional abuse, and economic control. This step involves reviewing police reports, protective orders, witness testimony, and psychological evaluations.
2. **Determine the evidence-basis for the impact on the child**. The model emphasizes assessing how the conflict or abuse might have affected the child's psychological well-being, development, and relationship with

each parent. Assessment would likely include evaluating trauma symptoms, attachment issues, and whether the child expresses fear or distress around a parent.

3. **Assess parenting capacity and development of protective measures**. Evaluators examine each parent's ability to provide a safe and nurturing environment. This includes assessing mental health issues, substance use, history of parenting behaviors, and willingness to coparent.

4. **Categorize risk and apply decision guidelines**. The model guides professionals in classifying cases based on risk levels (e.g., low, moderate, or high risk). Depending on the risk level, the decision tree provides recommendations regarding parenting time, restrictions, supervised visitation, and necessary interventions.

The decision-tree framework incorporates best practices for ensuring that parenting plan recommendations align with legal standards while prioritizing child safety. Using the structured decision-tree model encourages the use of trauma-informed forensic evaluation procedures in an ecological manner.

When using the Drozd et al. (2013) decision-tree model to assess PCCP, the evaluator needs to provide a clear, operational definition of the concepts being evaluated and then, identification of the specific factors to be assessed, which include the following:

- **Multiple levels of functioning within each family**. This would include assessment of individual level of behaviors, cognitions, affective experiences, and perception of others. The assessment would also include historical and current assessment of various dyadic relationships within the family, both within and across generations.

- **Family of origin factors**. These would include, but not be limited to, information about parenting models, discipline models, parent-to-parent communication models, parent-to-child communication models, power and control factors within and between generations, conflict resolution models, ethnic and cultural factors, and gender roles.

- **Family system factors**. Among the many factors that might be investigated at this level, one would examine past and present ways in which children and parents have been involved with each other. Another area is an historical exploration of parent–child alignments and parent–child alliances that have come and gone over time should be investigated. Data about each of these historical parent–child relationships needs to be seen through the eyes of each child as well as through the eyes of each parent. More data can be gathered from grandparents and others who have personal knowledge of the past and present family relationships.

- **Extrafamilial and community-based factors**. Religious, cultural, and ethnic involvement with community institutions, authority figures, and others who might influence the family are important to consider.

Clearly, this is not an exhaustive list of factors to consider. We believe that no matter how comprehensive of a list we can develop, there will be factors that need to be assessed in some families that we cannot anticipate. This limitation is part of the reason why developing a static model of assessing PCCP or alienation problems, or resist and refuse dynamics seems beyond our reach.

MILCHMAN'S MENTAL ABUSE POTENTIAL MODEL

Milchman (2022a) suggests that a significant limitation to the Drozd et al. (2013) model is the decision not to place weights on various factors, arguing that "there is no evidence that there is predictive value in organizing the data in any specifically weighted way" (Drozd et al., 2013, p. 26). Milchman's mental abuse potential (MAP) model assigns weight to four factors that are posited as "generally accepted psychological knowledge about two types of child abuse (sexual abuse, psychological maltreatment) adverse parenting, and alienation" (p. 113):

1. **CC and IPV.** The evaluator gathers information about whether one parent has engaged in patterns of CC, psychological abuse, or DV. Milchman views the IPV factor as the most important to assess because abuse has serious implications for child safety and parental fitness.
2. **Child maltreatment (i.e., abuse and neglect)**. The evaluator investigates whether the child has been subjected to physical, emotional, sexual abuse, or neglect by either parent. This is the second most important factor of investigating because child safety is paramount before considering other relational factors.
3. **Harmful parenting practices (i.e., adverse or deficit parenting)**. The evaluator examines suboptimal or harmful parenting that does not rise to the level of abuse but may still negatively impact the child. Adverse parenting might include concerns about parental poor emotional regulation, harsh discipline, or exposing the child to high-conflict interactions.
4. **Parental alienation, or ways in which a parent exercises undue influence over a child against a parent**. The assessment is focused on whether one parent has engaged in behaviors that wrongfully turn the child against the other parent, without justification. Milchman stresses that alienation should only be examined after ruling out abuse and harmful parenting, as genuine estrangement can be misinterpreted as alienation.

Factors one through three represent abuse and adverse parenting and need to be investigated before the evaluator examines the fourth factor that represents alienation. Milchman (2022a) acknowledges that there is no scientific basis for the weights she assigns to these factors. The factor weights are based upon her rational or logical analysis.

The MAP model focuses on assessing three broad areas: (a) mental abuse patterns such as identifying coercive, controlling, and psychologically abusive behaviors in family dynamics; (b) once identified, assess the validity of abuse claims; and (c) parent–child relationship dynamics (i.e., whether a child's rejection of a parent is due to actual maltreatment, undue influence, or another underlying factor). Milchman (2022a) believes that the model is particularly useful in cases where allegations of parental alienation, DV, or child psychological maltreatment arise. It provides evaluators with a systematic method for determining whether a child's rejection of a parent is based on legitimate harm (such as abuse or neglect) or whether undue psychological influence has distorted their perceptions.

Milchman (2022a) argues that "sequential assessment is an essential difference" (p. 114) between her MAP model and the Drozd et al. (2013) decision-tree model. Evaluators using the MAP model would conduct separate, structured interviews of parents and children to assess their narratives, perceptions, and emotional responses. Questions focus on the origins of the conflict, the child's reasoning for their feelings, and any signs of suggestibility or external influence. Evaluators would also review court and clinical records by examining past legal filings, protective orders, therapy records, and school reports to detect patterns of concern. Historical evidence of CC, threats, or emotional manipulation is given significant weight. Evaluators would also observe parent–child interactions. Direct observations of how the child and each parent interact can provide crucial insights into their emotional bond, attachment security, and relational dynamics. Evaluators look for indications of fear, distress, or exaggerated hostility that seem out of proportion to past events. Psychological assessments are conducted using standardized forensic tools used to assess parental influence, psychological well-being, and emotional distress. The MAP model supports integrating these findings into a comprehensive evaluation rather than relying solely on subjective narratives.

Conceptually interesting, we raise concerns about how Milchman (2022a) does not provide literature-based citations to support some of the ideas upon which the MAP model is based. For example, Milchman indicated that the MAP schema is based upon "generally accepted psychological knowledge" yet provides no citations to support her assertion. Furthermore, Milchman's discussion of areas of psychological maltreatment and adverse parenting factors to assess does not refer to the plethora of parenting behaviors and child responses to those behaviors that might be outside of the dominant culture in which most evaluators operate (see Chapter 8). What is viewed as maltreatment or adverse parenting behaviors in one culture might be viewed as normative in another culture. How a child interprets parental behaviors that might be viewed by people outside their culture as problematic is not addressed in her discussion. Milchman's framing of her argument as alienation theorists versus trauma theorists is troublesome as it continues what we believe to be a basic underlying problem in our field. Many move too quickly to polarize, pitting one theoretical model against another rather than looking for commonalities and seeking resolutions to bridge the conceptual differences.

Milchman's (2022a) binary argument about alienation versus trauma theorists, however, raised for us an important issue similar to issues raised earlier in this book. Evaluators need to clearly articulate the implicit theoretical assumptions that guide their thinking, data collection, and opinion formation. Assume that an evaluator embraces one of the trauma models to which Milchman refers in which recommendations from the evaluator are based upon the theoretical notion that healing of trauma should precede steps toward reunification. The judge, on the other hand, is a strong believer in the reunification first model that Milchman appears to argue comes from those who are more likely to embrace an alienation model.

Arguments over how best to address the PCCP might light up the courtroom because of these conflicting approaches to parent–child healing without recognizing that the basis of the argument is derived from different theoretical models that support very different pathways toward healing. We also raise concerns about framing psychological solutions to PCCP when a child has been abused as moral decisions (Milchman, 2022a, p. 115). Psychological expert witnesses are qualified to testify because of their specialized knowledge of the professional and scientific knowledge in their field. We are concerned that testimony based upon moral decisions is outside the scope of expert psychological testimony.

Framing psychological concerns in terms of moral decisions strongly suggests a binary choice associated with good versus bad, right versus wrong, and moral versus immoral. Framing psychological concerns in such binary choices continues the polarization in the field and implies, if not directly suggests, that there are right and wrong pathways without recognizing the substantial complexity that the field is struggling with in attempting to find reliable and effective solutions to these difficult PCCPs.

COMPREHENSIVE CHALLENGES IN PARENTING PLAN ASSESSMENTS: A MULTILEVEL APPROACH TO EVALUATING FAMILY DYNAMICS

Developing a comprehensive assessment procedure in family law presents several challenges that evaluators must address. One of the primary obstacles is the necessity for a clear and operational definition of the concept being evaluated. The evaluator must not only define the concept but also determine the specific factors that require assessment. Additionally, a rationale must be established, explaining how each of these factors relates to the overall concept, ensuring that the evaluation remains structured and meaningful.

Furthermore, a well-rounded assessment must consider multiple levels of functioning within a family. This includes an exploration of individual behaviors, cognitive patterns, emotional experiences, and perceptions of others. It is also essential to evaluate historical and current dynamics within various dyadic relationships across generations, as these interactions can significantly influence the present state of the family.

An additional challenge is the need to incorporate family-of-origin influences into the assessment. Evaluators must examine various aspects of parental beliefs and behaviors, such as the guiding principles behind their parenting, their disciplinary approaches, and their past and current communication patterns with both their coparent and their children. Moreover, insight into power dynamics within and across generations must be explored, as these can shape parenting styles and decision making. Conflict resolution abilities, as well as the influence of extended family, cultural traditions, and ethnic factors, must also be considered, as they contribute to the family's overall functioning.

Beyond individual and relational dynamics, the assessment must also analyze the family as a system. This involves examining historical and present interactions between children and parents, paying close attention to the development of parent–child alignments and alliances over time. The perspective of each child, as well as that of each parent, should be gathered to gain a comprehensive understanding of family history. Grandparents and other extended family members may also offer valuable insight into the evolution of these relationships.

Additionally, the evaluator must consider extra-familial and community-based influences that may impact family functioning. Elements such as religious, cultural, and ethnic involvement with institutions, as well as relationships with community figures and authorities, should be examined, as they often play a significant role in shaping family interactions and dynamics.

Overall, the complexity of conducting a thorough family assessment requires evaluators to navigate multiple layers of individual, relational, systemic, and cultural factors, ensuring that all relevant aspects are considered to provide a comprehensive and insightful evaluation.

No matter how comprehensive a list, there will be factors that need to be assessed in some families that we cannot anticipate. This limitation is part of the reason why developing a static model of gatekeeping, assessing PCCP and alienation problems, or resist and refuse dynamics seems beyond our reach.

The forensic model (Martindale & Gould, 2004) discussed throughout this book provides a robust, conceptual template for forensic psychological assessment. Similar to the indeterminant intention of best interest of the child standard (Mnookin, 1975), the forensic model provides for a flexible approach to comprehensive data gathering from multiple sources but does not suggest that these multiple data-gathering sources can be applied to only certain relevant areas of forensic psychological inquiry.

DOMINANT FACTOR VERSUS MULTIFACTOR MODEL

Over the past several years, the professional disagreements about PCCP have circled around three conceptually overlapping areas yet are represented in the literature most often as separate arguments. One argument is the continued and, in our view, outdated argument about whether alienation exists. Some authors appear fixed on kicking a dead horse involving the empirical basis for the original parental alienation syndrome formulation. Another argument that we believe is critically important to continue to debate involves the competing models of what Milchman (2022a) calls the alienation theorists and the trauma theorists. A third argument is the debate over which PCCP model best captures the family dynamics and investigative factors that need to be examined. This debate is often referred to as examining the respective explanatory power of the dominant factor v. multifactor theories. Although we believe that there are far more similarities between the models than are generally acknowledged, we provide a brief description of the five-factor model (FFM; Bernet & Greenhill, 2022; Bernet & Xu, 2022) of the dominant factor theory intended to help in understanding some of the theoretical arguments often made by those who advocate for and against the FFM. See the five factors listed in Chapter 19.

Many years ago, Warshak drew attention to the degree status of the individuals supporting various PCCP models. He noted that Gardner was a medical doctor trained in differential diagnoses. It made sense that Parental Alienation Syndrome and the FFM models might reflect a medical model approach to behavioral descriptions. Bernet and Freeman are medical doctors. Perhaps their training in differential diagnosis influences which PCCP models they support. In contrast, Joan Kelly was trained as a sociologist and Jan Johnston, Ben Garber, and the authors of this text were trained as psychologists influenced by family systems theories. Other factors that have influenced our thinking about the movement away from diagnostic labels include our focus on an ecological model, as well as our fascination with the hierarchal taxonomy of psychopathology and the alternative model of personality disorders described in Chapter 17. Categorical perspectives on behavior can be helpful in many ways but also run the risk of creating a confirmatory bias effect by seeking behaviors that support a particular diagnosis while ignoring and therefore not attending to behaviors outside of the diagnostic category yet relevant to the issues of concern.

When we have engaged in one-on-one dialogues with those who support the FFM, it quickly becomes clear that their understanding of PCCPs is more in-line with a more dimensional approach to these behavioral concerns than is often described in their writings.

GARBER'S RUBRIC MODEL

As Garber, Fidler, Bala, Warshak, and Milchman have reminded us, PCCP have a variety of sources and are often based upon very complex historical and current factors. How does one develop an assessment methodology robust enough to address the multiple issues that might be an area of concern in an evaluation?

Over the past several decades, Garber (2004, 2012) has drawn attention to the child's experience living in high conflict family systems. He has offered a variety of ideas for evaluators to consider, among them is critical attention to the need for children to develop and maintain secure attachments with both parents.

Garber (2012) argued that "we must instead perform the delicate balancing act of providing children with a developmentally appropriate opportunity to build a secure attachment with each of their parents from birth forward" (p. 467). He identified four points that need to be considered "within an evolutionary and developmental perspective":

- "The quality of a child's attachment relationship with Parent A is built both upon [their] direct experience of Parent A's sensitive and responsive care and upon [their] experience of Parent B's endorsement of Parent A as a sensitive and responsive caregiver."
- "Most children will benefit from a primary relationship with their mother from birth through the second or third year and may thereafter build a relationship with their father on the basis of their mother's endorsement."
- "The mutual disregard and acrimony characteristic of the high-conflict divorce population makes it exceedingly unlikely that a mother granted near-exclusive care of her infant will thereafter be willing or able to genuinely endorse the father so as to lay the foundation for the child's secure attachment with him."
- "Very young children of high-conflict parents may have the best opportunity to make and maintain a healthy relationship with both of their parents when they have frequent, developmentally informed, and carefully structured contact with both from their earliest days." (p. 467)

We add to the last point that it is extremely difficult to reestablish relationships with infants and young children when relationships have been disrupted (Lamb & Kelly, 2009).

Garber's (2024) structured rubric is designed to minimize bias, standardize evaluations, and encourage a more comprehensive assessment of PCCP. The rubric is divided into six domains of inquiry, each addressing different aspects of the child's resistance: incidental factors (such as disruptions in routine or sensory aversions), child-specific variables (including trauma history and personality traits), the relationship between the aligned parent and the child (examining enmeshment or undue influence), the relationship between the rejected parent and the child (considering past neglect or estrangement), systemic factors (such as interparental conflict or differing parenting styles), and external influences (like peer pressure or extended family involvement).

The rubric does not provide definitive answers but serves as a guide to ensure evaluators consider relevant factors when assessing a child's resistance or refusal. By offering a structured approach, it helps reduce bias factors that either dismiss parental alienation outright or assume it is the sole cause of PCCP. Garber's model aims to move beyond the adversarial alienation versus estrangement debate and encourage a more holistic, ecologically based evaluation that prioritizes the child's best interests. The framework is also designed to evolve with ongoing research and judicial perspectives, ensuring that assessments remain informed and relevant. We incorporate much of his model in our suggestions below.

Garber et al. (2022) provide the following definitions in their field guide:

- **Triangulation**: The triangulated child has been pulled into adult conflict to play a part in the conflict.
- **Enmeshment**: A developmentally and culturally inappropriate corruption of the boundaries between parent and child that works against the child's drive toward autonomy.
- **Estrangement**: The child resists contact with a parent for objectively justifiable reasons.
- **Polarized child**: A behavioral description without implication of causation; a child who is observed to strongly prefer proximity to/communications with Parent A and to avoid, resist, refuse, or reject proximity to and communications with Parent B.
- **Alienation**: A family systems dynamic characterized by the child's alignment with Parent A and resistance or refusal of contact with Parent B due to exposure to Parent A's (and their allies') unwarranted negative words, actions, or expressed emotions about Parent B.

OUR MODEL FOR ASSESSING PCCPS

Our model for assessing PCCPs is rooted in family systems theory and incorporates elements of multiple models presented above, including Garber's (2024) rubric. Using the ecological model we describe throughout this book, we analyze individuals, dyadic, and family systems in the following manner.

Individual Assessment of the Parents

Evaluators should conduct an individual assessment of each parent by examining their psychological, emotional, and behavioral functioning, as well as their parenting capacity. Key elements include

- **Parental history and functioning**: Evaluators should collect a comprehensive history, including childhood experiences, past relationships, mental health history, substance use, and significant life events. Understanding how past experiences influence their parenting style is critical (J. B. Kelly & Johsnton, 2001).
- **Parenting beliefs and styles**: Evaluators should assess parenting philosophies, disciplinary strategies, emotional responsiveness, and adaptability. Parents who display rigid, punitive, or overly permissive approaches may contribute to PCCP.

- **Emotional and psychological functioning**: Mental health evaluations are critical to assess for issues such as personality disorders, anxiety, depression, or trauma, which could impact parenting. An individual's ability to manage stress, especially within high-conflict custody disputes, should also be assessed (J. B. Kelly & Johnston, 2001).
- **Parent's insight and capacity for coparenting**: Parents should be evaluated on their ability to recognize their child's needs independently from their conflict with the other parent. Those who engage in polarized, zero-sum thinking may struggle to coparent effectively (Gould & Martindale, 2007).

Assessment of the Children

Evaluators should conduct child assessments using developmentally appropriate methods to understand the child's perceptions, attachment security, and the potential influence of parental behaviors:

- **Developmental and emotional needs**: The child's age, cognitive ability, and developmental stage should be considered when evaluating their responses to parental separation. Separation anxiety in young children is normal, while strong rejection of a parent may indicate external influence (J. B. Kelly & Johnston, 2001).
- **Child's perceptions and expressed views**: The child's statements should be analyzed for consistency, emotional congruence, and depth. Children influenced by an alienating parent may repeat adult language without nuance or personal experiences (J. B. Kelly & Johnston, 2001).
- **Assessment of false narratives**: Evaluators should assess whether the child has developed distorted or exaggerated negative views of one parent. If so, it is important to determine whether these views stem from actual experiences, suggestive questioning by a parent, or alignment with an anxious caregiver (Principe & London, 2022).

The Relationship Level: The Parents

The evaluator should analyze the dynamics between the parents, including conflict patterns, historical issues, and their ability to coparent effectively:

- **History of marital and coparenting relationship**: Evaluators should review the relationship history, including conflict patterns, past incidents of violence, and significant turning points that may have affected their ability to coparent (J. B. Kelly & Johnston, 2001).
- **Current level of conflict**: High-conflict coparents often fall into adversarial patterns where one parent's gain is perceived as the other's loss. Evaluators should assess the intensity, frequency, and themes of conflicts (Fidler & Bala, 2010).

- **Safety factors**: Evaluators need to examine both factors that contribute to risk and mitigate risk, affecting safety. It is important to identify protective and risk factors, parental insight into their respective contributions, and steps that might be taken to reduce risk or increase safety.
- **Parenting communication**: Evaluators should examine each parent's ability to communicate, make joint decisions, and manage conflicts related to child-rearing. Parents who rely on third-party mediation, legal intervention, or use children as messengers indicate dysfunction (Drozd & Olesen, 2004).
- **Gatekeeping behaviors**: Evaluators should assess whether one parent excessively restricts the child's relationship with the other parent through negative messaging, scheduling conflicts, or interfering with visitations (W. G. Austin, Fieldstone, & Pruett, 2013).
- **Power imbalances and systemic issues**: In cases of DV or CC (see next two chapters), evaluators must be cautious about recommending shared parenting, as one parent may use the system to maintain control over the other (Stark, 2023a, 2023b).

The Relationship Level: Parent–Child

The evaluator should assess the nature, quality, and history of the child's relationship with each parent before and after the separation:

- **Attachment security**: Evaluators should determine if the child's resistance to contact is due to a secure attachment with one parent, parental influence, or issues such as abuse, neglect, or maladaptive parenting (Drozd & Olesen, 2004). Evaluators should examine whether the child perceives one parent as a "safe haven" while rejecting or fearing the other parent (Madigan et al., 2024).
- **Observational assessments**: As described in Chapter 13, evaluators should observe the child's interactions with both parents to assess warmth, engagement, responsiveness, and any signs of fear, withdrawal, or excessive alignment (J. B. Kelly & Johnston, 2001).
- **Parental influence and conditioning**: Some children may reject a parent due to repeated negative messaging, while others may have rational concerns about their safety. Evaluators should differentiate between external influence and child-driven rejection (Garber, 2020b).
- **Parenting behaviors that impact relationship quality**: Evaluators should look for behaviors such as over-permissiveness, enmeshment, CC, or emotional distance, all of which can negatively affect a parent–child bond (Drozd & Olesen, 2004).
- **Parental behaviors and contributions to PCCP**: Evaluators should assess whether a parent engages in behaviors that could contribute to alienation or

estrangement, such as restrictive gatekeeping, undermining the other parent, or emotionally enmeshing with the child (Drozd & Olesen, 2004).

- **Conflict Exposure**: Children who have been exposed to high levels of parental conflict may develop negative coping strategies, such as aligning with one parent or withdrawing from both (J. B. Kelly & Johnston, 2001).

The Family System

Using Garber's (2024) rubric, the evaluator should assess the family system. By doing so, they can combine the data they have gathered above into the following:

- Incidental factors (such as disruptions in routine or sensory aversions)
- Child-specific variables (including trauma history and personality traits)
- The relationship between the aligned parent and the child (examining enmeshment or undue influence)
- The relationship between the rejected parent and the child (considering past neglect or estrangement)
- Systemic factors (such as interparental conflict or differing parenting styles)
- External influences (like peer pressure or extended family involvement)

The Context-Specific Level

At this level, the evaluator investigates extrafamilial and community-based factors that might affect each level of functioning. This level would include a social capital analysis. Religious, cultural, and ethnic involvement with community institutions, authority figures, and others who might influence the family are important to consider.

- **Extended family involvement**: Grandparents, stepparents, and other relatives can reinforce alienation or support reunification efforts. Evaluators should determine whether family members are acting as independent support systems or escalating conflict (Warshak, 2020a).

- **Cultural and religious influences**: Beliefs about parenting roles, family hierarchy, and discipline vary across cultures. Evaluators must recognize how cultural expectations shape behaviors and attitudes toward coparenting (J. B. Kelly & Johnston, 2001).

- **Legal and social context**: Family court procedures, protective orders, and child welfare involvement can affect the child–parent dynamic. Evaluators should determine whether legal interventions have exacerbated or alleviated PCCP (Milchman, 2022a).

- **Practical matters:** Distance between the homes, the temperament of the transitions between the homes, the child's connections in each household or neighborhood, and so on should be considered.

The Systemic Pressures

At this level, the evaluator investigates systemic pressures that might affect each level of functioning. Evaluators consider how the stressors associated with being involved in litigation and the social and economic pressures associated with litigation might affect the individual, a particular dyad, or the family system. Similarly, pressures might come from individuals involved in forensic psychological evaluations or the expectations of professionals working with the individual, dyad, or family system:

- **Litigation and court-ordered evaluations**: High-conflict custody battles often create systemic pressure, reinforcing adversarial positions rather than promoting coparenting solutions. Evaluators should be aware of how legal narratives shape family dynamics (Fidler & Bala, 2010).
- **Mental health and forensic professionals' influence**: Therapists, custody evaluators, and expert witnesses may unintentionally reinforce alienation dynamics by adopting polarized positions. Evaluators should use evidence-based assessments rather than subjective judgments (Garber et al., 2022).
- **Social and economic stressors**: Financial strain, job instability, and housing insecurity can exacerbate PCCP. Evaluators should recognize these external pressures when assessing each parent's ability to provide a stable environment (W. G. Austin, 2018b).

CONCLUSION

This chapter examines various conceptual frameworks that explain the causes of PCCP, distinguishing between enmeshment, estrangement, alienation, and developmental or contextual resistance. Rather than adhering to a singular diagnostic approach, contemporary research advocates for an ecological perspective that considers the interplay of child-specific factors, parental behaviors, systemic influences, and external pressures. A key theme emphasized throughout is the need to move beyond polarized debates, such as alienation versus estrangement, in favor of a multidimensional, child-centered approach. Professionals are encouraged to integrate structured decision-making tools, forensic assessment methodologies, and systemic analyses to evaluate both parental influence and child experiences. The chapter underscores that disruptions in parent–child contact rarely stem from a single cause but are instead the result of complex, interacting variables, including parenting behaviors, coparenting conflict, and a child's psychological responses to their family environment. Forensic evaluators are urged to move away from rigid diagnostic labels and instead focus on relational dynamics that impact a child's ability to maintain meaningful connections with both parents. Historical perspectives from Gould (1998) to Garber (2020a, 202b) reinforce this idea, emphasizing the importance of identifying patterns of behavior over diagnosing syndromes.

Ultimately, the chapter calls for a scientifically grounded, family-centered forensic approach—one that seeks to understand relationships and interactions rather than reducing complex family struggles to simple diagnostic terms. Seek out dynamics, not diagnosis!

21

Evolving Conceptualizations of Domestic Violence

This chapter has several aims. We discuss the various definitions of domestic violence (DV) and studies that have examined evaluator training in family violence assessment. We address myths and misconceptions about family violence and its effect upon family members, as well as whether parenting plan evaluators are adequately addressing family violence allegations. We then summarize several models of family violence that have been reported in the literature as useful assessment paradigms. We discuss children as witnesses, effects on children of exposure to DV, and effects on parent–child relationships related to exposure to DV. Lastly, we describe various assessment procedures.

DEFINITIONS: CHALLENGES AND AMBIGUITIES

We begin by providing an operational definition of DV used in this chapter. We designate the term *family violence* to refer to all types of physically, psychologically, and emotionally abusive behaviors within a family system. We chose the generic term family violence in order to differentiate specific forms of family violence that will be discussed below.

Family violence is a major social policy concern around the globe (Ackerman et al., 2019). More than 15 years ago, Ver Steegh and Dalton (2008) called attention to the "surprising lack of agreement about its nature, causes, frequency, and appropriate legal treatment" (p. 454). The field has both progressed

https://doi.org/10.1037/0000474-022
Parenting Plan Evaluations: An Evidence-Informed Approach to Child Custody, by J. W. Gould and C. M. Mulchay

and stood still in its attempts to reach a professional consensus about definition of terms and with empirical bases for distinctions between and among different types of DV, such as intimate partner violence (IPV) and coercive control (CC; K. A. Crossman & Hardesty, 2018).

We provide a cursory explanation of IPV and CC here and provide a more extensive discussion in the body of this chapter. Table 21.1 summarizes the key differences between the two concepts.

IPV refers to physical, sexual, psychological, or financial abuse that occurs within an intimate relationship, regardless of gender, marital status, or sexual orientation. IPV can be situational or patterned, and its severity varies. Characteristics of IPV include, but are not limited to, physical violence (e.g. hitting, pushing, strangulation) or psychological abuse (e.g. threats, gaslighting, humiliation). IPV might be situational (i.e. conflict-driven) or coercive (i.e. power-driven). One of the ways to distinguish conflict driven violence from coercive, power-driven violence is to assess its frequency and severity.

In contrast, CC is a strategic pattern of ongoing psychological and emotional abuse aimed at dominating, isolating, and regulating the victim's autonomy and freedom. Unlike episodic violence, CC does not always involve physical violence but instead relies on systematic manipulation. Characteristics of CC include, but are not limited to, monitoring and surveillance, isolation, threats and intimidation, gaslighting and psychological domination, and financial control.

The progress in the field has been reflected in more and better research designs used to examine family violence factors. The field has become better at discriminating different forms of family violence that include both acts of physical abuse as well as acts of emotional and psychological abuse. The profound consequences of the effects of different forms of family violence have been increasingly identified, and trauma-informed treatment approaches have continued to develop. As discussed earlier in this book, trauma-informed mental health forensic assessment has developed from the family violence literature.

TABLE 21.1. Key Differences Between IPV and Coercive Control

Factor	Intimate partner violence (IPV)	Coercive control (CC)
Nature	Can be situational or patterned	Chronic, systematic control
Physical violence	Often present but not always systematic	Not always physical; can rely on psychological abuse
Intent	Often arises from conflict or emotional dysregulation	Power and domination over victim
Psychological abuse	May be present but not always central	Primary mechanism of abuse
Isolation and monitoring	Sometimes present	Core feature of CC
Risk to victim	Injury risk varies; may escalate	Escalates over time; can lead to homicide

Research and scholarship describing increasingly more complex and sophisticated ideas of different forms of family violence have progressed from ideas about separation engendered violence (Johnston & Campbell, 1993) to the complexities of intimate partner violence (W. G. Austin & Drozd, 2012, 2013; Drozd, 2008; Holtzworth-Munroe et al., 2021) to the nuances of CC (Beck & Raghavan, 2010; Champion, 2022; K. A. Crossman & Hardesty, 2018; Hardesty et al., 2015, 2024; Hardesty & Ogolsky, 2020; E. Katz, 2022; E. Katz et al., 2020), which will be discussed in the following sections.

Similar to the conceptual development of thinking about parent–child contact problems that has moved from a categorical to a dimensional perspective, understanding the complexities involved in assessment of allegations of physical, emotional, and psychological abuse has moved from a categorical to a dimensional perspective. We define a dimensional perspective to include analyses of multiple factors that are likely to influence multiple variables within a family system. For example, using an ecological model as discussed throughout this book, dimensional assessment of allegations of family violence might include examination of individual psychopathology, dyadic relationships within the family between and within generational boundaries, family system relationships, extended family relationships, and cultural and community relationships.

There continue to be arguments among professionals who adhere to a particular model, claiming that their ideas about DV, IPV, or CC are the dominant or most reliable approach to the assessment of physical, emotional, and psychological abuse. We believe that there is value in examining different ideas about the nature, causes, assessment, and treatment of physical, emotional, or psychological abuse.

From a dimensional perspective, family violence in its various forms affects family systems, not just individuals. We find great value in the work of Hardesty & Ogolsky (2020) who are bringing the ecological model and dimensional analyses into understanding the complexities of family violence.

Family violence has been associated with deterioration of parenting skills in mothers (Günaydin & Zincir, 2024). It has been associated with increased depression, anxiety, and emotional distress in mothers and children (Holt et al., 2008; E. Katz, 2019, 2022). Adverse effects on children's brain development have been associated with exposure to DV (Tsavoussis et al., 2014) as well as a myriad of other emotional and psychological challenges (Callaghan, Fellin, & Alexander, 2017; Lourenço et al., 2013). There are concerns about the intergenerational effects of witnessing family violence among children (Forke et al., 2019).

A significant obstacle has been the lack of professional consensus regarding each of the terms used to describe different forms of family violence. Despite the lack of professional consensus around terms commonly used to describe family violence, reliance on the scientific process provides an avenue toward clarity: the operational definition.

An operational definition clearly defines the meaning of a term and their use within a specific context. Operational definitions provide a means by which other people are able to see how the specific terms are being applied in the particular case. It provides the reader with a clear definition of terms being used to describe the object of investigation. Operational definitions in evaluation reports and testimony are needed so that the consumer of the information knows exactly what is being discussed.

We emphasize the need for evaluators to provide clear operational definitions of the type of family violence they are investigating. Consistent with one of the *Daubert* factors, evaluators might cite a particular underlying theory of science as guiding their investigation. For example, the evaluator could describe the social isolation factor drawn from Stark's *coercive control model.* To ensure clarity, evaluators should

- identify a specific evidence-based model of CC,
- cite peer-reviewed literature supporting that model, and
- explain why the model is relevant to the case.

Evaluators would begin by citing Dr. Evan Stark's (2007) widely recognized coercive control theory and its description of CC as a *pattern of domination* that includes

- isolation (restricting access to friends, family, or support systems),
- monitoring (constant surveillance of a partner's actions, communication, or finances),
- threats and intimidation (verbal threats, destruction of property, harm to pets or children),
- deprivation of independence (controlling employment, transportation, or finances), and
- gaslighting and psychological manipulation (distorting the victim's sense of reality).

A parenting plan evaluator citing Stark's model would reference studies supporting its usefulness in family courts. The evaluator would then apply the model's factors to the specific case at hand. Evaluators should define each factor clearly (e.g., "monitoring behavior" means tracking phone calls, installing GPS, reading emails) and select measures that use the same or similar definitions of the terms that are being assessed by the assessment tool. Once the definitions are provided and appropriate measures are selected, the evaluator needs to show how the data from the assessment tool captures the relevant behaviors in the case.

For example, assume that a parent alleges that their ex-partner has isolated them from family and friends. Instead of making a vague claim, the evaluator would define the behaviors of concern (e.g., "The alleged perpetrator removed the victim's name from joint phone plans, blocked access to family contacts, and limited child visitation with extended relatives."). Next, the evaluator would compare the description of the behavior of concern to research-based CC indicators (e.g., "Studies indicate that forced social isolation is a primary strategy of coercive controllers."). A third step would be for the evaluator to assess the reliability of the data by showing how corroborating sources, such as text messages, emails, or witness statements, provide evidence of this behavior.

It is important to remember that evaluators must describe how they assessed each factor and identified the strengths and limitations of each assessment tool. This includes identifying the types of data collected (e.g., interviews, psychological testing, records review). It also includes how the evaluator has addressed the reliability and validity of both the assessment measures and the opinions drawn from those data (e.g., risk of bias, false allegations, memory distortions). Finally, the evaluator should address limitations on opinions, including describing their consideration of alternative hypotheses and why the opinion proffered to the court has the strongest basis in the facts of the case. A simple outline might help to organize the steps taken that resulted in the proffered opinion:

- **Methods**: Interviews with the alleged victim, analysis of text messages, police reports.
- **Strengths**: Multiple data sources allowed cross-validation.
- **Limitations**: Fear of retaliation may have caused the parent to downplay threats.
- **Expert opinion caveat**: "Due to the potential for victim underreporting, a lack of explicit threats does not necessarily indicate the absence of coercive control."

MISCONCEPTIONS AND MYTHS ABOUT FAMILY VIOLENCE AND VICTIMS

There are many misconceptions and myths about family violence and victims. In this section, we discuss several that have contributed to the difficulties in finding professional consensus regarding definitions of the various terms associated with family violence. For example, Jaffe et al. (2003) identified the following misconceptions held by many evaluators:

- **Misconception 1: Family violence is rarely a problem for divorcing couples involved in a child custody dispute**. The reality is that the majority of parents in high-conflict divorces involving child custody disputes report a history of family violence.
- **Misconception 2: Family violence ends with separation for abused women**. The reality is that abused women often face continuing risks from their partner after separation.

- **Misconception 3: As long as children are not abused directly, they are not harmed by exposure to family violence**. The reality is that children exposed to family violence may suffer from significant emotional and behavioral problems related to this traumatic experience.
- **Misconception 4: As family violence is behavior between adults, it is not relevant for the determination of child custody**. The reality is that family violence is highly relevant to the determination of child custody by the courts and court-related services.
- **Misconception 5: Family courts, lawyers, and court-related services such as mediation and custody evaluation can assess the needs of abused women and their children as well as the impact of the batterer**. The reality is that the significance of family violence is often overlooked by family courts, lawyers, and court-related services.
- **Misconception 6: Legal and mental health (counseling) services for abused women and their children separating from batterers are readily accessible and well-coordinated**. The reality is that abused women often experience difficulty accessing appropriate legal and mental health counseling services for themselves and their children.
- **Misconception 7: There are no apparent solutions and community strategies to the complex dilemmas posed by abused women and children separating from batterers**. The reality is that there are many emerging community and court innovations in responding to women and children separating from an abusive parent.

Other authors have proposed additional misconceptions individuals often hold about family violence (Sattler, 1998):

- **Misconception 1: It doesn't happen to someone like me**. **It happens to poor and uneducated people.** The fact is that family violence victims are found in all socioeconomic groups.
- **Misconception 2: Pregnant women are not battered**. Recent CDC (2024b) surveillance shows that about 5–6% of pregnant women in the U.S. experience intimate partner violence during pregnancy .
- **Misconception 3: Battering is a private affair**. **It isn't appropriate for health care providers to assess or intervene.** The fact is that health care providers are often legally, morally, or ethically compelled to help by diagnosing victims of battering and informing them of their rights and how to get help.
- **Misconception 4: If the victims wanted the abuse to end, they would leave or seek help**. The fact is that most women seek outside help from clergy, police, family, and health care providers, but are often encouraged to return home and to keep the family together because the "outside help" people are not trained to recognize the signs and ramifications of family

violence. Research demonstrates that as many as 75% of visits to the emergency room by battered women occur after separation (Cuthbert et al., 2002).

- **Misconception 5: The battered woman is masochistic.** The fact is that a woman only stays when she is economically and emotionally dependent, embarrassed, lonely, afraid of retaliation, or guilt-ridden. Many abused women leave as many as seven times before they leave for good. Tragically, 70% of the women killed in family violence situations have already left or are in the process of leaving.
- **Misconception 6: Only alcoholics and drug addicts abuse their partners.** The fact is that batterers do demonstrate high usage of alcohol, but that use is separate from violent behavior. Family violence is an issue of control and dominance over another person. Alcohol or other drugs do not cause violence or abuse but are contributing factors.
- **Misconception 7: Battering only occurs in heterosexual relationships.** The fact is that battering can occur and has been reported among gay and lesbian couples.
- **Misconception 8: Only women are battered.** Research over the past decades has demonstrated that viewing family violence as a unidirectional phenomenon does not address the various types of DV, some of which is male initiated, female initiated, or bidirectional.

ARE PARENTING PLAN EVALUATORS ADEQUATELY ASSESSING FAMILY VIOLENCE ALLEGATIONS?

Several years ago, concerns were raised about the adequacy of training of parenting plan evaluators. Over the past 2 decades, several state psychology licensing boards and state legislatures have required training in family violence. There is little published research examining the degree to which these mandated training programs are similar in content or the degree to which the programs have contributed to increases in the competence of evaluation procedures. However, the mandated programs provide opportunities for the dissemination of information about family violence and often require licensed professionals to take yearly or biannual continuing education updates.

A review of the research on whether parenting plan evaluators understand and assess family violence yields mixed results (Saunders et al., 2013, 2016). Saunders et al. examined the hypothesis that evaluators' belief in false allegations by the mother and their recommendations that perpetrators have custody or unsupervised visits would be positively associated with (a) being a male evaluator, (b) patriarchal norms, (c) not knowing a survivor of IPV, and (d) less knowledge of IPV. Saunders et al. also hypothesized that evaluators' belief in false allegations by mothers would be related to their recommendation that perpetrators have custody or unsupervised visits. Results supported most of the hypothesized relationships with particular support for the role of belief variables as predictors of evaluator recommendations.

Throughout this book, we have tried to point out instances in which bias factors might play a role in the findings upon which experts often base their opinions. We note the potential role of an anchor bias in the Saunders et al. study's formulation of hypotheses and the subsequent findings that supported the hypotheses. Anchoring bias occurs when individuals rely too heavily on an initial piece of information (the "anchor") when making decisions, even when new or contradictory evidence is presented. In the case of custody evaluators, preexisting beliefs about false allegations of IPV serve as an anchor that influences their decision making. These beliefs shape how they interpret evidence, even when the available data does not support them.

Saunders et al. found that some evaluators believe mothers frequently make false allegations of IPV. This belief anchors their assessment process, resulting in an increased likelihood that the researchers would be skeptical of abuse claims even when corroborating evidence exists. If a researcher starts with the belief that mothers commonly fabricate abuse claims, they might design investigative questions that dismiss warning signs of coercive control, gaslighting, or post-separation abuse. Said differently, when the research questions are formulated based upon a preexisting belief (i.e., the anchor), it is likely that the results of the data collection and the opinions that flow from those data will confirm the anchor.

As noted above, many jurisdictions require continuing education classes focused on family violence training. Bow and Boxer (2003) surveyed parenting plan evaluators for their education and exposure to family violence assessment and found 68.2% of their sample had no graduate courses addressing family violence. However, custody evaluators had taken continuing education courses on family violence. The average number of seminars on family violence was 7.4 (median = 4.0) and the median number of family violence books or articles read by evaluators was 18. Only 4.5% of the sample attended no seminars and 2.7% had read fewer than three books or articles (Bow & Boxer, 2003). They concluded that evaluators reported involvement in continuing education courses focused on family violence education. Bow and Boxer also found that 37% of custody evaluations involved allegations of family violence. About one-half (46%) of the allegations surfaced around the time of separation, about one-third (29%) were characterized as examples of episodic violence, and about one-quarter (24%) were characterized as chronic violence (Bow & Boxer, 2003).

About 50% of the violence was reported to be male initiated (51%), and 11% was reported to be female initiated. Within the custody context, 14% of intimate partner violence was found to be bidirectional. The most frequently reported types of family violence were, in order of frequency of occurrence: verbal or emotional abuse, physical aggression, coercion and threats, controlling finances, destruction of property, isolation, stalking, rape, and kidnapping children (Bow & Boxer, 2003).

Evaluators were found not to be using abuse-specific measures in their assessment protocols. Bow and Boxer reported that when specialized questionnaires were being utilized, they were used when assessing adults; 29% developed their own questionnaire, 20% used the Spousal Assault Risk Assessment Guide, 15% used the Psychopathy Checklist-Revised, 11% used the Historical-Clinical-Risk-Management-20, and 9% used the Conflict Tactics Scale (CTS; Bow & Boxer, 2003).

Use of trauma-specific measures such as the Trauma Symptom Inventory (Briere, 1995), the Trauma Symptom Checklist for Children (Briere, 1996), the Detailed Assessment of Post Traumatic Stress (Briere, 2001), or other such measures that might assist evaluators in assessing the magnitude of trauma reported by the alleged victims were not reported to have been used (Bow & Boxer, 2003).

Logan et al. (2002) conducted a content analysis of 82 PPEs and found that evaluators do not appear to investigate the nature or extent of family violence, and "more specifically, (evaluators) do not explore family violence as a way of attending to the child's safety interests" (p. 735). Examination of evaluator reports found that often parents were interviewed together despite having court documents indicating concern about allegations of family violence toward the mother. "[T]his practice could contribute not only to distorted information from victims but could also contribute to further harm through retribution for disclosures of violent acts or child endangerment" (Logan et al., 2002, p. 735). This concern is consistent with research over the past 20 years showing that abused women were more likely than nonabused women to report that the presence of the abuser in the courtroom may adversely influence their ability to be open during court proceedings because of their fear of possible future harm by the abuser (Newmark et al., 1995).

In contrast to Bow and Boxer, Logan et al. (2002) found that multiple methods were not used to examine the "best interests of the child." Just over half of the evaluations reviewed had obtained information from collateral interview sources. Only about 38% of reviewed reports included home visits, and even fewer reported reviewing collateral information from documents such as school records, criminal histories, medical records, counseling records, or other court records.

Fundamental aspects of the prevailing family violence paradigm clash with central tenets of current family courts; namely, the family court's emphasis on the increasing role of fathers, preferences for joint and shared custody and parenting plans, and the saliency of the friendly parent concept (Jaffe et al., 2003). There is some research supporting these claims (Hans et al., 2014).

These research findings, reports from the family violence community, and concerns from within the PPE community should have direct implications for selecting and training parenting plan evaluators (Drozd & Olesen, 2004). Drozd and Olesen wrote, "We find ourselves greatly concerned that there is a group of colleagues who are engaged in the practice of parenting plan evaluations who do not understand how to competently assess the dynamics of and effects upon children of family violence" (p. 68).

EVOLUTION OF MODELS FOR ASSESSING FAMILY VIOLENCE IN THE PARENTING PLAN FIELD

It is important to understand the development of DV and IPV research paradigms that began with attention primarily on heterosexual, married couples and has progressed significantly from those early days. Today, DV and IPV research has included lesbian, gay, bisexual, transgender, and queer (LGBTQ) relationships, cohabiting partners, and other nontraditional family structures. Many of these earlier studies shaped policy and interventions in ways that often-neglected nonheterosexual relationships. However, more recent research has attempted to bridge this gap, acknowledging that IPV occurs across all gender identities and sexual orientations. For example, Straus's (1979) seminal work that set the stage for early DV research focused on husband-wife relationships. Gelles's (1972) book, *The Violent Home: A Study of Physical Aggression Between Husbands and Wives* continued the research emphasis on domestic violence between married couples. R. E. Dobash and R. Dobash (1979) argued that domestic violence is rooted in patriarchal systems and was largely framed around heterosexual marriage dynamics. Johnson's (1995) important contribution that began examining domestic violence in terms of typologies was framed with the context of heterosexual relationships. The groundbreaking national survey of Tjaden and Thoennes (2000) was the first to bring to light IPV and was initially based upon heterosexual couples. Only later was discussion about same-sex relationships included. Many researchers, scholars, and clinicians have contributed to the development of various models to assist in the assessment of various forms of family violence. We have included a summary of those models that we believe have made the most significant contributions to the development of conceptual models and assessment procedures used to guide assessment of family violence.

We do not propose that we provide an exhaustive list of published models and the choices we have selected as most useful in guiding our thinking about assessment of family violence allegations in parenting plan disputes might tell you more about us, the authors, then we can anticipate. Selection from among a multidecade literature addressing family violence and its assessment reflects the biases of those doing the selection. We seek not to offend anyone by excluding from reference respected colleagues and their work. All expert opinions should be based upon adequate and sufficiently reliable data. We endeavor to explain the professional and scientific basis for our selection of the particular models described below. Unlike court testimony, however, we will not address reasonable alternative models simply because comparing and contrasting the nonselected model against the selected models would require significantly more space than we can accommodate in this book. Instead, we have dedicated two chapters. We begin with the Duluth model.

The Duluth Model

In the early 1970s, the *Duluth model* developed out of the Domestic Abuse Intervention Project in Duluth, Minnesota. Proponents of the Duluth model challenged the then-prevailing social context they viewed as accepting or condoning violence or "wife beating" (Pence et al., 2011). The Duluth model emphasized that confronting the power dynamics that operate in abusive relationships are central to protecting battered women. The Duluth approach spawned the "battered women's movement" that challenged deeply entrenched notions and practices concerning violence towards women (https://bwjp.org/).

In dealing with domestic abuse and violence cases within the Duluth model, the single most important factor to be considered is how the use of violence affects the distribution of power in abusive relationships (Pence et al., 2011). A basic assumption of the Duluth model is that the use of violence by men in marriage serves a social function and is intended to control and define women's lives.

The Duluth model drew attention to the cultural minimizing of the ways in which family violence was ignored or reframed as a normative aspect of marriage. The Duluth model focused attention on the minimizing language used to describe violence against women by their partners that served to mask the severity and the potentially lethal consequences of that violence. Euphemisms such as "domestic disputes" or "disturbances" in police reports, "marital conflict" in counseling files, and "incompatibility" in divorce pleadings trivialized the trauma women experienced. Gender bias, victim blaming, lack of resources, as well as the ambivalence, fear, and dependencies victims experience with their abusers make the prosecution of these cases extremely difficult (Ackerman et al., 2019; Zarling & Russell, 2022).

The *Power and Control Wheel* reflected a pictorial depiction of the power and control dynamics of the Duluth model. The central premise of the wheel is that battering is caused by a culturally supported belief that people have the right to control their partners. The internal spokes of the wheel reference eight control behaviors or dynamics of the perpetrators. A second circle surrounding the internal wheel and spokes identifies the physical and sexual violence as tactics used by the batterer to generate power and control over their victims (Dutton & Starzomski, 1997).

In the Duluth model, the view of family violence is built upon four assumptions:

1. DV is rooted in patriarchy and gender-based power imbalances. The Duluth model assumes that domestic violence is primarily a result of societal norms that support male dominance and female subordination.

2. Men use violence as a tool of control, not as a loss of control. The model posits that abusers do not act out of uncontrolled anger or stress but rather as a conscious strategy to maintain power over their partners.

3. Holding offenders accountable is key to stopping domestic violence. The model emphasizes that perpetrators must take full responsibility for their

abusive behaviors, rejecting excuses based on external factors such as substance abuse or childhood trauma.

4. Victims' experiences must be at the center of interventions. The model prioritizes survivor voices, advocating for community-based responses that support and empower victims rather than blaming them.

These four assumptions shape the Power and Control Wheel, a core tool of the model, which outlines the various ways abusers manipulate and exert control over their partners beyond physical violence, including emotional abuse, economic control, and isolation.

Dutton and Starzomski (1997) offered early criticism of the Duluth model. They investigated whether the Power and Control Wheel, which describes eight forms of power and control tactics, constituted a syndrome of intercorrelated actions. Tests were conducted of whether certain features of the abusive personality could accurately predict various octants of the Power and Control Wheel. With the exception of "using the children as pawns," all Power and Control Wheel dimensions of the abuse of power and control were significantly intercorrelated. Dutton and Starzomski (1997) interpreted these findings to suggest a possible syndrome of abuse of power and control. They found that personality disturbance was significantly correlated with all octants except using the children. Their conclusion was that their findings supported a comprehensive model of abusive uses of power and control tactics integrating both social and psychological influences.

Other alternatives to the original Duluth model have drawn attention to various systems of oppression (e.g., heterosexism, ageism, ableism, racism, spirituality and religion, classism, and sexism) that might affect the experiences of victims of IPV. Factors such as personal, cultural, and structural identities are viewed individually or in combination as potentially influencing women's experiences of intimate partner abuse. Chavis and Hill (2009) revised the Power and Control Wheel to incorporate these additional variables, calling their modification the *Multicultural Power and Control Wheel.*

As our field has begun to critically examine assumptions that have traditionally guided thinking about family violence assessment, among other areas of mental health, questions have been raised about the application of the Power and Control Wheel to non-White populations.

One form of family violence is sexual violence. A recent study examined customs, beliefs, and practices among individuals living in seven different Pacific cultures who represented ethnic groups different from those upon which the Duluth model was based (Rankine et al., 2017). The study's findings identified the brother–sister covenant and the sanctity of women as strong protective and preventive factors against sexual violence, expressed differently in each Pacific culture studied (i.e., people from Fiji, Niue, Samoa, Tokelau, Tonga, and Tuvalu in New Zealand).

Although study participants came from seven different island cultures, most participants viewed sexual violence as involving their extended families, village, and church communities, rather than solely the individuals concerned. Rankine et al. (2017) concluded that the communal values and practices of these seven Pacific cultures raise questions about the individualistic assumptions and the meaning of violence underlying the Power and Control Wheel and the Duluth model of domestic violence. Their findings might speak to differences in community, family, and individual perceptions among people from different cultures or ethnic groups in how best to address family violence and its treatment. The participants in this study came from a collectivist society rather than a culture based more on an individualistic culture such as those upon which the Duluth model was developed. The authors' findings raised questions about how an individualized model such as the Duluth model can help services effectively support women in these collective societies experiencing violence, and how it can contribute to Pacific community prevention of violence (Rankine et al., 2017).

Johnston and Campbell's Typology of Interparental Violence in Custody Cases

Johnston and Campbell's (1993) introduction of a family violence typology was a significant contributing factor in creating a paradigm change in the field of family violence theory and assessment. They defined family violence as the use of physical restriction, force, coercion or intimidation of force by one parent to force another parent to do something against their will. Included among their definition of violent behaviors were hitting, slapping, biting, choking, threat with a weapon, unlawful entry, destruction of property, physical injury, suicide, and murder.

Violent behavior was also defined to include psychological intimidation such as threats, control and inappropriate use of power tactics. Among the identified behaviors that characterized psychological intimidation were harassment, stalking, threats against children, and violence against pets or property. Johnston and Campbell (1993) did not include a definition of emotional abuse but note that emotional abuse often precedes, accompanies, or follows physically violent behaviors.

Although models of IPV and CC were not developed for several decades, it is easy to see the basis for these models evolving from the seminal work of Johnston and Campbell. The Johnston and Campbell model of domestic violence built upon earlier typologies of IPV by incorporating a forensic family law perspective and integrating insights from psychology and criminology. Their model refined previous understandings of DV by emphasizing the heterogeneity of abusive relationships, especially in the context of family court disputes and custody evaluations.

The first generation of early generalized theories of domestic violence (1970s–1980s) viewed IPV as a unitary phenomenon, primarily framed through three contrasting psychological theories of the times. The first of these categories is feminist theories (e.g., L. E. A. Walker, 1979) that emphasized patriarchal control and gendered power dynamics. A second was psychological perspectives focusing on personality disorders, attachment issues, and trauma. A third was social learning theories (e.g., Bandura, 1977) that highlighted intergenerational transmission of violence.

In the 1990s, Johnson (1995, 2008) challenged the singular view of DV by proposing different types of IPV, distinguishing between

- **Coercive controlling violence (intimate terrorism)**: severe, systematic control and violence,
- **Situational couple violence**: conflict-driven, bidirectional violence,
- **Separation-instigated violence**: violence occurring during breakups, and
- **Mutual violent control**: two partners using CC against each other.

At about the same time, Johnston and Campbell (1993) applied many of Johnson's ideas to the custody world, developing a custody-focused model. Johnston and Campbell developed a typology that helped custody evaluators differentiate types of IPV in high-conflict divorce and custody cases. This typology was forensically useful, helping courts assess risk, child impact, and coparenting potential. Their model was the first to bridge the gap between forensic psychology and family law, ensuring that IPV assessments in custody cases were scientifically grounded (i.e., building on Johnson's framework), trauma-informed (i.e., acknowledging victim vulnerability), and risk-sensitive (i.e., differentiating types of violence for court interventions).

Johnston and Campbell's (1993) model included five types of intimate partner violence:

1. Ongoing or episodic battering (severe, patterned coercive violence)
2. Female-initiated violence
3. Male-controlling interactive violence (male-driven but reactive)
4. Separation-engendered violence triggered by relationship breakdown (i.e., postdivorce trauma)
5. Psychotic and paranoid reactions leading to violence

Ongoing or Episodic Battering

In the Johnston and Campbell (1993) model, *ongoing or episodic battering* was defined as battering male–battered wife. It was hypothesized that the propensity for physical abuse and violence lies with the men in these relationships. Typically, these males demonstrated low frustration tolerance, poor impulse control, and a high need to dominate and control their female partners. These males showed signs of significant jealousy and possessiveness. They displayed traditional chauvinistic attitudes and an exaggerated view of their masculinity. About half of males identified as ongoing or episodic batterers were also found to engage in the use of drugs or alcohol as a precipitant or contributor to violence (Johnston & Campbell, 1993).

Men in this category typically display little impulse control when they act out their internal rage and frustration toward others. These men appear to want to hurt their partner as much as they want to control them. They also tend to deny or minimize their abuse or place the blame for their violence on their wives.

Women who separated from their partners were found to be at significant risk of harm because of the increased danger from the episodic male batterer. These men tend to stalk their former partners, terrorizing them with threats of or attempts at murder or suicide.

These men also begged for forgiveness and reconciliation, promising to change. Women in these relationships were at significant risk of harm years after separation.

Female-Initiated Violence

Johnston and Campbell (1993) researched women initiating aggression in heterosexual relationships. It is important to remember that this study was conducted when such research most often examined heterosexual, married relationships. Johnston and Campbell reported that these women were active, demanding, and emotionally intimidating to their husbands. Few of these women were reported to have done much physical damage with their violence. They were reported to throw objects, destroy possessions, and attack their partners (e.g., hitting, biting, kicking, and other methods of physical assault). These attacks were reported to have included threats to use weapons, especially when the security of the relationship was being threatened, most often during marital separation.

The male partners of these women often tried to prevent, contain, or restrain the aggressive behavior by passively fending off their attacks. Postseparation, these men ceased their attempts to contain or placate their wives' aggressive reactions. Johnston and Campbell (1993) characterized these men as passive, depressed, obsessive, intellectualizing, intimidated by their wives' aggressiveness, and embarrassed when pulled into the fight.

Compared with the episodic male batterer, female-initiated violence tends to result in less severe damage and injury (Johnston & Campbell, 1993). Episodic male-batterer violence typically results in more severe physical injuries, including bruises, fractures, and lacerations. There is a greater likelihood of internal injuries (e.g., organ damage from blunt force trauma) and concussions or head injuries from strangulation or blunt force. Female-initiated violence tends to be less severe, often resulting in scratches, slaps, or minor bruising. Often the injuries are defensive injuries (e.g., scratches on forearms, bites). There are also fewer incidents of concussions or broken bones. There are differences in the pattern of assault. Male-initiated violence (either episodic or CC) often involved repeated blows with greater force. The use of weapons is more frequent and included strangulation, a high-risk lethality indicator. Female-initiated violence was more often reactive rather than sustained. There is a lower frequency of the use of weapons, and physical aggression is more likely to involve defensive physical responses, such as pushing. Male batterers often exhibit CC behaviors (e.g., stalking, intimidation, financial control) while female-initiated violence more often occurs in self-defense or retaliation rather than as a sustained pattern of domination.

Male Controlling Interactive Violence

Johnston and Campbell (1993) found that male controlling interactive violence often resulted from increasing disagreements between the spouses characterized by escalating aggression beginning with verbal insults to verbal abuse to physical violence. Johnston and Campbell reported that the most outstanding aspect of this type of family aggression was the male's overwhelming need to assert control over his partner. Men were observed to use physical force in their attempts to dominate and overpower their wives, yet this aggressive behavior did not typically include sadistic acts or brutal beatings. Demonstrating the interactive aspect of this type of family violence, men were found to display varying amounts of control over their behaviors that were related to their perception of the level of resistance they perceived from their partners.

Psychological characteristics of these males were found to reflect traditional beliefs in authoritarian and dictatorial behavior as being part of an appropriate role within the family, including the use of acts of physical aggression as a way of resolving both intrafamilial and extrafamilial conflict. This physical aggression was found to spill over to hurting their children, their siblings, and their parents (Johnston & Campbell, 1993).

Parents within this category of violent behavior tended to blame one another for the frequency and intensity of aggressiveness. As more stress was placed on the divorcing couple, there was a greater chance of violence. When alcohol was involved, the violence tended to be more severe, and the perpetrator was unable to recall clear memories of the incident. Once separated and no longer able to provoke each other, Johnston and Campbell (1993) reported that the violence between spouses often ended.

Separation-Engendered Violence or Postdivorce Trauma

Johnston and Campbell (1993) found that *separation-engendered violence*, also called *postdivorce trauma*, is the type of family violence most likely to be found in custody disputes. In instances of separation-endangered violence, acts of violence were uncharacteristic of the divorcing couple's everyday lives, absent during their marriage. The aggressiveness of these couples was found to be directly related to the increased tension and distress associated with relationship dissolution. Family violence in these cases was unpredictable and infrequent.

The unpredictable nature of the physical aggression resulted in increased mistrust of the offending spouse precisely because the aggressive actions were unexpected. Johnston and Campbell (1993) reported that both men and women were able to acknowledge their aggression and expressed genuine shame over their loss of control and injury to their former partner. In general, the risk for further violence was small once the emotional and legal issues in the divorce were resolved.

Psychotic and Paranoid Reactions Leading to Violence

For a small number of parents involved in family dissolution, violent family behavior was found to be related to significant psychopathology. According to Johnston and Campbell (1993), "the marital separation often triggered an acute phase of danger wherein a disturbed spouse pieced together the rubble of their marriage and mentally rewrote history, perceiving their partner as having intentionally plotted to exploit them and cast them off" (pp. 197–198).

The disturbed partner was found to respond with aggressiveness to their perceived feelings of betrayal in the form of a preemptive strike against their partner. The abnormal behavior ranged from fleeting, incoherent ideas that were coupled with unpredictable outbursts of verbal and physical aggression to full blown paranoid delusions. When such paranoid delusions emerged, not only was the partner at risk, but also those who were perceived to be part of the conspiracy (Johnston & Campbell, 1993).

The victim spouses reportedly would respond in one of two ways. Either they perceived the danger in the threats and were frightened by it, seeking to avoid or calm the aggressor, or they appeared oblivious to or in denial of the significant danger perpetrated by their disturbed partner (Johnston & Campbell, 1993).

Summary of Johnston and Campbell's Model

Johnston and Campbell (1993) reported that boys' adjustment tended to be most significantly impacted in the male-batterer category. They were equally likely to be less disturbed in the male-controlling and female-initiated violence categories. Boys were equally likely to be least disturbed in the separation-trauma and nonviolent divorcing families.

Girls were found to be equally disturbed in male-batterer and male-controlling violent families. They were less disturbed in female-initiated and separation-trauma families. They were least disturbed in nonviolent divorcing families.

Johnston and Campbell (1993) spoke to the need to differentiate among the various types of family violence and how each type affects a family. Further, family violence is likely to affect parent–child relationships differently based upon a variety of factors that include, but are not limited to, the effects of different patterns of violence, frequency of violence, severity of violence, and age of the child.

Johnston and Campbell (1993) recommend that consideration of sole or joint custody is inappropriate with a father who has engaged in ongoing or episodic battering. Similarly, any parent who is psychotic or has paranoid delusions should not be awarded sole or joint custody. In fact, when the threat of violence is real, visitation may need to be supervised or suspended until the children's safety is assured. They also warned that spouses who left battering or psychotic relationships may have diminished capacity to parent children effectively as a function of their victimization. They may need assistance in rehabilitating their parenting competencies to a level of satisfaction.

According to Johnston and Campbell (1993), a careful examination of the parenting capacity of a mother who is a female-initiator is needed before considering placement of children under her care. It may be that the father is the more appropriate residential parent, however, he may be too passive and unavailable to his children because of his victimization. When considering a male-controlling aggressor, fathers may be found to need parenting skills to manage their children assertively. Similarly, the mother may also need such skills. Very clear, structured transition routines are needed to assure the safety of the children as well as effectively manage the potential for conflict between the parents.

Michael Johnson's Differentiation Theory

Johnson (1995) argued that there are two distinct forms of couple violence. Johnson noted that some families suffer from *common couple violence*, characterized by occasional outbursts of violence from either husbands or wives. Other families are terrorized by systematic male violence that he labeled *patriarchal terrorism*. Patriarchal terrorism has also been called intimate terrorism (Leone et al., 2007).

Johnson's (1995) differentiation theory explored differences found in data from national surveys and data coming from women's shelters across the country (p. 285). National survey data had found women as likely to utilize violence in response to couple violence as men (Gelles, 1972). This was markedly different from the power and control type of abuse involving men's subordination of women (Bancroft & Silverman, 2002).

Johnson's observations are early recognition of what today is referred to as coercive controlling behaviors. Patriarchal terrorism was defined by relationships in which men controlled "'their women' [through] systematic use of not only violence, but economic subordination, threats, isolation, and other control tactics" (Johnson, 1995, p. 285). Johnson argued that common couple violence, or situational couple violence, is the norm and much more frequent than patriarchal terrorism, which was rare.

Although parenting plan evaluators report that the majority of cases involve situational violence rather than violence characterized by power and control (Saunders et al., 2013), some fear that a widespread belief that those who litigate custody are not that different than the normal population reinforces a tendency to minimize the breadth and seriousness of abusive violence, leading to instances where allegations are not considered serious (Ver Steegh, 2005).

Dutton: Gender Neutral Approaches to Family Violence

Dutton and his colleagues (2010) challenged the then-prevailing gender-specific model by citing to research findings little empirical support for the notion that intimate partner violence should be framed as a gender-based issue in which men are overwhelmingly more likely to be perpetrators of family violence and women are more likely to be victims of family violence.

Dutton asserts that traditional models of family violence assume that males are the most likely perpetrators of family violence and females are most likely to be victims of family violence (Dutton, 2006a, 2006b). A primary assumption is that patriarchy and male privilege drive family violence. Assessment strategies that follow from a gender-based model of family violence place greater emphasis on characteristics of the abuser; that is, greater weight is placed on individual characteristics including impulsiveness, low frustration tolerance, narcissism, lack of empathy, and values and beliefs about the relationship between men and women based upon social and gender inequality (Dutton, 2006b).

The study of cognitive biases has become a crucial aspect of understanding human judgment, particularly in research methodology, forensic evaluations, and legal decision making. Although concepts such as confirmatory bias and anchoring effects were not explicitly defined when Dutton raised concerns about flawed methodologies, his observations laid the groundwork for recognizing the ways in which human cognition can shape, distort, or reinforce preexisting conclusions. In the early days of bias research, scholars primarily focused on errors in reasoning and judgment within controlled psychological experiments. However, over time, it became clear that these biases were not limited to experimental settings—they extended into scientific research, forensic evaluations, and even judicial rulings. The gradual incorporation of cognitive science into research methodology helped to expose systemic biases that could lead to incorrect conclusions about IPV, family law cases, and parenting plan assessments.

One of Dutton's primary concerns has been the presence of confirmation bias in IPV research, where studies selectively interpret data in a way that reinforces preexisting theories or ideological perspectives. He criticized the tendency for many IPV studies to focus predominantly on male-perpetrated violence, often disregarding female-perpetrated IPV or mutual violence. He raised concerns about how interpretation of ambiguous behaviors through a gendered lens often lead to one-sided conclusions. These confirmatory bias factors had the effect of minimizing or dismissing findings that contradicted mainstream IPV theories, particularly those showing bidirectional aggression in relationships.

Dutton (2006a) argued that an alternative research paradigm might be based upon analyses of relationship factors or family factors. He referred to his model as a gender-inclusive model. Primary assumptions in a gender-inclusive model are that both men and women are perpetrators and victims of family violence. Family violence and abusive behaviors in intimate relationships result from a variety of causes that are likely to frequently interact. Among the factors that need to be examined include relationships between and among family members, the type of abuse, and the real and perceived effects of familial violence on each member and their respective role in maintaining the dysfunction. It is possible, however, the causes of family violence lie in personality factors more representative of the gender-specific model.

CURRENT ASSESSMENT MODELS

The concept of family violence has moved from an initially undifferentiated concept viewed through the lens of gender-specific models to complex categorical models and, more currently, complex dimensional models. Among the models currently applied to parenting plan assessment are those examining IPV and CC (Palmer et al., 2024).

Intimate Partner Violence

Definition

IPV is abuse or aggression in a former or current relationship (Palmer et al., 2024). One distinction is that DV refers only to physical violence occurring between or among any members of a household, while IPV refers specifically to violence between partners (Drozd et al., 2020). Similar to other important concepts and constructs often used in family court related issues, the inconsistent definitions of IPV limit the ability of the field to speak in one voice about its precise definition, its reliable measurement, effective interventions and prevention programs, and how best to respond to this serious health and social problem (Breiding et al., 2015).

The specific subtype IPV has also been identified as a significant public health threat that affects millions globally (Hardesty & Ogolsky, 2020; Hardesty et al., 2024). Hardesty and Ogolsky's (2020) review provided the most comprehensive analysis of IPV available. They examined IPV at four ecological levels: Individual, relational, community, and sociocultural. At the individual and relational levels, they investigated the prevalence, directionality, typologies, predictors, and outcomes of IPV in pre- and postseparating families. They expanded their review of IPV to include a review of men's violence against women, women's violence against men, reciprocal violence between men and women, and IPV among same-sex partners (Hardesty & Ogolsky, 2020).

IPV has been reported to be more prevalent among couples with children (Hardesty & Ogolsky, 2020). Of couples reporting experiencing IPV, 60% have children living in the household (Hamby, 2014). Abuse and the risk for lethality often escalates following separation (Hardesty et al., 2024).

Studies have revealed that women are 10 times more likely to be victims of IPV than men, especially when abuse occurs after separation (Hardesty et al., 2024). Women who are separated and divorced report higher rates of IPV than married women. Hardesty points out that much of this research is cross-sectional making it virtually impossible to determine if separation occurred before or after the IPV (Hardesty & Ogolsky, 2020).

Prevalence

IPV and CC have been found to occur at similar rates for males and females whether examining the frequency of victimization or perpetration (Palmer et al., 2024). However, females suffer the greatest harm from IPV in terms of physical and psychological injury. Women who have been victims of IPV suffer more frequent and more severe injuries, experience higher levels of fear, stalking, and sexual assaults (Palmer et al., 2024).

According to the Centers for Disease Control and Prevention (CDC), IPV impacts approximately 41% of women and 26% of men, who have experienced sexual violence, physical violence, or stalking (CDC, 2024a). The CDC identifies IPV as a significant public health issue. About 75% of female and 50% of male survivors experience injury, furthermore, one in five homicide victims are killed by an intimate partner (CDC, 2024a). These statistics are likely an underestimation as "only a small fraction of all IPV victims ever seek help from either the criminal justice or health care system" (Breiding et al., 2015, p. 1). IPV survivors can experience a number of negative outcomes, including physical, behavioral, emotional, cognitive, academic, and social functioning (S.E. Evans et al., 2008; Holt et al., 2008; Hungerford et al., 2012).

IPV allegations are frequent in parenting plan disputes. "It is very rare for evaluators to obtain similar reports from parents regarding what, if any, domestic violence took place, including agreement on the main initiator and the victim" (Hynan, 2015). There is significant concern among DV, IPV, and CC advocates that parenting plan evaluators are not properly trained in identification and assessment and, as a result, continue the pattern of harm that brought them to the attention of the court and the evaluator's office in the first place (Rossi et al., 2016).

An intimate partner may be a current or former spouse, dating partner, or sexual partner. While there are different definitions and typologies, the CDC provides the following definitions:

> **Physical violence** is defined as the intentional use of physical force with the potential to cause death, disability, injury, or harm.
>
> **Sexual violence** is defined as a sexual act that is committed or attempted by another person without freely given consent of the victim or against someone who is unable to consent or refuse.
>
> **Stalking** is a pattern of repeated, unwanted attention and contact that causes fear or concern for one's own safety or the safety of someone else.
>
> **Psychological aggression** is the use of verbal and nonverbal communication with the intent to: (a) harm another person mentally or emotionally, or (b) exert control over another person.

These behaviors may vary in frequency, severity, directionality, pattern, intention, circumstance, and consequence. The Association of Family and Conciliation Courts (2016) Guidelines for Examining Intimate Partner Violence highlight the importance of context:

> In some relationships disagreements escalate into physical violence as the result of poor impulse control or poor conflict management skills. In other instances, violence is associated with substance abuse and/or mental illness. Sometimes, violence can be a reaction to the stress of separation or divorce without any history of violence or propensity for future violence. In some cases, violence is used

> to prevent or protect against real or perceived threats or risk of harm. In other relationships one partner exercises power to intimidate, isolate, denigrate, control and subordinate the other partner, frequently resulting in significant fear, trauma, disempowerment, and/or entrapment. (p. 4)

The guidelines encourage evaluators to effectuate the following principles:

- **Prioritize the safety and wellbeing of children and parents**. The overarching goal of the evaluation process is to achieve the best possible outcomes for families. An evaluator plays a key role in preserving, protecting, and promoting safe, healthy, and functional relationships and living arrangements during and following separation.
- **Ensure an informed, fair, and accountable process**. An evaluator plays a key role in informing the parties about the nature and purpose of the evaluation process, including how information will be used and to whom it will be disclosed. The evaluator establishes a fair and accountable process culminating in a written report that describes the information collected on intimate partner violence, explains how the information was analyzed and synthesized, and directly links the information to recommendations.
- **Focus on the individual family**. Another goal of evaluation is to respond to the particular needs and circumstances of individual families, without any preconceived ideas about whether or not intimate partner violence exists and if so, who has done what to whom, or what the implications of intimate partner violence might be for children, parenting, and coparenting. An evaluator plays a key role in screening for, and where appropriate, investigating, analyzing, and synthesizing information related to intimate partner violence on a case-by-case basis (Association of Family and Conciliation Courts, 2016).

An important differentiation, yet still not always acknowledged, is that the research often fails to distinguish between the more severe form of IPV with psychological control dynamics from situational, conflict-instigated, and more common IPV (W. G. Austin & Drozd, 2012; Johnson & Leone, 2005). "[B]ecause these types of violence have different psychological and social roots, interpersonal dynamics, and consequences for the victim, much of the empirical domestic violence literature is virtually meaningless" (Johnson & Leone, 2005).

A recent study sought to examine the relationship between emotional IPV and different forms of violence (e.g., stalking perpetration and victimization, physical IPV perpetration and victimization, sexual IPV perpetration and victimization, and controlling behaviors) using a meta-analysis (Palmer et al., 2024). Data from 188 studies, yielding 382 effect sizes, were used to compare the strength of correlates for IPV victimization versus perpetration, as well as gendered results (Palmer et al., 2024).

Palmer et al. (2024) reported that, in order of strength of effect sizes, controlling behaviors victimization, physical IPV victimization, physical IPV perpetration, sexual IPV victimization, stalking victimization, and sexual IPV perpetration were significantly associated with emotional IPV victimization.

Note that the strongest effect size was between emotional IPV and controlling behaviors, not physically violent behaviors.

Additional analyses found that, in order of strength of effect sizes, emotional IPV perpetration was positively associated with stalking perpetration, physical IPV perpetration, causing injury to a partner, controlling behaviors victimization, sexual IPV perpetration, physical IPV victimization, controlling behaviors perpetration, and sexual IPV victimization. Similar results are noted here revealing that emotional IPV perpetration had a larger effect size with stalking compared to acts of physically aggressive behavior.

Consistent with previous research examining gender differences, Palmer et al. (2024) report limited significant differences around gender, with physical IPV victimization approaching significance for emotional IPV perpetration for women.

Coercive Control

Our review of current peer-reviewed literature in the child arena suggests that considerable attention is being paid to the concept of CC. Some states have introduced statutes providing a legal definition of CC and identify specific factors that define the concept. For example, California governor Gavin Newsom signed Senate Bill 1141 that allows courts to consider CC as DV in family court matters. The law defined CC as "a pattern of behavior that unreasonably interferes with a person's free will and personal liberty." Several states have passed or are considering passing legislation defining CC and allowing its testimony in family law cases.[1]

Definition

CC is a subcategory of DV that is characterized by a persistent pattern of goal oriented, intentional tactics used to dominate, manipulate, and maintain authority over a current or former partner (Stark, 2023a). Tactics used by those who engage in CC include monitoring, isolating, intimidating, restricting resources, humiliating, and subordinating. Tactics can vary across relationships and over time within relationships and often target multiple domains (e.g., work, sexuality, support networks; Hardesty et al., 2024).

Manipulation and coercion are hallmarks of CC, whether it is overt or subtle. As it is applied to parenting plan disputes, an evaluator needs to investigate how a former intimate partner has engaged in coercive behaviors toward a former partner to force them to comply with their demands. Coercion might include physical, psychological, or emotional terror threats that carry with them credible threats of harm or punishment such as threats of violence, threats of financial vengeance, or threats to take children away (Hardesty et al., 2024).

[1]Ten states have adopted or are considering adopting legislation addressing coercive control (National Conference of State Legislatures, 2022).

Most research has examined CC when violence or threats of violence have been involved. Custody evaluators, however, are more likely to encounter CC tactics characterized by nonviolence actions such as stalking, harassment, and fear that might occur by showing up at unpredictable times or unscheduled activities (Hardesty et al., 2024).

Several researchers argue that CC, as well as IPV, must be understood through the assaults on the personhood, dignity, autonomy, liberty, and self-worth of the human being, and not just in terms of the physical bruises it leaves (E. Katz, 2022; Stark, 2023a, 2023b).

Recently, Emma Katz (as cited in Richards, 2023) suggested a way to distinguish situational couple violence from CC. She posited that situational couple violence occurs when parents argue and their arguments turn physical. It is the passion and heat of the moment that leads to the acts of aggression; acts that are not and have not been part of their daily lives. CC, on the other hand, is defined differently. Katz provided a definition of CC during a podcast:

> This is not just people being a bit controlling, controlling over one or two things. This is somebody who is being controlling over somebody's whole life, intruding on their normal levels of freedom and autonomy . . . their usual ability to carry out day to day activities that we would usually take for granted like decide where to go and how long to spend, . . . and what to wear and who we can see and who we can speak to and what sort of opinions we can express. (Richards, 2023, 2:25)

Emma Katz (2022) summarizes the tactics and behaviors of CC perpetrators: emotional and psychological abuse; control of time, space, and movement; monitoring and stalking; sexual abuse; economic abuse; isolation from sources of support; faith based and spiritual abuse; manipulating and grooming others; exploiting systems, institutions, and services; coercing criminal activity; intimidation and threats to commit acts of physical abuse, violence, and homicide; and physical abuse, violence, and homicide.

Emma Katz (2022) expands the traditional understanding of a child witnessing IPV to include the child's agency, which refers to the ability to use free will to make decisions and be an active participant in shaping one's life. The child's relational agency allows evaluators to assess the child's strengths, adaptive coping strategies, and maladaptive coping strategies. Assessing a child's agency places emphasis on understanding how a child's experience of coercive controlling behavior is more than just experiencing an event. Assessment of a child's agency focuses on understanding how the child's experience defines, in part, how they develop relations with others and engage in interactions with their parents (E. Katz, 2022).

Not only are the children impacted by their parents' behaviors, "children influence and affect the people with whom they interact, and so their agency extends to the relationships they have with the people in their lives" (E. Katz, 2022, p. 49). This is a shift from thinking about children as passive recipients of IPV or CC. As Katz (2022) concludes, "Children are victims and they are harmed, but they are also copers and survivors" (p. 55). Framed within the ecological model stressed in this book, children's experiences with parents who expose the child to coercive controlling behaviors reverberate throughout the multiple systems and relationships in which the child lives.

Mothers experiencing IPV face barriers to safety postseparation because they must negotiate coparenting arrangements and family court (Broughton & Ford-Gilboe, 2017). Researchers have voiced concern about the ways in which the effects of IPV and CC on parenting and child development are frequently minimized or underdetected in family court proceedings, which has lasting consequences for survivors; Meier, 2015).

Many authors assert that parents with minor children, legal systems and policies that regulate divorce, separation and custody are the central context influencing the ability to maintain safety following separation from an abusive partner (Broughton & Ford-Gilboe, 2017; Hardesty et al., 2024). They voice concerns that the family court context in and of itself creates conditions for the continuation of abusive and coercive controlling behaviors that are likely to play out during litigation and in postseparation contexts (E. Katz, 2022; Stark, 2023a, 2023b). They argue that family courts are ill-equipped to consistently account for the power and control dynamics of all forms of IPV and CC. Too often, it is argued, family courts' inattention to or minimization of the damage to families of a parent who engages in IPV or CC facilitate the very risk patterns that brought the family to the attention of the court in the first place. Some authors have argued that the minimization of harm results in shifting the focus away from the damaging behaviors of the perpetrators while placing blame on those experiencing abuse (Feresin et al., 2018; E. Katz, 2022; Stark, 2023a, 2023b). The takeaway for parenting plan evaluators is to be aware that how the family violence factors are framed, clearly explained, and tied into the empirical foundation of their risk to parent and child have significant implications for how it is understood by the court.

Emotional Intimate Partner Violence and Coercive Control

Palmer et al. (2024) appear to define emotional IPV in a manner similar to nonviolent CC. They define emotional IPV as occurring only within the context of intimate relationships and characterized by "insults, belitting, constant humiliation, intimidation (e.g., throwing things), threats of harm, and threats of taking away the children" (Palmer et al., 2024, p. 2).

They reported that emotional IPV is the most prevalent form of abuse, with nearly 50% of men and women reporting experiencing emotional abuse victimization. Individuals' lack of understanding of behaviors that constitute emotional abuse affects their ability to accurately perceive what accounts for emotional abuse and to accurately identify and report their victimization (Stern et al., 2019).

Exposure Reduction Hypothesis

Palmer et al. (2024) described the exposure reduction hypothesis. The basis of the exposure reduction hypothesis is that shortening the duration of time in a violent relationship would result in a reduction in other more severe forms of abuse. The more resources and opportunities an individual has that would allow escaping from an abusive relationship, the less likely they are to experience the negative outcomes of the abusive relationship. The longer a person stays in an abusive relationship, the greater the likelihood that the type, severity, and frequency of abusive acts will be targeted upon that person. The exposure reduction hypothesis highlights the importance of recognizing correlates early in abusive and violent relationships, such as characteristics of emotional IPV. By providing adequate resources and information, the risk of violence reaching the point of intimate partner homicide could be lessened, as well as utilizing early intervention tactics (Palmer et al., 2024).

One critique of the exposure reduction hypothesis is that often when leaving an abusive relationship, there is an increased risk for escalated violence. Although an individual leaving a violent relationship may be at greater risk for harm, providing adequate resources and early intervention could aid in a lower likelihood of further victimization in different forms of violence and abuse (Palmer et al., 2024).

Prior verbal abuse and prior physical harm early in a relationship predicts subsequent physical partner abuse (Schumacher & Leonard, 2005). Controlling behaviors and emotional forms of IPV have been found to escalate to more severe forms of IPV (Aizpurua et al., 2021). Controlling behaviors within the intimate context, including acts to constrain free mobility or access to friends and relatives, were found to predict moderate forms of violence and may be an indicator of more severe IPV (Aizpurua et al., 2021). Other studies found that being a victim of physical and emotional abuse is a precursor to subsequent development of victimization and perpetration of other forms of violence (Wagers et al., 2021).

Behaviors associated with emotional IPV perpetration were found to serve as a catalyst for the perpetration of other forms of violent behavior supporting early results from Follingstad (1990) who reported that acts of emotional IPV were experienced as the most detrimental form of abuse which lead to other forms of violence victimization.

Among the important conclusions of the Palmer et al. study is "the importance of ending violence before it escalates to more severe forms, such as severe physical violence or intimate partner homicide . . . Controlling behaviors are frequently associated with emotional IPV and therefore continue to be associated with emotional IPV perpetration as a factor in this form of detrimental IPV" (Palmer et al., 2024, p. 11).

Effects

After separation from an abusive partner, up to 90% of women report continued harassment, stalking, or abuse (Hardesty et al., 2012). There is little reliable research examining patterns of abusive behaviors following separation. There are few quantitative studies examining coercive or abusive tactics postseparation that include using children, threats, manipulation of visitation and coparenting schedules, and withholding child support (Toews & Bermea, 2017). There are also few, if any, studies that have examined how these tactics impact the health and well-being of children and families (Broughton & Ford-Gilboe, 2017).

One study examined mothers' experience of their abusive former partner's intrusion (i.e., unwanted interference from CC, custody and access difficulties, and mothers' depressive symptoms) and its effects on measures of family health and well-being after separation from said partner (Broughton & Ford-Gilboe, 2017). Among the results was that a mother's social support moderated intrusion effects on family health and well-being. Another finding was that the majority of women who had been separated from their abusive partners for an average of 2–5 years reported that they continued to experience CC.

Toews and Bermea (2017) found that "the violent and coercive behaviors men used during the marriage continued to influence the women's perceptions of the power and control their former husbands had over them postseparation. As a result, many of the women described how they gave up everything just to get out of their abusive marriages" (p. 2166).

Another study examined the priorities of women mothering children in the context of IPV (Broughton et al., 2024). Findings revealed that the "priorities of women mothering in the context of intimate partner violence are complex, shaped not only by what they want but by the limited options available to them given constraints such as income, employment, housing, and service responses. CC, structural inequities, and assumptions about mothering are important factors influencing mothers' priorities and experiences" (Broughton et al., 2024, p. 1520).

Although there is an emerging concern about early childhood exposure to IPV as a serious social and public health matter, there is little research (Lévesque et al., 2023). One area needing additional examination is a parent's underestimation of their children's exposure to IPV. One study found that the presence of adults' violent behaviors toward children was significantly associated with the mother's higher perceived awareness of early childhood exposure to IPV (Lévesque et al., 2023).

Empirical evidence for the effects of CC on victim parents or children—with or without physical violence—is relatively undeveloped due, in part, to the tendency for researchers to focus on incidences of physical violence, which can be easier to define and measure than CC (Lévesque et al., 2023). Limiting investigation of IPV to discrete incidents of physical violence without considering context (e.g., CC vs. situational conflict) and chronicity results in underestimates of the risks and harms associated with the insidious, daily nature of CC (Hardesty et al., 2024).

There are data to suggest that the effects of psychological abuse associated with CC has a more profound and longer lasting effect than the effects of past physical violence (Postmus et al., 2012). Chronic IPV that is more likely to involve CC (Johnson, 2008) appears to have unique negative impacts on parenting compared to past or isolated incidents (Adhia & Jeong, 2019; Jeong et al., 2020). Previous research has demonstrated associations between maternal experience of IPV and a range of adverse outcomes among women and their young children. Adhia and Jeong (2019) found that IPV victimization was negatively associated with early child development outcomes. Path analysis indicated that the direct association between IPV victimization and early child development outcomes was partially and independently mediated through maternal and paternal stimulation (Adhia & Jeong, 2019; Jeong et al., 2020).

THE NEED FOR RELIABLE ASSESSMENT PROCEDURES

The assessment of IPV using reliable data-gathering procedures presents unique challenges, particularly when evaluating the emotional and psychological aspects of abuse. Unlike physical violence, which can often be substantiated through medical records, photographs, or eyewitness accounts, psychological IPV is more elusive, relying heavily on self-reports, behavioral observations, and subjective interpretations. Given the high-stakes nature of PPEs, the necessity for reliable and valid assessment measures is paramount. However, even with strong assessment tools, forensic evaluators must remain acutely aware of the demand characteristics present in legal contexts that distinguish them from clinical evaluations.

Traditionally, psychological IPV has been assessed through self-report questionnaires, clinical interviews, and behavioral checklists. While these tools can provide valuable hypotheses, their reliability is often questioned in forensic settings, where litigation motives can influence responses. Victims may minimize or deny abuse due to fear, shame, or legal strategy, while perpetrators may distort or deny their actions to protect their interests. False allegations, though less common, also pose concerns that evaluators must carefully consider.

Forensic Versus Clinical Contexts: A Critical Distinction

As discussed throughout this book, a fundamental challenge in all aspects of forensic evaluation—including IPV assessment—is recognizing the stark differences between clinical and forensic settings. In clinical practice, mental health professionals prioritize treatment, support, and symptom relief, fostering a therapeutic alliance with their clients. In contrast, forensic evaluations are conducted with the goal of assisting legal decision making, often requiring evaluators to maintain a neutral stance and scrutinize the credibility of reports. The demand characteristics in forensic settings—meaning the factors that may influence how individuals respond to assessments—are substantially different from those in clinical environments. For instance, individuals involved in custody disputes may have incentives to exaggerate claims of IPV to gain a legal advantage. Conversely, victims may downplay or deny the extent of abuse out of fear of retaliation or losing custody of their children. Perpetrators may engage in impression management, portraying themselves as nonabusive while subtly undermining the victim's credibility.

Given these complexities, evaluators cannot rely solely on clinical assessment methods. Instead, they must adopt a multimodal approach, integrating multiple sources of information, including collateral reports from family, friends, teachers, or law enforcement who have personal knowledge of the behaviors of concern. The evaluator should review relevant court and medical records documenting prior incidents of abuse. Evaluators should not be limited to reviewing these court and medical records relating to recent behaviors. The history of aggressive behaviors is critical information to help in discriminating trait-type notions that are more difficult to respond to treatment intervention from separation related aggressiveness. Evaluators should conduct several behavioral observations during evaluations and interactions. As we will describe in the next chapter, they may also consider using structured and validated forensic assessment tools that minimize bias and demand effects.

The Role of Evaluator Expertise

Because forensic IPV assessments require a delicate balance between psychological science and legal scrutiny, evaluators must be well trained in both domains. A lack of expertise in forensic assessment can lead to misinterpretations that could significantly impact legal outcomes, affecting child custody decisions. Parenting plan evaluators must be skilled in identifying malingering (i.e., intentional exaggeration or fabrication) and impression management. They must have skill in recognizing and assessing trauma responses that may lead victims to appear inconsistent or emotionally dysregulated. Evaluators should work toward identifying specific behaviors that reliably differentiate IPV from other concerns by operationally defining behaviors that fit into the IPV category that are independent (or relatively independent) from behaviors that might be explained by other non-IPV factors. Finally, the evaluator must be skilled in communicating findings to the court in a way that is objective, clear, and legally relevant. Without evidence-based or evidence-informed evaluation methods, there is a risk that courts may dismiss legitimate IPV allegations or, conversely, act on unsubstantiated claims, leading to unjust rulings. This underscores the urgent need for specialized training for parenting plan evaluators in IPV-specific assessment.

UNRELIABLE ASSESSMENT PROCEDURES YIELDING UNRELIABLE PREVALENCE RATES

Despite the overwhelming evidence of the prevalence of IPV and CC in separating and divorcing families, reliable and valid methods of assessment are urgently needed. Stern et al. (2019) identified several risks resulting from poorly conducted evaluations. One risk is the lack of reliable and valid assessment tools developed to measure IPV and CC used in both clinical and forensic assessments. Although there are somewhat greater options to use assessment tools developed for clinical assessment, concerns exist about the use of such clinically developed instruments in a forensic context (Palmer et al., 2024; see also Chapter 15).

Another risk is due to evaluators' potential misunderstanding or lack of knowledge of the wide range of behaviors that fall under the working definition of the various types of abuse that might exist in a family (Palmer et al., 2024). Concerns have been raised about how to interpret the varying prevalence rate data examining gender differences or parity in IPV. The inconsistency in these results continues to be poorly understood. One approach is to explore whether differences in prevalence rates are associated with methodological concerns (i.e., method variance). For instance, Hamby (2016) investigated the effects of item wording on the CTS on gender patterns for victimization reports in a range of samples. Among the findings, Hamby reported that some item wordings yielded higher rates of female rather than male victimization. Similar patterns were reported across CTS forms for highly victimized women. Among Hamby's conclusions were that the CTS and similar behavioral checklists tended to be vulnerable to false positives. Self-report measures designed to minimize false positives produce results consistent with other IPV methodologies; that is, they do not demonstrate gender parity. She recommended the use of the partner victimization scale when a scale that has multi-method convergence with other IPV methodologies is desired (Hamby, 2016). Looking beyond the ways in which item wording might influence responses to measures that result in unreliable data regarding prevalence rates, Hamby (2017) found that choices regarding the operationalization of IPV in surveys have a substantial impact on gender patterns. That is, the lack of consensus regarding an operational definition of IPV is a significant confounding variable in attempts to understand IPV.

Almost 20 years ago, Gould and Martindale (2007) made a similar point, calling attention to the multiple definitions used by different professions such as law enforcement, state statutes, social service organizations, and mental health. Gould and Martindale referred to this as *definitional ambiguity* (p. 247). The lack of professional consensus among many important concepts frequently used in parenting plan assessment continues to be a concern. Rather than reaching professional consensus about a definition of a concept such as abuse, IPV, or CC, too often our research bases are drawn from studies that have operationally defined these terms that are not often similarly defined in subsequent studies. The result is that research findings give the impression of developing a reliable evidence-based foundation for expert opinions until one begins to look beyond the surface at the differences in definition, methodologies, and other factors that introduce potential error into the scientific integrity of those studies. Hamby's work is an excellent example of attempting to take the bull by the horns by addressing some of the methodological errors inherent in our current research studies.

Hardesty and her colleagues (2015) have also focused attention on establishing clearer definitions of CC and the factors associated with it. CC is central to distinguishing between Johnston's (2008) two main types of intimate partner violence: (a) coercive controlling violence and (b) situational couple violence.

To date, studies have examined the negative effects of violent CC, but few studies have examined CC without violence. Kimberly A. Crossman and her colleagues (2016) found that mothers experiencing emotional IPV reported more coping strategies, more risk, more harassment, and higher levels of perceived threat than mothers with no violence and no control. Findings also revealed that mothers experiencing emotional IPV reported similar levels of fear and control during marriage as mothers experiencing violent CC. These mothers also reported more postseparation fear than either the control group or the mothers experiencing violent CC (K. A. Crossman et al., 2016).

In another study, K. A. Crossman and Hardesty (2018) investigated how CC itself operates and is experienced as abusive. They also examined how the processes of control considered coercive differ from control dynamics that are part of all relationships remain uncertain. Their study revealed that felt or experienced constraint was central to the process of control, but two distinct patterns produced this phenomenon (K. A. Crossman & Hardesty, 2018). They distinguished constraint through commitment from constraint through force.

Constraint through commitment involved a process of being constrained by oneself or one's partner to uphold cultural conventions of heterosexual marriage and parenting. *Constraint through force* involved a process of being controlled wholly in a targeted and systematic way by one's partner (K. A. Crossman & Hardesty, 2018).

Early research focused on the number of controlling tactics used by the perpetrator. The diversity of tactics used by a male to dominate his partner has been historically viewed as among the most important data to gather in making a reliable determination. Evaluators might consider addressing the Hardesty et al. (2015) research findings that measuring the frequency of use of coercive and controlling behaviors yields more accurate descriptions of the degree of CC experienced by the women in the relationships of divorcing couples.

Mothers and children are frequently subject to postseparation abuse through coercive controlling behaviors of the former partner, and continued abuse tends to be facilitated and perpetuated by factors at the family (e.g., power differentials between intimate partners, stigma), community (e.g., legal system responses) and societal levels (e.g., gender and patriarchal norms).

HOW PEOPLE EXPERIENCE DOMESTIC VIOLENCE

Children as Silent Witnesses

Historically, children exposed to family violence have often been described as silent witnesses (Callaghan, Fellin, Mavrou, et al., 2017; Callaghan et al., 2018). The assumption was that if the children were not the victims of DV, then the psychological and emotional consequences of family violence would have little, if any, effect on the children.

Children have always been victims in family violence families regardless of which parent or caretaker was the victim or perpetrator. Davies and Cummings seminal work in the 1990s describing the theoretical structure of the emotional security hypothesis (Cummings & Davies, 1995; P. T. Davies & Cummings, 1994) described children's emotional reactions to experiencing parental conflict and DV. The emotional security hypothesis also predicted that children's exposure to marital conflict creates a template through which children's future responding is affected.

Emotional Security Theory

Patrick T. Davies and Cummings (1994) hypothesized that children's concerns about emotional security are involved in their regulation of emotional arousal and organization and in their motivation to respond in the face of marital conflict. "Over time these response processes and internalized representations of parental relations that develop have implications for children's long-term adjustment. Emotional security is seen as a product of past experiences with marital conflict and as a primary influence on future responding" (P. T. Davies & Cummings, 1994, p. 387).

Children's relationships and environments significantly influence their construction of the meaning of the social world around them (P. T. Davies & Cummings, 1994). This process is thought to occur through the development of children's internal working models, or general representations of self and others (Fivush, 2006). Two interrelated developmental theories—attachment theory and emotional security theory—identify the critical importance of the parent–child and parent-to-parent relationship, respectively, as fundamental building blocks in the development of a child's internal working models (Speidel et al., 2022).

Attachment theory identifies that the quality of early parent–child relationships form the basis for children's perceptions of their caregivers and others as secure bases that can be relied on for safety and comfort (Ainsworth et al., 1978). EST builds upon attachment theory by extending the importance of security in the parent–child relationship to the child's perception of security in the broader family context (Cummings & Davies, 2010).

It is important to remember that challenges to emotional security are related to exposure to parental conflict. Longitudinal emotional security theory research has supported the hypothesis that emotional insecurity is an explanatory mechanism for children's adjustment between childhood and adolescence. Emotional security has been found to be a multidimensional regulatory system between physiological and psychological indicators of emotional security theory (Cummings et al., 2014).

Some studies have found that interparental conflict predicted children's lower prosocial behavior and higher peer rejection. Peer rejection was predicted by children's emotional insecurity with their fathers (Lux & Walper, 2019).

More recent studies have examined whether interparental conflict was differentially related to different forms of emotional security (i.e., family, interparental, parent–child) and whether forms of emotional security were differentially associated with mental health problems for adolescents in married versus divorced or separated families (O'Hara et al., 2023). The patterns of association were similar across family structures. A high-quality parent–child relationship did not reduce the harmful effects of exposure to interparental conflict on children's reported level of emotional insecurity or in their reported mental health problems. O'Hara et al. (2023) concluded that "regardless of family structure, emotional security across multiple family systems may be a critical target for intervention to prevent youth mental health problems, in addition to interventions that reduce conflict and improve parent–child relationships."

Effects of Exposure to Parental Conflict on Children's Emotional Security

Children's exposure to interparental conflict characterized by high levels of hostility and escalating anger has been repeatedly shown to increase children's risk for developing psychological problems, including internalizing (e.g., depression, anxiety) and externalizing (e.g., aggression, attention-deficit hyperactivity disorder) symptoms (O'Hara et al., 2023). A challenge for evaluators is that, despite the risk posed by interparental conflict, many children who are exposed to high levels of parental conflict do not develop significant psychological difficulties over the course of their lives (O'Hara et al., 2023).

Evaluators should consider how research has found that children's encoding and processing of social and emotional cues and development of behavior problems are linked to their exposure to interparental hostility (P. T. Davies et al., 2016a). Evaluators might consider investigating a variety of factors associated with children's exposure to parental conflict.

One factor is the assessment of the frequency, severity, form, and type of exposure to which the children have been exposed to their parents' conflict. It is hypothesized that children's repeated exposure to parental conflicts containing hostility, violence, and escalating anger creates a toxic emotional environment that undermines children's abilities to feel safe and secure in both their physical and emotional relationships with parents. That is, children's security in the parent–child relationship and in the interparental relationship is undermined (P. T. Davies et al., 2016b).

A challenge for evaluators is that emotional security is an unobservable phenomenon. However, children's difficulties in maintaining emotional security in their home or in their parental relationships can be inferred through behavioral signs of heightened and prolonged distress reactions (e.g., freezing, anxious facial expressions, and verbal concern), avoidance (e.g., turning away from conflict, putting hands over ears), and involvement (e.g., mediating the conflict) in interparental discord (P. T. Davies et al., 2016b). Information obtained from third-party observers with direct, personal knowledge of the children and their relationship with each parent would be critical as a step toward verifying potential threats to children's emotional security.

An evaluator's attention needs to include the length of a child's exposure to parental conflict. It appears that the more often children are exposed to parental conflict, the more likely it is that they will have difficulty developing and maintaining a sense of security. Difficulties in developing and maintaining emotional security are tied into children's vulnerability to developing psychopathology (P. T. Davies et al., 2016b).

Effects of Children's Exposure to Parental Conflict on Parent–Child Relationships

Children not only have been found to witness and be exposed to parental conflict, but they also often become involved in the parental violence (Günaydin & Zincir, 2024). In our parenting plan assessments, we have observed some children attempting to stop their parents' conflict by physically inserting themselves between their parents. They have been observed attempting to divert their parents' attention toward their behaviors in an attempt to refocus their parents' anger toward protection of their children. Still other children take sides in the argument, increasing the likelihood of becoming a target of their parents' anger.

The quality of the parent–child relationship is often significantly affected by children's exposure to parental conflict. The victim's parent–child relationship is often affected differently than the perpetrator's parent–child relationship, however the child's relationship with each parent is often significantly affected and, not infrequently, damaged. Current research sheds light on the profound psychological and developmental consequences of IPV and high-conflict family dynamics. By examining both parental and child outcomes, the findings underscore the intergenerational transmission of trauma, and the long-term risks associated with exposure to family violence.

Parental Impact: The Struggle of Parenting in Violent Environments

Studies on parents who have experienced domestic violence, such as those by Günaydin and Zincir (2024), indicate that these parents report significantly lower levels of parenting satisfaction. This dissatisfaction could be attributed to multiple stressors, including the emotional and psychological toll of ongoing conflict, fear, financial instability, and, in some cases, posttraumatic stress resulting from exposure to violence.

For victimized parents, the impact appears even more pronounced. The Günaydin and Zincir (2024) study suggests that parents who experience family violence exhibit higher levels of internalizing symptoms, such as anxiety and depression. This is particularly concerning, as a parent's mental health is closely linked to their ability to provide a nurturing and stable environment for their children. When a parent is struggling with their own psychological distress, it can impair their capacity to engage in positive parenting practices, potentially leading to difficulties in attachment, inconsistent discipline, and emotional unavailability. Consequently, children in these households may not receive the emotional support necessary for healthy development.

Children and Adolescents: The Dual Burden of Internalizing and Externalizing Problems

The second major theme in the research concerns the effects of IPV exposure on children (Hungerford et al., 2012). Children of different ages are affected differently by exposure to parents' IPV, showing internalizing and externalizing behaviors (M. Lee et al., 2023). Internalizing behaviors refer to inward responses to stress that includes anxiety, depression, and anger. Externalizing behaviors refer to outward-directed responses to stress, including aggression, defiance, impulsivity, and conduct disorders. Children in violent households may model the aggressive behavior they observe, normalizing the use of hostility as a means of conflict resolution. In some cases, these children may struggle with authority figures, exhibit disruptive behaviors in school, or engage in delinquent activities later in adolescence (Bender et al., 2022).

The distinction between internalizing and externalizing symptoms is crucial because it highlights how children process trauma differently. Some children may become withdrawn and anxious, turning inward, while others may act out aggressively as a defense mechanism. Both pathways pose significant risks for long-term psychological and social development (Dessimoz et al., 2022).

Effects of Intimate Partner Violence Exposure by Developmental Stage

Infants (0–2 years) exposed to IPV are at risk for disrupted attachment. Infants depend on caregivers for security. IPV can disrupt attachment, leading to insecure or disorganized attachment styles, which may affect emotional regulation later in life. Infants often experience elevated stress responses (Schulz et al., 2024). Chronic exposure to IPV can lead to heightened cortisol levels (stress hormone), which can negatively impact brain development (Mueller & Tronick, 2019). Their sleep and feeding routines are often disrupted. Infants in violent households often exhibit irregular sleeping, feeding, and crying patterns, indicating distress. Infants exposed to IPV tend to show delayed developmental milestones. Exposure to violence can contribute to delays in cognitive, motor, and social development (Kaufman & Henrich, 2000).

Some of the long-term risks include interferences with the ability to develop appropriate emotional regulatory behaviors (Mueller & Tronick, 2020). Poor emotional regulation, difficulty forming secure relationships, increased risk of anxiety and depression in later years have also been reported (Ackerman et al., 2019).

Toddlers and preschoolers (2–5 years) are also significantly affected by exposure to IPV. These children frequently display heightened fearfulness and anxiety. Toddlers might display increased clinginess, separation anxiety, and excessive fear responses (Harper et al., 2018). Some children model violent behavior and may become physically aggressive toward peers, siblings, or caregivers. Toddlers exposed to IPV may exhibit bedwetting, thumb-sucking, and loss of previously acquired language skills. Similar to infants, toddlers and preschool children have been observed to display poor self-regulation (Bender et al., 2022). They display difficulty managing emotions, leading to frequent temper tantrums and difficulty soothing themselves. Sleep disturbances are common, often characterized by nightmares and trouble sleeping due to heightened anxiety (Insana et al., 2014). Research findings have found that there are long-term risks resulting from exposure to IPV. Young children tend to manifest behavioral problems, difficulties in social relationships, and increased likelihood of future emotional dysregulation (Bender et al., 2022).

School-age children (6–12 years) also suffer short- and long-term effects of exposure to IPV (Carpenter & Stacks, 2009). School-age children often internalize their emotional experiences. Children begin to experience anxiety, depression, low self-esteem, and social withdrawal. They show difficulties at school. Exposure to IPV correlates with attention problems, difficulty concentrating, and lower academic performance. Some school-age children externalize their distress through bullying, defiance, and rule-breaking behavior. They might display increased aggression or conduct problems (Zarling et al., 2013). Some children report headaches, stomachaches, and other physical symptoms due to psychological distress. School-age children are vulnerable to being placed in the middle of their parents' conflict. They may experience loyalty conflicts. They report feeling torn between parents, experiencing guilt and confusion over their family situation. The long-term risks include having social difficulties in and out of school, or repeating cycles of IPV in their own relationships (Bender et al., 2022).

Adolescents (13–18 years) are also likely to suffer from exposure to IPV (Savopoulos et al., 2023). They show a tendency toward increased risk-taking behaviors. IPV exposure is linked to substance use, early sexual activity, delinquency, and running away from home. They experience relationship issues. Teens may struggle with forming healthy relationships and are prone to becoming involved in dating violence or becoming involved in controlling relationships (K. E. Evans et al., 2022). Adolescents are prone to manifest mental health disorders. IPV exposure increases the risk of depression, anxiety, posttraumatic stress disorder (PTSD), and suicidal ideation (Louis & Reyes, 2023).

Teens may show reduced motivation, lower academic achievement, school truancy, or dropping out. They may display defiant or oppositional behaviors at home and at school. Adolescents often report experiencing anger, resentment, and difficulties respecting authority (Fong, Hawes, & Allen, 2019).

The long-term risks from exposure to parental IPV include higher risk of IPV victimization or perpetration in adulthood, substance abuse, criminal behavior, and chronic mental health challenges. Camacho et al. (2012) highlight that adolescents exposed to severe IPV are at increased risk of developing internalizing behaviors, which include symptoms such as withdrawal, anxiety, depression, and self-blame. The stress and fear associated with witnessing violence can disrupt emotional regulation, leading to difficulties in coping with adversity. Moreover, children who internalize their distress may struggle with self-esteem, social relationships, and academic performance.

Finally, adolescents exposed to IPV are at increased risk to engage in violent or physically aggressive behaviors in intimate relationships (K. E. Evans et al., 2022). They are also more likely to engage in bullying behavior in school and other social relationships (H. Lee et al., 2022).

Intergenerational Transmission of Trauma and Long-Term Consequences

The cumulative findings presented in the research point to an intergenerational transmission of trauma. Children who grow up in violent households are not only at risk for emotional and behavioral issues in childhood and adolescence, but they may also carry these effects into adulthood. Studies suggest that children who witness IPV may have a higher likelihood of experiencing or perpetrating violence in their own intimate relationships later in life. This cyclical nature of trauma underscores the importance of early intervention to break the pattern.

Furthermore, exposure to IPV during childhood has been linked to long-term mental health issues, including an increased risk for PTSD, substance abuse, and difficulty forming secure attachments in adulthood. As these children transition into adult roles—whether as parents, partners, or professionals—the unresolved trauma from their upbringing can manifest in new ways, perpetuating cycles of dysfunction and distress.

Short- and Long-Term Consequences of Parental Exposure to and Participation in Intimate Partner Violence

Parents from relationships characterized by IPV were at increased risk for parental PTSD and alcohol use disorder 2 years later, but not for major depressive disorder. Parental alcohol use disorder independently increased the risk for offspring externalizing behavior, but IPV continued to predict offspring externalizing independent of parental alcohol use. Parenting, particularly involving low satisfaction with the child, was significantly associated with both IPV and the child's externalizing behavior, but did not mediate the effects of IPV on externalizing. IPV predicted higher levels of aggression, hostile reactivity, and depressive mood in their offspring (Ehrensaft & Cohen, 2012).

One study examined the prospective association of parental reports of IPV involvement (perpetration and victimization) with offspring trauma symptoms an average of 6 years later and the moderating influence of positive and negative parenting (Ehrensaft et al., 2017). Whether a victim or perpetrator of IPV, IPV predicted child trauma symptoms. For fathers, but not mothers, this association held when controlling for stressful life events and psychopathology. IPV predicted lower positive and higher negative parenting practices among both victims and perpetrators of IPV. The authors concluded that positive parenting moderated the association of IPV with child trauma symptoms. Childhood exposure to IPV between parents appeared to increase the future risk for trauma symptoms. IPV was associated with more negative and less supportive parenting practices. Findings also suggested that positive parenting may be protective, though perhaps not at extreme levels of IPV (Ehrensaft et al., 2017).

Fathers' Beliefs About Their Motivation to Engage in Intimate Partner Violence

Few studies have investigated how men who perpetrate IPV experience being a parent. One qualitative study examined the beliefs of a small sample of fathers in treatment for IPV (N = 11) and the impact of their recollections of childhood experiences on their fathering. Two superordinate themes emerged from their interviews that described the participants' fathering experience. One theme was being a benign versus detrimental force in the child's life. The second theme was having the intention of not repeating and the actual repetition of harmful parenting (Mohaupt et al., 2021, p. 467). Fathers described being conflicted regarding being potentially damaging for their child's development. They pointed to a lack of stable positive relationships, both early in life and in the present, that would serve as positive role models. The authors concluded: "Partner-violent men's meaning making of their fathering seems to be influenced by their early-life experiences with their parents in several problematic ways. Fathers who use IPV may both accept and reject that they have been harmed by the parenting they received as children. Similarly, they may both acknowledge and discard that their use of violence harms their children" (Mohaupt et al., 2021, p. 467).

Wagers et al. (2021) examined emotional abuse among incarcerated men. They found that victimization and perpetration of emotional IPV were common experiences among the men in their study. Surprisingly, 73% of the sample report emotional IPV victimization and 70% report emotional IPV perpetration. Physical IPV was reported to occur less often than emotional IPV, with 44% of young men reporting being victims of physical IPV and 29% reporting perpetration of physical IPV. Wagers et al. (2021) found strong associations between IPV victimization and IPV perpetration.

Not surprising was the finding that IPV involvement as a victim or perpetrator is more common than not among young men involved in the justice system compared to the general population. Both emotional and physical forms of IPV were reported among men who witnessed and experienced violence during adolescence (Wagers et al., 2021).

Other recent research has focused on the fathering vulnerability hypothesis, which posits that fathers and their family relationships are particularly susceptible to the effects of destructive interparental conflict (Hoegler et al., 2024). This hypothesis provides a scientific framework for explaining fathers' responses to interparental conflict in custody related situations. Understanding how fathers are uniquely affected by destructive interparental conflict can help ensure fair and evidence-based custody determinations that prioritize child well-being. Expert witnesses should explain that fathers' withdrawal or distress does not indicate parental incompetence but may result from prolonged exposure to destructive conflict.

Given the fathering vulnerability hypothesis, evaluators should consider fathers' psychological responses to conflict. Some fathers reduce contact or withdraw due to repeated conflict-driven stress, not due to a lack of commitment to their child. If one parent diminishes or undermines the father's role (e.g., by making unilateral decisions, restricting communication), evaluators must document and address these dynamics. Fathers may experience heightened emotional distress (e.g., depression, anxiety, or learned helplessness) due to prolonged interparental conflict. Evaluators should screen for mental health issues related to ongoing litigation or conflict-driven parenting stress.

Destructive conflict often diminishes fathers' parenting involvement, especially if they experience gatekeeping behaviors from the other parent. Evaluators should explore whether a father's withdrawal from parenting is due to conflict dynamics rather than a lack of interest or ability. Some fathers may be unfairly viewed as less competent or less involved simply due to the effects of conflict rather than parenting capacity. Evaluators should differentiate between intentional disengagement and conflict-driven disengagement to provide a more accurate assessment. As discussed in earlier chapters, high-conflict custody cases often involve allegations of parental alienation, CC, or psychological distress. Fathers may be particularly vulnerable to allegations of alienating behaviors and false narratives due to their susceptibility to conflict. Evaluators should assess for factors affecting parent-child contact problems or undermining of the father's role. Fathers who experience chronic conflict may also struggle with legal advocacy due to emotional fatigue. Courts should be aware that distress-related disengagement does not equate to a lack of parental fitness.

CONCLUSION

This chapter has explored the evolving conceptualizations of DV and the challenges that persist in defining and assessing its impact on families. We have examined various models that contribute to a nuanced understanding of DV, including intimate partner violence (IPV) and CC. Parents in violent relationships struggle with decreased parenting satisfaction and increased internalizing symptoms, which in turn affects their ability to provide a stable environment for their children. Children exposed to IPV face heightened risks of developing both internalizing and externalizing behaviors, placing them at risk for long-term mental health and behavioral challenges. Understanding these patterns is essential for parenting plan evaluators. Furthermore, we have seen how different theoretical frameworks—from the Duluth model to Johnston and Campbell's typologies and Johnston's differentiation theory—offer valuable perspectives but also reflect limitations. A growing body of research calls for a more holistic, dimensional approach that considers the interplay of individual, relational, and sociocultural factors. Finally, the chapter emphasized the importance of acknowledging children as active participants in their experiences of DV, rather than as passive witnesses. The research reviewed underscores the profound effects of DV on family members, particularly children, whose exposure to interparental conflict can lead to lasting emotional and psychological consequences. The role of parenting plan evaluators is crucial in ensuring that assessments are conducted with rigor and reliability.

In the next chapter, we will continue our exploration of tools to assess for DV.

22

Tools to Assess for Domestic Violence

This chapter builds on a comprehensive review of the literature concerning the assessment of family violence allegations, delving into the various procedures employed during evaluations. Most of the tools used in domestic violence (DV) assessments have evolved primarily from clinical experience combined with evidence-informed, rational approaches that pinpoint critical areas for evaluation. These methods, although grounded in practical insights, often lack rigorous psychometric validation—a limitation acknowledged by the authors. Despite this shortfall, the tools remain instrumental, particularly as guides during in-depth forensic interviews where they help frame the conversation and identify key issues. They also serve as a foundation for hypothesis generation, assisting professionals in developing a deeper understanding of the complexities inherent in family violence cases. In essence, while the empirical robustness of these instruments may be limited, their practical application provides a valuable starting point for further investigation and supports more nuanced, evidence-based decision making in forensic contexts. The chapter thus emphasizes the dual need for both immediate, practice-based utility in DV assessments and ongoing research to strengthen the reliability and validity of these assessment tools.

https://doi.org/10.1037/0000474-023
Parenting Plan Evaluations: An Evidence-Informed Approach to Child Custody, by J. W. Gould and C. M. Mulchay

DISTINGUISHING TYPES OF VIOLENCE

Families experiencing violence differ greatly, with the types of abuse ranging from isolated incidents to long-term patterns of physical aggression that intensify and occur across multiple contexts. Beyond physical harm, family violence often encompasses emotional and psychological abuse—such as physical threats, sexual coercion, verbal insults, social isolation from friends and family, and financial control. A significant concern is that family courts frequently employ a one-size-fits-all response that may not effectively reduce future risks (Ver Steegh & Dalton, 2008). For example, using the history of physical violence as a sole predictor of future incidents or potential lethality can be misleading. Family violence is often intertwined with individual factors like mental illness or substance abuse, which can significantly influence both the impact on the victim and the perpetrator's motivations (Ver Steegh & Dalton, 2008).

Evaluators must, therefore, consider both individual characteristics and the broader interpersonal context when assessing allegations of family violence. It is crucial that such assessments evaluate not only the potential for lethal harm and the risk of continued violence but also other forms of intimidation that may be present. Parenting plan evaluators, in particular, are advised to consider various typologies of violence. Different typologies help differentiate between types of abuse by framing specific questions—such as whether the violence is used as a means of coercive control (CC), arises from interpersonal conflict, serves as a form of resistance or self-defense, results from separation, or is linked to severe mental illness or substance abuse (Ver Steegh & Dalton, 2008). This nuanced approach is essential for developing a comprehensive understanding of the dynamics at play and for tailoring interventions to effectively reduce future risks.

Distinguishing among different types of family violence not only improves the accuracy of identifying its presence but also helps pinpoint the most suitable interventions for each unique family situation (Ver Steegh & Dalton, 2008). Families affected by violence do not all benefit equally from a single intervention strategy. By categorizing family violence effectively, evaluators can tailor recommendations to address specific dynamics and needs, ensuring that the processes and services offered are truly individualized (Ver Steegh & Dalton, 2008).

In practice, evaluators are encouraged to include follow-up assessments in their recommendations to the court (Ver Steegh & Dalton, 2008). Depending on the specific circumstances, this might involve suggesting temporary orders or emergency parenting plans, arranging for ongoing monitoring during the case, or even conducting additional investigations before finalizing long-term parenting arrangements (Ver Steegh & Dalton, 2008).

At present, the field faces significant challenges due to the absence of reliable and valid tools for assessing risk and predicting the potential for effective coparenting among divorcing parents with a history of family violence. Additionally, the lack of standardized training for parenting plan evaluators means that myths and misconceptions about different forms of family violence can inadvertently influence how evaluators gather data and form their opinions. In this chapter, we review several commonly used tools and introduce a new tool designed to enhance the precision and effectiveness of family violence evaluations.

Potency, Pattern, and Primary Perpetrator Screening

In 2008, Jaffe and his colleagues introduced a transformative approach to assessing family violence—one that acknowledged not all instances of abuse are alike, and therefore, not every case requires the same response. They developed the potency, pattern, and primary perpetrator (PPP) screening tool, a methodical framework that guides evaluators through three critical dimensions: potency, pattern, and the identification of the primary perpetrator (see Exhibit 22.1).

EXHIBIT 22.1

PPP Screening Questions

Part A: Potency of violence (Level of severity, dangerousness, or risk of lethality)

1. Are there any threats or fantasies of homicide or suicide? Is so, does the person have a specific plan to act on them?
2. Are weapons available (guns, knives, etc.), indicating the means are accessible?
3. How extreme was any prior violence? Were injuries caused, and if so, how serious?
4. Is the person highly focused upon or obsessed with the specific victim as a target of blame?
5. Is there a history of mental illness—especially thought disorders, paranoia, or severe personality disorder?
6. Is the person under the influence of drugs or alcohol, indicating diminished capacity to inhibit angry impulses? Is there a history of substance abuse?
7. Does the person express a high degree of depression, rage, or extreme emotional instability (indicating a propensity to act irrationally and unpredictably)?
8. Is the party recently separated or experiencing other stressful events like loss of job, eviction from home, loss of child custody, severe financial problems, etc.?

Part B: Pattern of violence and coercive control

1. Is there a history of physical violence including destruction of property, threats (to hurt self or loved ones), assault, battery, sexual coercion, or rape?
2. Has there been disregard or contempt for authority (e.g., refusal to comply with court-ordered parenting plans, violation of protective orders, a criminal arrest record)?
3. How fearful or intimated is the partner?
4. Is there a history of emotional abuse and attacks on self-esteem?
5. Does one party make all decisions (e.g., about social, work, and leisure activities; how money is spent; how children are disciplined and cared for; household routines and meals; personal deportment and attire, etc.)?
6. Has the partner been isolated or restricted from outside contacts (e.g., with employment, friends, and family)?
7. Is there evidence of obsessive preoccupation with, sexual jealousy towards, or possessiveness of the partner?
8. After separation, have there been repeated unwanted attempts to contact the partner (e.g., stalking, hostage-taking, threats or attempts to abduct the partner or child)?
9. Have there been multiple petitions or litigation that appear to have the purpose of controlling and harassing?

(*continues*)

EXHIBIT 22.1. (*Continued*)

Part C: Primary perpetrator indicators: Who is the primary aggressor, if either?

1. Who provides a more clear, specific, and plausible account of the violent incident(s)? Who denies, minimizes, obfuscates, or rationalizes the incident? (The victim more likely does the former; the perpetrator the latter.)
2. What motives are used to explain why the incident(s) occurred? (Victims tend to use language that suggests they were trying to placate, protect, avoid, or stop the violence, whereas perpetrators describe their intent being to control or punish.)
3. What is the size and physical strength of each party relative to the amount of damage and injury resulting from the incident(s)? Does either party have special training or skill in combat? (Perpetrators who are better equipped are able to cause the greater damage.)
4. Are the types of any injuries or wounds suffered likely to be caused by aggressive acts (the perpetrator's) or defensive acts (the victim's)?
5. If the incident(s) involved mutual combat, were the violent acts or injuries by one party far in excess of those of the other? (Violent resistors tend to assert only enough force to defend and protect; when primary perpetrators retaliate, they are more likely to escalate the use of force aiming to control and punish.)
6. Has either party had a prior protective order issued against them—whether in this or a former relationship (indicating who was determined to be the primary aggressor in the past)?

Note. From "Custody Disputes Involving Allegations of Domestic Violence: Toward a Differentiated Approach to Parenting Plans," by P. G. Jaffe, J. R. Johnston, C. V. Crooks, & N. Bala, 2008, ***Family Court Review*, *46*(3)** p. 505 (https://doi.org/10.1111/j.1744-1617.2008.00216.x).

Imagine a family case where tensions have escalated over time. In one home, an incident of violence might initially appear to be an isolated outburst. However, when experts apply the PPP screening, they begin by evaluating the *potency* of the incident. They assess how severe and dangerous the behavior was—considering elements such as the force used, the presence of any weapons, and the potential for serious injury or even death. This step is crucial because even a single act of violence can carry significant risk if it is particularly intense or escalatory. The next step in the process is to examine the *pattern* of behavior. Evaluators look beyond the isolated incident to determine whether the violence is part of a recurring cycle. In our hypothetical case, they might discover that what seemed like a one-off event is actually one thread in a tapestry of repeated, coercive actions designed to control and intimidate. This recurring pattern, as research indicates, tends to inflict deeper, long-lasting trauma on everyone involved—especially the children, who are particularly vulnerable to the effects of sustained emotional and physical abuse. Finally, the screening tool directs attention to identifying the *primary perpetrator*. In the midst of conflict, it is often challenging to discern whether one party is predominantly responsible or if the violence is mutually exchanged. Through careful investigation, evaluators aim to pinpoint who is primarily instigating the abuse. This determination is vital because it influences decisions about who might be capable of providing a safe, nurturing environment for the child, and conversely, whose access might need to be limited to protect the child's well-being (Jaffe et al., 2008).

What makes the PPP screening particularly valuable is that it organizes the entire evaluation process, extending its influence beyond just the initial interviews. It creates a narrative that weaves together the severity of the violence, its repetitive nature, and the dynamics between the parties involved. This comprehensive approach ensures that every facet of family interaction is scrutinized, ultimately guiding the creation of parenting plans that are finely tuned to the unique realities of each case. In essence, the PPP screening tool does more than simply label an incident as violent—it provides a structured, nuanced method to understand and address family violence in a way that prioritizes the safety and long-term healing of all involved, especially the children.

Jaffe's PPP model, while offering a framework to understand DV dynamics, has not been without its detractors. Critics have raised concerns that the model tends to reduce the multifaceted nature of abusive relationships into a limited set of components, thereby oversimplifying what are often highly complex interactions (Lapierre et al., 2018). In doing so, it may neglect important situational factors or individual differences that contribute to the escalation or maintenance of violence.

Another significant criticism is that the model seems to lean heavily on a gendered analysis of power imbalances (Bates & Graham-Kevan, 2016; Straus, 2009). While it successfully highlights how control and dominance can shape abusive behaviors, this focus can inadvertently sideline cases that do not fit the traditional mold—such as instances of mutual violence or abuse in same-sex relationships. By anchoring its analysis primarily in gendered power dynamics, the model may not fully capture the diversity of experiences across different relational and cultural contexts. Additionally, concerns have been raised regarding the empirical underpinnings of their PPP model (Hardesty et al., 2015). The PPP model requires further rigorous validation across varied populations before it can be considered a universally reliable tool. Without robust empirical support, there is a risk that practitioners and policymakers might over-rely on its framework, potentially leading to interventions or legal decisions that do not adequately address the nuances of each case. Finally, critics also point to operational ambiguities within the model. The definitions of key constructs such as power imbalances or control tactics can sometimes be vague, which complicates their consistent application in both clinical practice and legal settings. This lack of clarity can result in subjective interpretations, undermining the model's utility in informing precise assessments and interventions (Jenkins, 2017).

In summary, while Jaffe's PPP model has contributed valuable insights into the dynamics of DV, the possibility it may oversimplify complex interactions, its gendered focus, questions surrounding its empirical validation, and ambiguities in its operational definitions remain points of criticism.

Johnson's Elaboration Upon Jaffe's Potency, Pattern, Primary Perpetrator Model

Building on the groundwork laid by Jaffe et al. (2008), Johnson and his colleagues recognized that understanding family dynamics in cases of violence requires an even broader perspective. They expanded the original PPP screening—which focused on the severity of the abuse (i.e., potency), its recurring nature (i.e., pattern), and the identification of the main aggressor (i.e., primary perpetrator)—by incorporating two additional elements: parenting problems and the child's preference or perspective.

Imagine a case where the physical acts of violence are just one part of a much larger picture. Beyond assessing how dangerous an incident is, the expanded 5P model delves into the day-to-day challenges parents might face. The fourth element, *parenting problems,* refers to the inherent difficulties in parenting practices that can affect a child's well-being. These issues might range from a parent's struggles with effective discipline or emotional regulation to broader challenges in managing stress and conflict. Even in the absence of overt violence, such problems can significantly influence the family's dynamics and the overall safety of the child.

The fifth element—*the child's preference or perspective*—brings the child's voice into the equation. Recognizing that children can often provide valuable insights into which environment feels safest or most nurturing, this component acknowledges that the child's own feelings and experiences are essential when designing a parenting plan. By listening to the child, evaluators can better gauge which living arrangements might offer them the most stability and support, ensuring that their emotional and psychological needs are met (Gould & Martindale, 2009a).

In this holistic approach, every P works together to create a comprehensive understanding of the family's situation. While the original three Ps help to clarify the nature and source of the violence, the additional considerations of parenting problems and the child's preference ensure that the final parenting plan addresses not only the immediate risks but also the underlying issues that might affect long-term safety and well-being. This more expansive model ultimately supports more informed and compassionate decisions, keeping the best interests of the child at the heart of the process.

Johnson's Lethality Assessment Model

Johnson (2006) presents a comprehensive framework for evaluating the risk of lethality in violent relationships, weaving together a series of interconnected factors that help predict potentially fatal outcomes. At the heart of his approach is the recognition that when a person expresses threats or even entertains fantasies of homicide or suicide, it signals a dangerous preoccupation with ending a life, whether their own or someone else's. This unsettling mindset is compounded when weapons like guns or knives are readily available, as these tools transform violent impulses into lethal possibilities. Johnson's model emphasizes that a history of violence—particularly one that is frequent and intensifying within the relationship—serves as a critical warning sign. Past behaviors often set the stage for future actions, revealing a pattern that may be difficult to break. Further elevating the risk, the presence of drug or alcohol abuse can exacerbate these tendencies by impairing judgment and reducing self-control, thereby fueling a cycle of violence.

Equally concerning is the role of obsessive, controlling, or possessive behavior. Such patterns, especially when they persist after separation in the form of stalking or continued harassment, reveal an unhealthy fixation that can escalate into more dangerous forms of violence. Alongside these behavioral markers, high degrees of depression and rage paint a picture of emotional volatility—a state in which impulsive actions may override reason. A history of mental illness also factors into the assessment, suggesting that underlying psychological issues might contribute to erratic or harmful behavior. Adding another layer to this multifaceted evaluation is the individual's attitude towards authority. Disregard or contempt for societal rules and prior court orders not only reflects a lack of respect for legal boundaries but also hints at a deeper resistance to accountability, which can intensify conflicts.

Finally, recent significant stressors—whether it be the loss of a job, the death of a loved one, or a recent separation—can act as catalysts that push an already tense situation toward a lethal outcome. In combining these elements, Johnson's list provides evaluators with a nuanced tool to identify those cases where the risk of deadly violence is not just theoretical but alarmingly real.

Johnson's (2006) list of factors to consider in the assessment of lethality include

- threats or fantasies of homicide or suicide;
- availability of weapons such as guns or knives;
- a history of violence, especially if it is within the relationship and more frequent and severe;
- concurrent drug and alcohol abuse;
- obsessive, controlling, or possessive behavior regarding the partner, especially if it includes postseparation behavior like stalking;
- high degrees of depression and rage;
- history of mental illness;
- disregard and contempt for authority, or disregarding prior court orders; and
- recent significant stressors (i.e., loss of employment, a death in the family, recent separation).

Johnson's lethality assessment model has drawn criticism over the years for several reasons. One common critique is that the model tends to oversimplify the multifaceted nature of DV (Hamby, 2009). By assigning specific weights to certain risk factors, the model can inadvertently downplay the complex interplay of psychological, situational, and contextual elements that contribute to lethal outcomes. This reductionist approach (Capaldi et al., 2005) may miss critical nuances, especially in cases where the dynamics of abuse are fluid and evolve over time. Critics have also questioned the model's predictive validity and its applicability across diverse populations (Graham-Kevan & Archer, 2009). Many of the studies used to develop and validate the model were based on specific demographic samples, raising concerns about whether its risk indicators can be generalized to all cultural, socioeconomic, and relational contexts (Kasturirangan et al., 2004). In practice, this means that the model might not fully capture risk factors unique to different communities or types of relationships, such as same-sex partnerships, where traditional gender assumptions do not apply.

Another area of concern is the reliance on self-reported information and historical data, which are inherently subject to bias (Bates & Graham-Kevan, 2016). In contentious and emotionally charged situations, individuals might underreport or misrepresent behaviors, either out of fear, shame, or an attempt to manipulate outcomes. Such biases can lead to inaccuracies in risk assessment—either by overestimating the danger and triggering unwarranted interventions or by failing to identify genuinely high-risk scenarios. Additionally, some critics argue that the model's focus on predetermined indicators can result in both false positives and false negatives. On one hand, an overemphasis on certain factors may inflate the perceived risk, potentially leading to excessive or even punitive measures. On the other hand, important emerging indicators of danger that fall outside the model's parameters might be overlooked, leaving some cases under-assessed and insufficiently protected (Saunders et al., 2016).

In summary, while Johnson's lethality assessment model has been influential in shaping risk assessment practices in DV cases, its limitations—ranging from oversimplification and potential bias to issues with generalizability and accuracy—underscore the ongoing need for more nuanced and context-sensitive tools in this critical area.

Bancroft and Silverman's Domestic Violence Assessment Model

Bancroft and Silverman (2002) have developed a model that identifies several factors that need to be evaluated when determining if family violence or abuse has occurred, to what extent it has occurred, and what needs to be done in response to these concerns. Their model suggests that we evaluate the following:

1. **General concerns**. Johnson cites three interrelated concerns about how familial violence is recognized and managed in cases involving parent–child contact. Together, these concerns point to the need for a more comprehensive and sensitive approach in both evaluating family dynamics and in public understanding—ensuring that all dimensions of abuse, not just the physical ones, are adequately considered and addressed:

    a. **Historical Patterns of Parent–Child Contact Problems**
    This concern reflects the recognition that a problematic history between parents and children can signal ongoing or future issues. When past interactions have been fraught with conflict or

dysfunction, there is an increased risk that current contact arrangements may continue to be harmful to the child's well-being.

b. **Evaluator Inattention to Familial Violence**
Here, the worry is that professionals tasked with assessing family situations—such as custody evaluators or child welfare experts—might not fully consider or even overlook signs of familial violence. This lack of attention can lead to underestimating the severity or even the presence of abuse, thereby compromising the safety and support provided to vulnerable family members.

c. **Misconception About the Nature of Familial Violence**
Many people tend to equate familial violence solely with physical aggression. However, a more nuanced view recognizes that abuse often involves an imbalance of power and control, manifesting as emotional, psychological, or even economic abuse. This misconception can lead to a failure to identify and address the subtler, but equally damaging, forms of abuse within families.

2. **Use of control**. The overarching characteristic of the batterer is the imposition of a pattern of control over their partner. This includes criticism, verbal abuse, economic control, isolation, cruelty, and an array of other tactics. Patterns of control typically emerge gradually and intensify during the early years of the marriage. Assessors should explore changes in imposition of power associated with marriage, pregnancy, birth of a child, and other life transitions. Areas of life that need to be assessed include arguments and decision making, household responsibilities, emotional care taking and attention, sexual relations, finances, childrearing, and outside social contacts.

3. **Entitlement**. The overarching attitudinal characteristic of the batterer is entitlement. Entitlement is the belief that one has special rights and privileges no one else may have. Entitlement leads to the belief that one is justified in protecting their special status in relationships through the use of physical violence and psychological control.

4. **Self-centeredness and selfishness**. Related to their sense of entitlement, batterers view their needs as of paramount importance in the family. They are often preoccupied with their own needs and, as a result, are either less available or unavailable to their children's needs. Their self-centered focus often interferes with their children's ability to move toward age-appropriate autonomy and independence. Assessors should explore whether the batterer is able to place the needs of the children ahead of their own, and explore the developmental movement of children toward age-appropriate autonomy and independence.

5. **Superiority**. Batterers believe themselves to be superior to others, especially their victims. The quality of communication between the batterer and their partner may reflect the batterer's attitude toward their partner as

being a willful and ignorant child whom they need to educate and improve. Batterers may show an attitude of contempt toward their partners. Superiority may lead to viewing the partner as an object, depersonalizing the relationship. They may refer to their partners not by their names but by terms such as "my girl" or "the wife," suggesting a degree of emotional distance indicative of not knowing their partners as people.

6. **Possessiveness**. Batterers often view their partners as their property. Owned objects may be used as the owner chooses, and this attitude may lead to unwanted advances and abusive actions aimed at forcing the partner not to resist the batterer's wishes and demands. Possessiveness often is observed in stalking behavior, limited social contact, and access to others.

7. **Fear of abandonment**. Batterers often have an inordinate fear of abandonment and are usually despondent after separation. At these times, the risk of violence to the partner or children is significantly increased.

8. **Confusion of love and abuse**. Batterers often confuse their strong feelings of love for their partners as a justification to abuse them. The batterer confuses the experience of anger with the expression of violence. It is the expression of anger through violent actions that is abusive.

9. **Manipulativeness**. Batterers use a wide range of manipulative tactics to coerce their partners to conform their behaviors to serve the needs of the batterer. It is important to remember that the vast majority of family violence offenders project a public image that is in sharp contrast to the private reality of their behavior and attitudes.

10. **Externalization of responsibility**. Batterers do not take responsibility for their actions and their effect on others. They blame others and attribute the reason for their behaviors on the influence others had upon them. They exhibit a pattern of justifying their actions and making excuses. They shift blame to their partners (e.g., "She knows how to push my buttons") or their children (e.g., "They deserve what they got"). They often are successful in manipulating other family members to take on the responsibility of the abuse.

11. **Denial, minimization, and victim blaming**. Batterers rarely disclose their violent behavior. They may deny that they perpetrate violence upon others in the family or indicate that they are the victims of someone else's violence. They often minimize their history of abuse and report less violence in the marriage than do their partners. Exploring denial and minimization is a critical component to a satisfactory evaluation.

12. **Serial battering**. Batterers often have a history of family violence with intimate partners. Interviewing former intimate partners and obtaining court complaints and orders and police complaints and records are critical components of a comprehensive evaluation.

13. **Authoritarian parenting style**. Batterers tend to employ an authoritarian parenting style.
14. **Under-involvement, neglect, and irresponsibility in parenting**. Batters may be under-involved and neglectful parents, placing all responsibility for parenting on their partners. They tend to show less physical affection and consider caring for their children to be the other parent's job. They often show a lack of knowledge about their children's lives, including their education, medical care, social involvements, and other relevant areas of child development. They are largely unaware of the effect of their violent and controlling behavior on their children's development.
15. **Undermining of the parenting authority when the family was together**. Batterers tend to consider themselves superior in all aspects of their family life and place little positive value on the other parent's parenting authority in front of the children. They also undermine the other parent's parenting competence by continual criticism.
16. **Undermining of parenting after separation**. Batterers will often create a postseparation home environment that is largely or entirely lacking in structure and discipline. Children who enjoy this freedom return to their other parent's home displaying an increased resistance to accepting their efforts to impose structure. The children have historically viewed the batterer as the disciplinarian and their other parent as inadequate or incompetent. Therefore, the children act defiant and oppositional and often ignore their parenting directives. The batterer uses these data that reflect their historical undermining of the other parent's parental authority as proof that they is incapable of parenting the children by themself and argues that the children need to be in their custody.
17. **Self-centeredness in relation to their children**. A batterer's parenting style is often characterized by self-centeredness in relationship to their children. The batterer is unwilling to modify their parenting style to suit the needs of their children and is insensitive to their children's feelings and experiences resulting from their rigid adherence to their own ways. Batterers are often unable to view their children as separate from themselves. Children are often viewed as objects and not as people with separate internal states and emotional needs.
18. **Manipulativeness with children**. Batterers are manipulative with their children in a manner similar to their manipulativeness with their partners.
19. **Ability to perform under observation**. Batterers are able to hold up a good, positive public image with their children. If seen in a parent–child observation for a custody evaluation, the batterer's power over the children to get them to comply with their expectations for good behavior may likely be observed. Evaluators need to be cautious about how they interpret the data obtained from the parent–child observation. Without collateral support, the generated data may tell us either about the child's respect

for their parent's abusive power or the child's positive relationship with the parent. Without additional information, there is no reliable way to distinguish one hypothesis from the other.

Bancroft and Silverman's Concerns About Batterers' Parenting Style

Although the Bancroft and Silverman model has faced criticism for its limited empirical support (Gould & Martindale, 2007), its clinically derived insights provide a useful perspective on how a batterer's parenting style might adversely affect children. The model, while not grounded in extensive quantitative research, draws from clinical observations that highlight a disturbing potential: the very behaviors exhibited by batterers in their roles as parents may sow the seeds of long-term emotional and psychological harm. These clinical ideas suggest that even beyond the immediate incidents of violence, the patterns of interaction—a combination of coercion, control, and inconsistency—can create an environment in which children feel unsafe and unsupported. Despite debates over the model's scientific underpinnings, its discussion remains vital because it underscores the importance of considering the nuanced ways in which a parent's behavior, particularly in violent contexts, can impact a child's development and overall well-being.

The parenting style of a batterer plays a crucial role in the risk of child abuse, as highlighted by Bancroft and Silverman's research (2002). Batterers often adopt an authoritarian parenting approach, characterized by rigid and harsh discipline methods, high demands for obedience and respect, and limited emotional warmth or nurturing. This style can lead to significant psychological harm and increases the risk of physical abuse. Paradoxically, many batterers also exhibit neglectful parenting behaviors. Their self-centeredness often results in inattention to children's needs, inconsistent involvement in childcare, and a lack of age-appropriate supervision. This neglect can result in both physical and emotional harm to children, creating a dangerous and unstable environment. A particularly damaging aspect of a batterer's parenting style is the tendency to undermine the other parent's authority. This can manifest in various ways, such as contradicting or overruling the other parent's decisions, encouraging children to disrespect or disobey them, and using children as a means to control or punish the other parent. Such behavior creates confusion and instability for children, increasing their vulnerability to abuse and emotional distress. Moreover, batterers model abusive behavior, which can have long-lasting effects on children. Children exposed to DV are at risk of learning and internalizing abusive behaviors, developing distorted views of relationships and conflict resolution, and experiencing a range of emotional and behavioral problems. Perhaps most alarmingly, batterers have a higher likelihood of directly abusing their children. Physical abuse rates are significantly higher among batterers, and sexual abuse of children is more common in homes with DV. Emotional abuse through intimidation, manipulation, and exposure to violence is also prevalent.

In conclusion, the batterer's parenting style elevates the risk of various forms of child abuse, both directly through their actions and indirectly through the toxic family dynamics they create. This multifaceted impact underscores the importance of considering parenting style when assessing the risk to children in situations of DV.

Criticism of the Bancroft and Silverman Model

Bancroft and Silverman's (2002) work on assessing risk to children from batterers has been influential in the field of DV, but it has not been without its critics. While their model is comprehensive and widely used, some professionals have raised concerns about various aspects of their approach. One of the primary criticisms is the lack of rigorous empirical validation (Gould & Martindale, 2007). Although the model is based on extensive clinical experience, some argue that it hasn't been subjected to large-scale, systematic studies to confirm its effectiveness and accuracy. This ties into another critique: the potential overreliance on the authors' clinical experiences rather than broader research findings. Gender bias is another point of contention. Critics suggest that the model may be skewed towards scenarios involving male perpetrators and female victims, potentially overlooking other DV dynamics (Dragiewicz, 2012). This bias could limit the model's applicability in cases that don't fit this typical pattern. Some professionals argue that the model may oversimplify the complex dynamics at play in DV situations (Bancroft et al., 2011). Family relationships and individual circumstances can be intricate, and there's concern that the model might not capture all the nuances of each unique case. Another criticism focuses on the model's limited emphasis on the potential for batterers to change their behavior (Bancroft & Silverman, 2002; Gondolf, 2002; Stark, 2007). While Bancroft and Silverman do address this to some extent, some argue that more attention could be given to rehabilitation and behavior modification (Stark, 2007). Cultural considerations have also been raised as a potential weakness. Bancroft acknowledges that their model may not adequately account for cultural differences in family structures and parenting styles, potentially leading to misinterpretations in diverse communities (Bancroft & Silverman, 2002; Raj & Silverman, 2002). Lastly, there are worries about the potential for misuse of the model, particularly in custody disputes (Bancroft & Silverman, 2002). If not applied carefully and in conjunction with other assessment tools, there's a risk that it could lead to unfair outcomes.

Despite these criticisms, it's important to note that Bancroft and Silverman's work remains widely utilized in the field of DV assessment and intervention. Their model has contributed to understanding the risks batterers pose to children.

The Domestic Violence in Child Custody Protocol

The domestic violence in child custody (DVCC) protocol, developed by Drozd (2008), is a valuable tool used to assess the ways in which partners handle conflict and the dynamics of power and control that are often present in cases of DV. With its 152 items, the protocol is designed to uncover underlying issues in family relationships that can lead to or signify family violence, including physical aggression, emotional manipulation, and even sexual abuse. This tool is not meant to provide conclusive evidence in and of itself, but rather to guide professionals in the early stages of their investigation into family violence. Drozd's careful consideration that the protocol should not offer "definitive findings" underscores the important role it plays in prompting further inquiry. Instead of acting as a stand-alone diagnostic device, the DVCC is intended to encourage evaluators to ask the right questions and score common behaviors and concerns that could signal the presence of abusive patterns.

By framing the issue in terms of power, control, and conflict management, the protocol helps evaluators understand the broader dynamics at play, particularly in cases where emotional and psychological abuse might remain hidden beneath more obvious signs of physical violence. One of the primary advantages of the DVCC is that it calls attention to diverse forms of familial violence that might otherwise be overlooked in a legal or custody dispute. The emotional and psychological abuse that can disrupt family structures is often insidious, hard to detect, or disregarded by evaluators, particularly when they have focused primarily on physical violence.

The tool can prompt evaluators to look beyond physical injuries, considering how the family's conflict resolution style, history of communication, and power imbalances could affect the safety and well-being of the child involved. Drozd's (2008) protocol aligns with a growing awareness that family violence is not confined only to physical aggression. DV in the context of child custody isn't merely about hitting or hurting; it is often about systematic control and manipulation. This distinction provides a more comprehensive understanding of the influence family violence may have on all members and lays the groundwork for more nuanced evaluations in the context of child custody decisions.

By framing familial violence as much broader than physical aggression, the tool enables evaluators to address necessary questions that extend beyond traditional evaluation methods, enhancing the safety net for children and families in extremely complex situations. In this way, the DVCC protocol serves as a preliminary but profound step in uncovering the layers of familial violence that might otherwise be missed in the rush to make conventional legal determinations, reshaping how such cases are approached and ultimately ensuring that a wider range of abuses is considered when evaluating child custody.

Drozd's (2008) development of the DVCC protocol represents a thoughtful and methodical effort to better understand and address the complex dynamics of family violence in custody disputes. Instead of providing a definitive verdict on whether abuse exists, the DVCC serves as an initial framework—an extensive list of questions aimed at uncovering how partners manage conflict and where power imbalances might be contributing to a pattern of violence. This self-report protocol invites respondents to share detailed accounts of their experiences, shedding light on aspects of abuse that might not be immediately visible in a courtroom setting.

Moreover, the DVCC protocol serves as a starting point for evaluators and triers of fact. Rather than delivering an unequivocal diagnosis, it prompts deeper inquiry—encouraging professionals to ask nuanced questions and consider a broader spectrum of abusive behaviors. In doing so, it equips those involved in child custody cases with a structured method to identify potential red flags and better understand the underlying issues. Ultimately, Drozd's (2008) DVCC protocol is less about delivering immediate conclusions and more about opening a dialogue that can lead to a more comprehensive evaluation of familial violence in contexts where the stakes are incredibly high.

The protocol includes

- obtaining civil and criminal complaints and judgments from police, courts, and other relevant venues;
- obtaining work records;
- assessing weapons access;
- examination of alcohol and substance use;
- formal risk assessment;
- collateral contacts, including former romantic partners;
- examination of power and control variables in relationship;
- examination of how parents argued (i.e., type of interaction);
- examination of how parents resolved arguments (i.e., methods of resolution);
- examination of triggers for fights;
- parents' understanding of fight triggers and how to avoid them;
- psychological variables that may contribute to propensity toward violence, for example, impulsiveness, low frustration tolerance, rigid versus flexible thinking, authoritarian worldview, sex role perspective;
- parental insight into their anger and its management;
- parental insight into the cycle of violence within their relationship—how it starts and what attributions each parent makes about the other's motivation;
- examination of psychological or emotional abuse variables;
- examination of financial or economic abuse variables;
- examination of sexual abuse variables;
- exposure of child to forms of violence and conflict;
- examination of child disciplinary techniques (i.e., what is used);

- examination of deployment of child disciplinary techniques (i.e., when it is used); and
- awareness of multiple disciplinary strategies sans corporal punishment.

Critics of the Drozd DVCC protocol have raised several concerns regarding its design and application in evaluating familial violence within child custody disputes. They are

- **Reliance on self-report**: One of the primary criticisms is its dependence on self-reported data (Fieldstone & Coates, 2008). In contentious custody situations, individuals may have strong incentives to either underreport or exaggerate certain behaviors. This can lead to responses that are influenced by social desirability or defensive posturing, thereby questioning the reliability of the information gathered.
- **Length and respondent fatigue**: The DVCC consists of 152 items, a length that some argue can overwhelm respondents. Extended questionnaires may lead to fatigue, reducing the accuracy and consistency of responses. We raise concerns that the length could result in incomplete or less thoughtful answers, undermining the protocol's ability to capture a clear and comprehensive picture of the family dynamics at play. The DVCC often takes more than 90 minutes to complete.
- **Cultural and contextual limitations**: While the protocol aims to capture physical, emotional, and sexual dimensions of abuse, some scholars suggest that it may not fully account for the subtleties of power imbalances across diverse cultural, socioeconomic, and familial contexts. The structured nature of the tool might not adequately reflect the complex and varied manifestations of abuse, particularly in cases where cultural norms influence the expression or perception of power and control (Gould & Martindale, 2013).
- **Ambiguity in legal applicability**: Drozd (2008) emphasizes that the DVCC is not a diagnostic tool but rather a starting point for inquiry. This inherent ambiguity can be problematic in legal settings, where clear, definitive evidence is often sought. Without explicit thresholds or interpretative guidelines, judges and legal professionals might find it challenging to draw concrete conclusions from the DVCC's findings, potentially leading to inconsistent or subjective applications in custody cases.
- **Need for further validation**: Another point of criticism concerns the empirical grounding of the tool. While the DVCC is built on a solid theoretical foundation, some critics argue that more extensive validation across diverse populations is necessary. Without robust evidence supporting its reliability and validity, there remains uncertainty about whether the instrument can consistently and accurately reflect the nuances of familial violence in all contexts.

In summary, while the DVCC protocol represents a significant step toward recognizing and interrogating the multifaceted nature of familial violence, its reliance on self-reporting, extensive length, potential cultural insensitivity, ambiguous legal utility, and the need for further validation are important areas of criticism that need addressing to enhance its effectiveness in real-world applications.

Austin's Frameworks for Testing Credibility, Risk, and Lethality

Austin's Six-Factor Test of Credibility

William G. Austin's (2000a) Six-Factor test of credibility offers a structured method for evaluating sensitive DV allegations. The test has various components: it examines objective verification of the claims, ensuring that there is a clear and consistent pattern in abuse complaints across time; whether other credible individuals can corroborate the allegations; if any credible third-party reports contradict the allegations; and it defines the psychological profiles of both the alleged perpetrator and the victim. The factors included in W. G. Austin's (2000a) Six-Factor test of credibility for investigating family violence allegations are

1. objective verification,
2. pattern of abuse complaints,
3. corroboration by credible others,
4. absence of disconfirming verbal reports by credible third parties,
5. psychological profile and past history of abusive behavior by the alleged perpetrator of marital violence, and
6. psychological status of the alleged victimized spouse.

The Six-Factor test provides an operational framework for understanding the reliability of abuse claims, helping ensure that accusations—whether true or false—are assessed with rigor and fairness. Equally important is the assessment of risk and lethality in custody cases where family violence is a factor. Austin offers another comprehensive framework designed to help courts predict the risks that may arise in these cases.

William G. Austin's (2000a) Six-Factor test accounts for both past and present patterns: For instance, is the violence in question a singular incident or part of a recurring pattern? When using the Six-Factor test, evaluators should consider the following:

- Is the violence bidirectional, where both partners engage in aggressive behavior?
- The severity of physical harm—from mild injuries to more profound trauma—is also a key component.

- Understanding whether the violence in question is verbal aggression or physical assault provides important context for potential harm in custody situations.

Risk factors, such as substance abuse or mental health disorders, are included in the model. It is also important to recognize that a parent's psychological or substance-related struggles might elevate the likelihood of violence within the household. Furthermore, an especially critical point is whether children have been exposed to violence, as this can add additional layers of risk and harm when determining the best parenting plan arrangements.

It is important to understand Austin's use of the term credibility. There is a difference between offering opinions about the truthfulness of an individual or an alleged event and gathering data that either supports or refutes the assertion. Assessment of credibility is the province of the court. Gathering data to support or refute an assertion or allegation is within the purview of forensic psychological investigations. Austin uses the term credibility to refer to gathering data to support or refute an assertion or allegation, not to offer an expert opinion about truthfulness.

Another caution is that the Austin model is not a test as the term test is defined in the psychological literature. Austin's model is a data-gathering procedure intended to assist in identifying relevant data that supports or refutes assertions or allegations.

Austin argues that establishing whether there is data to support or refute a party's allegations of family violence is a crucial part of the process. Austin operationally defined credibility in a custody evaluation to entail seeking third-party data that either confirms or refutes a parent's assertion. Information should be gathered from multiple, independent sources.

Austin's Framework for Assessing Risk and Lethality

William G. Austin (2001) also developed frameworks for assessing risk and lethality in child custody cases. Austin's focus is gathering data from multiple independent sources of information that can help the court best predict risk or harm to children involved in custody and access cases. The six dimensions of this protocol are

1. temporal pattern of violence (is it a single incident, multiple, bidirectional, chronic, or persistent?),
2. gender of the perpetrator and causal direction of violence (instigated by male or female, bidirectional-mutual, mostly male, mostly female),
3. severity of physical harm (mild, moderate, severe),
4. type of aggression (verbal or physical),
5. presence of major risk factors (alcohol, substance abuse, on-going mental disorder, major mental disorder), and
6. children's exposure or nonexposure to violence.

Criticism of Austin's Frameworks

Austin's models, including the Six-Factor test of credibility and the risk and lethality framework, has not been without their detractors. While the model offers a structured way to assess family violence in child custody cases, we are concerned that it tends to oversimplify the inherently complex and subjective task of evaluating credibility. By dividing evidence into predetermined categories such as objective verification, pattern of abuse complaints, and psychological profiles, the model may not fully capture the subtle nuances of each case. In practice, obtaining truly objective verification can be challenging, especially in high-conflict environments where family dynamics obscure clear-cut evidence.

We have raised concerns throughout this book about threats to reliability when data gathering is based upon subjective measures. Data gathered using Austin's models, such as assessing the psychological status of both the alleged perpetrator and victim, can introduce evaluator biases. Inconsistencies can arise when assessments depend heavily on professional judgment, leading to questions about the model's reliability across different cases and evaluators. Additionally, the model's focus on predefined dimensions like the temporal pattern of violence and specific risk factors (such as substance abuse or mental health issues) may fail to account for the varied and context-dependent nature of abuse (Gould & Martindale, 2013). This reductionist approach risks overlooking critical aspects of family violence that do not neatly fit into established categories. Moreover, we noted that there is no empirical validation of Austin's model. While it provides a useful framework, further research is needed to ensure its predictive accuracy and to verify that its criteria are applicable across diverse cultural, socioeconomic, and familial contexts.

In essence, while Austin's model represents a commendable attempt to bring structure to a complex issue, its potential for oversimplification, subjectivity, and limited generalizability remains a significant point of contention among scholars and practitioners alike.

The Spousal Assault Risk Assessment Guide and the Brief Spousal Assault Form for the Evaluation of Risk

The Spousal Assault Risk Assessment Guide (SARA) represents a concerted effort to ground the assessment of intimate partner violence (IPV) in a solid, empirical foundation. Developed initially in the 1990s and now in its third edition (SARA-V3), the instrument was designed by Kropp and Gibas (2021) to serve as a structured professional judgment tool. It provides a checklist of risk factors that have been systematically identified through extensive research, making its application "evidence-based, empirically guided, or empirically supported practice" (Kropp & Gibas, 2021).

The SARA includes 20 items within four general categories: criminal history, psychosocial adjustment, spousal assault history, and alleged current offense. Items were chosen based on empirical research linking the item to risk of spousal assault. Risks ratings are made after data collection on the 20 items.

Criminal history:

1. Past assault of family members
2. Past assault of strangers or acquaintances
3. Past violation of conditional release or community supervision

Psychosocial adjustment:

4. Recent relationship problems
5. Recent employment problems
6. Victim of or witness to family violence as a child or adolescent
7. Recent substance abuse or dependence
8. Recent suicidal or homicidal ideation
9. Recent psychotic or manic symptoms
10. Personality disorder with anger, impulsivity, or behavioral instability

Spousal assault history:

11. Past physical assault
12. Past sexual assault or sexual jealousy
13. Past use of weapons or credible threats of death
14. Recent escalation in frequency or severity of assault
15. Past violation of no-contact order
16. Extreme minimization or denial of spousal assault history
17. Attitudes that support or condone spousal assault

Alleged current offense:

18. Severe or sexual assault
19. Use of weapons or credible threats of death
20. Violation of no-contact order

The assessment process itself is methodical. Evaluators start by gathering comprehensive information about the case. Each risk factor is then rated on a three-point scale—categorized as present, possible or partially present, or not present. Following this, evaluators assess whether each factor might impact management planning, again using a three-point scale (yes, possible or partially, no). This step is crucial in linking the identified risks to concrete management strategies. For example, in a parenting plan evaluation (PPE), these strategies might include measures such as supervised visitations, supervised exchanges, monitored communication, tailored treatment programs, or staggered arrival and departure times. After the detailed rating process and risk scenario planning, the SARA-V3 culminates in summary risk judgments. Evaluators rate the overall case across four key areas: case prioritization, risk for serious physical harm, imminent violence, and any other risks. These summary ratings are given on a three-point ordinal scale—ranging from low or routine, through moderate or elevated, to high or urgent—providing a clear, standardized indication of the level of risk present.

In addition to the SARA-V3, a shorter version known as the Brief Spousal Assault Form for the Evaluation of Risk (B-SAFER) was developed. Based on SARA-V2 and parallel in structure to the SARA-V3, the B-SAFER offers a streamlined assessment that focuses on core perpetrator risk factors and victim vulnerability factors. This simplified instrument is designed for situations where a quicker yet reliable assessment is needed.

It is important to note a critical point regarding the SARA's and the B-SAFER's validity. Although the tools are built on a strong empirical base, much of its validity data comes from studies involving incarcerated men or individuals facing legal challenges. As Hynan (2015) notes, this raises questions about the tool's applicability in PPEs, where the dynamics and characteristics of the involved parties may differ substantially from those in the original validation samples.

Critics note that the dynamics and circumstances of individuals undergoing legal proceedings may differ substantially from the parties involved in PPEs. This difference raises questions about whether the models are fully applicable or accurate in such contexts. In child custody cases, for example, the relationship dynamics are often less extreme, with different motivations and forms of violence at play. Another criticism is the inherent subjectivity within the models.

Overall, the development of the SARA and its associated instruments marks a significant stride toward standardizing the risk assessment process in cases of spousal assault and IPV. By combining empirical research with structured professional judgment, these tools aim to assist evaluators in making informed, consistent, and actionable decisions in complex, high-stakes situations.

OUR ECOLOGICAL MODEL FOR ASSESSING DOMESTIC VIOLENCE

Using an ecological model (EM) informed by social learning theory (Bandura, 1977), biopsychosocial factors (Grych & Fincham, 1990), and attachment-based emotion regulation (Cummings & Davies, 1996; Cummings et al., 2009), we developed a structured and comprehensive approach to evaluation of DV. Our approach ensures that every aspect of DV—from individual emotional functioning to systemic pressures—is examined to develop a balanced and legally sound parenting plan evaluation. The process is as follows:

1. Explain how safety concerns will be addressed.
2. Screen for DV.

3. Evaluate each parent individually.
4. Evaluate the child.
5. Evaluate the parent–parent relationship.
6. Evaluate the parent–child relationships.
7. Evaluate the overall family system.
8. Evaluate broader systemic pressures.
9. Based on the data, develop a parenting plan.

In the following, we describe each step of the investigative process.

Explain How Safety Concerns Will Be Addressed

Evaluators should communicate how they will respond to safety concerns during the evaluation. Evaluators are well served to provide this information in the initial paperwork agreements and in initial conversations with the parents. An evaluator may need to reach out to the court for guidance, give prior notice before communicating, ensure a safety plan is established, and clarify the constraints of the evaluation process, results, and recommendations (Association of Family and Conciliation Courts, 2016).

Screen for Domestic Violence

After explaining safety protocols to parents, all parenting plan evaluators should conduct a screening for past and current exposure to or victimization of all forms of DV, including but not limited to IPV or CC. Screening is an ongoing process during the evaluation. The evaluator should continue to be attentive to the possibility of DV occurring during the evaluation. We have been involved in cases in which DV was initially denied, and then during the evaluation, one parent alleged DV had occurred in the past. We have also been involved in cases in which a mother's attorney told her client not to allege or disclose she was a victim of DV because it had occurred in the past.

SAFeR, produced by the Battered Women's Justice Project (Davis, 2015), is a screening instrument that begins with open-ended questions, which become more specific as the screen progresses. SAFeR involves screening for IPV, assessing the nature and context of IPV, focusing on the effects of IPV, and responding to IPV. Many evaluators use questionnaires to begin their evaluation (Garber et al., 2023), which should include screening questions for DV. If the evaluator does not use a questionnaire, we recommend they screen for DV in their early interviews.

As early as possible, the evaluator should review any documentation, such as protective orders or police reports, that may reference DV or safety concerns. If there are no concerns expressed, the evaluator momentarily pauses their DV assessment. We again encourage evaluators to remember that just because

FIGURE 22.1. Ecological Model Applied to Assessment of Domestic Violence

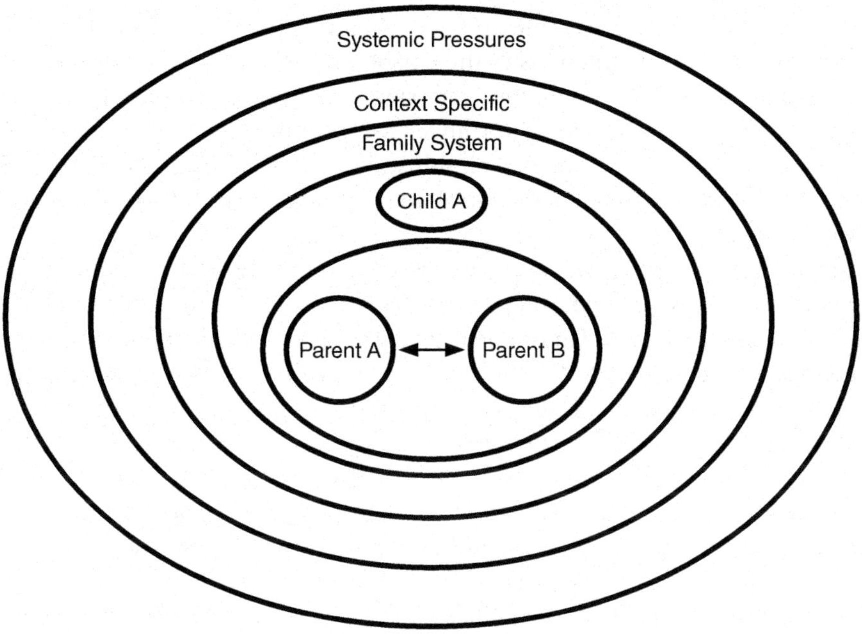

there is no data to support DV early on in the evaluation process, it does not mean their analysis is over. They need to be vigilant for DV dynamics throughout their evaluation. If, for example, there is no data to support DV early on in the evaluation, and then data arises later in the evaluation, we would then encourage the evaluator to follow the EM in Figure 22.1.

Evaluate Each Parent Individually

The next step is an assessment of each parent's individual emotional regulation skills and behaviors. The evaluator assesses the parent's past and current abilities to regulate their emotions and anger through psychological testing, interview protocols, record review, interviews with the other parent, and collateral interviews.

In their individual assessment of each parent, evaluators may administer the Minnesota Multiphasic Personality Inventory, Third Edition (MMPI-3). After assessing the validity scales, an analysis of a parent's test results begins with the higher-order scales. All three higher-order scales (emotional or internalizing dysfunction, thought dysfunction, and behavioral or externalizing dysfunction) may be relevant in a DV assessment. Of the restructured scales, evaluators should closely attend to dysfunctional negative emotions (RC7), antisocial behavior (RC4), and ideas of persecution (RC6). Of the internalizing scales, evaluators should assess anger proneness, stress, worry, and compulsivity. Of the externalizing scales, evaluators should attend to aggression, impulsivity, activation, and substance abuse. Moving next to the interpersonal scales, evaluators should attend to dominance and self-importance. Finally, under the personality psychopathology five subscales, evaluators should assess aggressiveness, psychoticism, disconstraint, and negative emotionality or neuroticism.

Evaluators may also administer the personality assessment inventory. After attending to the validity scales, the aggression scale assesses attitude and behavioral features relevant to aggression, anger, and hostility. Items on the personality assessment inventory that load on this scale range from "indicators of verbal assertiveness and poor anger control to violent and assaultive behaviors" (Morey, 2007).

Evaluators should attend to the mania scale, with particular attention to the activity level (MAN-A) and irritability (MAN-I) subscales. Noting that the paranoia scale may be elevated in response to litigation, evaluators should assess the parent's hypervigilance (PAR-H), persecution (PAR-P), and resentment (PAR-R). On the borderline scale, the affective instability (BOR-A) and identity problems (BOR-I) may be of interest. On the antisocial scale, both egocentricity (ANT-E) and stimulus-seeking (ANT-S) might be relevant.

If anxiety is raised, evaluators should assess physiological anxiety (ANX-P). Stress (STR) and nonsupport (NON) may also be of interest. Regarding the interpersonal scales, dominance (DOM) should be assessed. Regarding the supplemental indexes, evaluators should review the violence potential index (VPI), which incorporates risk factors such as explosive expression of anger, sensation seeking, substance abuse, and impulsivity.

Evaluators may also use a structured interview tool such as the Structured Clinical Interview for DSM Disorders or the Diamond. The evaluator should be aware of the threats to validity associated with asking the parent to self-report symptoms on measures that do not have response style indicators.

The evaluator should then interview collaterals, such as therapists, psychiatrists, and others in the community, who can provide observations of the parent's individual functioning. Note that although we begin with an individual assessment of the parent, our assessment does not end at the individual level. Next, we assess the child.

Evaluate the Child

Next, the evaluator assesses the child's individual behavior through interviews, observations, reports from the parents, psychological testing, and collateral contacts. The evaluator pays close attention to the child's ability to regulate their emotions in an age-appropriate manner. The evaluator assesses for the symptoms of trauma sequelae that may be associated with the child being exposed to DV.

The child may complete the Behavior Assessment System for Children, Third Edition, which can be used to develop hypotheses on the child's strengths and challenges. When the child's teacher and parents also complete this assessment, there are multiple data points to compare. Interviews with the teacher and the child's therapist may provide valuable data and should be prioritized.

Parenting the child may be a source of stress in the family system. Therefore, the evaluator should also assess the child's behavior to understand if the child's behavior is a source of frustration for the parents. The evaluator should also assess the child's strengths and vulnerabilities and assess the child's temperament and disposition.

Evaluate the Parent–Parent Relationship

The next step in our EM is to look at the relationship between the parents. Then we will assess the relationships between the parents and the children. In assessing the relationship between the parents, the evaluator assesses verbal arguments, destruction of property, threats of physical violence, physical violence, financial manipulation or control, sexual violence, and stalking.

The evaluator should assess for past and present safety concerns. The evaluator should review historical documents such as police reports and protective orders. Another information source is the parents' communication found in emails, text messages, and personal knowledge derived from collateral interviews.

The evaluator uses the SARA, B-SAFER, or Domestic Abuse Interview Guide to structure their data gathering. The SARA or B-SAFER also provide the evaluator with safety planning.

Evaluate the Parent–Child Relationships

After evaluating the parents' relationship, the evaluator evaluates the relationship between each parent and each child. The evaluator assesses the degree to which the children look toward the parent for safety and comfort.

The evaluator assesses the historical nature of the relationship between each parent and child, with special attention to relationship dynamics such as the quality of the attachment, enmeshment, estrangement, or resist and refuse dynamics (Garber et al., 2022). If there are concerns regarding enmeshment, estrangement, or resist and refuse dynamics, reference Chapters 19 and 20.

Evaluate the Overall Family System

At the next level the evaluator assesses the family system dynamics that lead to conflict.

The evaluator applies Jaffe et al.'s (2008) PPP screening questions or Johnson et al.'s (2009) 5P's (which added parenting problems and the child's preference or perspective) to their analysis.

Evaluate Broader Systemic Pressures

The outer layer of our EM incorporates an analysis of systemic pressures. These may include community, school, religion, climate change, or natural disasters. For example, the COVID-19 pandemic created systemic pressures on many families that impacted their individual emotional regulation, their relationships with one another, the family system, and led to context-specific conflicts.

Develop a Parenting Plan

Parenting plans incorporate a balance between the generally positive benefits of parent–child interactions while ensuring safety and security concerns for both the child and their parents (Hynan, 2018). The evaluator combines and organizes the gathered data and then develops a set of inferences about the meaning of the data. Choosing from among these inferences, the parenting plan should be based upon the findings that are more likely than not to provide the child with support for their psychological best interests.

Part of developing a parenting plan is determining whether or not physical safety measures are warranted. These can include supervised visitation, supervised communication, supervised parenting time exchanges, and protection orders. Determination of emotional safety measures are also critically important. Emotional safety protections might include structuring communication through an application like Our Family Wizard, monitoring communication by a therapist or parenting coordinator, defining a neutral place for parenting time exchanges, or staggering arrival and departure times for exchanges, therapy, and the child's activities. In those instances in which there are concerns about CC, the evaluator should also include ways to monitor economic security factors that may impact the family system.

After the evaluator assesses whether physical safety measures and emotional safety measures are warranted, the evaluator then makes a recommendation for how these measures can be implemented. Monitoring and enforceability vary greatly based on jurisdiction.

An evaluator may also recommend allocation or limitations of decision-making authority, however it is critical that the evaluator think through the profound constitutional issues raised when a parent's liberty interest in parenting is suspended or terminated (Gould et al., 2016a). The recommendation that parents may share decision making authority should include the following analysis:

- **Safe involvement between parents** is free from violence, threats of violence, and CC; stable and predictable; and focused on and responsive to the needs of the child.
- **Healthy parent–child relationships** are free from violence, threats of violence, and CC; age and developmentally appropriate; focused on and supportive of the child; based on mastery of basic parenting skills and parental decision making; and consistent with established rules and expectations.
- **Cooperation between parents** requires mutual responsibility and shared authority; absence of violence, threats of violence, exploitation, and coercion; willingness to consider alternate viewpoints; capacity to recognize and respond to others' needs (i.e., emotional maturity); and ability to compromise and

reach agreement on important issues. If other family caregivers are involved in parenting plans, these considerations would apply to them as well.

- **Effective communication between parents** is open and direct, civil and bidirectional, constructive (i.e., not harmful or damaging, and more than the mere sharing of information), and focused on the children.
- **Clear boundaries between partner and parental roles** means that parents are able to separate their role as parents from their role as partners; limits between partner and parental roles are clear and unambiguous. (Association of Family and Conciliation Courts, 2016)

CONCLUSION

The assessment of DV allegations in family court is both an art and a science—one that demands rigorous methodology, critical analysis, and a deep understanding of the nuanced interplay between individual behaviors and systemic influences. The integration of validated instruments like the SARA-V3 and B-SAFER, alongside structured frameworks such as the PPP Screening, provides evaluators with essential tools to navigate these complex cases. However, the journey is far from complete. Continued efforts to standardize training, enhance empirical validation, and mitigate systemic pressures are vital to ensuring that every evaluation genuinely reflects the best interests of the child.

Assessing allegations of DV in family court proceedings is a highly intricate task that requires evaluators to navigate a maze of data and frameworks. Evaluators draw on a variety of tools—ranging from psychological assessments and collateral interviews to direct behavioral observations—to systematically identify the presence, severity, and impact of family violence. Given the complex nature of DV in its various forms and its varied effect of its victims and the larger family system, these assessments cannot rely on one-size-fits-all approaches. Instead, they must adopt an individualized, evidence-informed methodology that carefully weighs risk factors, evaluates parental functioning, and prioritizes the safety and well-being of children. To achieve this, professionals are encouraged to utilize risk assessment instruments that offer a structured approach to data gathering that helps standardize the evaluation process and ensures that all relevant aspects of the case are considered. Our model emphasizes an ecological approach that is structured, evidence-informed, and provides transparency.

Ultimately, the primary goal of these assessments is to ensure that parenting arrangements foster the physical and emotional safety of the child while promoting outcomes that are in the best interests of the child. Parenting plan evaluators need to embrace the importance of applying a rigorous, evidence-based or evidence-informed approach to each step of the evaluation process while also recognizing the significant limitations that presently exist in the available assessment tools that have yet to be systematically examined for their use in parenting plan evaluations.

23

Forensic Assessment of Parental Requests to Relocate

Relocation is among the most challenging psycholegal dilemmas facing evaluators and the courts. Relocation pits the legitimate wishes of Parent A to relocate with the child away from the child's home community and Parent B against Parent B's desire to remain highly involved with the minor child. A large body of research shows that relocation is a general risk factor for children of divorce; in fact, some data suggest that the risk to children from relocation is similar to the risk from divorce itself (W. G. Austin, 2000b).

At its core, relocation cases involve a delicate balance between a parent's right to mobility and a child's need for stability and continued relationships with both parents. Courts and evaluators are tasked with making decisions that prioritize the best interests of the child while considering the legitimate personal, economic, and social reasons a parent may have for moving.

The task of the evaluator is at least twofold. One is to address, identify, and contain the risk of potential harm to the child–nonmoving parent relationship (W. G. Austin, 2015a, 2015b). The second task is to compare and contrast the nature and quality of social capital available to the child in each home and community in an effort to assist the court in developing a picture of the child's life in each location (W. G. Austin, 2015b). This chapter aims to provide a structured and research-informed framework for assessing parental relocation requests, emphasizing the importance of safeguarding the child's well-being while addressing the competing interests of both parents.

https://doi.org/10.1037/0000474-024
Parenting Plan Evaluations: An Evidence-Informed Approach to Child Custody, by J. W. Gould and C. M. Mulchay

PREVALENCE OF CHILD RELOCATION IN THE GENERAL POPULATION VERSUS DIVORCED FAMILIES

Current mobility data show that a significant number of individuals move during a given year. Some estimates of what is called the mover rate reveals that somewhere around 12% of the total population move in a particular year. There are interstate moves. There are intercounty moves. There are intrastate moves. There are international moves. Separated individuals were the most mobile group. More than 50% of separated individuals move. Never-married individuals move slightly less often than do those who have been separated (W. G. Austin, 2015a).

Young children have a high mobility rate. Approximately 45% of young children ages 5 to 9 move in a particular year among the separated group. The aid groups that are more likely to have younger children have higher moving rates. More than 65% of those parents ages 25 to 29 relocate and about 45% of young parents ages 30 to 34 years relocate. Among those who have been divorced, a little more than 25% relocate in a given year (W. G. Austin, 2015a).

Nearly half of children of divorce relocate after the divorce is finalized. Evaluators should become familiar with jurisdiction-specific statutory requirements and case law pertaining to relocation (W. G. Austin, 2000a, 2000b; W. G. Austin et al., 2016).

THE RELOCATION DILEMMA

The psycholegal relocation dilemma involves conflicting social policy goals and the constitutional rights of parents to both have the right to travel and have access to and involvement with one's children. Among the factors associated with the right to travel are a divorced parents right to pursue personal, social, vocational, or educational goals in order to improve that parent's quality of life (W. G. Austin, 2015a).

The reality is that relocation will likely alter the nature and the quality of the child's relationship with the nonmoving parent. Maternal relocation has been reported to be related to, but not necessarily a cause of, "negative impacts on children's long-term relationships with their fathers, their adjustment to their parents' divorce, and their ongoing experience of their parents' relationship" (W. G. Austin, 2015a). These findings have been found to be unrelated to parental conflict and domestic violence. Relocation does not necessarily reduce parent conflict. Even local moves substantially change the nature and the quality of the child's relationship with the nonmoving parent. This is particularly true when one parent wishes to move within a large urban metropolitan area. A within-county or within-state relocation often significantly affects drive time and the nonmoving parent's frequent involvement with the child's school and extracurricular activities (W. G. Austin, 2015a).

Furthermore, some findings reveal that relocation has been associated with serious behavior problems. Long-distance separation from biological fathers prior to age 12 was found to be related to serious behavior problems in adolescence and young adulthood. This study found that adolescent children and young adults who lived more than an hour away from their father displayed higher levels of anxiety and depression symptoms, and disturbed relationships with all three parental figures (i.e., biological fathers, mothers, and stepfathers; Stevenson et al., 2018). The authors reported that these associations were unrelated to mother–stepfather conflict and domestic violence, mothers' family income, and mother–biological father relationship quality (Stevenson et al., 2018).

Despite all the concern about risk of harm to a young child resulting from parental relocation postseparation, data also show that the nonresidential or noncustodial parent moves with considerable frequency, creating a risk for the child. Also, research findings support the view that considerable geographical distance has a negative effect on parental involvement in the child's activities and poses long-term adjustment challenges to the child when the geographical separation is caused by either parent moving.

The challenge for the evaluator, the court, and the parents is to find ways to effectively manage the risk of potential harm to the nonmoving parent–child relationship and the relocating parent–child relationship.

THREE HARMS

William G. Austin (2015a) has identified three types of potential harm resulting from a parent's relocation. First, there is relationship harm associated with less involvement and a qualitatively negative shift in the child's relationship with the nonmoving parent due to the practical limitations for frequent and continuous involvement. The second type of harm is developmental harm to the child that results from less frequent involvement would the nonmoving parent and the reduction in the child's access to the psychosocial resources and assets that the nonmoving parent brings to the life of the child. A third harm is the increased likelihood of parental conflict resulting from the relocation and the child's exposure to that parental conflict. Austin refers to this as "relocation engendered conflict." Relocation can turn a previously cooperative coparenting relationship into one characterized by increased conflict and mistrust.

The nonmoving parent often views the intention to relocate as the moving parent's motivation to reduce the child's involvement with the nonmoving parent. Nonmoving parents often raise concerns about the moving parent engaging in restrictive gatekeeping, as the very act of relocating is a form of restricting the child's access to the other parent. In contrast, the moving parent will often assert that the relocation will result in a better quality of life for parent and child. A challenge to the moving parent is an ability to demonstrate that there is a factual basis for asserting that the relocation will result in a better quality of life rather than speculation that the future is brighter in an unfamiliar or untested geographic community.

JURISDICTION-SPECIFIC LEGAL CONSIDERATIONS IN PARENTAL RELOCATION CASES

Given the complexity of these emotional and psychological issues, how does a parenting plan evaluator help the court? Beyond being competent in the evidence-based and evidence-informed literature in conjunction with a skillful application of that information in conducting evaluations, evaluators must also be familiar with the statutes, case law, and local rules in their jurisdiction. Jurisdiction-specific statutory requirements and case law provide essential guidelines for courts when evaluating parental relocation requests. By considering key evidentiary factors—including the child's best interests, the feasibility of alternative custody arrangements, and the impact on parental relationships—courts aim to make well-reasoned decisions that promote stability and positive developmental outcomes for children. Given the psychological complexities inherent in these cases, parenting plan evaluators play a crucial role in providing the court with evidence-based insights that inform judicial decision-making.

While the specific requirements may differ, courts generally consider a set of *evidentiary factors* that must be analyzed before ruling on a relocation petition. Not all states have statutory definitions of best interest although most, if not all states, have relocation statutes. The evidentiary factors most often refer to statutory factors that have the authority of the state's legislature. Many jurisdictions that have relocation statutes require courts to assess specific key factors defined in those statutes when determining whether a child's relocation should be permitted:

- **The best interests of the child**: The fundamental consideration in any custody or relocation case is the child's best interests. Courts analyze how the move will impact the child's emotional, psychological, educational, and social well-being.
- **Reason for the relocation**: Courts evaluate the relocating parent's motivation for moving. Acceptable reasons often include career advancement, financial improvement, remarriage, family support, or better educational opportunities for the child. If the move appears to be an attempt to interfere with the other parent's custody rights, it may be denied.
- **Impact on parent–child relationships**: The court examines whether relocation would negatively impact the child's bond with the nonrelocating parent and extended family. A move that significantly limits parenting time may raise concerns about maintaining a meaningful parent–child relationship.

- **Feasibility of a revised parenting plan**: Courts assess whether a long-distance parenting arrangement can be established that preserves the child's relationship with both parents. This may involve modifications to custody schedules, travel arrangements, and communication methods.
- **The child's adjustment and stability**: The impact of relocation on the child's routine, school, community ties, and support system is a crucial consideration. Courts assess whether the benefits of relocation outweigh the potential disruption to the child's stability.
- **The wishes of the child**: Depending on the child's age and maturity, courts may consider their preference regarding relocation. Some jurisdictions have laws specifying at what age a child's preference may be given greater weight.
- **Parental cooperation and ability to support relationships**: Courts examine whether the relocating parent is willing to facilitate the child's relationship with the other parent. A history of coparenting cooperation or parental alienation may influence the court's decision.
- **Economic and logistical practicality**: The financial implications of relocation, including the cost of travel for visitation, must be considered. The court may assess whether relocation creates an undue financial burden on the nonrelocating parent.
- **History of domestic violence or abuse**: If there is a history of domestic violence, abuse, or neglect, courts may consider whether relocation is necessary to protect the safety and well-being of the child and the relocating parent.

In addition to statutory guidelines, case law plays a crucial role in shaping how relocation cases are decided. Courts rely on prior judicial rulings to interpret statutory factors, establish legal tests, and set precedents for evaluating evidence in relocation cases. Some jurisdictions apply a presumption in favor of relocation if the moving parent has primary custody, while others require the relocating parent to provide substantial justification for the move.

There are several legal tests derived from case law, although the test most frequently used is best interest of the child. These tests are

- **Good faith standard**: Some courts require the relocating parent to demonstrate that the move is being made in good faith (e.g., for employment, education, or family support) rather than to limit the other parent's access.
- **Detriment versus benefit analysis**: Courts weigh the potential harm to the child's relationship with the nonrelocating parent against the benefits of the move.
- **Burden of proof considerations**: Some jurisdictions place the burden of proof on the relocating parent, while others require the opposing parent to prove that the move would be harmful to the child.

Even within the framework of statutory factors and case law, courts exercise *judicial discretion* in deciding relocation cases. Judges assess the unique circumstances of each case, considering expert evaluations, testimony from parents and children, and other relevant evidence. This case-specific approach ensures that decisions are made in a way that prioritizes the well-being of the child while respecting parental rights.

WHEN PARENTS MUST LIVE IN DIFFERENT CITIES

There are times when one parent needs to move to another city for legitimate reasons, other than just trying to spirit the children away from the other parent. Some jurisdictions provide the court with guidance about what is considered "legitimate," however our responsibility is to investigate the parent's reasons for leaving (W. G. Austin & Gould, 2006).

There are a number of parenting access plans that might be implemented to maximize the amount of contact between the nonplacement parent and the children. School schedules are such that much contact time is available during the school year. Teacher conferences, teacher planning days, teachers' conventions, Presidents' Day weekend, midwinter and spring breaks, and traditional holiday times allow for the opportunity for long weekends or extended time out of school. Often, 4-day weekends are made available to the nonplacement parent.

Among the many challenges facing families in which relocation is being considered is the ways in which the nonmoving parent's access to the child affects the child's developmental trajectory. As Austin has pointed out in his seminal work on relocation, children of different ages are at different levels of risk of harm. How the tension is balanced between the needs of a parent to have a strong and healthy relationship with their child and the needs of the child to develop and maintain roots in the school community, neighborhood community, peer group, and other developmentally appropriate areas of normal development is an ongoing challenge.

Referring back to our discussion of Lewis' (2021b) concerns about lack of generalizability of psychological research, we believe similar concerns exist about the degree to which research examining the effect on children of parental relocation lacks generalization. Most research studies examining how parental relocation affects children are based upon samples drawn from undergraduate and graduate student populations. Often there is little information that helps the reader to know specific characteristics of the sample or, more to the point we are making, little subsequent research examining different cohorts made up of different background factors that might help with the generalizability of the initial research findings.

In addition, the nonprimary placement parent should be encouraged to travel to where the children reside during the school year and become involved in the children's activities. The nonprimary placement parent should also be encouraged to interact with the children's friends and their families. The intention is for the nonplacement parent to become familiar with all aspects of the children's lives in their primary placement community.

A VERY BRIEF HISTORY OF RELOCATION DECISIONS

Some states have statutes or case law that articulate factors the court must consider in deliberations about a parent's request to relocate. Historically, among the most powerful court decisions was the 1996 California Supreme Court decision in *In re Marriage of Burgess*. The *Burgess* court found that a primary placement parent who wishes to relocate shall be permitted to do so without having to prove that the move is necessary. The California Supreme Court further ruled that it was not a substantial change of circumstances for the custodial parent to relocate. Their decision was based upon a belief that as long as the custodial parent has a "sound, good faith reason" to change their place of residence, that parent may do so unless, as a direct result, there will be significant detriment to the child. The trial court's ultimate decision also needs to consider this, as it does in all child custody matters, in the context of the child's best interests. The *Burgess* decision was viewed as a substantial change in policy from previous court decisions in most jurisdictions around the country and, at the time, influenced several states to adopt some or all of the *Burgess* reasoning.

The *Burgess* court based its decision, in significant part, on an amici curiae brief filed on behalf of Judith Wallerstein, PhD. Wallerstein's brief was based on her extensive longitudinal research with children in the San Francisco Bay Area, as well as two relocation cases that were studied in depth. Wallerstein notes that children are limited in their ability to travel to visit a distant parent, that children should not be made to travel a great deal during their developmental years, and that some parents relocate in bad faith and should be enjoined from doing so (Wallerstein & Tanke, 1996). Her bottom line, however, was predicted on the principle that

> [i]t is altogether reasonable to assume that a parent and child who have been living together as a family unit and sharing the same household for several years are likely to have a close attachment to each other that promotes a healthy sense of security and self-esteem in the child. It is reasonable to assume that more guidance and discipline from that parent will prepare the child for responsible participation in society. (p. 305)

The best interests of the child, she indicates, are "best served within the nurture and protection provided by high-quality parent–child relationships—the relationships, rather than geographical convenience, should be paramount in custody cases" (Wallerstein & Tanke, 1996, p. 320).

A substantial backlash developed against the *Burgess* decision, culminating in the filing of amici briefs by psychologist Richard Warshak et al.[1] and family law

---

[1]Amici, along with Warshak, in *In re Marriage of Lamusga (Navarro v. LaMusga)*, are Sanford L. Braver, PhD; Joan B. Kelly, PhD; James H. Bay; and William G. Austin, PhD.

attorney Leslie Ellen Shear et al.[2] in a case decided by the California Supreme Court in 2004: *In re Marriage of Lamusga (Navarro v. LaMusga)*. The essential position of both the Warshak et al. and Shear et al. briefs were that (a) Wallerstein's briefs in both *Burgess* and *LaMusga*[3] do not represent the views of the majority of experts on child development and child custody, (b) the California Supreme Court's decision in *Burgess* does not adequately permit trial courts to consider the individual needs of each child and what is in the best interests of that child, (c) the *Burgess* decision grossly underestimates the profound affect that relocation can have on a child and their development and welfare, and (d) relocation should be among the factors that are considered a change of circumstances requiring the trial court to make an assessment in the context of the best interests of the child (Ackerman et al., 2019).

Today, states appear to have adopted a best interest of the child analysis as the threshold standard when evaluating a parent's request to relocate with the party's children. A few states seek to establish who has been the primary parent and, once established, it is assumed that decisions made by the custodian parent are, by definition, in the best interests of the child. In such states, once a custodian parent is identified by the court, that parent may relocate unless the nonmoving parent can demonstrate significant risk of harm to the minor children.

RESEARCH FINDINGS TO CONSIDER IN FORENSIC RELOCATION ASSESSMENT

William G. Austin has articulated that the application of research findings in relocation assessment in child custody cases are likely more relevant than in any other child custody cases (W. G. Austin, 2015a, 2015b). Reliable research should be able to identify and predict potential risks to children of divorce who

[2]Amici, along with Shear, in Lamusga, are Marjorie G. Fuller, JD; Nancy Williams Olesen, PhD; Mamela Panasti Stettner, JD, CFLS; Michael E. Lamb, PhD; Dawn Gray, JD, CFLS; Joan B. Kelly, PhD; Lawrence E. Leone, JD, CFLS; William G. Austin, PhD; Constance R. Ahrons, PhD, MSW; Harold J. Cohn, JD, CFLS; Sanford L. Braver, PhD; Frieda Gordon, JD, CFLS; James M. Hallett, JD, CFLS, CFCLS; Sidner J. Brown, PhD; Lynette Berg Robe, JD, CFLS; Michael Gottlieb, PhD; Tammy-Lyn Gallarini, JD, CFLS; Richard A. Warshak, PhD; Kenneth C. Cochrane, JD, CFLS; Neil S. Grossman, PhD; David R. Lane, JD, CFLS; Maureen Stubbs, JD, CFLS; Fred Norris, PhD; Dianna Gould-Saltman, JD, CFLS; Carol Silbergeld, LCSW, BCD; Susan Ratzkin, JD; Jeffrey M. Lulow, PhD; Dale S. Frank, JD; Leslye Hunter, MA, LPC, LMFT; Ronald S. Granberg, CFLS; James R. Flens, PsyD; Rebekah A. Frye, JD; Renee A. Cohen, PhD; Tracey Duell-Cazes, JD, CFLS; Marnee W. Milner, JD; Jacqueline Singer, PhD; Erica L. Hedlund, JD; James Livingston, PhD; Josephine A. Fitzpatrick, JD, CFLS; Michael A. Fraga, PsyD; Timothy C. Wright, JD; CFLS; Avery Cooper, JD; CFLS; and Lawrence W. Thorpe, JD, CFLS.

[3]Amici, along with Wallerstein, in LaMusga, are Pauline F. Kernberg, MD; Joyanna Lee Silberg, PhD; Julia M. Lewis, PhD; John B. Sikorski, MD; and Stephanie Joan Dallam, RN, MSN, FNP Amici, along with Wallerstein, in Burgess are Trevor C. Thorpe, JD; Steven R. Liss, JD; Mark J. Warfel, JD; and John R. Schiller, JD, CFLS.

relocate. The effects on childhood adjustment among children who relocate after separation is similar to the effects on childhood adjustment resulting from divorce.

Austin has argued for more than 20 years that the legal standard that best fits a relocation analysis is the least detrimental alternative approach (W. G. Austin 2000a, 2015a, 2015b). His argument is based upon the substantial research evidence showing that children are best served by having frequent and continuous contact with each parent. Disruption to a child's ability to maintain frequent and continuous contact is a risk factor and also a necessary component of any parental relocation.

If a relocation is to occur and the relocation results in a disruption to the frequency of parent–child contact, then the evaluator's assessment focus must be to explore what, if any, least detrimental alternative is available that will support the child's relationship with the nonmoving parent with minimal disruption to the quality of the nonmoving parent–child relationship. The evaluator's task is, in part, to explore ways in which the child's relationship with the nonmoving parent is able to be supported while allowing the moving parent to establish a life in a geographically distant location. There will be changes to the nature and type of nonmoving parent–child relationship resulting from the relocation however, not all changes to routine or activities will have negative effects on the quality of the child's relationship with the nonmoving parent.

Note that we have focused our attention on the child's relationship with the nonmoving parent rather than focusing on the nonmoving parent's relationship with the child. Our experience is that the nonmoving parent is rightly concerned about the ways in which a relocation will change the usual and customary activities and experiences shared with the minor child prior to the relocation. Changes to these activities and experiences will be inevitable, however adopting new activities and experiences might provide reasonable alternatives to the child that would allow for the development of a rich, high-quality relationship with the nonmoving parent that minimizes risk of disruption to the child's relationship with the nonmoving parent.

RELOCATION AS AN ADVERSE CHILDHOOD EVENT

When we focus our attention on the child, we note that relocation, particularly in the context of family law disputes, can be classified as an adverse childhood event (ACE) due to its potential to cause significant stress, emotional upheaval, and long-term developmental consequences for children (Rodriguez-Perez & Castellanos, 2024). ACEs are defined as stressful or traumatic experiences occurring during childhood that have the potential to negatively impact psychological, emotional, and physical well-being throughout a person's life (Karatekin et al., 2023). Relocation often meets this definition, especially when it disrupts key attachments, routines, and support systems (Stevenson et al., 2018).

One of the core psychological risks associated with relocation is the disruption of secure attachments, particularly when a child is separated from a parent, extended family members, or a familiar caregiving environment (J. B. Kelly & Lamb, 2003). Children rely on consistent emotional bonds to develop a sense of security and trust in their surroundings (Rohmah & Purwanta, 2023). When relocation alters these relationships—especially in high-conflict custody cases—it can lead to attachment insecurity, anxiety, and emotional distress. Young children, in particular, may experience separation anxiety, difficulty adjusting to new caregivers or routines, and feelings of abandonment if they are relocated away from a primary attachment figure (J. B. Kelly & Lamb, 2003). Adolescents may struggle with identity formation and emotional regulation if they are removed from established peer groups, schools, and community connections (Stevenson et al. 2018).

Furthermore, relocation cases in family law are often highly contentious, with one parent opposing the move and legal battles creating an environment of prolonged parental conflict. High-conflict parental disputes are a well-documented ACE, as they expose children to ongoing stress, emotional manipulation, and sometimes coercive control dynamics (Drozd et al., 2019). A child caught in the middle of a relocation dispute may feel pressure to align with one parent or experience loyalty conflicts, which can lead to increased stress and internalized guilt. If the relocation is a consequence of domestic violence or coercive control, the child may experience significant emotional trauma from witnessing or being directly affected by abuse (Drozd et al., 2019).

Children thrive on predictability and consistency in their social environments. Relocation often disrupts a child's access to familiar support systems, including friends and peer networks, teachers and educational stability, extracurricular activities, and extended family members and community figures. This loss of social capital can contribute to social isolation, withdrawal, and difficulty adjusting to new environments (W. G. Austin & Rappaport, 2018). Research shows that childhood relocations are associated with higher rates of depression and anxiety, particularly if the child has already experienced multiple disruptions in living arrangements (Rodriguez-Perez & Castellanos, 2024).

Because relocation often means a change in schools, it can negatively impact a child's academic performance, social integration, and overall educational trajectory (J. B. Kelly & Emery, 2003; Rodriguez-Perez & Castellanos, 2024). Studies indicate that frequent moves during childhood are linked to

- lower academic achievement due to inconsistent curricula and lost instructional time,
- increased behavioral issues as children struggle to adapt to new classroom environments, and
- higher dropout rates in adolescents who experience multiple relocations.

For children with special needs or learning disabilities, relocation can create additional barriers to receiving consistent educational support services, exacerbating existing challenges (Pickar & Kaufman, 2019).

The stress associated with relocation can lead to chronic emotional distress, particularly if the move is involuntary (e.g., due to parental divorce, financial hardship, or court orders). Research on ACEs suggests that chronic stress during childhood can alter neurodevelopmental processes, increasing the risk of anxiety disorders, depressive symptoms, posttraumatic stress reactions (particularly in cases involving abrupt separations or loss of a parent), and behavioral problems, including aggression or withdrawal (Mosley-Johnson et al., 2021). Children who experience relocation due to custody disputes, parental estrangement, or family breakdown may also develop maladaptive coping strategies, such as avoidance, emotional suppression, or difficulty trusting caregivers (Stevenson et al., 2018).

ACEs, including relocation-related stressors, are associated with long-term health and psychological risks (Boullier & Blair, 2018), including

- increased risk of mental health disorders in adulthood,
- higher likelihood of relationship instability (due to attachment disruptions),
- elevated risk of substance use as a coping mechanism, and
- reduced overall life satisfaction and well-being.

The cumulative impact of relocation as an ACE is especially pronounced when combined with other adverse experiences, such as parental divorce, economic hardship, domestic violence, or neglect (Mosley-Johnson et al., 2021).

AUSTIN'S RELOCATION RISK ASSESSMENT MODEL

The most commonly utilized model applied to relocation and risk to children is W. G. Austin and colleague's (2016) relocation risk assessment (RRA) model. The RRA model (which we discuss in more depth later) is an empirically-based model consisting of risk and protective factors with empirical association with child outcomes. In those states in which there are relocation statutes, many, if not most, of the RRA factors are included in the factors judges must consider before opining on a parent's request to relocate with the party's minor children.

A related area of research relevant to forensic assessment of potential risk of harm to children from parental relocation is the gatekeeping literature (W. G. Austin & Rappaport, 2018). The parental gatekeeping literature (discussed in Chapter 19) is based upon extensive peer-reviewed literature examining coparenting behavior, gatekeeping behaviors, parental conflict, and empirical associations with parental involvement and child outcomes. Austin and Rappaport suggest that parental relocation is a form of restrictive gatekeeping. They argue that a justification analysis is required that examines the facts, context, reasons for moving, advantages or disadvantages, and legal factors (W. G. Austin & Rappaport, 2018).

More recent scholarship has helped to transform an earlier unidirectional view of gatekeeping (W. G. Austin & Drozd, 2013; W. G. Austin, Fieldstone, &

Pruett, 2013) into a more multidimensional view, recognizing the potential for each parent to engage in restrictive gatekeeping in different behavioral domains regarding parent–child contact while engaging in flexible gatekeeping in other behavioral domains. Further, a parent might be a more restrictive gatekeeper in some behavioral domains in which the other parent is a more flexible gatekeeper (W. G. Austin & Rappaport, 2018).

Parental gatekeeping is conceptualized as a continuous variable and occurs within *different behavioral domains* (W. G. Austin & Rappaport, 2018, p. 58). A custody evaluator can strive to identify the quality and specifics of gatekeeping within each domain. Examples of behavioral domains include information sharing about the child in various activities; parents' willingness to communicate with each other about child-related areas of interest and importance; compliance with the parenting time schedule and spirit of the parenting plan (which can include supporting parental involvement in extracurricular activities), including being flexible as needed; not being critical of other parent to the children or others (i.e., public criticism); not exposing the children to negative statements about the other parent; and showing to the child an appreciation of value in the contributions and importance of the other parent in the life of the child (W. G. Austin & Rappaport, 2018, p. 58).

When the evaluator's assessment does not identify reliable and sufficient data to support or justify the parent's relocation, questions might be raised about the parent engaging in restrictive gatekeeping. When it appears that the parent who seeks to relocate is unable to provide the evaluator with information sufficient to support the relocation, then questions need to be asked about a parent's motivation to engage in unjustified restrictive gatekeeping.

Restrictive gatekeeping is not a dichotomous variable. There are some instances in which a parent's restrictive gatekeeping is justified. Justified or protective restrictive gatekeeping is supported when a parent seeks to relocate to escape abuse or other threatening situations perpetrated by the child's other parent. There are also times when restrictive gatekeeping is understandable yet fails to reach a level of justified restrictive gatekeeping. A parent might seek to relocate to escape a reality-based historical fear of the other parent as a risk to self or the minor child yet has not explored whether trauma-informed psychotherapy might provide a useful tool to help manage the parent's fear, help create a safe environment, and avoid a significant disruption of the child's relationship with the other parent. Determining whether protective gatekeeping can be justified or unjustified is determined by the evidence-based reasons for the parent's concern about a risk of harm to themself or the child.

A fourth area is the child development literature addressing children's attachment, especially attachment needs of infant, toddler, and preschool age children. Relocations stress can often disrupt psychologically important parent–child relationships, which may have adverse consequences for children (J. B. Kelly & Lamb, 2003). Evaluators should be familiar with the literature addressing the development of attachment relationships in infants and toddlers and the ways in which relocation is likely to affect young children of different ages (Lamb, 2018).

Lamb, among others, has addressed the changing family roles and evidence that most infants form attachment relationships with both of their parents (Lamb, 2018). These findings contribute to a decades-long debate about parenting arrangements when the parents of infants and toddlers separate. Lamb argues that misunderstanding of attachment theory and the available empirical evidence have clouded rather than clarified evidence-based decision making about parenting access plans for young children. He argues that, consistent with attachment theory, the evidence suggests that children benefit when parenting plans are designed to provide young children with meaningful and positive relationships with both of their parents (Lamb, 2018).

A fifth area of peer-reviewed research focuses attention on the large research basis showing children of divorce do best when they have quality relationships with both parents. Substantial research has revealed that children of divorce have better long-term adjustment and well-being when they are able to maintain quality relationships with both parents. Children raised in families in which there is little to no parental conflict are more likely to maintain quality relationships with each parent and stay on healthy, age-appropriate developmental trajectories compared to children of divorce whose parents engage in on-going conflict. However, children benefit from quality contact with each parent even when parents cannot contain their conflict and the children's exposure to it (W. G. Austin, 2015a).

A sixth area of peer-reviewed research is the extensive literature about the positive contribution of father involvement to children. Research findings reveal that fathers' contributions to their children's short- and long-term development are different in kind from the contributions of mothers (Lamb, 2010, 2013; Pleck, 2010). A parallel area of research relevant to understanding the importance of fatherhood research is that which addresses the effect on children of a father's absence (Lamb, 1999; Lehr & MacMillan, 2001).

Modecki et al. studied the role of postdivorce paternal involvement with their adolescent children. Three profiles of father engagement were identified in their sample of mainly White, non-Hispanic divorced fathers: moderate involvement and low conflict, low involvement and moderate conflict, and high involvement and high conflict. Adolescent children of fathers characterized as moderate involvement/low conflict had the highest academic achievement and the lowest number of externalizing problems 9 years later compared to adolescent offspring whose fathers had profiles indicating either the highest or lowest levels of involvement but higher levels of conflict (Modecki et al., 2015). Results suggested that greater paternal psychosocial support and more frequent father–adolescent contact *did not* outweigh the negative impact of interparental conflict on youth outcomes in the long term (Modecki et al., 2015). Although the Modecki et al. study was not a relocation study, the results might speak to the challenges faced by older children whose parents are engaged in continuous conflict and also relocate.

A seventh area of peer-reviewed research is the evolving literature on the importance of social capital on children's development. Social capital is defined as the psychological, emotional, and social contributions that are provided to the child by the parents, extended family, peers, organizations, and groups (Coleman, 1990). The application of a social capital analysis to a child custody dispute allows for a comparative analysis of the expected types and degrees of social capital or human resources that will be available to the child in the two alternative residential living arrangements and with competing parenting time arrangements (Parkinson et al., 2016).

TWO COMPLEMENTARY MODELS FOR FORENSIC ASSESSMENT OF RELOCATION REQUESTS

Austin proposes that forensic assessment of a parent's request to relocate might be examine through the use of at least two different but complementary approaches: the RRA model and the social capital model.

The Relocation Risk Assessment Model

The RRA model is a research-based, actuarial model consisting of identified risk and protective factors supported by the research literature on the effects of the factors on children of divorce (W. G. Austin, 2000b, 2018a, 2018b). Survey data suggest that about 60% of child custody evaluators use the RRA risk assessment model (W. G. Austin, 2015a, 2015b).

Austin's RRA is a heuristic and not a test. It should not be subjected to *Daubert* challenges on the admissibility of expert testimony (W. G. Austin, 2018b). It might, however, be subject to a *Frye* challenge (i.e., a challenge of whether or not the relocation heuristic is generally accepted in the field). It would likely pass a *Frye* challenge as survey data reveal that it is the most commonly used approach to relocation assessment utilized by parenting plan evaluators (W. G. Austin, 2018b).

Each of the eight RRA factors should be thought of as continuous variables that are likely to vary in potential degree. For example, the factor of degree of past parental involvement with the child may show the nonmoving parent had been an involved father regarding activities around the house and shuttling the child to and from activities during the weekend but not during the week while the mother left work early during the weekday to attend to the child's activities. Upon separation, both parents might have adjusted their schedules to meet the demands of the separation and of the child. Parent A might have reduced their work hours to have greater availability during the workweek, while Parent B might have increased their work hours to have funds available for her new responsibilities.

Each of the RRA eight factors can serve as either a risk or protective factor, depending on where the data fall along the continuum for the variable (W. G. Austin, 2018b). For example, a mother might have a multiyear history postseparation of being consistently very supportive of the child's relationship with her father. The mother's proposed long-distance parenting time arrangement reflects the continued positive support reflecting an inclusive and liberal amount of parent–child access. In such cases, the mother's past and current support for the child's relationship with her father is viewed as a protective function for sustaining quality in the parent–child relationship. Alternatively, suppose there has been a history of restrictive gatekeeping with limited support and flexibility by the moving parent. In that case, the history of restrictive gatekeeping is a potential risk and a red flag of potential harm to the nonmoving parent–child relationship. In such cases, the nonmoving parent might view the moving parent's history of restrictive gatekeeping as evidence of the relocation being another attempt to marginalize the nonmoving parent's future role in the child's life (W. G. Austin, 2018b).

Eight Factors of the Relocation Risk Assessment Model

The relocation risk and protective factors consist of the following:

Age of the Child

Young children up until about age 6 are at high risk of harm to their evolving attachment relationships resulting from relocation. Attachment theory not infrequently may be overemphasized by evaluators as suggesting traumatic experience due to disrupted parent–child relationships associated with divorce and relocation because the child's development is so multi-determined by other factors. However, it will be difficult to sustain quality in the nonmoving parent–child relationship when there is disruption and resulting long-distance parenting. Challenges to developing and maintaining a healthy parent–young child relationship would include cognitive limitations of the very young child involving object permanence and memory (W. G. Austin, 2000b, 2018a, 2018b; Gould & Stahl, 2001; J. B. Kelly & Lamb, 2000; Lamb & Kelly, 2001).

After the age of 3 years and between the ages of 3 to 6 years, there is more flexibility in developing parenting access plans that can support a young child's health relationship with the nonmoving parent due to the more advanced cognitive growth, language competence, memory abilities, and social media factors that might facilitate more frequent and meaningful contact (W. G. Austin, 2000b, 2018a, 2018b; Gould & Stahl, 2001; J. B. Kelly & Lamb, 2000; Lamb & Kelly, 2001).

With older school-age children (e.g., 8–12 years), there is a hypothesis of a developmental window to better cope with the physical and psychological separation from the distant or nonresidential parent (W. G. Austin, 2018b). These children are in developmental stages where their memory capacity, more sophisticated language skills, and greater cognitive sophistication provide the developmental scaffolding to efficiently understand their relationship and emotional connection with the distant parent, usually the father. They can regulate their electronic contact with the father. They can enjoy extended blocks of parenting time with the father and separation from the mother (e.g., winter, spring, and summer school vacations).

Older school-age children (e.g., 12–18) are a high-risk group for very different reasons. The known difficulties associated with peer-group acceptance and membership are critical factors for children in this age group. Older children who relocate are faced with a myriad of factors associated with social acceptance that are less of a concern for younger children. These social acceptance factors are significant risk factors for children in this age group and often are a basis to consider maintaining the child in the nonmoving parent's home.

Relocating parents with children of different ages face additional challenges by the reality that there often may be two or more children potentially relocating with the moving parent. The children may be in different developmental stages with quite an age difference between the children (e.g., ages 3 and 9 years respectively; W. G. Austin, 2018b).

Geographical Distance of the Move and Travel Time

Empirical data show a correlation between distance and nonmoving parents' frequent and continuous level of involvement in the lives of the children who relocated (W. G. Austin, 2018b). A primary concern is that relocation would likely disrupt the previously established parent–child bond. The child experiences the nonmoving parent as less available and less involved in day-to-day activities. The nonmoving parent often becomes unfamiliar with the relocated child's friends, neighbors, teachers, activities, and so forth.

Psychological Stability of Relocating Parent and Parenting Effectiveness of Both Parents

Children's adjustment is correlated with parents' mental health and symptomatology (W. G. Austin, 2018b), especially research on the effects of the mother's depression on parenting behavior (Bornstein, 2019). Children have been found to display better adjustment when they have a quality relationship with at least one parent who shows an effective parenting style that includes showing warmth and responsiveness to the child's needs (J. B. Kelly & Emery, 2003).

The assumption drawn from these data is that a parent who relocates with children and who is healthy and psychologically resourceful would likely be better positioned to help themselves and the child adjust and cope with the changes associated with relocation (W. G. Austin, 2018b). Psychologically healthy parents who relocate are more likely to establish new social networks and sources of social capital for themself and child (W. G. Austin, 2018b).

Individual Resources and Individual Differences in the Child's Temperament and Special Developmental Needs

Children with difficult temperaments have been found to have more difficulties with divorce than children with more flexible temperaments (Hetherington, 1999). Children whose history shows them to be resilient have been found to have fewer difficulties resulting from relocation and are expected to cope better with relocation (Rutter, 2006). Higher cognitive ability is the strongest predictor of resiliency in children (Rutter, 2006).

The Austin RRA model has yet to address alternative resilience models (B. J. Ellis et al., 2017). Most theoretical models addressing adversity and resilience have been based on a deficit model. A deficit model asserts children exposed to adverse childhood experiences, of which divorce and relocation are two such experiences, are predictors of risk for impairments in learning and behavior. Interventions are structured to prevent, reduce, or repair the damage resulting from exposure to the adverse experiences (B. J. Ellis et al., 2017).

An alternative model is an evolutionary–developmental model (EDM) that emphasizes the coherent, functional changes that occur in response to stress over the life course (B. J. Ellis et al., 2017). The EDM posits that some individuals faced with adversity are able to leverage the unique strengths and abilities that develop in response to high-stress environments (B. J. Ellis et al., 2017).

The EDM asks, "What are the attention, learning, memory, problem-solving, and decision-making strategies that are enhanced through exposures to childhood adversity?" (B. J. Ellis et al., 2017, p. 561). Applied to a relocation analysis, the EDM would focus on how children faced with the adverse experience of relocation after divorce are able to work with, rather than against, these strengths to promote success in all phases of a child's life.

Degree of Involvement by the Nonresidential Parent

When nonmoving parents have been highly involved and enjoy a quality relationship with the child, then it creates higher risk of harm when the child relocates due to the loss in social capital and support for the child. Research shows the advantages when the child enjoys quality relationships with both parents (J. B. Kelly & Emery, 2003) and fathers (Lamb, 2013). Further, children of divorce benefit from relationships with fathers especially when there has been warmth and responsiveness in parenting style and more intensive involvement (Lamb, 2013).

Relocation would be expected to create more risk of relationship disruption to the nonmoving parent–child relationship when the child relocates. Paradoxically, a previously significantly involved nonmoving parent also becomes a protective factor. It is likely that the highly involved father with a meaningful relationship before relocation will be motivated to remain highly involved albeit in a long-distance relationship (W. G. Austin, 2018b).

Gatekeeping and Support for the Other Parent–Child Relationship

As discussed prior, facilitative or flexible gatekeeping in a long-distance parenting arrangement is predicted to be a primary protective factor in supporting the child's relationship with the nonmoving parent. The supportive residential or relocating parent with inclusive coparenting and responsible parental gatekeeping management skills will likely mitigate risk of in the nonmoving parent–child relationship.

Specific behavior domains associated with parental gatekeeping in the context of relocation have been previously described. Conversely, restrictive gatekeeping in the long-distance arrangement is predicted to disrupt the child's quality relationship with the nonmoving parent. When the residential parent does not proactively cooperate on electronic communication; not keeping the other parent well informed about the child's activities and needs; impeding electronic access; and not facilitating long-distance exchanges for parenting time, then the risk of detriment will result. Restrictive gatekeeping involving a very young child creates a high risk of relationship harm between the child and the nonmoving parent (W. G. Austin, 2018b).

Interparental Conflict and Domestic Violence

As discussed in Chapters 21 and 22, the terms "interparental conflict," "domestic violence," "intimate partner violence," and "violence and nonviolent coercive control" have strong emotional power. They conjure up physical fights, physical injuries, children crying in the corner of a room, parents yelling and hurting each other, children panicking over their exposure to parental conflict, and helpless about how to stop their parents from fighting.

Relocation is often a justifiable choice for a parent who seeks to escape from intimate partner violence (IPV). Relocation is also a justifiable choice for a parent who seeks to protect the children from the abusive behaviors of the other parent. Research findings have consistently shown that children's exposure to parental conflict places children at high risk for developing adjustment problems. Parents who are victims of abuse often develop psychological and emotional reactions that affect their parenting. Parents who are perpetrators of abuse often are unable or unwilling to recognize the abusive nature of their actions and, instead, externally blame others or refuse responsibility for their behavior. Children exposed to parental abusive behaviors often learn through incidental experiences dysfunctional behaviors such as emotional dysregulation, aggressive behavior to solve problems, and refusal to take responsibility for their behavior.

Among the challenges faced by evaluators is obtaining accurate, reliable information from independent third-party sources to support the assertions made by each family member. Many ideas drawn from the domestic abuse literature are poorly defined and have no reliable method of assessment. For example:

- What types of aggressive or coercive behavior must be present in order to justify a parent to relocate with the minor child away from the perpetrator? How frequently must an aggressive or coercive behavior occur in order to justify a parent to relocate with the minor child away from the perpetrator?
- What mental health interventions should be taken by a parent or perpetrator before a relocation is viewed as the only remaining option? What mental health interventions should be taken by the parent/victim before a relocation is viewed as the only remaining option?
- Is a parent or perpetrator who has never engaged in physical violence yet is engaged in coercive controlling behaviors over several years displaying behavior that should allow the other parent to relocate?

In some cases, there may be a compelling argument for a geographical barrier hypothesis (W. G. Austin, 2018b) that relocation may shield the children from exposure to enduring conflict between the parents. However, there is no professional consensus about a reliable methodology to use that would gather sufficient information to support such a recommendation.

There may be times when the evaluator can establish a pattern of coercive control where the aggressor parent has engaged in controlling, intrusive, authoritarian behaviors during the marriage and continues to show coercive controlling behaviors postseparation. In some jurisdictions, coercive control and other behaviors that introduce lack of safety for the parent or children may be sufficient for the court to grant the relocation request. The evaluator's task is to investigate and balance the potential issues of safety and violence risk.

When there are allegations of abuse or violence, the evaluator's task is to utilize a reliable methodology to assess safety and violence risk. As we discussed in Chapters 21 and 22, domestic violence assessment includes, at the very least, gathering data about the frequency, severity, intensity, and nature (i.e., kind) of the behavior. William G. Austin (2018b) reminds us that in some cases,

> the IPV may be minor in severity, perhaps one incident at the time of separation, and should not be viewed as terribly relevant to creating a parenting plan or the relocation issue. The most frequent pattern of IPV is the conflict-instigated, situational-specific type that most often would be interactive, or mutual in the dynamics. Evaluators report that the most IPV they encounter is one that is associated with the marital separation. (p. 216)

Recentness of Marital Separation

It is assumed that the combination of the recency of divorce coupled with the recency of relocation creates a significant risk of harm for the child. The assumption is based upon the idea that a child will cope better with relocation once the child has adjusted to life in the postseparation stage of family stabilization. However, many parents choose to relocate soon after divorce.

Limitations of the Relocation Risk Assessment Model

Saini and colleagues (2015) observed that the W. G. Austin (2008) RRA model's reliance on statistical language such as "actuarial predictive model designed to assist evaluators in organizing data for the complex relocation case" (p. 347) might suggest a great degree of science upon which the RRA is based. However, to date, there is no research to support any type of reliable ranking of the weight to be assigned to each of the RRA model factors. The RRA model is a way to organize information.

According to the *APA Dictionary of Psychology*, an *actuarial risk assessment* is

> a statistically calculated prediction of the likelihood that an individual will pose a threat to others or engage in a certain behavior (e.g., violence) within a given period. Unlike in a clinical risk assessment, someone conducting an actuarial risk assessment relies on data from specific, measurable variables (e.g., age, gender, prior criminal activity) that have been validated as predictors and uses

mathematical analyses and formulas to calculate the probability of dangerousness or violent behavior. (American Psychological Association, n.d.)

Saini et al. (2015) assert that there is no evidence-basis that can be relied upon to make mathematical analyses and formulas to predict whether a relocation will be beneficial or harmful in a given case. Currently, there is no empirical basis to allow for reliable statistical inferences about risk to children whose parents wish to relocate. The danger in using the statistical model language suggested by Austin are concerns that some colleagues might extrapolate from data points identified in the RRA model that are unable to make these predictions with any sort of numberical accuracy.

Saini et al. (2015) raise concerns about the degree to which courts have relied upon research that explores the impact of local moves on children in multiple contexts in the absence of empirical evidence on the impact of relocation specific to the context of separation and divorce. Some research has examined the effects of relocation on academic outcomes and specific developmental outcomes, yet caution is needed when applying these results to a separation and divorce context.

Social Capital Model

The second approach in a forensic assessment of a parent's request to relocate is based upon a social capital analysis. Social capital analysis is a descriptive concept that investigates the resources available to individuals that influence the quality of life in their respective environments (W. G. Austin & Gould, 2006; W. G. Austin & Rappaport, 2018). Social capital analysis captures the variety of family, social, community, educational, cultural, and associated activities to which the child might be exposed in a particular community. It is a useful way to conduct the fundamental comparison for the court so that the evaluator can better help the court visualize similarities and differences between communities in which the child might live.

Social capital analysis is intertwined with the concept of gatekeeping. Gatekeeping and the potential harm to the nonmoving-party relationship will be the central focus in virtually every relocation dispute and debate. A parent who engages in unjustified restrictive gatekeeping would be expected to diminish the nonmoving parent–child relationship. One way to diminish the nonmoving parent–child relationship is to interfere with the child's access to the social capital experiences offered by the nonmoving parent. For example, the unjustified restrictive gatekeeping parent would thwart the child's access to the nonmoving parent's extended family and that parent's psychosocial resources and contributions to the child. It is predicted that a parent who engages in unjustified restrictive gatekeeping will adversely affect the child's adjustment to a relocation and contribute to the disruption of the child's relationship to the nonmoving parent. On the other hand, it would be predicted that facilitative, flexible gatekeeping would open the gate for the child access to the nonmoving parent's resources that would serve to maintain the child's relationship to that parent.

Part of the social capital analysis needs to include practical considerations on issues such as each parent's availability to the child during and after school, the quality of the school system, the stability of the new home (e.g., if the relocating parent is remarrying), and so forth. Another part of the analysis would be to offer suitable alternative parenting plans that would provide the child with sufficient parenting time with the nonmoving parent to offset factors that might adversely affect the child's relationship with that parent.

Austin has talked about a bias against relocation. Austin identifies two general sources of bias against relocation. First is the "presence of explicit or implicit anti-relocation bias also will tilt the social capital analysis so that the parents are not starting out on 'equal footing' in the analysis of the facts and circumstance . . ." (W. G. Austin, 2018a). The relocating parent often will have difficulties showing the relative advantages and greater level of social capital available in the new community. This results in the evaluator having little reliable data upon which to make fundamental comparisons between the home and the relocating community.

The second form of bias involves confirmatory bias (see Chapter 7) usually in the form of antirelocation bias (W. G. Austin, 2018a). Austin believed that there was a widespread antirelocation bias held by evaluators, attorneys and judges that often interfered with the fair and balanced administration of justice in relocation cases. He warned: "Relocation is also unique in that it is a type of case in which it appears confirmatory bias by both evaluators and judges may be a widespread problem, usually in the form of anti-relocation bias" (W. G. Austin, 2018a, p. 42).

Combining the Relocation Risk Assessment and Social Capital Model

Relocation analyses examine both the potential risk of harm to the child's relationship with the nonmoving parent and social capital advantages and disadvantages to the child and the relocating parent. The RRA analysis focuses attention on evidence-informed based factors associated with potential risk of harm and protective factors to be considered. The social capital analysis focuses attention on specific advantages and disadvantages of the relocating parent's parenting plan. Among the factors to explore in a social capital analysis are the quality of schools, the degree of support from extended family in one location versus the other, as well as the differences in the cost of housing and employment opportunities (W. G. Austin, 2018a).

OUR ECOLOGICAL MODEL FOR ASSESSING RELOCATION REQUESTS

Our ecological model incorporates aspects of the RRA model and the social capital models to provide a structured framework for evaluating relocation requests. These models allow evaluators to assess key risk factors such as the child's developmental stage, the distance of the move, the relocating parent's ability to support the child's relationship with the other parent, and the presence of protective factors that may mitigate adverse effects. By systematically applying a structured analysis, evaluators can help courts make informed decisions. The process is as follows:

1. Assess for safety.
2. Evaluate each parent individually.
3. Evaluate the child.
4. Evaluate the parent–parent relationship.
5. Evaluate the parent–child relationships.
6. Evaluate the overall family system.
7. Evaluate the environment.
8. Evaluate broader systemic pressures.
9. Based on the data, develop a parenting plan.

Next we provide details on each step.

Assess for Safety

Evaluators should begin by assessing for safety as the reason for a parent's relocation (see Chapters 21 and 22).

Evaluate Each Parent Individually

A key step in the relocation assessment is evaluating each parent's psychological functioning, parenting capacity, and ability to support the child's relationship with the other parent postrelocation. This involves

- **Psychological testing**: Evaluators may use standardized tools such as the Minnesota Multiphasic Personality Inventory, Third Edition or Personality Assessment Inventory to develop hypotheses regarding emotional regulation, stress tolerance, aggression, impulsivity, and interpersonal functioning. Particular attention should be given to factors like anger proneness, externalizing behaviors, and dominance, which may indicate a history of coercive control or restrictive gatekeeping.
- **Parenting skills and emotional regulation**: Interviews with each parent, collateral contacts, and historical records help assess parenting history, coparenting dynamics, disciplinary strategies, and responsiveness to the child's needs.
- **Parental motivation for relocation**: Evaluators should assess whether the relocation request is based on valid reasons (e.g., job opportunities,

family support, education) or if it serves to limit the child's relationship with the nonrelocating parent.

Evaluate the Child

The evaluator should assess the child's psychological well-being, resilience, attachment security, and ability to cope with the transition. This involves

- **Interviews and observations**: Speaking with the child directly, observing parent–child interactions, and obtaining reports from teachers, therapists, or other caregivers.
- **Developmental considerations**: Evaluators should consider how the child's age, temperament, and social attachments will be affected by relocation. Younger children may struggle with disrupted attachment relationships, while adolescents may face social and academic difficulties.
- **Trauma and emotional adjustment**: If the child has a history of exposure to parental conflict or relocation-related instability, evaluators should assess potential risks of increased stress, anxiety, or behavioral problems.

Evaluate the Parent–Parent Relationship

Evaluators should examine the coparenting relationship and its history of cooperation or conflict. This includes assessing

- **Parental communication**: The extent to which parents can effectively communicate and make joint decisions about the child.
- **Conflict history**: Patterns of conflict, including verbal disagreements, legal disputes, and allegations of domestic violence or coercive control.
- **Gatekeeping behaviors**: Whether either parent engages in restrictive gatekeeping or facilitative gatekeeping, as well as the justifications for their gatekeeping.

Evaluate the Parent–Child Relationships

Evaluators should analyze the strength and quality of each parent's relationship with the child, particularly the nonrelocating parent. Key considerations include

- **Attachment security**: The child's reliance on each parent for emotional support, stability, and caregiving.
- **Parental involvement**: The history of each parent's role in daily caregiving, school involvement, and extracurricular activities.
- **Risk of relationship disruption**: Evaluators should assess whether relocation would significantly impair the child's bond with the nonrelocating parent and if alternative arrangements could mitigate these risks.

If there are concerns related to enmeshment, estrangement, or resist and refuse dynamics, evaluators should reference established frameworks for understanding parent–child relationships in high-conflict custody disputes (see Chapters 19 and 20).

Evaluate the Overall Family System

Relocation cases often involve broader family dynamics that influence the child's adjustment. Evaluators should assess social capital through

- **Extended family support**: The presence of relatives or support networks in both the current and proposed new locations.
- **Parental adjustment postseparation**: Whether either parent has demonstrated difficulty adapting to coparenting, which could affect relocation outcomes.
- **Impact on siblings**: If the child has siblings, evaluators should consider the impact of separation or relocation on sibling relationships.

Evaluate Environmental Stressors

Evaluators consider external factors that could influence the relocation decision, including

- **Extended community support**: The presence of therapists, coaches, mentors, and religious groups or supports.
- **Educational opportunities**: The quality of schools in both locations and their ability to meet the child's academic and social needs.
- **Financial stability**: The relocating parent's employment prospects and overall financial security.
- **Cultural and community ties**: Whether the child's cultural, religious, or social connections will be disrupted by the move.

Using the social capital model, evaluators compare the resources available to the child in both the current and proposed environments.

Evaluate Broader Systemic Pressures

The broader societal context may also play a role in relocation decisions. Evaluators should consider

- **Legal and policy frameworks**: State-specific relocation laws and legal precedents that shape judicial decisions.
- **Public health and safety issues**: Factors such as crime rates, healthcare access, and environmental concerns in each location.

- **Pandemic and natural disasters**: As seen with COVID-19, global crises can significantly impact relocation feasibility and coparenting arrangements.

Based on the Data, Develop a Parenting Plan

Here are some ideas that might be included in a parenting plan recommendation for the court considering a parent's request to relocate:

1. **Residential schedule**
   - Identify the primary residential parent and justify the recommendation.
   - Propose a balanced visitation schedule for the nonrelocating parent.
2. **Long-distance parenting time**
   - Outline holiday and school break schedules.
   - Address extended visitation options and the child's adaptability.
3. **Virtual contact**
   - Recommend an age-appropriate schedule for FaceTime or Zoom calls.
   - Clarify policies on phone contact considering parental cooperation and conflict history.
4. **Travel and transportation**
   - Suggest responsibility for travel costs without exceeding professional competency.
   - Provide guidelines for pick-up and drop-off logistics, including airline escorts if needed.
5. **Decision making and coparenting**
   - Recommend joint or divided decision making with dispute resolution mechanisms.
   - Ensure both parents have access to school and medical records.
6. **Transition support**
   - Suggest counseling if necessary, with provider recommendations.
   - Propose a gradual transition plan if feasible.
7. **Modification and review**
   - Recognize that parenting plans may need adjustments.
   - Recommend periodic reevaluation and a dispute resolution process based on parental history.

CONCLUSION

Parenting plan evaluations in relocation cases require a careful balance of psychological expertise, legal awareness, and a steadfast commitment to the best interests of the child. These cases are inherently complex, as they involve both present and predictive analyses of family dynamics, child adjustment, and the potential impact of a proposed move. Unlike standard custody disputes, where evaluators focus on optimizing coparenting arrangements within a shared geographic space, relocation evaluations demand a forward-looking approach that considers the long-term implications of a major environmental transition.

In this chapter, we explored the critical components of a comprehensive relocation evaluation, including the assessment of parent–child relationships, the feasibility of long-distance coparenting, the child's developmental needs, and the practical logistics of maintaining meaningful contact with both parents. By integrating scientific research, clinical judgment, and a methodologically sound assessment process, evaluators can provide courts with informed, child-centered data that aid in decision making.

Despite the structured framework outlined in our model, evaluators must recognize that relocation cases do not offer a one-size-fits-all solution. Each family's individual circumstances—such as parental involvement, the quality of relationships, the child's adaptability, and the broader social and economic context—must be carefully weighed. It is crucial that evaluators remain neutral, objective, and trauma-informed, particularly in high-conflict cases where allegations of parental alienation, coercion, or domestic violence may complicate the evaluation process.

As courts increasingly rely on psychological expertise to navigate the challenges of relocation disputes, parenting plan evaluators hold a profound responsibility to ensure that their assessments are evidence-informed, transparent, and legally relevant. Their findings and recommendations can shape the trajectory of a child's life, determining whether stability is best preserved through maintaining proximity to both parents or whether relocation offers greater opportunities for growth and well-being. Ultimately, the goal of a parenting plan evaluation in a relocation case is not simply to support or oppose a move, but to provide the court with a well-reasoned, research-informed analysis that prioritizes the child's long-term adjustment and developmental needs.

Epilogue: The Integration of Judgment, Data, and Science in Custody Evaluation

Throughout this book, we have encouraged evaluators to approach their role as explorers—open to complexity, humble in their conclusions, and grounded in both scientific rigor and clinical wisdom. The work of custody evaluation resists oversimplification. It calls for the integration of multiple forms of knowledge, methodological care, and ethical mindfulness. We end this book by returning to one of the most persistent challenges in the field: the relationship between data and opinion, and how to responsibly bridge the analytic gap between the two.

As we have discussed in the book, the analytic gap refers to the conceptual and evidentiary space between the data collected during the evaluation and the expert opinions proffered in the report or courtroom testimony. Courts and scholars alike have asked: When is the gap too wide to support a reliable, admissible opinion? And how can evaluators reduce that gap through transparent, defensible reasoning?

This tension between empiricism and clinical inference is not merely academic. It has direct implications for admissibility under *Daubert*, *Kumho*, and their progeny. Judges are gatekeepers, and the burden is on the expert to show that their conclusions are based on reliable methods applied to the facts of the case. The key, therefore, is transparency. Evaluators must show their work—articulating each step between data collection and expert opinion, including the literature that supports (or challenges) each methodological and interpretive decision.

https://doi.org/10.1037/0000474-025
Parenting Plan Evaluations: An Evidence-Informed Approach to Child Custody, by J. W. Gould and C. M. Mulchay

We reject the notion that expert opinions in custody cases must rely exclusively on empirical findings. The field lacks a sufficient research base to offer conclusive, generalizable prescriptions for every family. At the same time, we caution against overreliance on clinical experience in the absence of scientific grounding. Expert opinions must be tethered to the professional and scientific knowledge of the discipline, and framed in terms of probability, not certainty.

We caution against presenting expert opinions with undue certainty. Confidence should not be mistaken for credibility. Social science is inherently probabilistic. Findings are never absolute; they are provisional and context dependent. This means that expert testimony should be framed as more likely than not, and evaluators should demonstrate openness to reasonable alternative hypotheses. Overstated confidence can mislead the court and compromise the integrity of the judicial process. Judges and attorneys may seek experts who present with unwavering assurance, but the true mark of expertise is not certainty—it is transparency, intellectual humility, and fidelity to the limits of our knowledge.

We urge evaluators to be bold and cautious at once. Be bold in your commitment to scientific integrity, in your effort to understand the unique dynamics of each family, and in your articulation of well-reasoned, evidence-based, and evidence-informed opinions. Be cautious about the limits of your inferences, the potential for bias, and the temptation to speak with more certainty than your data can support.

Parenting plan evaluations are, at their best, a synthesis of scientific method and human understanding. The responsibility is immense, the impact profound. Our hope is that this work helps illuminate the standards of care, the questions worth asking, and the values worth upholding in this deeply consequential and professionally exciting field.

Go forth as explorers. Be students of both science and humanity. And always, always, show your work.

REFERENCES

Aboud, F. E., & Amato, M. (2001). Developmental and socialisation influences on intergroup bias. In R. Brown & S. L. Gaertner (Eds.), *Intergroup processes* (pp. 65–85). *Blackwell handbook of social psychology*. Blackwell Publishers.

Achenbach, T. M., McConaughy, S. H., & Howell, C. T. (1987). Child/adolescent behavioral and emotional problems: Implications of cross-informant correlations for situational specificity. *Psychological Bulletin, 101*(2), 213–232. https://doi.org/10.1037/0033-2909.101.2.213

Ackerman, M. J. (1995). *Clinician's guide to child custody evaluations*. John Wiley & Sons.

Ackerman, M. J. (2006). *Clinician's guide to child custody evaluations* (3rd ed.). John Wiley & Sons.

Ackerman, M. J., & Ackerman, M. C. (1997). Custody evaluation practices: A survey of experienced professionals (revisited). *Professional Psychology: Research and Practice, 28*(2), 137–145. https://doi.org/10.1037/0735-7028.28.2.137

Ackerman, M. J., Bow, J. N., & Mathy, N. (2021). Child custody evaluation practices: Where we were, where we are, and where we are going. *Professional Psychology: Research and Practice, 52*(4), 406–417. https://doi.org/10.1037/pro0000380

Ackerman, M. J., & Dolezal, S. (2006). Custody evaluators' views of controversial issues. *American Journal of Family Law, 20*(3), 200–205.

Ackerman, M. J., & Drosdeck, C. M. (2010). Should your infant spend the night? *Family Advocate, 33*(1), 12–15.

Ackerman, M. J., & Gould, J. W. (2015). Child custody and access. In B. L. Culter & P. A. Zapf (Eds.), *APA handbook of forensic psychology: Vol. 1. Individual and situational influences in criminal and civil contexts* (pp. 425–469). American Psychological Association. https://doi.org/10.1037/14461-013

Ackerman, M. J., & Kane, A. W. (1990). *Psychological experts in divorce, personal injury, and other civil actions*. Wiley Law Publications.

Ackerman, M. J., Kane, A., & Gould, J. W. (2019). *Psychological experts in divorce actions* (7th ed.). Kluwar.

Ackerman, M. J., Kane, A. W., & Gould, J. W. (2024). *Psychological experts in divorce actions* (7th ed., 2024 Supplement). Aspen Publishing.

Ackerman, M. J., & Pritzl, T. B. (2011). Child custody evaluation practices: A 20-year follow up. *Family Court Review, 49*(3), 618–628. https://doi.org/10.1111/j.1744-1617.2011.01397.x

Adhia, A., & Jeong, J. (2019). Fathers' perpetration of intimate partner violence and parenting during early childhood: Results from the Fragile Families and Child Wellbeing Study. *Child Abuse & Neglect, 96,* 104103. https://doi.org/10.1016/j.chiabu.2019.104103

Adler, L., Yehoshua, I., & Mizrahi Reuveni, M. (2023). Postpartum depression among gay fathers with children born through surrogacy: A cross-sectional study. *Journal of Psychiatric Practice, 29*(1), 3–10. https://doi.org/10.1097/PRA.0000000000000684

Ainsworth, M. D., Blehar, M., Waters, E., & Wall, S. (1978). *Patterns of attachment: Assessed in the strange situations*. Lawrence Erlbaum Associates.

Aizpurua, E., Copp, J., Ricarte, J. J., & Vázquez, D. (2021). Controlling behaviors and intimate partner violence among women in Spain: An examination of individual, partner, and relationship risk factors for physical and psychological abuse. *Journal of Interpersonal Violence, 36*(1-2), 231–254. https://doi.org/10.1177/0886260517723744

Alexander, P. C. (2015). *Intergenerational cycles of trauma and violence: An attachment and family systems perspective*. W.W. Norton & Company.

Alonso, D. J., Jordan, A. E., & Gülgöz, S. (2024). Children's attitudes about transgender identity disclosure and concealment. *British Journal of Developmental Psychology, 43*(2), 359–375. https://doi.org/10.1111/bjdp.12493

American Academy of Child and Adolescent Psychiatry. (1997). Practice parameters for child and adolescent forensic evaluations. *AACAP Official Action, 36*(10, Suppl.), 57S–68S.

American Academy of Child and Adolescent Psychiatry. (2011). Practice parameters for child and adolescent forensic evaluations. *Journal of the American Academy of Child & Adolescent Psychiatry, 50*(12), 1300–1312.

American Academy of Matrimonial Lawyers. (2011). *Child custody evaluation standards.*

American Academy of Matrimonial Lawyers. (2013). Child custody evaluation standards. *Journal of the American Academy of Matrimonial Lawyers, 25*(2), 251–294.

American Association for the Advancement of Science. (1993). *Project 2061: Benchmarks for science literacy*. Oxford University Press.

American Educational Research Association, American Psychological Association, & National Council on Measurement in Education. (1985). *Standards for educational and psychological testing*. American Psychological Association.

American Educational Research Association, American Psychological Association, & National Council on Measurement in Education. (2014). *Standards for educational and psychological testing*. American Educational Research Association.

American Professional Society on the Abuse of Children. (1997). *Practice guidelines: Psychosocial evaluation of suspected sexual abuse in children.*

American Psychological Association. (n.d.). Actuarial risk assessment. In *APA dictionary of psychology*. Retrieved March 3, 2026, from https://dictionary.apa.org/actuarial-risk-assessment

American Psychological Association. (1994). *Guidelines for child custody evaluations in family law proceedings.*

American Psychological Association. (2010). Guidelines for child custody evaluations in family law proceedings. *American Psychologist, 65*(9), 863–867. https://doi.org/10.1037/a0021250

American Psychological Association. (2013a). Guidelines for psychological evaluations in child protection matters. *American Psychologist, 68*(1), 20–31. https://doi.org/10.1037/a0029891

American Psychological Association. (2013b). Specialty guidelines for forensic psychology. *American Psychologist, 68*(1), 7–19. https://doi.org/10.1037/a0029889

American Psychological Association. (2015). *APA Task Force on Violent Media: Technical report on the review of the violent video game literature*. Retrieved from https://www.apa.org/pi/families/review-video-games.pdf

American Psychological Association. (2017a). *Ethical principles of psychologists and code of conduct* (2002, amended effective June 1, 2010, and January 1, 2017). https://www.apa.org/ethics/code/index

American Psychological Association. (2017b). *Multicultural guidelines: An ecological approach to context, identity, and intersectionality*. https://www.apa.org/about/policy/multicultural-guidelines.pdf

American Psychological Association. (2022). *APA guidelines for child custody evaluations in family law proceedings*. Retrieved from https://www.apa.org/about/policy/child-custody-evaluations.pdf

American Psychological Association Presidential Task Force on Evidence-Based Practice. (2006). Evidence-based practice in psychology. *American Psychologist, 61*(4), 271–285. https://doi.org/10.1037/0003-066X.61.4.271

Arizona v. Youngblood, 488 U.S. 51 (1988).

Ash, P., & Guyer, M. (1984). Court implementation of mental health professionals' recommendations in contested child custody and visitation cases. *The Bulletin of the American Academy of Psychiatry and the Law, 12*(2), 137–147.

Association of Family and Conciliation Courts. (1994). *Model standards of practice*.

Association of Family and Conciliation Courts. (2007). Model standards of practice for child custody evaluations. *Family Court Review, 45*(1), 70–91.

Association of Family and Conciliation Courts. (2016). *Guidelines for examining intimate partner violence*.

Association of Family and Conciliation Courts. (2018). *Guidelines for the use of social science research in family law.*

Association of Family and Conciliation Courts. (2022). *Guidelines for parenting plan evaluations in family law cases*.

Austin, J. L., & Kovera, M. B. (2015). Cross-examination educates jurors about missing control groups in scientific evidence. *Psychology, Public Policy, and Law, 21*(3), 252–264. https://doi.org/10.1037/law0000049

Austin, W. G. (2000a). Assessing credibility in allegations of marital violence in the high-conflict child custody case. *Family Court Review, 38*(4), 462–477. https://doi.org/10.1111/j.174-1617.2000.tb00585.x

Austin, W. G. (2000b). A forensic psychology model of risk assessment for child custody relocation law. *Family Court Review, 38*(2), 186–201. https://doi.org/10.1111/j.174-1617.2000.tb00569.x

Austin, W. G. (2001). Partner violence and risk assessment in child custody evaluation. *Family Court Review, 39*(4), 483–496. https://doi.org/10.1111/j.174-1617.2001.tb00627.x

Austin, W. G. (2008). Relocation, research, and forensic evaluation: Part 2: Research in support of the relocation risk assessment model. *Family Court Review, 46*(2), 347–365. https://doi.org/10.1111/j.1744-1617.2008.00205.x

Austin, W. G. (2011). Parental gatekeeping in custody disputes: Mutual parental support in divorce. *American Journal of Family Law, 25*(4), 148–153.

Austin, W. G. (2015a). Child custody evaluation and relocation, Part I of III: Forensic guideposts for the evaluator and court. *American Journal of Family Law, 29*(3), 156–170.

Austin, W. G. (2015b). Child custody evaluation and relocation: Part II of III: Options for a systematic approach to forensic evaluation. *American Journal of Family Law, 29*(2), 207–223.

Austin, W. G. (2018a). Child custody evaluation and relocation: Part III of III: Forensic consultation services and common errors by evaluators. *American Journal of Family Law, 30*(1), 32–45.

Austin, W. G. (2018b). Parental gatekeeping and child custody evaluation: Part III: Protective gatekeeping and the overnights "conundrum." *Journal of Divorce & Remarriage, 59*(5), 429–451.

Austin, W. G., Bow, J. N., Knoll, A., & Ellens, R. (2016). Relocation issues in child custody evaluations: A survey of professionals. *Family Court Review, 54*(3), 477–486. https://doi.org/10.1111/fcre.12224

Austin, W. G., Dale, M. D., Kirkpatrick, H. D., & Flens, J. R. (2011). Forensic expert roles and services in child custody litigation: Work product review and case consultation. *Journal of Child Custody, 8*(1-2), 47–83. https://doi.org/10.1080/15379418.2010.547444

Austin, W. G., & Drozd, L. M. (2012). Intimate partner violence and child custody evaluation, part 1: Theoretical framework, forensic model, and assessment issues. *Journal of Child Custody, 9*(4), 250–309. https://doi.org/10.1080/15379418.2012.749717

Austin, W. G., & Drozd, L. M. (2013). Judge's bench book for application of the integrated framework for the assessment of intimate partner violence in child custody disputes. *Journal of Child Custody, 10*(2), 99–119. https://doi.org/10.1080/15379418.2013.796850

Austin, W. G., Fieldstone, L., & Pruett, M. K. (2013). Bench book for assessing parental gatekeeping in parenting disputes: Understanding the dynamics of gate closing and opening for the best interests of children. *Journal of Child Custody, 10*(1), 1–16. https://doi.org/10.1080/15379418.2013.778693

Austin, W. G., & Gould, J. W. (2006). Exploring three functions in child custody evaluation for the relocation case: Prediction, investigation, and making recommendations for a long-distance parenting plan. *Journal of Child Custody, 3*(3-4), 63–108. https://doi.org/10.1300/J190v03n03_04

Austin, W. G., & Kirkpatrick, H. D. (2004). The investigation component in forensic mental health evaluations: Considerations for parenting time assessments. *Journal of Child Custody: Research, Issues, and Practices, 1*(2), 23–46. https://doi.org/10.1300/J190v01n02_02

Austin, W. G., Pruett, M. K., Kirkpatrick, H. D., Flens, J. R., & Gould, J. W. (2013). Parental gatekeeping and child custody/child access evaluation: Part I: Conceptual framework, research, and application. *Family Court Review, 51*(3), 485–501. https://doi.org/10.1111/fcre.12045

Austin, W. G., & Rappaport, S. (2018). Parental gatekeeping forensic model and child custody evaluation: Social capital and application to relocation disputes. *Journal of Child Custody, 15*(1), 55–75. https://doi.org/10.1080/15379418.2018.1431827

Axt, J. R., Ebersole, C. R., & Nosek, B. A. (2014). The rules of implicit evaluation by race, religion, and age. *Psychological Science, 25*(9), 1804–1815. https://doi.org/10.1177/0956797614543801

Baer, R. A., Wetter, M. W., & Berry, D. T. R. (1992). Detection of underreporting of psychopathology on the MMPI: A meta-analysis. *Clinical Psychology Review, 12*(5), 509–525. https://doi.org/10.1016/0272-7358(92)90069-K

Baerger, D. R., Galatzer-Levy, R., Gould, J. W., & Nye, S. (2002). A methodology for reviewing the reliability and relevance of child custody evaluations. *Journal of the American Academy of Matrimonial Lawyers, 18*(1), 35–73.

Baiocco, R., & Laghi, F. (2013). Sexual orientation and the desires and intentions to become parents. *Journal of Family Studies, 19*(1), 90–98.

Baker Valley Lumber, Inc. v. Ingersoll-Rand Co., 813 A 2d. 409 (N.H. 2002).

Bala, N. (2004). Assessments for postseparation parenting disputes in Canada. *Family Court Review, 42*(3), 485–510.

Bancroft, L., & Silverman, J. G. (2002). *The Batterer as parent: Addressing the impact of domestic violence on family dynamics*. Sage Publications.

Bandura, A. (1977). *Social learning theory*. Prentice-Hall.

Barber Rioja, V., & Rosenfeld, B. (2018). Addressing linguistic and cultural differences in the forensic interview. *International Journal of Forensic Mental Health, 17*(4), 377–386. https://doi.org/10.1080/14999013.2018.1495280

Bates, E. A., & Graham-Kevan, N. (2016). Is the presence of control related to helpseeking behavior? A test of Johnson's assumptions regarding sex differences and the role of control in intimate partner violence. *Partner Abuse, 7*(1), 3–25.

Bathurst, K., Gottfried, A. W., & Gottfried, A. E. (1997). Normative data for the MMPI-2 in child custody litigation. *Psychological Assessment, 9*(3), 205–211. https://doi.org/10.1037/1040-3590.9.3.205

Baumrind, D. (2013). Authoritative parenting revisited: History and current status. In R. E. Larzelere, A. S. Morris, & A. W. Harrist (Eds.), *Authoritative parenting: Synthesizing nurturance and discipline for optimal child development* (pp. 11–34). American Psychological Association. https://doi.org/10.1037/13948-002

Beavers, W. R., & Hampson, R. B. (1990). *Successful families: Assessment and intervention.* W. W. Norton & Co.

Beavers, W. R., & Hampson, R. B. (2003). Measuring family competence: The Beavers Systems Model. In F. Walsh (Ed.), *Normal family processes: Growing diversity and complexity* (3rd ed., pp. 549–580). The Guilford Press.

Bebes, A., Samarova, V., Shilo, G., & Diamond, G. M. (2015). Parental acceptance, parental psychological control and psychological symptoms among sexual minority adolescents. *Journal of Child and Family Studies, 24*(4), 882–890. https://doi.org/10.1007/s10826-013-9897-9

Beck, C. J. A., & Raghavan, C. (2010). Intimate partner abuse screening in custody mediation: The importance of assessing coercive control. *Family Court Review, 48*(3), 555–565. https://doi.org/10.1111/j.1744-1617.2010.01329.x

Bem, D. J. (1972). Self-perception theory. *Advances in Experimental Social Psychology, 6*, 1–62. https://doi.org/10.1016/S0065-2601(08)60024-6

Bender, A. E., McKinney, S. J., Schmidt-Sane, M. M., Cage, J., Holmes, M. R., Berg, K. A., Salley, J., Bodell, M., Miller, E. K., & Voith, L. A. (2022). Childhood exposure to intimate partner violence and effects on social-emotional competence: A systematic review. *Journal of Family Violence, 37*(8), 1263–1281. https://doi.org/10.1007/s10896-021-00315-z

Bengtson, V. L., Biblarz, T. J., & Roberts, R. E. L. (2007). How families still matter: A longitudinal study of youth in two generations. In S. J. Ferguson (Ed.), *Shifting the center: Understanding contemporary families* (pp. 323–336). McGraw-Hill.

Benjamin, G. A. H., Beck, C. J., Shaw, M., & Geffner, R. (2018). *Family evaluation in custody litigation: Promoting optimal outcomes and reducing ethical risks* (2nd ed.). American Psychological Association. https://doi.org/10.1037/0000071-000

Bennet, A., Kuchirko, Y., Halim, M. L. D., Costanzo, P. R., Martin, C. L., Stanaland, A., & Ruble, D. (2024). A 6-year longitudinal exploration of diversity in ethnically/racially minoritized children's early peer circles. *Social Development, 33*(4). https://doi.org/10.1111/sode.12744

Ben-Porath, Y. (2020). *An introduction to the MMPI-3 for forensic psychologists.* American Academy of Forensic Psychology.

Bente, G., Novotny, E., Roth, D., & Al-Issa, A. (2020). Beyond stereotypes: Analyzing gender and cultural differences in nonverbal rapport. *Frontiers in Psychology, 11.* https://doi.org/10.3389/fpsyg.2020.599703

Bergstrom-Lynch, C. (2020). Free to be you and me, maybe: Lesbian, gay, bisexual, and transgender parents doing gender with their children. *Journal of Gender Studies, 29*(3), 282–294. https://doi.org/10.1080/09589236.2019.1635000

Bernet, W. (2020). The Five-Factor Model for the diagnosis of parental alienation. *Feedback, 6*(Summer), 3–15.

Bernet, W., & Baker, A. J. (2024). Comments regarding "Looking beyond the sorting hat: Deconstructing the 'Five-Factor Model of Alienation," by Garber and Simon. *Family Transitions, 65*(1), 32–44. https://doi.org/10.1080/10502556.2023.2293386

Bernet, W., & Freeman, B. W. (2013). The psychosocial assessment of contact refusal. In D. Lorandos, W. Bernet, & S. R. Sauber (Eds.), *Parental alienation: The handbook for mental health and legal professionals* (pp. 47–73). Charles C. Thomas Publisher.

Bernet, W., & Greenhill, L. L. (2022). The Five-Factor Model for the diagnosis of parental alienation. *Journal of the American Academy of Child & Adolescent Psychiatry, 61*(5), 591–594. https://doi.org/10.1016/j.jaac.2021.11.026

Bernet, W., & Xu, S. (2022). Scholarly rumors: Citation analysis of vast misinformation regarding parental alienation theory. *Behavioral Sciences & the Law.*

Berry, J. W. (2023). Living together in culturally diverse societies. *Canadian Psychology, 64*(3), 167–177. https://doi.org/10.1037/cap0000362

Berry, J. W., & Hou, F. (2016). Immigrant acculturation and wellbeing in Canada. *Canadian Psychology, 57*(4), 254–264. https://doi.org/10.1037/cap0000064

Berry, J. W., & Hou, F. (2019). Multiple belongings and psychological well-being among immigrants and the second generation in Canada. *Canadian Journal of Behavioural Science / Revue Canadienne des Sciences du Comportement, 51*(3), 159–170.

Berry, J. W., Phinney, J. S., Sam, D. L., & Vedder, P. (2006). Immigrant youth: Acculturation, identity, and adaptation. *Applied Psychology, 55*(3), 303–332. https://doi.org/10.1111/j.1464-0597.2006.00256.x

Bettinsoli, M. L., Suitner, C., & Maass, A. (2021). Take a walk on the cultural side: A journey into embodied social cognition. In M. D. Robinson & L. E. Thomas (Eds.), *Handbook of embodied psychology: Thinking, feeling, and acting* (pp. 423–450). Springer Nature Switzerland AG. https://doi.org/10.1007/978-3-030-78471-3_19

Blasbalg, U., Hershkowitz, I., Lamb, M. E., & Karni-Visel, Y. (2021). Adherence to the Revised NICHD Protocol recommendations for conducting repeated supportive interviews is associated with the likelihood that children will allege abuse. *Psychology, Public Policy, and Law, 27*(2), 209–220. https://doi.org/10.1037/law0000295

Blizard, R. A., & Shaw, M. (2019). Lost-in-the-mall: False memory or false defense? *Journal of Child Custody, 16*(1), 20–41. https://doi.org/10.1080/15379418.2019.1590285

Bond, K. T., Mansour, M., Kershaw, T., & Flores, D. D. (2023). "Whenever you're ready to talk about it": Prompts and barriers to inclusive family sex communication with gay, bisexual, and queer sons. *American Journal of Sexuality Education, 18*(4), 569–593. https://doi.org/10.1080/15546128.2022.2141935

Bornstein, M. H. (Ed.). (2019). *Handbook of parenting: Children and parenting* (3rd ed.). Routledge/Taylor & Francis Group.

Borum, R., Otto, R., & Golding, S. (1993). Improving clinical judgment and decision making in forensic evaluation. *The Journal of Psychiatry & Law, 21*(1), 35–76. https://doi.org/10.1177/009318539302100104

Bottesi, G., Caudek, C., Colpizzi, I., Iannattone, S., Palmieri, G., & Sica, C. (2024). Advancing understanding of the relation between criterion a of the alternative model for personality disorders and hierarchical taxonomy of psychopathology: Insights from an external validity analysis. *Personality Disorders: Theory, Research, and Treatment, 16*(2), 198–204. https://doi.org/10.1037/per0000703

Boullier, M., & Blair, M. (2018). Adverse childhood experiences. *Paediatrics and Child Health (Oxford), 28*(3), 132–137. https://doi.org/10.1016/j.paed.2017.12.008

Bouris, A., Guilamo-Ramos, V., Pickard, A., Shiu, C., Loosier, P. S., Dittus, P., Gloppen, K., & Michael Waldmiller, J. (2010). A systematic review of parental influences on the health and well-being of lesbian, gay, and bisexual youth: Time for a new public health research and practice agenda. *The Journal of Primary Prevention, 31*(5-6), 273–309. https://doi.org/10.1007/s10935-010-0229-1

Bow, J. N. (2006). Review of empirical research on child custody practice. *Journal of Child Custody, 3*(1), 23–50. https://doi.org/10.1300/J190v03n01_02

Bow, J. N. (2010). Use of third party information in child custody evaluations. *Behavioral Sciences & the Law, 28*(4), 511–521. https://doi.org/10.1002/bsl.946

Bow, J. N., & Boxer, P. (2003). Assessing allegations of domestic violence in child custody evaluations. *Journal of Interpersonal Violence, 18*(12), 1394–1410. https://doi.org/10.1177/0886260503258031

Bow, J. N., Flens, J. R., Gould, J. W., & Greenhut, D. (2006). An analysis of administration, scoring, and interpretation of the MMPI-2 and MCMI-II/III in child custody evaluations. *Journal of Child Custody, 2*(4), 1–22. https://doi.org/10.1300/J190v02n04_01

Bow, J. N., Gottlieb, M. C., & Gould-Saltman, H. D. (2011). Attorneys' beliefs and opinions about child custody evaluations. *Family Court Review, 49*(2), 301–312. https://doi.org/10.1111/j.1744-1617.2011.01372.x

Bow, J. N., Gould, J. W., Flens, J.R., & Greenhut, D. (2006). Testing in child custody evaluations—Selection, usage, and Daubert admissibility: A survey of psychologists. *Journal of Forensic Psychology Practice, 6*(2), 17–38. https://doi.org/10.1300/J158v06n02_02

Bow, J. N., & Quinnell, F. A. (2001). Psychologists' current practices and procedures in child custody evaluations: Five years after American Psychological Association guidelines. *Professional Psychology: Research and Practice, 32*(3), 261–268. https://doi.org/10.1037/0735-7028.32.3.261

Bow, J. N., & Quinnell, F. A. (2002). A critical review of child custody evaluation reports. *Family Court Review, 40*(2), 164–176. https://doi.org/10.1111/j.174-1617.2002.tb00827.x

Bow, J. N., & Quinnell, F. A. (2004). Critique of child custody evaluations by the legal profession. *Family Court Review, 42*(1), 115–127. https://doi.org/10.1111/j.174-1617.2004.tb00637.x

Brand, B. L., Schielke, H. J., Brams, J. S., & DiComo, R. A. (2017). Assessing trauma-related dissociation in forensic contexts: Addressing trauma-related dissociation as a forensic psychologist, part II. *Psychological Injury and Law, 10*(4), 298–312. https://doi.org/10.1007/s12207-017-9305-7

Braunstein, L. J., & Wittmann, J. P. (2023). To recommend or not recommend: That is still the question. *Family Court Review, 61*(4), 782–800. https://doi.org/10.1111/fcre.12751

Breiding, M., Basile, K. C., Smith, S. G., Black, M. C., & Mahendra, R. R. (2015). *Intimate partner violence surveillance: Uniform definitions and recommended data elements.* Version 2.0. https://stacks.cdc.gov/view/cdc/31292

Briere, J. (1995). *Trauma symptom inventory: Professional manual.* Psychological Assessment Resources.

Briere, J. (1996). *Trauma symptom checklist for children (TSCC).* Psychological Assessment Resources.

Briere, J. (2001). *Detailed assessment of posttraumatic stress (DAPS) manual.* Psychological Assessment Resources.

Bricklin, B. (1995). *The custody evaluation handbook: Research-based solutions and applications.* Brunner/Mazel.

Brodsky, S., & Goldenson, J. (2022). Feedback in forensic mental health assessment. *Journal of Forensic Psychology Research and Practice, 50*(1), 1–13.

Brodzinsky, D. M. (1993). On the use and misuse of psychological testing in child custody evaluations. *Professional Psychology: Research and Practice, 24*(2), 213–219. https://doi.org/10.1037/0735-7028.24.2.213

Bronfenbrenner, U. (1977). Toward an experimental ecology of human development. *American Psychologist, 32*(7), 513–531. https://doi.org/10.1037/0003-066X.32.7.513

Bronfenbrenner, U., & Morris, P. A. (2006). The bioecological model of human development. In R. M. Lerner & W. Damon (Eds.), *Theoretical models of human development* (6th ed., pp. 793–828). *Handbook of child psychology.* John Wiley & Sons.

Broughton, S., & Ford-Gilboe, M. (2017). Predicting family health and well-being after separation from an abusive partner: Role of coercive control, mother's depression and social support. *Journal of Clinical Nursing, 26*(15-16), 2468–2481. https://doi.org/10.1111/jocn.13458

Broughton, S., Ford-Gilboe, M., & Varcoe, C. (2024). Understanding what shapes the priorities of women who are mothering in the context of intimate partner violence: A qualitative study. *Journal of Clinical Nursing, 33*(4), 1520–1532. https://doi.org/10.1111/jocn.16976

Brown, D., Walker, D., & Godden, E. (2021). Tele-forensic interviewing to elicit children's evidence—Benefits, risks, and practical considerations. *Psychology, Public Policy, and Law, 27*(1), 17–29. https://doi.org/10.1037/law0000288

Brown, D. A., & Lamb, M. E. (2019). Forks in the road, routes chosen, and journeys that beckon: A selective review of scholarship on children's testimony. *Applied Cognitive Psychology, 33*(4), 480–488. https://doi.org/10.1002/acp.3511

Bruck, M. (2009). Human figure drawings and children's recall of touching. *Journal of Experimental Psychology: Applied, 15*(4), 361–374. https://doi.org/10.1037/a0017120

Bruck, M., & Ceci, S. J. (1995). Amicus brief for the case of State of New Jersey v. Michaels presented by Committee of Concerned Social Scientists. *Psychology, Public Policy, and Law, 1*(2), 272–322. https://doi.org/10.1037/1076-8971.1.2.272

Bruck, M., Ceci, S., Kulkofsky, S., Klemfuss, Z., & Sweeney, C. (2008). Children's testimony. In M. Rutter, D. Bishop, D. Pine, S. Scott, J. Stevenson, E. Taylor, & A. Thapar (Eds.), *Rutter's child and adolescent psychiatry* (pp. 81–94). Wiley-Blackwell. https://doi.org/10.1002/9781444300895.ch7

Bruck, M., Ceci, S. J., & Francoeur, E. (1999). The accuracy of mothers' memories of conversations with their preschool children. *Journal of Experimental Psychology: Applied, 5*(1), 89–106. https://doi.org/10.1037/1076-898X.5.1.89

Bunting v. Jamison, 984 P.2d 467 (Wyo. 1999).

Burgamy, S., Argentino, J., & Benson, G. (2021, April 27). *Gender diversity and sexual orientation issues in contested custody cases* [Presentation]. New Jersey Association of Family and Conciliation Courts Annual Meeting and Seminar.

Burrow v. Arce, 997 S.W.2d 229 (Tex. 1999).

Butcher, J. N., Morfitt, R. C., Rouse, S. V., & Holden, R. R. (1997). Reducing MMPI-2 defensiveness: The effect of specialized instructions on retest validity in a job applicant sample. *Journal of Personality Assessment, 68*(2), 385–401. https://doi.org/10.1207/s15327752jpa6802_9

Callaghan, J. E. M., Alexander, J. H., Sixsmith, J., & Fellin, L. C. (2018). Beyond "witnessing": Children's experiences of coercive control in domestic violence and abuse. *Journal of Interpersonal Violence, 33*(10), 1551–1581. https://doi.org/10.1177/0886260515618946

Callaghan, J. E., Fellin, L., & Alexander, J. (2017). Beyond vulnerability: Working with children who have experienced domestic violence. In *Teaching critical psychology: International perspectives* (pp. 219–237). Routledge. https://doi.org/10.4324/9781315209319-11

Callaghan, J. E. M., Fellin, L. C., Mavrou, S., Alexander, J., & Sixsmith, J. (2017). The management of disclosure in children's accounts of domestic violence: Practices of telling and not telling. *Journal of Child and Family Studies, 26*(12), 3370–3387. https://doi.org/10.1007/s10826-017-0832-3

Camacho, K., Ehrensaft, M. K., & Cohen, P. (2012). Exposure to intimate partner violence, peer relations, and risk for internalizing behaviors: A prospective longitudinal study. *Journal of Interpersonal Violence, 27*(1), 125–141. https://doi.org/10.1177/0886260511416474

Camparo, L. B., Guzman, A., & Saywitz, K. J. (2018). Narrative elaboration technique. In J. L. Johnson, G. S. Goodman, & P. C. Mundy (Eds.), *The Wiley handbook of memory, autism spectrum disorder, and the law* (pp. 270–291). Wiley-Blackwell. https://doi.org/10.1002/9781119158431.ch14

Campbell, J. Y. (1996). Understanding risk and return. *Journal of Political Economy, 104*(2), 298–345. https://doi.org/10.1086/262026

Canadian Pediatric Society. (n.d.). *Gender identity.* Retrieved February 5, 2025, from https://caringforkids.cps.ca/handouts/behavior-and-development/gender-identity

Canadian Pediatric Society. (2019). Digital media: Promoting healthy screen use in school-aged children and adolescents. *Paediatrics & Child Health, 24*(6), 402–417. https://doi.org/10.1093/pch/pxz095

Capaldi, D. M., Shortt, J. W., & Kim, H. K. (2005). A lifespan developmental systems perspective on aggression toward a partner. In W. M. Pinsof & J. Lebow (Eds.), *Family psychology: The art of the science* (pp. 141–167). Oxford University Press.

Capra, D. J. (1998). The *Daubert* puzzle. *Georgia Law Review (Athens, Ga.), 32*(3), 699–782.

Carmichael v. Samyang Tire, Inc., 131 F.3d 1433 (11th Cir. 1997).

Carone, N., Mirabella, M., Innocenzi, E., Quintigliano, M., Antoniucci, C., Manzi, D., Fortunato, A., Giovanardi, G., Speranza, A. M., & Lingiardi, V. (2023). The intergenerational transmission of attachment during middle childhood in lesbian, gay, and heterosexual parent families through assisted reproduction: The mediating role of reflective functioning. *Attachment & Human Development,* 1–27. https://doi.org/10.1080/14616734.2023.2292053

Carone, N., Quintigliano, M., Speranza, A. M., Tanzilli, A., & Lingiardi, V. (2024). Parenting and psychological adjustment during middle childhood in lesbian, gay, and heterosexual parent families formed through assisted reproduction. *Psychology of Sexual Orientation and Gender Diversity*. Advance online publication. https://doi.org/10.1037/sgd0000744

Carpenter, G. L., & Stacks, A. M. (2009). Developmental effects of exposure to intimate partner violence in early childhood: A review of the literature. *Children and Youth Services Review, 31*(8), 831–839. https://doi.org/10.1016/j.childyouth.2009.03.005

Carr, G. D., Moretti, M. M., & Cue, B. J. (2005). Evaluating parenting capacity: Validity problems with the MMPI-2, PAI, CAPI, and ratings of child adjustment. *Professional Psychology: Research and Practice, 36*(2), 194. https://doi.org/10.1037/0735-7028.36.2.188

Carroll, J. E., Gruenewald, T. L., Taylor, S. E., Janicki-Deverts, D., Matthews, K. A., & Seeman, T. E. (2013). Childhood abuse, parental warmth, and adult multisystem biological risk in the Coronary Artery Risk Development in Young Adults study. *Proceedings of the National Academy of Sciences of the United States of America, 110*(42), 17149–17153. https://doi.org/10.1073/pnas.1315458110

Caspi, A., Houts, R. M., Belsky, D. W., Goldman-Mellor, S. J., Harrington, H., Israel, S., Meier, M. H., Ramrakha, S., Shalev, I., Poulton, R., & Moffitt, T. E. (2014). The P-factor: One general psychopathology factor in the structure of psychiatric disorders? *Clinical Psychological Science, 2*(2), 119–137. https://doi.org/10.1177/2167702613497473

Ceci, S., & Bruck, M. (2000). Why judges must insist on electronically preserved recordings of child interviews. *Court Review, 37,* 8–10.

Ceci, S., Hritz, A., & Royer, C. (2016). Understanding suggestibility. In W. T. O'Donohue & M. Fanetti (Eds.), *Forensic interviews regarding child sexual abuse: A guide to evidence-based practice* (pp. 141–153). Springer International Publishing.

Ceci, S. J., & Bruck, M. (1995). *Jeopardy in the courtroom: A scientific analysis of children's testimony*. American Psychological Association. https://doi.org/10.1037/10180-000

Ceci, S. J., & Bruck, M. (2006). Children's suggestibility: Characteristics and mechanisms. In R. V. Kail (Ed.), *Advances in child development and behavior* (pp. 247–281). Elsevier Academic Press.

Ceci, S. J., & Bruck, M. (2007). Loftus's lineage in developmental forensic research: Six scientific misconceptions about children's suggestibility. In M. Garry & H. Hayne (Eds.), *Do justice and let the sky fall: Elizabeth Loftus and her contributions to science, law, and academic freedom* (pp. 65–77). Lawrence Erlbaum Associates.

Ceci, S. J., Fitneva, S. A., & Gilstrap, L. L. (2003). Memory development and eyewitness testimony. In A. Slater & G. Bremner (Eds.), *An introduction to developmental psychology* (pp. 283–310). Blackwell Publishing.

Centers for Disease Control and Prevention. (2021). *Positive parenting tips.*

Centers for Disease Control and Prevention. (2023). *Fast facts: Preventing intimate partner violence*. U.S. Department of Health & Human Services.

Centers for Disease Control and Prevention. (2024a). *About intimate partner violence*. https://www.cdc.gov/intimate-partner-violence/about/index.html

Centers for Disease Control and Prevention. (2024b). Intimate partner violence and pregnancy and infant health outcomes—Pregnancy Risk Assessment Monitoring System, nine U.S. jurisdictions, 2016–2022. *Morbidity and Mortality Weekly Report, 73*(48), 1093–1098. https://www.cdc.gov/mmwr/volumes/73/wr/mm7348a1.htm

Cerqueira-Santos, E., Santos, J. J., & Lawrenz, P. (2021). Child development in families with gay and lesbian parents and beliefs about homosexuality. In N. A. de Morais, F. Scorsolini-Comin, & E. Cerqueira-Santos (Eds.), *Parenting and couple relationships among LGBTQ+ people in diverse contexts* (pp. 293–309). Springer Nature Switzerland AG. https://doi.org/10.1007/978-3-030-84189-8_17

Champion, K. (2022). Coercion in families and child resistance to contact with a parent after family separation. *Journal of Family Trauma, Child Custody & Child Development, 19*(3–4), 230–243. https://doi.org/10.1080/26904586.2022.2105273

Chandler, L. A. (2003). The projective hypothesis and the development of projective techniques for children. In C. R. Reynolds & R. W. Kamphaus (Eds.), *Handbook of psychological and educational assessment of children: Personality, behavior, and context* (2nd ed., pp. 51–65). Guilford Press.

Charman, S., Douglass, A. B., & Mook, A. (2019). Cognitive bias in legal decision making. In N. Brewer & A. B. Douglass (Eds.), *Psychological science and the law* (pp. 30–53). Guilford.

Chavis, A. Z., & Hill, M. S. (2009). Integrating multiple intersecting identities: A multicultural conceptualization of the power and control wheel. *Women & Therapy, 32*(1), 121–149.

Chen, Y., Haines, J., Charlton, B. M., & VanderWeele, T. J. (2019). Positive parenting improves multiple aspects of health and well-being in young adulthood. *Nature Human Behaviour, 3*(7), 684–691. https://doi.org/10.1038/s41562-019-0602-x

Chen, Y., Kubzansky, L. D., & VanderWeele, T. J. (2019). Parental warmth and flourishing in mid-life. *Social Science & Medicine, 220*, 65–72. https://doi.org/10.1016/j.socscimed.2018.10.026

Chevalier, C. S., Boccaccini, M. T., Murrie, D. C., & Varela, J. G. (2015). Static-99R reporting practices in sexually violent predator cases: Does norm selection reflect adversarial allegiance? *Law and Human Behavior, 39*(3), 209–218. https://doi.org/10.1037/lhb0000114

Chin, J. M. (2014). Psychological science's replicability crisis and what it means for science in the courtroom. *Psychology, Public Policy, and Law, 20*(3), 225–238. https://doi.org/10.1037/law0000012

Chin, J. M., Lutsky, M., & Dror, I. E. (2019). The biases of experts: An empirical analysis of expert witness challenges. *Manitoba Law Journal, 42*(4), 21–67. https://doi.org/10.29173/mlj1124

Choong, Y., Theofanos, M., Renaud, K., & Prior, S. (2019). Case study: Exploring children's password knowledge and practices, *Proceedings of 2019 Workshop on Usable Security (USEC)*, San Diego.

Choudhry, N. K., Fletcher, R. H., & Soumerai, S. B. (2005). Systematic review: The relationship between clinical experience and quality of health care. *Annals of Internal Medicine, 142*(4), 260–273. https://doi.org/10.7326/0003-4819-142-4-200502150-00008

Cicchetti, D., & Toth, S. L. (1995). A developmental psychopathology perspective on child abuse and neglect. *Journal of the American Academy of Child & Adolescent Psychiatry, 34*(5), 541–565. https://doi.org/10.1097/00004583-199505000-00008

Clauss-Ehlers, C. S., Chiriboga, D. A., Hunter, S. J., Roysircar, G., & Tummala-Narra, P. (2019). APA *Multicultural Guidelines* executive summary: Ecological approach to context, identity, and intersectionality. *American Psychologist, 74*(2), 232–244. https://doi.org/10.1037/amp0000382

Coffey, C. A., Batastini, A. B., & Vitacco, M. J. (2018). Clues from the digital world: A survey of clinicians' reliance on social media as collateral data in forensic evaluations. *Professional Psychology: Research and Practice, 49*(5-6), 345–354. https://doi.org/10.1037/pro0000206

Coleman, J. S. (1990). *Foundations of social theory.* Harvard University Press.

Commonwealth v. Lanigan, 641 N.E.2d 1342 (Mass. 1994).

Corey, D. M., & Ben-Porath, Y. S. (2020). Practical guidance on the use of the MMPI instruments in remote psychological testing. *Professional Psychology: Research and Practice, 51*(3), 199–204. https://doi.org/10.1037/pro0000329

Coyne, S. M., Radesky, J., Collier, K. M., Gentile, D. A., Linder, J. R., Nathanson, A. I., Rasmussen, E. E., Reich, S. M., & Rogers, J. (2017). Parenting and digital media. *Pediatrics, 140*(Suppl. 2), S112–S116. https://doi.org/10.1542/peds.2016-1758N

Crnic, K., & Low, C. (2002). Everyday stresses and parenting. In M. H. Bornstein (Ed.), *Handbook of parenting: Vol. 5. Practical issues in parenting* (2nd ed., pp. 243–267). Lawrence Erlbaum Associates.

Crossman, A. M., Powell, M. B., Principe, G. F., Gabrielle, F., & Ceci, S. J. (2002). Child testimony in custody cases: A review. *Journal of Forensic Psychology Practice, 2*(1), 1–32.

Crossman, K. A., & Hardesty, J. L. (2018). Placing coercive control at the center: What are the processes of coercive control and what makes control coercive? *Psychology of Violence, 8*(2), 196–206. https://doi.org/10.1037/vio0000094

Crossman, K. A., Hardesty, J. L., & Raffaelli, M. (2016). "He could scare me without laying a hand on me": Mothers' experiences of nonviolent coercive control during marriage and after separation. *Violence Against Women, 22*(4), 454–473. https://doi.org/10.1177/1077801215604744

Cummings, E. M., & Davies, P. T. (1995). The impact of parents on their children: An emotional security perspective. In R. Vasta (Ed.), *Annals of child development: A research annual* (Vol. 10, pp. 167–208). Jessica Kingsley Publishers.

Cummings, E. M., & Davies, P. T. (1996). Emotional security as a regulatory process in normal development and the development of psychopathology. *Development and Psychopathology, 8*(1), 123–139. https://doi.org/10.1017/S0954579400007008

Cummings, E. M., & Davies, P. T. (2010). *Marital conflict and children: An emotional security perspective.* Guilford Press.

Cummings, E. M., El-Sheikh, M., Kouros, C. D., & Buckhalt, J. A. (2009). Children and violence: The role of children's regulation in the marital aggression-child adjustment link. *Clinical Child and Family Psychology Review, 12*(1), 3–15. https://doi.org/10.1007/s10567-009-0042-7

Cummings, E. M., Koss, K. J., & Cheung, R. Y. M. (2014). Interparental conflict and children's mental health: Emerging directions in emotional security theory. In C. R. Agnew & S. C. South (Eds.), *Interpersonal relationships and health: Social and clinical psychological mechanisms* (pp. 179–201). Oxford University Press.

Cuthbert, C., Slote, K., Driggers, M. G., Mesh, C. J., Bancroft, L., & Silverman, J. (2002). *Battered mothers speak out: A human rights report on domestic violence and child custody in the Massachusetts family courts.* Wellesley Centers for Women.

Dale, M. D., & Gould, J. W. (2014). Science, mental health consultants, and attorney-expert relationships in child custody. *Family Law Quarterly, 49*(1), 1–43.

Dale, M. D., Gould, J. W., & Levine, A. M. (2021). Cross-examining experts in child custody: Applying cross-examination and review models to evaluators and evaluations. *Journal of the American Academy of Matrimonial Lawyers, 33*(2), 327–392. https://aaml.org/wp-content/uploads/MAT206.pdf

Dale, M. D., & Smith, D. (2021). Making the case for videoconferencing and remote child custody evaluations (RCCEs): The empirical, ethical, and evidentiary arguments for accepting new technology. *Psychology, Public Policy, and Law, 27*(1), 30–44. https://doi.org/10.1037/law0000280

Darom, N. (2023). "However I talk about it, my kids tell me I'm doing it wrong": U.S. mothers of cisgender children grapple with gender diversity. *Gender & Society, 37*(6), 827–854. https://doi.org/10.1177/08912432231194789

Daubert v. Merrell Dow Pharmaceuticals, Inc., 509 U.S. 579 (1993).

D'Augelli, A. R., Grossman, A. H., & Starks, M. T. (2008). Families of gay, lesbian, and bisexual youth: What do parents and siblings know and how do they react? *Journal of GLBT Family Studies, 4*(1), 95–115. https://doi.org/10.1080/15504280802084506

Davies, J. (2019). Developing a model for evidence-based clinical forensic interviewing. *International Journal of Forensic Mental Health, 18*(1), 3–11. https://doi.org/10.1080/14999013.2018.1508096

Davies, P. T., & Cummings, E. M. (1994). Marital conflict and child adjustment: An emotional security hypothesis. *Psychological Bulletin, 116*(3), 387–411. https://doi.org/10.1037/0033-2909.116.3.387

Davies, P. T., Hentges, R. F., Coe, J. L., Martin, M. J., Sturge-Apple, M. L., & Cummings, E. M. (2016a). The multiple faces of interparental conflict: Implications for cascades of children's insecurity and externalizing problems. *Journal of Abnormal Psychology, 125*(5), 664–678. https://doi.org/10.1037/abn0000170

Davies, P. T., Martin, M. J., Coe, J. L., & Cummings, E. M. (2016b). Transactional cascades of destructive interparental conflict, children's emotional insecurity, and psychological problems across childhood and adolescence. *Development and Psychopathology, 28*(3), 653–671. https://doi.org/10.1017/S0954579416000237

Davis, G. (2015). SAFeR: A four-part approach to decision-making in domestic violence-related child custody disputes. Minneapolis, MN: Battered Women's Justice Project.

Day, A., Woldgabreal, Y., & Butcher, L. (2023). Cultural bias in forensic assessment: Considerations and suggestions. In G. C. Liell, M. J. Fisher, & L. F. Jones (Eds.), *Challenging bias in forensic psychological assessment and testing: Theoretical and practical approaches to working with diverse populations* (pp. 245–258). Routledge.

De Finetti, B. (1968). Probability: Interpretations. In D. E. Sills (Ed.), *International encyclopedia of the social sciences* (Vol. 12, pp. 496–504). Macmillan.

De Los Reyes, A., Augenstein, T. M., Wang, M., Thomas, S. A., Drabick, D. A. G., Burgers, D. E., & Rabinowitz, J. (2015). The validity of the multi-informant approach to assessing child and adolescent mental health. *Psychological Bulletin, 141*(4), 858–900. https://doi.org/10.1037/a0038498

De Los Reyes, A., & Epkins, C. C. (2023). Introduction to the special issue. A dozen years of demonstrating that informant discrepancies are more than measurement error: Toward guidelines for integrating data from multi-informant assessments of youth mental health. *Journal of Clinical Child and Adolescent Psychology, 52*(1), 1–18. https://doi.org/10.1080/15374416.2022.2158843

DeMatteo, D., Burl, J., Filone, S., & Heilbrun, K. (2016). Training in forensic assessment and intervention: Implications for principle-based models. In R. Jackson & R. Roesch (Eds.), *Learning forensic assessment: Research and practice* (2nd ed., pp. 3–31). Routledge/Taylor & Francis Group.

DeMatteo, D., Marczyk, G., Krauss, D. A., & Burl, J. (2009). Educational and training models in forensic psychology. *Training and Education in Professional Psychology, 3*(3), 184–191. https://doi.org/10.1037/a0014582

DeMatteo, D., Marczyk, G., Krauss, D. A., & Burl, J. (2013). Education and training models in forensic psychology. In J. B. Helfgott (Ed.), *Criminal psychology: Vol. 1. Theory and research* (pp. 43–60). Praeger.

DePaulo, B. M., Charlton, K., Cooper, H., Lindsay, J. J., & Muhlenbruck, L. (1997). The accuracy–confidence correlation in the detection of deception. *Personality and Social Psychology Review, 1*(4), 346–357. https://doi.org/10.1207/s15327957pspr0104_5

DePaulo, B. M., Lindsay, J. J., Malone, B. E., Muhlenbruck, L., Charlton, K., & Cooper, H. (2003). Cues to deception. *Psychological Bulletin, 129*(1), 74–118. https://doi.org/10.1037/0033-2909.129.1.74

Dessimoz Künzle, L., Cattagni Kleiner, A., & Romain-Glassey, N. (2022). Suffering and care of 0–12 year-old children exposed to intimate partner violence: Making clinical forensic data talk. *Frontiers in Psychiatry, 13*.

Dickinson, J. J., Lytle, N. E., & Poole, D. A. (2021). Tele-forensic interviewing can be a reasonable alternative to face-to-face interviewing of child witnesses. *Law and Human Behavior, 45*(2), 97–111.

Dobash, R. E., & Dobash, R. (1979). *Violence against wives: A case against the patriarchy*. Free Press.

Donovan, T., & Mickey, R. M. (2019). *Bayesian statistics for beginners: A step-by-step approach*. Oxford University Press.

Dragiewicz, M. (2012). Family violence or woman abuse? In R. Alaggia & C. Vine (Eds.), *Cruel but not unusual: Violence in Canadian families* (pp. 43–62). Wilfrid Laurier University Press.

Dror, I. (2011a). A novel approach to minimize error in the medical domain: Cognitive neuroscientific insights into training. *Medical Teacher, 33*(1), 34–38.

Dror, I. E. (2011b). The paradox of human expertise: Why experts get it wrong. In N. Kapur (Ed.), *The paradoxical brain* (pp. 177–188). Cambridge University Press.

Dror, I. E., & Kukucka, J. (2021). Linear sequential unmasking–expanded (LSU-E): A general approach for improving decision making as well as minimizing noise and bias. *Forensic Science International: Synergy, 3*, 100161. https://doi.org/10.1016/j.fsisyn.2021.100161

Dror, I. E., Kukucka, J., Kassin, S. M., & Zapf, P. A. (2018). No one is immune to contextual bias—Not even forensic pathologists. *Journal of Applied Research in Memory and Cognition, 7*(2), 316–317.

Dror, I. E., & Murrie, D. C. (2018). A hierarchy of expert performance applied to forensic psychological assessments. *Psychology, Public Policy, and Law, 24*(1), 11–23.

Drozd, L., Saini, M. A., & Vellucci-Cook, K. (2019). Trauma and child custody disputes: Screening, assessment, and interventions. In L. R. Greenberg, B. J. Fidler, and M. A. Saini (Eds.), *Evidence-informed interventions for court-involved families: Promoting healthy coping and development* (pp. 260–281). Oxford University Press.

Drozd, L. M. (2008). DVCC protocol. *Journal of Child Custody: Research, Issues, and Practices, 4*(3–4), 19–31. https://doi.org/10.1300/J190v04n03_02

Drozd, L. M., Deutsch, R. M., & Donner, D. A. (2020). Parenting coordination in cases involving intimate partner violence. *Family Court Review, 58*(3), 774–792.

Drozd, L. M., Kuehnle, K., & Walker, L. E. A. (2004). Safety first: A model for understanding domestic violence in child custody and access disputes. *Journal of Child Custody: Research, Issues, and Practices, 1*(2), 75–103.

Drozd, L. M., & Olesen, N. W. (2004). Is it abuse, alienation, and/or estrangement? A decision tree. *Journal of Child Custody: Research, Issues, and Practices, 1*(3), 65–106.

Drozd, L. M., Olesen, N. W., & Saini, M. A. (2013). *Parenting plan and child custody evaluations: Using decision trees to increase evaluator competence and avoid preventable errors*. Professional Resource Press/Professional Resource Exchange.

Drozd, L. M., Saini, L., & Carson, C. (2022 , May 11–14). *An evidence-informed family systems decision tree for intervening in parent–child contact problems* [Conference presentation]. 59th Annual Conference of the Association of Family and Conciliation Courts, Chicago, IL, United States.

Drozd, L. M., Saini, M., & Olesen, N. (Eds.). (2016). *Parenting plan evaluations: Applied research for the family court* (2nd ed.). Oxford University Press.

Drozdek, A. (1994). Awe and arrogance in science. *The Midwest Quarterly, 35*(2), 136–151.

Dunbar, A. S., Perry, N. B., Cavanaugh, A. M., & Leerkes, E. M. (2015). African American parents' racial and emotion socialization profiles and young adults' emotional adaptation. *Cultural Diversity & Ethnic Minority Psychology, 21*(3), 409–419.

Dutton, D. G. (2006a). Domestic abuse assessment in child custody disputes: Beware the domestic violence research paradigm. *Journal of Child Custody: Research, Issues, and Practices, 2*(4), 23–42.

Dutton, D. G. (2006b). On comparing apples with apples deemed nonexistent: A reply to Johnson. *Journal of Child Custody: Research, Issues, and Practices, 2*(4), 53–63.

Dutton, D. G., Hamel, J., & Aaronson, J. (2010). The gender paradigm in family court processes: Re-balancing the scales of justice from biased social science. *Journal of Child Custody: Research, Issues, and Practices, 7*(1), 1–31.

Dutton, D. G., & Starzomski, A. J. (1997). Personality predictors of the Minnesota Power and Control Wheel. *Journal of Interpersonal Violence, 12*(1), 70–82.

Dweck, C. (2008). *Mindset: The new psychology of success.* Random House Digital.

Eagly, A. H., & Chaiken, S. (1993). *The psychology of attitudes.* Harcourt Brace Jovanovich.

Ebbinghaus, H. (1885). *Memory: A contribution to experimental psychology* (H. A. Ruger & C. E. Bussenius, Trans.). Teachers College, Columbia University.

Eberhardt, J. L. (2020a). *Biased: The new science of race and inequality.* William Heinemann.

Eberhardt, J. L. (2020b). *Biased: Uncovering the hidden prejudice that shapes what we see, think, and do.* Penguin Books.

Edmond, G., & Roach, K. (2011). A contextual approach to the admissibility of state's forensic science and medical evidence. *University of Toronto Law Journal, 61*(3), 343–409. https://www.jstor.org/stable/23018554

Ehrensaft, M. K., & Cohen, P. (2012). Contribution of family violence to the intergenerational transmission of externalizing behavior. *Prevention Science, 13*(4), 370–383. https://doi.org/10.1007/s11121-011-0223-8

Ehrensaft, M. K., Knous-Westfall, H., & Cohen, P. (2017). Long-term influence of intimate partner violence and parenting practices on offspring trauma symptoms. *Psychology of Violence, 7*(2), 296–305.

Eisenberg, N. (2020). Findings, issues, and new directions for research on emotion socialization. *Developmental Psychology, 56*(3), 664–670.

Ekman, P., & O'Sullivan, M. (1991). Who can catch a liar? *American Psychologist, 46*(9), 913–920.

Ellis, B. H., Abdi, S. M., & Winer, J. P. (2020). *Mental health practice with immigrant and refugee youth: A socioecological framework.* American Psychological Association. https://doi.org/10.1037/0000163-000

Ellis, B. J., Bianchi, J., Griskevicius, V., & Frankenhuis, W. E. (2017). Beyond risk and protective factors: An adaptation-based approach to resilience. *Perspectives on Psychological Science, 12*(4), 561–587. https://doi.org/10.1177/1745691617693054

Emery, R. (2024). Is the emperor naked? Questioning the alienation hypothesis. *Family Transitions, 65*(1), 45–48. https://doi.org/10.1080/28375300.2024.2326260

Emery, R. E. (2011). *Renegotiating family relationships: Divorce, child custody, and mediation* (2nd ed.). Guilford Press.

Emery, R. E., Otto, R. K., & O'Donohue, W. T. (2005). A critical assessment of child custody evaluations: Limited science and a flawed system. *Psychological Science in the Public Interest, 6*(1), 1–29.

Emery, R. E., Otto, R. K., & O'Donohue, W. (2008). Custody disputed. In S. O. Lilienfeld, J. Ruscio, & S. J. Lynn (Eds.), *Navigating the mindfield: A user's guide to distinguishing science from pseudoscience in mental health* (pp. 175–179). Prometheus Books; Rowman & Littlefield.

Epstein, J. (2009). Cross-examination: Seemingly ubiquitous, purportedly omnipotent, and at risk. *Widener Law Review, 14*(2), 427–451.

Epstein, S. B., & Fontana, F. C. (2010, June 2–5). *Constitutional rights and the best interests of children: Strange bedfellows* [Conference presentation]. 47th Annual Conference of the Association of Family and Conciliation Courts, Denver, CO, United States.

Erard, R. E., & Viglione, D. J. (2014). The Rorschach Performance Assessment System (R-PAS) in child custody evaluations. *Journal of Child Custody: Research, Issues, and Practices, 11*(3), 159–180.

Ericsson, K. A. (2004). Deliberate practice and the acquisition and maintenance of expert performance in medicine and related domains. *Academic Medicine, 79*(10, Suppl), S70–S81.

Evans, J. S. B. T., & Stanovich, K. E. (2013). Dual-process theories of higher cognition: Advancing the debate. *Perspectives on Psychological Science, 8*(3), 223–241. https://doi.org/10.1177/1745691612460685

Evans, K. E., Lee, H., Russell, K. N., Holmes, M. R., Berg, K. A., Bender, A. E., & Prince, D. M. (2022). Adolescent dating violence among youth exposed to intimate partner violence: A systematic review. *Journal of Family Violence, 37,* 1245–1262.

Evans, S. E., Davies, C., & DiLillo, D. (2008). Exposure to domestic violence: A meta-analysis of child and adolescent outcomes. *Aggression and Violent Behavior, 13*(2), 131–140.

Exner, J. E., McDowell, E., Pabst, J., Stackman, W., & Kirk, L. (1963). On the detection of willful falsifications in the MMPI. *Journal of Consulting Psychology, 27*(1), 91–94.

Eyde, L. D., Robertson, G. J., & Krug, S. E. (1993). *Responsible test use: Case studies for assessing human behavior*. American Psychological Association.

Faigman, D. L., Kaye, D. H., Sakes, M. J., & Sanders, J. (Eds.). (2002). *Modern scientific evidence: The law & science of expert testimony* (2nd ed., Vol. 1–4). West Publishing.

Faigman, D. L., Monahan, J., & Slobogin, C. (2014). Group to individual (G2i) inference in scientific expert testimony. *The University of Chicago Law Review, 81*(2), 417–480.

Faigman, D. L., Slobogin, C., & Monahan, J. (2016). Gatekeeping science: Using the structure of scientific research to distinguish between admissibility and weight in expert testimony. *Northwestern University Law Review, 110*(4), 859–904.

Faigman, D. L., Wagner, A., Bonnie, R. J., Casey, B. J., Davis, A., Hoffman, M. B., Jones, O. D., Montague, R., Morse, S. J., Raichle, M., Richeson, R. A., Scott, E. S., Steinberg, L., Taylor-Thompson, K., & Yaffe, G. (2017). *G2i knowledge brief: A knowledge brief of the MacArthur Foundation Research Network on Law and Neuroscience*. MacArthur Foundation Research Network on Law and Neuroscience.

Fanniff, A. M., York, T., & Gutierrez, R. (2023). Developing consensus for culturally informed forensic mental health assessment: Experts' opinions on best practices. *Law and Human Behavior, 47*(3), 385–402. https://doi.org/10.1037/lhb0000531

Fantus, S., & Newman, P. A. (2022). The procreative identities of men in same-sex relationships choosing surrogacy: A new theoretical understanding. *Journal of Family Theory & Review, 14*(2), 254–274. https://doi.org/10.1111/jftr.12456

Farm Bureau Mut. Ins. Co. of Ark., Inc. v. Foote, 14 S.W.3d 512 (Ark. 2000).

Farr, R. H., & Vázquez, C. P. (2020). Stigma experiences, mental health, perceived parenting competence, and parent–child relationships among lesbian, gay, and heterosexual adoptive parents in the United States. *Frontiers in Psychology, 11,* 445. https://doi.org/10.3389/fpsyg.2020.00445

Fazio, R. H. (2001). On the automatic activation of associated evaluations: An overview. *Cognition and Emotion, 15*(2), 115–141. https://doi.org/10.1080/02699930125908

Fazio, R. H. (2007). Attitudes as object-evaluation associations of varying strength. *Social Cognition, 25*(5), 603–637. https://doi.org/10.1521/soco.2007.25.5.603

Fazio, R. H., & Towles-Schwen, T. (1999). The MODE model of attitude-behavior processes. In S. Chaiken & Y. Trope (Eds.), *Dual process theories in social psychology* (pp. 97–119). Guildford Press.

Federal Rules of Evidence. (2024, December 1). U.S. Government Publishing Office. https://www.uscourts.gov/sites/default/files/2025-02/federal-rules-of-evidence-dec-1-2024_0.pdf

Feely, T. H., & Young, M. J. (1998). Humans as lie detectors: Some more second thoughts. *Communication Quarterly, 46*(2), 109–126. https://doi.org/10.1080/01463379809370090

Feinberg, J. M., & Gould, J. W. (2012, June 6–9). *The credible and helpful child custody report* [Conference presentation]. 49th Annual Conference of the Association of Family & Conciliation Courts, Chicago, IL, United States.

Feresin, M., Folla, N., Lapierre, S., & Romito, P. (2018). Family mediation in child custody cases and the concealment of domestic violence. *Affilia, 33*(4), 509–525. https://doi.org/10.1177/0886109918766659

Ferra, F., Blades, M., & Walsh, D. (2022). The effect of the number of interviewers on children's testimonies. *Psychology, Crime & Law, 28*(4), 372–389. https://doi.org/10.1080/1068316X.2021.1909017

Fidler, B. J., & Bala, N. (2010). Children resisting postseparation contact with a parent: Concepts, controversies, and conundrums. *Family Court Review, 48*(1), 10–47. https://doi.org/10.1111/j.1744-1617.2009.01287.x

Fieldstone, L., & Coates, C. A. (2008). High-conflict, domestic abuse or alienating behavior: How do you know? In W. M. Pinsof & J. Lebow (Eds.), *Innovations in interventions with high-conflict families* (pp. 1–45). Association of Family and Conciliation Courts.

Fisher, C. E., Faigman, D. L., & Appelbaum, P. S. (2015). Toward a jurisprudence of psychiatric evidence: Examining the challenges of reasoning from group data in psychiatry to individual decisions in law. *University of Miami Law Review, 69*(3), 685–754.

Fivush, R. (2006). Scripting attachment: Generalized event representations and internal working models. *Attachment & Human Development, 8*(3), 283–289. https://doi.org/10.1080/08912960600858935

Follingstad, D. (1990). Methodological issues and new directions for research on violence in relationships. In D. J. Besharov (Ed.), *Family violence: Research and public policy issues* (pp. 13–25). AEI Press.

Fong, V. C., Hawes, D., & Allen, J. L. (2019). A systematic review of risk and protective factors for externalizing problems in children exposed to intimate partner violence. *Trauma, Violence, & Abuse, 20*(2), 149–167. https://doi.org/10.1177/1524838017692383

Forke, C. M., Catallozzi, M., Localio, A. R., Grisso, J. A., Wiebe, D. J., & Fein, J. A. (2019). Intergenerational effects of witnessing domestic violence: Health of the witnesses and their children. *Preventive Medicine Reports, 15*, 100942. https://doi.org/10.1016/j.pmedr.2019.100942

Fortunato, A., Quintigliano, M., Carone, N., De Simone, S., Lingiardi, V., & Speranza, A. M. (2023). Parenting, dyadic coping, and child emotion regulation in lesbian, gay, and heterosexual parent families through assisted reproduction. *Journal of Reproductive and Infant Psychology*, 1–17. https://doi.org/10.1080/02646838.2023.2287678

Foulidi, X., & Papakitsos, E. C. (2022). The parental involvement in a multicultural educational context. *Journal of Research Initiatives, 6*(1), 8.

Francisquini, M. C. J., Silva, T. M. S., Santos, G. C. D., Barbosa, R. O., Dias, P. H. G., Ruiz, A. B., Silva, J. M. D., & Stabelini Neto, A. (2024). Associations of screen time with symptoms of stress, anxiety, and depression in adolescents. *Revista Paulista de Pediatria: Orgao Oficial da Sociedade de Pediatria de Sao Paulo, 43*(9). https://10.1590/1984-0462/2025/43/2023250

Frank, M. G., & Feeley, T. H. (2003). To catch a liar: Challenges for research in lie detection training. *Journal of Applied Communication Research, 31*(1), 58–75. https://doi.org/10.1080/00909880305377

Frank, M. G., Paolantonio, N., Feeley, T. H., & Servoss, T. J. (2004). Individual and small group accuracy in judging truthful and deceptive communication. *Group Decision and Negotiation, 13*(1), 45–59. https://doi.org/10.1023/B:GRUP.0000011945.85141.af

Franz v. United States, 707 F.2d 582 (D.C. Cir. 1983).

Freeman, B. W. (2020). The psychosocial assessment of contact refusal. In D. Lorandos & W. Bernet (Eds.), *Parental alienation: Science and law* (pp. 44–81). Charles C. Thomas Publisher, Ltd.

Fuhrmann, G. W., & Zibbell, R. A. (2012). *Evaluation for child custody*. Oxford University Press.

Gacono, C. B., & Smith, J. M. (2020). Issues to consider prior to using the R-PAS in a forensic context. *Journal of Projective Psychology and Mental Health, 28*(1), 4–13. https://psycnet.apa.org/record/2021-80090-002

Galatzer-Levy, R., Baerger, D. R., Gould, J. W., & Nye, S. (2002). Evaluating the evaluation: How to understand and critique custody evaluations. In R. Brown & L. Morgan (Eds.), *2003 Family Law Update* (pp. 139-211). Aspen Publishing.

Galatzer-Levy, R., Gould, J. W., & Martindale, D. A. (2009). From empirical findings to custody evaluations. In R. Galatzer-Levy, L. Kraus, & B. Galatzer-Levy (Eds.), *Scientific basis of child custody evaluations* (2nd ed., pp. 1–48). John Wiley & Sons.

Gammill v. Jack Williams Chevrolet, Inc., 972 S.W.2d 713 (Tex. 1998).

Ganrud v. Smith, 206 N.W.2d 311 (Iowa 1993).

Garber, B. D. (2004). Parental alienation in light of attachment theory: Consideration of the broader implications for child development, clinical practice, and forensic process. *Journal of Child Custody, 1*(4), 49–76. https://doi.org/10.1300/J190v01n04_04

Garber, B. D. (2007). Developing a structured interview tool for children embroiled in family litigation and forensic mental health services: The query grid. *Journal of Forensic Psychology Practice, 7*(1), 1–18. https://doi.org/10.1300/J158v07n01_01

Garber, B. D. (2009). Attachment methodology in custody evaluation: Four hurdles standing between developmental theory and forensic application. *Journal of Child Custody, 6*(1-2), 38–61. https://doi.org/10.1080/15379410902894841

Garber, B. D. (2012). Security by association? Mapping attachment theory onto family law practice. *Family Court Review, 50*(3), 467–470. https://doi.org/10.1111/j.1744-1617.2012.01461.x

Garber, B. D. (2014). The chameleon child: Children as actors in the high conflict divorce drama. *Journal of Child Custody, 11*(1), 25–40. https://doi.org/10.1080/15379418.2014.892805

Garber, B. D. (2016). Exploring a process-oriented forensic family observation protocol. *Family Court Review, 54*(2), 261–276. https://doi.org/10.1111/fcre.12217

Garber, B. D. (2020a). Dynamics, not diagnoses. *Family Court Review, 58*(2), 368–370.

Garber, B. D. (2020b). Sherlock Holmes and the case of resist/refuse dynamics: Confirmatory bias and abductive inference in child custody evaluations. *Family Court Review, 58*(2), 386–402. https://doi.org/10.1111/fcre.12478

Garber, B. D. (2024). A structured rubric for evaluating the many systemic variables that can contribute to parent–child contact problems (PCCP). *Family Court Review, 62*(2), 343–358. https://doi.org/10.1111/fcre.12785

Garber, B. D., Mulchay, C., & Knuth, S. (2023). Questionnaires in child custody evaluations: The forgotten ubiquitous medium. *Journal of Family Trauma, Child Custody & Child Development, 20*(1), 20–36. https://doi.org/10.1080/26904586.2022.2086657

Garber, B. D., Prescott, D. E., & Mulchay, C. (2022). *The family law professional's field guide to high-conflict litigation: Dynamics, not diagnoses*. American Bar Association, Family Law Section.

Garber, B. D., & Simon, R. A. (2018). Individual adult psychometric testing and child custody evaluations: If the shoe doesn't fit, don't wear it. *Journal of the American Academy of Matrimonial Lawyers, 30*(2), 325–341.

Garber, B. D., & Simon, R. A. (2024a). Looking beyond the sorting hat: Deconstructing the "five factor model" of alienation. *Family Transitions, 65*(1), 5–31. https://doi.org/10.1080/10502556.2023.2262359

Garber, B. D., & Simon, R. A. (2024b). Moving toward consensus: Joining Bernet and Baker, Emery, and Griffin to better understand the dynamics of parent–child contact problems (PCCP). *Family Transitions, 65*(1), 65–77. https://doi.org/10.1080/28375300.2024.2313376

Gardner, F. (2000). Methodological issues in the direct observation of parent–child interaction: Do observational findings reflect the natural behavior of participants? *Clinical Child and Family Psychology Review, 3*(3), 185–198. https://doi.org/10.1023/A:1009503409699

Gardner, R. A. (1985). Recent trends in divorce and custody litigation. [A Publication of the American Academy of Psychoanalysis]. *The Academy Forum, 29*(2), 3–7.

Gardner, R. A. (1987). *The parental alienation syndrome and the differentiation between fabricated and genuine child sex abuse*. Creative Therapeutics.

Gardner, R. A. (1992). *The parental alienation syndrome*. Creative Therapeutics.

Gardner, R. A. (1998). Recommendations for dealing with parents who induce a parental alienation syndrome in their children. *Journal of Divorce & Remarriage, 28*(3-4), 1–23. https://doi.org/10.1300/J087v28n03_01

Garrison, Y. L., Tang, S. S., & Lee, B. A. (2024). Liberation psychology perspectives for Asian American clients. *Journal of Health Service Psychology, 50*, 3–13. https://doi.org/10.1007/s42843-024-00098-z

Gato, J., Leal, D., Biasutti, C., Tasker, F., & Fontaine, A. M. (2021). Building a rainbow family: Parenthood aspirations of lesbian, gay, bisexual, and transgender/gender diverse individuals. In N. A. de Morais, F. Scorsolini-Comin, & E. Cerqueira-Santos (Eds.), *Parenting and couple relationships among LGBTQ+ people in diverse contexts* (pp. 193–213). Springer Nature Switzerland AG. https://doi.org/10.1007/978-3-030-84189-8_12

Gawande, A. (2011). The checklist manifesto: How to get things right. *Journal of Nursing Regulation, 1*(4), 64. https://doi.org/10.1016/S2155-8256(15)30310-0

Gawronski, B., & Bodenhausen, G. V. (2006). Associative and propositional processes in evaluation: An integrative review of implicit and explicit attitude change. *Psychological Bulletin, 132*(5), 692–731. https://doi.org/10.1037/0033-2909.132.5.692

Gawronski, B., & Bodenhausen, G. V. (2007). Unraveling the processes underlying evaluation: Attitudes from the perspective of the APE model. *Social Cognition, 25*(5), 687–717. https://doi.org/10.1521/soco.2007.25.5.687

Gawronski, B., Brannon, S. M., & Bodenhausen, G. V. (2017). The associative-propositional duality in the representation, formation, and expression of attitudes. In R. Deutsch, B. Gawronski, & W. Hoffman (Eds.), *Reflective and impulsive determinants of human behavior* (pp. 103–118). Routledge/Taylor & Francis Group.

Gawronski, B., LeBel, E. P., & Peters, K. R. (2007). What do implicit measures tell us?: Scrutinizing the validity of three common assumptions. *Perspectives on Psychological Science, 2*(2), 181–193. https://doi.org/10.1111/j.1745-6916.2007.00036.x

Gelles, R. J. (1972). *The violent home: A study of physical aggression between husbands and wives*. Sage Publications.

Gemberling, T. M., & Cramer, R. J. (2014). Expert testimony on sensitive myth-ridden topics: Ethics and recommendations for psychological professionals. *Professional Psychology: Research and Practice, 45*(2), 120–127. https://doi.org/10.1037/a0036184

General Electric Co. v. Joiner, 522 U.S. 136 (1997).

Giaimo v. Florida Autosport, Inc., 154 So.3d 385 (Fla. 1st DCA 2014).

Giannelli, P. C. (1980). The admissibility of novel scientific evidence: Frye v. United States, a half century later. *Columbia Law Review, 80*(6), 1197–1250. https://doi.org/10.2307/1122061

Gilbert v. Daimler Chrysler Corp., 685 N.W.2d 391 (Mich. 2004).

Gilovich, T., Lepper, M., Nisbett, R., & Ward, A. (2022). Lee D. Ross (1942–2021). *American Psychologist, 77*(2), 308–309. https://doi.org/10.1037/amp0000916

Gilstrap, L. L., Fraser-Thill, R. L., & Ceci, S. J. (2001). Children's source monitoring. *Imagination, Cognition and Personality, 21*(2), 176–180.

Giovanardi, G., Fortunato, A., Di Giannantonio, B., Nimbi, F., Carone, N., & Lingiardi, V. (2024). Closing circles: Family-of-origin reconciliations following the transition to parenthood in lesbian and gay parents through assisted reproduction. *Journal of Gay & Lesbian Mental Health*, 29(2), 204–231. https://doi.org/10.1080/19359705.2024.2310234

Glancy, G. D., & Saini, M. (2009). The confluence of evidence-based practice and *Daubert* within the fields of forensic psychiatry and the law. *The Journal of the American Academy of Psychiatry and the Law, 37*(4), 438–441.

Golanski, A. (2001). Why legal scholars get *Daubert* wrong: A contextualist explanation of law's epistemology. *Whittier Law Review, 22*(3), 653–721.

Goldberg, A. E. (2023). LGBTQ-parent families: Diversity, intersectionality, and social context. *Current Opinion in Psychology, 49,* 101517. https://doi.org/10.1016/j.copsyc.2022.101517

Goldberg, A. E., Silvert, L., & Farr, R. H. (2024). Family-building desires among adopted adolescents with lesbian, gay, and heterosexual parents. *Family Relations, 73*(4), 2392–2414. https://doi.org/10.1111/fare.13042

Goldberg, A. E., Toomey, R. B., & Abreu, R. L. (2024). "Don't say gay": Implications for outness and desire to move among LGBTQ+ parents in Florida. *Sexuality Research & Social Policy, 21*(3), 1189–1205. https://doi.org/10.1007/s13178-024-00982-9

Goldenson, J. (2024). Trauma-informed forensic mental health assessment of plaintiffs alleging harms from childhood abuse. In G. Young (Ed.), *Handbook of psychological injury and law.* Springer Nature Switzerland AG.

Goldenson, J., Brodsky, S. L., & Kukor, T. (in press). Aspirational forensic mental health assessment. *Journal of American Psychiatry and the Law.*

Goldenson, J., Brodsky, S. L., & Perlin, M. L. (2022). Trauma-informed forensic mental health assessment: Practical implications, ethical tensions, and alignment with therapeutic jurisprudence principles. *Psychology, Public Policy, and Law, 28*(2), 226–239. https://doi.org/10.1037/law0000339

Gondolf, E. W. (2002). *Batterer intervention systems: Issues, outcomes, and recommendations.* Sage Publications.

Gonzales v. Exec. Airlines, Inc., 236 F.R.D. 73 (D.P.R. 2006).

Goodman, D. (2011). *Promoting diversity and social justice: Educating people from privileged groups.* Routledge.

Gordon, S. (2016). Crossing the line: *Daubert,* dual roles, and the admissibility of forensic mental health testimony. *Cardozo Law Review, 37*(4), 1345–1399. https://cardozolawreview.com/wp-content/uploads/2018/08/GORDON.37.4.pdf

Gottman, J. M., Katz, L. F., & Hooven, C. (1996). Parental meta-emotion philosophy and the emotional life of families: Theoretical models and preliminary data. *Journal of Family Psychology, 10*(3), 243–268. https://doi.org/10.1037/0893-3200.10.3.243

Gould, J. W. (1998). *Conducting scientifically crafted child custody evaluations.* Sage Publications.

Gould, J. W. (1999). An interdisciplinary collaborative model for developing psycholegal questions in court ordered child custody evaluations. *Juvenile & Family Court Journal, 50*(1), 43–52. https://doi.org/10.1111/j.1755-6988.1999.tb01277.x

Gould, J. W. (2006). *Conducting scientifically crafted child custody evaluations* (2nd ed.). Professional Resource Press.

Gould, J. W. (2018). Challenges to the admissibility of child custody advisory reports: The *Daubert* challenge. In M. J. Ackerman, A. W. Kane, & J. W. Gould (2017). *Psychological experts in divorce actions* (6th ed., Suppl.). Aspen Publishing.

Gould, J. W., & Dale, M. (2022). Reviewing child custody evaluations: Using science to maximize reliability & minimize bias. In H. Hall & J. G. Poirier (Eds.), *Forensic psychology and neuropsychology for criminal and civil cases* (2nd ed., pp. 575–604). Taylor & Francis.

Gould, J. W., Dale, M., Fisher, N. B., & Gould, M. R. (2016). Scientific and professional knowledge for family court: Legal expectations of experts. In L. Drozd, M. Saini, & N. Olesen (Eds.), *Parenting plan evaluations: Applied research for the family court* (2nd ed., pp. 3–44). Oxford University Press. https://doi.org/10.1093/med:psych/9780199396580.003.0001

Gould, J. W., & Flens, J. (2020, November 9–13). *Thinking differently about the value of collateral information* [Conference presentation]. Association of Family & Conciliation Courts 14th Symposium on Child Custody, Las Vegas, NV, United States.

Gould, J. W., Flens, J., & Rappaport, S. (2018). Use of psychological tests in child custody evaluations: Effects of validity scale scores on evaluator confidence in interpreting clinical scales. In R. Rogers & S. D. Bender (Eds.), *Clinical assessment of malingering and deception* (4th ed., pp. 497–513). Guilford Press.

Gould, J. W., & Martindale, D. A. (2005). A second call for clinical humility and judicial vigilance: Comments on Tippins and Wittmann (2005). *Family Court Review, 43*(2), 253–259. https://doi.org/10.1111/j.1744-1617.2005.00025.x

Gould, J. W., & Martindale, D. A. (2007). *The art and science of child custody evaluations.* Guilford Press.

Gould, J. W., & Martindale, D. A. (2008). Custody evaluation reports: The case for references to the peer-reviewed professional literature. *Journal of Child Custody, 5*(3-4), 217–227. https://doi.org/10.1080/15379410802583700

Gould, J. W., & Martindale, D. A. (2009a). Including children in decision making about custodial placement. *Journal of the American Academy of Matrimonial Lawyers., 22*(2), 303–314.

Gould, J. W., & Martindale, D. A. (2009b). Specific questions guide child custody investigations. *The Matrimonial Strategist,* 1–3.

Gould, J. W., & Martindale, D. A. (2013). Child custody evaluations: Current literature and practical applications. In R. K. Otto (Ed.), *Handbook of psychology: Vol. 11. Forensic psychology* (2nd ed., pp. 101–138). John Wiley & Sons.

Gould, J. W., Martindale, D. A., & Flens, J. R. (2009). Responsible use of psychological tests in child custody assessment. In R. Galatzer-Levy, L. Kraus, & B. Galatzer-Levy (Eds.), *Scientific basis of child custody evaluations* (2nd ed., pp. 85–124). John Wiley & Sons.

Gould, J. W., Martindale, D. A., & Flens, J. R. (2013). Responsible use of psychological tests: Ethical and professional practice concerns. In D. Saklofske, C. Cecil Reynolds, & V. Schwean (Eds.), *The Oxford handbook of child psychological assessment.* Oxford University Press.

Gould, J. W., Martindale, D. A., Tippins, T. M., & Wittmann, J. P. (2011). Testifying experts and non-testifying trial consultants: Appreciating the differences. *Journal of Child Custody, 8*(1-2), 32–46. https://doi.org/10.1080/15379418.2010.547442

Gould, J. W., Mayefsky, A., & Stembleck, P. (2016). Constitutional rights and the expert opinions addressing parental access and decision-making. *Matrimonial Strategist.*

Gould, J. W., & Mulchay, C. (2023). Child custody evaluations. In D. DeMatteo & K. Scherr (Eds.), *Oxford handbook of psychology and law.* Oxford University Press.

Gould, J. W., & Mulchay, C. (in press). Importance and challenges of scientific & specialized knowledge in expert testimony. In L. Drozd, M. Saini, & N. Olesen (Eds.), *Parenting plan evaluations: Applied research for the family court* (3rd ed.). Oxford University Press.

Gould, J. W., & Nolletti, J. J. (2015). Preparing clients for custody evaluations: A call for critical examination. *Journal of the American Academy of Matrimonial Lawyers, 27*(2), 359–389. https://www.aaml.org/wp-content/uploads/MAT201_5.pdf

Gould, J. W., & Posthuma, A. (2017). The unsubstantiated claims of Turkat's Harmful effects of child custody evaluations on children.*Court Review: The Journal of the American Judges Association, 52*(4), 160–167. https://digitalcommons.unl.edu/cgi/viewcontent.cgi?article=1568&context=ajacourtreview

Gould, J. W. & Rappaport, S. (2016). Proper use of psychological test results in child custody evaluations. *Matrimonial Strategist,* 34(12), 1, 4.

Gould, J. W., & Stahl, P. M. (2000). The art and science of child custody evaluations: Integrating clinical and forensic mental health models. *Family Court Review, 38*(3), 392–414. https://doi.org/10.1111/j.174-1617.2000.tb00581.x

Gould, J. W., & Stahl, P. M. (2001). Never paint by the numbers: A response to Kelly & Lamb (2000), Solomon (2001), and Lamb & Kelly (2001). *Family Court Review, 39*(4), 372–376. https://doi.org/10.1111/j.174-1617.2001.tb00619.x

Graham, J. R. (2000). *MMPI-2: Assessing personality and psychopathology* (3rd ed.). Oxford University Press.

Graham, P. (2022). Transgender children and young people: How the evidence can point the way forward. *BJPsych Bulletin, 47*(2), 98–104. https://doi.org/10.1192/bjb.2022.3

Graham-Kevan, N., & Archer, J. (2009). Control tactics and partner violence in heterosexual relationships. *Evolution and Human Behavior, 30*(6), 445–452. https://doi.org/10.1016/j.evolhumbehav.2009.06.007

Greenberg, L. R., & Gould, J. W. (2001). The treating expert: A hybrid role with firm boundaries. *Professional Psychology: Research and Practice, 32*(5), 469–478. https://doi.org/10.1037/0735-7028.32.5.469

Greenberg, L. R., Gould, J. W., Gould-Saltman, D. J., & Stahl, P. M. (2003). Is the child's therapist part of the problem? What judges, attorneys, and mental health professionals need to know about court-related treatment for children. *Family Law Quarterly, 37*(2), 241–271.

Greenberg, S. A., & Shuman, D. W. (1997). Irreconcilable conflict between therapeutic and forensic roles. *Professional Psychology: Research and Practice, 28*(1), 50–57. https://doi.org/10.1037/0735-7028.28.1.50

Grigoropoulos, I. (2022). Gay fatherhood experiences and challenges through the lens of minority stress theory. *Journal of Homosexuality, 70*(9), 1867–1889. https://doi.org/10.1080/00918369.2022.2043131

Grisso, T. (1986). *Evaluating competencies: Forensic assessments and instruments*. Plenum. (Volume 7 of Perspectives in law & psychology).

Grob, G. N. (1991). Origins of DSM-I: A study in appearance and reality. *The American Journal of Psychiatry, 148*(4), 421–431. https://doi.org/10.1176/ajp.148.4.421

Gross, E. B., Fine, R. D., Gülgöz, S., Olson, K. R., & Gelman, S. A. (2024). Children's gender essentialism and prejudice: Testing causal links via an experimental manipulation. *Developmental Science, 27*(5), e13532. https://doi.org/10.1111/desc.13532

Gross, S. R., & Mnookin, J. L. (2003). Expert information and expert evidence: A preliminary taxonomy. *Seton Hall Law Review, 34*(1), 141–189. https://repository.law.umich.edu/articles/570/

Grossman v. State Board of Psychology, 825 A.2d 748 (Pa. 2003).

Grusec, J. E., & Hastings, P. D. (Eds.). (2015). *Handbook of socialization: Theory and research* (2nd ed.). Guilford Press.

Grych, J. H., & Fincham, F. D. (1990). Marital conflict and children's adjustment: A cognitive-contextual framework. *Psychological Bulletin, 108*(2), 267–290. https://doi.org/10.1037/0033-2909.108.2.267

Gülgöz, S., Alonso, D. J., Olson, K. R., & Martin, C. L. (2024). Memory biases for gender-typed images in a gender-diverse group of children. *British Journal of Developmental Psychology*, 43(2), 305–318. https://doi.org/10.1111/bjdp.12490

Günaydin, Y., & Zincir, H. (2024). The effect of child–parent relationship therapy-based play support on parental stress and acceptance, and child behaviours in children who witness family violence: Randomized controlled study. *Australian and New Zealand Journal of Family Therapy, 45*(3), 336–348. https://doi.org/10.1002/anzf.1579

Haack, S. (2013). A match made on Earth: Getting real about science and the law. *SSRN, 36*(1), 39–56. https://doi.org/10.2139/ssrn.2338103

Hahn, A., & Gawronski, B. (2019). Facing one's implicit biases: From awareness to acknowledgment. *Journal of Personality and Social Psychology, 116*(5), 769–794. https://doi.org/10.1037/pspi0000155

Haig, B. D. (2014). *Investigating the psychological world: Scientific method in the behavioral sciences*. Massachusetts Institute of Technology Press. https://doi.org/10.7551/mitpress/9780262027366.001.0001

Halim, M. L. D., Atwood, S., Osornio, A. C., Pauker, K., Dunham, Y., Olson, K. R., & Gaither, S. E. (2023). Parent and self-socialization of gender intergroup attitudes, perceptions, and behaviors among ethnically and geographically diverse young children. *Developmental Psychology, 59*(10), 1933–1950. https://doi.org/10.1037/dev0001586

Halim, M. L. D., Glazier, J. J., Martinez, M. A., Stanaland, A., Gaither, S. E., Dunham, Y., Pauker, K., & Olson, K. R. (2024). Gender attitudes and gender discrimination among ethnically and geographically diverse young children. *Infant and Child Development, 33*(3), e2482. https://doi.org/10.1002/icd.2482

Hamby, S. L. (2009). *Battered women's protective strategies*. National Resource Center on Domestic Violence and Pennsylvania Coalition Against Domestic Violence.

Hamby, S. (2014). Intimate partner and sexual violence research: Scientific progress, scientific challenges, and gender. *Trauma, Violence, and Abuse, 15*(3), 149–158. https://doi.org/10.1177/1524838014520723

Hamby, S. (2016). Self-report measures that do not produce gender parity in intimate partner violence: A multi-study investigation. *Psychology of Violence, 6*(2), 323–335. https://doi.org/10.1037/a0038207

Hamby, S. (2017). A scientific answer to a scientific question: The gender debate on intimate partner violence. *Trauma, Violence, and Abuse, 18*(2), 145–154. https://doi.org/10.1177/1524838015596963

Hammer, B. (2024). Legal decision-making. *Family Advocate, 47*(1), 24–27.

Hans, J. D., Hardesty, J. L., Haselschwerdt, M. L., & Frey, L. M. (2014). The effects of domestic violence allegations on custody evaluators' recommendations. *Journal of Family Psychology, 28*(6), 957–966. https://doi.org/10.1037/fam0000025

Hardcastle, V. G. (2020). Group-to-individual (G2i) inferences: Challenges in modeling how the U.S. court system uses brain data. *Artificial Intelligence and Law, 28*(1), 51–68. https://doi.org/10.1007/s10506-018-9234-0

Hardesty, J. L., Crossman, K. A., Haselschwerdt, M. L., Raffaelli, M., Ogolsky, B. G., & Johnson, M. P. (2015). Toward a standard approach to operationalizing coercive control and classifying violence types. *Journal of Marriage and Family, 77*(4), 833–843.

Hardesty, J. L., & Ogolsky, B. G. (2020). A socioecological perspective on intimate partner violence research: A decade in review. *Journal of Marriage and Family, 82*(1), 454–477. https://doi.org/10.1111/jomf.12652

Hardesty, J. L., Ogolsky, B. G., & Akinbode, T. D. (2024). Coparenting and intimate partner violence. *Family Court Review, 62*(1), 131–145.

Hardesty, J. L., Raffaella, M., Khaw, L., Mitchell, E., Hasweschwerdt, M., & Crossman, K. (2012). An integrative theoretical model of intimate partner violence, coparenting after separation, and maternal and child well-being. *Journal of Family Theory & Review, 4*(4), 318–331. https://doi.org/10.1111/j.1756-2589.2012.00139.x

Harper, B., Nwabuzor Ogbonnaya, I., & McCullough, K. C. (2018). The effect of intimate partner violence on the psychosocial development of toddlers. *Journal of Interpersonal Violence, 33*(16), 2512–2536.

Harris, M., & Fallot, R. D. (2001). Envisioning a trauma-informed service system: A vital paradigm shift. *New Directions for Mental Health Services, 89*(89), 3–22.

Harris-Brit, A., & Jones, A. (2022, November 10–12). *Diversity and the revised AFCC guidelines: Why one size does not fit all* [Conference presentation]. Association of Family and Conciliation Courts 15th Symposium on Child Custody, Las Vegas, NV, United States.

Hart, M., & Secunda, P. (2009). A matter of context: Social framework evidence in employment discrimination class actions. *Fordham Law Review, 78*(1), 37–70.

Hasel, L. E., & Kassin, S. M. (2009). On the presumption of evidentiary independence: Can confessions corrupt eyewitness identifications? *Psychological Science, 20*(1), 122–126. https://doi.org/10.1111/j.1467-9280.2008.02262.x

Hathaway, S. R., & McKinley, J. C. (1943). *The Minnesota Multiphasic Personality Inventory.* (Rev. ed.). University of Minnesota Press.

Heilbrun, K. (2001). *Principles of forensic mental health assessment*. Kluwer Academic/Plenum Press.

Heilbrun, K., DeMatteo, D., Marczyk, G., & Goldstein, A. M. (2008). Standards of practice and care in forensic mental health assessment: Legal, professional, and principles-based considerations. *Psychology, Public Policy, and Law, 14*(1), 1–26. https://doi.org/10.1037/1076-8971.14.1.1

Heilbrun, K., Grisso, T., & Goldstein, A. (2008). *Foundations of forensic mental health assessment*. Kluwer.

Heilbrun, K., Rogers, R., & Otto, R. (2002). Forensic assessment: Current status and future directions. In J. R. P. Ogloff (Ed.), *Taking psychology and law into the twenty-first century* (pp. 119–146). Kluwer Academic/Plenum Publishers.

Hembree-Kigin, T. L., & McNeil, C. B. (2013). *Parent–child interaction therapy*. Springer Science & Business Media.

Henry, C. S., Sheffield Morris, A., & Harrist, A. W. (2015). Family resilience: Moving into the third wave. *Family Relations, 64*(1), 22–43.

Herman, S. P., & the American Academy of Child and Adolescent Psychiatry. (1997). Practice parameters for child custody evaluation. *Journal of the American Academy of Child & Adolescent Psychiatry, 36*(10, Suppl.), 57S–68S.

Hershkowitz, I., & Lamb, M. E. (2020). Allegation rates and credibility assessment in forensic interviews of alleged child abuse victims: Comparing the revised and standard NICHD protocols. *Psychology, Public Policy, and Law, 26*(2), 176–184.

Hershkowitz, I., Lamb, M. E., Katz, C., & Malloy, L. C. (2015). Does enhanced rapport-building alter the dynamics of investigative interviews with suspected victims of intra-familial abuse? *Journal of Police and Criminal Psychology, 30*(1), 6–14. https://doi.org/10.1007/s11896-013-9136-8

Hershkowitz, I., Orbach, Y., Lamb, M. E., Sternberg, K. J., & Horowitz, D. (2006). Dynamics of forensic interviews with suspected abuse victims who do not disclose abuse. *Child Abuse & Neglect, 30*(7), 753–769. https://doi.org/10.1016/j.chiabu.2005.10.016

Hetherington, E. M. (1999). Should we stay together for the sake of the children? In E. M. Hetherington (Ed.), *Coping with divorce, single parenting, and remarriage: A risk and resiliency perspective* (pp. 93–116). Lawrence Erlbaum Associates.

Hoegler, S., Vetterly, S., & Cummings, E. M. (2024). Evaluation of a couple- and family-based intervention: Implications for the fathering vulnerability hypothesis. *Parenting: Science and Practice, 24*(1), 1–29. https://doi.org/10.1080/15295192.2023.2254344

Hofmann, W., & Wilson, T. D. (2010). Consciousness, introspection, and the adaptive unconscious. In B. Gawronski & B. K. Payne (Eds.), *Handbook of implicit social cognition: Measurement, theory, and applications* (pp. 197–215). Guilford Press.

Holland, R. W., Verplanken, B., & Van Knippenberg, A. (2002). On the nature of attitude-behavior relations: The strong guide, the weak follow. *European Journal of Social Psychology, 32*(6), 869–876. https://doi.org/10.1002/ejsp.135

Holmes, K., Whitman, M., Mulchay, C., & Ben-Porath, Y. (in press). *MMPI-3 in child custody and parental fitness settings*. Psychological Assessment.

Holt, S., Buckley, H., & Whelan, S. (2008). The impact of exposure to domestic violence on children and young people: A review of the literature. *Child Abuse & Neglect, 32*(8), 797–810. https://doi.org/10.1016/j.chiabu.2008.02.004

Holtzworth-Munroe, A., Beck, C. J., Applegate, A. G., Adams, J. M., Rossi, F. S., Jiang, L. J., Tomlinson, C. S., & Hale, D. F. (2021). Intimate partner violence (IPV) and family dispute resolution: A randomized controlled trial comparing shuttle mediation, videoconferencing mediation, and litigation. *Psychology, Public Policy, and Law, 27*(1), 45–64. https://doi.org/10.1037/law0000278

Hopwood, C. J. (2018). A framework for treating DSM-5 alternative model for personality disorder features. *Personality and Mental Health, 12*(2), 107–125. https://doi.org/10.1002/pmh.1414

Horton, C. (2023). Institutional cisnormativity and educational injustice: Trans children's experiences in primary and early secondary education in the UK. *The British Journal of Educational Psychology, 93*(1), 73–90. https://doi.org/10.1111/bjep.12540

Horvath, L. S., Logan, T. K., & Walker, R. (2002). Child custody cases: A content analysis of evaluations in practice. *Professional Psychology: Research and Practice, 33*(6), 557–565. https://doi.org/10.1037/0735-7028.33.6.557

Hsee, C. K., Yang, Y., & Li, X. (2019). Relevance insensitivity: A new look at some old biases. *Organizational Behavior and Human Decision Processes, 153*, 13–26. https://doi.org/10.1016/j.obhdp.2019.05.002

Hughes, D., Rodriguez, J., Smith, E. P., Johnson, D. J., Stevenson, H. C., & Spicer, P. (2006). Parents' ethnic–racial socialization practices: A review of research and directions for future study. *Developmental Psychology, 42*(5), 747–770. https://doi.org/10.1037/0012-1649.42.5.747

Huguley, J. P., Wang, M. T., Vasquez, A. C., & Guo, J. (2019). Parental ethnic–racial socialization practices and the construction of children of color's ethnic–racial identity: A research synthesis and meta-analysis. *Psychological Bulletin, 145*(5), 437–458. https://doi.org/10.1037/bul0000187

Hume, D. (1777 ed.). *An enquiry concerning the human understanding and concerning the principles of morals.*

Hungerford, A., Wait, S. K., Fritz, A. M., & Clements, C. M. (2012). Exposure to intimate partner violence and children's psychological adjustment, cognitive functioning, and social competence: A review. *Aggression and Violent Behavior, 17*(4), 373–382. https://doi.org/10.1016/j.avb.2012.04.002

Hynan, D. J. (2003). Parent–child observations in custody evaluations. *Family Court Review, 41*(2), 214–223. https://doi.org/10.1111/j.174-1617.2003.tb00885.x

Hynan, D. J. (2013). Use of the Personality Assessment Inventory in child custody evaluation. *Open Access Journal of Forensic Psychology, 5*, 120–133.

Hynan, D. J. (2014). *Child custody evaluation: New theoretical applications and research.* Charles C. Thomas.

Hynan, D. J. (2018). *Parenting plans: Meeting the challenges with facts and analysis.* American Bar Association.

Idaho v. Wright, 497 U.S. 805 (1990).

In re Marriage of Burgess, 913 P.2d 473 (Cal. 1996).

In re Marriage of Lamusga (Navarro v. LaMusga), 88 P.3d 81(Cal. 2004).

Insana, S. P., Foley, K. P., Montgomery-Downs, H. E., Kolko, D. J., & McNeil, C. B. (2014). Children exposed to intimate partner violence demonstrate disturbed sleep and impaired functional outcomes. *Psychological Trauma: Theory, Research, Practice, and Policy, 6*(3), 290–298. https://doi.org/10.1037/a0033108

Insel, T., Cuthbert, B., Garvey, M., Heinssen, R., Pine, D. S., Quinn, K., Sanislow, C., & Wang, P. (2010). Research domain criteria (RDoC): Toward a new classification framework for research on mental disorders. *The American Journal of Psychiatry, 167*(7), 748–751. https://doi.org/10.1176/appi.ajp.2010.09091379

Isaacs, M. B., George, C., & Marvin, R. S. (2009). Utilizing attachment measures in child custody evaluations: Incremental validity. *Journal of Child Custody, 6*(1-2), 139–162. https://doi.org/10.1080/15379410902894882

Jacobellis v. Ohio, 378 U.S. 184 (1964).

Jaffe, P. G., Crooks, C. V., & Poisson, S. E. (2003). Common misconceptions in addressing domestic violence in child custody disputes. *Juvenile & Family Court Journal, 54*(4), 57–67. https://doi.org/10.1111/j.1755-6988.2003.tb00086.x

Jaffe, P. G., Johnston, J. R., Crooks, C. V., & Bala, N. (2008). Custody disputes involving allegations of domestic violence: Toward a differentiated approach to parenting plans. *Family Court Review, 46*(3), 500–522. https://doi.org/10.1111/j.1744-1617.2008.00216.x

James, W. (1890). *The principles of psychology*. Henry Holt & Co.

Jenkins, K. (2017). Rape myths and domestic abuse myths as hermeneutical injustices. *Journal of Applied Philosophy, 34*(2), 191–205.

Jeong, J., Adhia, A., Bhatia, A., McCoy, D. C., & Yousafzai, A. K. (2020). Intimate partner violence, maternal and paternal parenting, and early child development. *Pediatrics, 145*(6), e20192955. https://doi.org/10.1542/peds.2019-2955

Johnson, M. P. (1995). Patriarchal terrorism and common couple violence: Two forms of violence against women. *Journal of Marriage and Family, 57*(2), 283–294. https://doi.org/10.2307/353683

Johnson, M. P. (2008). *A typology of domestic violence: Intimate terrorism, violent resistance, and situational couple violence*. Northeastern University Press.

Johnson, M. P., & Leone, J. M. (2005). The differential effects of intimate terrorism and situational couple violence: Findings from the National Violence Against Women Survey. *Journal of Family Issues, 26*(3), 322–349. https://doi.org/10.1177/0192513X04270345

Johnston, J. R. (2006). A child-centered approach to high-conflict and domestic-violence families: Differential assessment and interventions. *Journal of Family Studies, 12*(1), 15–35. https://doi.org/10.5172/jfs.327.12.1.15

Johnston, J. R., & Campbell, L. E. G. (1993). A clinical typology of interparental violence in disputed-custody divorces. *American Journal of Orthopsychiatry, 63*(2), 190–199. https://doi.org/10.1037/h0079425

Johnston, J. R., & Roseby, V. (1997). *In the name of the child: A developmental approach to understanding and helping children of conflicted and violent divorce*. Free Press.

Johnston, J. R., & Sullivan, M. J. (2020). Parental alienation: In search of common ground for a more differentiated theory. *Family Court Review, 58*(2), 270–292. https://doi.org/10.1111/fcre.12472

Joint Task Force for the Development of Telepsychology Guidelines for Psychologists. (2013). Guidelines for the practice of telepsychology. *American Psychologist, 68*(9), 791–800. https://doi.org/10.1037/a0035001

Judge, A., & Deutsch, R. M. (Eds.). (2016). *Overcoming parent–child contact problems: Family-based interventions for resistance, rejection, and alienation*. Oxford University Press.

Kahneman, D. (2011). *Thinking, fast and slow*. Farrar, Straus & Giroux.

Kalich, L., Carmichael, B. D., Masson, T., & Blacker, D. (2007). Evaluating the evaluator: Guidelines for legal professionals in assessing the competency of evaluations in termination of parental rights cases. *The Journal of Psychiatry & Law, 35*(3), 365–397. https://doi.org/10.1177/009318530703500307

Karatekin, C., Mason, S. M., Riegelman, A., Bakker, C., Hunt, S., Gresham, B., Corcoran, F., & Barnes, A. (2023). Adverse childhood experiences (ACEs): An overview of definitions, measures, and methods. *Handbook of adverse childhood experiences: A framework for collaborative health promotion*, 31–45.

Kasturirangan, A., Krishnan, S., & Riger, S. (2004). The impact of culture and minority status on women's experience of domestic violence. *Trauma, Violence & Abuse, 5*(4), 318–332.

Katz, E. (2019). Coercive control, domestic violence, and a five-factor framework: Five factors that influence closeness, distance, and strain in mother–child relationships. *Violence Against Women, 25*(15), 1829–1853. https://doi.org/10.1177/1077801218824998

Katz, E. (2022). *Coercive control in children's and mothers' lives*. Oxford University Press.

Katz, E., Nikupeteri, A., & Laitinen, M. (2020). When coercive control continues to harm children: Post-separation fathering, stalking and domestic violence. *Child Abuse Review, 29*(4), 310–324. https://doi.org/10.1002/car.2611

Katz, L. F., Maliken, A. C., & Stettler, N. M. (2012). Parental meta-emotion philosophy: A review of research and theoretical framework. *Child Development Perspectives, 6*(4), 417–422.

Kaufman, J., & Henrich, C. (2000). Exposure to violence and early childhood trauma. In C. H. Zeanah, Jr., (Ed.), *Handbook of infant mental health* (2nd ed., pp. 195–207). Guilford Press.

Kaushal, S. (2014). Different aspects of intercultural nonverbal communication: A study. *Asian Journal of Advanced Basic Science, 2*(2), 31–39.

Kellerman, J., Faruqee, S., Busch, B., & Krauss, D. (2018), Expert opinion: Hot tubbing as an alternative to adversarial expert testimony. Retrieved May 14, 2022, from http://ap-ls.wildapricot.org/resources/EmailTemplates/2018_04%20April%20AP-LS%20Newsletter/ExpertOpinionApril.pdf

Kelly, J. B., & Emery, R. E. (2003). Children's adjustment following divorce: Risk and resilience perspectives. *Family Relations, 52*(4), 352–362. https://doi.org/10.1111/j.1741-3729.2003.00352.x

Kelly, J. B., & Johnston, J. R. (2001). The alienated child: A reformulation of parental alienation syndrome. *Family Court Review, 39*(3), 249–266. https://doi.org/10.1111/j.174-1617.2001.tb00609.x

Kelly, J. B., & Johnston, J. R. (2005). Commentary on Tippins and Wittmann's "Empirical and ethical problems with custody recommendations: A call for clinical humility and judicial vigilance." *Family Court Review, 43*(2), 233–241. https://doi.org/10.1111/j.1744-1617.2005.00022.x

Kelly, J. B., & Lamb, M. E. (2000). Using child development research to make appropriate custody and access decisions for young children. *Family and Conciliation Courts Review, 38*(3), 297–311.

Kelly, J. B., & Lamb, M. E. (2003). Developmental issues in relocation cases involving young children: When, whether, and how? *Journal of Family Psychology, 17*(2), 193–205. https://doi.org/10.1037/0893-3200.17.2.193

Kelly, R. F., & Ramsey, S. H. (2009). Child custody evaluations: The need for systems-level outcome assessments. *Family Court Review, 47*(2), 286–303.

Kerber, A., Ehrenthal, J. C., Zimmermann, J., Remmers, C., Nolte, T., Wendt, L. P., Heim, P., Müller, S., Beintner, I., & Knaevelsrud, C. (2024). Examining the role of personality functioning in a hierarchical taxonomy of psychopathology using two years of ambulatory assessed data. *Translational Psychiatry, 14*(1), 340–353. https://www.nature.com/articles/s41398-024-03046-z

Kia-Keating, M., Ahmed, S. R., Guler, J., & Alshabani, N. (2023). Intergenerational relations. In S. C. Nassar, K. J. Ajrouch, F. J. Dallo, & J. Hakim-Larson (Eds.), *Biopsychosocial perspectives on Arab Americans: Culture, development, and health* (2nd ed., pp. 37–52). Springer Nature Switzerland AG.

Kiang, L., Supple, A. J., & Stein, G. L. (2019). Latent profiles of discrimination and socialization predicting ethnic identity and well-being among Asian American adolescents. *Journal of Research on Adolescence, 29*(2), 523–538.

Kim, S. A., & Stein, E. (2018). Gender in the context of same-sex divorce and relationship dissolution. *Family Court Review, 56*(3), 384–398.

King, H. E. (2013). Assessment in custody hearings: Child custody evaluations. In K. F. Geisinger, B. A. Bracken, J. F. Carlson, J.-I. C. Hansen, N. R. Kuncel, S. P. Reise, & M. C. Rodriguez (Eds.), *APA handbook of testing and assessment in psychology: Vol. 2. Testing and assessment in clinical and counseling psychology* (pp. 587–605). American Psychological Association. https://doi.org/10.1037/14048-034

Kirkpatrick, H. D. (2004). A floor, not a ceiling: Beyond guidelines—An argument for minimum standards of practice in conducting child custody and visitation evaluations. *Journal of Child Custody, 1*(1), 61–75.

Kleinman, T. G. (2021). Commentary: Use of the term "parental alienation" may be part of the problem. *Journal of Family Trauma, Child Custody, and Child Development, 18*(3), 217–220.

Klocke, U. (2024). Sexualization of children or human rights? Attitudes toward addressing sexual-orientation diversity in school. *Journal of Homosexuality, 71*(3), 600–631.

Knuth, S. B. (2020). Child custody litigation and psychological evaluation. In A. B. Batastini & M. J. Vitacco (Eds.), *Forensic mental health evaluations in the digital age: A practitioner's guide to using internet-based data* (pp. 143–168). Springer Nature Switzerland AG. https://doi.org/10.1007/978-3-030-33908-1

Koren-Karie, N., & Oppenheim, D. (2018). Parental insightfulness: Retrospect and prospect. *Attachment & Human Development, 20*(3), 223–236.

Korkman, J., Otgaar, H., Geven, L.M., Bull, R., Cyr, M., Hershkowitz, I., Mäkelä, J.M., Mattison, M., Milne, R., Santtila, P., van Koppen, P., Memon, A., Danby, M., Filipovic, L., Garcia, F.J., Gewehr, E., Gomes Bell, O., Järvilehto, L., Kask, K., . . . Volbert, R. (2024). White paper on forensic child interviewing: Research-based recommendations by the European Association of Psychology and Law. *Psychology, Crime & Law, 31*(8), 987–1030. https://doi.org/10.1080/1068316X.2024.2324098

Kotov, R., Jonas, K. G., Carpenter, W. T., Dretsch, M. N., Eaton, N. R., Forbes, M. K., Forbush, K. T., Hobbs, K., Reininghaus, U., Slade, T., South, S. C., Sunderland, M., Waszczuk, M. A., Widiger, T. A., Wright, A. G. C., Zald, D. H., Krueger, R. F., Watson, D., & the HiTOP Utility Workgroup. (2020). Validity and utility of hierarchical taxonomy of psychopathology (HiTOP): I. Psychosis superspectrum. *World Psychiatry, 19*(2), 151–172.

Kotov, R., Krueger, R. F., & Watson, D. (2018). A paradigm shift in psychiatric classification: The Hierarchical Taxonomy Of Psychopathology (HiTOP). *World Psychiatry, 17*(1), 24–25. http://doi.org/10.1002/wps.20478

Kotov, R., Krueger, R. F., Watson, D., Achenbach, T. M., Althoff, R. R., Bagby, R. M., Brown, T. A., Carpenter, W. T., Caspi, A., Clark, L. A., Eaton, N. R., Forbes, M. K., Forbush, K. T., Goldberg, D., Hasin, D., Hyman, S. E., Ivanova, M. Y., Lynam, D. R., Markon, K., . . . Zimmerman, M. (2017). The Hierarchical Taxonomy of Psychopathology (HiTOP): A dimensional alternative to traditional nosologies. *Journal of Abnormal Psychology, 126*(4), 454–477. https://doi.org/10.1037/abn0000258

Kroger Co. v. Betancourt, 996 S.W.2d 353 (Tex. Ct. App. 1999).

Kropp, P. R., & Gibas, A. (2021). The Spousal Assault Risk Assessment Guide (SARA). In K. S. Douglas & R. K. Otto (Eds.), *Handbook of violence risk assessment* (2nd ed., pp. 389–409). Routledge/Taylor & Francis Group.

Krueger, R. F., & Hobbs, K. A. (2020). An overview of the DSM-5 alternative model of personality disorders. *Psychopathology, 53*(3-4), 126–132.

Kuehnle, K. (1998). Child sexual abuse evaluations: The scientist-practitioner model. *Behavioral Sciences & the Law, 16*(1), 5–20.

Kuehnle, K., & Connell, M. (Eds.). (2009). *The evaluation of child sexual abuse allegations: A comprehensive guide to assessment and testimony*. John Wiley & Sons.

Kuehnle, K., & Connell, M. (2013). Child sexual abuse evaluations. In R. K. Otto (Ed.), *Handbook of psychology: Vol. 11. Forensic psychology* (2nd ed., pp. 579–613). John Wiley & Sons.

Kuehnle, K., Greenberg, L. R., & Gottlieb, M. C. (2004). Incorporating the principles of scientifically based child interviews into family law cases. *Journal of Child Custody: Research, Issues, and Practices, 1*(1), 97–114.

Kuehnle, K., Ludolph, P. S., & Brubacher, S. P. (2016). Allegations of child sexual abuse in parenting plan evaluations: Assessing children's memory and behavior. In L. Drozd, M. Saini, & N. Olesen (Eds.), *Parenting plan evaluations: Applied research for the family court* (2nd ed., pp. 279–307). Oxford University Press.

Kukor, T. (n.d.). *AAFP: Critical thinking in forensic psychological evaluation* [Conference presentation]. American Academy of Family Physicians Convention, Chicago, IL, United States.

Kukor, T. (2022, November 3). *Analytic habits of the master forensic thinker* [Conference presentation]. First Annual Conference of the American Academy of Forensic Psychology, Chicago, IL, United States.

Kukucka, J., Kassin, S. M., Zapf, P. A., & Dror, I. E. (2017). Cognitive bias and blindness: A global survey of forensic science examiners. *Journal of Applied Research in Memory and Cognition, 6*(4), 452–459.

Kumho Tire Co. v. Carmichael, 526 U.S. 137 (1999).

Kuppens, S., & Ceulemans, E. (2019). Parenting styles: A closer look at a well-known concept. *Journal of Child and Family Studies, 28*(1), 168–181. https://doi.org/10.1007/s10826-018-1242-x

LaFortune, K. A., & Carpenter, B. N. (1998). Custody evaluations: A survey of mental health professionals. *Behavioral Sciences & the Law, 16*(2), 207–224.

Lahey, B. (2021). *Dimensions of psychological problems: Replacing diagnostic categories with a more science-based and less stigmatizing alternative*. Oxford University Press.

Lamb, M. E. (1999). Noncustodial fathers and their impact on the children of divorce. In R. A. Thompson & P. R. Amato (Eds.), *The postdivorce family: Children, parenting, and society* (pp. 105–125). Sage Publications.

Lamb, M. E. (Ed.). (2010). *The role of the father in child development* (5th ed.). John Wiley & Sons.

Lamb, M. E. (2013). The changing faces of fatherhood and father-child relationships: From fatherhood as status to father as dad. In M. A. Fine & F. D. Fincham (Eds.), *Handbook of family theories: A content-based approach* (pp. 87–102). Routledge/Taylor & Francis Group.

Lamb, M. E. (2018). Does shared parenting by separated parents affect the adjustment of young children? *Journal of Child Custody: Research, Issues, and Practices, 15*(1), 16–25.

Lamb, M. E., Hershkowitz, I., Orbach, Y., & Esplin, P. W. (2018). *Tell me what happened: Structured investigative interviews of child victims and witnesses*. John Wiley & Sons.

Lamb, M. E., & Kelly, J. B. (2001). Using the empirical literature to guide the development of parenting plans for young children: A rejoinder to Solomon and Biringen. *Family Court Review, 39*(4), 365–371.

Lamb, M. E., & Kelly, J. B. (2009). Improving the quality of parent–child contact in separating families with infants and young children: Empirical research foundations. In R. M. Galatzer-Levy, J. Kraus, & J. Galatzer-Levy (Eds.), *The scientific basis of child custody decisions,* (2nd ed., pp. 187–214). John Wiley & Sons.

Lamb, M. E., Orbach, Y., Sternberg, K. J., Hershkowitz, I., & Horowitz, D. (2000). Accuracy of investigators' verbatim notes of their forensic interviews with alleged child abuse victims. *Law and Human Behavior, 24*(6), 699–708. https://doi.org/10.1023/A:1005556404636

Lapakko, D. (2015). Communication is 93% nonverbal: An urban legend proliferates. *Communication and Theater Association of Minnesota Journal, 34*(1), 7–19.

Lapierre, S., Côté, I., Lambert, A., Buetti, D., Lavergne, C., Damant, D., & Couturier, V. (2018). Difficult but close relationships: Children's perspectives on relationships with their mothers in the context of domestic violence. *Violence Against Women, 24*(9), 1023–1038.

La Rooy, D. J., Brown, D., & Lamb, M. E. (2013). Suggestibility and witness interviewing using the Cognitive Interview and NICHD protocol. In A. M. Ridley, F. Gabbert, & D. J. La Rooy (Eds.), *Suggestibility in legal contexts: Psychological research and forensic implications* (pp. 197–216). Wiley-Blackwell.

Leal, D., Gato, J., Coimbra, S., Freitas, D., & Tasker, F. (2021). Social support in the transition to parenthood among lesbian, gay, and bisexual persons: A systematic review. *Sexuality Research & Social Policy, 18*(4), 1165–1179.

Lee, C. M., & Hunsley, J. (2003). Evidence-based assessment of childhood mood disorders: Comment on McClure, Kubiszyn and Kaslow (2002). *Professional Psychology: Research and Practice, 34*(1), 112–113. https://doi.org/10.1037/0735-7028.34.1.112

Lee, H., Russell, K. N., O'Donnell, K. A., Miller, E. K., Bender, A. E., Scaggs, A. L., Harris, L. A., Holmes, M. R., & Berg, K. A. (2022). The effect of childhood intimate partner violence (IPV) exposure on bullying: A systematic review. *Journal of Family Violence, 37,* 1283–1300.

Lee, M., Kang, S., Uribe, A., Harvey, E. A., & Galano, M. M. (2023). Mediators and moderator of the effects of early exposure to intimate partner violence on children's mental health. *Development and Psychopathology*. Advance online publication.

Lehr, R., & MacMillan, P. (2001). The psychological and emotional impact of divorce: The noncustodial fathers' perspective. *Families in Society, 82*(4), 373–382.

Leone, J. M., Johnson, M. P., & Cohan, C. L. (2007). Victim help seeking: Differences between intimate terrorism and situational couple violence. *Family Relations, 56*(5), 427–439.

Leshin, J., Carter, M. J., Doyle, C. M., & Lindquist, K. A. (2024). Language access differentially alters functional connectivity during emotion perception across cultures. *Frontiers in Psychology, 14,* 1084059. https://doi.org/10.3389/fpsyg.2023.1084059

Lévesque, S., Julien, D., Joubert, K., Clément, M.-È., Lessard, G., & Flores, J. (2023). Exposure to intimate partner violence in children aged 6 months to 8 years: Factors associated with mothers' awareness of children's exposure to this violence. *Violence and Gender, 10*(2), 73–84.

Lewis, N. A., Jr. (2021a). Can we achieve "equality" when we have different understandings of its meaning? How contexts and identities shape the pursuit of egalitarian goals. *Psychological Inquiry, 32*(3), 155–164.

Lewis, N. A., Jr. (2021b). What counts as good science? How the battle for methodological legitimacy affects public psychology. *American Psychologist, 76*(8), 1323–1333. https://doi.org/10.1037/amp0000870

Lewy, J., Cyr, M., & Dion, J. (2015). Impact of interviewers' supportive comments and children's reluctance to cooperate during sexual abuse disclosure. *Child Abuse & Neglect, 43,* 112–122.

Liell, G. C., Fisher, M. J., & Jones, L. F. (Eds.). (2023). *Challenging bias in forensic psychological assessment and testing: Theoretical and practical approaches to working with diverse populations.* Routledge.

Liell, G. C., Fisher, M. J., Jones, L. F., & Hough, L. F. (2023). Forensic context assessment: Some current challenges. In G. C. Liell, M. J. Fisher, & L. F. Jones (Eds.), *Challenging bias in forensic psychological assessment and testing: Theoretical and practical approaches to working with diverse populations* (pp. 3–19). Routledge.

Lilienfeld, S. O. (2010). Can psychology become a science? *Personality and Individual Differences, 49*(4), 281–288. https://doi.org/10.1016/j.paid.2010.01.024

Lilienfeld, S. O. (2012a). Further sources of our field's embattled public reputation. *American Psychologist, 67*(9), 808–809. https://doi.org/10.1037/a0031015

Lilienfeld, S. O. (2012b). Public skepticism of psychology: Why many people perceive the study of human behavior as unscientific. *American Psychologist, 67*(2), 111–129. https://doi.org/10.1037/a0023963

Lilienfeld, S. O., Ammirati, R., & David, M. (2012). Distinguishing science from pseudoscience in school psychology: Science and scientific thinking as safeguards against human error. *Journal of School Psychology, 50*(1), 7–36.

Lilienfeld, S. O., Wood, J. M., & Garb, H. N. (2000). The scientific status of projective techniques. *Psychological Science in the Public Interest, 1*(2), 27–66.

Logan, T. K., Walker, R., Jordan, C. E., & Horvath, L. S. (2002). Child custody evaluations and domestic violence: Case comparisons. *Violence and Victims, 17*(6), 719–742.

London, K., Bruck, M., Ann Poole, D., & Melnyk, L. (2011). The development of metasuggestibility in children. *Applied Cognitive Psychology, 25*(1), 146–155.

Loso, H., Chaarani, B., Dube, S. L., Albaugh, M. D., Cheaito, A., Garavan, H., & Potter, A. (2023). Gender diversity associated with patterns of brain activation seen in populations that experience childhood stress. *Frontiers in Integrative Neuroscience, 17,* 1084748.

Louis, J. M., & Reyes, M. E. S. (2023). Prevalence, factors, and impact of exposure to parental intimate partner violence: A scoping review. *Clinical Child Psychology and Psychiatry, 28*(1), 354–366.

Lourenço, L. M., Baptista, M. N., Senra, L. X., Adriana, A. A., Basílio, C., & Bhona, F. M. D. C. (2013). Consequences of exposure to domestic violence for children: A systematic review of the literature. *Paidéia (Ribeirão Preto), 23*(55), 263–271.

Lux, U., & Walper, S. (2019). A systemic perspective on children's emotional insecurity in relation to father: Links to parenting, interparental conflict and children's social well-being. *Attachment & Human Development, 21*(5), 467–484.

Lyon, T. D. (1999). The new wave in children's suggestibility research: A critique. *Cornell Law Review, 84*(4), 1004–1087.

Lyon, T. D. (2001). Let's not exaggerate the suggestibility of children. *Court Review, 28*(3), 12–14.

Lyon, T. D. (2002a). Expert testimony on the suggestibility of children: Does it fit? In B. L. Bottoms, M. Bull Kovera, & B. D. McAuliff (Eds.), *Children, social science, and the law* (pp. 378–411). Cambridge University Press.

Lyon, T. D. (2002b). Scientific support for expert testimony on child sexual abuse accommodation. In J. R. Conte (Ed.), *Critical issues in child sexual abuse* (pp. 107–138). Sage Publications.

Lyon, T. D., McWilliams, K., & Williams, S. (2019). Child witnesses. In N. Brewer & A. B. Douglass (Eds.), *Psychological science and the law* (pp. 157–181). Guilford Press.

Madigan, S., Deneault, A. A., Duschinsky, R., Bakermans-Kranenburg, M. J., Schuengel, C., van IJzendoorn, M. H., Ly, A., Fearon, R. M. P., Eirich, R., & Verhage, M. L. (2024). Maternal and paternal sensitivity: Key determinants of child attachment security examined through meta-analysis. *Psychological Bulletin, 150*(7), 839–872.

Main, M., Hesse, E., & Kaplan, N. (2005). Predictability of attachment behavior and representational processes at 1, 6, and 19 years of age: The Berkeley longitudinal study. In K. E. Grossman, K. Grossmann, & E. Waters (Eds.), *Attachment from infancy to adulthood: The major longitudinal studies* (pp. 245–304). Guildford Press.

Maldonado, S. (2017). Bias in the family: Race, ethnicity, and culture in custody disputes. *Family Court Review, 55*(2), 213–242.

Manjra, I. I., & Masic, U. (2022). Gender diversity and autism spectrum conditions in children and adolescents: A narrative review of the methodologies used by quantitative studies. *Journal of Clinical Psychology, 78*(4), 485–502.

Martin, C. L., Xiao, S. X., DeLay, D., Fabes, R. A., Hanish, L. D., & Oswalt, K. (2024). Differing gender diverse children have differing experiences with same- and other-gender peers. *British Journal of Developmental Psychology, 43*(2), 376–395. https://doi.org/10.1111/bjdp.12500

Martindale, D. A. (2001). On the importance of suggestibility research in assessing the credibility of children's testimony. *Court Review, 38*(3), 8–10.

Martindale, D. A. (2005). Confirmatory bias and confirmatory distortion. *Journal of Child Custody: Research, Issues, and Practices, 2*(1–2), 31–48.

Martindale, D. A. (2017). *Interviewing, report writing, and testifying in child custody cases.* Two-day program offered under the auspices of the Forensic Training Academy of John Jay College of Criminal Justice and Concept Professional Training.

Martindale, D. A. (2019, June 17). Allegations of alienation or child sexual abuse in custody evaluations [Course webinar]. Palo Alto University. https://concept.paloaltou.edu/course/Allegations-of-Alienation-or-Child-Sexual-Abuse-in-Custody-Evaluations

Martindale, D. A., & Gould, J. W. (2004). The forensic model: Ethics and scientific methodology applied to child custody evaluations. *Journal of Child Custody, 1*(2), 1–22.

Martindale, D. A., & Gould , J. W.. (2007). Custody evaluation reports: The case for empirically-derived information. *Journal of Forensic Psychology Practice, 7*(3), 87–99.

Martindale, D. A., & Gould, J. W. (2012). Deconstructing custody evaluation reports. *Journal of the American Academy of Matrimonial Lawyers, 25*(2), 357–374.

Martindale, D. A., & Gould, J. W. (2013a). Ethical principles and professional competencies. In R. K. Otto (Ed.), *Handbook of psychology: Vol. 11. Forensic psychology* (2nd ed.). John Wiley & Sons.

Martindale, D. A., & Gould, J. W. (2013b). Ethics in forensic practice. In R. K. Otto (Ed.), *Handbook of psychology: Vol 11. Forensic psychology* (2nd ed. pp. 37–61). John Wiley & Sons.

Martinez, R. (2018). Professional identity, the goals and purposes of forensic psychiatry, and Dr. Ezra Griffith. *The Journal of the American Academy of Psychiatry and the Law, 46*(4), 428–437.

Martinez, R., & Candilis, P. (2020). Ethics in the time of injustice. *The Journal of the American Academy of Psychiatry and the Law, 48*(4), 428–430.

McClure, E. B., Kubiszyn, T., & Kaslow, N. J. (2002). Advances in the diagnosis and treatment of childhood mood disorders. *Professional Psychology: Research and Practice, 33*(2), 125–134. https://doi.org/10.1037/0735-7028.33.2.125

McConnachie, A. L., Ayed, N., Foley, S., Lamb, M. E., Jadva, V., Tasker, F., & Golombok, S. (2021). Adoptive gay father families: A longitudinal study of children's adjustment at early adolescence. *Child Development, 92*(1), 425–443. https://doi.org/10.1111/cdev.13442

McCurdy, A. L., & Russell, S. T. (2023). Perceived parental social support and psychological control predict depressive symptoms for lesbian, gay, bisexual, transgender, queer, or questioning youth in the United States. *Child Development, 94*(3), 691–705.

McCurley, M. J., Murphy, K. J., & Gould, J. W. (2006). Protecting children from incompetent forensic evaluations and expert testimony. *Journal of the American Academy of Matrimonial Lawyers, 19*(2), 277–320.

McGlynn, M. (2004). *The royal prerogative and the learning of the Inns of Court.* Cambridge University Press.

McGough, L. S. (1995). For the record: Videotaping investigative interviews. *Psychology, Public Policy, and Law, 1*(2), 370–386. https://doi.org/10.1037/1076-8971.1.2.370

McIntosh, J. E. (2011). Guest editor's introduction to special issue on attachment theory, separation, and divorce: Forging coherent understandings for family law. *Family Court Review, 49*(3), 418–425. https://doi.org/10.1111/j.1744-1617.2011.01382.x

McIntosh, J. E., Pruett, M. K., & Kelly, J. B. (2014). Parental separation and overnight care of young children, part 2: Putting theory into practice. *Family Court Review, 52*(2), 256–262. https://doi.org/10.1111/fcre.12088

McIntosh, J. E., Smyth, B. M., & Kelaher, M. (2013). Overnight care patterns following parental separation: Associations with emotion regulation in infants and young children. *Journal of Family Studies, 19*(3), 224–239. https://doi.org/10.5172/jfs.2013.19.3.224

McIntosh, J. E., Smyth, B. M., & Kelaher, M. A. (2015). Responding to concerns about a study of infant overnight care postseparation, with comments on consensus: Reply to Warshak (2014). *Psychology, Public Policy, and Law, 21*(1), 111–119. https://doi.org/10.1037/h0101018

McKee, A. (2022). "Is this your baby?": Gay fathered families' experiences navigating heteronormativity in the United States. *Journal of Homosexuality, 69*(4), 677–698. https://doi.org/10.1080/00918369.2020.1848149

Meier, J. S. (2015). Johnson's differentiation theory: Is it really empirically supported? *Journal of Child Custody: Research, Issues, and Practices, 12*(1), 4–24. https://doi.org/10.1080/15379418.2015.1037054

Melton, G. B., Petrila, J., Poythress, N. G., Slobogin, C., Otto, R. K., Mossman, D., & Condie, L. O. (2018). *Psychological evaluations for the courts: A handbook for mental health professionals and lawyers* (4th ed.). Guilford Press.

Mercer, J., & Drew, M. (Eds.). (2022). *Challenging parental alienation: New directions for professionals and parents.* Routledge.

Merchant, E. K. (2024). Parental meta-emotion philosophy: A review of the past decade of Research. *Psychology, 15*(3), 364–376.

Merriam-Webster. (n.d.-a). Ideographic. In *Merriam-Webster.com dictionary*. Retrieved March 10, 2025, from https://www.merriam-webster.com/dictionary/ideographic

Merriam-Webster. (n.d.-b). Nomothetic. In *Merriam-Webster.com dictionary*. Retrieved March 10, 2025, from https://www.merriam-webster.com/dictionary/nomothetic

Meyer, G. J., Finn, S. E., Eyde, L. D., Kay, G. G., Moreland, K. L., Dies, R. R., Eisman, E. J., Kubiszyn, T. W., & Reed, G. M. (2001). Psychological testing and psychological assessment. A review of evidence and issues. *American Psychologist, 56*(2), 128–165.

Meyer v. Nebraska, 262 U.S. 390 (1923).

Mihura, J. L., Meyer, G. J., Dumitrascu, N., & Bombel, G. (2013). The validity of individual Rorschach variables: Systematic reviews and meta-analyses of the comprehensive system. *Psychological Bulletin, 139*(3), 548–605. https://doi.org/10.1037/a0029406

Mikolajczak, M., Gross, J. J., & Roskam, I. (2019). Parental burnout: What is it, and why does it matter? *Clinical Psychological Science, 7*(6), 1319–1329.

Milchman, M. S. (2018). Commentary: Implicit cultural arguments affect the science of shared parenting. *Journal of Child Custody: Research, Issues, and Practices, 15*(3), 218–227.

Milchman, M. S. (2022a). Distinguishing parental alienation from child abuse and adverse parenting. In J. Mercer & M. Drew (Eds.), *Challenging parental alienation: New directions for professionals and parents* (pp. 107–137). Routledge.

Milchman, M. S. (2022b). Oversimplified beliefs about alienation rebuttals of child abuse allegations–practice issues. *Journal of Family Trauma, Child Custody, & Child Development, 19*(2), 101–118. https://doi.org/10.1080/26904586.2022.2049465

Milchman, M. S., Geffner, R., & Meier, J. S. (2020a). Ideology and rhetoric replace science and reason in some parental alienation literature and advocacy: A critique. *Family Court Review, 58*(2), 340–361.

Milchman, M. S., Geffner, R., & Meier, J. S. (2020b). Putting science and reasoning back into the "parental alienation" discussion: Reply to Bernet, Robb, Lorandos, and Garber. *Family Court Review, 58*(2), 375–385.

Millon, T., Davis, R., & Millon, C. (1997). *MCMI–III manual* (2nd ed.). NCS Pearson.

Millon, T., Grossman, S., & Millon, C. (2015). *MCMI-IV: Manual.* Pearson Assessments.

Mischel, W. (2008). Connecting clinical practice to scientific progress. *Psychological Science in the Public Interest, 9*(2), i–ii.

Mississippi Transp. Comm'n v. McLemore, 863 So.2d 31 (Miss. 2003).

Miyamoto, S., Dharmar, M., Boyle, C., Yang, N.-H., MacLeod, K., Rogers, K., Nesbitt, T., & Marcin, J. P. (2014). Impact of telemedicine on the quality of forensic sexual abuse examinations in rural communities. *Child Abuse & Neglect, 38*(9), 1533–1539.

Mnookin, R. H. (1975). Child custody adjudication: Judicial functions in the face of indeterminacy. *Law and Contemporary Problems, 39*(3), 226–293.

Mo, K., Anagnostou, E., Lerch, J. P., Taylor, M. J., VanderLaan, D. P., Szatmari, P., Crosbie, J., Nicolson, R., Georgiadis, S., Kelley, E., Ayub, M., Brian, J., Lai, M.-C., & Palmert, M. R. (2024). Gender diversity is correlated with dimensional neurodivergent traits but not categorical neurodevelopmental diagnoses in children. *Journal of Child Psychology and Psychiatry, and Allied Disciplines, 65*(9), 1223–1236. https://doi.org/10.1111/jcpp.13965

Modecki, K. L., Hagan, M. J., Sandler, I., & Wolchik, S. A. (2015). Latent profiles of nonresidential father engagement six years after divorce predict long-term offspring outcomes. *Journal of Clinical Child and Adolescent Psychology, 44*(1), 123–136.

Mohaupt, H., Duckert, F., & Askeland, I. R. (2021). How do memories of having been parented relate to the parenting-experience of fathers in treatment for intimate partner violence? A phenomenological analysis. *Journal of Family Violence, 36*(4), 467–480.

Monahan, J., & Walker, L. (1988). Social science research in law: A new paradigm. *American Psychologist, 43*(6), 465–472. https://doi.org/10.1037/0003-066X.43.6.465

Monahan, J., & Walker, L. (1991). Judicial use of social science research. *Law and Human Behavior, 15*(6), 571–584. https://doi.org/10.1007/BF01065853

Monahan, J., Walker, L., & Mitchell, G. (2009). The limits of social framework evidence. *Law Probability and Risk, 8*(4), 307–321. https://doi.org/10.1093/lpr/mgp020

Moran, J. A., & Weinstock, D. K. (2011). Assessing parenting skills for family court. *Journal of Child Custody, 8*(3), 166–188. https://doi.org/10.1080/15379418.2011.594726

Moreau, G. (2021). The pitfalls in the path of probabilistic inference in forensic entomology: A review. *Insects, 12*(3), 240–250. https://doi.org/10.3390/insects12030240

Morewedge, C. K., Yoon, H., Scopelliti, I., Symborski, C. W., Korris, J. H., & Kassam, K. S. (2015). Debiasing decisions: Improved decision making with a single training intervention. *Policy Insights from the Behavioral and Brain Sciences, 2*(1), 129–140. https://doi.org/10.1177/2372732215600886

Morey, L. C. (1991). *Personality Assessment Inventory professional manual.* Psychological Assessment Resources.

Morey, L. C. (2007). *Personality Assessment Inventory manual.* Psychological Assessment Resources.

Mosley-Johnson, E., Campbell, J. A., Garacci, E., Walker, R. J., & Egede, L. E. (2021). Stress that Endures: Influence of Adverse Childhood Experiences on Daily Life Stress and Physical Health in Adulthood. *Journal of Affective Disorders, 284,* 38–43. https://doi.org/10.1016/j.jad.2021.02.018

Motorola Inc. v. Murray, 147 A.3d 751 (D.C. 2016).

Mueller, I., & Tronick, E. (2019). Early life exposure to violence: Developmental consequences on brain and behavior. *Frontiers in Behavioral Neuroscience, 13,* 156. https://doi.org/10.3389/fnbeh.2019.00156

Mueller, I., & Tronick, E. (2020). The long shadow of violence: The impact of exposure to intimate partner violence in infancy and early childhood. *International Journal of Applied Psychoanalytic Studies, 17*(3), 232–245. https://doi.org/10.1002/aps.1668

Mulchay, C. & Knuth, S. (2021). Seven tips for gathering and interpreting social media data. *Association of Family and Conciliation Courts eNEWS, 16*(6).

Mulchay, C., & Knuth, S. (2022a, Novermber 11). *Gathering, interpreting, and archiving social media data* [Conference presentation]. 15th Association of Family and Conciliation Courts (AFCC) Symposium on Child Custody Evaluations: Breaking Through Conflict, Las Vegas, NV, United States

Mulchay, C., & Knuth, S. (2022b, May 11–14). *How to deal with social networking data: Authenticity and implications* [Conference presentation]. 59th Annual Conference of the Association of Family and Conciliation Courts, Chicago, IL, United States.

Mulchay, C., & Knuth, S. (2022c). *The use and misuse of mental health witnesses and experts in effective advocacy.* Interdisciplinary Forum on Mental Health and Family Law.

Mulchay, C., & Knuth, S. B. (2023a, May 31–June 3). *Applying Bayesian decision making to evaluations to improve decision making* [Conference session]. 60th Annual Conference of the Association of Family and Conciliation Courts, Los Angeles, CA, United States.

Mulchay, C., & Knuth, S. (2023b). Best practices in tele-forensic methods of gathering data. *Journal of Forensic Social Work, 7*(2), 3–17. https://doi.org/10.15763/issn.1936-9298.2023.7.2.3-17

Murrie, D. C., Boccaccini, M. T., Guarnera, L. A., & Rufino, K. A. (2013). Are forensic experts biased by the side that retained them? *Psychological Science, 24*(10), 1889–1897. https://doi.org/10.1177/0956797613481812

Myers, J. E. B. (1993). Expert testimony describing psychological syndromes. *Pacific Law Journal, 24*(3), 1449–1464.

National Center for Cultural Competence at Georgetown University. (n.d.). *Conscious & unconscious biases in health care (module 3).* https://nccc.georgetown.edu/bias/module-3/1.php

National Conference of State Legislatures. (2022, March). *Coercive control.* https://mgaleg.maryland.gov/cmte_testimony/2022/jud/17UK07nGbQXW6Y03IGiQi3oipDqyrEx2t.pdf

National Justice Compania Naviera SA v. Prudential Assurance [1993] FSR 563 at 565, [1993] 2 Lloyd's LR 68.

Navarro, J. L., & Tudge, J. R. (2023). Technologizing Bronfenbrenner: Neo-ecological theory. *Current Psychology, 42*(22), 19338–19354. https://doi.org/10.1007/s12144-022-02738-3

Neal, T. M. S., & Brodsky, S. L. (2016). Forensic psychologists' perceptions of bias and potential correction strategies in forensic mental health evaluations. *Psychology, Public Policy, and Law, 22*(1), 58–76. https://doi.org/10.1037/law0000077

Neal, T. M. S., & Grisso, T. M. S. (2014). The cognitive underpinnings of bias in forensic mental health evaluations. *Psychology, Public Policy, and Law, 20*(2), 200–211. https://doi.org/10.1037/a0035824

Neal, T. M. S., Lienert, P., Denne, E., & Singh, J. P. (2022). A general model of cognitive bias in human judgment and systematic review specific to forensic mental health. *Law and Human Behavior, 46*(2), 99–120. https://doi.org/10.1037/lhb0000482

Neal, T. M. S., Slobogin, C., Saks, M. J., Faigman, D. L., & Geisinger, K. F. (2019). Psychological assessments in legal contexts: Are courts keeping "junk science" out of the courtroom? *Psychological Science in the Public Interest, 20*(3), 135–164. https://doi.org/10.1177/1529100619888860

Neblett, E. W., Jr., Rivas-Drake, D., & Umaña-Taylor, A. J. (2012). The promise of racial and ethnic protective factors in promoting ethnic minority youth development. *Child Development Perspectives, 6*(3), 295–303. https://doi.org/10.1111/j.1750-8606.2012.00239.x

Neppl, T. K., Jeon, S., Diggs, O., & Donnellan, M. B. (2020). Positive parenting, effortful control, and developmental outcomes across early childhood. *Developmental Psychology, 56*(3), 444–457. https://doi.org/10.1037/dev0000874

Newmark, L., Harrell, A., & Salem, P. (1995). Domestic violence and empowerment in custody and visitation cases. *Family Court Review, 33*(1), 30–62. https://doi.org/10.1111/j.174-1617.1995.tb00347.x

Nichols, D. S., & Greene, R. L. (1997). Dimensions of deception in personality assessment: The example of the MMPI-2. *Journal of Personality Assessment, 68*(2), 251–266.

Nickerson, R. S. (1998). Confirmation bias: A ubiquitous phenomenon in many guises. *Review of General Psychology, 2*(2), 175–220. https://doi.org/10.1037/1089-2680.2.2.175

Nielsen, L. (2014). Woozles: Their role in custody law reform, parenting plans, and family court. *Psychology, Public Policy, and Law, 20*(2), 164–180. https://doi.org/10.1037/law0000004

O'Connell, M. E. (2009). Mandated custody evaluations and the limits of judicial power. *Family Court Review, 47*(2), 304–320. https://doi.org/10.1111/j.1744-1617.2009.01256.x

O'Hara, K. L., Cummings, E. M., & Davies, P. T. (2023). Interparental conflict and adolescent emotional security across family structures. *Family Process, 63*(1), 265–283. https://doi.org/10.1111/famp.12872

Olson, M. A., & Fazio, R. H. (2009). Implicit and explicit measures of attitudes: The perspective of the MODE Model. In R. E. Petty, R. H. Fazio, & P. Brinol (Eds.), *Attitudes: Insights from the new wave of implicit measures* (pp. 20–62). Lawrence Erlbaum Associates.

Oppenheim, D., & Koren-Karie, N. (2012). Parents' insightfulness: The importance of keeping the inner world of the child in mind for parenting evaluations. In L. Drozd (Ed.), *Parenting plan evaluations: Applied research for the family court* (2nd ed., pp. 25–46). Oxford University Press. https://doi.org/10.1093/med:psych/9780199754021.003.0002

Oppenheim, D., & Koren-Karie, N. (2014). Parental insightfulness and child–parent emotion dialogues: Their importance for children's development. In M. Mikulincer & P. R. Shaver (Eds.), *Mechanisms of social connection: From brain to group* (pp. 205–220). American Psychological Association. https://doi.org/10.1037/14250-012

Orbach, Y., Hershkowitz, I., Lamb, M. E., Sternberg, K. J., Esplin, P. W., & Horowitz, D. (2000). Assessing the value of structured protocols for forensic interviews of alleged child abuse victims. *Child Abuse & Neglect, 24*(6), 733–752. https://doi.org/10.1016/S0145-2134(00)00137-X

Orbach, Y., & Lamb, M. E. (2000). Enhancing children's narratives in investigative interviews. *Child Abuse & Neglect, 24*(12), 1631–1648. https://doi.org/10.1016/S0145-2134(00)00207-6

Orbach, Y., & Lamb, M. E. (2001). The relationship between within-interview contradictions and eliciting interviewer utterances. *Child Abuse & Neglect, 25*(3), 323–333. https://doi.org/10.1016/S0145-2134(00)00254-4

Otto, R. K., Edens, J. F., & Barcus, E. (2000). The use of psychological testing in child custody evaluations. *Family Court Review, 38*(3), 312–340. https://doi.org/10.1111/j.174-1617.2000.tb00578.x

Oxford English Dictionary. (2024). Monoculturalism. In *Oxford English Dictionary*. Retrieved from https://www.oed.com/dictionary/monoculturalism_n?tl=true

Padilla-Walker, L. M., & Coyne, S. M. (2011). "Turn that thing off!" parent and adolescent predictors of proactive media monitoring. *Journal of Adolescence, 34*(4), 705–715. https://doi.org/10.1016/j.adolescence.2010.09.002

Palmer, M. L., Keilholtz, B. M., Vail, S. L., & Spencer, C. M. (2024). The relationship between emotional intimate partner violence and other forms of violence: A meta-analytic review. *Family Process, 63*(4), 2291–2307. https://doi.org/10.1111/famp.12992

Palmore v. Sidoti, 466 U.S. 429 (1984).

Park, N., Schmitz, R. M., & Slauson-Blevins, K. (2020). "It takes a lot of planning": Sexual minority young adult perceptions of gay and lesbian parenthood. *Journal of Family Issues, 41*(10), 1785–1809. https://doi.org/10.1177/0192513X20925508

Parkinson, P., Cashmore, J., Taylor, N., Austin, W. G. (2016). Relocation, research, and child custody disputes. In L. Drozd & M. Saini (Eds.), *Parenting plan evaluations: Applied research for the family court* (2nd ed., pp. 431–459). Oxford University Press.

Patel, S. H., & Choate, L. H. (2014). Conducting child custody evaluations: Best practices for mental health counselors who are court-appointed as child custody evaluators. *Journal of Mental Health Counseling, 36*(1), 18–30. https://doi.org/10.17744/mehc.36.1.e00401wv7134w505

Pedraza, O., & van de Vijver, F. J. R. (2020). Bias, equivalence, and fairness. In O. Pedraza (Ed.), *Clinical cultural neuroscience: An integrative approach to cross-cultural neuropsychology* (pp. 252–275). Oxford University Press.

Pence, E., & Paymar, M. (2011). *Creating a process of change for men who batter: The Duluth curriculum*. Domestic Abuse Intervention Programs.

Pennington, N., & Hastie, R. (1990). Practical implications of psychological research on juror and jury decision making. *Personality and Social Psychology Bulletin, 16*(1), 90–105. https://doi.org/10.1177/0146167290161007

Pennington, N., & Hastie, R. (1991). A cognitive theory of juror decision making: The Story Model. *Cardozo Law Review, 13*(2-3), 519–557.

People v. Shreck, 22 P.3d 68 (Col. 2001).

Pettigrew, T. F., & Tropp, L. R. (2006). A meta-analytic test of intergroup contact theory. *Journal of Personality and Social Psychology, 90*(5), 751–783. https://doi.org/10.1037/0022-3514.90.5.751

Pettigrew, T. F., & Tropp, L. R. (2008). How does intergroup contact reduce prejudice? Meta-analytic test of three mediators. *European Journal of Social Psychology, 38*(6), 922–934. https://doi.org/10.1002/ejsp.504

Pherson, K. H., & Pherson, R. H. (2021). *Critical thinking for strategic intelligence* (3rd ed.). CQ Press.

Pherson, R. H., & Heuer, R. J. (2021). *Structured analytic techniques for intelligence analysis* (3rd ed.). CQ Press.

Pianowski, G., Carvalho, L. F., & Miguel, F. K. (2019). Investigating the Spectra constellations of the Hierarchical Taxonomy of Psychopathology (HiTOP) model for personality disorders based on empirical data from a community sample. *Brazil Journal of Psychiatry, 41*(2), 148–152. https://doi.org/10.1590/1516-4446-2018-0015

Pickar, D. B., & Kaufman, R. L. (2019). The special needs child after separation or divorce: Involving both parents in treatmnt and intervention planning. In L. R. Greenberg, B. J. Fidler, & M. A. Saini (Eds.), *Evidence-informed interventions for court-involved families: Promoting healthy coping and development* (pp. 325–354). Oxford University Press. https://doi.org/10.1093/med-psych/9780190693237.003.0013

Pierce v. Society of Sisters, 268 U.S. 510 (1925).

Pleck, J. H. (2010). Fatherhood and masculinity. In M. E. Lamb (Ed.), *The role of the father in child development* (pp. 27–57). John Wiley & Sons.

Poole, D. A. (2016). *Interviewing children: The science of conversation in forensic contexts.* American Psychological Association. https://doi.org/10.1037/14941-000

Posthuma, A. (2016). Current and new developments in psychological testing for child custody disputes. In M. L. Goldstein (Ed.), *Handbook of child custody* (pp. 67–84). Springer Nature Switzerland AG. https://doi.org/10.1007/978-3-319-13942-5_8

Postmus, J. L., Huang, C.-C., & Mathisen-Stylianou, A. (2012). The impact of physical and economic abuse on maternal mental health and parenting. *Children and Youth Services Review, 34*(9), 1922–1928. https://doi.org/10.1016/j.childyouth.2012.06.005

Priftis, N., & Panagiotakos, D. (2023). Screen time and its health consequences in children and adolescents. *Children, 10*(10), 1665. https://doi.org/10.3390/children10101665

Prime, H., Andrews, K., Markwell, A., Gonzalez, A., Janus, M., Tricco, A. C., Bennett, T., & Atkinson, L. (2023). Positive parenting and early childhood cognition: A systematic review and meta-analysis of randomized controlled trials. *Clinical Child and Family Psychology Review, 26*(2), 362–400. https://doi.org/10.1007/s10567-022-00423-2

Prince v. Massachusetts, 321 U.S. 158 (1944).

Principe, G. F., & London, K. (2022). How parents can shape what children remember: Implications for the testimony of young witnesses. *Journal of Applied Research in Memory and Cognition, 11*(3), 289–302. https://doi.org/10.1037/mac0000059

Pronin, E., & Kugler, M. B. (2007). Valuing thoughts, ignoring behavior: The introspection illusion as a source of the bias blind spot. *Journal of Experimental Social Psychology, 43*(4), 565–578. https://doi.org/10.1016/j.jesp.2006.05.011

Pronin, E., Lin, D. Y., & Ross, L. (2002). The bias blind spot: Perceptions of bias in self versus others. *Personality and Social Psychology Bulletin, 28*(3), 369–381. https://doi.org/10.1177/0146167202286008

Puhlman, D. J., & Pasley, K. (2013). Rethinking maternal gatekeeping. *Journal of Family Theory and Review, 5*(3), 176–193. https://doi.org/10.1111/jftr.12016

Raj, A., & Silverman, J. G. (2002). Violence against immigrant women: The roles of culture, context, and legal immigrant status on intimate partner violence. *Violence Against Women, 8*(3), 367–398.

Ramesh, R., & Ramana, G. V. (2023). Relationship between personality and parenting styles. *International Journal of Indian Psychology, 11*(1), 935–943.

Ramsey, S. H., & Kelly, R. F. (2004). Social science knowledge in family law cases: Judicial gatekeeping in the *Daubert* era. *University of Miami Law Review, 59*(1), 1–81.

Ramsey, S. H., & Kelly, R. F. (2006). Assessing social science studies: Eleven tips for judges and lawyers. *Family Law Quarterly, 40*(3), 367–380.

Rankine, J., Percival, T., Finau, E., Hope, L.-T., Kingi, P., Peteru, M. C., Powell, E., Robati-Mani, R., & Selu, E. (2017). Pacific peoples, violence, and the power and control wheel. *Journal of Interpersonal Violence, 32*(18), 2777–2803. https://doi.org/10.1177/0886260515596148

Rappaport, S., Gould, J., & Dale, M. (2018). Psychological testing can be of significant value in child custody evaluations: Don't buy the "anti-testing, anti-individual, pro-family systems" woozle. *Journal of the American Academy of Matrimonial Lawyers, 30*(2), 405–436.

Rappaport, S. R. (2022). "What we have here is a failure to communicate": The misuse of attachment and bonding in the courtroom: A call for definitions and explanations. *Family Court Review, 60*(1), 115–125. https://doi.org/10.1111/fcre.12563

Regier, D. A., Narrow, W. E., Clarke, D. E., Kraemer, H. C., Kuramoto, S. J., Kuhl, E. A., & Kupfer, D. J. (2013). DSM-5 field trials in the United States and Canada, Part II: Test-retest reliability of selected categorical diagnoses. *The American Journal of Psychiatry, 170*(1), 59–70. https://doi.org/10.1176/appi.ajp.2012.12070999

Reichardt, C. S. (1992). The fallibility of our judgments. *Evaluation Practice, 13*(3), 157–163. https://doi.org/10.1177/109821409201300302

Renaissance School of Medicine. (2024). *The Hierarchical Taxonomy of Psychopathology (HiTOP): About HiTOP.* Stony Brook University. Retrieved December 30, 2024, https://renaissance.stonybrookmedicine.edu/HITOP/AboutHiTOP

Reynolds, C. R., Altmann, R. A., & Allen, D. N. (2021). *Mastering modern psychological testing: Theory and methods* (2nd ed.). Springer Nature Switzerland AG. https://doi.org/10.1007/978-3-030-59455-8

Richards, L. (Host). (2023, January 27). Deconstructing coercive control and the impact on children with Dr. Emma Katz [Podcast episode]. In *Crime Analyst.* https://www.youtube.com/watch?v=Ayo6NuAeKdU

Rocchio, L. M. (2020). Ethical and professional considerations in the forensic assessment of complex trauma and dissociation. *Psychological Injury and Law, 13*(2), 124–134. https://doi.org/10.1007/s12207-020-09384-9

Rodriguez-Perez, C. J., & Castellanos, X. L. (2024). Residential instability and children's mental health: Emotional and behavioral consequences of frequent relocation. *Studies in Social Science & Humanities, 3*(9), 21–30. https://doi.org/10.56397/SSSH.2024.09.02

Roebers, C. M. (2002). Confidence judgments in children's and adults' event recall and suggestibility. *Developmental Psychology, 38*(6), 1052–1067. https://doi.org/10.1037/0012-1649.38.6.1052

Roebers, C. M., & Howie, P. (2003). Confidence judgments in event recall: Developmental progression in the impact of question format. *Journal of Experimental Child Psychology, 85*(4), 352–371. https://doi.org/10.1016/S0022-0965(03)00076-6

Roebers, C. M., Kälin, S., & Aeschlimann, E. A. (2020). A comparison of non-verbal and verbal indicators of young children's metacognition. *Metacognition and Learning, 15*(1), 31–49. https://doi.org/10.1007/s11409-019-09217-4

Rohmah, L., & Purwanta, E. (2023). Why should children have secure attachments? Literature review of the importance of attachment in child development. In M. Salimi, Gunarhadi, R. Hidayah, & D. A. Nugraha (Eds.), *Proceedings of the 6th international conference on learning innovation and quality education (ICLIQE 2022)* (Vol. 767, pp. 44–55). Atlantis Press.

Ross, M., & Sicoly, F. (1979). Egocentric biases in availability and attribution. *Journal of Personality and Social Psychology, 37*(3), 322–336.

Rossi, F. S., Holtzworth-Munroe, A., & Rudd, B. N. (2016). Intimate partner violence and child custody. In L. Drozd, M. Saini, & N. Olesen (Eds.), *Parenting plan evaluations: Applied research for the family court* (2nd ed., pp. 346–373). Oxford University Press. https://doi.org/10.1093/med:psych/9780199396580.003.0012

Rothblum, E. D., Bos, H. M. W., Carone, N., Koh, A. S., & Gartrell, N. K. (2024). Adults conceived via donor insemination by lesbian parents reflect on their own future parenting plans (and their own parents reflect on being grandparents). *LGBTQ+ Family: An Interdisciplinary Journal, 20*(1), 18–34. https://doi.org/10.1080/27703371.2023.2254270

Rubio, B., Vecho, O., Gross, M., van Rijn-van Gelderen, L., Bos, H., Ellis-Davies, K., Winstanley, A., Golombok, S., & Lamb, M. E. (2020). Transition to parenthood and quality of parenting among gay, lesbian and heterosexual couples who conceived through assisted reproduction. *Journal of Family Studies, 26*(3), 422–440. https://doi.org/10.1080/13229400.2017.1413005

Rudman, L. A. (2004). Sources of implicit attitudes. *Current Directions in Psychological Science, 13*(2), 79–82. https://doi.org/10.1111/j.0963-7214.2004.00279.x

Rumelhart, D. E. (1975). Notes on a schema for stories. In D. G. Brown & A. Collins (Eds.), *Representation and understanding: Studies in cognitive science* (pp. 211–236). Academic Press. https://doi.org/10.1016/B978-0-12-108550-6.50013-6

Rutter, M. (2006). Implications of resilience concepts for scientific understanding. In B. M. Lester, A. Masten, & B. McEwen (Eds.), *Resilience in children* (pp. 1–12). Blackwell Publishing. https://doi.org/10.1196/annals.1376.002

Sackett, D. L., Rosenberg, W. M. C., Gray, J. A. M., Haynes, R. B., & Richardson, W. S. (1996). Evidence based medicine: What it is and what it isn't. *BMJ, 312*(7023), 71–72. https://doi.org/10.1136/bmj.312.7023.71

Sager, C. J. (1976). *Marriage contracts and couple therapy: Hidden forces in intimate relationships*. Brunner-Routledge.

Saini, M. (2008). Evidence base of custody and access evaluations. *Brief Treatment and Crisis Intervention, 8*(1), 111–129. https://doi.org/10.1093/brief-treatment/mhm023

Saini, M., Allan-Ebron, D., & Barnes, J. (2015). A critical review of relocation research specific to separation and divorce. *Journal of Divorce & Remarriage, 56*(5), 388–408.

Saini, M., Laajasalo, T., & Platt, S. (2020). Gatekeeping by allegations: An examination of verified, unfounded, and fabricated allegations of child maltreatment within the context of resist and refusal dynamics. *Family Court Review, 58*(2), 417–431. https://doi.org/10.1111/fcre.12480

Saini, M., & Polak, S. (2014). The ecological validity of parent–child observations: A review of empirical evidence related to custody evaluations. *Journal of Child Custody, 11*(3), 181–201. https://doi.org/10.1080/15379418.2014.953661

Saini, M. A., Drozd, L. M., & Olesen, N. W. (2017). Adaptive and maladaptive gatekeeping behaviors and attitudes: Implications for child outcomes after separation and divorce. *Family Court Review, 55*(2), 260–272. https://doi.org/10.1111/fcre.12276

Sanders, J., & Turner, S. (2018). Parental communication and children's post-divorce adjustment: A meta-analysis. *Journal of Family Studies, 24*(1), 112–135.

Sargon Enters., Inc. v. Univ. of S. Cal., 288 P.3d 1237 (Cal. 2012)

Sattler, J. M. (1998). *Clinical and forensic interviewing of children and families: Guidelines for the mental health, education, pediatric, and child maltreatment fields*. Jerome M. Sattler Publisher.

Saunders, D. G., Faller, K. C., & Tolman, R. M. (2016). Beliefs and recommendations regarding child custody and visitation in cases involving domestic violence: A comparison of professionals in different roles. *Violence Against Women, 22*(6), 722–744. https://doi.org/10.1177/1077801215608845

Saunders, D. G., Tolman, R. M., & Faller, K. C. (2013). Factors associated with child custody evaluators' recommendations in cases of intimate partner violence. *Journal of Family Psychology, 27*(3), 473–483. https://doi.org/10.1037/a0032164

Savopoulos, P., Bryant, C., Fogarty, A., Conway, L. J., Fitzpatrick, K. M., Condron, P., & Giallo, R. (2023). Intimate partner violence and child and adolescent cognitive development: A systematic review. *Trauma, Violence, & Abuse, 24*(3), 1882–1907. https://doi.org/10.1177/15248380221082081

Saywitz, K. J. (1992). Enhancing children's memory with the Cognitive Interview. *APSAC Advisor*, 9–10.

Saywitz, K. J., & Camparo, L. (1998). Interviewing child witnesses: A developmental perspective. *Child Abuse & Neglect, 22*(8), 825–843. https://doi.org/10.1016/S0145-2134(98)00054-4

Saywitz, K. J., & Geiselman, R. E. (1998). Interviewing the child witness: Maximizing completeness and minimizing error. In S. J. Lynn & K. M. McConkey (Eds.), *Truth in memory* (pp. 190–223). Guilford Press.

Saywitz, K. J., Goodman, G. S., & Lyon, T. D. (2002). Interviewing children in and out of court: Current research and practice implications. In J. E. B. Myers, L. Berliner, J.

Briere, C. T. Hendrix, C. Jenny, & T. A. Reid (Eds.), *The APSAC handbook on child maltreatment* (pp. 349–377). Sage Publications.

Saywitz, K. J., Larson, R. P., Hobbs, S. D., & Wells, C. R. (2015). Developing rapport with children in forensic interviews: Systematic review of experimental research. *Behavioral Sciences & the Law, 33*(4), 372–389. https://doi.org/10.1002/bsl.2186

Saywitz, K. J., & Lyon, T. D. (2002). Coming to grips with children's suggestibility. In M. L. Eisen, J. A. Quas, & G. S. Goodman (Eds.), *Memory and suggestibility in the forensic interview* (pp. 85–113). Lawrence Erlbaum Associates.

Saywitz, K. J., Snyder, L., & Nathanson, R. (1999). Facilitating the communicative competence of the child witness. *Applied Developmental Science, 3*(1), 58–68. https://doi.org/10.1207/s1532480xads0301_7

Saywitz, K. J., Wells, C. R., Larson, R. P., & Hobbs, S. D. (2019). Effects of interviewer support on children's memory and suggestibility: Systematic review and meta-analyses of experimental research. *Trauma, Violence & Abuse, 20*(1), 22–39. https://doi.org/10.1177/1524838016683457

Schafersman v. Agland Coop., 631 N.W.2d 862 (Neb. 2001).

Schmidt, S., Heffernan, R., & Ward, T. (2023). Why dynamic risk factors cannot be applied universally: Their normative nature and the importance of cultural awareness in risk assessment and intervention. In G. C. Liell, M. J. Fisher, & L. F. Jones (Eds.), *Challenging bias in forensic psychological assessment and testing: Theoretical and practical approaches to working with diverse populations* (pp. 52–68). Routledge.

Schoppe-Sullivan, S. J., & Altenburger, L. E. (2019). Parental gatekeeping. In M. Bornstein (Ed.), *Handbook of parenting* (pp. 167–198) Routledge.

Schulz, M. L., Wood, C. E., Fogarty, A., Brown, S. J., Gartland, D., & Giallo, R. (2024). Intimate partner violence exposure during infancy and social functioning in middle childhood: An Australian mother and child cohort study. *Child Development, 95*(3), 817–830. https://doi.org/10.1111/cdev.14032

Schumacher, J. A., & Leonard, K. E. (2005). Husbands' and wives' marital adjustment, verbal aggression, and physical aggression as longitudinal predictors of physical aggression in early marriage. *Journal of Consulting and Clinical Psychology, 73*(1), 28–37. https://doi.org/10.1037/0022-006X.73.1.28

Schutz, B. M., Dixon, E. B., Lindenberger, J. C., & Ruther, N. J. (1989). *Solomon's sword: A practical guide to conducting child custody evaluations.* Jossey-Bass.

Sellbom, M., Flens, J., Gould, J., Ramnath, R., Tringone, R., & Grossman, S. (2022). The Millon Clinical Multiaxial Inventory-IV (MCMI-IV) and Millon Adolescent Clinical Inventory-II (MACI-II) in Legal Settings. *Journal of Personality Assessment, 104*(2), 203–220. https://doi.org/10.1080/00223891.2021.2013248

Sellier, A. L., Scopelliti, I., & Morewedge, C. K. (2019). Debiasing training improves decision making in the field. *Psychological Science, 30*(9), 1371–1379. https://doi.org/10.1177/0956797619861429

Semple, N. (2011). The "eye of the beholder": Professional opinions about the best interests of a child. *Family Court Review, 49*(4), 760–775. https://doi.org/10.1111/j.1744-1617.2011.01412.x

Seyyedadabi, A. A. (2006, November 19). *The muddled dream of returning to tradition: An interview with Abdulkarim Soroush* (N. Mobasser, Trans.) [Interview transcript]. http://drsoroush.com/en/the-muddled-dream-of-returning-to-tradition/

Shaw, M. (2019). Misperceptions and misapplications of research in family law cases: Myths of "Parental Alienation Syndrome" and implanted false memories. *Journal of Child Custody, 16*(1), 1–6. https://doi.org/10.1080/15379418.2019.1609384

Shenkman, G., & Abramovitch, M. (2021). Estimated likelihood of parenthood and its association with psychological well-being among sexual minorities and heterosexual counterparts. *Sexuality Research & Social Policy, 18*(2), 221–232. https://doi.org/10.1007/s13178-020-00451-z

Shuman, D. W., & Sales, B. D. (1999). The impact of *Daubert* and its progeny on the admissibility of behavioral and social science evidence. *Psychology, Public Policy, and Law, 5*(1), 3–15. https://doi.org/10.1037/1076-8971.5.1.3

Siegel, D. J. (2020). *The developing mind: How relationships and the brain interact to shape who we are*. Guilford Press.

Sims, T., Hogan, C., & Carstensen, L. (2015). Selectivity as an emotion regulation strategy: Lessons from older adults. *Current Opinion in Psychology, 3,* 80–84. https://doi.org/10.1016/j.copsyc.2015.02.012

Skafte, D. (1985). *Child custody evaluations: A practical guide*. Sage Publications.

Slaven, M. M. (2001). *Observational techniques in child custody evaluations*. Alliant International University.

Slobogin, C. (2006). *Proving the unprovable: The role of law, science, and speculation in adjudicating culpability and dangerousness*. Oxford University Press. https://doi.org/10.1093/acprof:oso/9780195189957.001.0001

Smart, C. (2002). From children's shoes to children's voices. *Family Court Review, 40*(3), 307–319. https://doi.org/10.1111/j.174-1617.2002.tb00842.x

Smart, C. (2004). Retheorizing families. *Sociology, 38*(5), 1043–1048. https://doi.org/10.1177/0038038504047186

Smith, E. R. (1998). Mental representation and memory. In D. T. Gilbert, S. T. Fiske, & G. Lindzey (Eds.), *Handbook of social cognition* (pp. 391–445). McGraw-Hill.

Smith v. Yang, 829 N.E.2d 624 (Ind. Ct. App. 2005).

Solomon, J., & Biringen, Z. (2001). Another look at the developmental research: Commentary on Kelly and Lamb's "Using child development research to make appropriate custody and access decisions for young children." *Family Court Review, 39*(4), 355–364. https://doi.org/10.1111/j.174-1617.2001.tb00617.x

Soto, C. J., & Jackson, J. J. (2013). Five-factor model of personality. *Journal of Research in Personality, 42,* 1285–1302

Speidel, R., Behrens, B., Lawson, M., Mark Cummings, E., & Valentino, K. (2022). Latent classes in preschoolers' internal working models of attachment and emotional security: Roles of family risk. *Development and Psychopathology, 35*(3), 1552–1569. https://doi.org/10.1017/S0954579422000293

Spiegel, A. (2005). The dictionary of disorder. *The New Yorker,* 56–63.

Spitzer, R. L., Endicott, J., & Robins, E. (1978). Research diagnostic criteria: Rationale and reliability. *Archives of General Psychiatry, 35*(6), 773–782. https://doi.org/10.1001/archpsyc.1978.01770300115013

Sroufe, L. A. (2005). Attachment and development: A prospective, longitudinal study from birth to adulthood. *Attachment & Human Development,* 7(4), 349–367. https://doi.org/10.1080/14616730500365928

Stahl, P. M. (1994). *Conducting child custody evaluations: A comprehensive guide*. Sage Publications. https://doi.org/10.4135/9781452243665

Stahl, P. M. (1999). *Complex issues in child custody evaluations*. Sage Publications. https://doi.org/10.4135/9781452229171

Stahl, P. M., & Simon, R. (2020). *Forensic psychology consultation in child custody litigation: A handbook for work product review, case preparation, and expert testimony*. American Bar Association.

Stahl, R. M. (2024). LGBTQ+ affirming practices for family court professionals. *Family Court Review, 62*(3), 640–652. https://doi.org/10.1111/fcre.12805

Stanovich, K. E., & West, R. F. (1998). Individual differences in rational thought. *Journal of Experimental Psychology: General, 127*(2), 161–188. https://doi.org/10.1037/0096-3445.127.2.161

Starck, A., Gutermann, J., Schouler-Ocak, M., Jesuthasan, J., Bongard, S., & Stangier, U. (2020). The relationship of acculturation, traumatic events and depression in female refugees. *Frontiers in Psychology, 11,* 906. https://doi.org/10.3389/fpsyg.2020.00906

Stark, E. (2007). *Coercive control: How men entrap women in personal life*. Oxford University Press.

Stark, E. (2023a). *Children of coercive control*. Oxford University Press.

Stark, E. (2023b). *Coercive control: How men entrap women in personal life*. Oxford University Press.

Stark, E., & Hester, M. (2019). Coercive control: Update and review. *Violence Against Women, 25*(1), 81–104. https://doi.org/10.1177/1077801218816191

State v. Brooks, 643 A.2d 266 (Vt. 1993).

State v. Coon, 974 P.2d 386 (Alaska 1999).

State v. Foret, 628 So.2d 1116 (La. 1993).

State v. Giese, 854 N.W.2d 687 (Wis. 2014).

State v. Hofer, 512 N.W.2d 482 (S.D. 1994).

State v. Kandutsch, 799 N.W.2d 865 (Wis. 2011).

State v. Mack, 292 N.W.2d 764 (Minn. 1980).

State v. Martens, 629 N.E.2d 462 (Ohio Ct. App. 1993).

State v. Moore, 885 P.2d 457 (Mont. 1994).

State v. McGrady, 787 S.E.2d 1 (N.C. 2016).

State v. Morel, 676 A. 2d 1347, 1355 (R.I. 1996).

State v. O'Key, 899 P.2d 663 (Or. 1995).

State v. Porter, 698 A.2d 739 (Conn. 1997).

State v. Rinmasch, 775 P.2d 388 (Utah 1999).

Stebbins, R. A. (2001). What is exploration? *Exploratory Research in the Social Sciences, 48*, 2–17. https://doi.org/10.4135/9781412984249.n1

Steensma, T. D., Kreukels, B. P., de Vries, A. L., & Cohen-Kettenis, P. T. (2013). Gender identity development in adolescence. *Hormones and Behavior, 64*(2), 288–297. https://doi.org/10.1016/j.yhbeh.2013.02.020

Steinberg, L. D. (2014). *Age of opportunity: Lessons from the new science of adolescence*. Houghton Mifflin Harcourt.

Stern, E., Gibbs, A., Willan, S., Dunkle, K., & Jewkes, R. (2019). 'When you talk to someone in a bad way or always put her under pressure, it is actually worse than beating her': Conceptions and experiences of emotional intimate partner violence in Rwanda and South Africa. *PLOS One, 14*(11), e0225121. https://doi.org/10.1371/journal.pone.0225121

Stevenson, M. M., Fabricius, W. V., Braver, S. L., & Cookston, J. T. (2018). Associations between parental relocation following separation in childhood and maladjustment in adolescence and young adulthood. *Psychology, Public Policy, and Law, 24*(3), 365–378. https://doi.org/10.1037/law0000172

Stockdale, L. A., Coyne, S. M., & Padilla-Walker, L. M. (2018). Parent and child technoference and socioemotional behavioral outcomes: A nationally representative study of 10- to 20-year-old adolescents. *Computers in Human Behavior, 88*, 219–226. https://doi.org/10.1016/j.chb.2018.06.034

Straus, M. A. (1979). Measuring intrafamily conflict and violence: The Conflict Tactics (CT) Scales. *Journal of Marriage and Family, 41*(1), 75–88. https://doi.org/10.2307/351733

Straus, M. A. (2009). Gender symmetry in partner violence: Evidence and implications for prevention and treatment. In D. J. Whitaker & J. R. Lutzker (Eds.), *Preventing partner violence: Research and evidence-based intervention strategies* (pp. 245–271). American Psychological Association. https://doi.org/10.1037/11873-011

Sue, D. W. (2001). Multidimensional facets of cultural competence. *The Counseling Psychologist, 29*(6), 790–821. https://doi.org/10.1177/0011000001296002

Sue, D. W. (2003). *Overcoming our racism: The journey to liberation*. Jossey-Bass. https://doi.org/10.4324/9780203829738

Sue, D. W. (2004). Whiteness and ethnocentric monoculturalism: Making the "invisible" visible. *American Psychologist, 59*(8), 761–769. https://doi.org/10.1037/0003-066X.59.8.761

Symons, D. K. (2010). A review of the practice and science of child custody and access assessment in the United States and Canada. *Professional Psychology: Research and Practice, 41*(3), 267–273. https://doi.org/10.1037/a0019271

Tamir, M., Ito, A., Miyamoto, Y., Chentsova-Dutton, Y., Choi, J. H., Cieciuch, J., Riediger, M., Rauers, A., Padun, M., Kim, M. Y., Solak, N., Qiu, J., Wang, X., Alvarez-Risco, A., Hanoch, Y., Uchida, Y., Torres, C., Nascimento, T. G., Afshar Jahanshahi, A., . . . García Ibarra, V. J. (2024). Emotion regulation strategies and psychological health across cultures. *American Psychologist, 79*(5), 748–764. https://doi.org/10.1037/amp0001237

Taylor, S. E., & Crocker, J. (1981). Schematic bases of social information processing. In E. T. Higgins, C. P. Herman, & M. P. Zanna (Eds.), *Social cognition: The Ontario symposium* (pp. 89–134). Lawrence Erlbaum Associates.

Tennessee v. Kiser., 284 S.W.3d 227 (Tenn. 2009).

Terzuoli, M. (2010). Relying on the unreliable: How a court rule could alleviate the problems inherent in the neutral mental health evaluation process in child custody cases. *Family Court Review, 48*(3), 571–582. https://doi.org/10.1111/j.1744-1617.2010.01331.x

Teti, D. M., Cole, P. M., Cabrera, N., Goodman, S. H., & McLoyd, V. C. (2017). Supporting parents: How six decades of parenting research can inform policy and best practice. *Social Policy Report, 30*(5), 1–34. https://doi.org/10.1002/j.2379-3988.2017.tb00090.x

Thompson, S. C., & Kelley, H. H. (1981). Judgments of responsibility for activities in close relationships. *Journal of Personality and Social Psychology, 41*(3), 469–477. https://doi.org/10.1037/0022-3514.41.3.469

Tippins, T. M. (2014, July 3). Custody evaluations: Quest for quality. *New York Law Journal*, 3.

Tippins, T. M., & Wittmann, J. P. (2005). Empirical and ethical problems with custody recommendations: A call for clinical humility and judicial vigilance. *Family Court Review, 43*(2), 193–222. https://doi.org/10.1111/j.1744-1617.2005.00019.x

Tjaden, P., & Thoennes, N. (2000). *Extent, nature, and consequences of intimate partner violence: Findings from the National Violence Against Women Survey*. U.S. Department of Justice, National Institute of Justice. https://doi.org/10.1037/e300342003-001

Toews, M. L., & Bermea, A. M. (2017). "I was naive in thinking, 'I divorced this man, he is out of my life'": A qualitative exploration of post-separation power and control tactics experienced by women. *Journal of Interpersonal Violence, 32*(14), 2166–2189. https://doi.org/10.1177/0886260515591278

Tolson v. State, 900 A.2d 639 (Del. 2005).

Tomšik, R., & Čerešník, M. (2017). Adolescent's personality through big five model: The relation with parenting styles. *Ad Alta: Journal of Interdisciplinary Research, 7*(2), 225–231. https://www.researchgate.net/publication/322357859_adolescent's_personality_through_big_five_model_the_relation_with_parenting_styles

Troxel v. Granville, 530 U.S. 57 (2000).

Tsavoussis, A., Stawicki, S. P. A., Stoicea, N., & Papadimos, T. J. (2014). Child-witnessed domestic violence and its adverse effects on brain development: A call for societal self-examination and awareness. *Frontiers in Public Health, 2*, 178. https://doi.org/10.3389/fpubh.2014.00178

Tull, M. T., & Aldao, A. (2015). Editorial overview: New directions in the science of emotional regulation. *Current Opinion in Psychology, 3*, iv–x. https://doi.org/10.1016/j.copsyc.2015.03.009

Turkat, I. D. (2016). Harmful effects of child-custody evaluations on children. *Court Review: The Journal of the American Judges Association, 52*(4), 152–158. https://digitalcommons.unl.edu/cgi/viewcontent.cgi?article=1572&context=ajacourtreview

Turkat, I. D. (2021). Why judges should not permit child custody evaluations. *American Journal of Family Law, 34,* 115–118.

Tversky, A., & Kahneman, D. (1973). Availability: A heuristic for judging frequency and probability. *Cognitive Psychology, 5*(2), 207–232. https://doi.org/10.1016/0010-0285(73)90033-9

Tversky, A., & Kahneman, D. (1974). Judgment under uncertainty: Heuristics and biases. *Science, 185*(4157), 1124–1131.

Tversky, A., & Kahneman, D. (2005). Judgment under uncertainty: Heuristics and biases. In M. H. Bazerman (Ed.), *Negotiation, decision making and conflict management* (Vol. 1–3, pp. 251–258). Edward Elgar Publishing.

TXI Transp. Co. v. Hughes, 306 S.W.3d 230 (Tex. 2010).

Umaña-Taylor, A. J., & Hill, N. E. (2020). Ethnic–racial socialization in the family: A decade's advance on precursors and outcomes. *Journal of Marriage and Family, 82*(1), 244–271. https://doi.org/10.1111/jomf.12622

Underwager, R., & Wakefield, H. (1998). *The taint hearing* [Presentation]. 13th Annual Symposium in Forensic Psychology, Vancouver, BC, Canada

Underwood, S. W. (2024). Gay dads to be: Reflections on gender, sexuality, family, and race in adoption and surrogacy. *LGBTQ+ Family: An Interdisciplinary Journal, 20*(5), 339–354. https://doi.org/10.1080/27703371.2024.2342419

United States v. Addison, 498 F.2d 741 (D.C. Cir. 1974).

van Houten, J. T., Tornello, S. L., Hoffenaar, P. J., & Bos, H. M. W. (2020). Understanding parenting intentions among childfree gay men: A comparison with lesbian women and heterosexual men and women. *Frontiers in Psychology, 11,* 430. https://doi.org/10.3389/fpsyg.2020.00430

Vera, L. M., Boccaccini, M. T., Laxton, K., Bryson, C., Pennington, C., Ridge, B., & Murrie, D. C. (2019). How does evaluator empathy impact a forensic interview? *Law and Human Behavior, 43*(1), 56–68. https://doi.org/10.1037/lhb0000310

Ver Steegh, N. (2005). Differentiating types of domestic violence: Implications for child custody. *Louisiana Law Review, 65*(4), 1379–1431.

Ver Steegh, N., & Dalton, C. (2008). Report from the wingspread conference on family violence and family courts. *Family Court Review, 46*(3), 454–475. https://doi.org/10.1111/j.1744-1617.2008.00214.x

Viglione, D. J., de Ruiter, C., King, C. M., Meyer, G. J., Kivisto, A. J., Rubin, B. A., & Hunsley, J. (2022). Legal admissibility of the Rorschach and R-PAS: A review of research, practice, and case law. *Journal of Personality Assessment, 104*(2), 137–161. https://doi.org/10.1080/00223891.2022.2028795

Vincent, G. M., & Viljoen, J. L. (2018). Racist algorithms or age-old systemic problems? The latest risk assessment debate. *Criminal Justice and Behavior, 47*(2), 1576–1584.

Vredeveldt, A., van Rosmalen, E. A., Van Koppen, P. J., Dror, I. E., & Otgaar, H. (2024). Legal psychologists as experts: Guidelines for minimizing bias. *Psychology, Crime & Law, 30*(7), 705–729. https://doi.org/10.1080/1068316X.2022.2114476

Vygotsky, L. S. (1934). *Thought and language.* MIT Press.

Wagers, S. M., Piquero, A. R., Narvey, C., Reid, J. A., & Loughran, T. A. (2021). Variation in exposure to violence in early adolescence distinguishes between intimate partner violence victimization and perpetration among young men involved in the justice system. *Journal of Family Violence, 36*(1), 99–108. https://doi.org/10.1007/s10896-020-00170-4

Walker, A. G., & Kenniston, J. (2013). *Handbook on questioning children: A linguistic perspective* (3rd ed.). American Bar Association.

Walker, A. G., & Warren, A. R. (1995). The language of the child abuse interview: Asking the questions, understanding the answers. In T. Ney (Ed.), *True and false allegations of child sexual abuse: Assessment and case management* (pp. 153–162). Brunner/Mazel.

Walker, D., Smith, K. A., & Vul, E. (2022). Reconsidering the "bias" in "the correspondence bias." *Decision, 9*(3), 263–284. https://doi.org/10.1037/dec0000180

Walker, J. (2007). Unresolved loss and trauma in parents and the implications in terms of child protection. *Journal of Social Work Practice, 21*(1), 77–87. https://doi.org/10.1080/02650530601173656

Walker, L., & Monahan, J. (1987). Social frameworks: A new use of social science in law. *Virginia Law Review, 73*(3), 559–598. https://doi.org/10.2307/1072923

Walker, L. E. A. (1979). *The battered woman.* Harper & Row.

Wallace, L. N. (2021). Differences in social media monitoring practices based on child and parent gender. *Family Relations, 70*(5), 1412–1426. https://doi.org/10.1111/fare.12568

Wallerstein, J., & Tanke, T. (1996). To move or not to move: Psychological and legal considerations in the relocation following divorce. *Family Law Quarterly, 30*(2), 305–332.

Ward, C. (1996). Acculturation. In D. Landis & R. S. Bhagat (Eds.), *Handbook of intercultural training* (2nd ed., pp. 124–147). Sage Publications.

Ward, T., & Durrant, R. (2022). Targets of explanation in correctional and forensic psychology: A black box model. *Aggression and Violent Behavior, 67,* 1–11. https://doi.org/10.1016/j.avb.2022.101782

Warren, A. R., & Woodall, C. E. (1999). The reliability of hearsay testimony: How well do interviewers recall their interviews with children? *Psychology, Public Policy, and Law, 5*(2), 359–371. https://doi.org/10.1037/1076-8971.5.2.355

Warren, A. R., Woodall, C. E., Thomas, M., Nunno, M., Keeney, J. M., Larson, S. M., & Stadfeld, J. A. (1999). Assessing the effectiveness of a training program for interviewing child witnesses. *Journal of Applied Developmental Psychology, 3*(2), 128–135. https://doi.org/10.1207/s1532480xads0302_6

Warshak, R. A. (2000). Blanket restrictions: Overnight contact between parents and young children. *Family Court Review, 38*(4), 422–445. https://doi.org/10.1111/j.174-1617.2000.tb00583.x

Warshak, R. A. (2015). Ten parental alienation fallacies that compromise decisions in court and in therapy. *Professional Psychology: Research and Practice, 46*(4), 235–249. https://doi.org/10.1037/pro0000031

Warshak, R. A. (2020a). *Resist and refuse: Only part of the problem.* Retrieved February 20, 2024, from https://www.facebook.com/permalink.php?story_fbid=2099896440155096&id=117275435083883

Warshak, R. A. (2020b). When evaluators get it wrong: False positive IDs and parental alienation. *Psychology, Public Policy, and Law, 26*(1), 54–68. https://doi.org/10.1037/law0000216

Weiner, I. B. (1989). On competence and ethicality in psychodiagnostic assessment. *Journal of Personality Assessment, 53*(4), 827–831. https://doi.org/10.1207/s15327752jpa5304_18

Weiner, I. B., & Kleiger, J. H. (2021a). Introduction to the psychological assessment of disordered thought and perception: Definitions and concepts. In I. B. Weiner & J. H. Kleiger (Eds.), *Psychological assessment of disordered thinking and perception* (pp. 3–13). American Psychological Association. https://doi.org/10.1037/0000245-001

Weiner, I. B., & Kleiger, J. H. (Eds.). (2021b). *Psychological assessment of disordered thinking and perception.* American Psychological Association. https://doi.org/10.1037/0000245-000

Weiss, R. A., & Rosenfeld, B. (2012). Navigating cross-cultural issues in forensic assessment: Recommendations for practice. *Professional Psychology: Research and Practice, 43*(3), 234–240. https://doi.org/10.1037/a0025850

Wesson, M. (1985). Historical truth, narrative truth, and expert testimony. *Washington Law Review, 60*(2), 331–354.

West, T. V., & Kenny, D. A. (2011). The truth and bias model of judgment. *Psychological Review, 118*(2), 357–378. https://doi.org/10.1037/a0022936

Westen, D., & Weinberger, J. (2004). When clinical description becomes statistical prediction. *American Psychologist, 59*(7), 595–613. https://doi.org/10.1037/0003-066X.59.7.595

Whitman, M. R., Holmes, K., Sue Elias, L., Cappo, B. M., & Ben-Porath, Y. S. (2024). Incremental validity of MMPI-3 and NEO PI-3 scores in public safety candidate pre-employment psychological evaluations. *Criminal Justice and Behavior, 51*(3), 331–352.

Widiger, T. A., & Crego, C. (2019). The Five Factor Model of personality structure: An update. *World Psychiatry, 18*(3), 271–272.

Widiger, T. A., & Hines, A. (2022). *The Diagnostic and Statistical Manual of Mental Disorders, Fifth Edition*, alternative model of personality disorder. *Personality Disorders, 13*(4), 347–355. https://doi.org/10.1037/per0000524

Wigmore, J. H. (1978). *Evidence in trials at common law* (Vol. 7). Little, Brown.

Wilt v. Buracker, 443 S.E.2d 196 (W. Va. 1994).

Wittmann, J. P. (2022). A three-factor ethical reasoning model for court-involved practitioners: Services, roles, and values. *Family Court Review, 60*(3), 507–529. https://doi.org/10.1111/fcre.12656

Woodward, K. E., Boeldt, D. L., Corley, R. P., DiLalla, L., Friedman, N. P., Hewitt, J. K., Mullineaux, P. Y., Robinson, J., & Rhee, S. H. (2018). Correlates of positive parenting behaviors. *Behavior Genetics, 48*(4), 283–297. https://doi.org/10.1007/s10519-018-9906-2

Wright, A. J. (2020). *Conducting psychological assessment: A guide for practitioners*. John Wiley & Sons. https://doi.org/10.1002/9781119687245

Wright, A. J., Vardanian, M. M., & Constantine, K. (2023). The Wright–Constantine Structured Cultural Interview (WCSCI) and integration of culture into case conceptualization. *The Counseling Psychologist, 51*(1), 36–61. https://doi.org/10.1177/00110000221127408

Yao, S., Xu, M., & Sun, L. (2023). Five-factor personality dimensions mediated the relationship between parents' parenting style differences and mental health among Medical University Students. *International Journal of Environmental Research and Public Health, 20*(6), 1–11. https://doi.org/10.3390/ijerph20064908

Yoon, H., Scopelliti, I., & Morewedge, C. K. (2021). Decision making can be improved through observational learning. *Organizational Behavior and Human Decision Processes, 162*, 155–188. https://doi.org/10.1016/j.obhdp.2020.10.011

Youngstrom, E. A., & Van Meter, A. (2016). Empirically supported assessment of children and adolescents. *Clinical Psychology: Science and Practice, 23*(4), 327–347. https://doi.org/10.1037/h0101738

Zablotsky, B., Arockiaraj, B., Haile, G., & Ng, A. E. (2024). *Daily screen time among teenagers: United States, July 2021–December 2023* (Brief No. 513). National Center for Health Statistics. https://www.cdc.gov/nchs/data/databriefs/db513.pdf

Zahn-Waxler, C., Duggal, S., Gruber, R., & Bornstein, M. H. (2002). Parental psychopathology. In M. H. Bornstein (Ed.), *Handbook of parenting* (Vol. 4, pp. 295–327). Psychology Press.

Zapf, P. A., Kukucka, J., Kassin, S. M., & Dror, I. E. (2018). Cognitive bias in forensic mental health assessment: Evaluator beliefs about its nature and scope. *Psychology, Public Policy, and Law, 24*(1), 1–10. https://doi.org/10.1037/law0000153

Zappala, M., Reed, A. L., Beltrani, A., Zapf, P. A., & Otto, R. K. (2018). Anything you can do, I can do better: Bias awareness in forensic evaluators. *Journal of Forensic Psychology Research and Practice, 18*(1), 45–56. https://doi.org/10.1080/24732850.2017.1413532

Zarling, A., & Russell, D. (2022). A randomized clinical trial of acceptance and commitment therapy and the Duluth Model classes for men court-mandated to a domestic violence program. *Journal of Consulting and Clinical Psychology, 90*(4), 326–338. https://doi.org/10.1037/ccp0000722

Zarling, A. L., Taber-Thomas, S., Murray, A., Knuston, J. F., Lawrence, E., Valles, N.-L., DeGarmo, D. S., & Bank, L. (2013). Internalizing and externalizing symptoms in young children exposed to intimate partner violence: Examining intervening processes. *Journal of Family Psychology, 27*(6), 945–955.

Zervopoulos, J. A. (2019). *How to examine mental health experts: A family lawyer's handbook of issues and strategies* (2nd ed.). American Bar Association, Family Law Section.

Zumbach, J., & Koglin, U. (2015). Psychological evaluations in family law proceedings: A systematic review of the contemporary literature. *Professional Psychology: Research and Practice, 46*(4), 221–234. https://doi.org/10.1037/a0039329

INDEX

A

E

N

O

P

Q

T

U

V

ABOUT THE AUTHORS

Jonathan W. Gould, PhD, ABPP, has been writing, teaching, and actively engaging in forensic psychological practice addressing child custody matters for more than 3 decades. He has conducted more than 350 court-appointed evaluations, consulted on over 3,500 family law matters, and conducted more than 2,400 work product reviews. He has testified nationally and internationally. He has served on the faculty of the National Family Law Trial Institute since 2002. He has been an associate editor of the *Journal of Child Custody* and a reviewer of manuscripts for more than a dozen peer-reviewed journals. He has published peer-reviewed articles in legal as well as mental health journals and has written several chapters about child custody procedures and specialized areas of custody assessment. Dr. Gould is on the Executive Committee of the North Carolina Chapter of the Association of Family and Conciliation Courts and is coauthor (with Marc J. Ackerman and Andrew W. Kane) of the sixth and seventh editions of *Psychological Experts in Divorce Actions*. He was the senior author of *The Art and Science of Child Custody Evaluations* and the sole author of the first and second editions of *Conducting Scientifically Crafted Child Custody Evaluations*. He is married to retired attorney (now artist) Nicki Fisher, has a blended family of six adult children (of whom three are married), and has six grandchildren.

Christopher M. Mulchay, PhD, ABPP, can frequently be found reading (often educating himself on best practices or innovative techniques), writing, and presenting. He has conducted more than 200 court-appointed evaluations and nearly 2,000 clinical evaluations, and he loves consulting on cases. He is a coauthor of *The Family Law Professional's Field Guide to High-Conflict Litigation*. With Jonathan W. Gould, he cowrote the chapters on child custody research and scholarship for *The Oxford Handbook of Psychology and Law* (2023) and for *APA Handbook of Forensic Psychology* (2026). They also wrote a chapter on scientific and specialized knowledge in expert testimony for the upcoming *Parenting Plan Evaluations: Applied Research for the Family Court, Third Edition*, to be published by Oxford University Press. Dr. Mulchay's work is focused on cutting-edge theories and technology. He has written or presented on artificial intelligence, digital evidence, social media, apps, and virtual reality. Dr. Mulchay has reviewed neuropsychological tests for the *Journal of Pediatric Neuropsychology* on dyslexia, dyscalculia, dysgraphia, and ADHD. Dr. Mulchay is board certified in forensic psychology by the American Board of Professional Psychology and a fellow in the American Academy of Forensic Psychology. Dr. Mulchay is honored to have served as president of both his local and state psychological associations and as the membership chair for his state psychological association. He is also proud to serve as the treasurer of the International Council of Psychologists. Outside of work, Dr. Mulchay enjoys spending time with his family and dog, whether on the water (surfing, paddling, swimming), hiking, or attending a concert.